Historical Dictionaries of Asia, Oceania, and the Middle East
Edited by Jon Woronoff

Asia

1. *Vietnam*, by William J. Duiker. 1989. *Out of print. See No. 27.*
2. *Bangladesh*, 2nd ed., by Craig Baxter and Syedur Rahman. 1996. *Out of print. See No.48.*
3. *Pakistan*, by Shahid Javed Burki. 1991. *Out of print. See No. 33.*
4. *Jordan*, by Peter Gubser. 1991
5. *Afghanistan*, by Ludwig W. Adamec. 1991. *Out of print. See No. 29.*
6. *Laos*, by Martin Stuart-Fox and Mary Kooyman. 1992. *Out of print. See No. 35.*
7. *Singapore*, by K. Mulliner and Lian The-Mulliner. 1991
8. *Israel*, by Bernard Reich. 1992
9. *Indonesia*, by Robert Cribb. 1992
10. *Hong Kong and Macau*, by Elfed Vaughan Roberts, Sum Ngai Ling, and Peter Bradshaw. 1992
11. *Korea*, by Andrew C. Nahm. 1993
12. *Taiwan*, by John F. Copper. 1993. *Out of print. See No. 34.*
13. *Malaysia*, by Amarjit Kaur. 1993. *Out of print. See No. 36.*
14. *Saudi Arabia*, by J. E. Peterson. 1993. *Out of print. See No. 45.*
15. *Myanmar*, by Jan Becka. 1995
16. *Iran*, by John H. Lorentz. 1995
17. *Yemen*, by Robert D. Burrowes. 1995
18. *Thailand*, by May Kyi Win and Harold Smith. 1995
19. *Mongolia*, by Alan J. K. Sanders. 1996. *Out of print. See No. 42.*
20. *India*, by Surjit Mansingh. 1996
21. *Gulf Arab States*, by Malcolm C. Peck. 1996
22. *Syria*, by David Commins. 1996
23. *Palestine*, by Nafez Y. Nazzal and Laila A. Nazzal. 1997
24. *Philippines*, by Artemio R. Guillermo and May Kyi Win. 1997

Oceania

1. *Australia*, by James C. Docherty. 1992. *Out of print. See No. 32.*
2. *Polynesia*, by Robert D. Craig. 1993. *Out of print. See No. 39.*
3. *Guam and Micronesia*, by William Wuerch and Dirk Ballendorf. 1994
4. *Papua New Guinea*, by Ann Turner. 1994. *Out of print. See No. 37.*
5. *New Zealand*, by Keith Jackson and Alan McRobie. 1996

Historical Dictionary
of Iraq

Edmund A. Ghareeb
With the assistance of
Beth Dougherty

*Historical Dictionaries of Asia,
Oceania, and the Middle East, No. 44*

The Scarecrow Press, Inc.
Lanham, Maryland, and Oxford
2004

SCARECROW PRESS, INC.

Published in the United States of America
by Scarecrow Press, Inc.
A wholly owned subsidiary of
The Rowman & Littlefield Publishing Group, Inc.
4501 Forbes Boulevard, Suite 200, Lanham, Maryland 20706
www.scarecrowpress.com

PO Box 317
Oxford
OX2 9RU, UK

Copyright © 2004 by Edmund A. Ghareeb

British Library Cataloguing in Publication Information Available

Library of Congress Cataloging-in-Publication Data

Ghareeb, Edmund.
    Historical dictionary of Iraq / Edmund A. Ghareeb. — 1st ed.
        p. cm. — (Historical dictionaries of Asia, Oceania, and the Middle East ; no. 44)
    ISBN 0-8108-4330-7
    1. Iraq–History. I. Title. II. Series.
DS70.9 .G47 2004
956.7–dc21   2003011526

⊗™ The paper used in this publication meets the minimum requirements of
American National Standard for Information Sciences—Permanence of
Paper for Printed Library Materials, ANSI/NISO Z39.48-1992.
Manufactured in the United States of America.

Contents

Editor's Foreword

Over the past decade or so, and especially since the Gulf War, there has been a tendency for the focus on Iraq to get narrower and narrower. Indeed, many foreign politicians, aided and abetted by the media, seem to equate it to one man: Saddam Husayn. Although he might not mind this, Iraq is infinitely larger and more varied. In fact, it is a fairly big country, with a substantial population coming from diverse origins and holding diverse views, whether or not they could be expressed openly. Indeed, more than might be expected, opposition does exist. And hidden dissension, not blind obedience, seems to have the longer tradition just as discord frequently overshadowed any cohesion. Now that a new, and hopefully happier, era has begun, it is time to look back on the past, with its countless twists and turns, to fathom how Iraq will evolve in the future.

The focus of this historical dictionary of Iraq is broad—impressively so. It reaches all the way back to the earliest civilizations and refers to the many, often less glorious periods that followed. It presents those who created empires and regimes, and those who overthrew or sought to undo them. It sheds lights on many social, religious, cultural, and economic groups and the institutions that were forged to hold them together, albeit not always effectively. And it culminates with the fall of the Ba'th regime.

This broad view is obviously more helpful than the old narrow focus. It is reflected through numerous dictionary entries on persons, places and events, organizations and institutions, and economic, social, and religious phenomena. The chronology, vital in this case, traces one of the world's longest histories. The bibliography permits even broader reading.

This impressively broad presentation of Iraq was written by Edmund Ghareeb and Beth Dougherty, who collaborated closely with him. As a journalist, Dr. Ghareeb followed and wrote on events in the Middle East, including Iraq. Since 1982, as an academic, he has been lecturing and writing on the same topics, with an emphasis on Kurdish studies. He has taught at the American University, where he is at present, along with Georgetown University and others.

Beth Dougherty is a professor of international relations at Beloit College, where she also specializes in Middle East affairs. Together they have formed an inimitable team who have produced this unique and very long-awaited *Historical Dictionary of Iraq*.

Jon Woronoff
Series Editor

Preface

The general purpose of this dictionary is to cover a number of diverse subjects ranging from the history of ancient Mesopotamia to the 'Abbasid Empire to present-day Iraq . It includes a historical overview, a country profile, the economy, oil, fauna, political institution, the Iran–'Iraq war, the Kuwait invasion, and the second Gulf War and other conflicts. It also covers the major ethnic groups such as the Kurds, the Turkumans and the Assyrians, Islam and Muslim sects, Christianity and Christian sects, as well as other religious groups. The dictionary highlights the main political, religious, and ideological parties, groups, and organizations; major historical personalities; languages; literature; culture; a comprehensive bibliography; and other topics. We have also dealt with a broad range of topics both ancient and modern.

Since the standard way of transliterating Arabic requires acute and grave accents and other diacritical marks that are not generally used by most Western writers and media, we have tried for simplicity's sake to avoid them. For the three Arabic vowels *a*, *i*, and *u* that are not usually written when they are short, we have used these letters. We also tended to write *Muslim* instead of *Moslem*, *Tariq* instead of *Tarik*, and *Husayn* instead of *Hussein*. The Arabic letter *'Ayn* is represented by an ' in words such as *'Abbas* or *Ba'th* but is omitted from names or words that are regularly used without it in the West or by the persons themselves. The *hamza*, a glottal stop, has generally been omitted. We have also tried to write words and letters in accordance with the standard Arabic pronunciation, such as the letter *q* instead of *k* for the letter *qaf*—for example, *Baqir*, not *Baker* or *Bakir*. The letters *gh* is used for the letter *ghayn* in *Baghdad* instead of *Bagdad*.

We would like to express our thanks to a number of colleagues, friends, and students far too numerous to mention each by name who have provided us with information or who typed part of the work. We are also grateful for the information provided by a number of Iraqi public and private figures, Arabs, Kurds, Assyrians, and Chaldeans as well as others. A special word of thanks goes to Jon Woronoff for his thoughtful comments, suggestions, and, more important, his patience.

Acronyms and Abbreviations

ALF	Arab Liberation Front
CENTO	Central Treaty Organization
CPA	Coalition Provisional Authority
GCC	Gulf Cooperation Council
IAEA	International Atomic Energy Agency
IAO	Islamic Action Organization
ICP	'Iraqi Communist Party
IGC	'Iraq Governing Council
IKF	'Iraqi Kurdish Front
IMK	Islamic Movement of Kurdistan
INC	'Iraqi National Congress
INOC	'Iraqi National Oil Company
IPC	'Iraqi Petroleum Company
ISP	'Iraq Socialist Party
KAR	Kurdistan Autonomous Region
KDP	Kurdistan Democratic Party
KRG	Kurdish Regional Government
NDP	National Democratic party
OPEC	Organization of Petroleum Exporting Countries
PKK	Kurdistan Workers' Party
PUK	Patriotic Union of Kurdistan
RC	Regional Command
RCC	Revolutionary Command Council
SAIRI	Supreme Assembly for the Islamic Revolution in 'Iraq
SPK	Socialist Party of Kurdistan
UAR	United Arab Republic
OFP	Oil-for-Food Program
UN	United Nations
UNESCO	United Nations Educational, Scientific, and Cultural Organization

UNR   United Nations resolution
UNSCOM   United Nations Special Commission on 'Iraq
UNMOVIC   United Nations Monitoring, Verification, and Inspection
             Commission

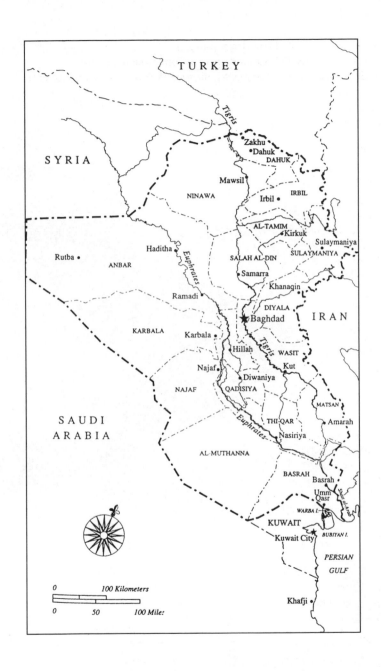

TURKEY

SYRIA

Tigris

•Zakhu
•Dahuk
DAHUK

Mawsil•

NINAWA   Irbil •   IRBIL

AL-TAMIM
•Kirkuk
                              Sulaymaniya
Rutba •   Haditha •   SULAYMANIYA
        ANBAR   SALAH AL-DIN
                    Euphrates
                    •Samarra
        Ramadi •   Khanaqin

                    DIYALA
                    ★Baghdad   IRAN

        KARBALA   Karbala •
                    •Hillah   Tigris
                              WASIT
                Najaf •   •Kut
                    •Diwaniya
        NAJAF   QADISIYA

SAUDI   MATSAN
ARABIA   THI-QAR   •Amarah
                    Euphrates
                    Nasiriya•

                AL-MUTHANNA

                    BASRAH   Basrah•
                              Umm
                              Qasr
                    WARBA I.   Shatt al-Arab

                    KUWAIT
                Kuwait City   BUBIYAN I.

                              PERSIAN
                              GULF

0   100 Kilometers
0   50   100 Miles   Khafji •

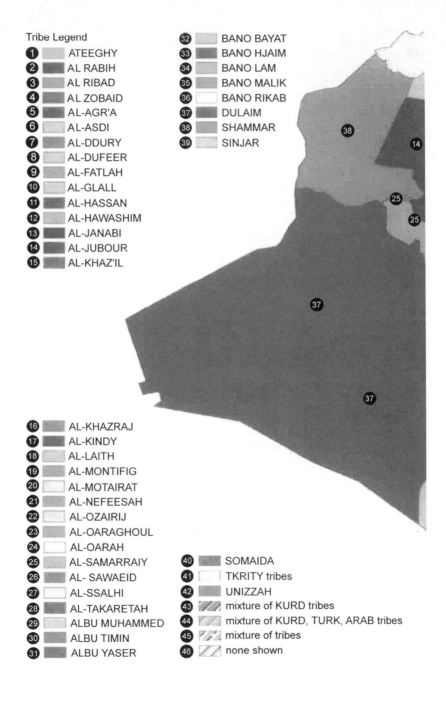

Tribe Legend

1 ATEEGHY
2 AL RABIH
3 AL RIBAD
4 AL ZOBAID
5 AL-AGR'A
6 AL-ASDI
7 AL-DDURY
8 AL-DUFEER
9 AL-FATLAH
10 AL-GLALL
11 AL-HASSAN
12 AL-HAWASHIM
13 AL-JANABI
14 AL-JUBOUR
15 AL-KHAZ'IL

32 BANO BAYAT
33 BANO HJAIM
34 BANO LAM
35 BANO MALIK
36 BANO RIKAB
37 DULAIM
38 SHAMMAR
39 SINJAR

16 AL-KHAZRAJ
17 AL-KINDY
18 AL-LAITH
19 AL-MONTIFIG
20 AL-MOTAIRAT
21 AL-NEFEESAH
22 AL-OZAIRIJ
23 AL-OARAGHOUL
24 AL-OARAH
25 AL-SAMARRAIY
26 AL- SAWAEID
27 AL-SSALHI
28 AL-TAKARETAH
29 ALBU MUHAMMED
30 ALBU TIMIN
31 ALBU YASER

40 SOMAIDA
41 TKRITY tribes
42 UNIZZAH
43 mixture of KURD tribes
44 mixture of KURD, TURK, ARAB tribes
45 mixture of tribes
46 none shown

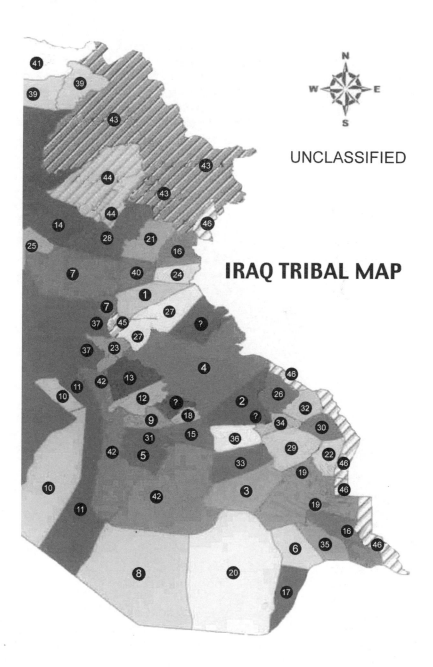

IRAQ TRIBAL MAP

UNCLASSIFIED

Chronology

A.D.

224–651 Sassanians rule

600–650 Muslim conquest begins

622 Year 1 of the Muslim calendar

632 Death of Muhammad

637 Battle of al-Qadisiyah, where the Arabs, outnumbered 6–1, defeat the Persians

661–750 Umayyad Caliphate

680 Husayn murdered

750 al-Abbas overthrows the Syrian Caliphate and moves the caliphate seat to Baghdad

750–1258 Abbasid Caliphate

762 Foundation of Baghdad set

830 Establishment of the House of Wisdom

1000–1400 Turco-Mongol centuries

1258 Hulaga Khan seizes Baghdad

1393 Timerlane occupies Baghdad

1401 Timerlane returns to Baghdad and destroys it

1508 Ismael Shah of the Safavid dynasty conquers 'Iraq

1514 Ottoman conquest of 'Iraq begins

1534 'Iraq conquered by Ottoman sultan Sulayman the Magnificent, marking the beginning of four centuries of Ottoman rule

1623 Shah Abbas of the Safavids seizes Baghdad from the Sublime Porte

1638 Ottomans retake Baghdad

1639 Treaty of Zuhab signed

1704 Mamluk rule in 'Iraq begins

1802 British establish a consulate in Baghdad

1831 End of Mamluk rule in 'Iraq as Ottomans regain administrative control

1869–1872 Midhat Pasha, governor of Baghdad, undertakes significant administrative and educational reforms

1888   German interests are granted the first foreign oil concession in 'Iraq

1899   German interests gain the concession for the Baghdad–Berlin railroad

1912   Turkish Petroleum Company (TPC) established

1914
November   British occupy southern 'Iraq

1917
11 March   British capture Baghdad

1920
28 April   'Iraq is awarded to Britain as a Class A Mandate at the San Remo Conference

June   The Mawsil Revolt, or *al-Thawra*, breaks out in response to the San Remo Conference; roughly one-third of the country passes from British control for three months

11 November   Provisional government formed

1921
March   Faysal nominated for the 'Iraqi throne at the Cairo Conference

July   Faysal overwhelmingly confirmed as king in a plebiscite

23 August   Faysal ascends the 'Iraqi throne

1922
10 October   Anglo–'Iraqi Treaty ratified by 'Iraq

1923
30 April   Protocol to the 1922 Anglo–'Iraqi Treaty modifies its duration from 20 to four years

1925
21 March   Faysal signs the Organic Law

1926
13 January   Anglo–'Iraqi Treaty signed

18 July   Mawsil *wilayet* becomes part of 'Iraq

1927
15 October   TPC's first major well comes in at Baba Gurgur

TPC renamed the 'Iraqi Petroleum Company (IPC)

1930
30 June   Anglo–'Iraqi Treaty signed that pledges Britain will nominate 'Iraq to the League of Nations in 1932

1932
3 October 'Iraq gains independence; is admitted to the League of Nations

1933
4–11 August The Assyrian Affair; hundreds of Assyrians are massacred

8 September King Faysal dies in Switzerland; Ghazi takes the throne

1934
January Central government passes a conscription law

1934–1935 Tribal uprisings in the mid-Euphrates region

Yazidis revolt against conscription

1935–1936 Kurdish uprising led by the Barzan tribe

Series of tribal uprisings, mainly in the south, largely precipitated by the enforcement of the Conscription law

1936
29 October The military successfully launches its first coup; another six coups would occur over the next five years

1937
May More uprisings in the mid-Euphrates region

4 July 'Iraq and Iran sign a frontier treaty governing the Shatt al-Arab

8 July Saadabad Pact signed by 'Iraq, Afghanistan, Iran, and Turkey

11 August General Bakr Sidqi assassinated

1939
4 April King Ghazi killed in an automobile accident; 'Abd al-Ilah becomes regent

1941 IPC group gains monopoly concession in all of 'Iraq
1–2 April Golden Square uprising brings Rashid Ali back into power

29 April Britain lands forces in Basra when Rashid Ali refuses its requests for the unconditional landing of its troops in 'Iraq

2 May Fighting breaks out between 'Iraq and Britain

29 May Rashid Ali government flees to Iran

30 May 'Iraq and Britain sign an armistice; 'Iraq remains under British occupation for the remainder of World War II

1943
January 'Iraq declares war on the Axis powers

1944 Ba'th Party founded in Damascus by Michel Aflaq and Salah al-Din Bitar

1945
March 'Iraq participates in the founding of the Arab League

December 'Iraq joins the United Nations (UN)

1948
15 January Portsmouth Treaty between 'Iraq and Britain signed in London by 'Iraqi prime minister Salih Jabr

16 January *Al-Wathbah*, the "Glorious Uprising," breaks out as student dissatisfaction spreads into rioting and demonstrations against the Portsmouth Treaty

27 January Jabr resigns; the new cabinet repudiates the Portsmouth Treaty

15 May State of Israel declared; first Arab–Israeli war erupts

1952 First Free Officer cell forms in the army
October Student strikes and demonstrations calling for direct elections begin

22 November Student unrest causes the fall of the 'Umari government; the demonstrations continue, leading to the declaration of martial law and the installation of a military government

1953
29 January The government is returned to civilian hands

2 May Faysal II reaches his majority and assumes constitutional powers as king

1955
24 February 'Iraq adheres to the Baghdad Pact

1956
29 October Tripartite attack against Egypt

University of Baghdad established

1958
14 February 'Iraq and Jordan form the Arab Federation in response to the formation of the United Arab Republic (UAR) by Egypt and Syria

14 July 'Iraqi Revolution; the monarchy is overthrown by a military coup led by 'Abd al-Karim Qasim and 'Abd al-Salam 'Arif; the royal family, 'Abd al-Ilah, and Nuri al-Sa'id are killed

August Mahdawi Court established

30 September Agrarian Reform Law is passed

September 'Arif is dismissed as deputy commander in chief on 10 September and stripped of his other political functions on 30 September; is sent to the Federal Republic of Germany as ambassador in October

5 November 'Arif, who returned to Baghdad on 4 November, is arrested for allegedly attempting to assassinate Qasim and overthrow the government

December 'Arif is put on trial and sentenced to death

9 December Rashid 'Ali plot to overthrow Qasim is discovered and foiled

1959
8 March An unsuccessful rebellion is launched in Mawsil by a group of Free Officers led by Colonel 'Abd al-Wahhab Shawwaf, who is killed during the fighting; in the aftermath of the rebellion, bloody confrontations between nationalists and Communists leave some 200 people dead

24 March 'Iraq withdraws from the Baghdad Pact

July Fighting breaks out in Kirkuk on the anniversary of the revolution in which scores of people are killed; blame is fastened on the 'Iraqi Communist Party

7 October A group of Ba'thists, including Saddam Husayn, make an unsuccessful attempt on Qasim's life

1959–1961 Dispute over the Shatt al-Arab reopens between 'Iraq and Iran

1960
September 'Iraq participates in the founding of the Organization of Petroleum Exporting Countries (OPEC)

1961
25 June Qasim lays claim to Kuwait and attempts to annex it

September Kurdish rebellion breaks out

11 December Public Law 80 proclaimed, expropriating 99.5 percent of the IPC concession

1963

8 February The "Ramadan Revolution"; Qasim overthrown by the Ba'th Party and 'Abd al-Salam 'Arif

9 February Qasim surrenders and is shot to death

7 April Agreement on unity between 'Iraq and the UAR is announced

30 September 'Iraq and Syria announce plans for federation

18 November 'Arif carries out a countercoup against the Ba'th Party

1964

February Public Law 11 establishes the 'Iraqi National Oil Company (INOC)

10 February A cease-fire in the Kurdish war is reached

14 July Nationalization laws passed, affecting numerous industries, including banking, insurance, cement, and cigarettes

1965

April Hostilities resume between the Kurds and the central government

1966 Iraqi and Syrian Ba'th parties split

13 April 'Arif and several ministers are killed in a helicopter accident

17 April 'Abd al-Rahman 'Arif is elected to succeed his brother as president

1967

5–11 June The Six-Day War; 'Iraq sends troops to Jordan and breaks relations with Britain and the United States

16 August Public Law 97 proclaimed, giving INOC the exclusive rights to the territories expropriated under Public Law 80

1968

17 July The Ba'th Party, in cooperation with military officers, overthrows the 'Arif regime

29–30 July Ba'thists stage a countercoup against the military officers with whom they had cooperated to seize power two weeks previously

1969

19 April Iran declares the abrogation of the 1937 treaty and announces it would make free use of the Shatt al-Arab

1970

11 March   The Ba'th issues the March Manifesto, an autonomy agreement with the Kurds

1971

15 November   The Ba'th proclaims a reform program called the National Action Charter

1972

7 April   Production begins at North Rumaila oilfield

9 April   'Iraq signs a Treaty of Friendship and Cooperation with the Soviet Union

1 June   'Iraq nationalizes most of the IPC and sets up the 'Iraq Company for Oil Operations (ICOO) under the provisions of Public Law 69

1973

20 March   'Iraq occupies a border post in Kuwait during a dispute over Warba and Bubiyan Islands

30 June   Security Chief Nazim Kazzar attempts a coup in which he kills Defense Minister Hammad Shihab and wounds Interior Minister Sadun Ghaydan; Kazzar is executed on 7 July 1973

July   Iraqi Communist Party joins the Ba'th Party in a National Front

7 October   'Iraq nationalizes the American and Dutch holdings in Basra Petroleum Company (BPC)

December   'Iraq nationalizes C. S. Gulbenkian's interest in BPC

1974

10 February   Border fighting between 'Iraq and Iran results in scores of casualties

11 March   Baghdad unilaterally enacts the Autonomy Law for the Kurds

March   Fighting between the Kurds and the central government breaks out again

1975

6 March   The Algiers Agreement between 'Iraq and Iran is announced; within 48 hours Iran withdraws its support for the Kurds, leading to the collapse of the Kurdish rebellion by April

8 December   'Iraq completes the nationalization of its oil industry

1977
5–6 February   Demonstrations break out in Najaf and Karbala during *Ashura*, and troops are dispatched to quell the disturbances; eventually a number of religious leaders are executed or imprisoned for their roles in the events

1978
May   The Ba'th executes 21 communists for allegedly organizing cells in the army

November   Baghdad Summit is held; 'Iraq takes lead in expelling Egypt from the Arab League in response to Egypt's signing of the Camp David Accords

7 November   'Iraq and Syria announce plans for union

1979
June   Riots break out in Najaf and Karbala

16 July   Ahmad Hasan al-Bakr steps down as 'Iraqi president; Saddam Husayn assumes the presidency

28 July   Union plans with Syria are cancelled; Saddam accuses Syria of plotting to overthrow his regime and executes 22 high-ranking party officials, including five members of the Revolutionary Command Council (RCC)

1980
April   Assassination attempts against Tariq 'Aziz and Latif Nusayyif Jasim lead to a crackdown on the underground Shi'i group al-Da'wa

Summer   'Iraq's leading Shi'i clergyman, Muhammad Baqir al-Sadr, and his sister are secretly executed

22 September   'Iraq invades Iran

1981
7 June   Israel bombs and destroys 'Iraqi nuclear reactor facility at Osiraq

Iranian forces cross into 'Iraq

1984
March   The tanker war starts

11 November   'Iraq resumes diplomatic relations with the United States

1985
May   The war of the cities begins

1986
9 February   'Iraq loses the Faw Peninsula to Iranian forces

March UN secretary-general Javier Perez de Cuellar accuses 'Iraq of using chemical weapons

1987
17 May 'Iraq accidentally attacks the U.S.S. *Stark*, killing 37 crewmen

July The UN Security Council passes UN Resolution 598, which calls for an end to the Iran–Iraq war

1988
16 March 'Iraq uses chemical weapons against Kurdish civilians at Halabja

8 August 'Iraq and Iran agree to a cease-fire

1989
10 February 'Iraq and Iran agree to direct peace talks

21 February Arab Cooperation Council formed

17 August A massive explosion takes place at an 'Iraqi military facility near Al Hillah; Western sources claim hundreds of people are killed in the accident

5 December 'Iraq successfully tests a missile capable of carrying a payload into space

1990
15 March 'Iraq hangs Farzad Barzoft, an Iranian-born journalist working for a British paper, on charges of spying for Israel

28 March U.S. Customs officials conclude a sting operation in London, arresting three people on charges of buying nuclear triggers said to be meant for shipment to 'Iraq

2 April Saddam Husayn threatens to use chemical weapons against Israel if Israel attacks 'Iraq

11 April British Customs officials seize eight steel pipes bound for 'Iraq, charging that they formed part of the barrel of a "supergun"; over the next several weeks other shipments are seized in Greece, Turkey, Italy, and West Germany.

30 May At a closed session of the Baghdad summit, Saddam accuses OPEC quota violators of waging "a kind of war against 'Iraq"

17 July Saddam warns that OPEC quota violators are harming 'Iraqi interests and that 'Iraq will use force if they do not abide by the production agreement

23 July 'Iraq moves troops to its border with Kuwait

1 August 'Iraq invades Kuwait

2 August The UN Security Council passes Resolution 660, condemning 'Iraq's invasion of Kuwait, demanding its immediate and unconditional withdrawal, and threatening to invoke sanctions. The United States, Britain, and France freeze 'Iraqi and Kuwaiti assets

6 August The UN Security Council imposes sanctions against 'Iraq

7 August The United States launches Operation Desert Shield, aimed at protecting Saudi Arabia from an 'Iraqi invasion

8 August 'Iraq announces its annexation of Kuwait; the UN Security Council declares the annexation to be null and void

15 August 'Iraq offers to accept Iran's terms for a peace settlement, including a return to the boundary provisions of the Algiers Agreement

28 August 'Iraq declares Kuwait as its 19th province and renames Kuwait City Kadhima

14 October 'Iraq and Iran resume diplomatic relations

29 November The UN Security Council passes Resolution 678, which authorizes members "to use all necessary means" to oust 'Iraq from Kuwait; the resolution establishes a 15 January 1991 deadline for 'Iraq to comply with all prior resolutions calling for its withdrawal

1991
9 January Iraqi foreign minister Tariq 'Aziz and U.S. secretary of state James Baker meet for six hours in Geneva; the talks do not produce progress toward a peaceful settlement of the Gulf crisis

17 January A multinational force led by the United States launches Operation Desert Storm, an air campaign against 'Iraq and its forces inside Kuwait

18 January 'Iraq launches seven SCUD missiles at Israel and one at Saudi Arabia; by late February, it has launched a total of at least 17 SCUDs against Saudi Arabia and 39 against Israel

24 February The multinational force launches a ground assault into Kuwait and southern 'Iraq

27 February Coalition forces gain control of Kuwait City; U.S. president George H. Bush declares that Kuwait has been liberated and announces that coalition forces will cease hostilities exactly 100 hours after the ground attack commenced. 'Iraq announces it will comply with all 12 UN resolutions dealing with its invasion of Kuwait

28 February   Soldiers returning from Kuwait ignite an uprising against the regime in southern 'Iraq

5 March   The uprising spreads to 'Iraqi Kurdistan

21 March   A UN team issues a report on postwar conditions in 'Iraq; the team says that the coalition had bombed 'Iraq into a "preindustrial" state and warns of famine and epidemics

3 April   Forces loyal to Saddam succeed in crushing the last vestiges of the uprising; thousands of refugees flee into Iran, Turkey, and Saudi Arabia

5 April   With one million refugees fleeing into surrounding countries, the United States begins airdropping supplies to Kurdish refugees along the 'Iraqi–Turkish border

16 April   The United States announces the formation of "safe havens" in northern 'Iraq to be enforced by U.S., British, and French troops

6 May   U.S. forces withdraw from southern 'Iraq

13 September   A UN report concludes that by the mid-1990s 'Iraq would have been capable of building two to three atomic devices a year if its program had not been uncovered

19 September   The UN Security Council authorizes the sale of $1.6 billion of 'Iraqi oil for the purchase of humanitarian supplies, with one-third of the proceeds to go toward reparations; Saddam refuses to accept the terms of the resolution on 4 February 1992

7 October   UN inspectors discover the Al-Atheer complex, the headquarters of 'Iraq's nuclear weapons program

1992
16 April   The UN Border Demarcation Commission announces changes in the 'Iraqi–Kuwaiti border that give Kuwait a larger share of the Rumaila oil field and part of the 'Iraqi port of Umm Qasr

22–24 May   The two major parties in Kurdistan, the Kurdistan Democratic Party (KDP) and the Patriotic Union of Kurdistan (PUK), each win 50 seats in the National Assembly; a runoff is to be held at a later date to determine the paramount leader after neither candidate—Mas'ud Barzani and Jalal Talabani—achieved a majority

16–19 June   The 'Iraqi National Congress (INC), an umbrella organization representing over 30 opposition groups, holds a conference in Vienna; SAIRI and al-Da'wa are not officially represented

5 July 'Iraq refuses to allow UN weapons inspectors access to the Agricultural Ministry; on 26 July the standoff is settled after the UN agrees to exclude members from countries that participated in Operation Desert Storm

6 August 'Iraq announces that it will not allow UN inspection teams into its Ministries

26 August The United States announces the establishment of a "no-fly" zone south of the 32d parallel, designed to protect the Shi'i from the 'Iraqi air force

23 September The 'Iraqi opposition begins a three-day meeting at Arbil; all factions, including those that boycotted the INC meeting in June, are present

2 October The UN Security Council votes to use up to $500 million in frozen 'Iraqi assets to pay for UN expenses in 'Iraq and for reparations

7 December Saddam announces the completion of the so-called Third River project

1993
4 January 'Iraq moves surface-to-air missiles into the southern no-fly zone, precipitating a series of military strikes against southern sites during January

10 January Baghdad refuses to allow a UN inspection team to fly into 'Iraq

11 January 'Iraq moves surface-to-air missiles into the northern no-fly zone

17 January The United States attacks a military complex in southern Baghdad with Tomahawk missiles; the lobby of the al-Rashid hotel is destroyed and several people are killed

19 January 'Iraq agrees to allow the UN inspection team into Baghdad and announces a cease-fire against Allied planes

7 May The Clinton administration announces it has evidence that during George H. Bush's April visit to Kuwait, 'Iraqi agents had planned to assassinate him

15 May 'Iraq invalidates its ID25 note in an effort to combat rampant inflation

26 June The United States attacks intelligence headquarters in Baghdad in retaliation for the alleged plot to assassinate Bush in April; several civilians are killed, including well-known artist Laila al- Attar

5 July UN weapons inspectors leave 'Iraq after Baghdad refused to allow the team to install cameras at two missile testing sites; a second team withdraws within a week

19 July 'Iraq agrees to accept long-term weapons monitoring, although it claims that the UN agreed to offer concessions on other issues, including the lifting of sanctions

27 July A UN team installs cameras at one of the two missile sites

26 October The dinar is traded on the black market for $1 = ID105, the first time the value of the dinar falls below $1 = ID100

18–20 November Between 500 and 600 civilians protest in Umm Qasr against the new UN-demarcated border between 'Iraq and Kuwait, which moved Kuwait's border northward by several kilometers

26 November 'Iraq tells the UN that it will accept Resolution 715—long-term weapons monitoring—and requests that sanctions be lifted

1994
5 February In an attempt to halt the precipitous drop in the value of the 'Iraqi dinar, the regime gives state banks permission to buy/sell hard currency outside the official rate ($1 = ID0.3)

17 February The PUK and Islamic Movement of Kurdistan (IMK) sign an agreement to end fighting that has left 200 dead

10 March The Central Bank announces that it will issue an ID50 note; the ID25 note had been the highest denomination in circulation

14 April Two U.S. helicopters are shot down over northern 'Iraq by two U.S. F-15 fighter jets; 26 people are killed

25 April The Central Bank announces it will issue an ID100 note; the dinar is trading at $1 = ID300 on the black market

29 May Because of the continuing economic crisis, Saddam Husayn dismisses Ahmad Khudayir and names himself prime minister

5 June The KDP and PUK open talks to resolve the differences that have fueled a month of fighting, which has left 400 people dead

20–21 August The Foreign Ministers of Iran, Syria, and Turkey meet in Damascus to discuss the 'Iraqi situation; they reaffirm their commitment to 'Iraq's territorial integrity

6 September 'Iraq and Kuwait meet to discuss the fate of 600 Kuwaitis missing since the Gulf War

25 September The government cuts rations on essential food items, including flour, rice, sugar, and cooking oil, leading to a doubling of prices on these items

27 September Tariq 'Aziz meets with French foreign minister Alain Juppe at the UN, the first high-level contact between a Western coalition power and 'Iraq since the Gulf War

5 October Saddam demands the UN lift the sanctions against 'Iraq or 'Iraq will cease to comply with its monitoring activities; two Republican Guard units begin moving to the Kuwaiti border

9 October The United States deploys 36,000 troops and 51 combat planes to the Gulf; Britain and France also commit military forces as Western intelligence reports estimate that 80,000 'Iraqi troops have massed in the Basra area

11 October 'Iraq begins withdrawing its troops from the border area; the United States deploys an additional 100 combat planes to the Gulf

12 October An allied force, including U.S., British, French, and Gulf Cooperation Council (GCC) contingents, arrives in Kuwait

15 October The UN Security Council passes Resolution 949, which demands that 'Iraq withdraw its military forces to their previous positions and forbids it from using its military forces to threaten its neighbors or UN operations

10 November The National Assembly and the RCC recognize Kuwait within its new UN-defined borders

mid–November Food prices continue to skyrocket; a kilo of flour reaches ID450, and a carton of eggs sells for ID1,350

13 November Tariq 'Aziz delivers a letter to the UN stating 'Iraq's official recognition of Kuwait within its new borders

24 November The KDP and PUK sign a 14-point peace plan promising elections in May 1995

20 December Ekeus reports that 'Iraq is falling far short of full compliance with UN resolutions requiring disclosure of its biological and chemical weapons programs

20 March Turkey sends 35,000 troops into northern 'Iraq in pursuit of PKK guerrillas; the forces withdraw by 4 May

25 March Americans William Barloon and David Daliberti are sentenced to eight years in prison for illegally entering 'Iraq; the two men accidentally strayed across the border from Kuwait; they are released on 16 July

14 April The UN proposes a plan to allow 'Iraq to sell $2 billion worth of oil for humanitarian purposes; 'Iraq rejects the UN "oil-for-food" plan on 17 April

20 May   The Sunni Dulaimi clan riots in Ramadi after one of its members is executed for alleged participation in a coup plot; 30 people died and 100 were wounded

1 July   'Iraq admits it developed biological weapons in 1989–1990 but claims it has since destroyed them

8 August   Husayn Kamil and Saddam Kamil Hassan Majid and their wives, both daughters of Saddam, defect to Jordan, where they are granted political asylum; 15 other military officials defect with them

12 August   Husayn Kamil calls for the overthrow of Saddam

17 August   'Iraq offers the UN new information on its nuclear and biological programs, which it claims had been withheld by Husayn Kamil

22 August   Ekeus announces that 'Iraq admitted arming missiles with chemical and biological agents

11 October   Ekeus reports that 'Iraq continues to withhold information about its weapons programs and therefore did not meet the requirements for the lifting of UN sanctions

15 October   Saddam is reelected president for another seven-year term, with 99.96 percent of the vote

31 October   A bomb explodes at the headquarters of the INC in Salah al-Din, leaving 25 people dead

8 November   UN sanctions are renewed a day after Ekeus revealed that 'Iraq attempted to build a nonexplosive nuclear weapon

1996
18 January   'Iraq agrees to negotiate with the UN over the April 1995 oil-for-food plan

20 February   Husayn Kamil, his brother Saddam, and their families return to 'Iraq

23 February   Husayn and Saddam Kamil are divorced by their wives and then killed by relatives who accused the brothers of disgracing the family with their defections to Jordan in August 1995

20 May   The UN and 'Iraq agree to a plan that will allow 'Iraq to sell $1 billion of oil every six months; proceeds would be divided between humanitarian purchases, compensation to Kuwait, and payments to Kurdish areas

18 July   The UN approves 'Iraq's revised version of how it will distribute the proceeds from the oil-for-food plan; after additional changes, it is approved on 8 August

31 August Iraqi forces enter the Kurdish autonomous zone in response to a request for assistance by the KDP; the combined KDP–Iraqi forces capture Arbil

1 September The UN suspends the oil-for-food agreement in response to 'Iraq's involvement in the KDP–PUK fighting

3 September The United States hits 'Iraqi air defense systems with cruise missiles and extends the no-fly zone from the 32nd to the 33rd parallel in response to 'Iraq's movement into the Kurdish enclave

4 September The INC reports that 'Iraqi government forces arrested 1,500 people in Arbil

10 September The United States warns 'Iraq to stop rebuilding the air defense sites damaged by U.S. missile strikes or risk another attack

10 December Under the oil-for-food plan, 'Iraq begins exporting oil via its pipeline through Turkey

12 December Uday Husayn, Saddam's son, is wounded in an assassination attempt

27 December France withdraws from Operation Provide Comfort

1997
19 March First shipment of food under UN oil-for-food program is delivered

9 Apri An 'Iraqi airliner flies to Jedda in violation of UN sanctions

16 October 'Iraq threatens to end cooperation with UNSCOM if new sanctions are imposed

23 October UN Security Council resolves to ban international travel by 'Iraqi officials unless 'Iraq cooperates with UNSCOM

29 October 'Iraq orders US members of UNSCOM to leave in one week; UNSCOM suspends its monitoring activities

4 November 'Iraq extends the deadline for the expulsion of U.S. members of UNSCOM but refuses to allow teams with U.S. members to search sites; 'Iraq threatens to fire on U.S. U-2 surveillance planes used by UNSCOM

10 November Iraqi civilians move onto grounds of presidential palaces, which 'Iraq refuses to allow UNSCOM to search, to act as human shields against anticipated U.S. military strike

12 November UN Security Council unanimously votes for new sanctions, including a travel ban

13 November 'Iraq expels UNSCOM

21 November   After talks with UN, 'Iraq permits UNSCOM to resume its work

15 December   'Iraq informs UNSCOM that it can never inspect the presidential palace sites

22 December   UN Security Council calls 'Iraqi refusal to open presidential palace sites "unacceptable"

1998

12 January   'Iraq refuses to cooperate with UNSCOM team led by American Scott Ritter, whom it accuses of espionage

14 January   UN Security Council demands "full, immediate and unconditional" access to all sites

21 January   U.S. president Bill Clinton says that the United States might take military action against 'Iraq with or without UN approval

20 February   UN Security Council doubles to $5.2 billion the amount of oil 'Iraq can sell every six months under the oil-for-food program; some of the funds were made available for oil industry infrastructure repair

23 February   After months of tension, 'Iraq and UN secretary-general Kofi Annan sign a news weapons monitoring agreement

17 April   UNSCOM tells the UN Security Council it has made virtually no progress in last six months

3–4 June   UNSCOM briefs the UN Security Council: 'Iraq has continuously concealed its biological and chemical weapons programs

19 June   UN Security Council approves plan to let 'Iraq spend $300 million to upgrade its oil facilities so it can actually produce the $5.2 billion of oil it is allowed every six months

21 July   Dennis Halliday, in charge of oil-for-food program, resigns in opposition to the humanitarian costs of sanctions

5 August   'Iraq ends all cooperation with UNSCOM until it is restructured; UNSCOM suspends its works as of August 9

9 September   UN Security Council votes to suspend sanctions reviews until 'Iraq cooperates with UNSCOM

31 October   'Iraq states it is ending all cooperation with UNSCOM, including closing down long-term monitoring; UN Security Council condemns this stand unanimously on 5 November

14 November   The United States aborts an air strike against 'Iraq, recalling the planes in the air after 'Iraq gives the UN a letter stating it would resume cooperation with UNSCOM, albeit with conditions. The United States calls these conditions unacceptable

16 November   UNSCOM returns to Baghdad

22 November   Izzat Ibrahim escapes uninjured from an assassination attempt in Karbala

15 December   UNSCOM head Richard Butler complains to the UN Security Council about 'Iraq's continuing lack of cooperation

16 December   The United States and Britain undertake Operation Desert Fox, four days of air strikes against suspected weapons sites, Republican Guard facilities, and intelligence sites; the United States reports that fewer than half of the targets are severely damaged

19 December   'Iraq declares an end to cooperation with UNSCOM

28 December   'Iraq fires on U.S. aircraft in the no-fly zone, and the United Sta5tes retaliates against 'Iraqi radar targets; from this point on, such incidents continue on an almost daily basis into 2002

1999
6 January   The United States admits that UNSCOM provided it with intelligence

17 July   Saddam grants younger son Qusay power to act as president in an emergency

17 December   UN Security Council creates new weapons monitoring body, UN Monitoring, Verification, and Inspection Commission (UNMOVIC), and creates a schedule for lifting sanctions; 'Iraq rejects the new body, vowing to refuse any weapons inspections until sanctions are lifted

2000
26 January   UN Security Council appoints Hans Blix as head of UNMOVIC

3 February   Kurds in Sulaymaniyya hold first elections in eight years

11 February   'Iraq states that UNMOVIC will not be allowed into 'Iraq

15 February   Jutta Purghan, head of the World Food program in 'Iraq, resigns, apparently to protest the humanitarian costs of sanctions

22 September   A French plane flies into Baghdad without the permission of the UN Security Council; this begins a slew of flights from Russia, Jordan, Tunisia, Syria, and Turkey over the next several months in violation of sanctions

2001

13 January   Over 70 Americans fly to 'Iraq in violation of UN sanctions carrying medical supplies

20 February   British prime minister Tony Blair calls Saddam "probably the most dangerous ruler at the present time anywhere in the world"

6 March   UN announces 'Iraq is illegally adding surcharges to each barrel of oil its sells under the oil-for-food program and placing the proceeds in a non-UN-monitored account

26 November   U.S. president George W. Bush warns 'Iraq to accept weapons inspectors or it will become the next target in the war on terrorism

2002

29 January   U.S. president George W. Bush labels 'Iraq part of an "axis of evil" that includes Iran and North Korea

13 February   Iraq rejects the return of UN weapons inspectors

14 May   UN Security Council approves "smart sanctions"

8 September   The United States begins a massive military buildup in the Persian Gulf amid war rumors

12 September   U.S. president George W. Bush delivers a speech to the UN, calling on the UN to prove its relevance by enforcing its resolutions demanding that 'Iraq disarm

16 September   Iraq unconditionally accepts the return of UN weapons inspectors

16 October   Saddam wins a new seven-year term as president with 100 percent of the vote

20 October   Saddam declares an amnesty for nearly all prisoners in 'Iraq, virtually emptying out the jails

8 November   By a 15–0 vote, the UN Security Council passes UNR 1441, which establishes an enhanced weapons inspections regime

13 November   Iraq agrees to UNR 1441

25 November   UN weapons inspectors arrive in 'Iraq

7 December   Iraq delivers a 12,000-page report to the UN declaring it has no weapons of mass destruction; UN quickly discovers it is essentially the same data presented in 1997

19 December   The United States declares the incomplete 'Iraqi report constitutes a "material breach" of UNR 1441

2003
28 January   First full report on the progress of weapons inspections delivered to the UN Security Council: 'Iraq is cooperating, but there are gaps in its accounting for chemical and biological weapons

14 February   Chief UN weapons inspector Hans Blix tells the Security Council 'Iraq has not fully cooperated

24 February   The United States, United Kingdom, and Spain propose a new resolution that would allow for the use of force against 'Iraq for its material breaches of UN resolutions; the resolution never comes to a vote in the face of strong opposition from other Security Council members

1 March   The Turkish parliament rejects U.S. request to base 62,000 troops in Turkey; force would open a northern front in 'Iraq

16 March   The United States, United Kingdom, and Spain hold an emergency summit, giving the UN 24 hours to enforce its resolutions against 'Iraq or the United States will lead a war against 'Iraq

17 March   UN orders all staff out of 'Iraq

18 March   U.S. president George W. Bush gives Saddam and his sons 48 hours to leave Baghdad or face war with the United States

19 March   The United States attempts to "decapitate" the 'Iraqi leadership with a precision air strike; President Bush announces the war has started

9 April   Saddam's regime collapses as U.S. forces take control of Baghdad; several days of severe looting follow

10 April   Abd al-Majid al-Khui, the head of the al-Khui Foundation is stabbed to death in Najaf by an angry crowd

28 April   At least 13 'Iraqis at a demonstration are killed by U.S. forces, which claimed they had been fired upon first

3 May   L. Paul Bremer becomes the top U.S. civilian authority in Baghdad

9 May Ayatullah Muhammad Baqir al-Hakim, the head of SAIRI, returns from exile in Iran

13 July 'Iraqi Governing Council holds its first meeting

22 July Uday and Qusay Husayn are killed by U.S. forces in a firefight at their safehouse in Mawsil

7 August At least 11 people are killed in a bombing at the Jordanian embassy in Baghdad

19 August A car bomb at UN headquarters in Baghdad kills top UN official Sergio Vieira de Mello and at least 22 others

22–24 August Violence between Kurds and Turkomen in Kirkuk leaves at least a dozen people dead

29 August A car bomb at the Imam 'Ali mosque in Najaf kills Ayatullah Muhammad Baqir al-Hakim; scores of people are killed in the blast

1 September 'Iraqi Governing Council names the first post-Saddam cabinet

11 September U.S. troops accidentally kill 10 'Iraqi police officers in Fallujah

21 September 'Iraqi Finance Minister Kamil al-Kaylani announces sweeping economic changes

14 October Turkish Embassy in Baghdad bombed, wounding 10

15 October Security Council resolution 1551 supports creation of 'Iraqi cabinet and preliminary constitutional committee, makes UN resources available to 'Iraqi government upon request, and authorizes a multinational force under unified command

26 October 'Iraqi resistance fighters fire a rocket salvo at the Rashid hotel in Baghdad, narrowly missing Paul Wolfowitz, the U.S. deputy defense secretary; an American colonel is killed and 18 people wounded

27 October Unprecedented and coordinated bombing wave in Baghdad targets the International Committee of the Red Cross and police stations on first day of Ramadan, killing about 40 people and wounding 200

2 November 19 soldiers die, 20 wounded when their helicopter is shot down by a missile

Introduction

'Iraq, the land of Hammurabi and Harun al-Rashid, has played a long and unique role in the history of human civilization. The oldest civilization known to humankind evolved on the shores of its twin rivers, the Tigris and the Euphrates. The great cities of antiquity—Uruk, Ur, Akkad, Babylon, Basra, Mawsil, and Baghdad—were major centers of high culture and political power for much of the course of human history.

The fertile valleys and plains of this land, known to the Greeks as *Mesopotamia,* witnessed the dawn of human civilization. It is where humans invented writing, theoretical and applied science, and developed irrigated agriculture. It is where they developed the principles of the rotary shaft and the application of heat to metal. It is here where humans established written laws, developed literature and music, and began keeping historical records.

The term *'Iraq* remains somewhat shrouded in historical mist. References to it are made in pre-Islamic Arab history and poetry. Some say it is derived from the country's ancient name *Araqi,* meaning "on the land of the sun." The Republican regime established in 1958 used the sun as its symbol, in part because of the sun's connection with this ancient name. Others believe that *'Iraq* is the Arabized version of *Irah*, which in ancient Asiatic languages meant "sea coast" or "riverside." The great eighth-century Arab historian al-Farahidi said that 'Iraq was given this name because it lay on the banks of the twin rivers that extended to the sea. In the Middle Ages the term *al-'Iraq al-Arabi* was used to refer to the southern delta area of Mesopotamia.

LAND AND PEOPLE

Although the boundaries of modern 'Iraq were cobbled together by the British after World War I, there has always been a geographic 'Iraq known to the Arabs since early Islamic days as lying roughly within the area between Baghdad and the Shatt al Arab, corresponding to the limits of ancient Mesopotamia. 'Iraq's premodern frontiers with the Arabian Peninsula to the southwest and with Iran to the east might not have been precisely defined, but natural boundaries of mountains and deserts did exist. Throughout history there have been periods when 'Iraq existed as a distinct political entity, particularly during the Sumerian and Akkadian eras. There have also been periods when 'Iraq as a distinct substate formed either the core or an integral part of larger empires.

Present-day 'Iraq is located in the northern part of the Arabian Peninsula and is part of Southwest Asia. It falls in the northern temperate zone between latitudes 29.5–37.25 and longitudes 38.45–45.48. It is bounded on the north by Turkey, on the east by Iran, on the southwest by Jordan and Saudi Arabia, and on the south by Kuwait and the Gulf. 'Iraq's boundaries extend 318 kilometers with Turkey, 144 kilometers with Jordan, 603 kilometers with Syria, 1,094 kilometers with Iran, 193 kilometers with Kuwait, and 925 kilometers with Saudi Arabia. Its shallow coastline on the Gulf extends only about 60 kilometers from Ras Bisha to Umm Qasr. 'Iraq's nearly landlocked position has contributed to long-standing border disputes and two destructive wars with Iran and Kuwait, respectively, since 1980.

The 1980–1988 conflict with Iran centered primarily on the issue of control over the Shatt al-Arab, which forms at the confluence of the Tigris, the Euphrates, and the Karun Rivers. The war ended in 1988, but a full diplomatic resolution was not achieved until just prior to the outbreak of the 1990 Persian Gulf War, when both parties agreed to return to the 1975 Algiers Agreement that placed the frontier along the thalweg line, or deepest part of the channel. The dispute with Kuwait centered around 'Iraq's access to the Gulf, conflicting claims to the islands of Warba and Bubiyan, and ownership of the Rumaila oil fields that straddle the Kuwaiti–'Iraqi border. Immediately after its invasion of Kuwait in August 1990, 'Iraq revived its claim to the whole of Kuwait.

In 1984, 'Iraq's borders with Jordan were demarcated, with 'Iraq ceding 50 square kilometers to Jordan. An agreement on boundaries was also reached with Saudi Arabia that divided up the diamond-shaped neutral zone that previously existed between the two countries. The eastern boundary with Iran was inherited by modern 'Iraq from an agreement reached between Iran and the Ottoman Empire in 1913. The northern boundaries were fixed as a result of an agreement reached between Turkey and the British Mandatory authorities in 1927, after prolonged negotiations that started in 1919.

'Iraq has an area of 447,964 square kilometers. The length of the country from Zakho in the north to al-Fao in the south is approximately 1,174 kilometers, and its width between al-Rutba in the west and Khanaqin in the east is 498 kilometers. 'Iraq offers the shortest land route between Europe and Southeast Asia and thus has served as a bridge between Asia, Africa, and Europe and between the Indian Ocean and the Mediterranean.

'Iraq's flat desert lands to the southwest and the presence of numerous passes through the northern and eastern mountains have made the country vulnerable to foreign invasions and migrations since the dawn of history. Its population reflects this, composed of a diverse mosaic of ethnic and religious groups such as Turkomans, Kurds, Shi'i and Sunni Arabs, Assyrians, and Sabeans. 'Iraq's diversity and its location on the boundary of a cultural and geographic divide between the Arab and non-Arab worlds have created a feeling of vulnerability to external threats to its security and sovereignty. Turkey and Iran have historically dominated or sought to dominate the country; during the Ottoman and Safavid periods, 'Iraq was an arena for their battles. Neighboring countries and other outsiders have also sought to exploit 'Iraq's internal divisions for their own ends.

The Tigris and the Euphrates are gifts to 'Iraq in the same manner as the Nile is a gift to Egypt. These twin rivers rise in the mountains of Turkey. The Euphrates is the longer but less complex of the two. Its headwaters meet at Kharput in central Anatolia and cross into Syria, where it is joined by the Khabur River before it enters 'Iraq at Abu Kamal. The Euphrates is 2,300 kilometers long, of which 1,213 kilometers are within 'Iraq. The Euphrates joins the Tigris at Qurna to form the Shatt al-Arab, which itself is joined by the Karun River coming from Iran, after which it flows into the Gulf.

The Tigris, rising in the Anti-Taurus Mountains of Turkey, is the faster and more uncontrollable of the two rivers. It is 1,718 kilometers long, 1,418 kilometers of which are within 'Iraq. Unlike the Euphrates, it receives sizeable amounts of water from a number of tributaries, including the Eastern Khabur, the Greater and Lesser Zab, the Udhaym, and the Diyala. The Khabur tributary, which rises inside Turkey and meets the Tigris at Fish Khabur, is about 160 kilometers long but only a small part of its basin is inside 'Iraq. At 392 kilometers in length, the Greater Zab rises in the Hakkari mountains of Turkey and meets the Tigris near the historic Assyrian city of Nimrud. It is the largest tributary of the Tigris and is in turn fed by other smaller tributaries flowing out of 'Iraq's Kurdish mountains. The Lesser Zab's principal streams start in Iran and are fed by other streams in 'Iraq. It is 400 kilometers long, of which 250 kilometers are within 'Iraq, and it meets the Tigris at al-Sharqat. Al-Udhaym rises inside 'Iraq and flows for 150 kilometers before it meets the Tigris near the town of Balad. The Diyala's main waters rise in Iran. It is 386 kilometers long, of which 300 kilometers are within 'Iraq. Another important river, the Karun, flows into the Shatt al-Arab from Iran and joins it about 80 kilometers from where the Shatt flows into the Gulf.

The volume and flow of these rivers vary greatly with the seasons and have recently been affected by dams and other water projects undertaken in Turkey and Syria. Conflicting claims to the water supplies have been made by the three countries. Although three-quarters of the Tigris-Euphrates water system flows inside 'Iraq, over 75 percent of the country's measurable water supply comes from outside the country. Extensive water irrigation and drainage projects have been undertaken by various 'Iraqi governments, and a number of man-made canals and lakes have been created.

Over the years, a number of dams and barrages have been built on the Tigris and Euphrates Rivers to avoid flooding. Dams were built for economic purposes such as irrigation, electricity, and fisheries. Politically, the dams also strengthen the authority of the central government. Al-Qadissiyya Dam is 260 kilometers north of Haditha. The Samarra Dam diverts water from the Tigris to the Tharthar depression. It is one of the largest dams in the world, with a capacity of 85 million cubic meters. The Saddam Dam was built in recent years near Mawsil. The Dirbandikhan Dam is on the Diyala River and the Dukan Dam is on the Lesser Zab. Other water sources include the al-Tharthar and the 'Abu Dibs depressions, and 'al-Habbaniya, 'al-Razzaza, and Sawa Lakes.

The marshes are vast expanses of shallow waters that at their height once extended all the way from the banks of the Tigris to the Euphrates and were fed by streams from Iran as well. They cover large areas and are found mainly in the three southern governorates of Thi Qar, Maysan, and Basra. Prior to draining some of the marshes for irrigation, as well as for security reasons during and in the wake of the two Gulf wars, their area extended over 9,000 square kilometers. The marshes are believed to have originally been formed after the waters of the Gulf began to recede to the south. Large forests of papyrus grow in many areas, and reeds rise to heights between three and six meters. A variety of water birds live in the marshes permanently or migrate to the area in winter. The marsh Arabs traditionally build their homes, whose attractive designs are believed to date back to ancient Mesopotamia, from reeds and reed mattings. They navigate the waterways that honeycomb the area in boats made from reeds and bitumen. Water buffaloes are widely raised, and rice is grown on the banks of the marshes. The best-known marshes are the Hawr 'al-Hammar, the even larger Hawr 'al-Huwaiza, and the Hawr 'al-Shuwayja. Prior to the recent wars, the population of the marshes was estimated between 125,000 and 150,000 people.

'Iraq was once the world's largest producer and exporter of dates, providing over 75 percent of the world's supply. But the recent wars in the Gulf have destroyed many palm groves, and the sanctions against 'Iraq have greatly increased the local consumption of dates, which are highly nutritious. Prior to 1980 there were 30 million date trees in 'Iraq—17 million in the Shatt 'al-Arab area alone—each producing about 1,000 dates during its fertile years. There are over 530 different kinds of dates that vary in size, taste, texture, and calories. The fruit is used to produce date molasses and a strong alcoholic drink known as 'Araq. Its leaves are also used for weaving. 'Iraqis refer to the date palm as "the eternal plant" and "the tree of life."

In addition to the date palm, oak, maple, ginger, and hawthorn trees grow in 'Iraq. In the mountainous areas pine trees can be found. Fig, pear, orange, grape, and numerous other kinds of fruit trees and vines are grown in various parts of the country. Large forests that once existed in the northern provinces have been decimated over the centuries by indiscriminate cutting for fuel and charcoal, overgrazing, and, more recently, war. Nevertheless, several thousand square kilometers of forested areas continue to survive.

In ancient times 'Iraq was rich in wild and domesticated animals. Lions, tigers, leopards, and bears were quite common in ancient Mesopotamia. Lions were last seen in 'Iraq around the beginning of the twentieth century, but they have become extinct along with other species due to over hunting with modern rifles and the destruction of their natural habitat. The oryx, wild donkey, and ostrich have rarely been seen in recent decades, and bears, leopards, wolves, and hyenas survive in decreasing numbers. Other wild animals native to 'Iraq include jackals, hyenas, gazelles, snakes, bats, lizards, and otters. The main domesticated animals raised in 'Iraq are camels, sheep, goats, water buffaloes, donkeys, mules, and Arabian horses. Migratory birds as well as ibis, herons, hubaras, vultures, and buzzards live in various parts of 'Iraq. A variety of fresh water fish can be found, including carp, barbus, catfish, eels, and shad. The lower reaches of the rivers also have species that migrate from the Gulf to spawn or feed, including anchovies, garfish, gobies, sharks, stingrays, and sea bream.

'Iraq is located in the warmer part of the Northern Temperate Zone. The summer and winter seasons dominate the climate. Hot and dry summers usually last from May to October, with average temperatures ranging between 36 and 43 degrees centigrade (C) in the central and southern regions and may reach a daytime maximum of 49 degrees C. Temperatures in the hilly and mountainous northern areas are generally cooler, ranging on average from between 28 to 31 degrees C and 4 to12 degrees C. Humidity is generally low except in areas close to rivers, lakes, or marshes. Winter usually lasts from November to early March, with an average temperature of 6 degrees C. Winter nights are usually very cold, while winter days are mild. The northern areas have longer autumns and springs. Rains usually fall in winter and spring and are heavier in the mountainous areas. The desert, central, and southern areas receive an average of 150 millimeters of rain annually. In the northeast heavier rains fall, ranging between 400 and 600 millimeters annually, making it possible for crops to be grown without irrigation. The mountains of Kurdistan receive about 1,000 millimeters of rain annually. During winter heavy snows usually fall in the high mountains.

'Iraq is divided into three main regions: the plains, the highlands, and the desert. The plains area may be divided into lower and upper regions. Lower 'Iraq is an area largely composed of marshes and swamps. It starts at the Jabal Hamran ridge located between Baghdad and 'al-Ramadi and stretches to the southeast toward Iran. The Tigris and the Euphrates flow into this area, which is characterized by rich alluvial soil as well as abundant oil and water resources. Upper 'Iraq, made up of two valleys formed by the Euphrates and Tigris, consists of foothills and steppes. It extends from the Syrian and Turkish borders toward the Jabal Hamran in the southeast. The topography of the highlands region in the northeast is varied and includes river basins, plateaus, plains, and mountains.

The mountainous area rises slowly, with some peaks near the Turkish and Iranian borders reaching heights of 2,400 to 3,000 meters. The southern and western desert areas extend from the Kuwaiti and Saudi Arabian borders in the southeast to the borders with Jordan and Syria in the west. This desert region consists of wide stony plains with some sandy areas. There is a wide pattern of water courses that are dry most of the year but briefly carry rains during the winter. Some wells exist in the areas once inhabited by Bedouin tribes.

The overwhelming majority of 'Iraq's people are Muslim Arabs. Nevertheless, 'Iraq also has a large number of other ethnic and religious communities, including the predominantly Sunni Kurds, who comprise 18 to 20 percent of the population. The Arab Muslims are divided into two sectarian religious communities, the Shi'is and the Sunnis. The Shi'is are a slight majority in the country, forming an estimated 55 to 60 percent of the population. There are also small Christian minorities, forming about 3 to 4 percent of the population, which include the Chaldeans, the Assyrians, the Syrian Orthodox or Jacobites, the Syrian Catholics, and the Armenian Orthodox Christians. Among other small minorities are the Yazidis, or so-called devil worshippers; the pre-Christian Mandeans; and a small community of Jews. Although the Jewish population of 'Iraq numbered close to 150,000 in 1950, with most living in Baghdad, today there are less than 1,000. The rest have since immigrated to Israel. Other ethnic and religious minorities include the Sunni Muslim Turkumen of northern 'Iraq, 1 to 1.5 percent of the population, the Sabeans, the Shabak, the Sarliyya, and the 'Ali Ilahis or Al al-Haqq.

Despite the heterogeneous nature of 'Iraq's population, it is important to note that the main differences are not ethnic as much as they are differing linguistic, religious, and cultural traditions resulting from 'Iraq's historic role as a magnet for migrants and invaders since prerecorded times. Semitic, Indo-European, and Mediterranean strains have mixed in 'Iraq over the centuries, but the dominant characteristics are those of the Semitic peoples who migrated from the Syrian Desert and the Arabian Peninsula both before and after Islam. There is a prevailing Arab cultural identification, which is seen as an heir to the earlier Mesopotamian civilizations.

The people of ancient Mesopotamia spoke Sumerian, a language not related to any other known language. The Akkadians used Sumerian as a religious language, while various Akkadian dialects, particularly Babylonian and Assyrian, flourished in Mesopotamia for over 2,000 years until they were replaced by Aramaic. The latter continued to dominate until after the early days of the Arab conquest, when it was gradually replaced by Arabic. Today, Arabic is the dominant language, spoken by 80 percent of the population. The majority of 'Iraqi Kurds, however, speak Kurdish, an Indo-European language that has been influenced by Arabic, Armenian, Aramaic, and Persian. The Aramaic dialect of Syriac continues to be used in the liturgy of 'Iraqi Christians and Sabeans, and it is actually spoken by some Assyrians and Chaldeans. A Turkic dialect is spoken by some of the Turkumen community. The Iranian communities living in 'Iraq prior to their expulsion in the 1970s spoke Persian.

EARLY CIVILIZATIONS

'Iraq played a unique role in the evolution of human civilization, with the oldest known communities of human settlement having been located on the banks of its twin rivers. The great cities of antiquity—Uruk, Ur, Nineveh, Akkad, Ashur, and Babylon—along with their successors—Hatra (the city of the Sun) Baghdad, Kufa, Mawsil, and Basra—have been major centers of culture and power for much of history. Mesopotamia witnessed the dawn of human civilization over 100,000 years ago when Paleolithic age man gathered in the fertile Mesopotamian plain. The abundant waters of the Tigris and Euphrates provided game, vegetation, and fish for these nomadic hunter-gatherers. The spring floods and summer dry season made permanent life on the plain difficult. Most lived in the mountains and foothills of the valleys. Human skeletal remains believed to be 45,000 to 60,000 years old have been found in the Shanidar cave in northern 'Iraq. These early Neolithic people are known to have left flowers on the graves of their dead and to have moved their camps seasonally in order to hunt wild animals and collect seeds, fruits, nuts, and wild grains.

These ancient hunter-gatherers were also the first to domesticate wild animals in order to use them for a constant supply of wool, meat, milk, and hides. The sheep, the goat, and the dog are believed to have been domesticated even before the cultivation of cereal. The ox, the donkey, and later on the horse were also domesticated. The late Neolithic age farmers became metal age farmers and understood the intricate relationship between agriculture and animal husbandry.

These developments led in turn to the construction of dwellings made from clay and the establishment of small, settled communities. Evidence of the first small, primitive villages of clay structures, dating to around 5000 B.C., has been excavated at Jarmo and other places. Agriculture began to spread down the river valleys, and by the sixth century B.C., villages such as Hassuna and Tal al-Sawan began to flourish, ultimately leading to the emergence of towns with paved streets and defensive walls.

Archaeologists and historians generally agree that the Sumerians built one of the oldest, if not the oldest, human civilizations beginning in approximately 4500 B.C. Despite surviving written records, the precise origins of the Sumerians are still a subject of debate. One theory argues that they came from the eastern Gulf, while another says they came from Transcaucasia. Still other theories claim they came from Anatolia or Iran. Regardless of where they came from, it is clear that they were preceded by other peoples who contributed to the social and political complexity of the region by the time of the earliest Sumerians. Also, it is not known whether the Sumerians were one people or a group of peoples whose name was given to all the inhabitants of the region at the time.

The Sumerians' major accomplishment was the invention of and the ability to communicate in a common language. They affixed signs to words and used reeds to make symbols in clay, enabling them to communicate in writing and leading to the establishment of the cuneiform script. It is strongly believed that the Sumerian language adopted parts of other writing systems in its later development. The Sumerians used a decimal system based on the alternating progression of sixes and tens (e.g., the number 100 was written as 60 + 40), which may have been adopted from a non-Sumerian culture.

Another notable Sumerian contribution was their role in the fourth-millennium shift from small villages to an urban society, represented by their construction of cities such as Eridu, Uruk, and Kish. These cities contained immense granaries, temples, and shrines devoted to their deities, and palaces for their kings, all of which were constructed by skilled laborers and craftsmen. Towers, known as *ziggurats*, were constructed of mud bricks and inscribed with information concerning their origin in a number of Sumerian cities. Temples, rooms, and painted pottery have been found inside these monuments.

The Sumerians were originally farmers and boatmen and had brought with them or obtained from their neighbors obsidian flakes for cutting skin, meat, and grain; jade and other stone axes for woodcutting; bronze for weapons; and gold, turquoise, and other precious metals for ornamental use. They developed the pottery wheel, which eventually led to the invention of the wheeled cart. The Sumerians also used fire to bake clay. They built sailing vessels that were widely used in commerce with the Gulf region.

The Sumerians also made major contributions in the areas of geometry, astronomy, geography, medicine, literature, music, and language and developed the first written laws. They left early clay records of their religion; administrative, economic, educational, and legal systems; literature; and scientific achievements. During the Sumerian period there existed a federation of Mesopotamian city-states with a common culture. Their records show a succession of ruling dynasties as well as the existence of political divisions among them.

Around 2316 B.C., the Akkadians under their leader Sargon (r. 2334–2279 B.C.) defeated the confederation of Sumerian city-states. They gave the name *Akkad* to the area around Baghdad and consolidated their control over northern 'Iraq and southern Anatolia. The Akkadians treated the conquered Sumerians with respect and joined forces with them. Consequently, Sargon was able to further expand his empire and to move into Asia Minor, Syria, Lebanon, and Palestine. His grandson Naram-Sin established the first Mesopotamian empire. He and his grandfather described themselves as the kings of four quarters of the world. After Naram-Sin's death, the empire declined and was later defeated by the Guti mountain tribes advancing from the north.

A Sumerian-Akkadian coalition emerged to expel the Gutians in 2120 B.C. and then established a creative and prosperous state; the earliest law code belongs to this era. This coalition was first dominated by the city of Uruk and later on by the city of Ur under the leadership of Ur-Nammu, founder of the Third Dynasty of Ur (2113–2006 B.C.). Attacks by the Elamites from the east and the Amorites from the west brought about the fall of Ur in 2006 B.C. Mesopotamia splintered into a number of kingdoms.

A new and powerful state, Babylonia, arose in Mesopotamia around 2000 B.C. The Babylonians were a Semitic people from the Syrian Desert who, under the leadership of Hamurabi (1792–1750 B.C.), unified all of Mesopotamia. In addition to being a great conqueror, Hamurabi is recognized as an important lawgiver. Originally called the *dinat mesharum*, "the verdicts of the just order," Hamurabi's Code of Law entails over 300 paragraphs and imposed a uniform social order over a diverse area. Listed within the code were 280 judgments of civil and criminal law covering theft, libel, administrative corruption, murder, negligence, slavery, ransom, and matters. These judgments offer a broad outline of legal obligations that the members of a civilized community should follow. The Babylonian Empire dissolved within 150 years of Hamurabi's death; the Hittites sacked Babylon in 1595 B.C.

Little is known about the subsequent period, when the Kassites controlled Mesopotamia (1595–1157 B.C.). The language and culture of the Sumerians and Akkadians survived under Kassite rule as a unified literary tradition revived by the scribes and priests who came to play an increasingly influential role in society. The most famous of the Kassite kings, Kurigalzu II (1345–1324 B.C.), was a great builder who founded 'Aqar Quf, the ruins of which have been excavated west of Baghdad. During the late stages of the Kassite period, Assyria, whose capital Ashur was located roughly 80 kilometers south of present-day Mawsil, began its ascendancy. Assyria was dominated by the kingdom of Mitanni, a feudal state of Hurrian origin. During the reign of Ashur-Uballit (1365–1330 B.C.), Assyria took over the collapsing Mitannian kingdom and acquired parts of northeastern Mesopotamia. Wars waged by a succession of Assyrian kings such as Enlil-Nirari (1329–1320 B.C.), Adad-Nirari (1307–1275 B.C.), and Shalmaneser I (1274–1245 B.C.) greatly expanded the kingdom's territory. Tukulti-Ninurta (1244–1208 B.C.) turned his armies against the Kassites and united all of Mesopotamia under Assyrian rule. The Kassites regained control after several years but came under renewed attack in 1160 B.C. by the Elamites. In 1157 B.C., the Elamites occupied Babylon, bringing the Kassite dynasty to an end.

A new, powerful Assyrian empire arose under Adad-Nirari II (911–891 B.C.) that would control Mesopotamia for the next three centuries. The Assyrian Empire made its contributions in the areas of administration, sculpture, architecture, and literature, in addition to its establishment of a ruthlessly efficient military force. Shalmaneser III (858–824 B.C.) expanded the empire and developed the concept of greater Assyria. But after his death, Assyria's fortunes again ebbed as nearly a century of internal difficulties weakened the empire. Tiglat-Pilaser III (745–727 B.C.) revitalized Assyria, turning it into the greatest power in the Middle East. He established a permanent army to consolidate his conquests and made Nineveh the Assyrians' new capital, with Babylon as their second city. Under his rule, subject nations were required to pay heavy taxes to finance Assyria's military machine. However, this policy ultimately backfired as it caused many of the subject nations to revolt against Assyrian rule. Other major Assyrian kings include Sargon II (721–705 B.C.), under whom Assyria reached its greatest political cohesion, and his son Sennacharib (704–681 B.C.), a brilliant military leader who is known for his destruction of Babylon in 689 B.C. as well as for his construction and expansion of Assyrian water projects. Ashurbanipal (668–627 B.C.) is famed for his support of literary and artistic endeavors. He gathered a large library at his palace in Nineveh, which included translations from Sumerian, Akkadian, and Babylonian written on clay tablets. More than 24,000 of these tablets have since been discovered.

The decline of the Assyrian Empire was primarily due to external military defeats as well as to prolonged internal strife. Upon Ashurbanipal's death, near–civil war broke out between his twin sons, both of whom claimed the throne; Sin-Shar-Ishkun eventually succeeded his brother in 623 B.C. In the meantime, the Chaldean king Nabopolassar of Babylonia had begun a series of attacks against Assyria in 626 B.C. An alliance struck between the Babylonians and the Medes led to Sin-Shar-Ishkun's defeat and the destruction of Nineveh in 612 B.C., which marks the end of the Assyrian Empire.

Nabopolassar's son, Nebuchadnezzer II (605–562 B.C.) ventured into Syria and Palestine often from 605 B.C. to 594 B.C. He conquered Jerusalem in 586, after which he took the Jews in captivity to Babylon, but he failed in his attempted invasion of Egypt. Although his immense armies required vast amounts of resources, he rebuilt Babylon into the largest city in the world, surpassing Nineveh, and one of the most prosperous regions in western Asia. The canal system was expanded, which provided more arable land and increased commerce. Nebuchadrezzer displayed his riches through immense architectural projects. A third wall was built around Babylon to increase protection of the city, and additional wings were constructed in the palace to expand its size. The walls of these newly built wings and inner courts were decorated with glazed tile bas-reliefs. Other decorative additions included the Hanging Gardens of Babylon, known as one of the seven wonders of the ancient world. Nebuchadrezzer devoted much attention to the construction of temples; it is during his reign that the famous Tower of Babel is built.

The Chaldean kings who succeeded Nebuchadrezzer were less successful rulers plagued by internal strife. In 539 B.C., Chaldea was conquered by Cyrus the Great, the ruler of the Achamenid Persians. The priest of Marduk, realizing Babylonia's weakness, negotiated an agreement with Cyrus for a peaceful surrender. During the initial period of Achamenid rule, Babylonia saw very little change in its daily administration. Cambyses, the son of Cyrus, was appointed viceroy of Babylonia in 538 B.C. and established his headquarters in Sippar. His death in 522 B.C. marked the end of a peaceful, stable era in Babylonian history.

Under the Achamenid ruler Xerxes, the quality of life in Mesopotamia began to change. The inability of Babylonians to regain their autonomy led to the deterioration of the city. There was no ruler residing in this region who could assure the upkeep of the canals, temples, palaces, parks, and gardens. From the start of Xerxes reign in 486 B.C. until the time of Alexander the Great's conquest of the region, buildings crumbled and the irrigation canals filled with sand.

The battle of Gaugamela in 331 B.C. cleared a path for Alexander's army to confront Persian troops in Babylon. Initially it appeared that this meeting would degenerate into a bloody battle, but the Persian troops instead surrendered without a fight. The Babylonians viewed Alexander as their liberator from Xerxes. Babylon became one of two capitals in Alexander's vast empire. Alexander, like Cyrus before him, realized that a ruler of a huge empire must win the approval of his subjects to succeed. He repaired most of the temples and performed sacrifices to the local deity, Marduk.

For 175 years after Alexander's death in 323 B.C., the Macedonian Seleucid dynasty continued to rule in Babylon, which retained its economic and cultural leadership. Characteristics of Seleucid rule such as Greek culture, tolerance, and concern for development far outlasted the demise of the dynasty itself. It was during this period that Berosus, the priest of Marduk, founded a school for astronomy and wrote what became an authoritative history of Babylon, which was translated into Greek.

The decline of the Seleucids around 150 B.C. placed Babylon under the control of the Parthian Empire. This led to the decline of Babylonian culture, as did the ongoing struggle for control of Mesopotamia between the Persian and Roman Empires. The use of the cuneiform script ended during the period of Greek rule, with the last-known use of this writing system dated to 75 A.D. Babylon's decline was hastened by the shifting of trade routes away from it and by the emergence of Ctesiphon as the new capital of the Sassanid Empire. Beginning around 54 B.C., Mesopotamia experienced a new wave of foreign invasions when the Romans, and later their Byzantine successors, sought to assert their control of the region, turning it into an arena for numerous wars between themselves, on the one hand, and the Parthian and Sassanid Persian Empires, on the other. Large areas of the country were repeatedly lost and recaptured by both sides until the coming of the Arab Muslims.

Around the third century A.D., the Sassanids began to use as a proxy force in 'Iraq the Arab Tannukh tribe, led by the Lakhmid family, the established kings of Hira, a city located on the Euphrates. Hira became a prosperous center of trade and Arab culture. Similarly, the Byzantines at this time enlisted the services of the Arab

Ghassanid tribe, who were rivals of the Lakhmids, to govern Byzantine Syria as their vassals. During this period, Nestorian Christianity, considered a heresy by the dominant Greek Orthodox church in Constantinople, flourished in Mesopotamia and parts of Persia. The Lakhmids ruled in 'Iraq until the death of their last king, al-Numan III, following which the Sassanids asserted a system of direct rule that lasted from 602 until their later defeat by the advancing Muslim armies.

In 633, 'Iraq witnessed the first arrival of Muslim Arabs from the recently established Arab-Islamic state on the Arabian Peninsula, in the form of raiding forces led by the famous military leader Khalid Ibn al-Walid. After defeating the Sassanids with the help of local Arab tribes, such as the Taghlib, Bakr, and Tamim, Khalid's forces laid siege to the Lakhmid city of al-Hira until it agreed to pay tribute. Khalid, however, was then called to Syria in order to assist the Arab Muslim forces there whose attempt at conquering the area was faltering. After Khalid's departure, Al Muthana ibn Haritha was left in charge of the Arab Muslim–occupied parts of 'Iraq. Al-Muthana relied upon his tribe, the Bakr, along with other powerful Arab tribes, such as the Taghlib and the Tamim, who were then living in the flat plains of lower Mesopotamia. The successful advance of the Arab forces proceeded for three years until their defeat by the Sassanids at the battle of al-Jisr. This temporary setback, however, was followed by al-Muthana's victory over the Sassanids at Buwayb. In 637, Arab Muslim forces under Sa'd ibn Abi Waqqas won a historic victory against the Persian Sassanids at al-Qadissiya. After this, the Sassanid cities of Hira and Nineveh were easily captured. The Sassanids suffered a final defeat at Nahawand, near the Zagros Mountains, in 642, which opened the way into Persia proper.

The Arab Muslims set up major military camps at Basra, on the Shatt al-Arab, and Kufa, on the Euphrates. These encampments later developed into major cultural, economic, educational, and religious urban centers. Much of subsequent Islamic history has been to some extent or other affected by developments and events occurring in these two cities. For example, captive prisoners and other spoils of war from Arab military campaigns in Persia and beyond were funneled through these two cities. Later they became the cultural depositories of accumulated Islamic literary, philosophical, historical, and scientific knowledge. However, they also witnessed the rise of much religious and political discord among the different Muslim factions.

Following the murder of the third caliph, Uthman ibn Affan, 'Ali ibn Abu Talib was declared his successor. 'Ali, the cousin and son-in-law of the Prophet Muhammad, faced opposition from Mu'awiya, the governor of Damascus and a cousin of the murdered caliph. He was also opposed by a group of influential Meccans who were led by 'Aysha, the widow of the Prophet Muhammad. Consequently, 'Ali moved his capital from Madina to Kufa, away from the centers of opposition to his rule. He was able to defeat his Hijazi opponents at the Battle of the Camel in 656 but was unable to subdue Mu'awiya before his assassination at the hands of a Kharijite fanatic in 661.

After 'Ali's death, Mu'awiya, who had already asserted his control over Syria and Egypt, was proclaimed caliph in the Hijaz and moved the empire's capital to Damascus. While under Umayyad rule from Damascus, several unsuccessful revolts were raised in 'Iraq by 'Ali's descendants and their followers, generally known at this time as the Alids but later referred to as Shi'is. In the area around Basra, the Kharijites who had opposed both 'Ali and Mu'awiya also continued to oppose the Umayyad government in Damascus. The Umayyad governors in 'Iraq harshly suppressed the Shi'i and Kharijite revolts. After Mu'awiya's death, his son Yazid ascended to the position of caliph, which the Umayyads for the first time converted into a hereditary office.

'Ali's second son, Husayn, was subsequently invited by partisans of 'Ali based at Kufa to lead the Alid struggle against the Umayyads. Shortly after raising the Alid flag of revolt, Husayn and a small group of companions were met by a much larger Umayyad force near Karbala, where they were massacred on the 10th of Muharam, or 10 October 680. This martyrdom of Husayn continues to be commemorated annually by Shi'is during 'Ashura. The defeat of Husayn, however, did not end opposition to the Umayyads in 'Iraq. Several more revolts broke out, some seeking to avenge Husayn, but each time the Umayyads succeeded in reasserting their control.

In 694, the Umayyad caliph 'Abd al-Malik appointed al-Hajjaj ibn Yusuf as his governor in 'Iraq. A wily and ruthless leader, al-Hajjaj succeeded in restoring order and caliphal authority. He established the city of Wasit, located between Basra and Kufa, as his new capital. He also undertook important public works projects, such as widening and digging irrigation canals and draining sewers, in order to promote economic development. Trade and development in 'Iraq progressed during this period. Following the death of al-Hajjaj, the Shi'is, the Kharijites, and the Abbasids led several unsuccessful uprisings and revolts against the Umayyads.

The Abbasids, who were also descended from the Prophet Muhammad's tribe of Quraysh, eventually launched a successful campaign to overthrow the Umayyads and avenge the Alids. In 749, Abu al-Abbas al-Saffah declared himself caliph in Kufa and went on to defeat the Umayyads in 750, after which he established the Abbasid dynasty in 'Iraq. The second Abbasid caliph, al-Mansur, succeeded in crushing Shi'i opponents, who felt betrayed by the Abbasids, as well as other failed uprisings. He established the new capital city of Baghdad, which was also known as *Dar al-Salam*, or the City of Peace. Under the Abbasids, Baghdad became one of the world's largest and most important trading and cultural centers. The new rulers encouraged trade and supported economic growth. They established new irrigation projects and developed metallurgy, textile, and paper industries. The developments further encouraged increased trade with the Far East, Europe, Byzantium, and Africa. Banks were also established during Abbasid rule.

Under the fifth Abbasid caliph, Harun al-Rashid (786–809), and his son al-Mamun (813–833), Baghdad became a magnet for men of science, literature, and art. Al-Mamun encouraged tolerance, dialogue, and learning. He established Bayt al Hikma, the "House of Wisdom," as a research center for the translation and study of scientific, literary, and philosophical works from the Sanskrit, Persian, Greek, and Syriac languages into Arabic. He brought translators from throughout the empire and paid each one an amount of gold equivalent to the weight of the books he translated. Bayt al-Hikma included a rich library and facilities for the study of astronomy. Al-Mamun adopted the Mu'tazilite doctrine, which was influenced by Aristotle's logic and aimed at harmonizing rational reason with religious faith while proclaiming that men had free will to make their own decisions. These views were, however, considered heretical by a majority of Sunnis and Shi'is.

Al-Mamun faced a number of uprisings by Kharijites, Zaydi Shi'is, and one in particular by Babik al-Kharmi and his Persian followers. Under the Abbasids, the Persian converts to Islam gained much influence, with a number of the Abbasids marrying Persian women whose children later turned toward Persia and organized their administration along Sassanid lines. The early Abbasid period was a golden age for Persian officials such as the Barmacids, who rose to high positions in the empire. While most of these influential Persians became culturally Arabized and were strong converts to Islam, others remembered the glories of past Sassanid rule and assumed hostile attitudes toward the Sunni Arab elite's dominance of the empire. Some Persians had reverted to their pre-Islamic Zoroastrian religion, leading to the rise of the so-called Shu'ubiyyah ethnic division between Arab and non-Arab Muslims. These developments led to confrontations that may have carried religious and or ethic undertones, as in the caliph al-Mahdil's suppression of al-Zandaiqah and of Harun al-Rashid's destruction of the Barmacids. The rivalry between al-Rashid's two sons, al-Amin and al-Mamun, has itself often been simplistically portrayed as an ethnic conflict between the Arab and the Persian camps because Al-Amin's mother was Arab while al-Mamun's mother was Persian.

After his rise to power as caliph in 833, al-Mutasim suppressed the Persian revolts and continued al-Mamun's previous battles against the Byzantines. He moved the capital to Samarra and, most notably, began the fateful policy of relying on Turkish slaves, or *mamluks*, to form the caliphs' guards. The Turkish influence on state affairs continued to increase under al-Wathiq (842). His successor, Al-Mutuwakkil (846), sought to weaken Turkish influence through several measures but was ultimately killed by his own Turkish guards in 861. His three successors were also killed by their Turkish mamluks.

Southern 'Iraq was shaken by a number of major revolts during this period, including the al-Zanj revolt by black slaves in the marshes of southern 'Iraq. The Zanj revolt lasted for 15 years and revealed the widening socioeconomic gaps among various segments of the population. This revolt greatly weakened the empire, drained its resources, and devastated much of southern 'Iraq before it was crushed in 883. Yet another major revolt was that of the Carmathians headed by the Ismaili Shi'i Hamdan Qurmut, which began in 890 and led to major defeats for the Abbasids in large areas of 'Iraq and Syria. The Carmathians established a state of their own in Bahrain and helped create Shi'i states in the Yemen and North Africa, all of which became independent of the Abbasids. The North African, or Maghrib, Shi'is founded the Fatimid dynasty, which eventually expanded its influence into Sicily, Egypt, Syria, and the Arabian Peninsula.

These factors contributed to the growing decline of the Abbasid Empire, which was forced to grant autonomy to some of the local rulers, such as the Aghlabites in Tunis and the Hamdanids in Aleppo, who later established their own emirate in Mawsil during the tenth century. In the meantime, the caliph continued to lose influence to his Turkish military commanders. For example, in 908 a Turkish commander appointed as caliph the 13-year-old boy al-Muqtadir, who in turn gave the mamluk warrior the title *Amir al-'Umara*, or "commander of the commanders." From that time onward, the Turkish commanders used this title to gain increasing control over the state administration and succeeded in becoming the real rulers in all but name. This diminution of the caliph's role led to rivalry among the Turkish commanders and other elements of the army. A state of anarchy and economic decline ensued within 'Iraq, which had by this time become the sole remaining territorial possession of the Abbasid caliphate.

In 944, caliph al-Mustakfi sought to end the influence of the Turkish military commanders by gaining the help of the Buyids, a Shi'i Daylami family from Persia. With the title of Amir al-'Umara given to them by the caliph, the Buyids gathered the actual control of state affairs in their hands and succeeded in restoring state control over much of 'Iraq. The Buyids encouraged trade, reorganized the postal service, built roads, dug canals, and fertilized the soil. However, they also introduced the practice of giving tax-paying lands to their commanders instead of paying them salaries. This ultimately had the effect of depriving the government of important tax revenues, which contributed to the eventual collapse of the state administration.

When a former high Buyid official rose to power in Baghdad and claimed to rule in the name of the Fatimid dynasty, the Abbasid caliph was forced to call on Toghrul Beg, leader of the Sunni Seljuk Turks, for assistance. Toghrul Beg entered Baghdad in 1055 and was given the titles of both sultan and king of the Amirs of East and West by the Abbasid caliph whose ultimate, although purely cosmetic, authority the Seljuks agreed in exchange to recognize. The Seljuks later extended their authority to parts of Persia, Anatolia, Syria, and Palestine. They founded schools and colleges to provide both secular and religious education. The Seljuks were overthrown in 1193 when the Abbasid caliph sought the help of another Turkish tribe, the Khawarizm Shahs, against the Seljuk leader Toghrul III. After deposing the Seljuks from power, the Khawarizm Shahs far exceeded their predecessors' demands on the caliph—for example, eroding his position to the point of inserting the name of their leader in the Friday sermon rather than that of the caliph himself.

Although the decline of Abbasid power was gradual and was largely generated by internal strife, it was an external military force—namely, the Mongols under the command of Hulagu Khan, the grandson of Genghis Khan—which brought about the ultimate destruction and collapse of the Abbasid Empire. In 1258, Hulagu unleashed his forces on Baghdad, which surrendered after a siege of seven weeks. The Mongols killed the caliph along with hundreds of thousands of his subjects, and in a relatively short period of time, they destroyed what it had taken five centuries to build. 'Iraq, the heart of the former Islamic Empire, was unable for centuries to rebuild what the Mongols devastated.

Until 1339, 'Iraq remained under the control of the Il-Khans, an Iranian-based Mongol dynasty founded by Hulagu. In 1355, Hassan Buzurg established the Jalarrid dynasty, which ruled in Persia and upper 'Iraq despite a series of rebellions in Baghdad that they successfully suppressed. Arriving suddenly from his Central Asian stronghold of Samarkand, Timur the Tatar and his army on horseback sacked Baghdad twice, in 1393 and again in 1401. He shocked the city with his brutal slaughter of many of its inhabitants. After Timur and his horsemen had departed as suddenly as they had come, the Jalarrids regained Baghdad briefly, only to lose it once again to the Kara Koyunlu, a Turkic tribe that ruled Asia Minor until 1468. Kara Koyunlu rule was challenged by tribal, political, and religious movements. In 1468, the Ak Koyunlu, yet another Turkic tribe, came from Tabriz to Baghdad where they ruled until 1508, when 'Iraq came under the control of the rising Shi'i Safavid dynasty of Persia.

In 1514, the Ottoman Sultan Selim I defeated the Safavids at Chaldiran and captured huge areas of Iran, 'Iraq, and Anatolia. Baghdad at this time still remained under Safavid control. In 1534, the Ottomans finally captured Baghdad itself but lost it again to the Persian Shah Abbas in 1623, only to regain it 13 years later. After this, Baghdad remained in Ottoman hands until its 1917 capture by the British in the course of World War I. The Ottoman period witnessed some revival of the city and some improvement in living conditions, but did not bring about true stability.

The Ottomans were unable to exercise much effective political control over 'Iraq until 1831, when Sultan Mahmud II asserted his direct rule by ousting from power in Baghdad the local Georgian mamluk dynasty. Prior to this time, 'Iraq had been divided into three vilayets—Baghdad, Basra, and Mawsil—each of which had its own local autonomous administration that was directly linked to Istanbul. Under this system, the three governorates had virtually no interaction with each other. The central Ottoman government concerned itself mainly with the collection of taxes, for which purpose it appointed local tribal and family leaders as their governors over the three vilayets. The existence of what amounted to three separate miniature substates, each exercising its own direct relations with Istanbul, prevented any political or economic integration of 'Iraq from taking place during this time.

Sultan Mahmud's 1831 reforms of provincial government were initially successful, but his gains were soon lost by his successors who were either inept or disinclined toward reform. Most of the many nineteenth-century Ottoman attempts at administrative and social reforms failed. However, under the enlightened governorship of the Ottoman reformer Midhat Pasha, from 1869 to 1872, 'Iraq did see the founding of new primary, secondary, and military cadet schools, as well as the establishment of new town councils, the enforcement of new administrative laws, the setting up of the first printing press, the publication in 1869 of a newspaper called *al-Zawra*, and honest attempts at land reform intended to help peasant farmers assume ownership of the fields they worked.

During the nineteenth century, 'Iraq was increasingly drawn into the world economy and international politics. Because of 'Iraq's strategic location astride the land routes to India and Britain's other Asian colonies, the British became more and more interested in 'Iraqi affairs. English, French, and Italian agencies and consulates opened offices in Basra, while a British steamship company established a near monopoly on Tigris River boat traffic between Basra and Baghdad. As it grew more interested in 'Iraq's economic and strategic potential for its own needs, Britain became increasingly concerned with growing German influence over the Ottoman Empire in general and 'Iraq in particular. The Turkish-German alliance resulted in a newly modernized Ottoman army with a highly educated officer corps (which coincidentally happened to contain a large number of 'Iraqis) trained by German military instructors and detailed plans for a modern railroad line to be constructed from Berlin to Baghdad. Thus, when Turkey took the fateful step of belatedly entering World War I on the side of the Central Powers in November 1914, a British Expeditionary Force from India, which had been ready and waiting for just such an occasion, landed at the 'Iraqi port city of Basra, where it established a beach head that eventually evolved into a full occupation of the country by the end of the war.

As early as the Sykes-Picot Agreement of 1916, Britain had obtained tacit consent from its wartime allies to occupy 'Iraq. British control was formalized in April 1920 at the San Remo conference of Allied powers, which granted Britain a mandate to establish a civil administration for the governing of 'Iraq, which had been under a British military occupation and administration since the end of 1918. Despite this vote of approval by the other Great Powers, a number of serious constraints were put on Britain's ability to govern 'Iraq effectively.

The British were faced with conflicting demands by a variety of groups within 'Iraq. The tribal shaykhs, for example, wanted confirmation of legal titles of ownership to tribal lands that traditionally had belonged collectively to the tribe as a whole but that the shaykhs were now attempting to claim as their own personal property. The tribesmen and peasants, on the other hand, wanted relief and protection from the exploitation they were already suffering at the hands of the tribal shaykhs and landlords. Sedentary villagers wanted security from plundering raids by nomads. Kurdish nationalists wanted the Mawsil walayet and practically all of 'Iraq north of Baghdad to be cut off and established as a separate, independent or autonomous Kurdish state, while Arab nationalists wanted an independent, Arab-dominated 'Iraqi state with all of 'Iraq's traditional territory, including Mawsil, unified under the rule of Baghdad.

The British at times encouraged different groups to make conflicting demands as a part of the policy of divide and rule and to strengthen their negotiating position with the 'Iraqi government. Within Britain there was a growing demand to cut back the financing of any commitment to 'Iraq, and much of British public opinion was in support of a complete British evacuation of the country. This current of opinion became more pronounced after the 'Iraqi revolt of 1920, which cost the British nearly £40 million and 2,500 lives before it was quelled. Furthermore, the mandate system was intended to prepare the country for eventual independent self-governance, rather than to serve as a means of permanent colonization.

British officials were aware of the tremendous financial burden necessary to keep an army of occupation in 'Iraq that could maintain internal security in the face of increasingly militant 'Iraqi nationalism. They also understood that there could be no permanent colonial status for 'Iraq. However, they were faced with the dilemma of finding a ruler for 'Iraq who would be acceptable to the local population but who would also be willing to allow them to preserve an influential role in the affairs of the country, especially in its foreign relations. At the March 1921 Cairo Conference, their choice fell on the Hashimite Amir Faysal, son of Sharif Husayn of Makka, newly proclaimed king of the Hejaz, who had proclaimed his anti-Ottoman Arab Revolt in 1916 at British behest. Faysal had a loyal following among 'Iraqi officers who had served under his leadership in the Arab Revolt and in his short-lived administration of Syria during 1919–1920. His Hashimite lineage made him acceptable to both Sunni and Shi'i Muslims, while at the same time his reputation for a liberal attitude of religious tolerance toward non-Muslims was welcomed by 'Iraq's other minorities. In 1921, Faysal became the first of the three Hashimite kings to sit on the throne of 'Iraq until the monarchy's violent overthrow in the 1958 revolution.

The British structured the 'Iraqi political system so that they could maximize their position and influence, while minimizing their commitment of financial resources and manpower. Modeled on the British political system, 'Iraq had a constitution that provided for the separation of powers into executive, legislative, and judicial branches of government. However, the balance of power was far from equal, as the monarch was given the right to appoint the prime minister, to dismiss parliament, and to veto parliamentary legislation, in addition to serving in the role as commander in chief of the armed forces.

The problem for Faysal and his successors was how to manage the delicate balance between British interests and those of 'Iraqi public opinion, which were frequently at odds. A significant gain for 'Iraqi nationalists came in 1930, when the British signed a new treaty of alliance with 'Iraq that agreed to end the mandate as soon as 'Iraq was accepted into the League of Nations. The treaty gave Britain an indirect, rather than direct, role in governing 'Iraq through the use of British advisers by the 'Iraqi government and army, but it contained clauses maintaining British control over 'Iraq's foreign affairs in ways such as the continued presence of British military bases on 'Iraqi soil and the requirement that 'Iraq provide every possible assistance to Britain in time of war. When the League of Nations admitted 'Iraq as a member state in October 1932, the mandate was formally ended, and 'Iraq officially became an independent state, although, as noted earlier, without full sovereignty over its own foreign policy and continued domestic interference by British advisers looking over the shoulders of every cabinet member.

A major source of instability was the untimely death of King Faysal I in 1933. Respected by almost everyone, Faysal had the capability and personality necessary to manage the internal social cleavages as well as to carry out a delicate balancing act between the British and the nationalists. Faysal was succeeded by his son Ghazi, who was popular with the public but an inexperienced leader. It was during Ghazi's reign (1933–1939) that the distinctive pattern for future 'Iraqi politics first became evident.

In 1936, the first of five military coups in as many years was successfully executed by the chief army officers. It was aimed at the prime minister and his cabinet rather than the king, who took an ambivalent attitude toward the whole proceeding. One of the main consequences of this first coup was that the army officer corps became accustomed to the regular use of military force to bring about changes in government policies and personnel. The other parallel trend was the splintering of 'Iraq's civilian politicians into a pro-British bloc headed by Nuri al-Sa'id and an anti-British group whose leading spokesman later became Rashid 'Ali al-Kaylani. Because it was anti-British, in the years immediately preceding World War II and during the 1941 'Iraqi revolt, this latter group received covert and overt support from Nazi Germany.

In 1939, the death of King Ghazi in a car accident placed the four-year-old King Faysal II on the throne, with Ghazi's brother-in-law, 'Abd al-Ilah, as regent and actual ruler of the country. Two years later, in 1941, the opportunistic civilian politician Rashid 'Ali served as the frontman for a group of nationalist military officers in a coup that temporarily succeeded in ousting from power Prime Minister Nuri al-Sa'id and Regent 'Abd al-Ilah, both of whom fled the country. The Rashid 'Ali regime sought freedom from British influence, tried to strengthen ties with the Germans, and attempted to nullify terms of the 1930 Anglo–'Iraqi Treaty that required 'Iraq to provide Britain with assistance in time of war. The British responded by invading 'Iraq and returning the regent 'Abd al-Ilah and other pro-British politicians to power once again.

From 1941 to 1958, the power structure of 'Iraqi politics remained relatively stable, despite outbursts of public protests against the regime in 1948 and 1952. King Faysal II officially assumed full powers from his uncle 'Abd al-Ilah in 1953, upon the former's eighteenth birthday, but the young king never exercised any real authority.

Nuri al-Sa'id emerged as the most powerful political figure in 'Iraq. He served as prime minister thirteen times during this period, and even when he was not occupying a formal position, he maintained his strong influence on the decision-making process. Nuri had developed a consistently pro-Western attitude early in his political career that he maintained until his assassination during the 1958 revolution. Having begun his career as a military officer, in which role he served under Faysal I during the Arab Revolt, he placed great emphasis on discipline, loyalty, and integrity. Nuri favored close cooperation with the West because in his view, 'Iraq's external security and internal preservation of order needed the help of friendly foreign military forces. He relied heavily on Britain to provide assistance in this area. This policy, however, ultimately contributed to the monarchy's downfall in the face of growing Arab nationalist and anti-British feelings.

Nuri was a veteran Arab nationalist, but he had different views on the issue than many other nationalists who were in opposition to his rule. He favored political cooperation, but not necessarily immediate unity, with other Arab states. Nevertheless, in the 1940s, he was influential in the creation of the Arab League and advanced his own plans for political unification of the Fertile Crescent. In early 1958, he reacted to the Egyptian-Syrian creation of the United Arab Republic (UAR) by proclaiming a federal state between the two Hashimite monarchies of 'Iraq and Jordan, which he invited Kuwait to join as well. The union never had much of a chance for development, however, because of the popular revolution that overthrew the monarchy five months later.

A number of interrelated reasons explain why Nuri and the monarchy were overthrown. The monarchy had concentrated on investing the first of 'Iraq's new oil revenues on long-term economic development programs such as flood control, while the majority of the population remained impoverished, especially those in the rural regions. Although the programs would have ultimately benefited them, these people were convinced that they were being exploited for the benefit of the wealthy merchant and land-owning classes. Many 'Iraqi's would have been happier with their government if it had invested more in social welfare, education, and health services for its citizens.

The political institutions of the 'Iraqi monarchy offered little room for participation in policymaking on the part of any individuals outside the ruling circle, which was centered around Nuri and the regent, to the point that even the parliament was excluded. Although Nuri had allowed five political parties to organize shortly after World War II, he effectively restricted their activity and finally outlawed them in 1954. The suppression of political parties left little room for peaceful opposition to or participation in the political system. Any individual who did voice concern over the government's decrees was likely to be jailed. It was estimated that at one time Nuri had jailed 10,000 political prisoners.

Although electoral laws were reformed numerous times, the legislative process continued to be controlled by the prime minister and regent. The parliament, formed largely of tribal shaykhs, landlords, and military officers, did not represent the varied economic, religious, or class structure of society, nor was it an effective check on the executive power.

Nuri himself contributed to the collapse of the Hashimite kingdom. His penchant for public order justified in his mind the need for coercion. His harsh methods in dealing with the opposition and his links with Britain made him one of the most hated men in the country. Although these methods pale in comparison to the far more brutal repression used by successive regimes, even his friends were frustrated by his intransigence and stubborn personality.

He and the monarchy were vulnerable to the charge of being tools of imperialism. With nationalist sentiment growing, the population was uniformly anti-British in attitude. The cordial relationship maintained between the governments of 'Iraq and Britain widened the rift between Nuri and the people he ruled. Moreover, when the Baghdad Pact was signed in 1955, by 'Iraq, Pakistan, Turkey, Iran, and Britain (with the United States as an observer), Nuri was publicly criticized by a great many other Arab states. President Nasir of Egypt was so outraged that he called for the 'Iraqi people to overthrow their prime minister. Relations with the more radical Arab states were further strained when France and Britain sided with Israel and invaded Egypt in 1956.

Disaffection with the regime came to a head in 1958. On 14 July, troops under General 'Abd al-Karim Qasim and Colonel 'Abd al-Salam 'Arif moved on Baghdad, and a bloody revolution ensued that culminated with the massacre of the entire royal family and the killing or suicide of Nuri al-Sa'id. Following the overthrow of the monarchy, 'Iraq became a republic, and a ruling three-man Council of Sovereignty was established. Qasim became acting prime minister and minister of defense. 'Arif was given the positions of deputy prime minister and minister of interior.

The goals of the Free Officers included the following: republican government, parliamentary democracy, a limited policy of agrarian reform, and a neutralist foreign policy. Most of the officers also sought closer cooperation with other Arab countries, particularly the UAR, and a greater measure of social justice. The officers approved of the Kurds' demand for self-government within a decentralized framework but did not countenance autonomy, which they feared might lead to secession.

The July revolution, which was welcomed by a majority of the people, represented an important milestone in modern 'Iraqi history. On the domestic level, the revolution brought an end to the monarchy and introduced a number of important social and economic reforms. These included the Agrarian Reform law, which aimed at limiting the size of individual landholdings, distributing land to the peasants and ending the feudal structure in the rural area; the Personal Status Act, which gave women equal rights; the withdrawal from the Sterling Zone and the end of ties between the dinar and the British banks; the proclamation of Law No. 80, which returned to 'Iraqi control over 99.5 percent of the concessionary areas of the 'Iraqi Petroleum Company (IPC); the undertaking of industrial, agricultural, and housing projects; the offering of large-scale services in the areas of health, education, and social affairs; the granting of permission for political parties to resume normal activity; and the release of all political prisoners and amnesty to all exiles.

Externally, 'Iraq withdrew from the Baghdad Pact in August 1959, abrogated the 1954 military agreement with Britain, recognized the People's Republic of China, and resumed diplomatic relations with the Soviet Union, which was followed by the first commercial and cultural agreements between the two countries.

The July revolution did not, however, succeed in advancing Arab unity or in bringing prosperity and stability to 'Iraq. The period from 1958 to 1968 was marked by political chaos, instability, and violence. A struggle for power ensued between Qasim and 'Arif, in which the Arab nationalists, the 'Iraqi Communist Party (ICP), and the Kurdistan Democratic Party (KDP) were involved. Within two months of the revolution, Qasim dismissed and later arrested his deputy 'Arif, who had aligned himself with the Nasirists and Ba'thists, and declared his support for union with the UAR. Qasim, who had emerged from obscurity to lead the revolution, is widely believed to have been an 'Iraqi patriot with no particular ideology. He sought to maintain himself in power by attempting to balance the various political groups with divergent interests. Qasim's unwillingness to join the UAR alienated him from the Arab nationalists and led Qasim to place greater reliance on the ICP and the Kurds, whose leader, Mulla Mustafa al-Barzani, had been allowed to return after a twelve-year exile in the USSR. The ICP increased its power by infiltrating and seeking to control the various professional student, labor, and peasant organizations and through the Popular Resistance Militia, organized to protect the regime.

The growing influence of communists, Qasim's failure to join the UAR in March 1959, and his suppression of Arab nationalists led to a poorly planned and executed coup against him in Mawsil under the leadership of Colonel 'Abd al-Wahhab al-Shawaaf, one of the Free Officers and an ardent Arab nationalist. The revolt was crushed by the government with the help of the Communist

Party and Mulla Mustafa's Kurdish partisans. Both groups took part in the massacre of Arab nationalists during and following al-Shawaaf's revolt. The communists and their allies set up their own courts, which passed summary sentences against Pan-Arabists, officers of the division leading the uprising and Turkumans. Some of those condemned to death were hanged on lamp posts, and some of those assassinated were dragged in the streets. The Kurds and the communists also participated in the anti-Turkuman, Kirkuk massacres in July 1959. The negative ramifications of these events led Qasim to denounce communist activities and to encourage splits within the ICP. The ICP, however, continued to support Qasim since the only serious alternative to his rule was the Arab nationalists who favored unity with the UAR.

In the face of growing popular disenchantment, Qasim sought to widen his base of support by accelerating economic development programs and social reforms. These programs led nowhere because of mismanagement, agricultural setbacks, and the growing economic, political, and military cost of the Kurdish revolt, which further undermined the stability of the Qasim regime. The Kurdish leader Barzani claimed that Qasim had not fulfilled his promises for some form of autonomy. Having revolted in the 1930s and 1940s the Kurds again rebelled, and with military aid from the Soviets, they effectively engaged a large segment of the 'Iraqi army, greatly intensifying the divisions within the country.

Another problem facing Qasim was the 'Iraqi claim to Kuwait that he renewed in 1961 when Kuwait became independent. His position alienated virtually every Arab country and left 'Iraq hopelessly isolated. It also cost him domestic support that he could ill afford to lose when opponents claimed he should have moved militarily to take Kuwait.

In summary, Qasim fell from power because he was unable to produce the democratic society that he had promised. He antagonized both the West, by withdrawing from the Baghdad Pact, and the Arab nationalists, by refusing to join the United Arab Republic and by his cooperation with the communists while being sucked into a no-win war against the Kurdish rebels.

On 8 February 1963, Qasim was ousted in a coup led by the 'Iraqi Ba'th Party together with sympathetic army officers and pan-Arab groups. Colonel 'Abd al-Salam 'Arif was appointed president, and a Ba'thist general, Ahmad Hasan al-Bakr, became prime minister. A National Revolutionary Command Council was formed with the Ba'thists in control of all important positions, and the first action it took was to execute Qasim, followed by a purge of the army and government of all communists and their sympathizers. Although the new regime was devoted to Arab unity, a split occurred between moderate and radical Ba'thists and between them and the Nasirites who wanted unity with Egypt. Nine months later, President 'Arif staged his own coup following dissention in the ranks and established a new Revolutionary Command Council.

'Arif's views on Arab nationalism and unity with the UAR underwent a major transformation following his seizure of power. He became more interested in maintaining his control over the country than achieving unity with Egypt. 'Arif declared the Ba'th Party illegal and arrested most of its supporters, especially after an attack on his life on 5 September 1964. 'Arif adopted economic, political, social, and information policies similar to those adopted by Egypt, the object of which was to prepare the ground for uniting the two countries in 1966. However, as merger time approached, his enthusiasm for union appeared to wane, leading his Nasirite prime minister, General 'Arif 'Abd al-Razzaq, to try an unsuccessful coup to overthrow him. 'Arif also sought to weaken the influence of the military by appointing a civilian, 'Abd al-Rahman al-Bazzaz, as prime minister and by following a policy of neutralizing the various rival factions within the military. He also accepted a cease-fire proposed by Kurdish leader al-Barzani, to end the Kurdish war.

'Arif's tenure in office came to an end when he died in a helicopter crash in 1966. He was succeeded by his older brother, 'Abd al-Rahman 'Arif. Razzaq and other Nasirite supporters made an unsuccessful overthrow attempt against the new regime in June 1966. The military, however, became restive. Poor crops, unsuitable development policies, and the high cost of the newly resumed Kurdish rebellion promted al-Bazzaz to announce a twelve-point program to resolve the Kurdish problem. Al-Bazzaz offered amnesty to the rebels, recognition of Kurdish as an official language, and special educational, health, and municipal institutions for the Kurds. The military, which opposed Bazzaz's Kurdish policy and his attempt to seek improved ties with Turkey and Iran, brought pressure on President 'Arif to replace Bazzaz with Colonel Naji Talib. 'Iraq's participation in the 1967 war and its aftermath created a deep sense of humiliation and disenchantment with the regime. Cabinet reshuffles and public demonstrations in which Ba'thists played a major role paved the way for the bloodless overthrow of the government on 17 July 1968.

After the Ba'th fell from power in 1963, an internal conflict between radical leftists and nationalists virtually crippled the party. In 1964, Ahmad Hasan al-Bakr, an army officer highly respected by the party, was elected leader and put an end to internal dissension. By July 1968, for the second time since the overthrow of the monarchy in 1958, the Ba'thist military and civilian wings, in alliance with two influential non-Ba'thist officers, launched a bloodless and successful coup. Colonel 'Abd al-Rahman al-Dawud and Colonel 'Abd Razzaq al-Nayif, leaders of the military officers, offered to cooperate with the Ba'th Party in its seizure of power. The Ba'thists reluctantly accepted their help as a means to achieve power and to avoid any premature leaks of their plans, but they intended to drive them out at the earliest possible moment. It was agreed that al-Bakr, the Ba'th leader, would be president, al-Nayif prime minister, and the cabinet a coalition of various shades of opinion.

The coup, led by al-Bakr, took place on 17 July 1968. The first official step was the establishment of the Revolutionary Command Council (RCC), which assumed supreme authority. The Ba'th leaders had already decided to remove the Nayif-Dawud group. On 30 July 1968, a group of party activists led by Saddam Husayn, a rising civilian Ba'th leader, arrested Nayif. He agreed to resign, and Dawud, on a mission in Jordan, agreed to remain there.

Al-Bakr assumed the post of premier in addition to the presidency and presided over the RCC and the Regional Command. A temporary constitution, defining the regime as democratic and socialist, was issued on 21 September. All powers were entrusted to the RCC until the calling of a National Assembly. The party itself, already highly organized, began to place its members into various branches of the government and almost all national organizations.

Fearful of a repetition of its ouster from power in 1963 by the military, the party succeeded in maintaining control over the military and in preventing coups in a country where they had become almost routine. This goal was achieved by improving the power and raising the standard of the military and by maintaining constant surveillance over its activities. Moreover, the party moved quickly to retire or remove those officers who were known for their hostility to the Ba'th Party while seeking to infuse the military with younger officers who were recruited from the party militia and given crash training courses. Ba'thist units were established to instruct the military in Ba'thist teachings.

The Ba'thists succeeded in warding off attempted coups and serious threats to the regime. In 1973, the party faced its most serious threat. Colonel Nazim Kazzar, chief of security, plotted to kill al-Bakr and Saddam. When the attempt went awry, Kazzar fled toward the Iranian border with two hostages, Defense Minister Hammad Shihab and Interior Minister Sa'dun Ghaydan. Kazzar was eventually captured, but not before he killed Shihab and wounded Ghaydan. Kazzar and 34 others were executed.

The 'Iraqi leadership not only relied on harsh security measures to maintain its authority but moved to create the prerequisites for stable rule. From 1969 to 1972, it took several major actions to broaden its base of support by advancing the implementation of some of its economic and social goals. The Ba'th took the initiative to establish a united front with the ICP and the KDP, as well as smaller independent and nationalist political groups. On 15 November 1971, the National Action Charter was drafted and presented for discussion to the ICP, KDP, and other political groups and figures. The charter outlined some of the actions that should be taken, such as promulgation of a permanent constitution, granting autonomy to the Kurds, and implementation of programs aimed at raising the standard of living of the peasants and workers. In foreign affairs, the charter called for a policy that would support "Arab rights and interests" and for close cooperation with the socialist countries, because of their support for these "rights and interests."

The regime pursued a policy of trying to create the prerequisites for stability in the 1970s by nationalizing its oil wealth and using the increased prices to expand its development programs and to greatly improve the standard of living of its people, through various social, economic, educational, and health programs. New laws enacted benefited women, workers, and peasants. The government by the mid-1970s appeared as if it had begun to achieve some of its goals at home and a growing regional role abroad. Nevertheless, the regime continued to face opposition from Shi'i religious groups and Kurdish groups.

The Ba'thists were determined to resolve the Kurdish problem, which they saw as "the most difficult and complex problem facing the party and the revolution." The Kurds, an ancient people who inhabit the rugged mountainous areas of 'Iraq as well as parts of Iran, Turkey, and Syria, were latecomers to the concept of nationalism that had spread widely in the Middle East in the nineteenth and twentieth centuries. After World War I, some of their leaders waged a series of rebellions in Turkey and Iran to preserve their traditional tribal authority, for religious reasons or for Kurdish autonomy. They were harshly suppressed. Several tribal uprisings occurred in 'Iraq in the 1920s and 1930s, but most did not begin to take nationalist tones until the 1940s. These uprisings were quelled, and Barzani, leader of the last uprising, ended up in exile in the Soviet Union following the collapse of the Mahabad Kurdish Republic in Iran, to which he had offered his military support.

After the 1958 revolution, Qasim allowed Barzani to return. His policy of wooing the Kurds and his advocacy of Arab Kurdish partnership alienated the pan-Arabists without giving satisfaction to Kurdish demands. The growing influence and military independence of Barzani's forces aroused Qasim's suspicions. When Barzani refused to heed the government's orders, Qasim took a tough stand and accused the Kurdish movement of harboring "secessionist" designs backed by "imperialism" and led by a "reactionary" Kurdish clique. Barzani established de facto control in the most rugged mountain areas near the borders with Turkey and Iran and waged a tough guerrilla campaign against the government. The Kurdish rebellion continued, with occasional periods of cease-fires and negotiations, until the Ba'th returned to power.

Following the 1963 experience, the Ba'th had come to realize that the protracted conflict with the Kurds was weakening the regime internally and externally and that a solution had to be found. In 1969, the government adopted several measures aimed at encouraging Kurdish reconciliation. Saddam negotiated a settlement with Barzani and the KDP that was concluded in the Autonomy Law announced on 11 March 1970. This manifesto included 15 articles, including a recognition of the "Kurdish personality" of areas where the Kurds formed a majority and an admission that the 'Iraqi people consisted of two main nationalities, Arab and Kurdish. The Kurdish language was given official status, and Kurds were to be taken into the government in accordance with their numbers in the population. A Kurdish vice president and five Kurdish ministers were to be appointed to the government, an amnesty was granted to Kurdish rebels, and Kurdish detainees were to be released. The government also promised to help in the reconstruction of the North. In return, the Kurds promised to disband their army, the *pesh mergas*, and to hand over their heavy weapons and radio transmitters to the government. The manifesto offered the Kurds the opportunity to run their own local affairs through autonomous government administrations. The manifesto and the Autonomy Law of 1974, however, limited Kurdish control over natural resources and placed internal security, defense, and foreign affairs in the hands of the central government. The law made it clear that the 'Iraqi government considered the "Kurdistan area" and its people to be an indivisible part of 'Iraq.

The attempts to reconcile the Kurdish leadership's demands and aspirations with those of the Ba'thist government foundered over a number of issues. The underlying conflict was one between a central government anxious to preserve its political survival and territorial integrity and Kurdish leadership whose desire for autonomy was exploited by foreign interests that sought to promote the instability, if not the destruction, of the Ba'thist government.

Encouraged by promises of aid from the United States, Iran, and Israel and suspicious of Ba'thist goals following two attempts on his life, Barzani escalated his demands. He insisted that oil-rich Kirkuk be included in the Kurdish area and that the Kurds have the authority to maintain their own forces and establish contacts with foreign powers. When the negotiations failed, the government unilaterally implemented the manifesto in 1974 in the areas under its control.

Heavy fighting ensued in the spring, summer, and fall of 1974. The 'Iraqi armed forces, better trained and equipped than the Kurdish irregulars, made costly but steady advances against Barzani's men. These victories pressured Iran to increase its aid to Barzani. But when the limited increase proved insufficient, Iran was forced to consider either a substantial increase in military aid to Barzani or to do nothing, thereby allowing the 'Iraqis to win. The increasing gravity of the situation led to new mediation efforts by the leaders of Algeria, India, and Jordan. Saddam Husayn and the shah of Iran reached an agreement on 6 March 1975 in Algiers.

The Algiers Agreement resulted in gains for both sides. 'Iraq accepted Iranian demands that the Shatt al-Arab boundary run along the thalweg line and agreed to end its support of the religious, leftist, and ethnic opponents of the Shah. Iran in return withdrew its support for the Kurdish rebellion. Both sides thus avoided a costly conflict and established a strong front within OPEC for higher oil prices. Following the signing of the agreement, the 'Iraqi army was able to quell the Kurdish revolt within a matter of weeks. Barzani and some of his supporters and their families took refuge in Iran. Mulla Mustafa himself later went to the United States, where he died of cancer in 1979.

In the aftermath of the rebellion, Baghdad followed a policy that combined brutality with leniency in dealing with the Kurds. It began implementing major economic development programs in the area designed to win the Kurds by transforming the economic structure of the Kurdish area and to improve the living standards of the people by establishing hospitals, schools, anti-illiteracy centers, factories for light industry, and tourist centers. It undertook land reform programs and established cooperatives to weaken the traditional structure that provided the base of support for Barzani. At the same time, the government implemented tough security measures in which tens of thousands of Kurds were deported and resettled in the Arab areas of 'Iraq, or in other areas of 'Iraqi Kurdistan, leading to the creation of a strategic border zone stretching along the borders with Iran. The regime also benefited from intra-Kurdish divisions, particularly between Barzani and Jalal Talibani, and from the successful recruitment of tens of thousands of Kurdish fighters, mainly from tribes hostile to the Kurdish leaders.

As a result of the growing Kurdish opposition to the resettlement policy, some Kurdish groups began to take arms against the regime. Kurdish guerrilla activity, however, remained isolated and ineffective until the eruption of the war with Iran in 1980, when Iranian support and 'Iraqi preoccupation with the war led to an increase in antigovernment Kurdish activity.

In July 1979, Saddam Husayn formally assumed power from al-Bakr. Within two weeks, Saddam announced that he had uncovered a Syrian-backed plot to overthrow his regime, although the circumstances surrounding this plot are still unclear. Twenty-two top party and government leaders, including five RCC members, were executed for their roles. One theory is that the victims were opponents of Saddam's tough line toward Iran, while another theory states that these individuals objected to Saddam's assumption of the presidency. Regardless, it is obvious that Saddam's emergence at the head of the 'Iraqi state combined with Ayatollah Khumaini's leadership of a revolutionary government in Iran created an explosive situation.

As it entered the 1980s, 'Iraq appeared poised to establish itself as a regional power, if not a contender for leadership of the Arab world. The decades-long Kurdish insurrection had finally been extinguished; 'Iraq's oil wealth had fueled an expanding economy, complete with excellent educational and medical sectors and a growing middle class; and these socioeconomic achievements had in turn brought a measure of political stability. A moderation of its radical leanings had also allowed 'Iraq to enjoy closer ties with the Arab Gulf monarchies and to capitalize on Egypt's expulsion from the Arab League.

However, 'Iraq's promise was never fulfilled, as Saddam plunged the country into two ruinous wars that destroyed virtually all of the progress the Ba'thist regime had achieved. Driven by fears that the Ayatollah Khumaini's virulent brand of political Islam would infect 'Iraq's Shi'i population, as well as by calculations that Iran was desperately weak, Saddam ordered an invasion of Iran in September 1980. The 'Iraqi forces made quick initial progress, but by December, the war had bogged down into a war of attrition that would drag on for another eight years. Iraq largely fought a high-tech war, relying on its superior weaponry against the human wave attacks of the Iranians. This strategy implicitly recognized the still fragile nature of the Iraqi polity—the regime did not want to endanger itself by asking its largely Shi'i conscript army to take heavy casualties. The Shi'i did not in fact side with Iran, but the Kurds took this opportunity to renew their war against Baghdad with Iran's help.

In the early years of the war, Saddam's regime attempted to pretend that all was well; it continued to spend heavily on development projects and shielded the population of Baghdad as much as possible from higher prices or shortages of essential goods. But the strain of funding a "guns-and-butter" effort proved to be too much. 'Iraq spent most of its foreign reserves, and then began to borrow heavily from the Gulf kingdoms, the West, especially France, and the Soviet Union. 'Iraq's financial situation deteriorated further when the price of oil, already low thanks to a prolonged market glut, plummeted dramatically in the spring of 1986.

Desperate to end this draining war, Saddam employed a variety of tactics designed to force Iran to the bargaining table. In the so-called war of the cities, 'Iraq began lobbing missiles into Iranian population centers, to bring the war home to the Iranian people and thus pressure Tehran to agree to a cease-fire; it used its long-range bombers in an unsuccessful attempt to cut Iranian oil exports; it attacked ships in the Persian Gulf carrying Iranian-origin cargo, touching off the tanker war; and, eventually, it began to widely employ chemical weapons against Iranian forces and their 'Iraqi Kurdish allies. This last tactic, coupled with Iran's deepening isolation and economic crisis, turned the tide of the war in 'Iraq's favor, and during the final year of the fighting, 'Iraq captured huge quantities of Iranian equipment as its forces swept the battlefields. The two exhausted belligerents finally agreed to a cease-fire on 8 August 1988.

Despite the tremendous human, physical, and financial costs of the war, Saddam emerged in a relatively strong position. 'Iraq had stemmed the tide of revolutionary Iranian fervor, protecting not just the Gulf kingdoms but also Jordan, another conservative Arab monarchy. Baghdad expected gratitude and financial largesse for its efforts, and Saddam clearly hoped to stake his claim to leadership of the Arab world now that the Iranians were defeated. Western firms were eager to help 'Iraq in its reconstruction efforts, seeing Baghdad as a good credit risk because of its enormous oil reserves. Saddam's war-time reconciliations with Egypt and the United States consolidated 'Iraq's international and Arab backing. Once more, 'Iraq appeared to be a rising power.

Saddam's ambitions soon began to unravel. 'Iraq's financial position eroded steadily; oil revenues could not keep up with reconstruction costs, debt servicing, import of necessities such as foodstuffs, and Saddam's secret and expansive efforts to develop weapons of mass destruction. Kuwait and Saudi Arabia refused to offer 'Iraq the consideration to which Baghdad believed it was entitled, continuing to consider their wartime aid to 'Iraq as loans even as 'Iraq slid deeper into financial trouble. Kuwait earned even more of Saddam's ire by steadfastly rejecting 'Iraqi efforts to gain control of the islands of Warba and Bubiyan, which belonged to Kuwait but blocked 'Iraq's vital access to the Persian Gulf. 'Iraq's financial woes also began to erode its standing in the West, as various countries cut their loans and credits to Baghdad. Matters worsened in the spring of 1990 when 'Iraq was caught out in two separate arms scandals, one involving its attempt to purchase "nuclear triggers" and the other involving the seizure in some eight different European countries of components for an alleged 'Iraqi "supergun." The arms scandals, coupled with 'Iraq's dreadful human rights record and Saddam's threat to make Israel "burn with fire" if Israel attacked 'Iraq, all but dried up 'Iraq's access to Western credit.

By late May, ominous rumblings issued from Baghdad directed at Kuwait. In addition to Kuwait's other transgressions, the kingdom's overproduction of oil was driving down the market price, costing 'Iraq dearly at a time when other sources of funding were increasingly unavailable. Baghdad charged that Kuwait was conspiring with Western imperialism against 'Iraq and warned that such behavior amounted to an economic war against 'Iraq. The crisis deepened in July as 'Iraq mobilized tens of thousands of troops to its border with Kuwait in anticipation of an OPEC meeting to deal with overproduction issues. Although Kuwait and the other overproducers agreed to abide by their OPEC quotas, Kuwait again refused to lease Warba and Bubiyan to 'Iraq, despite the presence of nearly 100,000 'Iraqi soldiers on the border.

'Iraq invaded and occupied Kuwait on 1 August 1990, touching off another war even more devastating in its consequences than the conflict with Iran. The UN immediately imposed comprehensive economic sanctions against 'Iraq, and the United States quickly mobilized forces to protect Saudi Arabia. With 'Iraq in full control of Kuwait, and the United States building a thirty-state coalition to support military action to reverse that control, the situation moved inexorably toward war. The coalition forces, with the support of the UN, launched Operation Desert Storm on 17 January 1991, beginning with a six-week air campaign against 'Iraq and its forces inside Kuwait. The ground war began 24 February, lasting only 100 hours. 'Iraqi forces were routed, and retreating soldiers quickly touched off an uprising against the regime in southern 'Iraq.

Although the major coalition powers such as the United States and Britain had made no secret of their desire to see Saddam removed from power, the coalition forces did not intervene in the spreading civil war in 'Iraq. The UN mandate had authorized only the liberation of Kuwait, and any effort to enter the 'Iraqi civil war threatened to destroy the coalition as the Arab members in particular would not countenance the dismemberment or occupation of 'Iraq by Western forces. By early March, the uprising spread to 'Iraqi Kurdistan, which quickly liberated large swathes of the North from Baghdad's control. Saddam's regime fought desperately for its survival, and the Republican Guard units that had largely escaped Kuwait intact ruthlessly suppressed the uprising in the South before turning their attention to the Kurdish areas. Terrified of Saddam's revenge, the Kurds began a massive exodus from 'Iraq into Turkey and Kuwait in early April as the Republican Guard moved into the area. The uprisings were crushed by 3 April.

A major humanitarian crisis resulted from the failed 'Iraqi uprisings. Over a million Kurdish and Shi'i refugees crowded into Iran, Turkey, and Saudi Arabia, and the Kurdish refugees in particular needed massive assistance, suffering from hunger and exposure as they climbed through the mountains with little more than the clothes on their backs. With close to 1,000 refugees a day dying, and Turkey's political stability threatened by the influx of Kurds, the United States and its major coalition allies were forced to take action. On 16 April, the United States announced the creation of "safe havens" in northern 'Iraq, areas outside Baghdad's control, patrolled by Western planes, to which the Kurds could return.

The safe havens became one of several efforts used by the Western powers, especially the United States, to keep Saddam "in a box" over the next decade. Sanctions continued, to be lifted only when 'Iraq made a full accounting of and destroyed its weapons of mass destruction programs. UN arms inspectors supervised 'Iraq's progress through repeated and invasive inspections and subsequent monitoring activities. No-fly zones were established and periodically enlarged in both the north and south, until 'Iraqi planes could only operate in a narrow band of the country around Baghdad. Whenever 'Iraq challenged the no-fly zones, either by scrambling 'Iraqi planes into the zones or by subjecting Western planes patrolling the zones to antiaircraft fire, the Western powers would retaliate by bombing 'Iraqi radar and antiaircraft sites. The safe havens evolved into the Kurdish Autonomous Zone, where the United States sponsored elections in 1992. The Kurdish zone also became the headquarters of the 'Iraqi opposition, with significant funding and assistance from the United States. Turkey violated 'Iraq's territorial integrity with impunity, launching several large-scale incursions into the Kurdish areas in an effort to root out the Turkish Kurdish insurgent group, the Kurdistan Workers Party (PKK). In the numerous confrontations between the UN and 'Iraq, mainly over arms inspections and the continuation of the punishing sanctions, the United States and Britain did not hesitate to use force, including the 26 June 1993 U.S. raid on 'Iraqi intelligence headquarters in Baghdad, in retaliation for an alleged 'Iraqi plot to assassinate former president George H. Bush, and Operation Desert Fox, four days of bombing in December 1998 undertaken when 'Iraq suspended all cooperation with the UN arms inspectors. There were almost daily bombings of 'Iraq even after the formal end to Desert Fox. In the face of all these efforts to undermine him, Saddam tightly clung to power.

The consequences of Operation Desert Storm and a decade of sanctions dev-astated 'Iraqi society and its people. The 1990–91 war reduced 'Iraq, a highly urbanized and mechanized society, to the preindustrial age. Coalition bombing destroyed the electrical grid and large parts of 'Iraq's transportation and communications infrastructure. Further damage to housing and other buildings occurred during the uprisings; Basra, newly rebuilt after suffering tremendous damage during the Iran–'Iraq war, was again heavily hit. Sanctions prevented 'Iraq from repairing its oil facilities, and capacity continued to hover well below prewar levels. Inflation and unemployment were rampant, the dinar's value plunged, and the middle class joined the ranks of the newly poor as its members sold off their possessions to buy food. High levels of malnutrition plagued 'Iraq's children, and the country's once-vaunted medical system now staggered under the burden of caring for patients without adequate infrastructure, equipment, or medicines. Preventable diseases began killing large numbers of people, especially children and the elderly, and diseases previously unknown in 'Iraq, related to chronic and persistent malnutrition, appeared.

Recognizing the horrendous costs of the sanctions to ordinary 'Iraqis, the UN proposed an oil-for-food deal to Saddam's regime in February 1992 and again in April 1995 that would have allowed 'Iraq to sell a certain amount of oil to pay for food and other humanitarian imports. Both times Baghdad refused the plan as a violation of its sovereignty and called on the UN to lift the sanctions. Finally, the two sides reached an agreement in August 1996 whereby 'Iraq would be permitted to sell $1 billion of oil every six months, with the proceeds divided among humanitarian purchases, compensation to Kuwait, and payments to the Kurdish area. The UN controlled the revenues and approved all purchases requested by 'Iraq. Occasional adjustments raised the ceiling on the amount of oil 'Iraq was allowed to sell and changed the percentage distribution of the funds. Despite the oil-for-food program, the health of 'Iraq's population continued to suffer, and several high-ranking UN officials, including the director of the UN humanitarian office in Baghdad, resigned in protest at the human costs of the sanctions.

Humanitarian considerations contributed to a steady erosion of support for the sanctions, including among France and Russia, both Security Council members. The United States and Britain remained steadfast in refusing to consider lifting the sanctions until 'Iraq had proven it has met its disarmament obligations. 'Iraq's argument that it had done so was weakened by the regime's decades-long effort to conceal the true nature of its programs. 'Iraq claimed in 1991 that while it had chemical and ballistic missile programs, it did not have biological or nuclear programs. Several months later the regime admitted to attempts to produce enriched uranium and made additional disclosures about its nuclear and biological programs in August 1995, including that it had armed missiles with chemical and biological agents. Throughout their respective tenures, the heads of the UN arms inspection teams, Rolf Ekeus and Richard Butler, reported that 'Iraq systematically and consistently attempted to conceal information about its programs. The UN was unable to monitor 'Iraqi compliance from December 1998 until the resumption of inspections under Hans Blix in late 2002.

Almost immediately following the attacks of 11 September 2001, 'Iraq entered into the U.S. debate over where and how to respond to the terrorist attacks. A group of neoconservative intellectuals, from the Project for a New American Century, responded by sending a letter to President George W. Bush expressing their support in the wake of the attacks and advocating for a U.S.-led invasion of 'Iraq. Secretary of Defense Donald Rumsfeld raised the issue of 'Iraq at the Pentagon and at the first meeting of the principals after 11 September. Support for including 'Iraq in the United States' response to 9/11 was strongest in the Pentagon, with both Secretary Rumsfeld and Deputy Secretary of Defense Paul Wolfowitz endorsing the idea.

Immediate attempts to include 'Iraq in the response to the terrorist attacks on New York and Washington, D.C., centered on linking 'Iraq to al-Qaeda. Former director of the Central Intelligence Agency (CIA) James Woolsey was sent by Wolfowitz on an unofficial visit to Britain in an attempt to find evidence linking 'Iraq to al-Qaeda. Richard Perle, a neoconservative writer, gave several speeches and wrote articles detailing the possible link between Saddam Husayn and al-Qaeda. The revelation by a Czech government official that 9/11 hijacker Mohammad Atta had visited Prague to meet with an 'Iraqi intelligence officer provided fuel for this argument. This meeting is disputed by the CIA and the Federal Bureau of Investigation (FBI), which believe Atta was in the United States at the time of this meeting. Absent convincing evidence of collusion between 'Iraq and al-Qaeda, the focus turned to 'Iraq's weapons of mass destruction (WMD) programs and Saddam's continuing refusal to allow UN inspectors to return to 'Iraq.

Over the past few years 'Iraq had begun to open up a bit to the outside world and started steps to improve relations with its neighbors, other Gulf states, and the Arab world. 'Iraq's efforts were met by positive responses, leading to a slow erosion of the sanctions imposed on 'Iraq. Many countries appeared willing to enter into business with Baghdad in defiance of the UN sanctions, and several others allowed for the resumption of chartered regular flights to Baghdad. This raised concerns in the United States, leading to an attempt to repackage sanctions on 'Iraq by the new Bush administration. These "smart sanctions" were an attempt by the United States to garner international support for sanctions on 'Iraq by easing trade in nonmilitary goods, while maintaining strict sanctions on equipment with possible military applications.

During the late 1990s, the 'Iraqis shifted their strategy; instead of hunkering down as they had during most of the decade, the regime embraced a rapprochement strategy while maintaining a strong grip on power internally. Attempts at dialogue with the UN over the return of weapons inspectors remained hostage to policies pursued by the United States, Britain, and 'Iraq. 'Iraq continued to suffer as a result of sanctions, albeit with some improvement due to an increase in the amount of oil 'Iraq could sell under the oil-for-food program. The United States was also able to stop the 'Iraqi regime's practice of forcing oil companies to pay a surcharge on every barrel of oil sold, thus decreasing the amount of money available to the regime. Inflation continued to be a problem in 'Iraq, and the regime's efforts at stopping it were unsuccessful. Overall, though, 'Iraq was beginning to show some signs of life. Daily life in 'Iraq improved somewhat in the late 1990s as more food and goods become available. In 2002, the 'Iraqi government released a development plan aiming for 11 percent annual growth. The plan called for diversifying 'Iraq's economy and moving away from the country's historical dependence on oil revenues.

Although 'Iraq's economy was showing some signs of life, the country continued to face a general deterioration in health, water, sewage, housing, and electricity. 'Iraq's oil industry continues to suffer from a lack of investment in infrastructure and a lack of proper maintenance on its existing equipment. The OFP restrictions have prevented the rebuilding of vital sectors of 'Iraq's economy. In addition, many of 'Iraq's best and brightest are leaving the country, resulting in a significant brain drain and thus further complicating 'Iraq's efforts to rebuild.

The 'Iraqi regime remains centered around the person of Saddam Husayn, who exercises wide-ranging constitutional powers. Saddam and his regime withstood severe pressures over the past decade and are faced with severe test to their continual survival. Saddam undertook a number of initiatives to maintain his grip on power. In the fall of 2002, the regime orgainzed an election for another seven-year term for Saddam. Supposedly 99.9 percent of the 'Iraqi public voted to approve keeping him power. Saddam also continued to cultivate important constituencies in 'Iraq. Essential to survival had been the traditional elite that supported the regime, Izzat Ibrahim, Taha Yasin Ramadhan, Tariq 'Aziz, the loyalty of the Ba'th Party, various Sunni and Shi'i tribes, the Special Republican Guard, and the Republican Guard. In recent months efforts had been made to keep in contact with military and party officials, tribal leaders, and scientists, meeting with some of these groups on a regular basis. Consequently, there were few signs that the regime's power had weakened internally. Saddam was effective in using policies of co-option and intimidation to counter any challenges to his rule. He was able to infiltrate opposition groups, especially those with ties to the 'Iraqi military, and for a short period of time the country had begun to overcome instability. The death of Ayatollah Muhammad Al-Sadr, whose death was blamed on the regime, led to disturbances in a number of areas and some bombings. In 2001 and 2002, additional bombings by opposition groups took place in 'Iraq.

Despite the reported rivalry between Saddam's two sons, Qusay seemed to have greatly strengthened his position and emerged as Saddam's successor. In May 2001, Qusay was elected to the Regional Command of the Ba'th Party. Several younger members were elected along with Qusay, including Huda 'Ammash, a woman activist and the daughter of a rival to Saddam during the early 1970s. Qusay was also appointed deputy to Saddam in the secretariat of the Ba'th Party's Military Bureau. This was seen as a very powerful position, superior even to the minister of defense. In addition, Qusay headed the Republican Guard; supervised the National Security Council, which was composed of the ministers of defense and interior; and headed the intelligence and security agencies. In contrast to his older brother Uday, Qusay avoided public attention and maintained good relations with his staff. Reportedly that Qusay was behind the emergence of some new faces in the 'Iraqi regime who showed increased pragmatism and sophistication in dealing with mounting U.S. pressure. One was the new foreign minister, Naji Sabri, who was well known for his pragmatism and is considered a good communicator with the outside world. He comes from a Ba'thist family with a history of opposition within the party to Saddam Husayn. The emergence of General 'Amir al Sa'di, the scientific adviser to the president, as an effective interlocutor and spokesman for the regime was another example that the regime sought to have a new discourse, even if for only tactical reasons, and to gain greater support on the Arab and international levels.

Three new vice presidents were appointed, along with a new minister of the interior. Thiyab al-Ahmad replaced Muhammad Abd al-Razzaq, who was assigned to party work after being criticized in the National Assembly because of accusations of corruption, rising crime, smuggling, the forgery of passports, and corruption within the police ranks. However, the regime continued with its old policies of appointing relatives and trusted figures to high positions. As tensions continued to escalate with the United States in spring 2003, 'Iraq was divided into four regions, with loyal officers sent to administer each of these areas in case of an American attack. If communications were disrupted by an American attack, each area was authorized to act independently of central control.

The regime appeared to be moving to acquire greater popular support. This was reflected in a number of steps that were taken by the regime, including emphasizing the religious identity by supporting religious activities and programs and thus balancing the regime's secular image. This move occurred at a time when many citizens turned to religious values and practices in part because of the two Gulf wars, the effects of the sanctions, and the ongoing crisis facing the country. The 'Iraqi government banned the sale of liquor and closed nightclubs. Attempts were made to reach out to the Shi'i population by rebuilding holy shrines at Najaf and Karbala and through visits by Saddam to

Shi'i holy areas. The Shi'a were given increased freedom to commemorate 'Ashura, and 'Iraq's students were asked to memorize at least part of the Koran prior to graduation. 'Iraqi officers, in order to be promoted, had to study the Koran, and the Husayn regime undertook a project to build new mosques, including the biggest in the world. The regime also emphasized the need for tolerance between the Shi'i and Sunni communities. In addition, it highlighted its role as protector of 'Iraq's sovereignty and dignity and as a defender of the faith. Saddam appeared to win some support from 'Iraq's clergy. In the Shi'i holy center of Najaf, Ayaat Allah al-Sistani and al-Najafi, two of the highest-ranking Shi'i marja' issued fatwas forbidding contact with any foreigners who try to harm 'Iraq. Sunni Mufti Al-Muddariss issued a similar warning, and they all called for support of the regime.

Surprisingly, the regime did not jam the new U.S. Radio Sawa beaming into 'Iraq. Some Internet cafés were reopened, along with the rebuilding of universities and institutes destroyed during the Gulf War. As war loomed with Washington, the Internet cafés were closed. The government continued to implemented the oil-for-food program, which provided the average citizen with basic amounts of food including wheat, sugar, tea, and occasionally chicken. The government distribution of the food was given high marks by UN officials. Every month, the ration card gave everyone 2 kilograms of rice, 9 kilograms of flour, 5.1 kilograms of butter, 1 kilogram of dry beans, 1 kilogram of chickpeas, 1 kilogram of dry milk, 2 kilograms of sugar, 300 grams of tea, soap, and milk for infants. In addition, domestic food production of fruits, vegetables, dates, eggs, and meat also increased. Previously, 'Iraq relied on imports for some of these products.

The 'Iraqi opposition continued to be disunited and to suffer from conflict between its various groups. Efforts by Washington and London to hold meetings brought a semblance of unity to the opposition; however, it continues to suffer from structural problems and a lack of trust between members. The opposition was unable to come to an agreement on the possible future of 'Iraq after the removal of Saddam Husayn. Its lack of presence in 'Iraq continued to hamper its activities, while the ties of some opposition elements to external powers, regional or otherwise, undermined their credibility. Nevertheless, serious efforts were made to unify, especially under the group of four consisting of the Supreme Assembly for the Islamic Revolution in 'Iraq (SAIRI), the KDP, the Patriotic Union of Kurdistan (PUK), and Al-Wifaq.

In the Kurdish area of northern 'Iraq, the two leaders Mas'ud Barzani and Jalal Talabani met twice and eventually reached an agreement in 2003 to resolve their differences. They reunited the Kurdish parliament, deciding on 49 members for the PUK, 51 for the KDP, and 5 for the Assyrians. The two decided to unify their military forces, to hold parliamentary meetings, and to have new elections. The two main parties agreed to open offices in each other's territory, and they formed joint commissions to reach agreements in four areas. On federalism, they agreed that 'Iraq should be divided into two areas, one Arab and one Kurdish, with Arabic the official language of the whole union, but with Kurdish the official language of the Kurdish region. An agreement was also to be reached on matters of mutual security concern and to normalize relations between the PUK and the KDP. Finally, both sides agreed to adopt common positions on the possible war between the United States and 'Iraq. A new legal body was established in northern 'Iraq, while the Kurds continued to receive 13 percent of the revenues from the OFP. Nevertheless, the two sides failed to unite their forces. However, both Kurdish governments are functioning well into 2003. Hospitals and clinics had been established. Water and electric networks had been rebuilt along with roads, some small factories, and many of the destroyed villages. Newspapers, magazines, and satellite TV channels published and broadcast in Kurdish, Arabic, Syriac, and Turkish. Al-Jazeera and Abu Dhabi TV channels opened offices in the Kurdish region and were followed by some Western news networks.

The Kurds worried that all their progress was tenuous and that they were living on borrowed time. The current situation was quite an improvement over the pre-1991 years. A majority of Kurds wanted to see an end to the 'Iraqi regime, yet they were worried about change. The Kurds were concerned that they were being used in the struggle against 'Iraq and demanded guarantees from Washington and London for any kind of participation in the future. Turkish and Iranian designs on northern 'Iraq and their history of conflict with the Kurdish people also worry the Kurds.

Continued tensions remain with the remnants of the PKK now known as Kadek, still operating in Northern 'Iraq (estimated 5,000 fighters). Also, new Islamic groups had emerged as the third largest force in Kurdish politics. In the 1992 election, Kurdish Islamic groups won 6 percent in regional elections. As a result of cooperation between the PUK and the Islamic movements these groups gained limited control, the Islamic groups established Islamic rule. some of them received support from Saudi Arabia to build hospitals and mosques in their areas.

There were splits in the Islamic movements and new groups emerged. In 2001, new battles erupted between the PUK and some Kurdish Islamic groups. The Islamic Unity Movement and Hamas entered into violent confrontations with the PUK. These groups joined the Islamic Tawhid, a salafi or traditionalist movement, some of whose leaders fought in Afghanistan or Chechnya. This group, with about 500 fighters, attempted to establish Islamic rule in the few villages under its control. A new group, Jund al-Islam (Soldiers of Islam) emerged from the union of the Tawhid Front and the Soran group. This group is believed to have ties with al-Qaeda, and its leaders have accused the Kurdish secularist parties of blasphemy and refuse to cooperate with them. They also called for the unity of all Islamic groups, the rejection of any non-Islamic rule, destroyed some Kakai temples, and assassinated some moderate clergy and PUK opponents.

The Dictionary

– A –

'ABBADI, ARKAN AL-. A Shi'i (q.v.) tribal shaykh of the al-Bu Fatla tribe in the south, educated at the London School of Economics. A competent if not necessarily dynamic politician, he served as minister without portfolio between 1953 and 1954, and as minister of social affairs in 1954 and again between 1957 and 1958. He was the son-in-law of Jamil al-Midfa'i (q.v.).

'ABBUD, LINA (1975–). A women's rights advocate and a member of the 'Iraqi Governing Council (IGC) (q.v.), she is also a gynecologist. She had recently been invited to join the government by U.S. Administrator for 'Iraq Paul Bremer.

'ABD AL-MALIK IBN MARWAN. Umayyad caliph (q.v.), r. 685–705. *See also* AL-HAJJAJ BIN YUSUF.

ABIZAID, JOHN. U.S. Army general who was appointed on 7 July 2003 as commander (CINC) of U.S. Central Command (CENTCOM), the section of the U.S. Department of Defense in charge of military operations and personnel in 'Iraq. Prior to his appointment as CENTCOM CINC, General Abizaid was the deputy commander of Operation Iraqi Freedom. During the 1990–1991 Gulf War, he was deployed to northern 'Iraq. In his civilian studies, he earned an M.A. in area studies at Harvard University and was an Olmstead Scholar at the University of Jordan in Amman.

ABU. Arabic term that means "the father of." It is an honorable title in 'Iraq as well as in other parts of the Arab world to be called the father of one's first son. It is generally used by close acquaintances.

'ABU-DULAMA (?–778). An Abyssinian slave who was famed for his wit, amusing stories, knowledge of literature (q.v.), and poetic talents.

AFLAQ, MICHEL (1910–1989). One of the most influential Arab nationalists, theoreticians, and writers of modern times. Along with Salah al-Din al-Bitar, Aflaq cofounded the Arab Ba'th Party (q.v.) in 1947, which despite its waning appeal and its failure to achieve its Arab unionist objectives, continued to provide legitimacy for the Ba'thist regimes in Baghdad (q.v.) and Damascus for decades. Aflaq was born to an Arab Christian (q.v.) family from Damascus and grew up at a time when the Arab world was experiencing intense nationalist activity and struggling for independence and unity. His early years greatly influenced his intellectual and political outlook. Aflaq, like many of his generation, was greatly disappointed by the post–World War I colonial settlements, which frustrated nationalist aspirations to unite the Arab East and placed much of the Arab world under colonial rule.

After completing secondary study in Syria, Aflaq and Bitar attended the Sorbonne University in Paris. Upon their return to Syria, they became high school teachers and began their political activities by organizing a group called "Youth for Arab Revival," which later came to be known as *al-Ba'th al-'Arabi*, or the Arab Renaissance. They organized support for Rashid 'Ali al-Kaylani's (q.v.) anti-British government in 'Iraq in 1941 and for the Palestinian nationalists opposed to British and Zionist policies and activities. In 1947, the Ba'th Party was established. Its main goals were the achievements of Arab unity, freedom, and a mild form of socialism. In 1953, Akram al-Hawrani and his Socialist Party joined, and the party name changed to the Arab Ba'th Socialist Party.

Aflaq saw his movement as the means to reawaken the "Arab Nations" through the inculcation of new values and the regeneration of the Arab individual. He blamed the traditional political elite and the colonial powers for many of the ills facing Arab society at the time, and he called for the radical transformation of Arab society by overcoming backwardness and injustice and struggling to achieve unity and independence. He advocated Arab nationalism as a unifying idea and emphasized the importance of language, culture, and the Islamic message and experience as major unifying elements. Nationhood was defined by the commonality of language, history, culture, and "message." It was both the substance and vehicle of history, literature (q.v.), and religion. The Arabic language for Aflaq provided for unity of thought and culture. He also favored democratic change, which proved to be elusive when the party came to power.

Jamal Abd al-Nasir's pan-Arab message appealed to Aflaq's hopes for Arab unity. Aflaq supported the union of Egypt and Syria in the United Arab Republic in 1958. The political problems that resulted in Syria from this union greatly disillusioned some Ba'thists and led to a deep split between military and civilian Ba'thists. Aflaq's sharp disagreement with military Ba'thists forced him to flee to Syria. He later went to Lebanon and then to Europe and South America after he was sentenced to death by the new Syrian Ba'th regime in 1966. His absence from the Arab world lasted until the Ba'th Party returned to power in 'Iraq in 1968. Aflaq was invited to 'Iraq, where he later served as general secretary of the Ba'th National Command (q.v.), although he had little say in day-to-day politics. His presence in 'Iraq gave the 'Iraqi Ba'th prestige and some rhetorical ammunition in its feud with the Syrian Ba'th over legitimacy. Aflaq continued to play a role as a teacher and theoretician of Ba'thist ideas until his death. He also wrote several novels and plays that celebrate Arabic literary themes and style.

AGHA, TAWFIQ MAHMUD (1867–1950). Kurdish writer and poet, also known as Pira Mird. His grandfather was minister under the last Baban prince. He received a religious education in Sulaymaniyyah and graduated from the Law College in Istanbul. He published a Turkish-language magazine, *Rasmali Kitab*, for four years. Pira Mird was one of the founders of the Kurdish Society for Cooperation, Progress, and Advancement and in charge of its magazine. He later became the mayor of the city of Amasiya. Pira Mird returned to 'Iraq in 1924 and devoted himself to journalism and Kurdish literature (q.v.). He published a weekly called *Jayan* (Life), from 1924 to –1950, which played a major role in advancing the Kurdish language.

AGRICULTURE. 'Iraq's agricultural sector has been a source of continuing disappointment to its revolutionary regimes. The country's primary economic activity under the monarchy, agriculture's contribution to gross domestic product (GDP) has steadily declined for over four decades. In 1960, agriculture accounted for 17 percent of GDP; in 1976, it accounted for 8.4 percent; and by 1989, agriculture contributed only 5.1 percent of GDP.

'Iraq's agricultural difficulties are both natural and man-made. Much of 'Iraq's cultivable land is affected by high levels of salinity. A variety of man-made problems, including incomplete attempts at land reform, the imposition of inefficient socialist forms of agricultural organization, and the UN sanctions (q.v.), have contributed to the sector's poor performance. The huge rural-urban migration 'Iraq witnessed beginning in the 1960s reduced the pool of agricultural laborers. During the 1990s, agriculture was badly neglected. The government devoted few resources to the sector, and the sanctions regime meant machinery went unrepaired or unreplaced and important inputs were difficult to import, including fertilizer, plant parts, high-quality seeds, animal vaccines, and pesticides.

Only 12 percent of 'Iraq's land is arable; one-third of its cultivable land is rain fed, and the other two-thirds is irrigated. A major problem is the high level of salt found in irrigated lands, the result of inadequate drainage. Roughly two-thirds of 'Iraq's irrigated land is affected by high salinity. By the early 1970s, 20 to 30 percent of irrigated land had been abandoned because of this problem, prompting the Ba'thist regime to embark on an expensive campaign of land reclamation.

'Iraq's primary crops are wheat, barley, rice, sugar beets, tomatoes, vegetables, and cotton. Winter crops—primarily wheat and barley—are grown in the northern, central, and southern districts, and summer crops—rice, dates, and cotton—are cultivated in the central and southern districts only because of inadequate levels of rainfall in the north. Wheat is produced mainly in the north and east of 'Iraq. Barley is mainly produced in the northern districts of Mawsil, Arbil, and Kirkuk (qq.v.), and the mid-Tigris–Euphrates (qq.v.) region. There has been a steady growth in the production and yields of barley because of its greater resistance to salinity, even while the percentage of land devoted to barley cultivation has fallen. Rice is a summer crop, grown in Amarah district and along the lower Euphrates. The area of cultivation, yields, and production of rice have all declined considerably. Dates are 'Iraq's most important commercial crop, followed by cotton. 'Iraq once produced 80 percent of the world's dates. Fighting during the Iran–'Iraq war (q.v.) destroyed many of 'Iraq's date groves, which line the Shatt al-Arab (q.v.) and reach inland as far as two kilometers. The number of date palms fell from 30 million in the 1960s to fewer than 13 million in 1985. 'Iraq has some 130 varieties of dates, but the Halawi, Sayir, and Zahidi are the most widely grown. Dates were promoted in 'Iraq as a sugar substitute to help alleviate the impact of the sanctions. Sheep, goats, and cattle are the main farm animals in 'Iraq. There are also significant numbers of water buffalo, camels, horses, mules, and donkeys.

The first major attempt at land reform took place under the Qasim (q.v.) regime. Influenced by Egypt's land reform law, the regime passed the Agrarian Reform Law (Law 30 of 1958) in September 1958. Under Law 30, holdings were restricted to 625 acres of irrigated land and 1,250 acres of rain-fed land. The expropriated land was to be distributed to the peasants in lots of 20 to 40 acres of irrigated land and 40 to 80 acres of rain-fed land. Land would be expropriated and distributed over a five-year period, and compensation was provided for. Peasants paid for the land and were required to join cooperatives, which were supposed to provide the inputs and services previously supplied by the landlord, such as seeds, credit, irrigation, and storage, transport, and marketing facilities. Agricultural productivity dropped sharply following the implementation of Law 30 and never fully recovered. Because the Qasim and later the 'Arif regimes (q.v.) lacked the trained administrators required to oversee the expropriation and distribution process, land reform was never completed. Between 1958 and 1963, 2.8 million acres of land were expropriated; however, only a third of the land was distributed to roughly 55,000 beneficiaries. The Ministry of Agrarian Reform thus became 'Iraq's largest landholder. Under Qasim, the ministry would lease sequestered land; an amendment to Law 30 during the 'Arif regimes allowed landlords the continued use of sequestered land until the government was able to distribute it.

The inability of cooperatives to play the role traditionally filled by the landlord also hurt productivity. The government lacked skilled personnel to staff the cooperatives, and the peasants were basically uninterested in and suspicious of cooperatives. Cooperatives were supposed to supply peasants with the necessary inputs and services, but by 1968, only 443 cooperatives had been formed when nearly double that number were required.

Following its 1968 seizure of power, the Ba'th Party (q.v.) continued the process of agrarian reform in keeping with its socialist doctrines. Demonstrating the importance the Ba'th placed on implementing socialism in the agricultural sector, it vested primary responsibility for agrarian reform in a party organization, the Higher Agricultural Council (HAC), and not with the Ministry for Agriculture and Agrarian Reform. Established in 1980, the HAC had 14 members, most of whom were Ba'thists, and was headed by 'Izzat Ibrahim al-Duri (q.v.), an influential party member from Tikrit. The HAC focused its efforts on the establishment of collective farms.

The Ba'th regime passed a new land reform law in 1970. Under Law 117, the ceilings on landholdings were lowered, and the basic categories of irrigated and rain-fed land were broken down into 11 subcategories. Individuals could hold 25 to 375 acres of irrigated land and 620 to 1,240 acres of rain-fed land, depending on the subcategory of the land being distributed. Membership in a cooperative was still required of beneficiaries, but after 1975, peasants no longer had to pay for the land they received. The new law did not provide compensation for expropriated land.

The same problems plagued the Ba'th's attempts at agrarian reform that had damaged earlier efforts. The lack of trained personnel slowed the distribution process, forcing farmers to lease land from the Ministry of Agriculture and Agrarian Reform, which controlled millions of acres of sequestered land. Between 1958 and 1975, 6.3 million acres were expropriated; 2.6 million acres under Law 30 and 3.7 million acres under Law 117. During the same period, 3.7 million acres were distributed to 157,862 beneficiaries. The government also established collective and state farms and hoped to eventually transform cooperatives into collectives. (Peasants possessed usufruct rights in cooperatives, and as members of collectives, they received tiny individual plots for their homes and private gardens. State farms were modeled along Soviet lines and were responsible for supplying cooperatives with inputs or for the production and processing of a single crop.) By 1979, nearly 2,000 cooperatives had been formed with a membership of 400,000 farmers; there were 77 collective farms, and another 300 were called for in the 1976–1980 Development Plan; and there were 8 state farms.

Socialized agriculture performed dismally. Agriculture's share of 'Iraqi GDP steadily declined from 1958; despite the emphasis the Ba'th Party placed on the agricultural sector in the 1976–1980 Development Plan, agriculture accounted for less than 10 percent of GDP in 1979. The Ba'thist goal of self-sufficiency in food was far from being met; continuing shortages meant the regime had to spend $1.4 billion importing food in 1980. Under the pressures of the war with Iran, the regime began to devote 15 percent of its budget for imports to food. By 1990, foodstuffs accounted for 25 percent of total imports.

Once Saddam Husayn (q.v.) assumed the presidency in July 1979, the regime gradually moved to privatize agriculture. In 1980, the HAC was abolished, removing control of agricultural policy from the party. Saddam decided in early 1981 to dismantle cooperatives, citing their unpopularity with the peasantry and noting that the cooperative system had not contributed to the development of the agricultural sector. By 1983, the number of cooperatives had fallen to 811 from nearly 2,000 in 1979. The number of collectives also fell off drastically during the same period, from 77 in 1979 to 10 by 1983.

The Ninth Regional Conference of the Ba'th Party in 1982 roundly criticized socialized agriculture and went so far as to recognize "both the legitimacy and the importance of the private sector in the economic field." Collectives and state farms were labeled economically worthless, and state interference in agriculture at all levels was viewed as having burdened agricultural development. The conference recommended that private activity with nonexploitative ownership should be left to its own initiative.

During 1983, the regime moved closer to privatization. It passed Law 35 of 1983, allowing individuals or companies to lease land from the Ministry of Agriculture and Agrarian Reform for up to 10 years with no ceiling on the size of the holding. New marketing rules permitted producers to bypass the State Organization for Agricultural Marketing and to sell direct to public wholesale markets or licensed private markets. In 1985, the regime announced that it would no longer accept unprofitable state agricultural schemes, and two years later it put all state farms up for sale or lease. Signaling the end of agrarian reform as a priority of the regime, the Ministry of Agriculture and Agrarian Reform became simply the Ministry of Agriculture in May 1987. In July, the Ministries of Agriculture and Irrigation were merged and reorganized. By 1989, agriculture was being fully run by the private sector with the exception of the state-run central markets. With the imposition of sanctions in 1990, the government tried to compensate for the loss of food imports by increasing domestic production, and the area under cultivation expanded. Nonetheless, harvests generally fell well short of the levels recorded prior to 1990. Under the UN oil-for-food program, 'Iraq imported large quantities of agricultural goods. Following the 2003 Gulf War, the Coalition Provisional Authority (CPA) (q.v.) began working to rehabilitate the agricultural sector. *See also* ECONOMY.

AHALI, JAMA'T AL- (THE PEOPLE'S GROUP). A major liberal society established in 1932 by a group of college-educated intellectuals, many of whom were greatly influenced by the democratic principles of the French Revolution and by European socialism, especially Fabianism. Its main founders were Kamil al-Chadirchi, Muhammad Hadid, Husayn Jamil (qq.v.), 'Abd al-Fattah Ibrahim, and 'Abd al-Qadir Isma'il, all of whom had studied or traveled abroad.

Al-Ahali was one of the few organizations in 'Iraq in the 1930s to adopt a coherent social and economic ideology. Its ideology was called *sha'biyya* (populism); it stressed welfare for all regardless of class, ethnicity, or religion. Al-Ahali's reform program reflected the interests of the peasants and the workers, emphasizing the need to achieve social transformation and calling for limitations on land ownership. The organization called for formal political education to bring 'Iraq out of its depressed political situation. Although sha'biyya recognized patriotism as an important force, it rejected nationalism, especially chauvinistic nationalism, which it saw as having a history full of blood, tyranny, and hypocrisy.

Although al-Ahali emphasized "the people" rather than the individual, it did call for the protection of essential human rights, especially liberty, private property, and equality of opportunity. It also believed that the state must give special attention to the health and education of the individual and recognize the individual's right to employment. The organization played an important role in influencing the economic and political thought of the next generation of political activists in 'Iraq. Al-Ahali ultimately broke down into three political parties, all of which continued to oppose the monarchy.

AHL AL-BAYT (FAMILY OF THE HOUSE OF THE PROPHET). The members of the Hashimites (q.v.) who are descended from the prophet Muhammad and his immediate descendants through his daughter Fatima and his son-in-law and cousin Imam 'Ali Ibn Abi Talib.

AHL AL-HAQQ (ALI ILAHIS). A small religious group, mostly Kurds (q.v.), which venerates Ali and some believe they deify Ali. Others say that they are influenced by the ancient religion of Yarsanism along with some ancient Babylonian, Persian, Christian (q.v.), and Muslim beliefs. They mostly live in Iran, and tiny communities of them live in northern 'Iraq among the Bajilan, Shabak, and Sarliyas (qq.v.).

AHL AL-KITAB (PEOPLE OF THE BOOK). A term used by Muslims to refer to non-Muslims who possessed earlier recorded revelations and scriptures of their own. The term refers to Christians, Jews (qq.v.), Sabeans, and Zoroastrians, who are treated differently from polytheists and idolators. The "Peoples of the Book" were generally considered to be *dhimmis* (protected people) and at times fared well under Muslim governments. Nevertheless, the failure of the dhimmis to accept Islam led to persecutions that varied in degree, depending on the tolerance of the particular ruler.

AHMAD, MIR HAJ (d. 1988). Kurdish politician and officer born in 'Aqra. He was a leading member of the Hewa Party (q.v.), which he represented at the founding meeting of the Komala Party (q.v.), another Kurdish nationalist party. He joined the al-Barzani revolution in 1944 and stayed with Mulla Mustafa al-Barzani (q.v.) during his trip to Iran in 1945. Ahmad served in the Mahabad Republic and after its collapse in 1946, he fled with Barzani to the Soviet Union. He returned with al-Barzani to 'Iraq after the 1958 revolution (q.v.). Ahmad retired from the 'Iraqi army as a full colonel.

AHMAD, MUHAMMAD AL- (1943-). Ba'th Party (q.v.) activist from Ninawa province. He joined the party in 1959, serving in its military, as well as its culture, information, and workers' bureaus. He eventually became the head of the bureau of political guidance and governor of al-Muthanna province (1987–1991). He became a member of the Regional Command (q.v.) in September 1991, although he was not reelected in May 2001.

AHWAR, AL- (THE MARSHES). A remote, secluded area in the southeast of the country stretching between 'Amara and Basra (q.v.) in the area where the Tigris River (q.v.) meets the Euphrates (q.v.). At one time, the region was one of the great bird sanctuaries in the world. The region has been adversely affected by the Iran–'Iraq war (q.v.), Desert Storm (q.v.), and the regime's efforts to drain the area for economic and political reasons. *See also* MARSH ARABS.

'ALAM AL-AKHDHAR, AL-. Arab student league established in Istanbul c. 1912 to strengthen the relations among Arab students studying in Turkey and to advocate the rise of the Arab nation. It published two magazines: *al-Lisan al-Arabi* (The Arab Language), followed by *al-Muntada al-Arabi* (The Arabic Club). This group had a tremendous impact on the Arab nationalists of that generation.

ALGIERS AGREEMENT. The long-simmering boundary dispute between 'Iraq and Iran along the length of the Shatt al-Arab (q.v.) came to the fore again in 1969, when Iran abrogated the 1937 Frontier Treaty (q.v.). Iran wanted the boundary to follow the river's *thalweg* (midpoint). A series of military clashes took place along the border from 1971 to 1974. Iran also supported the Kurdish rebellion then raging in northern 'Iraq. Under the pressure of the Kurdish rebellion, which was threatening the survival of the 'Iraqi regime, 'Iraqi vice president Saddam Husayn (q.v.) signed a new border agreement with the shah of Iran on 6 March 1975. The Algiers Communique, concluded with the good offices of the Algerian government, reaffirmed the land boundary as delimited by the 1913 Constantinople Protocol (q.v.) and the 1914 Proces Verbaux (q.v.), but it established the thalweg as the boundary of the Shatt al-Arab. The communique also pledged that the parties would halt all subversive acts against one another and that Iran would return to 'Iraq small areas previously controlled by Iran but claimed by 'Iraq. Within 24 hours of the communique, Iran withdrew its support for the Kurdish rebellion; the revolt collapsed by the end of April 1975. *See also* BAGHDAD TREATY; IRAN–'IRAQ WAR.

'ALI, SALAH 'UMAR AL- (1937–). A Ba'thist and more recently an opposition politician. He was born in Harba village near Tikrit and educated at the Teacher's College in Baghdad (q.v.). He joined the Ba'th Party (q.v.) during the late 1950s. He was elected to the Regional Command (q.v.) in 1966 and became a member of the Revolutionary Command Council (q.v.) in 1969, but he was dismissed from both posts in 1970. In 1970, he was named the editor of *al-Thawra* newspaper. 'Ali served briefly as minister of agriculture (1970) and held the position of minister of culture and information from 1970 to 1977. He was relieved of his position after criticizing members of the Ba'th hierarchy in 1980. He was made an ambassador to Sweden and Spain and served with the United Nations. In 1982, 'Ali resigned from his ambassadorship as a protest against the 'Iraqi regime, moved to London, and became involved in business activities. After the Iran–'Iraq war (q.v.), he established the 'Iraqi National Alliance, an opposition group.

'ALI, TAHSIN (1891–1977). 'Iraqi politician during the monarchy. He was born in Baghdad (q.v.). He graduated from the Military College in 1911 and was appointed to the police force in Baghdad. During World War I, 'Ali initially fought on the Ottoman side but then deserted and joined the Arab forces in Hijaz. He went to Syria with Faysal (q.v.) and was appointed governor of one of Syria's provinces. 'Ali returned to Baghdad after the establishment of the 'Iraqi government in 1920. He became secretary to the minister of defense in 1921 and commander of the police in Mawsil (q.v.). He also served as governor of Kut and several other regions. 'Ali held a number of cabinet posts: minister of education (1941–1943), minister of defense (1944), and minister of works (1944–1946).

'ALLAQ, 'ALI JA'FAR AL- (1945–). Writer, critic, and editor. He was born in southern 'Iraq and educated in both Baghdad (q.v.) and Britain, where he obtained a Ph.D. in Arabic literature (q.v.) from the University of Exeter. 'Allaq has served as editor in chief of the respected literary magazine, *al-Aqlam* (Quills) and has published several collections of poems, including *A Homeland for Water Birds* and *Family Tree*. He has also written a book of literary criticism, *Gypsy Kingdom*.

'ALLAWI, IYAD (1946–). Leader of the 'Iraqi National Accord (INA) (q.v.) and a member of the 'Iraqi Governing Council (IGC) (q.v.). 'Allawi was trained as a neurologist at the University of Baghdad. He later worked as a businessman and also as an intelligence official. He left 'Iraq in 1971 to live in the United Kingdom. In 1990, he was one of the main founders of the INA, which included many defectors from the Ba'th Party and the 'Iraqi military. A Shi'a Muslim, 'Allawi was a rising star in the Ba'th Party and a former intelligence chief before he defected in 1990. During his years in exile, the INA maintained close ties with the CIA and MI6 and is said to have received support from the United States and some Arab governments. 'Allawi worked for the World Health Organization (WHO) and in private business. He led a coup attempt against Saddam Husayn (q.v.) in the mid-1990s and is reported to have survived an assassination attempt by 'Iraqi agents. He has close ties to Ba'thists, former Ba'thists, and former military officers who opposed Saddam's government.

ALUSI, MANAL YUNIS AL- (1929–). One of the most influential women in 'Iraq under Saddam's regime as head of the General Union of 'Iraqi Women. A lawyer from Baghdad (q.v.), she joined the Ba'th Party (q.v.) in 1962 and served in a number of party posts, including membership in the leadership council of the Ba'th's Professionals' Office. Alusi played an aggressive role in advocating equal rights for women and their integration into all professions in 'Iraqi society.

'AMARA, LAMI'A ABBAS (1928–). A prominent poet of Sabean origin. She belongs to the generation of free verse poets that includes 'Abd al-Wahhab al-Bayati and Badr Shakir al-Sayyab (qq.v.). She graduated from the Baghdad Higher Teachers College in 1950 with a degree in Arabic language and literature (q.v.). She was a teacher for several years. Amara's work focuses on the issues facing women in 'Iraqi and Arab society. Her poetry (q.v.) collections include *The Empty Corner*, *'Iraqi Women*, and *Had the Fortune Teller Told Me*. She currently lives in the United States.

AMIN, MUHAMMAD, AL-. Abbasid caliph (q.v.), r. 809–813. Al-Rashid (q.v.) had designated that his three sons—al-Amin, al-Mamun (q.v.), and al-

Mu'tasim (q.v.)—would succeed him in that order. He had his will hung on the walls of his castle so that none of his sons would dare alter it. But this did not dampen the rivalry between al-Amin and al-Mamun, who represented not only two brothers competing for high office but also two main nationalities within the empire competing for dominance. Al-Amin was born to an Arab mother from the family of Abbas; al-Mamun's mother was Persian. Al-Amin had been tutored by an Arab in the Arab political heritage, and al-Mamun had been tutored by al-Fadl bin Sahl, the noted statesman of Persian origins. Governor of Khorasan since 808, al-Mamun was all but independent of Baghdad (q.v.), which inevitably aroused the suspicions of his brother.

Upon his assumption of the caliphate in 809, al-Amin tore down the document of succession. He ordered al-Mamun to remit some of Khorasan's revenues to Baghdad and informed him of his desire to replace certain high officials in Khorasan. Finally, al-Amin ordered al-Mamun to relinquish his right of succession to the caliphate. Heavy fighting immediately broke out, which ended with al-Amin's death in 813. His head was taken to al-Mamun, and his body dragged through the streets of Baghdad.

AMIR AL-MUMNIN. A term that literally means "commander of the faithful" and is generally reserved for the caliph (q.v.), as the successor to the prophet Muhammad's temporal authority. The term has been used by the caliphs since the rule of Caliph 'Umar Ibn al-Khattab. The Shi'is (q.v.) apply the term to 'Ali and usually refer to the leaders of their community as "Imam."

'AMIRI, HASAN 'ALI AL- (1938–). A Shi'i (q.v.) Ba'thist activist and technocrat. He was born and educated in Baghdad (q.v.). He received a law degree from the Baghdad Law College and joined the Ba'th Party (q.v.) before 1963. He is one of the first companions of Saddam Husayn (q.v.); they were imprisoned together in 1964. Amiri became the secretary-general for Popular Action (a Ba'th front organization) and a member of the 'Iraq–Egypt–Syria union study committee in 1963. He held a succession of posts in the early 1970s: he became responsible for the Workers Bureau; in 1971, he became the head of the Public Foundation for Textiles; in 1972, he served as the secretary-general of the Arab Economist Union; and in 1973, he served as secretary of the National Front.

After the Kazzar coup attempt in 1973, 'Amiri was one of the two inspectors of the Revolutionary Command Council (q.v.) with responsibility for internal security. He served on the Special Tribunal that tried the Shi'is who had participated in the 1977 insurrections. He might have taken a tougher line in the tribunal against the Shi'is than the other members because they were dismissed from their posts while he remained in power. 'Amiri held the posts of minister of internal trade (1974–1977), acting minister of foreign trade (1977), and minister of trade (1979–1987). He was a member of the

Regional Command (q.v.) (1977–1991) and Revolutionary Command Council (q.v.) (1977–1991). After he lost reelection to the Regional Command in 1991, he was appointed as a presidential adviser.

'AMMASH, HUDA (1958–). A prominent microbiologist, educator, and Ba'thist activist and the daughter of General Salih Mahdi 'Ammash (q.v.). 'Ammash is the first woman to be elected to the party's Regional Command (q.v.) in May 2001. She is a graduate of the University of Missouri and the Pasteur Institute in France. She taught at the University of Baghdad (1990–1995) and then became dean of the College of Education for Women and dean of the college (1995–1997). She headed the 'Iraqi Society of Microbiologists. She has published works on microbiology and genetic engineering and was a command member of the party's Baghdad (q.v.) branch prior to her election to the powerful Regional Command. She was accused of working on the development of chemical and biological weapons for the government of 'Iraq. She was taken into custody by U.S. forces on 5 May 2003. She is still being held.

'AMMASH, SALIH MAHDI (1925–1979). A Ba'thist politician and military officer. He was born in Baghdad (q.v.) to a peasant family. He attended the Baghdad Military College and the Staff College. In 1952, he became one of the first military figures to join the Ba'th Party (q.v.), and he joined the Free Officers (q.v.) in 1956. 'Ammash was arrested several times for antiregime activities by the 'Abd al-Karim Qasim (q.v.) government. He helped plan the February 1963 coup that brought the Ba'th to power. During the 1963 Ba'th government, he served as minister of defense and attempted to reconcile the opposed factions in the cabinet. 'Ammash held membership in the ruling Revolutionary Command Council, as well as the Regional and National Commands (qq.v.), respectively, of the Ba'th Party. When 'Abd al-Salam 'Arif (q.v.) came to power in the November 1963 countercoup, 'Ammash left the country and did not return until 1968.

In 1966, he was reelected to the Regional Command, and following the Ba'th's seizure of power in 1968, he regained membership in the National Command. He also became a member of the Revolutionary Command Council (RCC) (q.v.) and held the post of minister of the interior (1968–1970). 'Ammash represented the civilian wing of the Ba'th, and he engaged in a serious struggle with Hardan al-Tikriti (q.v.), the minister of defense, for leadership of the military. His rivalry with al-Tikriti ultimately contributed to their combined ouster and to the weakening of the military's influence over the Ba'th and the state. In April 1970, both al-Tikriti and 'Ammash gave up their positions to accept the vice president positions created for them to avoid any factional disputes. Frustrated by his demotion, 'Ammash became critical of the regime. By late 1971, his criticism of the Ba'th leaders and his disagreements with the civilian factions of the party led to his removal from the vice presidency and the RCC. 'Ammash held a succession of diplomatic posts in the 1970s: ambassador to the Soviet Union (1971–1974), ambassador to France (1974–1976), and ambassador to Finland (1976). Upon his return to Baghdad, he became active in cultural affairs. He is the author of a number of works on Arab military and strategic topics.

ANBAR, AL-. 'Iraq's largest province, characterized by its general desert environment. Its inhabitants reside by the Euphrates River (q.v.), which stretches along the province. It was once the center of the Abbasid caliphate. The region is known for its production of phosphate, glass, cement, and stones.

ANBARI, 'ABD AL-AMIR (1934–). Diplomat and lawyer. He was educated at Harvard University, where he received an M.A. in economics and a doctorate in Law. He joined the 'Iraqi diplomatic service and served as the chief of the Organization of Petroleum Exporting Countries' Legal Affairs Department, head of the 'Iraqi National Oil Company, and director-general of oil affairs in the Ministry of Oil. Between 1978 and 1985, Anbari was the chair of the 'Iraqi Fund for External Development, the governmental body that gives loans to developing countries. He served as ambassador to Britain from 1985 to 1987 and then as ambassador to the United States in 1987. From August 1989 until 1992, Anbari served as 'Iraq's permanent representative to the United Nations. He is considered an able lawyer, economist, and administrator.

ANFAL, AL-. Campaign by Saddam Husayn's (q.v.) regime to eliminate the Kurds (q.v.) as a threat to the government once and for all. The term *Anfal* is taken from the eighth *sura* of the Koran (q.v.) and means "spoils." The Kurds cooperated with Iran during the Iran–'Iraq war (q.v.), and Baghdad (q.v.) was determined to exact a heavy price for this latest act of rebellion. The campaign lasted from March to September 1988. It had eight separate stages, each one concentrated on a specific swath of territory. The first seven stages were directed against areas controlled by the Patriotic Union of Kurdistan (PUK) (q.v.), and the final stage swept through the strongholds of the Kurdistan Democratic Party (KDP) (q.v.).

'Ali Hasan al-Majid (q.v.) was granted virtually unlimited emergency powers in Kurdish areas as the official in charge of Anfal. The campaign was marked by mass executions and disappearances; the total destruction of 2,000 villages and over a dozen larger towns; the forced displacement of hundreds of thousands of Kurds who were offered no compensation and no assistance in their new locations; the destruction of the rural Kurdish economy and infrastructure; and some 40 documented cases of the use of chemical weapons. An estimated 50,000 to 100,000 Kurds were killed or disappeared. Human Rights Watch and other human rights organizations have called the Anfal campaign a genocide.

ANGLO–'IRAQI SPECIAL AGREEMENT OF 1955. Signed on 4 April 1955, the Special Agreement terminated the 1930 Anglo–'Iraqi Treaty (q.v.). Regarded as a supplementary agreement to the Baghdad Pact (q.v.), the treaty provided for close cooperation in defense between Britain and 'Iraq, including planning, combined training, and provision of facilities. The terms of an attached note returned to 'Iraqi control the air bases at Habbaniya and Shuaybi granted to Britain in the 1930 treaty. Britain announced that the Special Agreement had lapsed following 'Iraq's 1959 withdrawal from the Baghdad Pact.

ANGLO–'IRAQI TREATY OF 1922. The 1922 treaty established the form of the relationship between Britain and its Class A mandate, 'Iraq, as that of an alliance. In substance, however, the treaty reproduced most of the provisions of the mandate:

> *Article I*: Britain pledged to provide 'Iraq with advice and assistance through the offices of a high commissioner.
> *Article III*: 'Iraq agreed to draw up an Organic Law providing for freedom of religion and taking into account the "rights, wishes and interests of all populations inhabiting 'Iraq."
> *Article IV*: 'Iraq agreed to be guided by British advice "on all important matters affecting the international and financial obligations and interests" of Britain. 'Iraq further agreed to consult with the high commissioner on what was conducive to sound financial and fiscal policy.
> *Article VI*: Britain promised to secure the admission of 'Iraq to the League of Nations as soon as possible.
> *Articles VII, IX, and XV*: These provided for (respectively) separate military, judicial, and financial agreements.
> *Article XVIII*: This established the duration of the treaty as 20 years, to come into force as soon as it was ratified by both parties and had gained the acceptance of the 'Iraqi Constituent Assembly.

'Iraq had greeted the 1920 announcement of its status as a British mandate with a revolt, *al-Thawrah* (q.v.), against British control. Sir Percy Cox, Britain's representative in Baghdad (q.v.), realized in the aftermath of the revolt that the mandate would receive little support and settled on a

'ANI, YUSUF AL- (1927–). Playwright and actor. His work focuses on the social, economic, and political issues facing 'Iraqi society. While his writing re-
lies much on local color, he explores issues of basic human values. A unique
feature of his work is his reliance on the colloquial 'Iraqi dialect, which al-'Ani
believes can both support his ideas about the future and allow for psychological creativity. More important, coming from a socialist orientation, he works in
the language that is closest to that of the common people. Al-'Ani's best-known
plays include *I Am Your Mother, Shakir, The Cost of Medicine,* and *The Key*.

ANKARA, TREATY OF. Signed on 5 June 1926 by Britain, 'Iraq, and
Turkey, the Treaty of Ankara established the long-disputed frontier between
'Iraq and Turkey. The League of Nations had established a provisional frontier between 'Iraq and Turkey—the so-called Brussels Line—on 29 October
1924 that placed Mawsil (q.v.) province within 'Iraqi territory; the Treaty of
Ankara accepted this line as the frontier. 'Iraq also agreed to pay Turkey over
a 25-year period 10 percent of all the royalties received from the Turkish Petroleum Company (TPC) or from other persons or companies that exploited
the oil concession granted to the TPC.

ANTI-ZIONIST LEAGUE ('USBAT MUKAFAHAT AL-SAHYUNIYA). A
communist organization composed mostly of 'Iraqi Jews (q.v.). The idea for
the group emerged in 1945, and it became an official party in 1946 when the
government allowed the formation of political parties. The league's organizers requested a permit, saying that Zionism posed a threat to Jews as well as
to Arabs and their national unity. It stated that 'Iraqi Jews opposed Zionism
because they are Jews and Arabs at the same time. One of its founders was
Yahuda Siddiq, a member of the Central Committee of the 'Iraqi Communist
Party (q.v.). Other founding members included Yusuf Zalkha, Masru Qattan,
and Yusuf Zalluf. The league issued a newspaper, *al-'Usbat*. It was dissolved
in 1947 when the government banned political parties.

'AQRAWI, 'AZIZ (1924–199?). A Kurdish nationalist activist and military
commander from Aqra. He graduated from the 'Iraqi military academy and
the Staff College. He served in the Politburo of the Kurdistan Democratic
Party (q.v.) and led forces on a number of successful engagements against
'Iraqi troops. 'Aqrawi broke with Mulla Mustafa al-Barzani (q.v.) in 1973
over al-Barzani's rejection of the 'Iraqi government's autonomy plan. He
served as minister of state (1974–1976, 1977–1979) and as minister of transport and communications (1977). 'Aqrawi later fled the country to Syria,
where he joined the 'Iraqi opposition. He reportedly left Syria for the United
States and is not currently involved in political activities.

'AQRAWI, HASHIM (1926–). A Kurdish nationalist politician. He became involved in Kurdish nationalist activities as a young man and was elected to the Central Committee of the Kurdistan Democratic Party (KDP) (q.v.). He broke with Mulla Mustafa Barzani (q.v.) in 1973 over al-Barzani's rejection of the 'Iraqi government's autonomy plan. He became secretary general of the KDP faction that broke with al-Barzani. 'Aqrawi served as the speaker of the first executive council for the Kurdish autonomous region established by the government in 1974. He held a number of administrative positions, including governor of Babil and Dahuk provinces and general director of Kurdish Culture.

'AQRAWI, MATTA (1901–1982). A leading educator, historian, and international civil servant. 'Aqrawi was born to a prominent Christian family in Mawsil (q.v.). He graduated from the American University of Beirut (AUB) and later received his Ph.D. from Columbia University. He returned to 'Iraq where he taught and became director-general of the Ministry of Education. He later joined UNESCO and subsequently became its deputy director. A major part of his work was initiating, planning, and supervising compulsory education throughout the world. 'Aqrawi left UNESCO briefly in 1957–1958 to become the first president of the University of Baghdad. In 1963, he headed the Department of Education at AUB and Kuwait University. He also advised numerous governments, particularly in the third world, on their educational policies. He published numerous works in the areas of education, history, and democracy.

ARABIAN NIGHTS (ALF LAYLA WA LAYLA). A fascinating compilation of stories of Indian, Persian, and Arab origins about a king, his daughter, and his wazir, also known as *The Thousand and One Nights*. Some of the stories in the anthology were translated into Arabic from Persian, although some stories are believed to be based on earlier translations from Indian and perhaps Chinese sources. A number of 'Iraqi and Egyptian stories were added later. The stories were finally completed in the post-Abbasid period. The first Western translation was done by Antoine Galland in the 18th century. *The Arabian Nights* make numerous references to the reign of Harun al-Rashid (r. 786–809) (q.v.) although parts of the stories also refer to events occuring under the *Mamluk* ruling slave dynasty of Egypt. The stories offer a guide as to the kinds of life and entertainment that prevailed during those periods of Islamic life. *The Arabian Nights* have been widely translated into other languages; the most famous are by Lane, Burton, and Mardrus.

ARAB LEAGUE. A pan-Arab organization headquartered in Cairo, Egypt. Several Arab states, including Egypt, 'Iraq, Jordan, Lebanon, Saudi Arabia, Syria, and Yemen, met in May 1945 to establish the league. In 1950, after the

1948–1949 Arab–Israeli war, the Joint Defense and Cooperation Treaty was signed in order to maintain peace and security in the region and to coordinate Arab military power for defense against aggression. The Arab League entails a council that is composed of representatives from each state with one vote for each; a general secretariat for organizing the work of the league; and a number of committees to deal with cultural, social, economic, and other matters. It holds regular meetings in March and September at the level of heads of state or foreign ministers. The goal of the league is to strengthen ties among member states, coordinate political plans in order to achieve cooperation, and work to safeguard the independence and sovereignty of the member states as well as to preserve peace and security in the Arab world. Contrary to Arab nationalist aspirations, the league has failed to form a permanent Arab union or a federal state.

ARAB LIBERATION FRONT (JABHAT AL-TAHRIR AL-'ARABIYA). A Palestinian commando movement organized in April 1967 by the 'Iraqi Ba'th Party (q.v.). Its purpose was to establish a front that had a revolutionary, nationalist ideology that would lead the struggle against Zionism. Backed by the Ba'th and the 'Iraqi government, it sent fighters against Israel in the late 1960s. The movement participated in the Palestine National Council and the Executive Committee of the Palestine Liberation Organization. It was involved in the conflicts between the Lebanese and Jordanian governments and the Palestinian commando movement in the late 1960s and in 1970, respectively. 'Abd al-Rahman Ahmad acted as secretary general. It published a magazine, *The Arab Revolutionary*.

ARAB–OTTOMAN BROTHERHOOD (AL-IKHA AL-'ARABI AL-'UTHMANI). One of the first Arab groups to be formed after the 1908 Ottoman Revolution, the Arab–Ottoman Brotherhood operated openly and actively in the Arab East as well as in Istanbul. Its primary goal was to strengthen the new Ottoman constitution and to achieve the equality of ethnic groups within the Ottoman Empire. It also favored the use of the Arabic language in education and the preservation of the Arabic language and culture. It published a newspaper, *al-Ikha* (The Brotherhood). It enjoyed some support from Arab immigrant communities abroad, especially in the United States. Disagreements among its members led to its collapse.

ARAB UNION (AL-ITTIHAD AL-ARABI). The 1958 union between Jordan and 'Iraq. It was primarily aimed to correspond to the union between Egypt and Syria under President Gamal 'Abd al-Nasir and reflected the conflict that was taking place in the Middle East between the conservative monarchies and the Arab nationalists led by the United Arab Republic. It also reflected the Hashimite (q.v.) regime's desire to continue the idea of the Hashimite-led Fertile Crescent, a plan formulated by Nuri al-Sa'id (q.v.) and the Greater Syria plan promoted by King Abdullah of Jordan. The union came to an abrupt end when the 'Iraqi military revolted in 1958, bringing an end to the Hashimite monarchy. *See also* REVOLUTION, 1958.

ARAMAIC (SYRIAC, SURYANI). A Semitic language of the Middle East. The alphabets of Arabic and Hebrew, also Semitic languages, were influenced by Aramaic. Aramaic was introduced into the Fertile Crescent by the Arameans around the second century B.C. It quickly became the language of culture and commerce in the area and was also given special status in the Persian Empire. It was the language spoken by Jesus, and it remained the language of the rural population long after the coming of Islam and the Arabs. Over time it was replaced by Arabic. Many Aramaic-speaking Christians (q.v.) contributed to the intellectual life of the Abbasid Empire as the authors of philosophical, scientific, and literary texts and as the translators of Greek, Persian, and Syriac texts into the Arabic language. Religious and intellectual traditions survived in the major religious monasteries such as Mar Matta in 'Iraq and Dayr al-Za'farer in Anatolia. The Mongol invasions in the 13th and 14th centuries nearly destroyed the Aramaic-speaking Christian communities in 'Iraq, Persia, and Anatolia. The intolerance of Seljuk Turkish rulers further contributed to the decline of Aramaic as a spoken language and as a language of religious literature (q.v.). Today dialects of Aramaic are still spoken by a small number of Christian Chaldeans (q.v.) and Assyrians (q.v.) in 'Iraq and Syria. In 'Iraq, it remains the liturgical language of Nestorians, Chaldeans, Sabeans (q.v.), and Syrian Orthodox Christians. In the early 1970s, the 'Iraqi government recognized Syriac along with Kurdish and Turkish as official languages.

ARBIL. City and province in 'Iraq. Arbil, which in ancient Assyrian means "the city of the four gods," is one of the oldest inhabited cities in the world. It was built during the time of the Sumerians in c. 5200 B.C. The city was incorporated into the empire of the Third Ur dynasty (2004–2112 B.C.). It was linked by a network of roads with Iran, Syria, and Turkey and was a trading and agricultural center. In recent years, it has been the capital of the autonomous Kurdish region and has become the capital of the Kurdish administration established by the Western allies following Operation Desert Storm (q.v.). It is currently the seat of the Kurdish Regional Government led by the KDP (q.v.).

'ARIF, 'ABD AL-RAHMAN (1916–1982). President (q.v.) from 1966 to 1968 and older brother of 'Abd al-Salam 'Arif (q.v.), who preceded him as president. He attended the Baghdad Military College and the Staff College. From January 1957, he was a member of the Supreme Committee of the Free Officers, but 'Abd al-Karim Qasim (q.v.) forced him to retire. When the Ba'th Party (q.v.) seized power in February 1963, 'Arif was recalled and appointed as a division commander. He served as acting chief of staff during his brother's presidency (1963–1966.) When 'Abd al-Salam died in April 1966, 'Abd al-Rahman was put forward as a candidate for the presidency. He secured election on the second ballot when the civilians swung their vote behind him. He briefly held the post of prime minister (May–June 1967) but appointed Tahir Yahya (q.v.) to the post when he found the pressures of holding both offices to be too great in the aftermath of the June 1967 war. 'Arif was overthrown by the Ba'th and allowed to leave the country in 1968. He lived in Turkey until the eruption of the Iran–'Iraq war (q.v.), when he was allowed to return to 'Iraq.

'ARIF, 'ABD AL-SALAM (1921–1966). President (q.v.) from 1963 to 1966 and younger brother of 'Abd al-Rahman 'Arif (q.v.), who succeeded him as president (1966–1968). He graduated from the Baghdad Military College in 1942 and went on to the Staff College. As a Free Officer (q.v.), his forces captured Baghdad (q.v.) during the 1958 revolution (q.v.). He was appointed deputy commander in chief, deputy prime minister, and minister of the interior. But 'Arif and 'Abd al-Karim Qasim (q.v.) seriously clashed over the question of 'Iraqi union with Egypt. 'Arif, as a supporter of Gamal 'Abd al-Nasir, favored such a move, while Qasim opposed it. Consequently, Qasim relieved 'Arif of his duties on 30 September 1958 and sent him to Bonn, West Germany. 'Arif returned to 'Iraq on 4 December without Qasim's permission, and he was arrested the next day. He was tried before the People's Court chaired by al-Mahdawi on charges of attempting to assassinate Qasim and incite an uprising against the regime. In February 1959, he was found guilty and sentenced to death. However, he was acquitted of all charges in November 1961.

'Arif became president following the Ba'th Party's (q.v.) successful coup in February 1963. The Ba'th did not plan to allow 'Arif any real power; it needed someone with proven nationalist credentials and political status to head its regime. 'Arif turned the tables on the Ba'th, launching a counterrevolution in November 1963 in which he purged his cabinet of most of its Ba'th members. His ardor for union with Egypt cooled after his assumption of the presidency. He was known for his strong Sunni-oriented views and for his antipathy toward Shi'is (q.v.) and Christians (q.v.); in fact, he removed several of them from important posts during his presidency. 'Arif died in a helicopter crash on 16 April 1966.

ARSLAN, MUZAFFAR (1936–). 'Iraqi Turkuman (q.v.) from Kirkuk (q.v.) and leader of the Turkuman National Movement. He graduated from medical school in Turkey and received a specialty in anesthesiology in Germany. He became very active in the 'Iraqi student movement in Turkey and Germany. Arslan founded the Turkuman National Movement in 1988 in Ankara and then moved to northern 'Iraq following the collapse of central government control there in 1991. The movement's goal is to promote the cultural and national rights of the Turkumen in 'Iraq, and it calls for democracy and political pluralism.

ASH'ARI, ABU HASAN AL- (873–935). Prominent Sunni (q.v.) theologian. He used reason to construct arguments supporting Orthodox theology. He was an advocate of the Mu'tazilite (q.v.) school until his adoption of Sunni beliefs and views.

'ASHURA. The 10th day of the month of Muharram (in accordance with the Islamic calendar), it is the anniversary of the martyrdom of Husayn and a day of mourning for Shi'is (q.v.). Husayn, the grandson of the prophet Muhammad, was killed on 10 October 680 at the Battle of Karbala.

ASIL, NAJI AL- (1895–1963). Politician and diplomat. Born in Mawsil (q.v.), he studied in Istanbul and Beirut. Although he earned a degree in medicine, he never practiced his profession. He joined the Arab nationalist movement in the Hijaz and became a close friend of Sharif Husayn. He represented Sharif Husayn in London after World War I until the fall of the Hashimites (q.v.) in the Hijaz. Al-Asil returned to 'Iraq in 1926, where he became a professor and later dean of the Higher Teachers College. He joined the 'Iraqi Foreign Ministry and served in Iran. In 1936, he was appointed director of ceremonies in the Royal Palace. Al-Asil served as minister of foreign affairs from October 1936 until August 1937. He then retired from politics. In 1944, he became director general of antiquities, a post he held until his death.

'ASKARI, 'ALI (1937–1978). Kurdish politician and military leader born to a well-known family in the village of Askar. He was voted a member of the central committee of the Kurdish Democratic Party (KDP) (q.v.) at its first official meeting. He was the military commander for the Bahdinan area during the Kurdish uprising of 1961 and led the Khebat forces in Sulaymaniyya. 'Askari sided with Jalal Talabani (q.v.) and Ibrahim Ahmad against Mulla Mustafa al-Barzani (q.v.) during the 1964 split in the KDP. He escaped to Iran after an unsuccessful confrontation with the al-Barzani forces. Following a rapprochement between the two groups, he was allowed to return with some of his comrades in 1966, but they were placed under house arrest and prevented from political activity. He later fled with Talabani and went underground. 'Askari remained one of the leaders of the Talabani-Ahmad faction until its reunification with the al-Barzani faction in 1970. He led the defense of al-Barzani's headquarters during the 1974–1975 Kurdish revolt. Following the revolt's collapse in 1975, he retreated with al-Barzani's forces to Iran. Upon his return to 'Iraq, he was exiled to the south and prevented from contacting his comrades.

'Askari escaped from his exile in the south in August 1976 and joined the Patriotic Union of Kurdistan's (PUK) (q.v.) forces. During the first Congress of the PUK, he was appointed a member of the Politburo and the general commander of their forces. In the summer of 1977, contacts occurred with the Ba'th Party (q.v.) to find a peaceful solution to the Kurdish problem. Because of disagreements on the autonomy process and other factors, political tensions increased between the PUK and the KDP. A major clash between KDP (q.v.) and PUK (q.v.) forces led to the death of 'Askari along with Husayn Babal (q.v.) and Khalid Sa'id in 1978. The confrontation between the PUK and the KDP continued until 1986 when the two sides reached an agreement to end their differences.

'ASKARI, JA'FAR AL- (1885–1936). Founder of the 'Iraqi army and a politician. He was born in the Kurdish village of Askar; his father was a retired general in the Turkish army. He studied at the Military School in Baghdad (q.v.) and the Military Academy and Military Staff College in Istanbul, graduating as a lieutenant in 1904. Al-'Askari also studied for a brief period in Germany, specializing in military mobilization. He participated in the uprisings in al-Qasim in 1904–1905 and served in the army in 'Iraq.

During World War I, he volunteered to fight against Italian forces in Tripoli. He also fought against the British, who attempted to block his fighters from reaching Libya. Al-'Askari was wounded, taken prisoner, and escaped. He joined Sharif Husayn in 1917 and became the commander of Faysal's (q.v.) northern army. A courageous soldier, al-'Askari received the German Iron Cross and the British medal of St. Michael and St. George. He was appointed the military governor of Aleppo during Faysal's rule in Syria. He followed Faysal to London and then to 'Iraq after the collapse of the Syrian government.

One of Faysal's most trusted men, al-'Askari played a leading role in the creation of the 'Iraqi national army. He repeatedly served as minister of defense (1920–1922, 1930–1932, 1935–1936) and also served as a delegate to the League of Nations. He twice held the position of prime minister (1923–1924, 1926–1928). In 1936, he was assassinated en route to Bakuba as he carried a letter from King Faysal I (q.v.) to Bakr Sidqi (q.v.), leader of the military coup, informing him of a proposed change in the government and asking him to arrange for the cessation of violence. Viewing the mission as an effort to oppose the coup, Sidqi ordered four soldiers to kill al-'Askari. This assassination contributed to the newly formed government's collapse. Al-'Askari was considered to be intelligent, thoughtful, and an excellent administrator.

ASMA'I, AL- (?–831). A celebrated grammarian, philologist, and historian born in Basra (q.v.). He is well known for his transmission of oral history, anecdotes, amusing and unusual stories, and rare expressions of Arabic, of which he was considered a master. He was famed for his prodigious memory and knowledge of various sciences of his day. He wrote treatises on numerous subjects and was said to be the source for resolving doubtful points of literature (q.v.) and for his knowledge of the idiom of desert Arabs. It was believed that he knew by heart 16,000 pieces of verse composed in the Rajaz meter alone.

ASSASSINS. Also known as the Isma'ilis. An extremist Shi'i (q.v.) sect led by Hasan al-Sabah that rebelled against both the Seljuks (q.v.) and the Abbasids in c. 1090. Al-Sabah organized a secret society whose members came to be known as Assassins. The Assassins' main task was to identify and assassinate those individuals who were considered to be enemies. They sought shelter in the mountains and traveled in disguise to slay their enemies. The Assassins succeeded in killing a number of prominent officials and religious scholars.

ASSOCIATION OF 'IRAQI DEMOCRATS. An organization that is part of the 'Iraqi National Congress (q.v.). Not a political party per se, it includes a number of 'Iraqis who share similar principles and ideas and who have mostly democratic, liberal views. It favors the establishment of a democratic regime in Baghdad (q.v.).

ASSYRIANS. Christian community also known as Nestorians, Ashuris, Athuris, and Syriacs. The Assyrians and the Roman Catholic Chaldeans (q.v.) were known until the 15th century as the Church of the East or as the Assyrian Church. They have also been referred to as the Church of the Nestorians or the Church of the Persians. The tiny Assyrian community in 'Iraq and Iran is the remnant of an ancient Christian (q.v.) community. It has witnessed periods of great intellectual flowering and growth and periods of religious persecution and internal divisions. The community was nearly eradicated by massacres during the Mongol invasions of the 13th–14th centuries and then later at the hands of Kurdish princes and Ottoman officials in the 19th and early 20th centuries.

The modern-day Assyrians trace their origins to the ancient Assyrians, and while it is difficult to substantiate this link, it is generally recognized that the

Assyrians along with other Syriac-speaking communities in 'Iraq are the descendants of the ancient Aramaic-speaking (q.v.) people who have lived in the area since pre-Christian and pre-Islamic times. Since the 13th century, the Assyrians have mostly lived in the mountain region of the Mesopotamian plain, between Lake Van in the west and Lake Urmia in the east, an area that was later divided among 'Iraq, Iran, and Turkey. They trace their conversion to Christianity to the first century A.D. when the Apostle Thomas is said to have preached to Mesopotamia on his way to India. Christianity began to spread widely under Mar Adi and his students, leading to the birth of the Assyrian Church. By the third century, about 20 bishoprics were organized spreading from 'Iraq to Oman and Yemen. The headquarters was in Cteisphon (q.v.). The converts appear to have accepted the new faith with enthusiasm and remained loyal to it despite persecutions by the Persian rulers in the fourth century.

Mesopotamian Christianity was greatly influenced by the religious currents and controversies of the time. A major split occurred between the supporters and opponents of Nestorius, the patriarch of Constantinople from 428 to 431, who advocated that God could not physically become man and so Jesus Christ had to have had two natures; Mary was the mother of Christ, and Christ died on the cross as a man, but not as God. The emperor called a conference at Ephesus in 431 in order to resolve the conflict. The conference condemned Nestorius's teachings, and his followers were branded as heretical. The Assyrian Church in 'Iraq refused to condemn Nestorius and gave safe haven to some of his followers. It was this decision that led to the erroneous description of Assyrians as Nestorians. Another split occurred between the Monophysite church of Antioch, which was also opposed to the official church, and the church in Mesopotamia. The Monophysites (the Jacobite [q.v.], Armenian, and Coptic churches) accepted the indivisibility (*mono-*) of the nature of Christ (*-physite*), in contrast to the Assyrians, who believed in the dual nature of Christ. The Assyrian Church in Mesopotamia has been independent since the fifth and sixth centuries, and it came to be described as the Nestorian church or the church of Persia.

With the coming of Islam (q.v.), Mesopotamian Christians, both Arabs and Assyrians, supported the Muslim Arab armies against the Persian Empire which had been persecuting them. The Mesopotamian Christians (Jacobites and Assyrians) were generally tolerated and thrived under the early caliphs. They greatly contributed to the intellectual, scientific, and administrative life of the empire, and since they were not allowed to proselytize in the empire, they spread their teachings to Indonesia, China, central Asia, and India. During this period, the Assyrian community produced great scientists, translators, and physicians such as Hunayn Bin Ishaq (q.v.), the Bakhtishu family, al-Kindi, Ibn Masawayh, and many others. Despite important scientific and cultural contributions, the Assyrians suffered some persecution under the rule of the latter-day Abbasid caliphs. They were spared from Hulagu Khan's worst persecution because the church was led during this period by Patriarch Yahhub Allah, a Mongol. But they were almost totally exterminated by Timur Lame, who destroyed churches and monasteries and killed many of their members. A tiny community fled to the Kurdish mountains, and two other groups fled to Cyprus and India, where another Assyrian community existed.

The groups that fled to the Hakkari Mountains in Turkey were divided along tribal lines and were led by Mar Shimun, their patriarch. The mountain Assyrians were divided into clans headed by a chief known as Malik. They spoke a dialect of Aramaic and used it in their liturgy. Many also spoke Arabic and Kurdish. The Assyrian tribesmen were courageous warriors who had to fight often to defend themselves against raiding Kurds (q.v.) or Ottoman soldiers.

Under the Ottomans, the mountain Assyrians who were organized into tribes enjoyed a certain autonomy, and relations with the government was through their patriarch, who was recognized as their spiritual and temporal leader. The office of the patriarch was held in the same family from the 15th century with the position going from uncle to nephew or to a cousin. This practice was abolished in 1923. In the 16th century, internal divisions and Catholic missionaries seeking to convert the Assyrians to Catholicism led to a series of conflicts and splits. A branch of the church was united with Rome in 1553. In the 18th and especially 19th centuries, and with the decline in the Ottoman government's reach, British and American Protestant missionaries began to open missions and schools among the Assyrians and won some converts. Western missionary activity among the Assyrians was greatly resented by Ottoman officials and by some of their Muslim neighbors, who turned their wrath on the small Assyrian community. Contact with the missionaries might have contributed to the belief among some of the Assyrians that they are a separate nation and deserve different treatment. This perception along with the fact that many Assyrians had pinned their hopes for safety and justice on the intervention of European diplomats further aggravated relations with the government and with fanatical Kurdish princes such as Badr Khan, who massacred more than 10,000 Assyrians in one campaign during the 1840s. The Kurdish princes of Julamerkand and the Birwar chiefs also persecuted the Assyrians. Consequently, the Assyrians increasingly came to rely on the Western powers for protection.

During World War I, the Assyrians were encouraged by the Allies to fight on their side. The patriarch and other leaders had been heavily influenced by Western missionaries and diplomats to support the "Christian powers," and they hoped that the Allies would help them establish their own homeland and end their persecution. The Assyrians joined the Russian forces as the Russians advanced into parts of eastern Anatolia. However, when the Russians withdrew from the area, many Assyrians were subjected to severe reprisals. Renewed attacks by some of their Kurdish neighbors and by some Turkish forces led the Assyrians to flee to Iran in 1915–1916. More than half of the Assyrian community was massacred during this period. In 1918, the patriarch was killed by an Iranian Kurdish tribal chief, Ismail Agha, resulting in further flight into 'Iraq.

After World War I, the British settled approximately 50,000 Assyrians in refugee camps in 'Iraq. They also promised to help them return to their original areas in the Hakkari Mountains and to establish their own autonomous homeland. The settlement of the Mawsil (q.v.) question in 1925 by the League of Nations left the Hakkari in Turkish hands and ended Assyrian dreams of establishing a homeland for all the Syriac-speaking communities in northern 'Iraq and southeastern Turkey. The British also failed to deliver on the promise to settle the Assyrians as a community in one area where they would be able to defend themselves as was recommended by the Mawsil Commission of the League of Nations in 1924. The Assyrians were encouraged to believe that their good relations with the authorities in 'Iraq were likely to continue since they had served in the British-led 'Iraqi Levies as military police. This activity further alienated them from some of their Arab and Kurdish neighbors, particularly because these levies were used to put down Shi'i (q.v.) and Kurdish tribal uprisings against the British.

When the British mandate ended in 'Iraq in 1932, many of the Assyrians were still refugees and demanded that they be settled in an area of their own in northern 'Iraq. The nationalist 'Iraqi government and much of the public were opposed to these demands and saw the Assyrians as agents of the British. Tensions escalated in 1933 when the 'Iraqi government placed their patriarch under house arrest and demanded that he surrender his temporal powers. The government also made a proposal to the Assyrian tribes and warned unless they accepted it, they had to leave the country. Some of the tribes refused and moved to Syria. French Mandatory officials welcomed them but told them they had no chance of establishing a homeland.

In August 1933, the Assyrians returned from Syria and clashed fiercely with the 'Iraqi army. The following days witnessed attacks by soldiers and Kurdish and Arab tribesmen on Assyrian villages, many of which had not been involved in the clashes. The widespread massacres of Assyrian peasants and their families led King Faysal I (q.v.), who was receiving medical treatment in Europe, to return home to calm the situation. The attacks led to an exodus of Assyrians, with 6,000 settling in Syria, 4,000 in the United States, and smaller numbers settling in Lebanon and Sweden. Those who remained in 'Iraq numbered around 30,000.

The Assyrian population in 'Iraq today is estimated at roughly 60,000 to 80,000. The Assyrian patriarch Mar Dinkha IV has worked to establish closer ties with other Christian churches and more recently with Rome. The 'Iraqi government has recognized the Syriac language and culture and encouraged research in this area. The Assyrian church has 3 of its 123 bishoprics in 'Iraq.

'ATIYYAH, GHASSAN AL-. Politician and director of the Center for 'Iraqi Studies in London. Dr. 'Atiyyah is also editor-in-chief of *al-Malaf Al 'Iraqi* (the 'Iraqi File). He has lectured extensively at various 'Iraqi universities and has worked with the League of Arab States and the Research Center at Baghdad University. He has written and published many political papers and articles, primarily in Arabic, in the field of international affairs and Middle East politics and 'Iraq in particular. Dr. 'Atiyyah holds a Ph.D. in political science from the University of Edinburgh.

ATRUSHI, 'ABD AL-WAHHAB AL- (1936–). A Kurdish politician from the Shikhan district of northern 'Iraq. He attended school in Baghdad (q.v.) and graduated from the police academy. Al-Atrushi was active in the Kurdish movement led by Mulla Mustafa al-Barzani (q.v.) and served as adviser to the Revolutionary Command Council's (q.v.) Committee for Northern Affairs after the collapse of the Kurdish uprising in 1975. He also served as governor of Arbil (q.v.) and al-Anbar (q.v.) provinces.

'AWAD, GWORGIS (1908–199?). Intellectual, historian, and librarian. Born in Mawsil (q.v.), he studied there and in Baghdad (q.v.). In 1936, he became the director of the library of the 'Iraqi Museum and wrote the index of manuscripts held by the library. He was elected to the Arab Academy in Damascus. 'Awad wrote a number of works on 'Iraqi history and on works by ancient Islamic and non-Islamic writers.

'AYISH, MUHAMMAD (1934–1979). A Ba'thist labor activist. He joined the party in 1958 and was active in Ba'th Party (q.v.) affairs in the early 1960s, when he was arrested by 'Abd al-Salam 'Arif's (q.v.) government. He played an active role in both the 1963 and 1968 Ba'thist coups. He was a member of the Union of Workers and of the Ba'th Party's Workers' Central Office. 'Ayish was also involved in various Arab and international organizations, including the Committee for Solidarity with the Lebanese National Movement, which he headed. In 1977, he was appointed as a minister of state, appointed to the Revolutionary Command Council (q.v.), and elected to the Regional Command (q.v.). He also held the post of minister of industry (1978–1979). 'Ayish was executed in 1979 for involvement in the "pro-Syrian plot" to overthrow Saddam Husayn's (q.v.) government.

AYUBI, 'ALI JAWDAT AL- (1886–1969). Prime minister and diplomat during the monarchy. He was born in Mawsil (q.v.) to a Kurdish father and an Arab mother. Upon his graduation from the Military College in Istanbul, he joined the General Staff in Baghdad (q.v.). Jawdat joined the Arab Revolt in 1916 as a member of the Camel Corps, the vanguard of the Arab army that occupied Damascus in 1918. During Faysal I's (q.v.) rule in Syria, he served as military governor of Aleppo and then of the Biqa region, and as director general of the Police. He was a delegate to the 'Iraqi Congress in Damascus in 1920, which called for the appointment of Amir 'Abdullah as king of 'Iraq. He also organized nationalist activities to liberate 'Iraq from British rule.

After the collapse of Faysal's government in Syria, Jawdat returned to 'Iraq. He began his political career as an ally of Ja'far al-'Askari (q.v.), an avowedly pro-British Sharifian officer, but then began to cooperate with the opposition National Brotherhood Party (q.v.) of Yasin al-Hashimi and Rashid 'Ali al-Kaylani (qq.v.). Despite his opposition to the 1930 Anglo–'Iraqi Treaty (q.v.), Jawdat was considered a loyal pro-Hashimite (q.v.) with pro-British leanings.

Jawdat served in a number of positions. He served as prime minister three times (1934–1935, 1949–1950, 1957). He held the portfolios of interior (1923–1924, 1934–1935), finance (1930), foreign affairs (1939–1940, 1941, 1948–1949), and deputy prime minister (1953). In 1933, he was appointed chief of the Royal Palace. Jawdat was speaker of Parliament in 1935, and then accepted several diplomatic posts: ambassador to Britain (1935–1937), ambassador to France (1937–1939), and ambassador to the United States (1944–1948). He was appointed to the Senate during 1948–1949. Following the July 1958 revolution (q.v.), Jawdat went to Lebanon.

AYYUBIDS. A Sunni (q.v.) state founded by Salah al-Din al-Ayyubi that controlled 'Iraq, Egypt, Palestine, Nubia, Syria, and parts of Arabia and the Maghrib. The Ayyubids eliminated the centers of Shi'i (q.v.) thought in Egypt, closing al-Azhar University for five years and transforming it into a Sunni center of learning. They encouraged Sufism (q.v.) to fill the void left by the disappearance of Shi'i thought. After Salah al-Din (q.v.), the administration of the state was decentralized, and strong local authority was given to Ayyubid rulers in Aleppo, Ba'albeck, Banyas, Basra (q.v.), Damascus, Hama, Hims, and Yemen. The last Ayyubid ruler Quturan (1249–1250) was killed in 1250, and the slave dynasty of the *mamluks* took over the state. *See also* ZANKID STATE.

'AZIZ, GHANIM KHADDURI (1937–). Deputy speaker of the 'Iraqi National Assembly (q.v.) and Ba'thist activist. He graduated from the College of Economics and Commerce. 'Aziz joined the Ba'th Party (q.v.) in 1956 and worked as both a businessman and government official. He participated in the activities of the Society of 'Iraqi Economists and the Accountants Union and headed the General Foundation for Grain. 'Aziz has represented 'Iraq at a number of international conferences, including a diplomatic visit to the United States a few months prior to 'Iraq's August 1990 invasion of Kuwait (q.v.).

'AZIZ, 'IZZAT 'ABD AL- (?–1949). Kurdish military leader. He was born in 'Imadiyya to a well-known family. He completed his higher military education in Britain and served as an officer in the 'Iraqi army. 'Aziz was a leading member of the Hewa Party (q.v.). He helped form the Mahabad Republic's army and fought to defend it against the Iranian army. He also participated in the formation of the Kurdistan Democratic Party (q.v.) in 1946. After the collapse of the Mahabad Republic in 1946, 'Aziz returned to 'Iraq. He was executed in 1949.

'AZIZ, MUHAMMAD. First secretary of the 'Iraqi Communist Party (ICP) (q.v.) until 1993–1994. He was born to a Kurdish family and joined the ICP at an early age. He played an important if at times unsuccessful role in mending differences between top party leaders. He led the ICP–Central Committee faction after the ICP broke in two in 1967 due to differences with al-Hajj 'Aziz (q.v.). During the 1970s, the ICP leadership sought refuge in the areas of northern 'Iraq controlled by Mulla Mustafa al-Barzani (q.v.). 'Aziz then led an effort, with Soviet blessings, to negotiate and reconcile differences with the Ba'th Party (q.v.) in the wake of the split with al-Hajj 'Aziz. The subsequent alliance with the Ba'th, which lasted from 1972 to 1978, led to the participation of ICP members Mukarram al-Talabani (q.v.) and Amir 'Abd Allah in the 'Iraqi cabinet. Following the Ba'th's break with the ICP, he went into exile. During the Iran–'Iraq war (q.v.), he cooperated with other opposition groups in launching antigovernment campaigns in the Kurdish areas and declared support for Kurdish self-rule aspirations.

'AZIZ, SHAYKH 'ALI BIN 'ABD AL- (1929–). Head of the opposition Kurdistan Islamic Movement (q.v.). He was born in Halabja (q.v.) to a family of religious leaders. He studied in religious schools and was influenced by his brother 'Uthman. From 1956 to 1958, 'Aziz taught in various schools in 'Iraqi Kurdistan and then he headed mosques in Sulaymaniyya and Halabja. In 1973, the 'Iraqi government tried to arrest him and he was forced to go underground. He fled to Iran, where he established the Kurdistan Islamic Movement.

'AZIZ, TARIQ (1936–). Ba'thist intellectual, editor, and politician from Mawsil (q.v.). He has been considered the dean of 'Iraqi diplomacy since 1981 and is the regime's most visible senior member, as well as the only Christian (q.v.) represented in the inner circle. He received a B.A. in English language and literature (q.v.) from Baghdad University in 1958 and speaks English as well as French. 'Aziz edited the *Socialist*, a clandestine paper in the late 1950s. After the 1958 revolution (q.v.), he became the editor of *al-Jumhurilya* and moved onto *al-Jamahir* in 1963. After the 1963 collapse of the Ba'thist regime, he went to Syria and worked as an editor of the Syrian Ba'thist paper. 'Aziz's opposition to the military faction of the Syrian Ba'th led to his arrest after the 23 February 1966 coup in Syria that brought that faction to power. He returned to Baghdad (q.v.) after the 1968 revolution (q.v.) and became the editor of *al-Thawra* as well as the deputy head of the Ba'th Party's (q.v.) Office of Culture and National Information. In 1974, he was elected candidate member of the Regional Command (q.v.) and named director general of state radio and television. 'Aziz has held a number of cabinet positions: minister of information (1974–1977), deputy prime minister (1979–2003), and minister of foreign affairs (1983–1991). He headed the 'Iraqi team that met with U.S. secretary of state James Baker before the launching of Operation Desert Storm (q.v.). He was later appointed deputy prime minister and a member of the Revolutionary Command Council (q.v.). In April 2003, he surrendered to U.S. forces. He is still being held.

'AZZAWI, HIKMAT IBRAHIM AL- (1934–). An economist and Ba'thist activist from Diyala province. He graduated from the college of Commerce and Economics. He was an early convert to the Ba'th Party (q.v.), joining in 1953. He was dismissed from his job at the Central Bank for his party activities in the 1950s and was arrested during 'Abd al-Karim Qasim's (q.v.) regime. 'Azzawi was also arrested by 'Abd al-Salam 'Arif's (q.v.) regime after the countercoup in 1963. He became the superintendent of the Central Bank and an auditor of the director of stores and warehouses of the State Company of Electrical Instruments and Equipment between 1966 and 1968. He served in numerous economic posts under the Ba'th, including the director of the general establishment of trade (1968) and as a member of the board of directors of the Central Bank (1969). 'Azzawi was acting minister of the economy in 1969 and a deputy secretary-general of the Baghdad (q.v.) branch of the Ba'th. He held the posts of minister of the economy (1972–1976), minister of foreign trade (1976–1977), and minister of state for Kurdish affairs (1977). He was elected to the Regional Command (RC) (q.v.) in 1977 and also gained membership in the Revolutionary Command Council (RCC) (q.v.). In 1979 'Azzawi became secretary general of the party's southern organization and headed the RCC's Office for Economic Affairs.

He was relieved of his memberships in the RC and RCC in 1982 and appointed as an adviser to the RCC. He briefly headed the party bureau for students, peasants, and youth. In 1985, 'Azzawi became head of the 'Iraqi Central Bank. 'Azzawi was appointed Minister of Finance in 1995 and deputy prime minister in 1999. He was captured by 'Iraqi police in Baghdad and handed over to U.S. forces on 19 April 2003.

– B –

BABAL, HUSAYN (SHAYKH AL-YAZIDI) (1941–1978). The son of the prominent Yazidi (q.v.) family. He was a member of the Kurdish Democratic Party (KDP) (q.v.) and was captured early on in the Kurdish rebellion in the 1960s. Upon his release in 1964, he rejoined the uprising. Babal headed the Shaykhari District and commanded a small unit of *pesh mergas* (q.v.). After the collapse of the revolt, he fled to Iran with Mulla Mustafa al-Barzani (q.v.). After a brief stay in 'Iraq, he went to Syria where he was placed in charge of the Bahdinan branch of the Patriotic Union of Kurdistan (PUK) (q.v.). In the spring of 1977, Babal returned with a group of pesh mergas to Kurdistan. He was killed along with 'Ali al-'Askari (q.v.) and Khalid Sa'id in 1978.

BABAN, AHMAD MUKHTAR (1900–1976). Prime minister and cabinet official during the monarchy. He was born to a Kurdish family in Baghdad (q.v.). His mother was a member of the Baban family, a princely Kurdish family that maintained its autonomy until the middle part of the 19th century. Baban graduated from college in 1918 and received a law degree in 1923 from the Baghdad Law College. He was appointed governor of Mawsil (q.v.) in 1926 and later became governor of al-Kut. He held a number of cabinet posts as well as serving in various posts in the Royal Diwan: minister of social affairs (1942–1943, 1946), minister of justice (1943–1946), head of the Royal Diwan in 1946 and in 1953, deputy prime minister (1954, 1955–1957), minister without portfolio (1954–1955), acting minister of education (1957), and minister of defense (1957). Baban was prime minister when 'Abd al-Karim Qasim (q.v.) overthrew the monarchy in July 1958. He was arrested, tried, and found guilty by the Mahdawi People's Court. He was condemned to death, but the sentence was commuted. Baban was released in 1961 and went to Lebanon, where he remained until the outbreak of the Lebanese civil war in 1975, when he returned to Baghdad. Baban died in Germany, where he had gone to seek medical treatment.

BABAN, JALAL (1892– 199?). Cabinet minister during the monarchy. He was born to the princely Kurdish family of Baban. He graduated from the Military

College in Istanbul and served during the Balkan wars on the Ottoman side. After World War I, Baban returned to 'Iraq, where he took part in Kurdish nationalist activities against the British, for which he was exiled to Hinjan, an island in the Persian Gulf. However, he was not considered a radical Kurdish nationalist, and he came to be seen as pro-British. Baban held numerous cabinet positions: minister of works (1932–1933, 1937–1938, 1939–1940, 1941, 1948, 1949), minister of defense (1933), minister of education (1934), minister of finance (1943, 1949), and minister of social affairs (1948–1949).

BABAN, JAMAL (1893–1965). Lawyer and former minister of justice (1930–1932, 1933–1934) who was a member of a prominent Kurdish family. Baban served as a reserve officer in the armed forces and was elected to the parliament several times. One of his sons later became a bodyguard and close confidante of Saddam Husayn (q.v.).

BABIL. A governorate named after the ancient city of Babylon that lies south of Baghdad (q.v.). The governorate contains the ruins of the ancient city of Babil.

BABYLONIAN PYTHAGOREAN THEOREM. In 1962, a baked clay tablet was uncovered in Tal al-Dhiba', the Hill of the Hyenas, in Baghdad (q.v.), which revealed a diagram and a mathematical text showing a striking theoretical application of the Pythagorean theorem from the days of the early Babylonian kingdom, 1,250 years before Pythagoras. The tablet showed that early Mesopotamians not only mastered arithmetic but also had a sense of algebra and geometric laws.

BAGHDAD. The capital, and largest city, of 'Iraq. The city stretches along both sides of the Tigris River (q.v.), with an estimated population of 5 million people. Built in 762 by Caliph al-Mansur (q.v.), it reached its peak under Harun al-Rashid (r. 786–809) (q.v.) and his successors. It became a center of learning and intellectual activity throughout the world. Its population during the Abbasid period reached a peak of 1.5 million people. In 830, Caliph al-Mamun (r. 813–833) (q.v.) established a major university and library called *al-Bayt al-Hikma* (the House of Wisdom) (q.v.), in Baghdad. The mostly native Aramaic- (Syriac-) (q.v.) speaking Christian (q.v.) and Sabean scholars there translated classical Greek, Persian, Sanskrit, and Syriac works into Arabic. However, most of the buildings from the period were destroyed as the empire weakened in a series of conflicts. Baghdad regained some influence after the Seljuks (q.v.) occupied the city in 1055. This led to the rebuilding of a number of important monuments and mosques. The revival was short-lived, and Baghdad plunged into a long period of decline.

In 1258, the Mongols, led by Heluga Khan, occupied and thoroughly sacked Baghdad. By the time the Ottoman Empire gained control in 1638, the city's population had fallen to a few thousand. The city remained a backwater of the Ottoman Empire, although it revived some under the rule of Midhat Pasha in the 19th century. It became 'Iraq's capital in 1921. Windfall oil profits after 1973 funded extensive development of the city, but the fiscal austerity brought on by the Iran–'Iraq war (q.v.) halted virtually all such projects after 1983. The city's infrastructure sustained tremendous damage in the 1991 coalition bombing campaign of Operation Desert Storm (q.v.); the nearly dozen bridges crossing the Tigris and 80 percent of the electricity grid were destroyed, the water system was unusable, and many government and civilian structures were damaged or destroyed.

Baghdad is the center of governmental, industrial, educational, and cultural life in 'Iraq. All the major ministries, government institutions, and foreign embassies are located there. The city's economy is based on oil refining and the production of leather, carpets, textiles, cement, and tobacco products. There are three universities in the city: the country's oldest university, Baghdad University (founded 1958); al-Mustansiriyya University; and the University of Technology. The city boasts of many outstanding museums, including the 'Iraqi Museum, whose collection runs from prehistoric times through the Abbasid period; the Museum of Popular Heritage, featuring local handicrafts; the Costume and Folklore Museum, with a gorgeous collection of 'Iraqi costumes; and the Saddam Art Center, with a mostly modern collection. The center of the city is Tahrir Square (Liberation Square), and fabled Rashid Street is the main avenue, holding the financial district and bazaar areas. Two of Baghdad's most famous monuments are the 54-meter-high Baghdad Tower and the Saddam Husayn (q.v.) Victory Arch, two enormous hands holding swords over a parade ground. During the war of 2003, the capital suffered further damage as a result of the bombing and looting after the fall of the Ba'th regime. Some of the treasures at the National Museum, the National Archives, and other museums suffered major losses from looting and destruction after the fall of Baghdad.

BAGHDAD–BERLIN RAILROAD. A railroad line that links Berlin to Basra (q.v.), through Istanbul and Baghdad (q.v.), and on to Kuwait. In 1899, a German company was able to get the contract to extend the railway from Istanbul to Basra with the support of the German government. The new line, called the Baghdad–Berlin line, was completed in 1903. It extended to the city of Sammarra (q.v.). In 1914, another line was linked connecting Baghdad and Basra. Germany was interested in this project as part of its industrial rise and its search for spheres of influence and sources of raw materials as well as for markets for its industry. The construction of the railroad was also part of Germany's cooperation with the Ottoman state and the expansion of Germany's influence into the Middle East. The railroad was opposed by Russia and Britain, which saw in the German presence a threat to their influence in the region.

BAGHDAD MODERN ART GROUP. A group of young 'Iraqi artists led by Jawad Salim (q.v.) who sought to modernize and revitalize art in 'Iraq. It was considered one of the most unique arts movements in the Middle East in the post–World War II era.

BAGHDAD PACT. The Baghdad Pact, officially known as the Middle East Treaty Organization, was concluded on 24 February 1955 between 'Iraq and Turkey. Article V provided for the accession of other interested states; Britain joined on 5 April 1955, Pakistan on 23 September 1955, and Iran on 3 November 1955. The United States, which had made several unsuccessful bids to set up a Middle East defense organization, did not formally join the group but acted as a shadow member. Aimed at the Soviet Union, the pact provided for mutual cooperation in security and defense matters, noninterference, and the peaceful settlement of disputes.

The Baghdad Pact was widely opposed within 'Iraq, especially among Arab nationalist circles, and violently attacked from outside. Egyptian president Gamal 'Abd al-Nasir had resisted the establishment of a mutual defense organization in the Middle East because in his eyes it represented an infringement on the newly won sovereignty of the Arab states. Moreover, it focused on the wrong enemy—the Soviet Union instead of Israel. Nasir's calls for positive neutrality clashed head long with 'Iraqi prime minister Nuri al-Sa'id's (q.v.) pursuit of a pro-Western policy, making the Baghdad Pact one of the prime sources of 'Iraqi–Egyptian enmity during this period. Membership in a Western-inspired defense pact severely discredited Nuri's government in the wake of the Tripartite attack against Egypt in 1956, contributing to the eventual overthrow of the monarchical regime in 'Iraq in 1958 by Colonel 'Abd al-Karim Qasim (q.v.). 'Iraq withdrew from the Baghdad Pact on 24 March 1959.

BAGHDAD, TREATY OF 1975. Signed on 13 June 1975, this treaty formalized the provisions of the Algiers Agreement (q.v.) and added a fourth element: A breach of any of the pieces of the overall settlement would be considered clearly incompatible with the spirit of Algiers. Citing alleged Iranian attempts to subvert the 'Iraqi government following the seizure of power by the Ayatollah Khumaini, Saddam Husayn (q.v.) abrogated the Baghdad Treaty on 17 September 1980 and declared the Shatt al-Arab (q.v.) to be a wholly Arab river. Five days later, 'Iraq invaded Iran. The boundary along the Shatt al-Arab was one of the prime factors in precipitating the war and would become the most contentious issue in the peace negotiations that began in 1988. 'Iraq insisted that the Shatt al-Arab lay entirely within its territory and that the Baghdad Treaty was a dead letter, while Iran just as vociferously insisted that the abrogation of the Baghdad Treaty was illegal and therefore the boundary lay at the *thalweg* (midpoint). Following its invasion of Kuwait in August 1991, 'Iraq accepted the provisions of the Baghdad Treaty in order to reach a settlement with Iran, thus formally ending their state of war. *See also* IRAN–'IRAQ WAR.

BAHRI, YUNIS AL- (1901–1978). Controversial journalist. He was born Salih al-Juburi to a well-to-do land-owning family. He studied in Istanbul and lived there for a period. He then began a tour of Europe and South America, where he was very active in the Brazilian–Arab cultural movement. He also traveled in the Far East, where he was connected with the anti-Dutch nationalist movement. Bahri adopted the nickname "the Sailor" (after Sinbad the Sailor) upon his return to Baghdad (q.v.). He worked as a correspondent for a number of 'Iraqi and Egyptian papers and wrote articles about his experiences. He published a newspaper, *al-'Uqab*, which published anti-British articles. He also worked with King Faysal I's (q.v.) radio station, Qasr al-Zahur, which broadcast nationalist and cultural programs.

In 1939, Bahri traveled to Germany. He worked in the Eastern Arab Bureau in Berlin, where he broadcast pro-Nazi programs. He was the first individual in the Arab world to use a microphone to launch political attacks against various governments. He went to France after World War II, where he published an Arab newspaper from 1947 until 1956. After the 1956 Tripartite attack against Egypt, Bahri went to Beirut and worked with a number of newspapers. He returned to 'Iraq, where he broadcast propaganda against Egyptian president Gamal 'Abd al-Nasir. He eventually moved to Abu Dhabi, where he died in 1978.

BAKR, AHMAD HASAN AL- (1914–1982). President (q.v.) from 1968 to 1979. He was born in Tikrit to a landed notable family. After attending the Teacher's Training College (1929–1932), he taught primary school for six years before attending the Baghdad Military College (1938–1942). A member of the 'Iraqi Free Officers (q.v.), he was forced to retire after 'Abd al-Karim Qasim (q.v.) came to power in 1958. Al-Bakr joined the Ba'th Party (q.v.) in 1960. During the short-lived Ba'thist government in 1963, he was a member of the National Council of the Revolutionary Command as well as prime minister. He also became a member of the Regional and National Commands (qq.v.) in 1963. Following 'Abd al-Salam 'Arif's (q.v.) counterrevolution in November 1963, al-Bakr was appointed vice president. 'Arif eased al-Bakr from the cabinet in January 1964 by abolishing the position of vice president.

When the Ba'th regained power in 1968, al-Bakr became president of the new regime and chair of the Revolutionary Command Council (q.v.).

The following year, he became the secretary general of the Regional Command. Al-Bakr also held the post of minister of defense from 1973 to 1977. He enjoyed widespread respect in the military and helped ensure civilian supremacy over the military within the Ba'th. His government reached an accord with the Kurdish rebels that guaranteed the Kurds (q.v.) limited autonomy, nationalized the 'Iraqi oil industry, and established a popular front coalition that survived a number of years. Al-Bakr's regime also signed a Treaty of Friendship and Cooperation (q.v.) with the Soviet Union in 1972 and the Algiers Agreement (q.v.) with Iran that ended the 1974–1975 Kurdish revolt. He held power in 'Iraq for 11 years, although Saddam Husayn (q.v.) gained more and more influence as time went on. Al-Bakr resigned his posts in July 1979, ostensibly for poor health, and transferred power to Saddam. He is believed to have urged a softer line toward Iran after the 1979 revolution.

BARRAK, AHMAD AL-. A Shi'ite tribal shaykh and human rights activist from the al-Bu-Sultan from Babil. He is the head of the union of lawyers and human rights league in this central city. He has also worked with UN programs in 'Iraq.

BARZANI CLAN. A major Kurdish tribal and religious family that has played an important role in the modern political history of the Kurds (q.v.). The clan derives its name from the village of Barzan, which lies in the remote, inaccessible mountainous region of northeastern 'Iraq. The poverty and impregnability of the place produced fierce and tough warriors. The Barzanis descend from Shaykh Mahmud Muhammad, a prominent religious leader of the Naqshabandiyya Sufi (q.v.) order, who moved from Iran to Sulaymaniyya and then to Barzan in the early part of the nineteenth century.

His piety led some of the tribes in the region to follow his order. After his death, his son 'Abd al-Rahim stepped into his position, occupying the town of Barzan and building a *takiyya* (religious center) for himself and his followers. 'Abd al-Rahim had five sons, including 'Abd al-Salam, Ahmad, and Mulla Mustafa. 'Abd al-Salam became the shaykh of Barzan and the head of the takiyya after his father's death, as well as the possessor of its lands. He gathered followers who lived in the takiyya and were supported by its lands. His influence spread and he was able to impose taxes on some of the neighboring tribes who came to follow him fanatically.

He became de facto ruler of the area after defeating a number of Ottoman units in 1908. However, his ambitions put him in a recurring confrontation with the powerful Zibari tribe, which controlled the neighboring region. He made peace with the Ottomans but then reentered into confrontation with them when he refused to join the Ottoman army in World War I or to pay taxes and began to call for tax and educational reform and for improving the condition of the Kurds. The Ottomans sent a force against him, and he was arrested, tried, and executed in 1914. His brother Shaykh Ahmad (q.v.) became the leader of the clan. Leadership passed to Mulla Mustafa (q.v.), who led the Kurdistan Democratic Party (KDP) (q.v.) until his death in 1978. Mulla Mustafa's sons, Idris (q.v.) and Mas'ud (q.v.), in turn took control of the KDP. Mas'ud continues to serve as head of the party and is the most powerful figure in 'Iraqi Kurdistan today.

BARZANI, IDRIS AL- (1944–1987). The leader of the Kurdistan Democratic Party (KDP) (q.v.) from 1978 until 1987 and the son of Mulla Mustafa al-Barzani (q.v.). He was educated by private tutors and studied at religious centers. He left school to join his father and became very active in the KDP. Barzani joined the executive council of the Kurdish Revolution in 1968. He represented his father in 1974 during the last phase of negotiations with the 'Iraqi regime. The failure of these talks led the Barzanis to launch a military campaign against the government. Barzani played a major role in commanding operations in the last phases of the 1974–1975 revolt.

Upon his father's death in 1978, Barzani assumed leadership of the KDP. When Ayatollah Khumanyni's regime came to power in Iran, he favored cooperation with Iran. During the 1980s, Idris spent most of his time near the Iranian border dealing with Iranian officials, while his brother, Mas'ud (q.v.), spent most of his time inside 'Iraqi Kurdistan. However, the Barzanis antiregime activities during the Iran–'Iraq war (q.v.) contributed to the regime's harsh repression of the Barzanis as well as to the depopulation and destruction of Kurdish villages. Idris' son, Nawshirwan (q.v.), has emerged as a leading figure in the KDP and works closely with Mas'ud as the prime minister of the KDP's regional government.

BARZANI, MAS'UD AL- (1946–). President of the Kurdistan Democratic Party (KDP) (q.v.) and the head of one of the two Kurdish regional governments in 'Iraqi Kurdistan. A member of the 'Iraqi Governing Council (IGC) (q.v.), he was born in Mahabad, Iran, the same day his father Mulla Mustafa al-Barzani (q.v.) and others founded the KDP. His mother was a member of the al-Zibari tribe, one of the Barzanis' traditional rivals. He received a mostly private education. Barzani has devoted his adult life to goals enunciated by the KDP. He began his activities as secretary to his father. In 1963, he joined the *pesh mergas* (q.v.). In 1970, he was a member of the Kurdish team that negotiated the March Manifesto (q.v.) with Baghdad. After the party's Ninth Congress, he headed the party's security department.

By 1973, he and his brother Idris (q.v.) were the dominant figures in the Kurdish movement, along with their father. They exercized political power along with a small number of advisers, especially as Mulla Mustafa became ill and more detached. Mas'ud became the youngest member of the KDP Central Committee when he was elected in 1975, when he also was elected to the KDP Politburo. After the collapse of the Kurdish movement in 1975, Mas'ud played a key role in reorganizing the KDP and resuming opposition to the 'Iraqi regime. From 1976 until 1979, he lived in the United States. He returned to Iran after the overthrow of the shah's regime in 1979. From 1979 to 1988, he led a military and political struggle against the 'Iraqi regime and other Kurdish factions, particularly Jalal Talabani's (q.v.) Patriotic Union of Kurdistan (q.v.). Mas'ud assumed leadership of the KDP upon the death of his brother Idris in 1987.

Despite the tension between Barzani and Talabani, the two groups have managed to work more closely together since 1988. Following Operation Desert Storm (q.v.), Barzani coordinated and led the March 1991 uprisings in Kurdistan. In April 1991, Barzani's KDP and several other Kurdish parties initiated talks with the 'Iraqi government. When these talks failed to produce an agreement, he favored holding elections in the Kurdish area for a Kurdish regional assembly. Since the elections in May 1992, which produced a virtual tie between the KDP and PUK, Barzani and Talabani have shared power in Kurdistan. However, serious clashes between KDP and PUK followers killed hundreds of Kurds in the spring and summer of 1994. The rift between the two parties continues to persist. In recent years, both parties have begun to cooperate. Mas'ud enjoys respect for his moderation among 'Iraqi Kurds and Arabs. He was named to the 25-person 'Iraqi Governing Council in July 2003.

BARZANI, MULLA MUSTAFA AL- (1903–1979). The legendary leader of the Kurdish movement in 'Iraq from the early 1940s until his death. He belonged to the Barzani clan (q.v.), a religious clan of the Sunni (q.v.) Naqshabandi Sufi (q.v.) order, which had become involved in the Kurdish uprisings in the 1930s. Mulla Mustafa played a major role in the founding of the Kurdistan Democratic Party (KDP) (q.v.) and the Kurdish Mahabad Republic in Iran in 1946. He became a general in the army of the Mahabad Republic, which collapsed when the United States and Britain supported Iran against the Kurds (q.v.), who had the backing of the Soviet Union at that time.

Barzani sought asylum in the Soviet Union, where he remained until the 1958 revolution (q.v.), when he returned to 'Iraq. He was initially treated as a hero, but tensions eventually surfaced between Barzani and the government of 'Abd al-Karim Qasim (q.v.). Barzani moved to the Kurdish areas of 'Iraq and launched a rebellion in 1960, which continued off and on until its final defeat in 1975. In 1966, he reached an agreement with prime minister 'Abd al-Rahman al-Bazzaz (q.v.) that recognized some Kurdish rights and aspirations, but al-Bazzaz was removed before the agreement took effect.

Barzani was challenged in the 1960s by a more secular, urban, leftist, intellectual faction led by Ibrahim Ahmad and Jalal Talabani (q.v.), who criticized Barzani for being conservative and tribal. In 1964, Barzani succeeded in expelling Ahmad and his faction from the KDP.

In 1970, Barzani reached a historical unprecedented agreement with the 'Iraqi government, known as the March Manifesto (q.v.), which promised autonomy for the Kurds. Barzani was later encouraged by Iran, Israel, and the United States to escalate his demands against the regime. He was also motivated by a desire to establish either a federal republic within 'Iraq or an autonomous state of Kurdistan. He launched another revolt in 1974, which was eventually suppressed in 1975 following the withdrawal of Iranian support. Barzani moved to Iran after the collapse of the revolt and then went to the United States for medical treatment, where he died of cancer.

The dominant figure in Kurdish politics for decades, Barzani had an influence stemming from the strength of his character and personality, his experience as a military commander, and his family's leadership of the Naqshabandi order. His two sons, Idris (q.v.) and Mas'ud (q.v.), took command of the KDP after his death.

BARZANI, NECHERVAN (NAWSHIRWAN) (1966–). Prime minister of the Kurdish Regional Government in Arbil (q.v.) led by the Kurdistan Democratic Party (KDP) (q.v.) under the leadership of Mas'ud al-Barzani (q.v.). Nechervan is the grandson of the legendary Kurdish leader Mulla Mustafa al-Barzani (q.v.). In 1975, his family was forced into exile in Iran. He often accompanied his late father, Idris al-Barzani (q.v.), on official visits to Middle Eastern and European countries, which helped prepare him for his future political career. In 1984, he enrolled at the University of Teheran to study political science but withdrew three years later following his father's sudden death. He took up an active role in Kurdish politics, working in KDP youth organizations. Barzani was elected to the KDP's central committee during its 10th Congress in 1989 and was reelected at the 11th Congress in 1993, when he assumed a position on the political bureau of the KDP. After the 1991 Gulf War, he participated in the negotiations with the 'Iraqi government. In 1996, he was appointed deputy prime minister of the Kurdistan Regional Government in Arbil and in 1999 became prime minister. He has worked very hard to rebuild the Kurdish region's educational institutions and infrastructure, and to modernize the Kurdish region.

BARZANI, SHAYKH AHMAD AL- (1896–1969). Leader of the Barzanis (q.v.), who inherited political power after his elder brother 'Abd al-Salam was killed by the Turks. He burst on the scene in 1920 when he joined the Zibaris in killing a British official and his aide and attacking the cities of 'Aqra and 'Imadiyya. The British separated Barzan from the 'Aqra district to reduce the tensions between the Zibaris and the Barzanis. However, this led to a new confrontation between the Barzanis and the powerful shaykh of the Shirwani tribes, Rashid Lulan. Both sides frequently attacked and burned the other's villages.

Ahmad opposed Britain's attempt to extend civil administration to Barzan. The British used Assyrian (q.v.) levies to control the area but eventually withdrew. Ahmad used this opportunity to strengthen his influence in the region, and he replaced Shaykh Mahmud al-Barzinji (q.v.) as the most prominent Kurdish leader in 'Iraq. However, he was often accused by his enemies of religious fanaticism and deviation, which contributed to tribal strife. By 1932, the 'Iraqi government tried to extend its administrative control over the region, but Ahmad resisted. In the ensuing battles, the government was supported by a number of powerful tribes opposed to the Barzanis.

Ahmad retreated to Turkey, where he surrendered to the government. Turkey turned him over to the 'Iraqi authorities, who placed him in internal exile in the southern part of 'Iraq. At this time, Ahmad's brother, Mulla Mustafa (q.v.), began to emerge as a powerful figure. Ahmad was allowed to return to Kurdistan after several years, and he and Mulla Mustafa became active in antigovernment activities in 1943. In 1944, Mulla Mustafa reached an agreement with the government that resulted in a quieting of tensions. After 1944, the brothers led an uprising before fleeing to Iran, where they joined the Mahabad Republic. Ahmad was allowed to return to Barzan after the 1958 revolution (q.v.). Ahmad remained loyal to 'Abd al-Karim Qasim (q.v.) when Mulla Mustafa and his forces rebelled in 1961. He believed the Kurdish revolt had no purpose. He continued to exercise some religious influence over the Barzanis until his death in 1969, but he no longer played a major role politically.

BARZANI, 'UBAYD ALLAH AL- (1927–1980s). Cabinet minister and eldest son of Mulla Mustafa al-Barzani (q.v.). He was a close aide to his father and was jailed from 1945 to 1955 after his father's unsuccessful uprising against the 'Iraqi government. He had a falling out with his father over family and political affairs, officially breaking with Mulla Mustafa in 1973. 'Ubayd Allah supported the 'Iraqi government's Kurdish autonomy plan against which his father took up arms. He was appointed minister of state in 1974, a position he held until his reported execution in the early 1980s.

BARZINJI, AL- (SHAYKH MAHMUD AL-HAFID) (1884–1956). One of the early Kurdish nationalists. He was a member of the family of Shaykh Kaka Ahmad, a prominent Kurdish religious leader following the decline of the Baban family. Ahmad's grandson, Shaykh Sa'id, led many revolts against the Ottomans. After the fall of 'Abd al-Hamid's government in 1908, the Young Turks, with an eye to reducing Sa'id's influence in Sulaymaniyya, banished him to Mawsil (q.v.), where he was later killed. Shaykh Mahmud returned to Sulaymaniyya, where he enjoyed widespread religious support as the descendant of Kaka. The Turks gave him money and arms during World War I, but with the advance of the British in 'Iraq, he cooperated with them. He was appointed governor of Sulaymaniyya and the surrounding areas. He revolted in 1919, proclaiming himself king and declaring the establishment of a Kurdish state in 'Iraq. British forces shelled his headquarters, and he was forced to surrender. He was then exiled to India.

In 1922, when Mahmud's brother Shaykh Qadir cooperated with the Turks and occupied 'Imadiyya and Koisanjaq, Britain allowed Shaykh Mahmud to return. He again declared himself king of Kurdistan. 'Iraqi and British forces suppressed his government and he fled to Iran. He remained there until 1927, when the British allowed him to return. The Kurds (q.v.) wanted the 'Iraqi government to guarantee certain minority rights in the 1930 Anglo–'Iraqi Treaty (q.v.). Shaykh Mahmud resorted to violence when Kurdish demands were not met. His revolt was again suppressed and he was exiled to Nasiriyya in southern 'Iraq in 1931. He was later placed under house arrest in Baghdad (q.v.). The Rashid 'Ali al-Kaylani (q.v.) government freed him in 1941. He returned to Sulaymaniyya, where he remained until his death in 1956.

BASHIR, MUNIR (1930–1997). Internationally acclaimed musician and supreme master of the *'ud* (lute). Bashir belonged to an old family of musicians from Mawsil (q.v.). He was considered a leading representative of the musical tradition characterized by the Maqam and was widely viewed as an artist who found ways to create something new without destroying the typically authentic. He viewed his music as part of a continuous 'Iraqi tradition starting with the ancient Babylonian through to the pre- and post-Islamic Arabic musical traditions. Bashir also wrote extensively on the musical traditions and instruments that sprang from Mesopotamia and then spread to the rest of the world. He performed his music throughout the world and received numerous international decorations and medals. He served in various capacities, including vice president of UNESCO's International Music Council, director of the International Society of Music Education, president of the National Music Committee of 'Iraq, and secretary general of the Academy of Arab Music. He edited several musical journals and magazines.

BASRA, AL-. 'Iraq's second largest city, its main port and the capital of the province of Basra. It is located on the right bank of the Shatt al-Arab (q.v.), some 113 kilometers from the head of the Persian Gulf. Its population is estimated at 1.5 million people. Basra is divided into three main areas: al-Ashar, which runs along the Shatt al-Arab and contains the commercial district and the bazaar; al-Ma'qil, where the port is located, and Basra proper, the old residential section.

The city includes a number of important ruins and historical sites, including the Aljami, the Masjid, and the burial places of al-Zubayr and Talha, companions of Muhammad who sided with his wife, 'Aysha, at the Battle of the Camel (q.v.). It was founded by 'Iraq's Muslim conquerors in 638 and became a great market town and port, famous for its mosques and its library. Watered by canals from the Shatt al-Arab, it was also an important agricultural city. It was the site of major rebellions against the Umayyads in the eighth century as well as against the Abbasids. In 923, the city was damaged by attacks and was destroyed in the 13th century. In 1500, another settlement with the same name was built a few kilometers above the old city. Basra regained some of its commercial prominence during Ottoman rule, when it was also frequently the site of battles between the Persians and the Ottomans. Its commercial role expanded as Europe became interested in trading with India in the 19th century.

The discovery of oil in southern 'Iraq, and the development of an oil export infrastructure geared to exporting through the Persian Gulf in the 1960s and 1970s, vastly increased the importance and prosperity of Basra. However, because of their proximity to the front lines, both the city and port sustained terrible damage during the Iran–'Iraq war (q.v.); the government spent nearly $6 billion to rebuild Basra once the cease-fire was reached in 1988. Two museums are dedicated to remembering the sacrifices of the Iran–'Iraq war, the Floating Navy Museum and the Museum for the Martyrs of the Persian Aggression. Basra again sustained heavy damage during Operation Desert Storm (q.v.) and the subsequent uprisings in early 1991, from which it has yet to recover. Basra suffered further physical damage as a result of the sanctions and, more recently, of the 2003 Gulf War.

BASRI, MIR. Economist, intellectual, and writer. He was born to a Jewish family in Baghdad (q.v.). He was educated in 'Iraq and in France, where he majored in economics, world history, and literature (q.v.). He served as editor of the *Mayallat* magazine of the Baghdad Chamber of Commerce. Basri was also a member of the administrative board of Baghdad province. A member of the PEN Club and the Royal Asiatic Club in London, he has written a dictionary of economic trends in 'Iraq in Arabic, English, and French as well as short stories and biographies of prominent 'Iraqi intellectuals and politicians.

BASSAM, SADIQ AL- (1899–). Cabinet minister during the monarchy. He was born in Baghdad (q.v.), where he studied at the Law College. He served as a reserve officer in the Ottoman army and spent some time in Asia Minor. After World War I, he pursued a variety of activities: He practiced law, edited a newspaper, served as headmaster of a school, and engaged in trade. Al-Bassam was elected to Parliament in 1930 as a deputy for Kut and later was elected as a deputy for Diwaniya. He eventually joined the Senate. He was appointed director general for state domain and oversaw the lands and property of the government.

Al-Bassam held numerous cabinet portfolios. He served as minister of education (1935–1936, 1940–1941, 1946–1947), minister of the economy (1939–1940), minister of justice (1941–1942), minister of works (1943–1944), minister of finance (1948), minister of defense (1948), and minister without portfolio (1950–1952). He worked closely with Nuri al-Sa'id, Rashid 'Ali al-Kaylani, and Taha al-Hashimi (qq.v.). Al-Bassam was considered energetic, intelligent, and above sectarian politics.

BA'TH PARTY. The Ba'th is a pan-Arab, socialist party founded in Damascus in 1940 by Michel Aflaq (q.v.) and Salah al-Din Bitar. A highly organized pyramidal party, the Ba'th operates on the principle of democratic centralism. It is one of the few political parties with a comprehensive ideology and political doctrine to emerge in the Arab world, summed up in its slogan: "One Arab nation with an eternal mission." The literal translation of *Ba'th* means "resurrection" and also "to rise, to excite, to put in motion." This idea came to be very useful for a party that aspired to be dynamic, activist, and revolutionary. The Ba'th Party has achieved power in 'Iraq (1963, 1968–2003) and in Syria (1963–present).

'Aflaq, a Syrian (Antiochian) Orthodox Christian, and Bitar, a Sunni (q.v.) Muslim, studied at the Sorbonne in the 1930s. Upon returning to Syria, they taught in government schools and began spreading their ideas about Arab nationalism and the need to give rebirth to the Arab nation. They founded the Movement of the Arab Ba'th in 1940 with a handful of supporters. The word *party* was not used until 1944–1945. On 17 April 1947, the First Party Congress was held, attended by about 200 Ba'thist youths. The constitution was approved at this congress, making it the official date of the founding of the party. The party became known as the Ba'th Arab Socialist Party after it was joined by Akram Hawrani's Socialist Party in 1953.

The smallest unit of the Ba'th is the cell, which proved well suited to the party's early clandestine existence. At the top are the Regional Command (q.v.), covering an entire country in which the Ba'th has a party organization, and the National Command (q.v.), which represents all the regions. Since the acrimonious split between the 'Iraqi and Syrian regions in 1966, there have been competing National Commands. The Ba'th has influential regional parties in other Arab countries, particularly Jordan, Yemen, Lebanon, Sudan, and Mauritania.

The three principles in the Ba'th party slogan are unity, liberty, and socialism. The party maintains that the Arabs form one nation that constitutes an indivisible political unit. It condemned colonialism and pledged itself to gather all the Arabs into a single state. The Ba'th calls for a revitalization of Arab society by taking the path of *al-inqilab*, or the transformation of the people and the system.

The Ba'th's concept of liberty has two facets: internal and external. Internal liberty is the freedom of the individual from all psychological, social, and political restraints. From this liberty emerges the external one, the freedom of the individual from foreign control and influence and from social and economic exploitation. Because the human need for liberty has been overemphasized in the past, a system balancing the individual's rights and the community's interest must be provided.

Although socialism comes third in the Ba'th Party slogan, the Ba'th became one of the main exponents of socialism in the Arab world. The Ba'th Party constitution states that socialism is a necessity that springs from the heart of Arab nationalism. Socialism is also the system that will best allow the Arab people to fulfill its potential. The party calls for a redistribution of wealth; the nationalization of natural resources, public utilities, transportation and large industries; and land reform. The party was officially dissolved by the Coalition Provisional Authority (CPA) (q.v.) after the fall of Baghdad. Some elements of the party are believed to be active in the resistance against the Coalition forces.

BATTLE OF THE CAMEL. The Battle of the Camel occurred near Kufa, 'Iraq, in 656 following a revolt against 'Ali's assumption of the caliphate by two companions of the prophet Muhammad, Talha and al-Zubayr. They were allied with the Prophet's widow, 'Aysha. This alliance moved from Medina to 'Iraq and then sent a contingent of warriors to attack 'Ali's supporters in Basra (q.v.). 'Ali's army marched to meet the rebel forces at Kufa to put down the revolt. 'Aysha rode into battle on a camel, inciting her supporters against 'Ali (hence the battle's name). Talha and al-Zubayr were killed in battle, and 'Aysha was grievously wounded. 'Ali sent 'Aysha back to Makka, where she continued to live until her death in 678. Although 'Ali's victory assured him of the support of 'Iraqi Arabs, his forces were weakened for the next campaign, the Battle of Siffin (q.v.).

BATTLE OF SIFFIN. A major battle in 657 between 'Ali's army and the supporters of Mu'awiya, the Umayyad governor of Syria who had refused to accept the caliphate of 'Ali. Mu'awiya sought revenge against the killers of the caliph (q.v.) 'Uthman. He mustered a strong army of supporters and moved his troops toward 'Iraq, while 'Ali marched his troops from Kufa. The two armies met at Siffin, a village west of the Euphrates River (q.v.) near the border between Syria and 'Iraq. For months, the two sides engaged in a series of quarrels, rhetorical debates, and duels, but there was little actual fighting. 'Ali attempted to get Mu'awiya to accept his leadership and thus avoid further bloodshed, but Mu'awiya refused unless 'Ali surrendered the killers of 'Uthman. Tough fighting ensued, leaving hundreds of Muslims dead on both sides. As the fighting continued, increasing resentment at the killing of fellow Muslims built in both camps.

With 'Ali's troops close to military victory, one of Mu'awiya's advisers, 'Amr ibn al-'As, had Mu'awiya's troops hold up copies of the Koran (q.v.) on the tips of their spears. This halted the fighting, and arbitration was undertaken to determine whether 'Uthman had been killed unjustly. Mu'awiya sent 'Amr to represent him and 'Ali sent Abu Musa al-Ash'ari. 'Ali suffered two setbacks. The arbiters decided against him, but he refused to accept the verdict, vowing to continue the fighting. In addition, some of 'Ali's supporters broke away from him, angered that he had submitted his divinely vouchsafed office to human negotiations and deliberations. The Kharijites (q.v.), or "Seceders," withdrew to Nahrawan and demanded that 'Ali resign. 'Ali moved against the Kharijites, crushing them in 659.

During the month of Ramadan (q.v.) in 659, the arbiters met at Athruh. Al-Ash'ari agreed to a proposal denying the caliphate to both 'Ali and Mu'awiya and referring the whole matter to the people. With al-Ash'ari and 'Amr before a huge crowd, al-Ash'ari announced the deposition of 'Ali, calling on the people to choose a new caliph (q.v.). 'Amr followed him and nominated Mu'awiya for the caliphate. Al-Ash'ari immediately denounced this nomination as a betrayal. Arbitration collapsed and the fighting resumed. A Kharijite assassin killed 'Ali in 661 at the door of the mosque in Kufa. Mu'awiya, who had proclaimed himself caliph in 660, convinced 'Ali's son Hasan to give up his claim to the caliphate. Thus Mu'awiya became the first caliph of the Umayyad dynasty. The Battle of Siffin led to a split in Islam between 'Ali's followers, the Shi'is (q.v.) or partisans of 'Ali, and Mu'awiya's supporters, the Sunnis (q.v.).

BAYYATI, 'ABD AL-WAHHAB AL- (1926–1999). A prominent and prolific poet who is considered, along with Nazik al-Malaika (q.v.) and Badr Shakir al-Sayyab (q.v.), one of the leaders of the free verse movement. He was known for his innovative works that depart from classical Arab poetry (q.v.) in substance as well as in structure. He was educated at the Teachers Training College and was a teacher from 1950 to 1953, but he was later dismissed and arrested for his leftist political views and his opposition to the monarchy. Al-Bayyati left 'Iraq for Syria and Egypt in 1955 and settled in Cairo, where he became a member of the editorial staff of *al-Jumhuriyya*. After the 1958 revolution (q.v.), he returned to 'Iraq and became the director of translation at the Ministry of Education and later became a cultural attaché to Moscow and Madrid. He also served as lecturer at the Asian Peoples Institute in Moscow and cultural adviser to the Ministry of Culture and Information in 'Iraq.

Al-Bayyati was profoundly influenced and affected by the economic and political developments in the Arab world, particularly the victimization and injustice that prevailed in 'Iraq and other places. His work reflects his belief that the poet has a duty to resist oppression and seek political freedom. He has published numerous poetry collections, including *Broken Pitchers*, *The Books of Poetry and Revolution*, *Love Poems on Seven Gates of the World*, *Glory to Children and Olives*, *Poems in Exile*, and *Trial in Nishapur*, as well as a prose book called *My Poetic Experience*. He has also translated the poetry of Nazar Hikmat and Louis Aragon into Arabic. He died in Jordan.

BAYKAS, FAYIQ (1905–1948). Kurdish nationalist and poet who is better known as Fayiq 'Abdallah Hima. He was born in Sulaymaniyya, where he studied to become a teacher. He contributed to the deepening of Kurdish national consciousness through his political poetry (q.v.). Baykas was one of the most prominent leaders of the 6 July 1930 uprising in Sulaymaniyya, which demanded that an article on the rights of the Kurdish people be included in the 1930 Anglo–'Iraqi Treaty (q.v.). He was arrested, fired from his job, and exiled because of his nationalist stands and political poetry.

BAYT AL-HIKMA, AL- (HOUSE OF WISDOM). Translation center established by Caliph al-Mamun (q.v.) in Baghdad (q.v.) in 830 where Greek, Persian, Sanskrit, and Aramaic (Syriac) (q.v.) works were translated into Arabic. In addition to Hunayn bin Ishaq (q.v.) and Yuhanna bin Masaway, a number of important translators and literary figures worked at al-Bayt al-Hikma. These included Abu Bishir Matta (d. 940), who was one of the greatest authorities on logic of his time; Qusta ibn Luqa (d. 900), who was considered to be Ishaq's equal in the learning and mastery of Greek; Ibn Naima al-Haimsi (d. 835), who translated some of Aristotle's works; and Thabit bin Qura (d. 901), the Sabean philosopher from Harrin who became famous for his mastery of astronomical and mathematic writings and translations.

BAYYATI, HAMID AL-. A representative of the Supreme Council for Islamic Revolution in 'Iraq (SCIRI) (q.v.) in the United Kingdom. He received his Ph.D. in politics from Manchester University in 1990. al-Bayati participated in 'Iraqi opposition conferences in Beirut in 1990 and in Salah al-Din, northern 'Iraq, in 1992. He is the author of several books, including *The Terrorism Game: 11 September Attacks and New Alliances*, *The Shi'a of 'Iraq: Between Sectarianism and Suspicions in British Secret Documents*, and *The Coup of 8 February 1963 in 'Iraq in British Secret Documents*.

BAYYATI, HAMID MAJID MUSA AL- (1942–). Secretary-general of the 'Iraqi Communist Party (ICP) (q.v.) and a longtime activist in its ranks. Bayyati, an economic expert, was born in Hilla and became active in student politics as a cadre of the Communist Party. He was arrested for these activities in the mid-1960s. He was elected to the ICP's Central Committee in 1976. In 1993, he was elected secretary-general. He lived in 'Iraqi Kurdistan from 1991–2003. He was appointed to the 'Iraqi Governing Council (IGC) (q.v.).

BAZZAZ, 'ABD AL-RAHMAN AL- (1913–1973). Prominent lawyer, educator, and politician from Baghdad (q.v.). He graduated from the Baghdad Law College in 1934 and also received a law degree from the University of London. An ardent Arab nationalist, he sought in his writings to interpret Arab nationalism on an Islamic basis. To him, Islam was not hostile to Arab nationalism but a component of it. Al-Bazzaz was arrested and jailed for his activities by the British following the collapse of the Rashid 'Ali al-Kaylani (q.v.) movement in 1941. He remained in jail until the end of World War II. Al-Bazzaz became the dean of the Baghdad Law College, a position he lost in 1956 for protesting the suppression of free speech by Nuri al-Sa'id's (q.v.) government. He was arrested and banished from Baghdad and was arrested again for pan-Arab activities in February 1959 by the 'Abd al-Karim Qasim (q.v.) government. Following his release, he went to Cairo, where he stayed until the overthrow of Qasim. He held a series of diplomatic posts: ambassador to the United Arab Republic (1963), ambassador to Britain (1963–1964), and secretary general of the Organization of Petroleum Exporting Countries (OPEC) (1964–1965). Following the ouster of Tahir Yahya (q.v.) as prime minister in September 1965, al-Bazzaz returned to Baghdad to join the cabinet of 'Arif 'Abd al-Razzaq (q.v.). He held the positions of deputy prime minister, minister of foreign affairs, and minister of oil. When 'Abd al-Salam 'Arif (q.v.) suppressed a coup attempt by al-Razzaq two weeks later, he appointed his old friend al-Bazzaz as prime minister (1965-1966). Al-Bazzaz also held the foreign affairs portfolio. When 'Arif died in a helicopter accident in April 1966, al-Bazzaz was the civilian candidate for president (q.v.). He withdrew his name after the first ballot, and 'Abd al-Salam's brother, 'Abd al-Rahman 'Arif (q.v.) became president. Al-Bazzaz was appointed prime minister, and he also took on the post of minister of interior (1966) in the new cabinet.

During his two tenures as prime minister, al-Bazzaz brought about a settlement of the Kurdish war that had been dragging on for years. He was one of the leading advocates of the need to resolve the Kurdish problem peacefully. He pushed for a mixed economy that emphasized raising productivity levels as well as redistributing wealth. This moderate stance earned him the enmity of the Nasirites, who considered his policies to be reactionary. Unable to work with 'Abd al-Rahman and without the support of the Nasirites or the army, al-Bazzaz resigned his posts on 6 September 1966. He did not have close relations with the Ba'th Party (q.v.) and was arrested in 1968 along with a number of other former officials, accused of conspiring against the government. He was later released for health reasons in 1970.

BAZZAZ, SA'D AL- (1951–). Journalist and editor of *al-Zaman*, a newspaper published in London after the fall of the regime in Baghdad and Basrah. He was born in Mosul and received his B.A. in political science from the

University of Baghdad, an M.A. in international relations from the Arab League Institute for Research and Studies, and a second M.A. in modern history from the Faculty of Law and Politics, University of Baghdad. Before his defection he was the editor of the government newspaper *al-Jumhuriyya*. He is the author of numerous works of fiction, history, and contemporary Middle East politics in Arabic, including *A War Gives Birth to Another: The Secret History of the Gulf War*, published in 1992 by Ahliya House in Amman, Jordan, and *Kurds in the 'Iraqi Question: Statements and Dialogues*, published by Ahliya House in 1996.

BELL, GERTRUDE (1868–1926). Famous traveler, archeologist, and British intelligence officer who became a secretary to the British high commissioner in 'Iraq. She studied Oriental history and politics at Oxford University. She traveled extensively in the Arabian Peninsula, 'Iraq, Syria, and Turkey during Ottoman rule. Bell spoke fluent Arabic and Persian and played a major role in Britain's administration of 'Iraq after World War I. At the Cairo Conference, which dealt with British policy in the Arab world, she supported Faysal I's (q.v.) ascension to the throne of 'Iraq. Bell wrote extensively about the region, including a report on 'Iraq. Two volumes of her letters were published after her death.

BID'A. A term that refers to religious innovations, or to those practices and beliefs that are not recognized as having precedence in orthodox Islam and that were borrowed from non-Muslim systems. In recent times, the term has also been used in a political sense to refer to opponents who espoused Marxist or Western political concepts or concepts viewed as hostile and alien to Islamic culture and traditions.

BIDAWID, RAPHAIL I (1922–). The patriarch of the Chaldean (q.v.) Catholic Church, the largest Christian church in 'Iraq. He was born in Mawsil (q.v.) and attended parochial schools, including Shimun al-Safa Institute, where he studied for the priesthood. He later went to Rome, where he studied al-Ghazali's (q.v.) religious philosophy. Bidawid received a Ph.D. in philosophy in 1945 and a Ph.D. in theology in 1947. He returned to 'Iraq and taught philosophy and theology. He later served as the bishop of 'Imadiyya in 'Iraqi Kurdistan. He was then transferred to Beirut, where he served until he was elected to the patriarchal seat in 1989. Bidawid has authored a number of works, including studies on al-Ghazali, 18th-century Mawsil, and Christians (q.v.) in the Middle East. He was instrumental in establishing the Council of 'Iraqi Patriarchs and Bishops, which all 'Iraqi churches joined. He was also the founder of the College of Babylon, which is part of Baghdad University.

During the second Gulf War, Bidawid worked hard for a peaceful resolution of the conflict and has been active in seeking humanitarian assistance for needy 'Iraqis of all sects. He has been active in promoting unity between the Chaldean and Assyrian (q.v.) branches of the Eastern Church and has met with the patriarch of the Assyrian Eastern Church, Yuhanna Dinkha IV. He was also successful in his efforts to regain control of some of the nationalized church schools and institutions.

BOULOUS, SARGON (1944–). A prominent avant-garde poet and writer from Habaniyya. He left 'Iraq in 1967, where he had been working as a journalist and writer. He emigrated to the United States in 1968. Boulous studied comparative literature (q.v.) at the University of California, Berkeley, and sculpture at Skyline College in San Mateo, California. He has published his poetry (q.v.) and fiction in a number of Arab and international magazines. A selection of his poems, *Arrival in Where-City*, was published in the United States in 1982. Some of his works have been translated to English and other languages.

BREMER, L. PAUL, III. Appointed by President George H. W. Bush as presidential envoy to 'Iraq. Ambassador Bremer serves as the senior Coalition official in 'Iraq and is head of the Coalition Provisional Authority (CPA) (q.v.). He reports to Secretary of Defense Rumsfeld and advises the president, through Rumsfeld, on the situation in 'Iraq. Before his appointment, Ambassador Bremer was the chairman and CEO of Marsh Crisis Consulting and was previously managing director of the Kissinger Group. Prior to this, he served 23 years in the U.S. Foreign Service and served as ambassador to the Netherlands as well as ambassador-at-large for counterterrorism. A counterterrorism specialist, Bremer has little previous involvement in Arab affairs or with reconstruction projects. But U.S. officials say his appointment appealed to both the State Department and the Pentagon because of his diplomatic experience, his belief in aggressive action to deal with terrorism, and his close ties to prominent U.S. neoconservatives.

BROTHERHOOD OF PURITY (IKHWAN AL-SAFA). A remarkable fraternity of philosophers and encyclopedists based in Basra (q.v.) around the 10th century who wrote and explained their beliefs through essays and monographs. This group of Mu'tazilites (q.v.) attempted to reach some reconciliation between religion and science, and between *Sharia* (q.v.) and Greek philosophy. They wrote some 50 separate essays and treatises covering a whole range of mathematical and philosophical sciences known at the time. The Brothers of Purity spent a great deal of time studying mathematics, which they considered to be important in gaining knowledge of self and ultimately of God. They believed in the transmigration of souls and proclaimed unity among various religious and philosophical truths contained in Greek philosophy, Islam, Judaism, and Christianity. This group described themselves as seekers of truth and are considered one of the most tolerant religious groups in Islam.

BUTTI, RUFAYIL (1901–1956). Publisher and intellectual. He was born in Mawsil (q.v.) to a poor Christian (q.v.) family. He studied at the Teachers College in Baghdad (q.v.) and earned his living by assisting newspaper editors. An article he sent to *'Iraq* newspaper impressed Razzuq Ghannam, the paper's publisher, who asked Butti to continue to write for the newspaper. In 1924, Butti started a magazine, *al-Hurriya* (Freedom), which attracted the work of prominent Arab writers.

In 1930, he published a newspaper, *al-Bilad*, supporting the opposition National Brotherhood Party (q.v.). Yasin al-Hashimi (q.v.), one of the leaders of the National Brotherhood Party, greatly admired Butti's talents and encouraged his career. *Al-Bilad* became the leading paper in 'Iraq and gained the support and contributions of prominent political and intellectual figures. Butti was frequently attacked and sometimes even imprisoned as a result of his articles. In 1934, he was elected to Parliament and held the seat for three terms. His support of Rashid 'Ali al-Kaylani's (q.v.) coup in 1941 led the British authorities to take strong action against *al-Bilad* after they regained power. Butti was arrested and jailed for over a year. In 1952, he was appointed as press counselor at the 'Iraqi embassy in Cairo, where he served for a year before returning to Baghdad. He was the first minister of state for information in 'Iraq, a position he held in two cabinets in 1953–1954.

In addition to Arabic, Butti mastered English, French, and Aramaic (Syriac) (q.v.) and was an authority on Arab literature (q.v.). The well-known Lebanese American writer and traveler Amin al-Rihani was so impressed with Butti's knowledge of Arab literature and history that he named Butti "Ibn Khallikan of 'Iraq," after the famous historian and biographer.

BUWAYHIDS (BUYIDS). Rulers of 'Iraq from 946 to 1055. The Buwayhids were of non-Arab origin and came from a tribe that lived in Daylam, southwest of the Caspian Sea. Some scholars believe the tribe had Kurdish or Persian origins. They gained prominence in the service of the Samanids, a Persian dynasty that ruled in Khorasan and Transcaucasia from 910 to 999. In 940, Caliph al-Muttaqi invited one of Buwayh's sons to enter Baghdad (q.v.) with his forces. The Turkish mercenaries who had usurped the power of the caliph (q.v.) defeated al-Muttaqi (r. 940–944) before the Buwayhid forces could reach Baghdad. 'Ali, the chief Buwayhid ruler in Persia, sent his brother Ahmad at the head of another army to capture Baghdad, this time at the invitation of Caliph al-Mustakfi (r. 944–946). The Buwayhid forces took Baghdad in 945, bringing to an end the control of the Turkish mercenaries. Al-Mustakfi asked the Buway-hids to rule as his administrators, granting 'Ali the title *Rukn al-Dawla* (Pillar of the State) and Ahmad the title *Mu'izz al-Dawla* (Glorifier/Strengthener of the State). Realizing the weakness of the Abbasid state, the Buwayhids dismissed al-Mustakfi and appointed a puppet caliph, al-Muti' (r. 946–974). The caliph was reduced to functioning as titular head of state.

Buwayhid rule brought security and relative peace to 'Iraq. Trade flour-ished, as did jurisprudence, literature (q.v.), and philosophy. The role of reli-gion also increased tremendously under their rule. The first Buwayhid rulers were so powerful that Muslim worshippers mentioned their names along with that of the Abbasid caliph during Friday prayers. The Buwayhids stamped coins bearing their own names instead of that of the caliph. 'Ali and his brother Ahmad worked closely, but their sons were unable to maintain the level of harmony and cooperation that had prevailed during their fathers' rule. The Buwayhid dynasty in Persia came to an end with the defeat of their forces by Mahmud of Ghazni in 1029. In 1055, Tughril Beg, a Seljuk (q.v.) Turkish officer, asked permission to visit Baghdad with his forces as they traveled to the Hijaz on a pilgrimage. He camped near Baghdad, sparking riots and demonstrations against his forces in the city. Tughril Beg's troops entered Baghdad and took control, bringing the Buwayhid regime in 'Iraq to an end.

– C –

CALIPH. Comes from the Arabic word *khalifa*, which literally means "the successor to the Prophet." Abu Bakr was the first caliph and was known as the "successor of the messenger of God." 'Umar, the second caliph, was known as "The Successor to the Successor of the Messenger of God." The term ultimately accepted was that of *al khalifa*. Caliphs were also known as the *imam* (religious leader) or *amir al-muminin* (commander of the faithful). These three terms give an indication of the role of the caliph: He was the head of the religious community, deriving his authority from God, as well as military commander and political leader. The caliph was charged with pro-tecting Dar al-Islam, "the Abode of Islam." He had the authority to appoint or depose the governors of the provinces, and all officials were responsible to him.

The caliphs were generally chosen by the leaders of the community and Muhammad's supporters, the Muhajirin. According to Arab custom, the lead-ers of the tribes pledged their allegiance and gave their full authority to the head of the state. Abu Bakr became caliph by general acclamation. Abu Bakr designated 'Umar as his successor. 'Umar appointed a council to name his successor, which voted for 'Uthman. Although three different methods were used to select the first three caliphs, one feature was common to all. Regardless of whether the selection was by acclamation, designation, or consultation, a declaration of allegiance was necessary to confirm the caliph in his high office. Mu'awiya (r. 661–680), the first Umayyad caliph, wanted to maintain the caliphate in his own clan and designated his son Yazid as his successor. Mu'awiya asked the leaders of the community to pledge allegiance to the caliph-designate during his lifetime. Thus he added two new features to the process: He limited designation to his own family and required that the pledge of allegiance take place before the new caliph assumed office. (*See also* BATTLE OF SIFFIN.)

The Orthodox, or Rightly Guided, caliphs ruled from 632 to 661, with the seat of the caliphate located in Madina. The Umayyad caliphs ruled from 661 to 750, and Damascus was the capital of the empire. The Abbasid caliphs ruled from 750 to 1258, centered in Baghdad (q.v.). The title was later used by the Ottoman sultans, who claimed that it had transferred to their line when Sultan Salim displaced the last Abbasid caliph, who had been exiled in Cairo. The caliphate was abolished after World War I in Turkey by Mustafa Kemal (Ataturk).

CENTRAL TREATY ORGANIZATION (CENTO). The official name of the Baghdad Pact (q.v.) after 'Iraq withdrew from the group. The name *Baghdad Pact* was no longer suitable after the withdrawal of 'Iraq on 24 March 1959, and thus the pact had to be renamed.

CHADIRCHI, KAMIL AL- (1897–1964). A leading leftist politician, journalist, and pamphleteer from a wealthy and prestigious family. His father was the mayor of Baghdad (q.v.) under the Ottomans. He was elected to the parliament in 1927 and again in 1936. He also served as minister of works (1936–1937) but resigned in protest against the army's interference in governmental affairs. In 1954, he entered Parliament for the last time. He was an idealist and one of the leaders of Jam'at al-Ahali (q.v.) and later the leader of the National Democratic Party (NDP) (q.v.).

Al-Chadirchi advocated a non-Marxist but democratic socialist system of government. He is believed to have been one of the handful of civilians who knew in advance of the timing of the 1958 revolution (q.v.). There was speculation that he would get a high position in 'Abd al-Karim Qasim's (q.v.) government, but he preferred to delegate NDP representation to other party members, such as Husayn Jamil (q.v.) and Muhammad Hadid (q.v.). Subsequently, he began to criticize Qasim in newspaper and magazine articles. Qasim sent a message to al-Chadirchi warning him to stop his public criticism of the regime or risk being imprisoned.

Despite his opposition to the use of force and his support of the democratic process, al-Chadirchi allowed the groups he led to participate in military coups in 1936 and 1958, which greatly undermined these parties. He favored the cohesion and solidarity of a smaller body rather than tolerating differences among many followers. Consequently, despite his strength of character and liberal philosophy, his lack of flexibility and unwillingness to work with other groups and leaders to form broader political organizations greatly limited his influence.

CHADIRCHI, NASIR KAMIL AL- (1933–). A member of the 'Iraqi Governing Council (IGC) (q.v.), he is a lawyer from Baghdad and is the son of Kamil al-Chadirchi (q.v.), founder of one of the first democratic parties in 'Iraq. His father had a key role in 'Iraq's democratic movement before the Ba'th Party came to power. He was educated in Baghdad and Cairo and managed several agricultural companies. He was the Sunni representative at the Nasiriya conference of former opposition leaders and also headed the National Democratic Party. He has lived in 'Iraq since his studies in Cairo.

CHALABI, 'ABD AL-HADI AL-. Cabinet minister during the monarchy. He was born to a prominent Shi'i (q.v.) family that was considered one of the three wealthiest families in 'Iraq in 1958. He was a senator (vice president of the Senate), minister of education, and minister of public works between 1946 and 1947. Several members of his family also served in cabinet positions. Al-Chalabi was politically close to Nuri al-Sa'id (q.v.) and was a member of his Constitutional Union Party (q.v.).

CHALABI, 'ABD AL-RAHIM AL-. Academic and cabinet minister during the monarchy. He served as minister of supply and minister of works in 1946, and as minister of agriculture in 1952. He is the brother-in-law of 'Abd al-Hadi al-Chalabi (q.v.).

CHALABI, 'ABD AL-RAHIM AL- (1942–199?). Influential technocrat from Baghdad (q.v.). He received his early education at al-Hikma Jesuit School in Baghdad and received a degree in petroleum engineering in the United Kingdom. In 1975, he was appointed president of the State Organization for Oil Projects. In 1983, al-Chalabi became the undersecretary and chair of the 'Iraq National Oil Company. He played an important role in strengthening oil cooperation with a number of countries, including Turkey and the Soviet Union. He served as minister of oil from March 1987 until October 1990, when he became the scapegoat for a scheme to ration petroleum in 'Iraq. Al-Chalabi is reported to have attempted to flee 'Iraq following his dismissal, but he was caught and executed.

CHALABI, AHMAD (1944–). A member of the 'Iraqi Governing Council (IGC) (q.v.), a leading opposition figure, and head of the 'Iraqi National Congress (INC) (q.v.) before the third Gulf War. A Shi'a Muslim, he was born to a wealthy merchant family in Baghdad (q.v.) and left 'Iraq in 1956. He earned a B.S. degree from the Massachusetts Institute of Technology, and a Ph.D. in mathematics from the University of Chicago. Following the completion of his Ph.D., Chalabi was an assistant professor of mathematics at the American University of Beirut (AUB). He later was appointed the assistant dean of arts and sciences at AUB. In 1977, he became the deputy chair and general manager of Jordan's Petra Bank. Chalabi was named the president of the bank and CEO of the Petra International Banking Corporation in 1981, positions he held until his dismissal in a banking scandal in 1989. Forced to leave Jordan as a result of the scandal, he went to London and gained British citizenship. While in London, he founded the INC, an umbrella group to the other opposition forces. Jordan convicted him in absentia to 22 years in prison on fraud charges stemming from the collapse of the Petra Bank, although Chalabi insists the charges are false. He accused the Ba'th regime of plotting to frame him.

Since the end of the second Gulf War, he has been one of the leaders of the 'Iraqi opposition. Chalabi was reportedly the primary financier of the INC and the chair of its executive council. In the mid-1990s he tried to organize an uprising in Kurdish-controlled northern 'Iraq.

As war between 'Iraq and the U.S. loomed in late 2002, Chalabi actively lobbied for the formation of an 'Iraqi government in exile. However, although he has strong support from influential figures in the White House, Pentagon, and Congress, the Central Intelligence Agency and the State Department distrust him. His detractors point to his long absence from 'Iraq, his lack of an internal power base, and accounting irregularities in the INC's use of U.S. funding. Chalabi returned to northern 'Iraq in January 2003 and was airlifted to Nasiriyya by U.S. forces in April 2003 as Saddam's regime collapsed. Chalabi was named to the 25-person 'Iraqi Governing Council in July 2003.

CHALABI, FADHIL JA'FAR AL- (1929–). Economist. Born in Baghdad (q.v.), he received a B.A. in law from Baghdad University and a Ph.D. from the Université de Paris in oil economics. He was appointed the director of oil affairs in the Ministry of Oil in 1968 and permanent undersecretary of oil in 1973. Al-Chalabi served as the assistant secretary general to the Organization of Arab Petroleum Exporting Countries (1976–1978). In 1978, he became the deputy secretary general of the Organization of Petroleum Exporting Countries (OPEC) (q.v.), a post he held until 1988. From 1983 to 1988, he also served as acting secretary general of OPEC. Al-Chalabi is the author of a number of books and articles on OPEC and energy economics.

CHALABI, RUSHDI AL-. Cabinet minister during the monarchy. He served as minister without portfolio (1954–1955), minister of agriculture (1955–1957), minister of the economy (1958), and minister of transport in 1958. He was arrested briefly after the 1958 revolution (q.v.) and later released. He is 'Abd al-Hadi al-Chalabi's (q.v.) eldest son.

CHALDEANS. The largest Christian (q.v.) community in 'Iraq. Their numbers are estimated at between 400,000 — 600,000. The Chaldeans are the branch of the Assyrian (q.v.) church that united with Rome while retaining its own liturgy and traditions. Although most experts argue that the name *Chaldean* was given by the pope to distinguish this group from the Assyrian Church of the East, earlier references were made to the Syriac-speaking Christian community by Arab and Muslim historians who described them as the descendants of the ancient Chaldeans or as Chaldeans.

Following the Mongol massacres, a group of Assyrian Christians fled to Cyprus, where they came to unite with the Roman Catholic Church. Contacts occurred between the Assyrian church and Rome and emissaries were sent during the 13th century. More Catholic missionaries entered the area in the 15th century, bringing with them their own ideas and doctrines and winning some converts. In the 16th century, disputes arose over the appointment of a new patriarch, leading a group of church leaders to nominate a patriarch who sought unity with Rome. In 1553, the pope declared him head of the Chaldean church, making it the first Eastern church to reunite with Rome. The new patriarch was strongly opposed by his rival and the majority of the church. He was arrested and killed by an Ottoman official in 1555. The final schism occurred in 1683 when Bishop Yusuf of Diyarbakr was recognized by the pope and by the Ottoman sultan as patriarch over the Chaldean community.

In 1830, Pope Pius appointed as the new patriarch Bishop Yohanna Hurmus of Mawsil (q.v.), and he was given the title Chaldean patriarch of Babylon. In 1950, the seat was moved from Mawsil to Baghdad (q.v.). Although the Chaldeans, like the Syriacs (q.v.) and the Assyrians, were also massacred in the 19th century, they did not suffer to the same extent as the others, particularly in the period after World War I. They have not actively sought establishment of a separate state. The Chaldeans have generally been well integrated into 'Iraqi society. Many of their members are businessmen and technocrats, and a few have assumed high government positions. In addition to 'Iraq, Chaldean communities are found in the United States, Turkey, Syria, Iran, and Lebanon. A branch of the church also exists in India.

CHARTER OF NATIONAL PRINCIPLES. Declaration of 'Iraqi, Arab, and regional policy pronounced by Saddam Husayn (q.v.) in 1978. It entailed a number of points: the banning of any foreign military presence in the Arab world; the rejection of the use of force as a means of settling Arab conflicts; the banning of the use of force in settling disputes with neighboring countries except in self-defense; solidarity with Arab states against all foreign aggression; respect for international laws and customs regarding the use of waterways and air space; commitment to nonalignment and neutrality in international conflicts; the development and strengthening of a common base to strengthen Arab economies. 'Iraq committed itself to these principles and expressed a willingness to open a dialogue concerning them. This charter was an elaboration of 'Iraq's stated policies at a time when 'Iraq was seeking a rapprochement with its neighbors and pursuing a leading regional role. It was an attempt to formulate a common Arab strategy and to offer the Arab world a way to deal with the countries of the region and the superpowers. However, the failure of this policy was reflected by the war with Iran in 1980 and the 1990 invasion of Kuwait (q.v.).

CHIAWUK, MA'RUF (1885–1985). A writer, judge, and Kurdish nationalist activist. He was born in Baghdad (q.v.) and received a law degree in Istanbul. He was active in the Kurdish nationalist resistance to the British during and after World War I and was exiled to Burma. After the establishment of the 'Iraqi state, Chiawk returned to Baghdad. He served as a judge and was elected to Parliament. He is well known for his Kurdish nationalist views and authored several books on Kurdish language, literature (q.v.), and history.

CHRISTIANS. Christianity in 'Iraq dates back to the first century A.D., and its adherents are a tiny remnant of what was once a great and powerful religious body. Over the centuries, 'Iraqi Christians have clung to their faith despite religious persecution, enticements to convert, and political repression. Tradition has it that either Thaddeus, an emissary of the apostle Thomas, or the apostle Thomas himself brought the new faith to Edessa. From there it spread to Assyria and Babylonia, where the Church produced a great literature (q.v.) of its own and an Aramaic (q.v.) Bible. In the beginning the people of Mesopotamia may have adopted Christianity not so much out of faith as a desire to protest against the oppression of the Persian and Roman Empires or as a means of expressing their distinct identity and independence within these empires. Arbil (q.v.) became a bishopry, and during the early fifth century, Cteisphon (q.v.) became the seat of the patriarch of the Syriac Church in the Persian Empire.

In the fifth century, Mesopotamian Christians divided into two main autonomous churches: the Nestorian (q.v.) (today, known as the Syrian Apostolic Church of the East or simply the Church of the East) and the Monophysite, or the Syrian Orthodox Church of Antioch. These Eastern churches were considered schismatic by the Western Latin and Byzantine churches, and both suffered further splits and schisms through the influence of the Ro man Catholic Church as well as Protestant churches.

The new churches are the Syriac Catholic Church and the Chaldean (q.v.) Church. They have maintained their own liturgies, rites, and traditions but are in communion with the Vatican. In addition to these churches, there are very small numbers of converts to various Protestant denominations in 'Iraq, mainly adherents to the Baptist and Congregational Churches. A small number of Antiochian Orthodox Christians, Armenian Orthodox, Armenian Catholics, and Protestants also live in 'Iraq. Most of the Armenians originally came from Anatolia as a result of persecution by the Ottomans. The total number of Christians in 'Iraq today is estimated at between 3 and 4 percent of the population. Many Christians, particularly Assyrians, have left 'Iraq in recent years.

CLEMENCEAU-LLOYD GEORGE AGREEMENT. Signed in December 1918 by British prime minister David Lloyd George and French prime minister Georges Clemenceau, this agreement stipulated that the Mawsil (q.v.) province would fall within the British sphere of influence; under the provisions of Sykes-Picot (q.v.), Mawsil was included within the French zone. In return, Britain granted France a free hand in Syria and promised it a share in the oil (q.v.) deposits located in Mawsil.

COALITION PROVISIONAL AUTHORITY (CPA). Organization overseen by the U.S. Department of Defense which has been mandated to run 'Iraq until a new 'Iraqi government is elected. CPA is headed by L. Paul Bremer III (q.v.), a former Department of State official. Although primarily staffed by Americans from the Departments of State, Treasury, Agriculture, the U.S. Agency for International Development (USAID), and the White House's Office of Management and Budget (OMB), the United Nations and nongovernmental organizations have coordinated closely with CPA. Before Bremer's appointment by President Bush, the civilian leadership team that had been in charge of 'Iraq was the Office for Reconstruction and Humanitarian Assistance (ORHA), which was headed by retired Lieutenant-General Jay Garner (q.v.). ORHA is now part of CPA. CPA has sought to restore conditions of security and stability, rebuild 'Iraq's economy and infrastructure, and bring wanted Ba'th officials and terrorists to justice.

COMMITTEE FOR NATIONAL COOPERATION (LAJNAT AL-TA'AWUN AL-WATANI). Established in 1948 to oppose the signing of the Portsmouth Treaty (q.v.) between the Salih Jabr (q.v.) government and Britain. This treaty triggered widespread opposition and a mass uprising, *al-Wathba* (q.v.), that brought down Jabr's government. The public had lost confidence in the government and was increasingly unhappy with events in Palestine, particularly Britain's role in the loss of Arab rights in Palestine. The

Committee for National Cooperation included the 'Iraqi Communist Party (ICP) (q.v.), the Independence Party (q.v.), the National Democratic Party (q.v.), the People's Party (q.v.), and the Kurdish Democratic Party (q.v.). These parties agreed on the need to oppose Jabr's policies and to share a common national goal. An attempt to formulate a plan for coordinated action failed due to serious disagreements between the ICP and the Independence Party. In many ways, this committee laid the foundation for the subsequent creation of the National Front (q.v.).

CONSTANTINOPLE PROTOCOL. Concluded on 17 November 1913, the Constantinople Protocol describes in detail the boundary between the Ottoman Empire and Persia based on the 1847 Second Treaty of Erzurum (q.v.) and previous conventions. In a significant change, the anchorage off of Muhammara was included as part of Persian territory. A Delimitation Commission was established; in the event of disagreements, Britain and Russia had arbitral power. The outbreak of the World War I halted efforts to erect boundary pillars, although the length of the present-day 'Iraq–Iran border had been demarcated by that time. *See also* PROCES VERBAUX.

CONSTITUTIONAL UNION PARTY (HIZB AL-ITTIHAD AL-DUS-TARI). A unionist, constitutionalist party organized in 1951 by Nuri al-Sa'id (q.v.) that included large landowners and tribal leaders. Members included Khalil Kanna (q.v.) and Dhiya Ja'far. Its establishment followed Nuri's unsuccessful attempts to form a united political party with the Independence party. Its primary purpose was to strengthen the position of Nuri against the influence of the regent, 'Abd al-Ilah (q.v.), and the Salih Jabr (q.v.) bloc. The party called for the general reform of 'Iraq's political, social, economic, and cultural life; opposed sectarianism, regionalism, and isolationism; supported the strengthening of the links of brotherhood and understanding between Arab nations and peoples; and sought to strengthen the rule of law. It issued a newspaper, the *Constitutionalist Union*, in Baghdad (q.v.) and another one in Mawsil (q.v.) called the *Constitution*. The party was abolished in 1952.

COVENANT PARTY (HIZB AL-'AHD). A conservative political party founded by Nuri al-Sa'id (q.v.) when he became prime minister in 1930. Its purpose was to gain support for the passage of the 1930 Anglo–'Iraqi Treaty (q.v.). When Nuri resigned in October 1930, the party disappeared.

COVENANT SOCIETY (JAM'YAT AL-'AHD). A political group organized in 1913, mainly by 'Iraqi officers serving in the Ottoman military. Most of these officers would serve in Sharif Husayn's army during the Arab Revolt and later in Faysal's (q.v.) Syrian army. It called for the independence of 'Iraq, with Amir 'Abdullah, son of Sharif Husayn, as king and Prince Zayd as his deputy; and the eventual union of 'Iraq with Syria. Later on, it sought technical and economic support from Britain as long as this aid did not hamper or undermine true freedom. The group held its first meetings in Damascus and then established a number of branches in other Arab areas, including 'Iraq, notably in Baghdad (q.v.) and Mawsil (q.v.). It published a magazine, *al-Lisan*. Its 'Iraqi members included Yasin al-Hashimi, Nuri al-Sa'id, Ja'far al-'Askari, and Jamil al-Midfai (qq.v.). It also gained the support of T'alib al-Naqib (q.v.), who provided financial as well as moral support for its activities.

Following the ouster of Faysal's Arab government from Syria in 1920, the group transferred its headquarters to Aleppo and Dayr al-Zur to continue to seek the establishment of an Arab government for 'Iraq. However, Faysal's collapse had greatly weakened the group, and its activities ceased soon after.

CTEISIPHON. Ancient Parthian city located on the Tigris River (q.v.) to the southeast of Baghdad (q.v.). The city was once the winter capital of the Parthian Empire and is famous for the ruins of a gigantic vaulted hall, the Taq Kisra, which is believed to have been the palace of the Sasanian king Khosrow I (r. 531–578 B.C.). At one time it was also a Greek army camp, but the subsequent Roman occupation extinguished Greek culture in the area. When the Parthians annexed Babylonia in 129 B.C., they found it to be a convenient location and thus made it their winter capital. The Cteisiphanian monarchy that came to power c. 220 A.D. also favored the city. When the Arabs occupied the area in 637, they used the palace as an improvised mosque. The city was deserted when al-Mansur (q.v.) founded Baghdad in 762.

– D –

DAFTARI, 'ALI MUMTAZ AL- (1901–199?). Cabinet minister during the monarchy. He was born to a well-connected Baghdad (q.v.) family and is Yasim al-Hashimi's (q.v.) son-in-law. He served in various government posts, including minister of works and transportation (1946–1947), minister of finance (1948–1957), and acting minister of foreign affairs (1957). He was recognized as a brilliant administrator and political figure.

DA'WA, AL-ISLAMIYYA, HIZO (CALL PARTY). A leading 'Iraqi Shi'a (q.v.) opposition group. Al-Da'wa is believed to be composed of four religious groups. There have been wide disagreements as to when it started. Some believe it was founded in Najaf (q.v.) in late 1957 or 1958; others say it started in the early 1960s. It is generally believed that Nasirism in Egypt led the 'Iraqi Shi'a leaders to consider starting a movement, although they later became dissatisfied with Nasir after he began to crack down on the Muslim Brotherhood. Other scholars believe that the al-Da'wa rose in response to the growing influence of the 'Iraqi Communist Party (q.v.) in 'Iraq after the 1958 revolution (q.v.). During these periods, there were general meetings to organize a movement among the Shi'a. Many scholars believe that Muhammad Baqir al-Sadr (q.v.) organized the movement.

Al-Da'wa's original goal was to develop cultural activities among Muslims. The group initially favored the strategy of the Islamization of society instead of launching military action, and it has rejected Iranian leadership for this reason. It has sought to lead the Islamic movement, although it has not accepted the concept of the government of the jurisprudent. Contrary to other Islamic organizations that accepted Ayatollah Khumayni's leadership, many in al-Da'wa supported Ayatollah Shari'at Madari after the Iranian Revolution. In 1977, it is believed to have organized two major protests and later launched attacks on leading Ba'thist leaders and institutions leading to the arrests and executions of many of its members. After 1980, the party came to favor coalition activity with other parties that oppose the Ba'th (q.v.) government in 'Iraq. It is reported to have attempted to assassinate Saddam Husayn (q.v.) in 1982 and 1987. Al-Da'wa took part in the 'Iraqi National Congress (INC) (q.v.) organized opposition assembly in 1990 but briefly pulled out in 1995 and expressed reservations for the idea of a federal 'Iraq. The first rotating president of the 'Iraqi Governing Council (IGC) (q.v.) was al-Da'wa leader Ibrahim al-Ja'fari (q.v.). The party splintered into four factions in the 1980s. *See also* SUPREME ASSEMBLY OF THE ISLAMIC REVOLUTION IN 'IRAQ.

DAWLA. The state, government, or arena of politics. The term refers to any activity related to administrative, judicial, economic, political, financial, or social organizations.

DAWUD, IBRAHIM 'ABD AL-RAHMAN AL-. A leading military officer and politician from al-Ramadi. He headed the Republican Guard at the time of the 1968 revolution (q.v.). He was one of two military officers who cooperated with the Ba'th Party (q.v.) to overthrow the 'Abd al-Rahman 'Arif (q.v.) regime. Following the successful takeover, he became the minister of defense and a member of the Revolutionary Command Council (RCC) (q.v.). The Ba'th quickly maneuvered to rid itself of al-Dawud so that it could rule unhindered. He was sent to Jordan for a brief visit on 29 July 1968; once he arrived in Amman, he was instructed to remain there as the head of the 'Iraqi military mission, and he was dropped from the RCC.

Al-Dawud was appointed ambassador in residence abroad and retired from service in 1970.

DAWUD PASHA (1767–1851). The last of the major *mamluk* governors of 'Iraq, the slave soldiers who ruled 'Iraq under the Ottomans from 1729 to 1831. Dawud Pasha ruled 'Iraq in an absolute manner patterned on the rule of Muhammad 'Ali Pasha of Egypt. He gained control in 1817 and launched some important reforms. He attempted to end the system of capitulations in 1821 but was unsuccessful due to the protests of the East India Company to the Ottoman government. He also attempted to increase 'Iraq's financial resources in order to modernize and reorganize his own military as Muhammad 'Ali had done in Egypt. Dawud Pasha sought to monopolize the right to buy and export 'Iraqi products, particularly agricultural products like wheat, dates, salt, and barley, and he claimed ownership over merchant ships. He met with only limited success.

Dawud Pasha tried to create a strong central administration; he used repression and harsh military measures in order to undermine autonomous, regionalist, and tribal influences. He removed or exiled tribal leaders not loyal to him and placed a number of his supporters at the heads of the tribes. His war against the Kurdish tribes faced opposition from Iran, contributing to the mounting tensions between the Ottomans and the Persians. The two empires went to war from 1821 to 1823, and the Persians were victorious. However, the First Treaty of Erzurum (q.v.), signed in 1823, left Kurdistan under Ottoman control.

Dawud Pasha rebelled against the Ottoman government following the defeat of the Turks at the hands of the Russians in the 1828–1829 war. The Sultan sent an army against him headed by 'Ali Pasha, the governor of Aleppo, who defeated Dawud Pasha in 1831. This victory by the Ottoman government put an end to the autonomy of mamluks in Baghdad. Dawud Pasha was exiled by 'Ali Pasha, but he was later rehabilitated and named to a variety of posts. He was appointed Guardian of the Holy Shrines of Medina in 1845, a position he held until his death in 1851.

DESERT STORM. *See* KUWAIT, INVASION OF.

DHIA, 'IMAD (1952–). An engineer, political activist leader of IRDC, and a top 'Iraqi advisor to the U.S. administration in 'Iraq. He left 'Iraq in 1982, after his aunt, a prominent doctor, was arrested and then assassinated on release two years later. He lived in Plymouth, Michigan, and is on leave of absence from the Pfizer pharmaceutical company in Ann Arbor, Michigan. He served as the leader of the 'Iraqi Forum for Democracy (established in 1998), which played a leading role in the State Department's project on the "future of 'Iraq." He worked with the Pentagon to select other 'Iraqi members of the ORHA team, many of whom were drawn from his forum.

DIN, BAHA AL- (1950–). A Sunni Islamic intellectual with close ties to the Kurdistan Islamic Union Party (KIU) and the Muslim Brotherhood, he studied Islamic jurisprudence. He helped organize the KIU in 1991 and became its secretary-general in 1994. It is said that the KIU is the third most powerful force in Kurdish-dominated northern 'Iraq.

DIN, DARA NUR-AL- (1953–). A judge who was condemned to three years in jail under Saddam Husayn (q.v.) for ruling that one of his edicts on confiscating land was unconstitutional. A Sunni, he served eight months of his eight-year sentence before being released under general amnesty in October 2002.

DIN, SALAH AL- The founder of the Ayyubid (q.v.) state. He was born in Takrit of Kurdish origins. He became a great military hero to the Arabs and Muslims after his forces inflicted a number if defeats on the Crusaders, regaining much of the territory that the Crusaders had taken, including Jerusalem in 1187. Salah al-Din succeeded his uncle Shirkuh as Egypt's viceroy. He ended the Fatimid dynasty in Egypt by refusing to allow a successor to be named after the death if the last king. In addition to northern 'Iraq, Egypt, and Syria, Salah al-Din controlled the western part of Arabia, Nubia and part of the Maghrib.

Salah al-Din is also an 'Iraqi governorate whose capital is Takrit, the home area of many of Saddam Husayn's (q.v.) family. It has many imortant agricultural and irregation projects, including Samira Dam, the Ishaq project, the Ray al-Awjah, and Ray Dijla. The province is known for its pharmaceutical laboratories, dairy products, and plastics and food production factories.

DIRA. Area where a tribe grazes its flocks or cultivates crops. The area is commonly owned and collectively defended, and any produce is shared in accordance with the number of men in the family and their service to the tribe. The shaykh gets the largest share of the produce and crops.

DIXON, ZUHUR (1933–). Poet and writer. She was born in Abu al-Khasib, south of Basra (q.v.), and is largely self-taught. Her work addresses the position of women in a highly traditional society, while conveying the need for freedom and individuality. She has published several collections of poetry (q.v.), including *Cities Have Another Awakening* and *A Homeland for Everything*.

DURI, 'IZZAT IBRAHIM AL- (1942–). A Ba'thist politician and vice president of the Revolutionary Command Council (RCC) (q.v.). He was born in al-Dur to a poor peasant family. He studied in 'Amara and Baghdad (q.v.) and joined the Ba'th Party (q.v.) in 1958. He was arrested in 1959 and in 1962 for his political activities, in 1963 after the fall of the Ba'thist government, and again in 1967.

After the 1968 revolution (q.v.), Ibrahim was appointed to the Higher Committee for Public Works, a post he held until 1970. He became a member of the Regional Command (q.v.) in 1968 and the RCC in 1969. He served as minister of agriculture and agrarian reform (1969–1972), minister of agriculture (1972–1974), and minister of interior (1974–1979). Ibrahim headed the tribunal that tried Nazim Kazzar (q.v.) in 1973 after his abortive coup. After Saddam Husayn's (q.v.) assumption of power in 1979, he became deputy chair of the RCC and deputy secretary-general of the Regional Command. Ibrahim has visited a number of other countries and led a number of special missions abroad, including heading the 'Iraqi team at the 'Iraqi–Kuwaiti negotiations in Saudi Arabia immediately prior to 'Iraq's 1990 invasion of Kuwait (q.v.). Ibrahim's family has intermarried with Saddam's— Uday Husayn (q.v.) is married to Ibrahim's daughter. He reportedly disagreed with the regime's harsh policy in Kurdistan and is said to have threatened to retire from politics in 1970 if the army's tough methods in the north of 'Iraq did not change. Ibrahim served as deputy commander in chief of the armed forces, and on the eve of the 2003 U.S. attack, Saddam named him as military commander of the northern region. Al-Duri was reported to be leading the resistance against U.S. forces after the Ba'th's fall while other reports said he was seriously ill with leukemia. He remained at large as of September 2003.

DUR KURIGALZU ('AQARQUF). The site of the capital city of the Kassite kingdom (1595–1171 B.C.), located about 24 kilometers to the west of Baghdad (q.v.). The Kassites initially settled in Babylon and acquired much of Mesopotamian culture, before moving to establish their own capital, which they named after their king. One of the remaining landmarks of the city is the towering ziggurat, which is one of the largest in the area. When the ziggurat was first excavated in the mid-19th century, it was believed to have risen over 70 meters, although now archeologists estimate its height at roughly 57 meters.

– E –

EASTERN COMMAND. An organization of Jordanian, 'Iraqi, and Syrian forces established in 1968 with an 'Iraqi officer as its leader. The organization sent troops to Syria and to Jordan. Officially it was part of the Supreme Arab Unified Command, organized in 1964 and led by an Egyptian officer.

The Eastern Command was not very effective because of disagreements on a variety of issues between the governments involved. The 1970 civil war in Jordan dealt a death blow to the organization when the 'Iraqi troops in Jordan supported the Jordanians and the Syrian army supported the Palestinians. After this incident, the Jordanian and Syrian armies returned to the command of their respective national leaders, and the Eastern Command collapsed.

ECONOMY. 'Iraq's once-strong economy has been ravaged by the aftermath of three wars in 23 years and by 13 years of UN sanctions (q.v.). The economy is dominated by the oil (q.v.) sector. Oil is responsible for 95 percent of 'Iraq's export earnings and 50 to 60 percent of 'Iraq's gross domestic product (GDP). 'Iraq was producing 2.5 million barrels a day (mbd) in 2003, well below its pre-1991 level of 3.5 mbd. It possesses the world's second-largest reserves of oil, an estimated 112 billion barrels, and 110 trillion cubic feet of natural gas. 'Iraq's key nonoil industries prior to 1990 were sulfur, fertilizers, cement, and petrochemicals. Although the government has devoted billions of dollars to agricultural and industrial development since the mid-1970s, there has been little rise in the productivity of either sector.

'Iraq's major sources of imports before the August 1990 economic sanctions were the United States, West Germany, Turkey, Britain, Romania, Japan, France, and Italy. Its major export partners were the United States, Brazil, Turkey, Japan, France, Italy, Spain, and the Netherlands. Since the beginning of the oil-for-food program (OFP) (q.v.) in 1996, France, Russia, China, and the United States have all engaged in significant trade with 'Iraq; Egypt, Jordan, Syria, Turkey, and the United Arab Emirates participate in legal trade as well the lucrative black market trade. Its currency is the 'Iraqi dinar; once a strong gold-backed currency, the dinar is almost worthless now. Real GDP (GDP adjusted for inflation) fell 75 percent between 1991 and 1999, to a level equivalent to real GDP in the 1940s. 'Iraq's estimated GDP was $13.3 billion in 1999. GDP per capita was estimated around $2,400 in 2002.

'Iraq appeared to have a bright future in 1980. It had the region's fastest-growing economy, its oil revenues reached an all-time high of $26 billion, and it possessed $35 billion in foreign reserves. However, the outbreak of war with Iran in September 1980 seriously compromised 'Iraq's economic prospects. Within a week of the invasion, 'Iraq lost its ability to export oil through the Persian Gulf, and exports fell from 3 million barrels per day (b/d) in 1980 to between 600,000 and 900,000 b/d in 1981. The regime refused to curtail development plans, though, moving ahead with projects already under construction as well as awarding new contracts. 'Iraq funded both war and development by drawing down its foreign reserves and relying on loans

(which 'Iraq maintains were grants) from its Persian Gulf neighbors, especially Kuwait and Saudi Arabia.

In 1982, the regime was forced to abandon the "war and development"
strategy. Its foreign reserves rapidly were being exhausted, it had acquired
an estimated $30 to $40 billion debt, and oil prices were soft. To exacer-
bate matters, Syria closed down 'Iraq's Banias pipeline in April 1982, resulting in a drop in 'Iraqi exports to 300,000 to 400,000 b/d. Average exports did not climb above the 1 million b/d mark until 1984, and the oil
sector's contribution to GDP hovered at only one-third for several years.
The near-collapse of the oil market in April 1986 dropped 'Iraqi revenues
that year to $7 billion, although revenues rebounded to $12 billion in 1988.
Nearly a third of that revenue went to debt servicing. The economic situation had stabilized by the end of 1986, and Saddam Husayn (q.v.) began introducing sweeping economic reforms in 1987. He reorganized the bureaucracy, completely eliminating the state organization layer, which was
directly below the ministries. The union movement in the state sector was
disbanded, more decision-making power was invested in the heads of state
companies, and incentives, including profit sharing, were introduced. 'Iraq
also moved away from collectivist agriculture (q.v.), selling or leasing all
state farms in 1987.

'Iraqis expected the 1988 cease-fire with Iran to produce a "peace div-
idend," but conditions did not improve. Weak oil prices kept revenue at
between $13 and $15 billion annually; unemployment and inflation, estimated at a rate of 40 to 50 percent, plagued the economy; and debt servicing consumed $6 to $7 billion a year. Moreover, the regime continued
to devote $5 billion annually to military spending. International concerns
about 'Iraq's creditworthiness gathered strength, especially in the aftermath of disclosures in 1989 that 'Iraq had secured over $3 billion in unau-
thorized loans from the Atlanta branch of Italy's Banca Nazionale del
Lavaro. France completely halted its credit facilities to 'Iraq in 1990,
Britain cut its credit line by $90 million, and the United States only ap-
proved half of 'Iraq's credit request. 'Iraq's Gulf neighbors were unwill-
ing to offer Baghdad new credit or to forgive the $34 billion in war-related
loans/grants.

Beginning with a closed-session speech by Saddam Husayn on 30 May
1990, 'Iraq began to issue ominous statements concerning its desperate economic situation. 'Iraq charged Kuwait and the United Arab Emirates of waging economic war against it by overproducing oil and driving down prices.
Oil prices had dropped by 30 percent over the course of the spring of 1990,
resulting in a horrendous revenue gap. By July, 'Iraq's earnings were falling
$8 to $10 million a day below what it had anticipated at the beginning of the
year, and Baghdad began repeatedly charging that it was losing $1 billion a
year for every dollar drop in the price of a barrel of Organization of Petro-

leum Exporting Countries (OPEC) oil. It is against this backdrop that 'Iraq invaded Kuwait in August 1990.

The United Nations immediately imposed comprehensive sanctions. Allied bombing during Operation Desert Storm (q.v.) reduced 'Iraq to the preindustrial age, according to a 1991 UN Report. Further damage was sustained during the uprisings against the regime in the south and in Kurdistan. During the bombing, 90 percent of 'Iraq's national power grid was destroyed, severely disrupting sanitation and water purification facilities; the transportation and communications networks were all but destroyed; and oil-related facilities were heavily damaged, especially refineries and pumping stations.

'Iraq's efforts to repair and rebuild were severely hampered by the ongoing UN embargo and the weight of its foreign debt. Shortages of electricity and fuel, spare parts, industrial and agricultural inputs, and raw materials have crippled the economy. Many of the repairs that were made in 1991 drew on existing stocks of spare parts, which were mostly exhausted prior to the 2003 Gulf War, or on parts cannibalized from other facilities. Before the 2003 Gulf War, the public sector amounted to the production and refining of oil for domestic use and, since 1996, for export, and the rest of the economy was informal and subsistence based. At this time, many people have tried to survive by selling their personal possessions, leaving even the middle class destitute. A significant "brain drain" has further weakened the economy.

Under the old regime, rampant inflation was a continuing problem. The price of staple foods such as wheat flour, rice, vegetable oil, and sugar exploded; by mid-June 1993, vegetable oil cost 106 times what it had in August 1990, and sugar had become 149 times more expensive. In an effort to halt spiraling prices, the regime closed its borders and then invalidated the 25 'Iraqi dinar (ID) note in May 1993. This wiped out the savings of many 'Iraqis, particularly those abroad or in Kurdistan as they were unable to enter 'Iraq and exchange the notes prior to the invalidation. However, this failed to halt the deterioration in the dinar's value, which began a precipitous drop in October 1993. By 2003, U.S.$1 equaled 2,600 ID; it had traded at U.S.$1 = 1.5 ID prior to the invasion of Kuwait.

Economic conditions improved with the advent of oil-for-food program in December 1996 and higher oil prices in the late 1990s. Real GDP grew between 11 and 12 percent in 1999 and 2000, and per capita incomes rose. However, growth dropped to 3.2 percent in 2001 and remained stagnant into 2003. By 2003, 'Iraq earned $12 billion a year from legal oil sales, and illegal trading brought in $7 to $12 billion between 1998 and 2002. Furthermore, 'Iraq has substantial debts that are a tremendous drag on its economy. Its external debt is estimated at $130.5 billion, and reparations paid through the UN Compensation Commission could total $320 billion. Thus far, nearly $200 billion in claims have been settled or filed. After the fall of the regime, the Coalition Provisional Authority (CPA) (q.v.) introduced a free-market system to 'Iraq. The CPA and the 'Iraqi Governing Council's (IGC) (q.v.) finance minister announced significant economic aid and financial reform measures dealing with tax and tariff regimes, foreign investment, and the banking sector. *See also* INDUSTRY.

ERZURUM, FIRST TREATY OF. Boundary treaty between the Ottoman and Persian empires. Fighting along the Ottoman–Persian frontier broke out again in 1821. The fighting was partly the result of Dawud Pasha's (q.v.) attempts to gain control over the Kurdish tribes in 'Iraq, which were being supported by the Persians. This treaty, concluded on 28 July 1823, reaffirmed the boundary arrangement established by the Treaties of Zuhab (1639) (q.v.) and Kurdan (1746) (q.v.), respectively. *See also* ERZURUM, SECOND TREATY OF.

ERZURUM, SECOND TREATY OF. Boundary treaty between the Ottoman and Persian empires. The First Treaty of Erzurum (1823) (q.v.) temporarily halted fighting along the contentious Ottoman–Persian frontier, but in 1837 the Ottomans moved against Muhammara, and the Persians followed suit by attacking Sulaymaniyya in 1840. Under the auspices of Britain and Russia, a joint Turko–Persian Commission was established in 1843 to settle the border question. The commission concluded the Second Treaty of Erzurum on 31 May 1847. According to this agreement, Persia ceded its claim to Sulaymaniyya. The Ottomans formally recognized Persian sovereignty over the city and port of Muhammara (Khoramshahr), the island of Khidhr (Abadan), and the anchorage and land on the eastern bank of the Shatt al-Arab (q.v.). As with all previous boundary treaties, this left the entirety of the Shatt al-Arab within Ottoman 'Iraq. Persian vessels, though, were guaranteed the right to navigate on the Shatt al-Arab from its mouth to the point of contact of the two parties' frontiers. A Delimitation Commission was established, on which Britain and Russia had mediation powers. The commission functioned from 1848 until the outbreak of the Russo–Turkish War in 1876. An Explanatory Note to the Treaty, signed on 26 April 1847, stated that Persia would not be entitled to put forward claims to those regions on the right bank of the Shatt al-Arab or to the territory on the left bank, which belonged to Turkey. The Persian government would later contend that its delegates lacked the authority to sign this Note. *See also* CONSTANTINOPLE PROTOCOL.

EUPHRATES RIVER (AL-FURAT). One of two major rivers in 'Iraq, the other being the Tigris (q.v.). It is the largest and longest river in western Asia. The land between the two rivers is known as Mesopotamia. The river is

2,700 kilometers long. It is formed in southeast Turkey by the Murat and Karasha Rivers, crosses Turkey to enter Syria near Jarablus, and then enters 'Iraq below Abu Kamal. In Syria it is joined by two tributaries, al-Bulaykh and al-Khabur. The river continues in 'Iraq for 1,015 kilometers. The confluence of the Euphrates and the Tigris forms the Shatt al-Arab (q.v.) near Karmat 'Ali, north of Baghdad (q.v.), which flows into the Arab/Persian Gulf. The river is heavily dammed in 'Iraq for hydroelectric and irrigation purposes. Irrigation systems along the Euphrates date to ancient times. As the river flows south in 'Iraq, it loses a large portion of its water due to irrigation canals and Lake Hammar.

– F –

FADHAL, MUNTHIR AL- (1950–). Senior advisor to the 'Iraqi Justice Ministry. He was born in Najaf, of Shi'a parentage. He was visiting associate professor of Middle Eastern Law at the International College of Law in London and a legal adviser in Stockholm. From 1979 to 1981, he served in the 'Iraqi Justice Ministry. He also taught civil law at the University of Annaba in Algeria (1982–1985), the University of Baghdad (1986–1991, 1993), and the University of al-Zaytuna in Amman (1994–1997). He serves as a member of the U.S. State Department working group on the future of 'Iraq for which he has drafted a replacement 'Iraqi constitution. He is published in Arabic, Swedish, English, and Kurdish. He seems to be close to the 'Iraqi National coalition

FAHD, YUSUF SALMAN YUSUF (1901–1949). A well-known and charismatic leader of the 'Iraqi Communist Party (ICP) (q.v.). He was born in Baghdad (q.v.) to a Christian (q.v.) family originally from the north. His family moved to Basra (q.v.), and he attended the Syriac and then the American school. In 1916, he worked as a clerk for the British forces that occupied Basra. In 1935, Fahd helped found the 'Iraqi Communist Party and became a member of its Central Committee. After a government crackdown on the party, he left for Syria and Lebanon, where he established close ties with local communist parties. He traveled to France and then to Moscow, where he attended a Comintern-sponsored school. Fahd returned to 'Iraq in 1937–1938 and reorganized the ICP with Husayn al-Shibibi, Dawud Sayigh, Zaki Nassim, and Amina al-Rahhal. The party, however, was beset by internal divisions and rivalries. Nevertheless, Fahd's strong personality and Moscow's support guaranteed the supremacy of his group, and he was able to reunite most of the rival factions. The 'Iraqi government arrested Fahd in 1947, dealing a heavy blow to the party. He was executed in 1949. Fahd was widely respected for his intelligence, leadership, integrity, and dedication to his principles.

FA'IQ, SALAH (1945–). A journalist and free verse poet from Kirkuk (q.v.). He is largely self-taught, having left school at 15 years old. He has worked as a journalist and as the literary editor of the weekly *al-Dustur*, published in London. Fa'iq has published two collections of prose poetry (q.v.), *Hostages* and *That Country*.

FARAH, ELIAS (1928–). A leading educator and Ba'th Party activist and intellectual. He was born in Aleppo and received a Ph.D. in Switzerland. One of the earliest members of the Ba'th Party (q.v.), he joined the party in 1947 and was later arrested for his party activities. Farah remained loyal to the Michel Aflaq (q.v.) Salah al-Din Bitar wing of the party even after its ouster from power in Syria in 1966. He moved to 'Iraq in 1968 and was elected to the National Command (q.v.). He was subsequently reelected several times. Since 1978, he has devoted most of his time to writing and teaching at the party school and chronicling the history and ideology of the Ba'th. A devoted disciple of Aflaq's, Farah has written extensively on Aflaq's thought. He continues to live and work in 'Iraq.

FARMAN, GHAIB TU'MA (1927–). Novelist and writer. He wrote *The Palm Tree and the Neighbors*, which is generally considered one of the first serious 'Iraqi novels, and *Five Voices*, a realistic portrait of 'Iraq before the 1958 revolution (q.v.). He also wrote short stories. Most of Farman's characters are drawn from the intellectual and middle classes.

FATTAH, SAMI. Military officer and cabinet minister during the monarchy. An air force general, he served as minister of interior (1957–1958), minister of state for defense (1958), and minister of social affairs (1958). He also headed the Basra Port Authority. He was arrested and narrowly escaped hanging following the 1958 revolution (q.v.).

FAYSAL I (1855–1933). King of 'Iraq from 1921 to 1933 and the founder of the modern 'Iraqi state. He was the third son of Sharif Husayn of Makka and the military leader of the Arab Revolt during World War I. He was born in al-Ta'if and spent his early childhood and youth in Istanbul, where he was privately educated. After the 1908 constitutional movement, he was elected to Parliament. During this period, he began his Arab nationalist activities as a result of the growing suppression by the Young Turks.

Faysal increased his political activities after the hanging of a number of Arab nationalists in Syria and Lebanon. He established contacts with representatives in the parliaments in Syria and Lebanon, and they began to agitate for Arab independence. Faysal played a major role in the Arab Revolt launched by his father in 1916. Lawrence of Arabia served as Faysal's adviser and worked closely with him. Faysal led the northern army, and his forces occupied 'Aqaba in 1917 and Damascus in 1918. After the collapse of the Ottoman military and the end of World War I, Faysal represented his father at the Paris, Peace Conference in 1918. He traveled to London and then to Paris, again seeking to gain Arab rights.

During this period, Faysal reportedly signed an agreement with Chaim Weizmann, which dealt with Jewish settlements in Palestine. The agreement has continued to be disputed. Faysal returned to Damascus in 1920 after the Syrian Congress declared him king. However, his kingdom was destined not to last. The French continued to hold ambitions in Syria and Lebanon. French troops attacked the Syrian army at Maysalun in July 1920 and defeated and occupied Damascus. Faysal left Syria and went to Palestine, Italy, and later Britain, calling on the allies to recognize Arab rights.

At the San Remo Conference (q.v.) in 1920, the League of Nations had given Britain mandatory powers over 'Iraq. 'Iraqis greeted the announcement of the mandate with a full-scale revolt, al-Thawrat (q.v.). The British were forced to announce that they intended to form an independent Arab government in 'Iraq under British trusteeship. In an attempt to assuage popular feeling, the British chose Faysal to become king of 'Iraq at the 1921 Cairo Conference. Although the 'Iraqi throne had been promised by Britain to Faysal's older brother, 'Abdullah, British officials decided Faysal was a better choice. His appointment was welcomed by a majority of 'Iraqis. He was confirmed as king in a plebiscite in July 1921 and crowned the following month.

Faysal's kingdom lacked the most basic governmental infrastructures, including a constitution. The Ottomans had not only left behind a stagnant economy and deep-seated sectarian cleavages but also failed to develop any unifying political institutions or a viable central administration. Deeply aware of the ethnic and religious makeup of 'Iraq and worried about the possibilities for fragmentation and division, Faysal wrote a secret memo to his closest advisers expressing his concerns about the future of 'Iraq. He faced increasing demands from 'Iraqi and Arab nationalists who desired full independence, while simultaneously facing Britain's attempts to preserve and maintain its hold over 'Iraq. Moreover, Faysal had to deal with tribal uprisings and the question of the Mawsil (q.v.) province.

Faysal and 'Abd al-Rahman Naqib (q.v.) rejected the Anglo–British agreement that legitimized Britain's hold over 'Iraq. He worked diligently to gain full 'Iraqi independence and established a constitutional assembly and a cabinet in 1922. His aspirations and attempts to establish an independent state met with pressure and opposition from the British government, which imposed tough conditions on 'Iraq before it could join the League of Nations. However, his policy of quiet diplomacy pleased neither the radical nationalists nor the British, who both accused him of supporting and cooperating with the other. He continued to maneuver to gain the most concessions from the British and sought to resolve 'Iraq's disputes with neighboring states to smooth 'Iraq's admission to the League of Nations. 'Iraq gained its independence and League membership on 30 October 1932.

Faysal died in Switzerland on 8 September 1933, and his son Ghazi took the throne. He was a strong advocate of the establishment of a government of laws, and he faced 'Iraq's difficulties with wisdom, humility, and intelligence. *See also* HASHIMITES; SHARIFIAN ARMY.

FAYSAL II (1935–1958). Faysal II was the son of Ghazi (q.v.) and the king of 'Iraq from 1939 to 1958. He succeeded the 'Iraqi throne following Ghazi's death in an automobile accident in 1939. Because Faysal was only three, his uncle 'Abd al-Ilah (q.v.) was named as his regent. Faysal was educated in 'Iraq and at Harrow College in Britain. He assumed power in 1953. Although popular, he had little political influence and was greatly influenced by the regent and Nuri al-Sa'id (q.v.). He was killed on 14 July 1958 during the revolution (q.v.) along with nearly all of the members of the Hashimite family (q.v.). He might have been killed to deprive his supporters of a rallying symbol.

FERTILE CRESCENT. A geographic definition referring to 'Iraq, Syria, Jordan, Lebanon, and Palestine (now Israel). This region was controlled by the Ottoman Empire before the end of World War I and divided into mandates at the San Remo Conference (q.v.) in 1920. The Hashimites (q.v.) in both Jordan and 'Iraq advanced several plans to unite this area. The Syrian Socialist Nationalist Party of Anton Sa'ada also advocated the unity of the Fertile Crescent in the 1930s. Advocates of Fertile Crescent union believed that the unity of the area would be more natural than having greater Arab unity because of the common characteristics of the Fertile Crescent peoples.

FINANCIAL AGREEMENT OF THE 1922 ANGLO–'IRAQI TREATY. Under Article XV of the 1922 Anglo–'Iraqi Treaty (q.v.), 'Iraq and Britain concluded a separate agreement governing their financial relations, signed on 25 March 1924. 'Iraq assumed the full cost of its civil administration, including the expenses and costs of the high commissioner and his staff (Article XIII), and pledged to take over the full cost of its defense spending as soon as possible (Article I). Britain transferred a number of public works to 'Iraq—roads, bridges, the irrigation system, and the postal, telegraph, and telephone systems—for which 'Iraq was obligated to repay Britain at 5 percent interest over the next 20 years (Articles V, VI, and VII). 'Iraq also accepted a share of the Ottoman Public Debt (Article XVII).

FIQH. The technical term for the science of Islamic law or jurisprudence. It seeks to implement God's law through detailed codes of conduct and rules that cover religious, political, and civil life. The sources of *fiqh* are the Koran (q.v.), the practices and sayings of the Prophet (*sunna*), analogy (*qiyas*), and consensus (*ijma*). Shi'is (q.v.), as well as some Sunni (q.v.) scholars, also consider *ijtihad*, independent reasoning and interpretation from first principles, as a source of law.

FOLKLORE. After the Ba'th Party (q.v.) took power in 1968, there was an immediate call for the revival of 'Iraqi and Mesopotamian culture and folklore, and a book about folklore began to appear in 1969. The revival had several aims. First, recalling traditional customs would be a reminder of what shaped 'Iraq as a nation, and this was important in forming a national identity. Second, the revival of traditions through festivals and cultural education made the various groups within 'Iraq feel that their folklore was rich and diverse, therefore instilling more national pride in their country. Third, the revival of folklore was also intended to show the 'Iraqi people that their modern society was directly linked to an ancient culture and tradition.

Poets would read their poems in their own particular dialect, and their works mainly glorified the government and political leaders. Poetry festivals were important in times of political crisis, and the government viewed them as a way of unifying the fractious population. For instance, during the Iran–'Iraq War (q.v.), a poetry festival was held in the south in order to assure the unity of the Shi'is with the government. Many of the poems of the poetry festivals of the 1980s stressed the themes of Pan-Arabism and some denounced the regime of Ayat Allah Khumayni in Iran.

In architecture, the call for preservation of older buildings was made, and the government allocated a large amount of funds to restore some older, damaged buildings. Folklore museums were established and expanded, exhibiting previous lifestyles, housing styles, ways of eating, traditional crafts, and scenes from the social life of Baghdad.

THE FOLLOW-UP AND ARRANGEMENT COMMITTEE (FUAC). A precursor to the 'Iraqi Governing Council (IGC) (q.v.), 65 individuals were selected to be on the Follow-Up and Arrangement Committee (FUAC) of the 'Iraqi opposition during the London conference of 14–17 December 2002. FUAC was originally scheduled to meet for the first time in 'Iraqi Kurdistan on 15 January 2003; this was then pushed back to 27 February 2003, when 54 of its members met in Salah al-Din for 4 days. At this meeting, a six-member leadership council was elected and a final statement was agreed upon. The leadership council was comprised of Ahmad Chalabi (q.v.), Mas'ud al-Barzani, Jalal Talabani, Adnan Pachachi, Iyad 'Allawi, and 'Abd al-'Aziz al-Hakim. The meeting also established 14 committees to correspond to the work of separate ministries.

FRANCO–BRITISH CONVENTION OF 1920. Signed on 23 December 1920, this agreement details the boundary between 'Iraq and Syria. It established a Franco–British commission to demarcate the actual boundary on the ground, with disputes to be referred to the League of Nations for a final decision. Attempts to trace the boundary in 1921 and 1929 failed, and the question went to the League in November 1931. A neutral commission was appointed to recommend a frontier line; the boundary was finally established on 25 November 1932.

FREE 'IRAQ COUNCIL. An opposition group based in London, formed in early 1991 by a group of former intellectuals and politicians whose families were active under the monarchy. It is headed by Sad Jabr, who had earlier established the New Umma Party. It advocates the rebuilding of 'Iraq on a pluralistic, democratic basis and the building of a solid economy.

FREE PARTY (AL-HIZB AL-HURR). A conservative political party with pro-British leanings. Muhammad Mahmud al-Naqib established the Free Party in 1922 to support the cabinet of his father, T'alib al-Naqib (q.v.).

FRONT FOR THE DEFENSE OF PALESTINE (JABHAT AL-DIFA'AN FILASTIN). The creation of this group in 1947 by a number of different leftist and nationalist political parties reflected the growing concern about the future of Palestine among 'Iraqis. Its main objective was to combat what it saw as a Zionist conspiracy to separate Palestine from the Arab world and to protect and promote Arab rights in the face of the Zionist movement. The front was weakened by the government's suppression of the People's Party (q.v.) and the National Union Party (q.v.) and the unexpected stand of the 'Iraqi Communist Party (ICP) (q.v.) on the 1947 United Nations' plan to partition Palestine. The ICP initially saw partition as a colonial plan that would prevent cooperation and understanding between Arabs and Jews (q.v.). But when the Soviet Union voted in favor of partition, the ICP reversed its position and supported the plan. The loss of its left wing caused other parties to begin operating on their own and the front collapsed.

FRONTIER TREATY OF 1937. Boundary treaty between 'Iraq and Iran. In 1932, Iran requested that its border with 'Iraq along the Shatt al-Arab (q.v.)

be recognized as the *thalweg* (midpoint) of the river, rather than as the left bank, as specified in previous boundary conventions. 'Iraq took the dispute to the League of Nations in 1934; after several delays in the League's Council, 'Iraq and Iran undertook direct negotiations. The parties signed a treaty on 4 July 1937. The treaty recognized the validity of the 1913 Constantinople Protocol (q.v.) and the 1914 Proces Verbaux (q.v.), with one exception: Article II moved the boundary from the left bank to the thalweg for the eight kilometers in front of Abadan, a territorial gain for Iran. The agreement also established a commission to erect boundary pillars. *See also* ALGIERS AGREEMENT.

– G –

GARNER, JAY (1938–). Retired U.S. Army lieutenant-general appointed by President Bush in January 2003 to serve as the head of the Office of Reconstruction and Humanitarian Assistance (ORHA), also known as the "Garner Group" a precursor to the Coalition Provisional Authority (CPA) (q.v.). Some have speculated that Garner was removed because ORHA, which was later put under the control of CPA, was unable to control civil unrest and restore order in 'Iraq. As the deputy commanding general of the U.S. Army's V Corps, Garner ran Operation Provide Comfort in the Kurdish area of northern 'Iraq in 1991. Prior to his appointment to ORHA, Garner worked for SY Technology.

GHAFUR, HUMAM 'ABD AL-KHALIQ 'ABD AL- (1945–). Scientist and Ba'thist official from al-Ramadi. He earned a degree in physics in 1966–1967 in Baghdad (q.v.), an M.A. in nuclear physics in 1970 in London, and a Ph.D. in science and technology management in Paris. He was appointed a member of the Atomic Energy Commission in 1974, chief of the Nuclear Research Center in 1978, deputy chair of the Atomic Energy Organization in 1981, and chair (with rank of minister) of the Atomic Energy Organization in 1988. Ghafur has served as Minister of Higher Education and Scientific Research since July 1992. He was captured by U.S. forces in April 2003.

GHANIMA, YUSUF (1885–?). Administrator, politician, historian, and journalist during the monarchy. He was born in Baghdad (q.v.) to a well-known Christian (q.v.) family. He attended missionary schools and then studied history and economics in Beirut and France. After World War I, he quit the business he had been associated with since 1906 and entered politics. Ghanima was elected to the Administrative Council of Baghdad in 1922 and became a member of the Constitutional Assembly in 1923. He was elected as a deputy in the first 'Iraqi parliament.

A capable administrator, he held a variety of governmental positions. Ghanima served as the minister of finance (1928–1929, 1934–1935, 1946, 1947–1948), director-general of revenue (1932), director general of finance (1934–1935), chairman of the Agricultural and Industrial Bank (1934–1941), director-general of antiquities (1941), and minister of supply (1944–1946). Ghanima was close to the opposition National Brotherhood Party (q.v.). He also edited the newspaper *al-Siyasa* (The Politics) and wrote several books and articles including a history of 'Iraq's foreign trade, a history of 'Iraqi Jews (q.v.), and a history of 'Iraqi cities.

GHAYDAN, SA'DUN (1930–1985). Politician and military and intelligence officer. He was born in Baghdad (q.v.) and attended the Baghdad Military College. He commanded a tank battalion in the Republican Guards and played a major role in overthrowing 'Abd al-Rahman 'Arif (q.v.) and bringing the Ba'th Party (q.v.) to power in 1968.

Although not a Ba'thist, he held several prominent positions following the party's takeover in 1968. Ghaydan became a member of the Revolutionary Command Council (RCC) (q.v.) in 1968 and was appointed commander of the Baghdad garrison (1968–1970). He became the minister of the interior in April 1970, a position he held until November 1974. During his tenure as minister of the interior, Ghaydan was taken hostage and wounded in a coup attempt by Nazim Kazzar (q.v.) in June 1973. He became minister of communications in November 1974 and deputy prime minister in July 1979. He was relieved of his cabinet post and his membership in the RCC in June 1982 during a major cabinet shakeup.

GHAZALI, ABU HAMID AL- (1059–1111). A celebrated scholar of the Shafi'i school of Islam. He held a professorship at the famed Nizamiyya school. He was known for his use of reason to combat the Mu'tazilite (q.v.) school and other philosophies and ideas that he considered to be undermining religious orthodoxy. He authored numerous works, the most famous of which is *Tahafut al-Falsifa*, which was in turn refuted by the famous philosopher Ibn Rushid in his book *Tahafut al-Thafut*.

GHAZI I (1912–1939). Ghazi became the king following his father's death on 8 September 1933. He was born in Makka and was raised by his grandfather, Sharif Husayn, until he was brought to 'Iraq in 1924 where he was proclaimed crown prince. He attended the military school and also studied at Harrow College in London, England. Ghazi was generally considered a nationalist but was close to military officers who began to interfere in political affairs during his rule. Unlike his father, he did not have a strong personality and lacked experience as was manifested in his handling of the Assyrian crisis in 1933 when his father was out of the country. Under his rule there were numerous tribal uprisings that led to the fall of various governments including the first coup by General Bark Sidqi in 1936. He was the first 'Iraqi ruler to call for unity between Kuwait and 'Iraq. He was later killed in a car accident, which many 'Iraqis believe was a conspiracy to remove him from power.

GHILGAMISH. The best known of the heroes and epics of ancient Mesopotamia. Numerous stories were told about him in the Akkadian language; the best-known text of this epic was found on 12 incomplete tablets in Ninevah. The tablets were found in the library of the Assyrian king, Ashur Banipal (r. 668–627 B.C.). Some of the gaps in the tablets have been filled by fragments found in other places. The epic poem, about 3,500 lines long, is at least 1,500 years older than Homer's *The Iliad*. It is based on the myth of the god-king Ghilgamish and his amazing adventures, and it was written and rewritten in the languages of the ancient Middle East. Gilgamish became one of the ancient world's dominant epic figures and may have been the prototype for Hercules.

The epic tells the story of Ghilgamish from his early life as an arrogant youth to his days as the king of Ur. The people of Ur begged the gods for help against their oppressive king. The gods responded by creating Inkidu, a wild man of great strength who roamed with the beasts. He was enticed by a courtesan, who brought him to Ghilgamish. Ghilgamish prevailed after a long, fierce battle, and the two quickly became friends. They went on an adventure in the distant cedar forests, where Ghilgamish encountered and killed the fire-breathing guardian of the cedar mountains, Huamaba. The two then killed the Bull of Heaven, which had been sent by the goddess Ishtar, who wanted revenge on Ghilgamish for spurning her. The gods decided that Inkidu must die for killing the Bull. Ghilgamish was greatly anguished by the fate of his friend and feared he would share a similar fate unless he found the secret of immortality. He journeyed far and wide to meet with Utrapishtum, who told him that the secret of immortality lay in the fragrant and thorny Plant of Youth at the bottom of the sea. Although Ghilgamish succeeded in getting the plant, he lost it and his quest for immortality to a serpent.

GOLDEN SQUARE. The four colonels: Salah al-Din al-Sabbagh, Fahmi Sa'id, Kamil Shabib, and Mahmud Salman (qq.v.). They played a major role in bringing down the government of Jamil al-Midfa'i (q.v.) and installing Rashid 'Ali al-Kaylani (q.v.) in power in the 1941 revolt. When 'Abd al-Ilah (q.v.), the regent, fled to Jordan after the Rashid 'Ali coup, the Golden

Square appointed Sharif Sharaf as regent, a Hashimite (q.v.) who was not believed to be overly sympathetic to the British. This sparked a confrontation between the government and the British.

After a month of fighting between the 'Iraqi army and British forces sent from Palestine, the government collapsed, and its members fled 'Iraq. A truce was signed between 'Iraq and Britain in May 1941. The regent returned with Nuri al-Sa'id (q.v.) to Baghdad (q.v.), and Jamil al-Midfa'i was again named prime minister. However, al-Midfa'i's refusal to take harsh actions against the rebels led to his resignation, and subsequent governments took a hard line against the rebels. All four members of the Golden Square were executed, and Rashid 'Ali was imprisoned.

GUARDIANS OF INDEPENDENCE GROUP (JAM'YAT HARAS AL-ISTIQLAL). A secretive, clandestine political group established in early 1919 to oppose the British occupation of 'Iraq following World War I. Ja'far abu al-Timman (q.v.) was its main organizer and leader. The Guardians of Independence used both nationalist and religious rhetoric against the British presence and contributed greatly to the rise of emotions that led to the 1920 revolt, al-Thawrat (q.v.). It called for 'Iraqi and Syrian independence, the establishment of a constitutional monarchy, and the rejection of technical or economic assistance from the British. It concentrated most of its activities in the central Euphrates (q.v.) area and in Baghdad (q.v.). Its leadership included a number of prominent religious and political figures: Muhammad al-Sadr (q.v.), Shakir Mahmud, Hikmat Shawkat, Jalal Baban (q.v.), and Muhammad Baqir al-Shabibi. *See also* ANGLO–'IRAQI TREATY OF 1922.

– H –

HABBUBI, AHMAD AL-. One of the leading figures of the National Democratic Assembly, composed of the Unionist Socialist Party, 'Iraqi Free Officers (q.v.), and the Democratic Unionist Assembly. Born in Najaf, he obtained a law degree from Baghdad University in 1955 and later did graduate work in law at the University of Cairo. Al-Habbubi was a member of the Independence Party (q.v.) from 1946–1960 and later founded the Arab Socialist Party. He founded the National Democratic Assembly while in Egypt. He served as minister of rural affairs in 1965. He was arrested in Baghdad (q.v.) in 1968 and left 'Iraq in 1970 for Egypt.

HABBUBI, MUHAMMAD AL- (?–1916). Poet. Born in the mid-19th century in Najaf, he is considered one of the great poets of the old school. He is noted for his *Ghazals*, many of which had religious overtones, and he also wrote

Muwashahat, stanza poetry (q.v.). Al-Habbubi's work has been compared to that of the prominent Arab poet al-Ma'arri; both were suspected of atheism in some of their verse. A strong nationalist, he died resisting the British occupation of 'Iraq in 1916.

HADD. The term, which literally means "limit," is used in Islamic law to refer to the punishment prescribed for crimes by the Koran or the *sunna*, the practices and sayings of the prophet Muhammad.

HADDAD, NA'IM (1933–). Ba'thist minister. Born to a Shi'i (q.v.) family in Nasiriyya, he joined the Ba'th Party (q.v.) in the late 1950s. A one-time governor of Diyala province, he served as a member of the Regional Command (1974–1986) (q.v.) and the Revolutionary Command Council (RCC) (1977–1986) (q.v.). He held a series of cabinet positions: minister of youth (1974–1977), minister of state (1977), and deputy prime minister (1979–1980). In 1979, Haddad headed the special tribunal that tried the alleged plotters in the July 1979 "pro-Syrian plot." Twenty-two top Ba'thist officials, including five members of the RCC, were executed. He resigned as deputy prime minister upon his election to Parliament in 1980, where he served as speaker for many years. He was removed from all of his positions in 1986.

HADI, AL-. Abbasid caliph (q.v.), r. 785–786. Al-Hadi attempted to have his brother Harun al-Rashid (q.v.) disqualified from the succession to the caliphate in favor of his son Ja'far. Consequently, al-Rashid became a virtual fugitive until the death of al-Hadi. Al-Hadi reversed the policies of his father al-Mahdi (q.v.) and harshly persecuted the 'Alids and the Umayyads, jailing their leaders and confiscating their properties. He is perhaps best known for his massacre of 'Alid princes following their unsuccessful uprising in 786. Al-Hadi reportedly was poisoned by al-Khayzaran, the mother of al-Rashid, and died within a year of his assumption to the caliphate. Hadi became the deputy chairman of the RCC, and Saddam Husayn (q.v.) named him as the military commander of the central Euphrates' region on the eve of war with the United States in 2003. He was captured by U.S. forces in July 2003.

HADI, MIZBAN KHIDHR (1930–). A Shi'i (q.v.) Ba'thist activist from the Diyala district. He graduated from the Teachers College in 1963. He joined the Ba'th Party (q.v.) in 1958–1959 and was arrested by 'Abd al-Karim Qasim's (q.v.) government for antiregime activities. He was also arrested following the November 1963 countercoup against the Ba'th by 'Abd al-Salam 'Arif (q.v.). Hadi became a member of the Regional Command (q.v.) in 1982 after a period of party activity in Wasit, Najaf, and Diyala. He served as minister without portfolio (1982–1991) and was named to the Revolutionary

Command Council (q.v.) in October 1991. He played an important role in suppressing antigovernment uprisings in the wake of Operation Desert Storm. He surrendered to the Coalition Provisional Authority (CPA) (q.v.) in July 2003. *See also* KUWAIT, INVASION OF.

HADID, MUHAMMAD (1906–). Politician and cabinet minister. His father was believed to be one of the richest men in Mawsil (q.v.), and Hadid married the daughter of another millionaire. He studied at the London School of Economics and the American University of Beirut. He was one of the most influential civilians during the early days of 'Abd al-Karim Qasim's (q.v.) regime, holding the post of minister of finance (1958–1960). Hadid was one of the founders of Jam'at al-Ahali (q.v.) and the number two figure behind Kamil al-Chadirchi (q.v.). He also was a member of the National Democratic Party (q.v.). In May 1960, however, he broke relations with Chadirchi over the issue of how to deal with Qasim as Qasim leaned toward the communists. Hadid later formed the National Progressive Party. He was a prominent industrialist from 1939 and eventually became the director of the Vegetable Oil Extraction Company, in which he was also an important shareholder. Some believe he was responsible for getting Qasim to pass Law 80 (q.v.) and to join the Organization of Petroleum Exporting Countries (OPEC).

HADITHI, ANWAR AL- (1926–). A military officer and politician. He was educated at the Military College in Baghdad (q.v.). He played an active role in the 1958 revolution (q.v.) and in the 1963 Ba'thist coup. He served as secretary general of the Revolutionary Command Council (q.v.) in 1963. After 'Abd al-Salam 'Arif's (q.v.) countercoup in 1963, al-Hadithi was imprisoned for three years. He held the positions of minister of labor and social affairs (1968–1970, 1972–1976) and minister of transportation (1970–1972). He then served as ambassador to Czechoslovakia. He has retired from politics.

HADITHI, MURTADHA AL- (1939–1980). A Ba'thist activist and official. He received a degree in natural sciences in 1966 from the Teacher's College at Baghdad University. He led strikes and demonstrations against 'Abd al-Karim Qasim (q.v.) that led to his arrest in 1963. He led a military detachment during the 1968 Ba'th takeover. Following the coup, al-Hadithi held the posts of minister of labor and social affairs (1970–1972) and minister of foreign affairs (1972–1974). He held membership in the Regional Command (1966–1974) (q.v.) and the Revolutionary Command Council (1969–1974) (q.v.).

Al-Hadithi was relieved of his cabinet post and his membership in Ba'th Party organs in 1974. He was appointed ambassador to the Soviet Union and then ambassador to Spain. He was reportedly arrested upon his return to 'Iraq in 1979, although he was later released. Al-Hadithi reportedly died in Baghdad (q.v.) in 1980.

HAFIZ, YASIN TAHA (1943–1996). Poet and editor from Baghdad (q.v.). He attended the School of Education and taught English for a number of years. He was the editor of *Foreign Culture* magazine. Hafiz's published works include *Memory and the Beasts* (1969), *al-'Araf* (The Tower), and *'Abdallah and the Darwish*. He has also translated the works of a number of Western poets, including W. H. Auden and Dylan Thomas, into Arabic.

HAIDARI, BULAND AL- (1926–1996). A free verse poet of Kurdish origin. He was born and educated in Baghdad (q.v.). He worked as the editor of various literary magazines and was one of the leaders of the free verse movement that revolutionized the content and form of modern 'Iraqi poetry (q.v.). He has published several collections of poetry, including *Throb of Clay*, and contributed to free verse magazines in Lebanon, including *Shi'r* and *Mawaqif*. Al-Haidari lived in exile in Beirut from 1963 to 1976 and then returned to Baghdad. He currently lives in England, where he regularly contributes to Arabic-language publications.

HAIRI, KAZIM AL- (1938–). Al-Hairi is a prominent Mujtahid, follower of Muhammad Baqir al-Sadr (q.v.), and an ally of Muhammad Sadiq al-Sadr (q.v.). He was born in Karbala and studied there and in Najaf under Mahmud Shahrudi and Muhammad Baqir al-Sadr. In 1973, he left 'Iraq for Qum in Iran where he has taught at one of its seminaries. He has recently called on 'Iraqi Shi'is to support the stands of Muqtada al-Sadr (q.v.).

HAJJ 'AZIZ, AL-. A communist politician and intellectual of Kurdish origin from Baghdad (q.v.). He graduated from the Higher Teachers College and began his career as a teacher. He joined the 'Iraqi Communist Party (ICP) (q.v.) in 1945 and was arrested and sentenced to life imprisonment in 1946. After the 1958 revolution (q.v.), he was released and resumed his political activity in the ICP as the editor of its newspaper. In 1959, 'Aziz went to Moscow to further his education. He opposed the cooperation between the ICP and 'Abd al-Salam 'Arif's (q.v.) government in 1964.

After he returned to 'Iraq in 1966, he was elected to the Politburo of the ICP. His differences with the ICP leadership led to a major split in the party in 1967. 'Aziz headed the ICP–Central Command faction and served as its secretary general. The ICP–Central Command violently opposed the regime of 'Abd al-Rahman 'Arif (q.v.) and continued its opposition after the Ba'th Party (q.v.) regained power in 1968. 'Aziz was arrested again in 1968.

In 1969, he recanted his opposition to the regime in newspaper articles and gave up all organized political activity. In 1971, he became 'Iraq's representative to UNESCO and was elected to its executive council in 1978. 'Aziz has authored a number of books on Kurdish and 'Iraqi history as well as his memoirs.

HAJJAJ BIN YUSUF, AL- (660–714). A famous Arab military commander, political leader, and orator during the reign of Caliph 'Abd al-Malik (r. 685–705). He belonged to the tribe of Thaqif and grew up in al-Ta'if. As commander of the police in Damascus, al-Hajjaj gained a reputation as an orator and a tough politician. 'Abd al-Malik, facing serious internal challenges to his rule, named al-Hajjaj commander of his army. Al-Hajjaj was sent to put down the rebellion of 'Abd Allah bin al-Zubayr (622–692), who had proclaimed himself caliph (q.v.) in Makka after the death of Husayn in 680. Al-Zubayr was recognized as caliph by Arabia, 'Iraq, and Persia. Al-Hajjaj besieged Makka, even bombarding the city with catapults. He defeated the rebels in 692, and al-Zubayr was killed during the fighting. 'Abd al-Malik appointed al-Hajjaj commander of Makka, Madina, and al-Ta'if; within two years, he had brought the region completely under Umayyad control again.

'Abd al-Malik also faced uprisings in 'Iraq by the Shi'i (q.v.) and the Kharijites (q.v.). He appointed al-Hajjaj governor of 'Iraq in 695. Al-Hajjaj entered Kufa at the head of a tiny force. He delivered a fiery speech from the pulpit of the mosque, beginning, "Oh, people of 'Iraq! I see among you heads ripe for harvest. The time of harvest has arrived and I am the harvester. Blood will soon flow below the turbans and above the beards." Al-Hajjaj defeated the Kharijites in 696 and gained the complete acquiescence of the people of 'Iraq through a reign of terror. Eventually, al-Hajjaj was made viceroy of the entire eastern half of the empire, a position he continued to hold under 'Abd al-Malik's successor, al-Walid. Al-Hajjaj built the city of Wasit in 702, located between Basra (q.v.) and Kufa, which became the headquarters of the Umayyads in 'Iraq. He died and was buried in Wasit in 714.

HAKIM, 'ABD AL-'AZIZ AL-. Recently became leader of the Supreme Council for the Islamic Revolution (SAIRI) (q.v.) after the assassination of his brother, Ayat Allah Muhammad Baqir al-Hakim (q.v.), who was killed in a Najaf car bombing in 2003. Hakim, a Shi'a, returned to 'Iraq after 20 years living in exile. Previously, he commanded the group's military wing, the Badr Brigades, and was involved in dealing with other opposition groups. In addition, he participated in some of the initial contacts between SAIRI and U.S. officials. He has said that he does not seek to establish an Iranian-style government in 'Iraq.

HAKIM, AYAT ALLAH MUHAMMAD BAQIR AL- (1939–2003). He was a Shi'a leader of the Supreme Council for the Islamic Revolution in 'Iraq and candidate for a role in the U.S.-appointed 'Iraqi Governing Council (IGC) (q.v.). He was imprisoned and tortured as an opposition leader by the Ba'th Party regime during the 1970s and went into exile in Iran, where he lived for

23 years. Ayatollah al-Hakim advocated strict adherence to a hard-line interpretation of the concept "walayat al-faqih" in which ultimate authority rests with a supreme spiritual leader.

His relations with the United States were uneasy, partly because he held the United States responsible for the failure of the Shi'a uprising in southern 'Iraq in 1991. The presence in 'Iraq of Sciri's armed militia of 12,000–15,000 men, the Badr Brigade, led to further tensions with the U.S.-led occupation authority, which demanded that the group disarm. Before his return to 'Iraq, Ayatollah al-Hakim said the 'Iraqi nation would "use any legitimate means to resist foreigners' occupation of 'Iraq, should they decide to remain," but he softened his stance, ruling out violence as a means of resisting the U.S. occupation and declaring that the Badr Brigade be transformed into a civilian organization.

Despite Iranian support and a high international profile, it remains unclear how much political influence he wielded. His younger brother, Abd al-'Aziz al-Hakim, has been named as a potential U.S. nominee for the governing council.

HAKIM, MUHAMMAD AL-. Senior advisor to the Ministry of Planning. He supervises provincial affairs.

HAKIM, MUHAMMAD BAQIR AL- (1939–2003). A prominent Shi'i *mujtahid* (religious scholar who interprets religious law) (qq.v.) and the leader of the Tehran-based opposition to Saddam Husayn (q.v.). He was assassinated in Najaf (q.v.) after his return from Iran. He was the first ayatollah (Ayat Allah) for the Supreme Assembly of the Islamic Revolution in 'Iraq (SAIRI) (q.v.) when it was under the leadership of Sayyid Mahmud al-Hashimi. With the support of Ayatollah Khumaini, he assumed leadership of SAIRI. Al-Hakim is a university professor and one of the prominent figures in the Shi'i religious circles in Najaf (q.v.). He is an expert in Islamic jurisprudence and the interpretation of the Koran (q.v.). There are reports that he was asked by Muhammad Baqir al-Sadr (q.v.) to lead the movement. He was arrested for anti-regime activities in 1972 and 1977, the second time serving a year and a half in prison before intense external pressure led the Ba'th regime to release him in July 1979. Following the execution of al-Sadr and the outbreak of war with Iran in 1980, al-Hakim fled to Iran. The 'Iraqi regime arrested numerous members of his family to punish him for his activities in exile, and executed a number, including six of his brothers.

Al-Hakim made a triumphant return to 'Iraq on 9 May 2003, and settled in Najaf. He was killed by a powerful car bomb that exploded outside the Imam 'Ali Mosque in Najaf on 29 August 2003 as he was leaving Friday prayers. Widely viewed as a moderate and stabilizing force among 'Iraq's

Shi'i, his death dealt a severe blow to the already troubled security situation in post-Saddam 'Iraq.

HALABJA. A Kurdish town in northern 'Iraq that suffered a chemical weapons attack widely believed to be at the hands of the government of Saddam Husayn (q.v.) in March 1988. During the Iran–'Iraq war (q.v.), the Kurdish *pesh mergas* (q.v.) fought against the 'Iraqi forces; one group of pesh merga helped Iranian forces gain control of Halabja. Several days later, 'Iraqi planes dropped mustard gas and the nerve agent sarin on the town of 70,000, killing around 5,000 immediately; perhaps as many as 12,000 over the ensuing years succumbed to complications from their exposure to the gases. The attack on Halabja was in retaliation for allowing Iranian forces into the town, but it took place during the wider 'Iraqi campaign known as al-Anfal (q.v.) that was aimed at destruction of Kurdish opposition. (q.v.). Although not the only instance of the use of chemical weapons against the Kurds by Saddam's regime, it is the best known. Halabja is a stronghold of the Islamic Kurdish parties, notably the Islamic Movement of Kurdistan (q.v.)

HALLAJ, AL-HUSAYN IBN MANSUR, AL- (858–922). A controversial Sufi (q.v.) mystic during the reign of Caliph al-Muqtadir (r. 910–932). He embraced the doctrine of *fana'* (oneness with God) and traveled as far as India spreading his views on how one could bridge the gap between God and man. He claimed to have reached the state of complete unity with God: "I am whom I love and whom I love I am. We are two souls in one body. If you have seen me you have seen Him, and if you see Him you have seen both of us." He was arrested by al-Muqtadir in 922 and tried and found guilty of infidelity to Islam. Al-Hallaj was killed, his corpse burned and thrown into the Tigris River (q.v.). Some of his followers claimed that it was not al-Hallaj, but rather someone who resembled him, whom the caliph (q.v.) had murdered. His tomb is in Baghdad (q.v.). His only surviving book is *al-Tawasin.*

HAMDANI, 'ADNAN HUSAYN AL- (1940–1979). Ba'thist official and cabinet minister. Following the Ba'th Party's (q.v.) seizure of power in 1968, he was appointed general director of the affairs of oil companies within the ministry of oil. He served as head of the President's Office in 1970 and was a member of the Board of Administration of the National Oil and Minerals Company. Al-Hamdani was a member of the Regional Command (q.v.) in 1974 and later served as secretary-general of the follow-up committee on oil affairs and agreements. In 1972, he participated in the negotiations between 'Iraq and the oil companies that led to the nationalization of the 'Iraqi oil industry. He served as head of Saddam Husayn's (q.v.) office when he was vice chair of the Revolutionary Command Council (RCC) (q.v.) in 1976. Al-

Hamdani became a member of the RCC in 1977 and later served as chief of the President's Office and deputy prime minister. He served as minister of higher education in 1978. Despite his close friendship with Saddam, who had promoted him and helped him along in his career, he was accused of participation in the alleged 1979 "pro-Syrian plot" and was executed.

HAMDANIS, AL-. A semiautonomous state established under the Abbasids that lasted from 929 to 1115. It is named after Hamdan bin Hamdun, who belonged to Taqhlib, a famous Arab Christian (q.v.) tribe that converted to Islam much later than other tribes and that eventually adopted Shi'i (q.v.) Islam. Its capital was established in Mawsil (q.v.) under Nasir al-Dawla al-Hasan (r. 929–968). Under Sayf al-Dawla and 'Ali Abu al-Hasan, the state was extended to include Aleppo and Homs in Syria. The rulers of al-Hamdaniyyun encouraged intellectual activity: it was during their rule that al-Mutannabi (915–965), one of the best-known Arab poets, flourished. The state declined and collapsed during the struggle against the Byzantines and the Fatamids. Murtadha al-Dawla Mansur surrendered the state to the Fatamids in 1015.

HAMDUN, NIZAR (1944–2003). A leading 'Iraqi diplomat and 'Iraq's former ambassador to the United Nations and the United States. He attended the Jesuit-run al-Hikma University (q.v.), received a degree in architecture from the University of Baghdad, and later served in the 'Iraqi military. He was one of 'Iraq's leading experts on Syria and worked in the National Command of the Ba'th Party (q.v.) on Syrian affairs from 1970 until 1981. Hamdun was a deputy minister in the Ministry of Culture and Information until 1983, when he was sent to head the 'Iraqi interest section in Washington, D.C. He was ambassador to the United States from 1985 through 1987. During his tenure in Washington, he cultivated influential figures in Congress, the media. and the business community. He served as undersecretary in the Ministry of Foreign Affairs from 1987–1992. Hamdun was appointed 'Iraq's ambassador to the United Nations in 1992, a position he held until 1998 when he returned to 'Iraq to act as an advisor to Tariq 'Aziz (q.v.). He retired from service in 2001. Hamdun died in New York City in July 2003 after a long illness.

HAMID, MUHSIN 'ABD AL-. An Islamist intellectual and author of more than 30 books on interpreting the Koran. Hamid is the secretary-general of the 'Iraqi Islamic Party, founded in 1960 and banned in 1961, which is closely linked with the Muslim Brotherhood. He is a Sunni Muslim.

HAMID, MUHYI AL-DIN 'ABD AL- . 'Iraqi Free Officer (q.v.). He was born in Baghdad (q.v.) and attended the Baghdad Military College, the Staff College, and the Baghdad Law College. He was one of the seven Free Officers involved in the decision to overthrow the monarchy. He became minister of education and later minister of social affairs after the 1958 revolution (q.v.).

HAMID, SA'ID (1941–). Poet and editor. He studied Arabic literature (q.v.) at Baghdad University and worked for some time as a teacher. He served as editor of *al-Thawra* and headed the Radio and Television Broadcasting System. A committed Ba'thist, Hamid has written about his own experiences, merging the national with the personal in highly symbolic fashion. His poetry (q.v.) collections include *An Eighth Reading*, *Book of Gypsy Songs*, and *The Fires of Presence*.

HAMMADI, HAMAD YUSUF (1935–). A Ba'thist functionary and minister. He was born in Baghdad (q.v.) and received his higher education in The Netherlands. He held the positions of director-general of the Office of the Presidency and secretary to the president (q.v.). He was appointed as minister of culture and information in March 1991.

HAMMADI, SA'DUN (1930–). Former prime minister, National Assembly speaker, and leading Ba'thist theoretician, technocrat, and politician. He was arrested on 29 May 2003. He was born in Karbala (q.v.) to a middle-class Shi'i (q.v.) family. He graduated from the American University of Beirut with a degree in commerce and business administration, and he received a Ph.D. in economics from the University of Wisconsin in 1957. Hammadi joined the Ba'th Party (q.v.) in 1949 and is believed to have organized the first cell in Karbala. He organized a branch of the Ba'th in Lebanon in 1951 and another in the United States in 1953. He was exiled to Libya in 1959; upon his return to Baghdad (q.v.) in January 1963, he was arrested. The successful Ba'th coup the following month led to his appointment as minister of agrarian reform.

Hammadi worked as an adviser to the United Nations' Planning Institute in Syria in 1965–1966. He became president of the 'Iraq National Oil Company (q.v.) in 1968 and was appointed minister of oil and minerals in 1970. He held the post of minister of foreign affairs from 1974 until January 1983, when he resigned because of poor health. He then became minister of state for presidential affairs. Hammadi was elected chair of Parliament in 1984. He held membership in the Regional Command (q.v.) in 1957–1958, 1963, and 1982–1991. He also held membership in the Revolutionary Command Council (q.v.) from 1986 to 1991.

Hammadi was called on by Saddam Husayn (q.v.) in March 1991 to form a new cabinet after 'Iraq's disastrous defeat in Desert Storm (q.v.). He was chosen for several reasons: his background, his skill as a technocrat, and because he favored reconciliation with the outside world in the aftermath of Desert Storm. He was removed on 13 September 1991 purportedly because he lacked the support of the Ba'th Party and had been unable to convince the United Nations to lift its sanctions (q.v.). He is considered an economic liberal and favors a mixed economy. Hammadi is one of 'Iraq's leading experts on Iran. He is the author of a number of books and articles, including *Views about Arab Revolution*, *Toward Socialist Agricultural Reform in 'Iraq*, and *Memoirs and Views about Oil*. Hammad was arrested following the fall of the regime.

HAMMUDI, JA'FAR QASIM (1931–). Journalist and Ba'thist activist. He graduated from Baghdad University with a degree in economics and commerce. He became active in political and nationalist activities as a youth, joining the Ba'th Party (q.v.) in 1950. He participated in party intellectual and organizational activities and was frequently jailed under the monarchy and subsequent regimes. Hammudi was involved in both of the Ba'thist coups (1963, 1968). He served as minister of state (1977) and held membership in the Revolutionary Command Council (1977–1982) (q.v.) and the Regional Command (1977–1982) (q.v.).

HAMULA. The relationship that exists among several extended related families with a common ancestor. Usually this unit is next to the immediate family. It usually includes parents, children, grandparents, married sons and wives, unmarried sons, and unmarried daughters. Sometimes it includes orphaned and female relatives.

HAMURABI (1892–1750 B.C.). Babylonian king who established the famous code of laws. Under Hamurabi, the Babylonian kingdom reached its peak. Hamurabi began his rule by launching major attacks against the Sumerians, annexing southern Sumer to his kingdom and then rapidly annexing the other states of Mesopotamia. He rebuilt the old Babylonian empire and extended his rule to the entire Fertile Crescent (q.v.). The Babylonians rallied to his rule since he was a strong leader who commanded their religious as well as national allegiances. Non-Babylonian peoples within the empire were treated as subject people during his rule; this would continue for the next two centuries. Hamurabi undertook important reforms and spread Babylonian civilization and culture to the regions that he occupied. He launched a number of projects, especially in irrigation, that ensured the spread of prosperity within the empire.

Hamurabi is known as one of the first lawgivers in history. His code of laws is seen as the first that seriously attempted to pinpoint criminal responsibility in a world that was previously ruled by force or by the ruler's whim. Its importance has been widely acknowledged not just because of its revelations about the nature of justice in Babylonia itself but because it presented new and much more sophisticated concepts of justice than had existed at that time.

HAMZA, KHIDIIR. A well-known 'Iraqi nuclear scientist who is the author of "Saddam's Bombmaker," which describes how 'Iraq continued to build up its nuclear capabilities and was posing an imminent threat to U.S. security. He was often interviewed by the United States and media and was close to the neoconservative faction pushing for regime change in 'Iraq.

HAQQI, SA'ID (1945–). Senior advisor to the Ministry of Health. He comes from a Shi'a Kurdish (Fayli) family. From 1979–1983, he taught at the University of Baghdad and served as a senior assistant to 'Iraq's minister of health. From 1985, he worked as a doctor for the Veterans Affairs Medical Center in Florida and assistant professor of urology at the University of South Florida. He did not returned to 'Iraq until 2003 and has become a U.S. citizen.

HASAN, BARZAN IBRAHIM AL- (1949–). A Ba'th Party (q.v.) and security official, and half-brother of Saddam Husayn (q.v.). He was arrested following the fall of the regime. He joined the Ba'th in the late 1960s and worked for General Intelligence abroad after 1968. In 1977, he was appointed head of the President's Bureau and deputy director general of general intelligence. He became director of general intelligence in 1979. Al-Hasan was removed from this position around 1983 and dropped from sight for a while. He apparently believed he would marry Saddam's daughter Ragha, which created ill will when she married Saddam's cousin, Husayn Kamil (q.v.), instead. In January 1989, he went to Geneva as 'Iraq's representative to the United Nations. Al-Hasan was one of the participants in the January 1991 talks between U.S. secretary of state James Baker and 'Iraqi foreign minister Tariq 'Aziz (q.v.). He was known to be ruthless, greedy, and corrupt. He has three brothers, Ghadhon, Sab'awi (q.v.), and Watban (q.v.). He was captured by American forces in April 2003.

HASAN, SAB'AWI IBRAHIM AL-. Prominent security official and half-brother of Saddam Husayn (q.v.). He received a Ph.D. in law from Baghdad University. He was appointed head of general security in 1989. He has three brothers, Barzan (q.v.), Ghadhon, and Watban (q.v.).

HASAN, WATBAN IBRAHIM AL- (1952–). A Ba'th Party (q.v.) and security official, and half-brother of Saddam Husayn (q.v.). He graduated from Baghdad University's Department of Law and Politics in 1977. He assumed the post of director-general of the Office of the Revolutionary Command Council (q.v.) in 1980 and also served as vice chair and secretary of the North Affairs Committee. Al-Hasan was appointed an adviser to the Office of the President in 1988 and later named as undersecretary in the Ministry of

Interior and governor of Salah-al-Din province in 1991. He served as minister of the interior from November 1991 until he was replaced by Muhammad Ziman 'Abd al-Razzaq in the late 1990s. In August 1995, Uday Husayn (q.v.) severely wounded him in a shooting incident. He has three brothers, Barzan (q.v.), Ghadhan, and Sib'awi (q.v.). He was captured by U.S. forces in April 2003.

HASANI, 'ABD AL-RAZAQ AL- (1903–1997). A prominent 'Iraqi historian, writer, journalist, and civil servant. After graduating from the Teachers College, he worked for *al-Mufid* newspaper, which allowed him to travel extensively all over 'Iraq and to publish a book about his travels. He later established his own literary-historical magazine, *al-Fadhila*, and *al-Fayha* newspaper before joining the Ministry of Finance. After Rashid 'Ali al-Kaylani's (q.v.) coup in 1941, Hasani lost his job and was imprisoned for four years because of his involvement with the coup makers. He was allowed to return to the government and joined the staff of the cabinet. He is the author of more than 30 books and monographs as well as a number of articles and other historical and literary works.

HASHIMI, AQUILA AL- (?–2003). Al-Hashimi was appointed to the 'Iraqi Governing Council (IGC) (q.v.) by the Coalition Provisional Authority (CPA) (q.v) after the fall of the Baghdad regime. A Shi'a, diplomat and foreign affairs expert, she served as a close aide to Tariq 'Aziz when he was in charge of foreign affairs under Saddam Husayn (q.v.). She previously headed the public affairs section of the foreign ministry. Aquila held a doctorate in French literature. She was assassinated in the summer of 2003.

HASHIMI, TAHA AL- (1898–1961). A leading military and political figure, and the brother of Yasin al-Hashimi (q.v.). Born in Baghdad (q.v.), he studied at the military school and then at the Military College in Istanbul. He served as an officer in the Ottoman army from 1909 to 1918. Al-Hashimi participated in the Balkan wars and fought against the British in World War I. Although he was a member of Arab nationalist societies such as the Covenant Society (q.v.), he did not join the Arab Revolt. As the commander of seven Ottoman divisions, he was arrested and imprisoned at the end of World War I.

He joined Faysal I's (q.v.) government in 1920 and served as director of general security. After the collapse of Faysal's Syrian government, al-Hashimi returned to Istanbul, where he was appointed the head of the military history department in the Turkish General Staff school. In 1922, he returned to Baghdad. He served in a variety of posts: chief of staff of the army (1923–1924), chief of the census department (1926), and director of education (1928). Al-Hashimi returned to his position as chief of general staff at the Ministry of Defense in 1929 and held the post until 1936. In 1935, he was appointed acting director-general of education. He was visiting Turkey during the Bakr Sidqi (q.v.) coup; he was retired by the new regime and prevented from returning to 'Iraq.

After the assassination of Bakr Sidqi in 1937, al-Hashimi returned to Baghdad and was elected to Parliament. He also formed the Society for the Defense of Palestine. He enjoyed close relations with the Golden Square (q.v.) nationalist officers, cooperating with them to oppose Jamil al-Midfa'i's (q.v.) cabinet. He became the minister of defense in the cabinet Nuri al-Sa'id (q.v.) formed following the collapse of al-Midfai's government, a post he held in five consecutive cabinets between 1938 and 1941. Al-Hashimi became prime minister in February 1941, paving the way for Rashid 'Ali al-Kaylani's (q.v.) return to power.

When Rashid 'Ali's government collapsed later that year, he fled to Turkey, where he remained until 1946. In 1948, he served as a military adviser to the Arab committee coordinating the struggle in Palestine. In 1951, he established the opposition National Front Party. He served as vice chair of the 'Iraqi Development Board from 1953 to 1958. He was seen as a professional military man and an honest and incorruptible political leader. He was elected as a corresponding member of the Arab Academy in Damascus. He was the author of a number of books on Japan, military mobilization, the history of war, the military, geography of 'Iraq, and other topics.

HASHIMI, YASIN AL- (1884–1937). A leading military and nationalist figure during the monarchy. He was born in Baghdad (q.v.), where he also attended school before entering the military school in Istanbul. He graduated from the Staff College in 1905. He returned to 'Iraq and served with the army both in 'Iraq and in the Balkan wars. A devout Arab nationalist and member of the Covenant Society (q.v.), al-Hashimi promoted Arab nationalist ideas among the youth in Mawsil (q.v.). Following his promotion to general, he commanded the Eighth Army in Jordan and served as chief of staff under Faysal I's (q.v.) government. His Arab nationalist activities led to his arrest and imprisonment in 1919 by the British. After the collapse of Faysal's Syrian government, he went to Beirut and then on to Baghdad in 1922. Al-Hashimi was elected to Constituent Assembly and became deputy to the head of the chamber. In 1924, he formed a cabinet in which he also held the portfolios of defense and foreign affairs. His cabinet resigned in 1925 and he was elected again to the Parliament. He served as minister of finance in a number of cabinets (1926–1928, 1929–1930, 1933).

He formed the National Brotherhood Party (q.v.) in 1930 to oppose the policies of Nuri al-Sa'id (q.v.), especially Nuri's support for the 1930 Anglo–'Iraqi Treaty (q.v.). The party was dissolved in 1935 when al-Hashimi became prime minister again. He was forced to resign in 1936 after the Bakr Sidqi (q.v.) coup.

He left Baghdad for Damascus, where he lived until his death in 1937. Al-Hashimi was seen as a brilliant military commander and a tough politician who placed 'Iraq's national interest above personal and political interests. He was an ardent nationalist who sought 'Iraq's independence and Arab unity and who favored a democratic constitution and government for 'Iraq.

HASHIMITES. The family of Sharif Husayn bin 'Ali, the sharif of Makka and king of Hijaz (1854–1931). The Hashimite family ruled in 'Iraq (1921–1958) and has ruled in Jordan since 1921. According to the Hashimites, the Banu Hashim are the family of the Quraysh tribe from which the prophet Muhammad is descended. The family traces its descent from Muhammad through his daughter Fatima and his cousin and son-in-law 'Ali and their son al-Hasan. Sharif Husayn became the Amir of Makka in 1908. After an exchange of messages with the British high commissioner in Egypt, Sir Henry McMahon, he proclaimed the Arab Revolt in 1916 and declared himself king of Hijaz. In 1924, Sharif Husayn took steps to declare himself caliph (q.v.), but he was compelled to resign the same year in order to save the throne for his family. His son 'Ali (1879–1935) succeeded him, but 'Ali was driven out of the Hijaz by ibn Saud in less than a year. Sharif Husayn's second son 'Abdullah (1882–1951) became king of Jordan, and his third son Faysal (1885–1933) became king of Syria (1920) and then of 'Iraq (1921–1933). The Hashimite dynasty was overthrown in 'Iraq in the 1958 revolution (q.v.). *See also* HUSAYN–MCMAHON CORRESPONDENCE.

HASSAN, FAYIQ (1912–). One of 'Iraq's leading painters and sculptors. He believed that artists in this era must be internationalists because national styles only exist in a historical sense. He studied in Paris where he was influenced by French art. After a period of impressionist painting, Hassan's works became more and more abstract. His work focused extensively on local color, such as figures in country costumes and Bedouin shaykhs.

HATIM, ABU ('ABD AL-KARIM MAHOUD MUHAMMADAWI) (1958–). A prominent militia leader in the southern marshes of 'Iraq where he waged guerrilla activities against the regime, he is known as the "Lord of the Marshes." Hatim was jailed by the regime for seven years until 1986. He fought Saddam Husayn's (q.v.) regime for 13 years. Hatim controls much of the 'Amarah area, and the British allow his Hizb Allah group to maintain checkpoints on local roads. He is reported to believe his long opposition to Saddam Husayn entitles him to a significant role in postwar 'Iraq.

THE HAWZA. A powerful Shi'i religious institution, it traces its roots back to the 10th century and trains the Shi'i clergy. It is comprised of around 150 schools, universities, and seminaries, with over 5,000 students. Ayat Allah Sistani issued a religious ruling, or fatwa, in June 2003 opposing the formation of a constitutional council by the American occupation authorities, saying 'Iraqis should elect those who draft their constitution. His ruling was the most significant political pronouncement in the postwar period by the cleric, who urged 'Iraqis to push for general elections for a constitutional assembly, followed by a referendum on a draft constitution.

HAYDAR, RUSTUM (1889–1940). Arab nationalist and cabinet official under the monarchy. He was born in al-Biqa' in Lebanon to a prominent Shi'i (q.v.) family. He graduated from the Sorbonne and the Royal College of Istanbul. During World War I, he taught history and economics in Jerusalem and headed a private Islamic college, where he taught Arab history and literature (q.v.). Haydar was among the earliest promoters of Arab nationalist ideas; he began his nationalist activities among Arab students while he was in Paris. He joined the Arab Revolt, serving as Faysal I's (q.v.) secretary. He followed Faysal to 'Iraq, where he became chief of the Royal Diwan and Faysal's private secretary in 1921. Haydar served in a number of diplomatic and cabinet positions. He was sent to Tehran as minister plenipotentiary in 1929, and he succeeded in producing the first agreement between Faysal and the shah. He became a member of the Senate in 1931. He served as minister of finance (1930–1932, 1938–1940) and minister of works (1933–1934).

Although Haydar was recognized as one of the most knowledgeable and competent figures in the government, he was always very conscious of the fact that he was of non-'Iraqi origin. He worked closely with Nuri al-Sa'id and Taha al-Hashimi (qq.v.), especially after the 1936 Bakr Sidqi (q.v.) coup. Because of his background, Haydar had a number of opponents in 'Iraq and was assassinated in January 1940.

HAYDAR, ZAYD (1929–). A Ba'th Party (q.v.) activist and 'Iraqi diplomat. He was born in Lebanon and raised in Syria, where he studied at Damascus University. He received a Ph.D. in Yugoslavia in political economy. He joined the Ba'ths in the 1940s and became active in Arab nationalist politics. His activities in support of the Algerian Revolution led to his arrest and expulsion from France. Following the February 1966 coup, which brought Salah Jadid to power in Syria, Haydar was arrested and imprisoned for his support of the Michel Aflaq (q.v.) faction. He remained in prison until 1968. From 1968 to 1970, he served as a member of the National Command (q.v.) of the Ba'th Party and as secretary-general of the Arab Liberation Front between 1969 and 1970. He was responsible for the foreign relations of the National Command. Haydar joined the 'Iraqi diplomatic service and served as ambassador to Belgium.

HEWA PARTY. Kurdish political party. A group of students at Baghdad University founded the secret Hewa Party in 1939, whose objective was to promote the freedom of the Kurdish people and the liberation of Kurdistan. The party's size and influence grew very quickly among Kurds (q.v.) in 'Iraq, Iran, Turkey, and Syria. Rafiq Hilmy (q.v.), highly respected throughout the Kurdish community, was chosen to lead the party. The party had a military branch in which most of the high-ranking Kurdish officers of the 'Iraqi army were members. Due to the party's efforts, the 1943 uprising in Barzan grew from a tribal rebellion into a full-scale national uprising with clear goals. Hewa also contributed to the inception of the Komala, a Kurdish nationalist party in Iranian Kurdistan, which led to the establishment of the state of Mahabad. Differences arose between the leftists and the rightists in the Hewa Party regarding the Barzan uprising and toward external forces. These differences grew and eventually led to the demise of the party in 1944. *See also* BARZANIS.

HIKMA UNIVERSITY, AL-. School established in 1932 by a group of American Jesuits. The initial permit allowed the Jesuits to build a secondary school. Over the next three decades, over 1,000 students were enrolled. In 1955, the Ministry of Education granted the Jesuits permission to establish a university. The university quickly gained a reputation for high standards and took its name from al-Bayt al-Hikma (House of Wisdom) (q.v.), a center of learning established by the caliph (q.v.) al-Mamun (q.v.) in 830. 'Iraqi Christians (q.v.) played a prominent intellectual and administrative role at al-Hikma. The school was nationalized following the 1958 revolution (q.v.).

HILMY, RAFIQ (1898–1960). Kurdish nationalist leader and writer. He was born in the city of Kifri and attended the Military College in Istanbul. He later studied engineering. He mastered several languages, including Arabic, Turkish, Persian, and French, and he wrote poetry (q.v.) in Turkish. Hilmy was close to Shaykh Mahmud (q.v.). He often wrote political articles in the various Kurdish newspapers. He became a member of the leadership of Jamiyat Kurdistan, which was headed by Mustafa Yamalki (q.v.) in 1922. After the return of Shaykh Mahmud, he became the director of the school. Hilmy and several others went on a trip to Turkey as representatives of Shaykh Mahmud to negotiate with the Kemalists about organizing the relationship between the government of Turkey and that of Kurdistan. After the failure of Shaykh Mahmud's second revolt, Hilmy became a math teacher. He also led the Hewa Party (q.v.). He was a very capable writer in Turkish, Kurdish, and Arabic. His most important work was the six volumes of his memoirs that looked into the uprisings of Shaykh Mahmud. After the 1958 revolution (q.v.), he was appointed cultural attaché to Turkey. Hilmy was among the founding members of the 'Iraqi Communist Party (q.v.).

HIRA. Ancient city located in the Karbala governate south of al-Kufa. It was originally a military encampment and the capital of the Lakhmids, the rulers of Arab 'Iraq, and the vassals of the Sassanians of Iran in the fifth and sixth centuries. The Lakhmids were entrusted with keeping the tribes in check and guarding the borders against the Byzantines and their Arab vassals, the Ghassanids. The city was an important center of political, military, and diplomatic activities in the Arabian Peninsula, Byzantium, and Persia. It served as an important station on the trade route between Arabia and Persia. It is believed that the Arabic script was developed in Hira. The city also played a leading role in the development of Arab Christianity, since the city was the seat for Nestorian Christianity (q.v.). Hira began to decline in the seventh century, as the Persians successfully undermined and weakened the Lakhmid dynasty. It was captured by the Muslim Arab armies in 633.

HISQAIL, SASUN (1860–1932). Administrator and a prominent politician. He was born in Baghdad (q.v.) to a wealthy Jewish family. His father, Rabbi Hisqail, was the son of a prominent Jewish religious scholar who established a synagogue in Baghdad in 1909. Hisqail studied in the Jewish alliance school and went to Istanbul in 1877 in the company of Menachim Sallah, who had been elected as a representative to the Ottoman Parliament from Baghdad. He studied at the Royal College and then attended the Diplomatic College in Vienna. He traveled to Berlin and London, returned to Istanbul, and earned a law degree. Hisqail then returned to Baghdad where he served as a government translator.

Hisqail was a member of the Ottoman Parliament from 1908 to 1918 as a deputy from Baghdad and chaired the Budget Committee. In 1920, he returned to Baghdad and took the portfolio of finance in the first 'Iraqi cabinet (1920–1921). He would serve as minister of finance four more times (1921–1923, 1924–1925). Along with Ja'far al-Askari (q.v.) and Sir Percy Cox, Hisqail attended the 1921 Cairo Conference, which established the kingdom of 'Iraq. He was elected to the 'Iraqi Parliament as a representative from Baghdad in 1925 and was twice reelected. He headed the Finance and Economics Committee in Parliament. Hisqail was considered a competent and tough administrator, known for his legalistic point of view.

During the oil (q.v.) negotiations between 'Iraq and the Turkish Petroleum Company (TPC) in 1925, he insisted on government participation in the TPC and also ensured that the company agreed to make its payments to 'Iraq in gold, a step that was to prove very beneficial to the 'Iraqi government. He was also known for having one of 'Iraq's best libraries. He died in Europe in 1932, where he had gone for medical treatment.

HUSAYN–MCMAHON CORRESPONDENCE. Consisting of 10 letters exchanged in 1915 and 1916 between Sharif Husayn of Makka and British high commissioner of Egypt Sir Henry McMahon, the correspondence established a quid pro quo. Britain pledged "to recognize and support the independence of the Arabs in all the regions lying within the limits demanded by the Sharif of Makka," with the exceptions of portions of Syria west of Damascus, Homs, Hama, and Aleppo and the districts of Mersin and Alexandretta. The regions included were the Levant and the Arabian Peninsula. Thus, 'Iraq was to be part of this independent Arab state. In return, Sharif Husayn launched the Arab Revolt against the Ottoman Empire on 5 June 1916. Husayn's son Faysal (q.v.) played a leading role in the Arab Revolt and the Arab nationalist cause; eventually he would become 'Iraq's first king. *See also* HASHIMITES.

HUSAYN, QUSAY (1966–2003). The youngest son of Saddam Husayn (q.v.) and the head of 'Iraq's intelligence services and of the Republican Guards. Qusay was elected to the Regional Command (q.v.) and the Revolutionary Command Council (q.v.) of the Ba'th Party (q.v.) in May 2001 and was considered one of the most powerful men in 'Iraq. Rumors said he was being groomed to succeed his father. He studied political science and law at Baghdad University as well as a specialized course in administrative and military affairs prior to entering governmental affairs.

He emerged on the scene in 1992 as the head of the Republican Guards. He later was appointed to the powerful Ba'th Party Military Bureau, which oversees the military and became head of the Special Security forces and of the intelligence apparatus. He married the daughter of a prominent general, 'Abd al-Rashid, but the couple reportedly separated when the general fell from favor in the late 1980s. He had three sons. Qusay was killed in a fierce firefight with U.S. forces in the city of Mosul, along with his young son, his brother Uday, and a bodyguard. A relative is believed to have informed about their whereabouts.

HUSAYN, SADDAM (1937–). President (q.v.) of 'Iraq and the most influential figure in 'Iraq's modern history since King Faysal I (q.v.). Saddam was born to a poor peasant family in the village of al-'Awja near the ancient city of Tikrit, an important center for nationalistic and anti-British policies. According to published biographies, his father died before he was born and he was raised by his strong-willed mother Sabha and his paternal uncle Ibrahim al-Hassan, who married his mother.

His family wanted him to become a shepherd and farmer like themselves, but Saddam had other interests. The harsh early childhood life in a small peasant village had an impact on Saddam, who later wrote, "I was born and grew up stubborn, sad, independent, and angry." He did not attend school in the village but became interested in going to school after his cousin on his mother's side, Adnan Khayralla (q.v.), told him that he could learn to read and write at school. His uncle objected to Saddam attending school; Saddam took his first rebellious step by leaving home in the middle of the night for his uncle Khayralla Talfah's house in Tikrit. Talfah was an Arab nationalist army officer like many Tikritis who had joined Rashid 'Ali's (q.v.) anti-British revolt. Talfah took him in and treated him like one of his children. Saddam went with his uncle when he moved to Baghdad (q.v.), where Saddam completed his primary and secondary school. Talfah might have had the greatest influence on Saddam's political consciousness at this stage, infusing him with nationalist, anticolonialist, and antiregime sentiments.

Saddam grew up at a time of upheavals in 'Iraq and the rest of the Arab world, particularly with the rise of Nasirism and the Suez crisis. He became active in student politics, attracted to Gamal 'Abd al-Nasir's independent pan-Arab vision and particularly to the Ba'thist ideas and the writings of Michel Aflaq (q.v.). He joined the party in 1957. During the conflict between General 'Abd al-Karim Qasim's (q.v.) regime and the Ba'th and other Arab nationalist parties, Saddam became involved in antiregime activities and was sent to jail. He later agreed to participate in a plan approved by the 'Iraqi branch of the Ba'th Party to assassinate Qasim. The assassination failed, and Saddam was wounded in the leg. Afraid to seek medical attention, he is said to have dug the bullet out himself with a pocket knife and then escaped to his village. He later fled to Syria and from there to Egypt, where he completed his secondary education and entered Cairo University to study law. Saddam's stay in Egypt was the only opportunity Saddam had to live outside 'Iraq.

Saddam returned to 'Iraq when the Ba'th Party seized power in February 1963. He was soon in charge of the party's military organization and of the Peasant Bureau. These offices helped Saddam build an important constituency within the party. But the Ba'thists were ousted from power nine months later by 'Abd al-Salam 'Arif (q.v.). In 1964, Saddam secretly attended the party's seventh congress in Damascus, where he strengthened his ties to Michel Aflaq. This period was important in Saddam's life. He married his cousin, Sajida Talfah, and politically reestablished close ties with senior Ba'thist politician and military man, General Ahmad Hasan al-Bakr (q.v.).

Saddam was arrested for antiregime activity and sentenced to two years in jail. In prison, he continued his political activities and resumed his interrupted education, which he completed after the 1968 Ba'th coup. He used to smuggle letters to the outside world in the clothes of his son Uday (q.v.)

when his wife would come to visit him in jail. In 1966, Saddam fled from jail to find the Ba'th deeply splintered between the pro- and anti-Aflaq factions. The pro-Aflaq and Bitar wing was favored by Saddam, who played a major role in reorganizing and rebuilding the party in 'Iraq slowly and with stubborn determination. The ouster of the Ba'th Party from power in November 1963 coupled with Saddam's subsequent underground life left an important impression on his tactics, behavior, and manner of operations that he carried with him to the presidency. He was forced to become self-reliant, to be wary of others, to keep a close eye on opponents, and to oppose continued internal party bickering, and he was intolerant of divisions once a policy was adopted. He also became aware of the need for a strong, well-organized party with a strong leadership. He played a leading role in organizing along with al-Bakr and the other Ba'th leaders for the overthrow of the regime in 1968.

During the early years of the second Ba'th government, Saddam gradually strengthened his power base in the party. He was appointed assistant secretary-general of the Regional Command (q.v.) and a member of the Revolutionary Command Council (q.v.), the country's highest executive and legislative body. To create the prerequisites for a stable government, Saddam championed party unity, a strong military, an end to the Kurdish rebellion that had plagued 'Iraqi governments since 1961, and a modernized society with better standards of living for the people. To begin to tackle the Kurdish issue, Saddam pursued a strategy of conciliation that was opposed by some leading Ba'thists. His effort culminated in the 1970 March Manifesto (q.v.), which made important concessions to the Kurdish leadership. When the policy failed, he pursued a tough campaign that led to a deal with Iran and to the collapse of the Kurdish insurgency in 1975.

To help resolve the Kurdish conflict and accomplish other objectives, Saddam badly needed financial resources. 'Iraq's oil (q.v.) wealth was the main source for income. In 1970, he visited the Soviet Union, and later the two countries signed a Treaty of Friendship and Cooperation in 1972 (q.v.). 'Iraq moved to nationalize the 'Iraqi oil industry, and he played a major role in the mobilization of public and Arab support for his policies. Following the nationalization and the rise of oil prices, Saddam continued to consolidate and strengthen his and the party's position and to eliminate rivals. He also favored a policy of rapid economic development, education, land and labor reform, and granting women a larger role in society. He placed a great emphasis on advancing 'Iraq technologically including the acquisition of nuclear technology.

By the time of the 11th Party Congress in 1977, it was obvious that Saddam was the man slated to lead 'Iraq after the aging al-Bakr. In 1979, al-Bakr relinquished his position of president in favor of Saddam. A few weeks later in a still-murky event, Saddam purged his party and executed a number of top party officials. It is not clear whether they had simply challenged Saddam's ascendancy to the presidency or whether, as was claimed by the regime, they had conspired—some with Syrian authorities—against Saddam.

Since his early days as president, Saddam set himself up as a model to be emulated by his comrades in the party and the public when he said he would not ask them to do or not to do anything he himself would not do or refrain from doing. Saddam also developed a cult of personality and sought to foster his image both as a modern man and as a man of the people. He was at times shown visiting remote Kurdish villages wearing traditional local dress, although usually appearing wearing fashionable Western clothes.

After the Iranian revolution in 1979 and the rise of a theocratic Islamic regime to power in Tehran that sought to export its ideology to neighboring countries, relations rapidly deteriorated between the two countries. Inside the Ba'th leadership, divisions emerged on how to deal with Iran. One group favored patience and conciliation with the nonaligned anti-Israel revolutionary regime in Tehran, while the other faction, led by Saddam, believed the new regime posed a serious threat to 'Iraq's internal stability and favored confrontation. Soon, the two countries entered into eight years of bloody and costly war. 'Iraq ultimately emerged as the victor, albeit an exhausted one. In the meantime, the regime waged a harsh campaign against Kurdish insurgents who had cooperated with Iran during the war and that culminated in the destruction of numerous Kurdish villages and towns near the borders, the forced resettlement of their inhabitants, the use of chemical weapons at Halabja (q.v.), and the killing of thousands of suspected opponents.

During this time, 'Iraq made significant strides in absorbing modern technology, as well as linking its industrial and military production. Major modifications were made in the areas of artillery, missiles, as well as in chemical and nuclear programs. It also launched a space satellite named *al-Abid*. These developments, coupled with the way the Iran–'Iraq war (q.v.) ended, alarmed many inside and outside the region.

The 'Iraqi leadership came to believe that Israel, some regional players, Britain, and the United States were unhappy with 'Iraq's victory over Iran and 'Iraq wanted to punish for its independent stand and its attempt to build a military arsenal not sanctioned by the superpowers. At the February 1990 Arab summit, Saddam warned Arab leaders that the United States had emerged as a victor in the Cold War and was pursuing a policy favoring Israel and its interests, seeking to control Arab oil and increasing its military presence in the region. He warned that "unless the sons of the Gulf and all Arabs were alert, the Arab Gulf area will be ruled by the U.S." because the United States will be able to operate outside normal international constraints.

In the spring of 1990, two issues were of concern to Saddam: the Western campaign against 'Iraq and the immigration of Russian Jews (q.v.) to Israel. He was also concerned about Kuwait's increased oil production, which he viewed as a threat to 'Iraq's economy (q.v.).

His invasion of Kuwait (q.v.) and the second Gulf War revealed Saddam's temperament and his understanding of history. His high ambition and self-confidence allowed him to consult widely, but he ultimately made decisions alone. At times, he took initiatives and gambles, regardless of the results and possible losses. Saddam fought two major wars, one against Iran that he won, albeit at great cost, and one that he lost in devastating fashion against a 30-state coalition led by the United States. Over the past decade, he waged a war for the survival of his regime and to maintain 'Iraq's territorial unity and sovereignty. He ultimately lost the battle to stay in power following the 2003 U.S.–British invasion of 'Iraq.

Aware of the ethnosectarian structure of 'Iraqi society, Saddam adopted a secular policy seeking to avoid any politicization of religion. He also sought to link and emphasize 'Iraq's unique character and history. Although very proud of the country's Islamic and Arab culture and civilization, he also recognized the pre-Islamic ancient civilizations of Mesopotamia and made references in some of his speeches to Gilgamish and Hamurabi (qq.v.), among others. He also appropriated money for archeological research about the country's history, culture, and traditions.

His image in the outside world has generally been associated with brutality and rule, with the building and modernization of 'Iraq (although much of the infrastructure he built was destroyed in the Gulf wars), and with disastrous conflicts that 'Iraq entered under his leadership. Yet, he also transformed 'Iraq and raised issues that Arab public opinion continues to aspire to: national independence, Palestinian rights, and a fairer distribution of Arab wealth. He was motivated by tribal and village concepts of honor, dignity, and bravery that have influenced his outlook and dealings with others at home and abroad.

In foreign policy, Saddam sought a nonaligned role for 'Iraq and hoped to lead the nonaligned movement. He rejected alliances and foreign bases on 'Iraqi soil and pursued an independent policy between the United States and Soviet Union. Although he did not put the two on the same level, he opposed a policy of dependency on either. He favored establishing close cooperation with Europe and particularly with France to balance the superpowers.

Saddam has little acquaintance with the outside world and harbors many of the grievances carried by Arabs of his generation against Western colonization. For his survival, he relied on the military, different security agencies, loyal Ba'thists, relatives, and people from his region, and more recently tribal forces in the south and center, and until the Kurdish uprising in 1991 on some Kurdish tribes as well. Following the 1990–1991 Gulf War, some cracks appeared in the wall of support, such as the defection of his sons-in-law and some other officials in 1996. Saddam enjoyed acceptance as well as support from important segments of the population. He was a master at balancing the ambitions of his supporters. Until 2003 when his regime fell to advancing U.S. forces, Saddam had outmaneuvered those seeking to kill or oust him, be they fellow Ba'thists, tribal or religious opponents, ambitious military officers, or allied leaders. Repression, however, was not the only weapon he used to stay in power. His survival was essential also for some of his supporters who believed that their survival was also at stake if he was ousted. The excesses of the 1991 uprisings only served to cement this view.

For many 'Iraqis, especially those born since 1968, Saddam was the only leader they know. They witnessed sweeping social and economic transformations under his rule. 'Iraq achieved major industrial, technological, and educational progress. 'Iraqis also witnessed the destruction of most of their infrastructure and the loss of many lives under his regime. Yet, the devastating sanctions (q.v.) that were widely felt by the overwhelming majority of the population and the diminishing of 'Iraqi sovereignty as a result of no-fly zones and other interferences in internal 'Iraqi affairs were used by the regime to effectively argue that the targets are 'Iraq and the 'Iraqis and not just Saddam and his supporters. This view helped build support for the regime and allowed it to survive. And although many in and out of the region predicted Saddam's fall from power after the second Gulf War, he was able to maintain an iron grip on power until the fall of his regime.

On December 13, 2003, American forces captured Saddam during a nighttime raid on Adwar, a small village roughly 15 kilometers from Tikrit. Close questioning of Saddam's former bodyguards and members of his family produced the intelligence that led to the raid. He was living in a two-room mud shack, with a small hole in the ground outside disguised with styrofoam and dirt.

When soldiers uncovered the spider hole, Saddam emerged with his hands raised, stating he was the 'Iraqi president and wanted to negotiate. He was armed with a pistol; soldiers also recovered $750,000 in one hundred dollar bills and two AK-47 rifles. To prove to 'Iraqis that Saddam was in custody, footage of him undergoing a medical examination was released. He appeared haggard and exhausted, with a long beard and disheveled hair. Jubilant 'Iraqis took to the streets to celebrate, although many simultaneously expressed a sense of humiliation at the failure of their former leader to defend himself.

Despite the capture of Saddam, the insurgency continued to inflict almost daily casualties on American and international troops as well as 'Iraqi civilians. During initial questioning by coalition military and intelligence personnel, Saddam continued to deny that 'Iraq had weapons of mass destruction. An Iraq tribunal for genocide, crimes against humanity, and war crimes was established to try him.

'HUSAYN, SHARIF ALI BIN AL- (1956–). Sharif Ali is the head of the Constitutional Monarchy Movement (CMM), which was launched in 1993, and a leading claimant to the 'Iraqi throne. He is a political activist and was elected a member of the collective leadership of the 'Iraqi National Congress (INC) (q.v.) after joining its ranks in 1999. Sharif Ali is the son of Sharif al-Husayn Bin Ali and first cousin to the late King Faisal II, the last monarch of 'Iraq. The late Crown Prince Abd al-Ilah (q.v.) was his uncle. Following the 1958 military coup, Sharif Ali was taken into exile in Lebanon. He completed his higher education in the United Kingdom, obtaining a B.A. in economics and an M.A. in development economics. On completing his education, he joined an investment banking firm. The goal of the CMM is to reestablish the monarchy in the framework of a democratic, pluralistic, constitutional system of government. Sharif Ali is the patron of CMM and works toward the day when all 'Iraqi citizens can freely choose the system of government they desire. The CMM was one of seven organizations named in the 1998 'Iraqi Liberation Act. Sharif Ali is head of the King Faisal II (q.v.) Charitable Foundation.

HUSAYN, UDAY (1964–2003). Eldest son of Saddam Husayn (q.v.). He was married to the daughter of 'Izzat Ibrahim al-Duri (q.v.). In August 1995, he shot Watban Ibrahim al-Hasan (q.v.) during a family argument, severely injuring him. In October 1988, he killed his father's bodyguard and food taster, Kamil Jejo. Saddam had Uday arrested and jailed; after an investigation by the Ministry of Justice, the charges against him were dropped. He lost his positions as head of the 'Iraqi Olympic Committee and the 'Iraqi Football Federation, and he left 'Iraq for Switzerland in January 1989. He quickly returned to 'Iraq and was reappointed to his former positions in February 1990. He was seriously wounded in an assassination attempt in January 1997 and apparently suffered some paralysis of his legs. He also ran the Baghdad daily *Babil* and the shabab T.V. and commanded Saddam's Fedayin militia. Uday was widely accused of brutality and corruption. He was killed with his younger brother Qusay (q.v.) in firefight with U.S. forces in 2003.

HUSRI, SATI' AL- (1880–1970). One of the founders of Arab nationalism and an intellectual, educator, and political figure. He was born in Sana in Yemen of Syrian parents, and his father was a judge in the Ottoman courts. He spent much of his childhood traveling with his father to various parts of the Ottoman Empire, including Istanbul, Tripoli, Ankara, and the Balkans. Al-Husri studied management, political science, and the natural sciences and was fluent in Arabic, French, and Turkish. He worked as a high school science teacher and served in the Ottoman administration. After the Arab Revolt, he joined Faysal I's (q.v.) government in Syria. He became a member of Parliament, served on the Director's Council, and was minister of communication when Syria became independent in 1920. Al-Husri witnessed the Battle of Masalun, where the French defeated the fledgling Syrian army. In 1935, he published his book *The Day at Masalun*, containing vivid descriptions of the battle, an analysis of colonial interests in the region, and a blueprint for the Arab nationalist movement. He spent a year studying in Cairo while Faysal sought Western support in the aftermath of the collapse of the Arab government in Syria. Following Faysal's 1920 ascension to the throne in 'Iraq, al-Husri served as an adviser on foreign affairs.

Over the next two decades he played an important role in the politics of 'Iraq. He served as undersecretary at the Ministry of Foreign Affairs and taught at the Higher Teachers College. He was involved in the reorganization of 'Iraq's educational system and played a leading role in the coordination of the educational, intellectual, and scientific movement. His support of the Arab nationalists, especially during the Rashid 'Ali al-Kaylani (q.v.) movement, resulted in his expulsion from 'Iraq and the withdrawal of his passport. Al-Husri lived in Lebanon for four years and worked as an educational adviser to the Syrian government from 1944 to 1947.

He moved to Egypt, where he served as an educational adviser to the Arab League in 1948 and taught at the Arab Educational Academy. He founded an Arab studies academy in 1953–1954, which was attached to the Arab League. Al-Husri resigned from the academy because he believed it was not serving its intended goals and that it had become too bureaucratic. He dedicated the rest of his life to research and writing. In 1965, he was granted 'Iraqi citizenship and he returned to 'Iraq, where he remained until his death in 1970. He was one of the leading advocates of a secular Arab nationalism, the theme of many of his major works.

– I –

IJTIHAD. The exercise of opinion in legal decisions based on the prophet Muhammad's traditions, known as the *hadiths*. *See also MATHHAB*.

'ILMIYYA, AL-HAWZA AL-. The circle of scholars and students that forms the center of Shi'i (q.v.) religious and educational institutions. The number of these institutions is said to have increased after a decline during the early decades of the 20th century. The increase was partly due to the belief among some religious scholars that it was necessary to combat the rising influence of secular and atheistic movements like the 'Iraqi Communist Party (q.v.) in the late 1950s and early 1960s. The Shi'is expanded these educational institutions because the Ottomans had discriminated against them and refused to allow young Shi'is into their schools or give them positions in the government. Thus the Shi'is began to increasingly rely on their own religious institutions that were run by the religious scholars under the guidance of the *mujtahids* (q.v.) and the *marja'*, especially under the *marja' al-taqlid al-mutlaq* [the source of absolute interpretation, also known as the Grand Ayatollah (Ayat Allah) who issued edicts, religious interpretations, and guidance for the faithful].

ILAH, AL-AMIR 'ABD AL- (1913–1958). Regent of 'Iraq, 1939–1953. He was born in Hijaz, the only son of Sharif 'Ali, who was the eldest son of Sharif Husayn. He attended Victoria College in Alexandria, Egypt, for three years. Following Ibn Saud's conquest of the Hijaz, 'Abd al-Ilah accompanied his father to Baghdad (q.v.) in 1925. When King Ghazi (q.v.) died in 1939, he became the regent of 'Iraq, backed by Nuri al-Sa'id and Taha al-Hashimi (qq.v.). Neither of these men wanted Prince Zayd, who had seniority among the Hashimites (q.v.), to become regent. They started a propaganda campaign against Zayd, even warning that the army might revolt unless 'Abd al-Ilah got the position. 'Abd al-Ilah remained regent until Faysal II (q.v.) attained his majority in 1953, when he became the heir presumptive. He was not a shrewd politician and was seen as someone who did not want much responsibility. He allowed the Sharifian officers (q.v.) like Nuri al-Sa'id to run the affairs of the state. He did come to play a more active role after the end of World War II.

'Abd al-Ilah was strongly pro-British and this led to frequent tensions with the anti-British faction headed by Rashid 'Ali al-Kaylani (q.v.). When Rashid 'Ali seized power in 1941 with the help of the Golden Square colonels (q.v.), 'Abd al-Ilah fled to Jordan. When British troops drove out Rashid 'Ali's government, he returned to 'Iraq and continued his collaboration with Nuri. Despite his ties with Nuri, he also maintained relations with opponents of Nuri's such as Salih Jabr (q.v.). During the 1950s, 'Abd al-Ilah was interested in the throne of Syria, but none of 'Iraq's interferences in Syrian politics realized this goal.

When the army surrounded the palace during the July 1958 revolution (q.v.), 'Abd al-Ilah chose not to try to escape. He ordered his bodyguards to hold their fire and offered to leave the country with his family. The commanding officer lined the whole family up with their servants and opened fire, massacring them all. His body was dragged through the streets and later nailed to the door of the Defense Ministry. 'Abd al-Ilah paid little attention to domestic affairs, and was caught unaware by the discontent in the military. He relied on aides to tell him what was happening and was ultimately unable to take sufficient action when word reached him that three officers were planning a coup against the monarchy in 1958.

INDEPENDENCE PARTY (HIZB AL-ISTIQLAL). An influential nationalist party whose origins can be traced to the *Nadi al-Muthana* (q.v.) club of the 1930s. When the regent 'Abd al-Ilah (q.v.) announced his intent in December 1945 to establish political parties and democracy, Faiq al-Samarra'i (q.v.) promoted the idea of forming a nationalist party that supported 'Iraqi independence. A number of political activists including Muhammad Mahdi Kubba (q.v.), Khalil Kanna (q.v.), Khayralla Talfah (q.v.), and Shukri Zaki then organized the *Istiqlal*. In 1956, it joined the National Front (q.v.). The *Istiqlal* called for Arab unity, support for Palestine, the strengthening of the military, as well as social, educational and judicial reforms. It published a newspaper: *Liwa al-Istiqlal* (The Flag of Independence).

The *Istiqlal* cooperated with the 'Iraqi Free Officers (q.v.) from 1953 to bring about reforms and ultimately a change in the regime. It enjoyed influence among the officer corps because some of its members had participated in the Rashid 'Ali al-Kaylani (q.v.) movement against Britain in the 1940s. Faiq al-Samarra'i and Muhammad Sadiq Shanshal (q.v.) were asked by the Free Officers to prepare the first statement after the 1958 revolution (q.v.).

INDUSTRY. Industry's share of 'Iraqi GDP rose slowly from 1970 to 1990 but has not shown growth commensurate with the level of investment. Industry accounted for 7.8 percent of GDP in 1976 and 11.6 percent by 1989. The Iran–'Iraq war, the invasion of Kuwait, and sanctions (qq.v.) all dealt major blows to the development and growth of 'Iraqi industry. 'Iraq's key nonoil industries prior to 1990 were sulfur, fertilizers, cement, and petrochemicals. It possesses 500 million tons of sulfur reserves at Mishraq, near Mawsil (q.v.). Mining began in 1972, and by 1990, Mishraq was producing 1.5 million tons of sulfur per year. 'Iraq's plentiful phosphate reserves, estimated at 10,000 million tons, allowed it to become self-sufficient in fertilizer and to export it. The world's largest phosphate field is located at Akashat, northwest of Baghdad (q.v.), and 'Iraq built a huge fertilizer complex at al-Qaim. 'Iraq also was a major producer and exporter of cement before Desert Storm, producing 17 million tons of cement annually.

Industry remained small-scale and local until the revolutionary regimes came to power. Main 'Iraqi industries in the first half of the century were bricks, cigarettes, textiles, distilleries, and vegetable oils and soaps. Development efforts from 1950 to 1958 focused on agriculture (q.v.). Industry never received more than 20 percent of the development budget and sometimes did not receive any money at all, and it remained the weakest sector of the economy (q.v.). The sector received more attention during the Qasim (q.v.) and 'Arif regimes. Qasim did not subject industry to his nationalization policies, and the sector showed modest growth.

'Abd al-Salam 'Arif (q.v.) reversed this policy, nationalizing over two dozen of 'Iraq's largest industrial firms in July 1964. 'Arif's policies slowed industrial growth and there was little diversification of the sector. The Ba'th Party (q.v.) wanted to restructure and rapidly develop 'Iraqi industry through an import-substituting industrialization strategy. The nationalization of the 'Iraqi Petroleum Company (q.v.) in 1972 and the fourfold increase in oil (q.v.) prices the following year made significant expenditures possible. The 1975–1980 Five Year Plan focused on iron and steel, petrochemicals, and fertilizer projects. However, 'Iraq's underdeveloped infrastructure and lack of skilled managers handicapped its efforts. Moreover, the emphasis on producing primary products allowed bottlenecks to develop because 'Iraq did not have the capability to produce intermediate products.

The Iran–'Iraq war disrupted industrial development. During the first two years of the conflict, the regime attempted to pursue both war and development; it continued to offer contracts on new projects and to work on existing ones. But in 1982, with 'Iraq's foreign reserves running out, the regime was forced to tighten its belt. It fell into arrears on many of its existing contracts and insisted that companies provide their own financing on new projects. The regime repeatedly emphasized that it would not forget those who had stood by 'Iraq during the war, and many companies did try to continue their projects in the hopes of being able to capitalize on reconstruction contracts when the war ended. As the war dragged on, 'Iraq devoted its efforts to projects that had military applications. The Military Industries Commission, headed by Husayn Kamil (q.v.), took on increasing importance. The regime also attempted to increase the productivity and efficiency of the industrial sector by reorganizing the ministries that dealt with it.

Once the Iran–'Iraq war ended in August 1988, the regime moved ahead with the projects that it had been forced to abandon during the war. It undertook several multibillion-dollar projects, notably petrochemical plant 2. Major efforts were undertaken to expand 'Iraq's iron, steel industries, and fertilizer industries and to move into the manufacture of cars, trucks, and buses. As became clear in the aftermath of 'Iraq's invasion of Kuwait, enormous sums of money were being poured into military industrialization. Saddam Husayn (q.v.) in 1987 used the military industrialization projects as examples of how the rest of industry should work in 'Iraq. In July 1988, the Ministry of Industry was merged with the Military Industries Commission to create the Ministry for Industry and Military Industrialization, again headed by Husayn Kamil.

With the imposition of sanctions and the devastation wrought by Desert Storm, 'Iraqi industry has all but ceased to exist with the exception of small, domestic consumption industries. The industrial sector suffered further during the 2003 war and the subsequent looting and destruction that followed.

IRAN–'IRAQ WAR. On 22 September 1980, 'Iraqi forces struck across the border into Iran, culminating a year-long escalation of propaganda and border incidents between the two states. The roots of the conflict can be divided into two main categories: historical rivalry relating to questions of religion and territory, and tensions that resulted from the leadership changes in 1979. The religious split between 'Iraq and Iran dates to the seventh-century split in Islam between Sunnis and Shi'is (qq.v.). Although 'Iraq for centuries was under the control of Sunni rulers, Iran adopted Shi'sm.

The divide gained enormous salience after the 1979 Iranian Revolution, when a Shi'i government in Tehran confronted a Sunni minority government in 'Iraq, where 55 to 60 percent of the population was Shi'i. The territorial dispute also had deep roots; the status of the Shatt al-Arab (q.v.) had been at issue since the 15th century, although with the exception of the anchorage off Abadan, the entirety of the waterway remained in 'Iraqi hands. In the late 1960s, the shah of Iran began to pressure 'Iraq into moving the boundary of the Shatt to the *thalweg*, or midline, of the channel. Iranian support for the 1974–1975 Kurdish rebellion, which threatened to topple the ruling Ba'th (q.v.) government, forced Baghdad (q.v.) to accept the thalweg in the 1975 Algiers Agreement (q.v.). 'Iraq, however, was determined to regain control of the Shatt.

The leadership changes in 1979 brought to power two governments that were at ideological loggerheads. Saddam Husayn (q.v.) represented a secular, minority Sunni government that based its legitimacy on Arab nationalism, whereas Khomeini represented a theocratic, Shi'i government that rejected the idea of nationalism. Saddam saw in Khomeini's Iran a threat to his rule over heterogeneous and restive 'Iraq, a perception heightened by calls for Saddam's overthrow issued from Tehran. The revolutionary Islamic fervor emerging from Tehran also threatened the conservative Arab monarchies, particularly in the Persian Gulf. Moreover, the forces unleashed by the revolution had greatly weakened Iran; ethnic strife, military purges, economic paralysis, and government disorganization made Iran appear vulnerable. An invasion of Iran could simultaneously solve 'Iraq's territorial dispute, remove or at least reduce the threat the revolution posed to Saddam's rule, and bolster 'Iraq's claim to Arab leadership by demonstrating its role as protector. Given the chaotic atmosphere in Iran, an invasion looked to be a low-cost, short-term venture.

'Iraqi forces made rapid advances in the early days of the fighting, and Saddam offered a cease-fire less than two weeks after the invasion. Iran's refusal to accept a cease-fire and its surprisingly tenacious defense halted 'Iraq's advances by December 1980, and the fighting settled into a war of attrition. The tide of the war shifted dramatically in July 1982, when Iranian forces crossed into 'Iraq and drove to within 16 kilometers of Basra (q.v.), 'Iraq's second-largest city.

As the war dragged on, 'Iraq became increasingly desperate to end the conflict, but Khomeini refused to accept a cease-fire, saying there could be no compromising with infidels. Thus, 'Iraq pursued a number of strategies aimed at bringing the war to a close: economic strangulation of Iran, which it attempted through repeated bombing campaigns against Iranian oil export facilities and, beginning in 1984, by attacking tankers visiting Iranian ports; the war of the cities, which was waged off and on from 1984, designed to bring the war home to the Iranian population that then presumably would pressure the government to end the fighting; use of chemical weapons, which demoralized Iranian forces; and internationalization of the war, which 'Iraq hoped would cause the superpowers to pressure Iran into coming to the negotiating table. 'Iraq's fortunes suffered another blow in February 1986 with the loss of the al-Fao Peninsula to Iran.

The international community finally became more involved in 1987, and the tide of the war began to shift in 'Iraq's favor. In March, both the United States and the Soviet Union agreed to reflag Kuwaiti tankers, and in July, the United Nations passed Resolution 598, which called for a cease-fire. 'Iraq accepted the resolution immediately, but Iran rejected it. The U.S. reflagging operation led U.S. forces into a series of naval confrontations with Iran between September 1987 and July 1988, in which Iran's navy was decimated. Iran faced hard times on other fronts as well: 'Iraq recaptured al-Fao in April 1988; the American-led Operation Staunch had greatly restricted the arms supply to Iran, which found itself short of weapons and supplies; the intensification of the war of the cities was demoralizing the domestic population; and 'Iraq's use of chemical weapons was demoralizing Iranian troops. Iran finally accepted Resolution 598 in July 1988, and a cease-fire went into effect on 20 August 1988.

As the war drew to a conclusion, the 'Iraqi government moved against the Kurdish insurgents allied with Iran. In March 1988, Iranian and Kurdish forces accused 'Iraq of using chemical weapons against civilians in the Kurdish town of Halabja (q.v.), leaving several thousand dead. But regardless of which of these reports was accurate, the events at Halabja horrified international public opinion, and the incident was used in the effort to dehumanize Saddam's regime before and during the second Gulf War. 'Iraq launched the Anfal campaign against Kurdish guerrillas from 1987 through 1988, leading to new charges of use of chemical weapons, and more than 50,000 Kurds fled across the border to Turkey.

'Iraq had little to show for eight years of conflict. It had suffered an estimated 420,000 casualties (120,000 dead and 300,000 wounded; Iran suffered 300,000 dead and 450,000 wounded); it had spent its foreign exchange reserves and accumulated an estimated $60 billion debt; it was unable to export oil via the Persian Gulf; and the Shatt al-Arab remained closed, clogged with over 70 ships and years of debris and silting. The negotiations at Geneva remained at a stalemate for two years, with the delegations unable to agree even on the exchange of POWs.

In April 1990, Saddam moved to break the deadlock. In a letter to Iranian president Hashemi Rafsanjani, he proposed direct talks, but the Iranian response was not encouraging. However, in the immediate aftermath of its August 1990 invasion of Kuwait (q.v.), 'Iraq agreed to settle the outstanding issues on Iran's terms. On 8 August 1990, Saddam informed Rafsanjani that

'Iraq accepted the validity of the Algiers Agreement, thus leaving the thalweg as the boundary in the Shatt al-Arab, that 'Iraq would begin withdrawing from Iranian territory it still occupied on 17 August and that 'Iraq would commence a POW exchange on 20 August. 'Iraq and Iran restored diplomatic relations in October 1990.

'IRAQ NATIONAL OIL COMPANY. *See* LAW 11 OF 1964.

'IRAQI BA'TH PARTY. The pro-Syrian wing of the Ba'th Party (q.v.). A small, divided group mainly in exile in Syria, its members opposed the Ba'thists who took power in 'Iraq. Its members include Mahdi Alabidi.

'IRAQI COMMUNIST PARTY (ICP) (AL-HIZB AL-SHUYU'I AL-'IRAQI). Political party founded in March 1934 by a group of socialist and Marxist representatives in Baghdad (q.v.) who established a committee to combat imperialism and exploitation. Asim Fulayh was elected secretary-general of this organization. It also included some of the most prominent 'Iraqi leftists and communists, including Yusuf Salman, whose nom de guerre was Fahd (q.v.), Zaki Khairi, and Nuri Rufayil. The committee changed its name to the 'Iraqi Communist Party in 1935 and began publishing a newspaper, *The People's Struggle*, in July 1935.

The ICP was quickly discovered by the government, leading to the arrest of many members, including the secretary-general, and the banning of the party newspaper. Many of its leaders fled 'Iraq; some went to Iran and Syria, where they joined the local communist parties. Fahd went to Syria and eventually to the Soviet Union, where he lived and studied for several years. Fahd returned to 'Iraq in 1938 and reestablished the ICP. The party, though, was beset by internal conflict and rivalries, and a number of factions emerged. Dhu al-Nun Ayyub and Aycob Cohen led one such group, which had its own publication, *Ila al-Imam* (Forward). Dawud al-Sayigh, another rival of Fahd's, eventually split with the ICP and established the League of 'Iraqi Communists. The league opposed Fahd's leadership and survived until al-Sayigh's arrest in 1947. In 1944, Yusuf Harun Zilkha's faction established the Organization of the 'Iraqi Communist Party—Unity of Struggle. This group later agreed to rejoin the ICP under Fahd's leadership.

Despite its small membership in these years, Fahd was able to transform the ICP into an effective popular organization. The ICP supported Rashid 'Ali al-Kaylani (q.v.) against the British in 1941 and maintained a close relationship with him. After the defeat of Rashid 'Ali's movement, the ICP supported the Allies against Germany in World War II. Its opposition to the pro-British government after the war led to a crackdown. Prime minister Nuri al-Sa'id (q.v.) accused the ICP of receiving support from the Soviet Union and establishing contacts with the communist parties of Iran and Syria. The party's leaders, including Fahd in 1947, were arrested and sentenced to death, although the sentences were later commuted to life imprisonment. Under interrogation, some ICP leaders later broke down and provided the government with new information about Fahd's role in the party. He was retried, along with Zaki Basim and Muhammad al-Shabibi, and they were executed in February 1949.

After Fahd's arrest, the ICP was led by Yahuda al-Siddiq and Malik Sayif. The party established close relations with the Kurdistan Democratic Party (KDP), the Peoples' Party, and the National Democratic Party (NDP) (qq.v.). Its participation in *al-Wathba* (q.v.), the anti-Portsmouth treaty (q.v.) demonstrations in 1948, increased its popularity. However, the ICP's endorsement of the 1948 partition plan for Palestine, while in line with the Soviet position, created deep hostility between the party and the Arab nationalists.

The ICP faced serious setbacks following Fahd's execution. Its leaders were frequently arrested, and the party was unable to play a major role in 'Iraqi politics for several years. It regained some influence in the mid-1950s through its opposition to the Baghdad Pact (q.v.) and its participation in the antiregime National United Front (q.v.). Its membership in the National Front also led to an opening of relations with the 'Iraqi Free Officers (q.v.). (*See also* FRONT FOR THE DEFENSE OF PALESTINE.)

After the 1958 revolution (q.v.), the ICP gained considerable power. It sided with 'Abd al-Karim Qasim (q.v.) in his split with 'Abd al-Salam 'Arif (q.v.); participated in demonstrations calling for better relations with the Soviet Union; and proposed a federal union among 'Iraq, Egypt, and Syria instead of the unitary union for which the Arab nationalists were working. The ICP opposed the Arab nationalist position on union because it feared the creation of a powerful regime and because it believed such a union would favor the Arab nationalists. The party's strength was bolstered by Qasim's regime, which leaned heavily on the ICP for support to combat the influence of the Arab nationalists. Qasim permitted the establishment of Popular Resistance Forces, which were frequently led by ICP members, released party members from jail, and appointed communists to sensitive positions in the government. He provided the ICP additional posts after the communists helped suppress the Arab nationalist-supported Shawwaf revolt (q.v.) in Mawsil (q.v.) in March 1959. The ICP also strengthened its relations with the KDP and NPD during this period.

Opposition to the ICP's activities and growing power increased, especially after the Shawwaf revolt, in which the communists had killed large numbers of Arab nationalists, and the July 1959 Kirkuk massacres, in which communists had participated in massacres of Turkuman (q.v.). Religious leaders, both Christian (q.v.) and Muslim, began to warn against the communists' activities. The ICP's support for Kurdish aspirations also contributed to public disenchantment with the party. Popular discontent with the ICP forced Qasim to move to decrease the party's power. He limited the role of the Popular Resistance Forces, removed communists who held information positions, and tried to limit communist influence in the military. Qasim also arrested a number of communists and tried to control the activities of ICP-controlled unions.

Internal conflicts began to emerge within the ICP. The authority of Husayn al-Radhi, the secretary-general, was limited and a new leadership was established, including Baha al-Din al-Nuri and Hadi al-Adhami. The regime refused to allow the ICP under al-Rahdi to operate openly, while backing a political organization to set up an independent communist party under the leadership of Dawud al-Sayigh. This maneuver only served to weaken Qasim's friends within the ICP as al-Rahdi was able to regain his authority. The communists continued though to support Qasim's government and to provide military support to it.

Following the February 1963 Ba'thist coup, the communists were harshly suppressed; many of their leaders were arrested, some of whom were executed or died in prison. The party was led by 'Amir 'Abdullah and Baha al-Din al-Nuri, and their calls for popular resistance against the Ba'th regime led to increased repression. Once again the party was plagued by factionalism. The main party was known as the ICP–Central Committee, while a breakaway faction led by 'Aziz al-Hajj (q.v.) called itself the Communist Party–Central Leadership. Persecuted and divided, the party withdrew from Baghdad and concentrated its activities in the Kurdish areas, where it established close relations with the Kurdish leadership. This resulted in the increasing influence of Kurds (q.v.) in the party leadership, including 'Aziz Muhammad, a Kurd who became secretary-general of the party. (In 1976, the party reelected 'Aziz Muhammad as secretary general.)

Under the 'Arif regimes, the ICP reorganized itself and began following a more radical line. 'Aziz al-Hajj officially broke with the party and adopted a neutral position in the Sino-Soviet split. He called for armed struggle against the government, launching a guerrilla movement in the countryside, centered in the southern part of 'Iraq.

After the 1968 revolution (q.v.) returned the Ba'th to power, the ICP called on the nationalists and all progressive forces to adopt political positions in the new government. The Ba'th regime released a number of political prisoners, and some communists were permitted to return to 'Iraq. However, al-Hajj's group rejected cooperation with the ICP and the government and continued its uprising. Al-Hajj was arrested, and in a stunning about-face, he announced his support for the regime and was subsequently appointed 'Iraq's ambassador to UNESCO. Relations between the Ba'th and the ICP continued to improve. A number of communists entered the Ba'th Party in 1972, the same year 'Iraq signed a Treaty of Friendship and Cooperation (q.v.) with the Soviet Union. Mukarram al-Talabani and Amir 'Abdullah, both communists, were appointed as ministers of state, and the ICP's newspaper was published and distributed throughout 'Iraq. In 1973, the ICP became a legal party for the first time since its founding in 1934. The Ba'th and the ICP signed the National Action Charter, which called for the establishment of a progressive, nationalist, and democratic party that would include the Ba'th, the ICP, and the KDP. As part of this agreement, the ICP acknowledged that only the Ba'th Party could recruit members within the armed forces.

Serious splits eventually emerged between the ICP and the regime, concurrent with a cooling of 'Iraqi–Soviet relations over Soviet support to the Ethiopian government and because of growing concern over Soviet interference in Afghanistan. Twenty-one communists were executed in 1978 for forming cells in the army, a clear violation of its agreement with the Ba'th. Hundreds of other communists were either arrested or detained for questioning. In 1979, the Ba'th suppressed the ICP's newspaper, purged 29 communists from the army, and dismissed al-Talabani and 'Abdullah from the cabinet. Within a year, the ICP had been driven underground. Many of its cadres and members moved to the Kurdish region where it also had a Kurdish branch. The party has suffered from factionalism. One communist group is the Workers Communist Party, which was the first party to publish a newspaper after the fall of Saddam.

'IRAQI DEMOCRATIC ACCORD. An opposition group that is not a member of the 'Iraqi National Congress (q.v.). Based in London, it is headed by Salah 'Umar al-'Ali (q.v.), a Tikriti and former member of the Revolutionary Command Council (q.v.) who fell out with Saddam Husayn (q.v.) in the early 1970s. It works for the removal of Saddam and the inner core of his regime, although it favors giving the Ba'th Party (q.v.) a role to play in a post-Saddam government.

'IRAQI DEMOCRATIC MOVEMENT. A small opposition movement that consists of a number of exiled 'Iraqis. It is a member of the 'Iraqi National Congress (q.v.).

'IRAQI FASHION HOUSE (Dar al-Azya al-'Iraqiya). The 'Iraqi Fashion House was founded in 1970 to promote and protect the traditional forms of attire. The dress styles of the past were studied and duplicated, and the collection of garments traveled throughout 'Iraq and the world. Many of the designs were based on ancient 'Iraqi drawings. Its offices were looted and burned after the fall of Baghdad in 2003.

'IRAQI FREE OFFICERS. An opposition group connected with Hasan al-Naqib (q.v.) of the 'Iraqi Independent Alliance (q.v.). The group attempted to establish close links with 'Iraqi military officers and claims to have attempted to assassinate Saddam Husayn (q.v.). Its membership includes Husayn al-Jiburi.

'IRAQI GOVERNING COUNCIL (IGC). Formed on 13 July 2003, the IGC is the chief representative of the 'Iraqi people to the Coalition Provisional Authority (CPA) (q.v.) and the international community. Comprised of 25 members, the IGC represents the wide diversity of 'Iraqis. The IGC is expected to play a role in the formation of an 'Iraqi constitution and the gradual transfer of the administration of 'Iraq back to the 'Iraqi people.

'IRAQI INDEPENDENT ALLIANCE. An opposition group composed of a number of independent 'Iraqi nationalists. It is led by Hasan al-Naqib (q.v.), a moderate nationalist based in Damascus who is the Sunni (q.v.) member of the 'Iraqi National Congress's (q.v.) executive council. Al-Naqib was reported to have returned to Baghdad in 2003.

'IRAQI ISLAMIC PARTY (AL-HIZB AL-ISLAMI AL-'IRAQI). The 'Iraqi Islamic Party was primarily an offshoot of the Muslim Brotherhood, a group that spread to 'Iraq from Egypt shortly before World War II. It began to increase its activities shortly before the 1958 revolution (q.v.), especially in northern 'Iraq and later on in the Central Euphrates area and Baghdad (qq.v.). Two of its main leaders were 'Abdullah al-Mima, a prominent Mawsil (q.v.) religious figure, and Muhsin al-Hakim (q.v.), a prominent Shi'i *mujtahid* (qq.v.). It remained active after the 1958 revolution and opposed the regime of 'Abd al-Karim Qasim (q.v.) because of his cooperation with the communists. The party applied to the Interior Ministry in 1960 for a license, but the request was denied. The ministry reversed itself later the same year in response to rising criticism of the Qasim government for disbelief and atheism. The party did not have a specific official program, although it adopted a strong line against secularism and atheism. It criticized the neglect of religious education and called for the banning of the 'Iraqi Communist Party (q.v.). Its license was eventually withdrawn. Muhsin 'Abd al-'Aziz (q.v.), the party's secretary general, was appointed to the 'Iraqi Governing Council (IGC) (q.v.) in 2003.

'IRAQI–KUWAITI AGREEMENT OF 1963. Signed on 4 October 1963 by Kuwaiti prime minister Sabah al-Salim al-Sabah and 'Iraqi prime minister Ahmad Hasan al-Bakr (q.v.), this agreement restored friendly relations between 'Iraq and Kuwait. Under President 'Abd al-Karim Qasim (q.v.), 'Iraq laid claim to Kuwait in 1961, precipitating the landing of British troops in Kuwait to protect the newly independent sheikdom. Qasim's government refused to recognize Kuwait, asserting that 'Iraq had a historical claim to the territory dating back to the time of the Ottoman Empire. When the Ba'th Party (q.v.) seized power in 'Iraq in February 1963, it moved to normalize relations. In the 1963 agreement, 'Iraq recognized the independence and complete sovereignty of Kuwait, with the frontier as specified in a 1932 exchange of notes between the two countries. Saddam Husayn (q.v.) would revive claims to Kuwait in an attempt to justify 'Iraq's 1990 invasion and annexation of its southern neighbor. *See also* KUWAIT, INVASION OF.

'IRAQI NATIONAL ACCORD (WIFAQ). A former opposition party that had many former members of the Ba'th Party (q.v.), as well as some former military. Based in London, it was led by Ayyad Allawi (q.v.) officers and is part of the 'Iraqi National Congress (INC) (q.v.). It has many good contacts with officials and officers inside 'Iraq. The party was represented in Europe, Syria, and Turkey and had supporters in Saudi Arabia as well. It worked for the overthrow of Saddam Husayn's (q.v.) regime from within the Ba'th Party and the army. It published an opposition paper, *Baghdad*. Its members included General 'Adnan Nuri of the Republican Guard, Dr. Tahsin Mu'ala who had tended to Saddam's wounds after the 1959 failed assasination attempt on Qasim, and Nuri al-Badran, a former academic and diplomat, who is a member of the 'Iraqi cabinet and a brother-in-law of 'Allawi. It also included former UN Ambassador Salah-Umar al-Ali.

'IRAQI NATIONAL CONGRESS (INC). The main opposition group to Saddam Husayn's (q.v.) regime. The 'Iraqi National Congress (INC) was established in June 1992 in Vienna by over 200 representatives of various Kurdish, Shi'i (q.v.), Arab nationalist, independent, and socialist parties, organizations, and individuals. Its goals are the establishment of a constitutional, pluralist, democratic, and federal 'Iraq. The INC is also committed to sweeping reforms in the economic sector. At the Vienna meeting, it endorsed a free market economic system; privatization of economic sectors, including agriculture (q.v.), that had been nationalized by the Ba'th Party (q.v.); the conversion of the military-industrial complex to civilian use; and self-sufficiency in food production. The INC met in Salah al-Din in Kurdish-controlled 'Iraq in October 1992 and elected executive and legislative bodies. Mas'ud al-Barzani (q.v.), Hasan al-Naqib (q.v.), and Muhammad Bahr al-Ulum (q.v.) comprise the presidential council.

Muhammad Baqir al-Hakim (q.v.), the leader of the Supreme Assembly of the Islamic Revolution in 'Iraq (SAIRI) (q.v.), was nominated to the presidential council but declined. SAIRI opposed the division of the council along ethnic lines, with one seat each for the Kurds, Sunnis (qq.v.), and Shi'is, arguing that this reinforced divisions, underrepresented the numerically superior Shi'i population, and excluded minority groups like the Turkumen and Assyrians. A 26-person executive council was established, chaired by Ahmad Chalabi (q.v.), in which SAIRI did participate. The 281 delegates at the Salah al-Din meeting became the general assembly of the INC, which meets annually. The executive council was recently expanded to give the Sunnis and Shi'is greater representation. A constitutional advisory council, with between 37 and 50 members, was established at the same time. Chaired by 'Arif 'Abd al-Razzaq (q.v.), the advisory council was created to allow representation to groups that were not represented on the executive council. Chalabi played a large role in organizing and funding the INC and continues to run its day-to-day operations.

The INC has several weaknesses. There are persistent questions about the sources of the INC's wealth, it suffered from the perception that it is backed by foreign powers, and most of its constituent members lack strong support within 'Iraq. Finally, there were tensions between the Kurdish and Shi'i groups as well as between various Arab groups and leaders within the INC. SAIRI believes that the Kurds are overrepresented in the INC and remains suspicious of Kurdish calls for a federated 'Iraq. Chalabi and Bahr al-'Ulum became members of the IGC.

'IRAQI NATIONAL PARTY (AL-HIZB AL-WATANI AL-'IRAQI). A nationalist, anti-British party established in 1922 by Ja'far Abu al-Timman (q.v.) that had similar views to the al-Nahda group. The party called for free elections and an end to British interference in 'Iraqi internal affairs. It also condemned British activities, such as the closing of the newspapers *al-Mufid* and *al-Rafidian* and the aerial bombardment of the tribal forces supporting these newspapers. The party dissolved in 1933 when Rashid 'Ali al-Kaylani (q.v.) became prime minister.

'IRAQI PEOPLE'S PARTY (HIZB AL-SHA'B AL-'IRAQI). An opposition party founded by Yasin al-Hashimi (q.v.) in 1925 after he resigned as prime minister. The party opposed the 1926 Anglo–'Iraqi Agreement (q.v.). It brought down the second government of 'Abd al-Muhsin Sa'dun (q.v.) when its candidate to head Parliament, Rashid 'Ali (q.v.), defeated Sa'dun's candidate, Hikmat Sulayman (q.v.). It published a newspaper, *Mida al-Sha'b*, which suspended operations in 1927. The party's influence declined once several of its leaders assumed political positions.

'IRAQI PETROLEUM COMPANY (IPC). The IPC, originally known as the Turkish Petroleum Company, was established in 1912. It gained a concession from the 'Iraqi government in 1925 and struck oil (q.v.) at Baba Gurgur in 1927. The IPC had two subsidiary companies, the Mawsil Petroleum Company and the Basra Petroleum Company. It had five shareholders: Anglo–Persian Oil Company; Compagnie Française des Petroles; Dutch Shell Group; Near East Development Corporation, composed of five U.S. oil firms; and C. S. Gulbenkian. The four corporations each held 23.7 percent of the shares under a 1928 arrangement, with Gulbenkian holding the remaining 5 percent. The IPC lost 99.5 percent of its concession under the provisions of Law 80 of 1961 (q.v.), including the rich Rumaila field, but it continued to monopolize the production of 'Iraqi oil for the next decade. 'Iraq nationalized the IPC in 1972 under Law 69 (q.v.). *See also* ECONOMY; 'IRAQI–SOVIET TREATY OF FRIENDSHIP AND COOPERATION.

'IRAQI RECONSTRUCTION AND DEVELOPMENT COUNCIL (IRDC). In late February 2003, the Pentagon established the 'Iraqi Reconstruction and Development Council (IRDC), made up of 'Iraqis who would be part of a temporary government after the ousting of the Ba'th regime. After being based in suburban Virginia, its leading members were transported to Baghdad in late April 2003. Senior members of IRDC hold positions at each of 23 'Iraqi ministries, where they work closely with U.S. and British officials under the head of the Office of Reconstruction and Humanitarian Assistance (i.e., 'Iraq's civil administrator). Their official task is to rebuild the structures of a government that would then be handed over to the new 'Iraqi authority. The team is headed by 'Imad Dhia. (q.v.).

Members of the IRDC are officially employed by a San Diego–based contractor, Science Applications International Corporation (SAIC), whose vice president, until October 2002, was David Kay, the former UNSCOM (q.v.) inspector and the current head of the effort to investigate 'Iraq's weapons of mass destruction. SAIC also runs the "Voice of the New 'Iraq," the radio station established on 15 April 2003 at the city of Umm Qasr and funded by the U.S. government.

'IRAQI SOCIALIST PARTY (ISP). A small opposition party that is part of the 'Iraqi National Congress (q.v.). It is composed of Arab nationalists who were originally members of the Joint Action Committee, an earlier opposition group led by Dr. Mubdir al-Ways.

'IRAQI–SOVIET TREATY OF FRIENDSHIP AND COOPERATION. Signed on 9 April 1972, this treaty was widely seen as marking 'Iraq's entry into the Soviet sphere of influence. Modeled after the 1971 Egyptian–Soviet agreement, the treaty provided for Soviet military aid to 'Iraq, constant high-level consultations, and the promotion of bilateral relations, especially in the political, oil (q.v.), and trade spheres. It stipulated that neither side could join an alliance directed against the other, engage in hostile acts directed against the other, or permit the use of its territory for military acts directed against the other.

The timing of the agreement was linked to 'Iraq's long-standing battle with the foreign-controlled 'Iraqi Petroleum Company (IPC) (q.v.). In February 1972, with talks with the IPC deadlocked, 'Iraqi vice president Saddam Husayn (q.v.) flew to Moscow, apparently seeking Soviet assistance in the development of its oil industry if 'Iraq decided to nationalize the IPC. The day after the Treaty of Friendship and Cooperation was signed, Soviet premier Alexei Kosygin cut the ribbon at 'Iraq's Rumaila oil field, which the Soviets would help develop. In June 1972, 'Iraq nationalized nearly all of the IPC's holdings. The treaty also brought about a temporary honeymoon between the Ba'th Party (q.v.) and the long-suffering 'Iraqi Communist Party (ICP) (q.v.), which had been the target of numerous Ba'thist purges. In July of 1973, the ICP joined the National Front with the Ba'th Party. However, following the Soviet invasion of Afghanistan in 1979, Saddam accused the communists of forming cells in the armed forces and, despite Soviet objections, executed 22 people, bringing to an end cooperation between the two parties.

'IRAQI–TURKISH TREATY OF FRIENDSHIP AND NEIGHBORLY RELATIONS. Signed on 29 March 1946 between 'Iraq and Turkey, this pact reaffirmed the frontier as laid down in the 1926 Treaty of Ankara (q.v.) and pledged the two governments to noninterference in one another's affairs, the peaceful settlement of disputes, and mutual consultation in foreign affairs. It replaced the defunct 1937 S'adabad Pact (q.v.) and established a precedent for the 1955 Baghdad Pact (q.v.).

ISBAHANI, ABU AL-FARAJ AL- (897–967). One of the most distinguished and eminent scholars of Arab history and literature (q.v.). His *Kitab al-Aghani* (Book of Songs) has few rivals, and it was said that it took him 50 years to compile it. Sahib Ibn Abbad, a minister famed for his learning and erudition, supposedly substituted the *Book of Songs* for the 30 camel-loads of books he carried with him on his travels. Al-Isbahani also wrote numerous other works of poetry (q.v.) and prose. He was a descendent of the last Umayyad caliph.

ISHAQ, HUNAYN BIN (?–873). One of the greatest scholars in the history of the translation movement in Islam and one of the leading intellectuals of his era. He was a student of Yuhanna bin Masaway, the first abbot of al-Bayt al-Hikma (the House of Wisdom) (q.v.), which was established by the caliph al-Mamun (qq.v.) as a center of translation and research in 830. Both Hunayn and Yuhanna were 'Iraqi Christians (q.v.). Hunayn greatly improved methods of translation by putting it on a scientific footing. A large group of scholars worked under his supervision, including his son Ishaq, his nephew Hubaysh, and his disciple Isa bin Yahya. His philosophical and medical translations are believed to have been made with the highest standard of linguistic criticism and analysis. Ishaq is generally believed to have collected as many copies of a manuscript as possible so that he could determine the most correct text before he translated it. He translated a number of Aristotle's works into Arabic and Syriac, and he is also responsible for most of the Arabic translations of Plato's and Hippocrates' works.

'ISHTAR. The ancient Babylonian and Assyrian (q.v.) goddess of love and fertility. She is the counterpart to the Phoenician goddess, Astarte. Ishtar fell in love with Tammuz.

ISLAM. The dominant religion in 'Iraq. Islam, which means "submission to God's will," was founded by the prophet Muhammad, who was born around 570 A.D. in the city of Makka. There are two major sects in Islam: Shi'i (q.v.) Islam and Sunni (q.v.) Islam. These two sects were created following a major dispute over the line of the Prophet's succession following his death. Historically, Sunni Islam closely follows the original practices and traditions of the Prophet. Sunnis are less likely to accept interpretation and innovation, especially when it comes from other religions or cultures. The Sunnis also hold that the caliphate must be an elected office.

Sunnis are the largest Muslim sect overall; however, in 'Iraq the Shi'i are more numerous. There are Arab, Kurdish, and Turkuman (q.v.) Sunnis in 'Iraq, accounting for roughly 40 percent of the population. The majority of Kurds (q.v.) are Sunni. The Shi'i account for roughly 60 percent of the population. Most of the 'Iraqi Sunnis live in Baghdad (q.v.) and the north of the country, although there are also concentrations in some southern cities, such as Basra (q.v.), Nasiriyya, Suq al-Shyukukh, and al-Khamasia. 'Iraqi Sunni are in many different occupations, but historically they provided most of the military officer class and native officials under the Ottoman Empire. They continue to be dominant in the military, upper echelons of the civil service, and in the media.

ISLAMIC ACCORD MOVEMENT. An Islamic opposition party, mainly composed of *Islamic mujahhidin* and people who were expelled from 'Iraq. Originally based in Tehran, it has moved its base to Damascus after disagreements with the Iranians.

ISLAMIC ACTION ORGANIZATION (MUNAZMAT AL-'AMAL AL-ISLAMI). A Shi'i (q.v.) opposition group founded in 1982 by Hujjat Muhammad Taqi al-Islam al-Mudarrisi, the nephew of Ayatollah Muhammad al-Shirazi, who was assassinated in Lebanon. Al-Mudarrisi, now an Ayat-Allah, returned to 'Iraq in the spring of 2003. The movement was founded in Karbala (q.v.). It is believed to have been responsible for the assassination attempt on Tariq 'Aziz (q.v.) in 1980. The organization opposed the need to establish an alliance with the secular opposition for a long time. However, it met with representatives of the Kurdish and communist movements at the opposition conference held in 1991. It coordinated activities with Iran and Syria and was involved in the 1991 uprising. Ridha Jawad Taqi leads its activities. *See also* SUPREME ASSEMBLY OF THE ISLAMIC REVOLUTION IN 'IRAQ.

ISLAMIC BLOC. A Sunni (q.v.) opposition group led by Muhammad al-Alusi that is closely tied to the Muslim Brotherhood. Some of its members led an abortive uprising against Baghdad (q.v.) in 1970.

ISLAMIC LIBERATION PARTY. Sunni (q.v.) fundamentalist party with close ties to the Muslim Brotherhood that became active in 'Iraq in the 1950s.

ISLAMIC MOVEMENT OF KURDISTAN (IMK). Islamic political party believed to have been founded in 1986. It is led by two brothers, Shaykhs 'Uthman and 'Ali 'Abd al-'Aziz, who come from a prominent religious family of the Naqshabandiyya Sufi (q.v.) order in Halabja (q.v.). They are influential in the areas around Kirkuk (q.v.) and Halabja. The party is believed to have received support from Iran and to a lesser extent from Saudi Arabia. It became active in the ranks of the Kurdish refugees who had fled to Iran during the Iran–'Iraq war (q.v.).

In the May 1992 Kurdish elections, the party failed to gain the 7 percent vote threshold needed to gain entrance into Parliament, although it finished third in the voting behind the Kurdistan Democratic Party (KDP) (q.v.) and the Patriotic Union of Kurdistan (PUK) (q.v.). The IMK entered into military confrontations with the PUK in the fall of 1993 and the spring of 1994, leading to hundreds of deaths. It did not, however, move against the KDP and improved its ties with Mas'ud Barzani (q.v.). It currently has good relations with both the PUK and KDP. The IMK includes among its *pesh mergas* (q.v.) individuals who fought against the Soviets in Afghanistan and have since returned to Kurdish areas. The movement witnessed several breakups: the IMK had two members in the PUK regional government.

ISLAMIC MOVEMENT OF 'IRAQ. A mostly Shi'i (q.v.) opposition movement led by Shaykh Mahdi al-Khalisi, a member of the Coordinating Committee for Dialogue and Follow-up.

ISTIQLAL, AL-. *See* INDEPENDENCE PARTY.

– J –

JACOBITES (SYRIAC CHURCH). A small Christian (q.v.) community in 'Iraq. The name *Jacobite* refers to Jacob Baradai, who in the fifth century organized a faction of the Monophysite church of Syria. (Monophysites believe that Jesus Christ has a single nature, or a single composite nature that is part divine and part human.) The name *Jacobites* refers usually to the Syrian Orthodox Church in the Middle East. Other Monophysite churches in the

Middle East are the Coptic and Armenian Churches. The Jacobites welcomed the Muslim Arabs when they invaded Syria and 'Iraq and liberated them from the domination of the Persians, who had persecuted them. Jacobites reached high positions in the Abbasid state as scholars, physicians, and court administrators and were generally esteemed by the court in Baghdad (q.v.). The Jacobites flourished until the 12th century, numbering close to two million people in 'Iraq, Syria, Cyprus, and parts of Persia, with some 20 metropolitans and 103 bishops. The Jacobite patriarch claimed the title of patriarch of Antioch, although his seat was later held in various monasteries, and he exercised jurisdiction over Persia and 'Iraq. Internal splits, the Mongol invasions, and subsequent religious fanaticism and massacres greatly weakened the church, and by the 17th century, the church had only 17 bishops. During the 19th and early 20th centuries, the majority of the Jacobites lived in 'Iraq, Turkey, Syria, and India, where missionaries had carried the faith. Many Jacobites in Turkey fled persecution and massacres in the 19th century and during World War I, seeking refuge in Syria, Lebanon, and later Armenia and Sweden. The patriarch, who holds the title of mar ignatius, moved from Mardin to Mawsil (q.v.) in 'Iraq, and later to Homs in Syria and finally to Damascus. He has jurisdiction over Jacobites in 'Iraq, Syria, Lebanon, India, and the United States.

JABBARI, MAJID RASHID AL- (1947–). A progovernment Kurdish Revolutionary Party activist. He served as vice president of the General Union of 'Iraq Labor Unions. He is a Politburo member of the Kurdistan Democratic Party (q.v.) and a member of the Kurdish Cultural Society.

JABHA AL-SHA'BIYYA, AL-. A bloc formed by opposition members in Parliament, the National Democratic Party (NDP) (q.v.), and the Liberal Party (q.v.). The NDP initiated the efforts to form the bloc, but the government refused to extend it a license because the law allowed only individuals to establish parties. Consequently, the NDP withdrew its participation. When an independent politician was granted a license for the bloc in May 1951, the NDP cooperated with it. The bloc's platform included the distancing of 'Iraq from external alliances and an insistence that 'Iraq not become a base to threaten or attack Iran or any other country. It called for Arab cooperation and the preservation of the Arabness of Palestine. It emphasized the need for full 'Iraqi sovereignty and independence as well as for the establishment of a democratic constitution. It published a newspaper, *al-Difa'*, owned by Sadiq al-Bassam (q.v.). Muhammad Ridha al-Shabibi (q.v.) headed the executive committee. Other members included Husayn Jamil and Muhammad Hadid (qq.v.). Following disagreements among members after the 1952 elections, the bloc was dissolved in 1954.

JABR, SALIH (1896–1957). Politician and jurist during the monarchy. He was born in Nasiriyya and graduated from Baghdad Law School. He served as a judge from 1926 to 1930 and was elected to Parliament. He held a number of cabinet and administrative posts: minister of education (1933–1934, 1938–1940), governor of Karbala (1935–1936), minister of justice (1936–1937), director-general of customs and excise (1937–1938), minister of social affairs (1940), governor of Basra (q.v.) (1940–1941), acting minister of foreign affairs (1941–1943), and minister of finance (1942–1943). He was the first Shi'i (q.v.) to be prime minister (1947–1948). Jabr negotiated the 1948 Portsmouth treaty (q.v.), which superceded the Anglo–'Iraqi Treaty of 1930 (q.v.). While it was an improvement over the old treaty, it was denounced by the public and rival politicians. Violent protests and demonstrations, known as *al-Wathba* (q.v.), broke out causing rival political parties to demand the immediate resignation of Jabr's government and the repudiation of the treaty. He resigned on 27 January 1948, and the treaty was scrapped. He held the post of minister of interior in 1950. In 1951, he established the 'Iraqi Nation's Party, which stood in opposition to Nuri al-Sa'id (q.v.). Jabr was known for his sympathy to British policy. His son Sa'd was active in the opposition to Saddam. *See also* COMMITTEE FOR NATIONAL COOPERATION.

JA'FAR, HASAB AL-SHAYKH (1942–). Poet, translator, and journalist from Maysan. He studied literature in Moscow and worked as the director of the languages section at 'Iraqi television and radio stations. Historical and cultural themes abound in his poetry. He has published a number of collections, including *Visit to the Sumerian Lady* and *In the Mirror across the Wall*.

JA'FAR, MAJID 'ABD (1942–). A Ba'thist technocrat and cabinet minister from Diyala. He received an M.S. from Birmingham University in Britain in 1975. He has held the positions of director-general in the Ministry of Planning, director-general of the Central Organization of Statistics in the Ministry of Finance, and director-general of the budget in the Ministry of Finance. He served as minister of finance from March 1991 through July 1992.

JA'FARI, IBRAHIM AL- (1947–). A representative of the Shi'i al-Da'wa party (q.v.), which he joined in 1966, and a member of the 'Iraqi Governing Council (IGC) (q.v.). Al-Da'wa was responsible for assaults on a series of high-ranking Ba'thist officials during the Saddam era. Among other acts, it claimed responsibility for an assassination attempt on Saddam Husayn's (q.v.) eldest son Uday (q.v.) in 1996. Like its ideological opposite, the 'Iraqi Communist Party (ICP) (q.v.), its power inside 'Iraq was broken during the 1980s, and subsequently the organization split into various groups based, until recently, in Iran, Syria, and the United Kingdom. Ayatollah Muhammad Baqir al-Sadr (q.v.), the group's spiritual leader, was assassinated by the regime in 1999 in Najaf.

The party was banned in 1980, and al-Ja'fari fled the country to Iran and later to London. He attended Mosul University and is a medical doctor. Al-Ja'fari was the first to take the rotation chairmanship of the IGC in August 2003.

JAHIZ, AL- (c. 776–868). A major literary figure, one of the most masterful writers of Arabic prose, and the founder of the Mu'tazilite (q.v.) school. The grandson of a black slave, he was born in Basra (q.v.). Although he grew up in modest circumstances, he managed to gain a very good education. He moved to Baghdad (q.v.) during the reign of caliph al-Mamun (r. 813–833) (q.v.) and remained at court until a few years before his death in 868. Al-Jahiz is the author of 200 works on an extraordinary range of topics. Some of his most famous works include *The Book of Animals*, an anthology of animal anecdotes; *The Book of Clarity and Clarification*, which covers topics such as history and natural science; *The Book Misers*, an insightful and humorous study of human psychology; and *The Superiority of Blacks over Whites*. He outlined a unique political theory in a series of books submitted to al-Ma'mun. Al-Jahiz contended that people need an imam to guide them in their best religious and secular interests. He defined the main goals of the imam as warning the populace to avoid evil deeds and combating corruption. He believed that the imam had the responsibility to unite the people, to provide them with basic necessities, to protect them against their enemies, and to protect the weak against the strong. Al-Jahiz emphasized the need for a single leader because a multiplicity of leaders would ultimately lead to conflict among them. The imam must be brave, knowledgeable, patient, truthful, tough, wise, and generous without being wasteful. The basis of the imam's leadership is consultation; he must consult those close to him but not the general public because the general public does not understand the imamate. Al-Jahiz was a bold thinker greatly interested in all the sciences. He gave his name to one of the sects of the rationalists and founded a new ornamental style of literature known as *Adab*, which relied on poetry (q.v.), oratory, history, myths, and the sayings of the early Arabs. He died in Basra in 868; legend has it that he was crushed to death by a stack of falling books in his study.

JALIL, GHANIM 'ABD AL- (1938–1979). Ba'thist official and cabinet minister. He was born in Baghdad (q.v.) and graduated from the School of Law and Political Science in 1965. He became a member of the Ba'th Party (q.v.) in 1953. He was appointed governor of Kirkuk in 1970 and governor of Diyala in 1971. After serving as general manager of 'Iraqi ports in 1971, al-Jalil was asked to direct the 'Iraqi Company for Oil Operations after the nationalization of oil (q.v.) in 1972. He was elected a member of the Regional Command (q.v.) in 1974 and also became the head of the office of the Revolutionary Command Council (RCC) (q.v.). He served as minister of higher education and scientific research (1974–1977) and as minister of state (1977). In 1976, al-Jalil was given the responsibility for coordinating political activities between the central government in Baghdad and the executive and legislative institutions of the Kurdish autonomous region. He gained membership in the RCC in 1977. He was accused of participating in the alleged "pro-Syrian" plot in 1979 and summarily executed.

JAMALI, FADHIL AL- (1903–1997). Cabinet official, diplomat, and academic from Kadhimiya. He trained in Baghdad (q.v.) to be an elementary school teacher. He taught for four years and then was sent abroad by the Ministry of Education to study at the American University in Beirut. He studied philosophy and psychology before returning to Baghdad. After a stint as a teacher at the Baghdad Teachers College, al-Jamali went to the United States. He earned an M.A. and a Ph.D. in education from Columbia University. He was a lecturer on education at the Higher Teachers Training College in Baghdad from 1936 to 1947. Al-Jamali served in numerous diplomatic, administrative, and ministerial posts. He occupied a number of positions in the Ministry of Education (1932–1942), including supervisor general, inspector general, and director-general. He was appointed director general of foreign affairs and later held the portfolio of foreign affairs in seven different cabinets (1946–1948, 1949, 1952–1953, 1954). He served briefly as prime minister in 1954. He signed the United Nations' Charter in San Francisco on behalf of the 'Iraqi government and headed the 'Iraqi delegation to the UN General Assembly from 1947 to 1958. Al-Jamali was minister to Egypt and permanent representative to the UN in 1950. He was one of the most active 'Iraqi diplomats at the UN, acting as chair of the General Assembly three times in its first 11 plenary sessions. Following the 1958 revolution (q.v.), al-Jamali was arrested, tried, and sentenced to death by the Mahdawi Court. He spent three years in prison and was released in July 1961. He went to Tunis, where he became a professor of education at the University of Tunis. He was granted Tunisian citizenship. He is the author of several books.

JAMIL, HUSAYN (1908–199?). Cabinet minister, politician, and intellectual during the monarchy. He was born to one of the oldest and most prominent Baghdad (q.v.) families and trained as a lawyer. He came to be convinced that social, economic, and political reforms were badly needed in 'Iraq. An associate of Kamil al-Chadirchi (q.v.), Jamil was cofounder of al-Ahali (q.v.) and the National Democratic Party (q.v.). He served as minister of social affairs (1949–1950) and minister of guidance (1959).

JASIM, FULAYIH HASAN (1940–). A Ba'th Party (q.v.) activist and politician. He was born to a Shi'i (q.v.) family from the Diyala province and attended the Teachers College. He was arrested several times under the 'Abd al-Karim Qasim and 'Abd al-Salam 'Arif (qq.v.) regimes and was eventually dismissed from his teaching position because of his party activities. In 1974, Jasim was named governor of the Ninevah province; in 1975, he became acting deputy minister of interior. He served as minister of industry (1976–1977) and minister of state (1977). He was removed from his positions in March 1977 for his alleged lenience toward antiregime Shi'i protestors.

JASIM, LATIF NUSAYYIF (1941–). Ba'thist activist and longtime minister of culture and information. He was born in al-Rashidiyya to a Shi'i (q.v.) family and graduated from Baghdad University's College of Sciences in 1966. He joined the Ba'th Party (q.v.) in 1957 and served prison terms during the 'Abd al-Salam 'Arif regimes (q.v.). In 1963, Jasim went to Moscow as an aide to the 'Iraqi cultural attaché. Following the Ba'th's seizure of power in 1968, he became the deputy chair of the Central Peasant's Bureau, a post he held for 10 years. He has held a variety of positions within the government: chief editor of *Voice of the Peasant*; director-general of state radio and television (1974); minister of agrarian reform (1977); minister of culture and information (1979–1991); and minister of labor and social affairs (1993–1996). A member of the Regional Command (q.v.) since 1982, Jasim was not reelected to the position in 1991 and was appointed as a presidential adviser. He was elected a member of the Revolutionary Command Council (q.v.) in the 1990s and served as the deputy chairman of the Ba'th Party Military Bureau, positions he held until April 2003. Jasim was captured by American forces in June 2003.

JAWAHIRI, MUHAMMAD MAHDI AL- (1900–1996). One of the leading 'Iraqi poets who continued to write in the traditional style. He was born in Najaf (q.v.) to a family known for its literary interests. His first poem was published in 1921, after which his work began to appear regularly in 'Iraqi newspapers and magazines. Al-Jawahiri worked as a teacher in Baghdad (q.v.) in 1924 but was removed because a poem he wrote was critical of the government. Although he was reinstated, he resigned in 1927. Despite his criticisms of conditions under the monarchy, he managed to maintain a good relationship with the royal family. He was employed in the royal court for several years and held several positions in the Ministry of Education, although he was often expelled or resigned. Al-Jawahiri then took up journalism. He edited no fewer than 12 newspapers, most of which were short-lived due to their political content. In 1937, he was jailed for publishing an article critical of the regime. He went into self-imposed exile in 1956, living in Damascus and Czechoslovakia before returning to Baghdad. Through his poetry (q.v.), he played a major role in the politics of his times. Al-Jawahiri rejected political decadence and compromise, and his poetry is marked by social and political protests that emphasize his leftist views. His poetry collections include *Diwan al-Jawahiri*, *Return Post*, and *To Sleeplessness*. He has been honored by various Arab governments, including the Saddam Husayn (q.v.) regime.

JAWWAL, AL-. A literary and cultural society in the 1930s and 1940s. Its members included prominent Muslim and Christian (q.v.) intellectuals, officers, and educators, 'Iraqi as well as non-'Iraqi. Among the 'Iraqi officers who became members was Khayralla Talfah (q.v.), the brother of Saddam Husayn's (q.v.) mother and one of the figures who had a major impact on his politics.

JEWS. The 'Iraqi Jewish community, whose members today number less than 100, is but a remnant of a much larger and deeply rooted community that played an important role in the economic, political, and social life of the country from independence until the 1940s, when the majority of Jews left for Israel. 'Iraqi Jews are generally believed to be descendants of the Jews who were taken captive during the Babylonian Captivity. The first was taken captive under Shalmanassar around 721 B.C., but the largest group was taken under King Nabuchadnassar between 597 and 586 B.C. Their numbers increased as a result of successful proselytism during the Babylonian Captivity. A number of Jews returned to Palestine under the leadership of Nehemiah, but most of them remained in Babylon. The unsuccessful Jewish rebellions in Palestine in 66–70 A.D. and 132–135 A.D. added to the numbers of Jews in 'Iraq, which became a center of opposition to Roman emperors. The mostly urban Jewish community flourished in 'Iraq, and Mesopotamia became an important educational, religious, commercial, and cultural center for world Jewry. Great universities and seminaries were established at Nahr Di'a, Sura, and Powpithada, where scholars composed the Babylonian Talmud and worked out the rabbinical system.

Under Islamic rule, Jews, whose numbers were a little under a hundred thousand when 'Iraq came under Muslim rule, were treated well as a "People of the Book." The Jews of Baghdad (q.v.), particularly those with learning and expertise, found favor with many of the caliphs (q.v.), especially al-Ma'mun (q.v.). Baghdad alone boasted 10 rabbinical schools and several synagogues. During the 12th century, 'Iraqi Jews and Christians (q.v.) suffered discrimination under caliph al-Mutawakil (q.v.), but the situation improved under caliph al-Mu'tadhid. 'Iraqis of all religions suffered during the massacres and destruction that accompanied Mongol rule beginning in the mid-13th century. (*See* AHL AL-KITAB [PEOPLE OF THE BOOK].)

The condition of 'Iraqi Jews, whose numbers had dwindled to 20,000 to 30,000, improved under Ottoman rule, and a number of them began to trade with India and the Far East. The community was reorganized in accordance with the millet system and led by a member of the prominent Sassoun family. However, 'Iraqi Jews did not benefit from the Westernizing influence of the Sephardic Jews who fled into the Ottoman empire in 1492. Beginning in 1869, the opening of schools by the French Alliance Israelite Universelle helped the spread of modern education and the learning of French and English. Few Jews in 'Iraq had any contact with trends in Western thought, and there was little contact with or knowledge of Zionist activities. During the 19th century, though, prominent Jews such as Sasun Hisquail (q.v.) and Menahim Dawil represented 'Iraq in the Ottoman Parliament.

A somewhat different Jewish community lived in northern 'Iraq. These Jews, known as *Kurdish Jews*, numbered 20,000 by 1948. Their origins go back to the tribe of Benjamin and the early settling of the northern tribes. Unlike their coreligionists in 'Iraq, who had spoken Arabic since the Arab conquests, these Jews also spoke Syriac, a dialect of Aramaic (q.v.) also spoken by the Assyrians (q.v.). This community was not as centralized, organized, or educated as the other 'Iraqi Jewish community. About half lived in Mawsil (q.v.), and the rest lived in Kirkuk (q.v.), Zakho, Sulaymaniyya, Arbil (q.v.), and Dohuk. This group was generally indistinguishable from their Kurdish and Assyrian neighbors in terms of way of life and customs.

During the Mandate, the 'Iraqi Jewish community numbered roughly 120,000, with 60 to 65 percent living in Baghdad. Jews represented 2.5 percent of 'Iraq's population and 25 percent of Baghdad's. The post–World War I period witnessed a demographic and social expansion from Baghdad toward al-Hilla and Basra (q.v.) where smaller communities lived. Jews also began to move out of traditionally Jewish quarters into multireligious neighborhoods. By the 1930s, Baghdad had 60 synagogues and 1,000 students in Jewish schools. Under the new 'Iraqi state, a number of Jews served in important positions, including Hisqail, who became the first minister of finance, and Dawud Jamra, vice president of the 'Iraqi Court of Appeals. Others served in high posts in their respective ministries, such as Ishaq Hayim (Justice), Ibrahim al-Kabir (Finance), Salim Tarzi (Transportation), Moshe Shohit (Administration of Railroads), and Ezra Eliahu (Public Works). Jews established several newspapers and publications such as *al-Haris* (1920), *al-Misbah* (1924), *al-Bustan* (1939), and *al-Barid al-Yawmi* (1948). A number of prominent poets, novelists, and short story writers emerged, including Anwar Shawul, Murad Mikhail, Salim Darwish, Yaqub Balbul, Salim al-Katib, Mir Basri (q.v.), and Salim Qattan.

The community also thrived economically and financially. Jewish merchants handled up to 95 percent of all 'Iraqi imports and 10 percent of all exports. Most of 'Iraq's commercial agents, small bankers (35 of the 39 registered in Baghdad), jewelers, silversmiths, and goldsmiths were Jews. Several important banks were established by Jewish businessmen, including Bank

Zalkha, Bank Kharit, Bank Edward Abbudi, and the Lawi (Levi). Business families of 'Iraqi Jewish origin outside the country included the Sassouns, the Khadhuris (Keddouries), the Zalkhis, and the Saatchis. It was one of the wealthiest Jewish communities in the Middle East, although the wealth was not evenly distributed. The middle class mostly entailed retailers, civil servants, doctors, and lawyers, while the poorer members of the community were small shopkeepers, artisans, and domestic workers. As late as 1946, 25 percent of 'Iraq's middle class were Jews.

Jewish life in 'Iraq was greatly affected by the rise of Zionism, the growing conflict between Jews and Arabs in Palestine, and increasing hostility to British hegemony in 'Iraq. 'Iraqi independence, the growth of the nationalist movement, the death of King Faysal I (q.v.), the 1936–1939 Arab Revolt in Palestine and the subsequent arrival in 'Iraq of al-Haj Amin al-Husayni, the Mufti of Jerusalem, and the increase in Zionist activity by a handful of 'Iraqi Jews had a very negative impact on the life of the Jewish community. Most 'Iraqi Jews either were not active politically or opposed Zionism. Some Jewish activists, like Ya'cub Rujman and Na'im Tuwaya, joined the 'Iraqi Communist Party (q.v.) or other leftist parties. In 1941, following the suppression of the nationalist regime of Rashid 'Ali al-Kaylani (q.v.), the public's anti-Jewish feelings were exploited by the desire for looting. A riot erupted, leading to the destruction and looting of Jewish shops and businesses and the deaths of 110 people. This was the first directly anti-Jewish action rather than anti-British or anti-Zionist action. Anti-British feeling, growing Arab nationalist fervor, and the rise of German influence all contributed to the 1941 events, spurring an increase in Zionist activities by a very small segment of 'Iraq's Jewish population.

In 1946, a leftist group comprising anti-Zionist 'Iraqi Jews formed the Anti-Zionist League (q.v.). As late as 1946, the league's newspaper, al-'Usbat, had a daily distribution of around 6,000. Soviet support for Zionism and the international community's subsequent recognition of Israel confused and weakened anti-Zionist groups, while radical nationalists escalated their attacks on Zionism and communism. From 1947 onward, life for 'Iraqi Jews became difficult. The Dayr Yasin massacre, the 1948 Arab–Israeli war, and the influx of Palestinian refugees into 'Iraq inflamed anti-Jewish feelings. Legal restrictions were placed on Jews seeking to leave the country; they had to pay 2,000 dinars and promise not to go to Palestine. Between 1946 and 1948, only 65 Jews were allowed to emigrate, although 1,532 Jews left during the 1948 war. Jewish merchants' share of trade declined to 50 percent after World War II and to 20 percent by 1950. Their share of export trade dropped to 2 percent after World War II.

In 1949, all 'Iraqi Jews who had emigrated to Palestine were tried in absentia, and no Jews were given exit visas. A number of Jews were arrested and tried on charges of spying for the Soviet Union or for pro-Zionist activities; some of them were hanged. Nuri al-Sa'id (q.v.) subsequently forced the minister of defense, who was responsible for the harsh sentences, to resign, and the situation improved somewhat for the Jewish community. In 1950, the 'Iraqi government passed a law lifting the citizenship of Jews who had left the country or registered to do so. By 1952, the majority of 'Iraqi Jews had left the country. About 11,000 Jews remained behind, mostly members of the wealthier families. After the 1958 revolution (q.v.), life became intolerable for many of the remaining Jews, who left the country by legal or illegal means. Today only a tiny number of Jews remain in 'Iraq.

JIDDU, RAMZI (1944–). Senior advisor to the Ministry of Industry. He is a Chaldean (q.v.) Christian and a Baghdadi chemist and government official. He moved to the United States in 1978 after 'Iraqi police questioned him about his lack of affiliation to the Ba'th party. A leading member of the 'Iraqi Forum for Democracy, based in Superior Township, Detroit, Michigan, he worked as director of business development and new products for Biotherapies Inc., in Ann Arbor, Michigan.

JUDICIAL AGREEMENT OF THE 1922 ANGLO–'IRAQI TREATY. Under Article IX of the 1922 Anglo–'Iraqi Treaty (q.v.), 'Iraq and Britain concluded a separate agreement safeguarding the interests of foreigners in judicial matters, signed on 25 March 1924. The agreement stipulated that 'Iraq would employ British legal experts in its court system and grant them judicial powers; foreigners were granted a broad range of instances in which they could be tried in front of such judges (Article II). 'Iraq also agreed to submit all draft laws affecting the court system and the appointment of judges to the high commissioner for his views and advice on how the proposed laws affected the interests of foreigners (Article III).

JUND AL-IMAM. *See* SOLDIERS OF THE IMAM.

– K –

KAMAL, IBRAHIM. Cabinet minister during the monarchy. He was born to a prominent family from Mawsil (q.v.) and served as an Ottoman officer. He held the posts of minister of justice (1941) and minister of finance (1937–1938, 1941) and was considered a financial expert. The regent, 'Abd al-Ilah (q.v.), wanted him to become prime minister in 1942, but he was unable to form a cabinet. From the 1930s, Kamal was an opponent of Nuri al-Sa'id (q.v.).

KAMALI, SHAFIQ AL- (1929–1984). A prominent writer, poet, and Ba'th Party (q.v.) activist from Ramadi province. He graduated from the College of Literature in Baghdad (q.v.) in 1955 and received a graduate degree from Cairo University in Arab literature (q.v.). He taught at the College of Arts and Sciences at Baghdad University. Al-Kamali joined the Ba'th in the 1950s and was active in anti-British, antigovernment activities as a high school and college student. He was one of the first organizers of Ba'thist student groups and published underground leaflets and pamphlets. During the 1958 revolution (q.v.), he lost his teaching position but was appointed director-general of the Ministry of Culture and Information by the 1963 Ba'thist government. After its collapse, he was arrested and tortured. In 1969, al-Kamali gained membership in the National Command, Regional Command (as a reserve member), and the Revolutionary Command Council (qq.v.). He was appointed minister of youth in 1970. When conflicts with party leaders led to his dismissal, Ba'th Party founder Michel Aflaq (q.v.) urged that he be reappointed. In 1975, he was appointed deputy chair of the Arab Writers Union, an organization he later chaired. From 1977 to 1979, al-Kamali served as minister of information, followed by a stint as ambassador to Spain (1979–1980.) He was elected to Parliament in 1980. He was reportedly arrested in 1983 for seeking to arrange the escape of his imprisoned son so that he could avoid military service. He published several collections of poems that relate to ancient and contemporary Arab history and a volume on poetry (q.v.) among the Bedouin. Al-Kamali published and edited an important historical, political, and cultural magazine in the 1970s, *Afaq'Arabiyya* (Arab Horizons). He also wrote the 'Iraqi national anthem, which expresses support for Saddam Husayn (q.v.).

KAMIL, HUSAYN (1954–1996). Security official and former head of 'Iraq's military industrialization program. He was a cousin of Saddam Husayn (q.v.) and 'Ali Hasan al-Majid (q.v.) and married Saddam's daughter Raghad. Born in Tikrit, he joined the military in 1968. In 1982, he presided over the expansion of the Republican Guards from Saddam's bodyguards to the elite core of the army. Kamil headed general security for several years in the 1980s and established special security in 1987. As minister of industry and military industrialization from 1988 to 1991, he was responsible for 'Iraq's efforts to import and develop military technology, including ballistic missile capabilities, the supergun, and nuclear, chemical, and biological weapons. He also served as acting minister of oil (1990–1991) and minister of defense (1991). Considered the second-most powerful person in 'Iraq from 1988 to 1991, Kamil was removed from all his positions in November 1991. He was appointed a presidential adviser and then minister of industry and minerals in 1993. He was admitted to a hospital in Jordan in February 1994, where he reportedly underwent surgery for a brain tumor. Unlike most of the top members of Saddam's regime, Kamil did not serve on either the Revolutionary Command Council (q.v.) or the Regional Command (q.v.). On 10 August 1995, Kamil defected to Jordan with his brother Saddam Kamil (q.v.), their wives, and 15 other military officials. He reportedly provided top secret information on 'Iraq and its weapons capabilities to the UN and to the Central Intelligence Agency. Two days later, he called for the overthrow of Saddam. Shunned by the 'Iraqi opposition, Kamil decided to return to 'Iraq and seek Saddam's forgiveness. He and his family arrived in Baghdad (q.v.) on 20 February 1996. Three days later, Qusay and his brother were divorced from their wives. They were killed by relatives for disgracing the family by their defections. Other reports said they were killed on Saddam's order.

KAMIL, SADDAM. (?–1996). One-time head of Saddam Husayn's (q.v.) personal security detail and the brother of Husayn Kamil (q.v.). He was married to Saddam's daughter Rana. On 10 August 1995, he defected to Jordan with his brother Husayn Kamil, their wives, and 15 other military officials. He returned with his brother to 'Iraq on 20 February 1996. Rana divorced him three days later, and he was subsequently killed along with his brother and several other family members by relatives for disgracing the family by their defections.

KANNA, KHALIL. Cabinet minister under the monarchy. He was considered a strong, capable, skilled, and intelligent administrator. He was arrested and jailed in 1941 after Rashid 'Ali al-Kaylani's (q.v.) coup. He became a protégé of Nuri al-Sa'id (q.v.), to whom he was related by marriage. Kanna served as minister without portfolio (1950), minister of education (1950–1952, 1953, 1954–1955), and minister of finance (1955–1957). He was jailed after the 1958 revolution (q.v.). He published an autobiography that shed some light on the politics and personalities under the monarchy.

KANNU, YOUNADIM YUSUF. The lone Christian in the 'Iraqi Governing Council (IGC) (q.v.). He is an engineer who served as a minister for transport and communications in the first Kurdish regional cabinet in Arbil in 1992 and later served as minister of industry and trade in 1996. He was born in Dahuk in the Kurdish region but lives in Kirkuk.

KARBALA. One of 'Iraq's oldest and holiest Shi'i (q.v.) cities. It is also the capital of the governorate that bears its name and is about 55 kilometers south of Baghdad (q.v.). It contains the graves of Imam al-Husayn and his brother al-'Abbas. Al-Husayn was martyred at Karbala in his struggle against the caliph Yazid in 680, an event that Shi'is commemorate at 'Ashura (q.v.). It is also famed for its gardens, orchards, and date groves that are watered by the Husayniyya canal. The province also contains important archeological remains such as the fortress of the Ukhaidar Palace. Karbala is known for its fruit and citrus products and for its pine trees. It includes the oasis of 'Ayn al-Tamr and al-Razaza Lake, which is about 60 kilometers long.

KARIM, KHAIRALLAH 'ABD AL- (?–1949). An officer in the 'Iraqi army and a prominent leader of the Kurdish Hewa Party (q.v.). He participated in the 1943–1945 uprising led by Mulla Mustafa al-Barzani (q.v.) and fled with the Barzanis to Iran in 1945. He helped form the Kurdistan Democratic Party (q.v.) and the army of the Mahabad republic. Al-Karim was executed upon his return to Baghdad (q.v.) in 1949.

KARIM, SAM (SAM KAREEM) (1947–). Senior advisor to the Ministry of Transportation and Telecommunication. He was born in Baghdad and attended al-Sharqiyya High School from 1971 to 1974. He trained as an electrical engineer at the University of Baghdad (1974–1978) and left 'Iraq in February 1982 to train at the computer studies department at the University of Essex, United Kingdom. He has since worked as a computer consultant based in Detroit. Karim started the 'Iraq.net website in 1995. According to the U.S. Department of State in 1989, "his father was imprisoned by the 'Iraqi intelligence service and was tortured."

KARIM, TAYIH 'ABD AL- (1933–). Ba'thist politician, diplomat, and cabinet minister. He was born in Ana. Following his graduation from the Teachers College in 1951, he became a member of the Ba'th Party (q.v.) and was arrested several times in the 1950s for his political activities. Al-Karim received a degree in economics in 1959 and a law degree in 1969. He worked as a teacher from 1956 to 1959. He served as a senior official in the Ministry of Interior in 1963 and was appointed ambassador to Sudan in 1968. In 1970, al-Karim served as deputy minister of education. He was appointed director of the Office of Economic Affairs and to the Bureau of Arab Affairs in the Revolutionary Command Council (RCC) (q.v.) in 1972. He served as minister of oil from 1974–1982. In 1974, he became a member of the Supreme Agricultural Committee. Al-Karim was elected to the Regional Command (q.v.) in 1974 and gained membership in the RCC in 1977. He was relieved of all responsibilities and appointed senior adviser to the RCC in 1982.

KARMALY, ANASTAS MARY AL- (1866–1947). Famed linguist, author, and Catholic clergyman. He was born Peter Michael Yusuf to a Lebanese father and an 'Iraqi Chaldean (q.v.) mother. He attended Catholic schools in 'Iraq and Jesuit schools in Beirut and then joined a Carmelite monastery in Belgium, specializing in theology and philosophy. After visits to Andulusia and Spain, he returned to Baghdad (q.v.) in 1894 and taught Arabic and French at the Carmelite school. A prominent linguist and historian, al-Karmaly mastered Arabic, French, Latin, and Greek and had a good command of Syriac, Persian, English,

Italian, and other languages. He established the magazine *Lughat al-Arab* in 1911, which focused on language, history, and literature. He was elected a member of the Arab Academy in Damascus at its founding and became a member of the Cairo Arab Academy and the 'Iraqi Academy. His books covered such diverse topics as 'Iraqi history, ancient linguistics, and Arab coins. Al-Karmaly also authored an Arab dictionary and conducted linguistic research on a number of languages. He had a significant impact on the cultural and linguistic studies of his time. He held a weekly gathering at his home that was attended by leading linguists and intellectuals from the Arab world and 'Iraq.

KAYLANI, 'ABD AL-RAHMAN AL- (c. 1841–1947). Prime minister during the monarchy. He was born in Baghdad (q.v.) to a wealthy family that traced its descent to Shaykh 'Abd al-Qadir, who had come to Baghdad from Persia in 1095. His family had for centuries provided the leader of the Ashraf of Baghdad, a position that al-Kaylani himself held. He headed the provisional government in 'Iraq (1920–1921) and served as prime minister in the first two cabinets under the monarchy (1921–1922). Al-Kaylani was a traditional leader; he told Gertrude Bell (q.v.) that if the people were allowed to choose their own government in 'Iraq, a great deal of disorder would ensue. He believed that Britain had sufficient power and wealth to rule 'Iraq. He did not favor the assumption of the 'Iraqi throne by the Hashimites (q.v.), and his government resigned in 1921 once Faysal (q.v.) became king.

KAYLANI, RASHID 'ALI AL- (1892–1965). Politician, lawyer, and political leader from a prominent Sunni (q.v.) family in Baghdad (q.v.). He graduated from the Law College in Baghdad and worked as a judge. An ardent Arab nationalist, he cofounded the National Brotherhood Party (q.v.), which opposed the British. Rashid 'Ali served as minister of justice in 1924 and as a member of Parliament in 1925 and 1926. He was prime minister for seven months in 1933 and minister of interior in 1935 and 1936. He cooperated with the nationalist Golden Square colonels (q.v.) and with Hajj Amin al-Hussaini, the Mufti of Jerusalem who was in 'Iraq at the time. On the eve of World War II, Rashid 'Ali saw an opportunity for 'Iraq to achieve real independence from Britain by allying 'Iraq with the Axis powers. The Golden Square officers helped make him prime minister again in March 1940, and 'Iraq entered into a confrontation with Britain over relations with Italy and Germany. The British forced Rashid 'Ali out in January 1941, but he was brought back in a semicoup in April. He dismissed the pro-British regent 'Abd al-Ilah (q.v.) and appealed for German help against the British. Britain landed troops in Basra (q.v.) in late April, leading to several weeks of fighting between forces loyal to the nationalist government and the advancing British troops. Rashid 'Ali's government fled to Iran on 29 May 1941, and he eventually fled to Saudi Arabia and then to Egypt. After the 1958 revolution (q.v.), Rashid 'Ali hoped 'Iraq would join the United Arab Republic, headed by Egyptian president Gamal 'Abd al-Nasir. Disappointed by 'Abd al-Karim Qasim's (q.v.) anti-Nasir stance, he joined the opposition. He was arrested for involvement in a Nasirite plot and sentenced to death. He went into exile in Egypt and Lebanon. He was eventually pardoned and did not play a role in politics after that.

KAZZAR (KZAR), NAZIM (?–1973). Ba'thist security chief. He was born in al-Amara to a Shi'i (q.v.) family and educated at the Technological Institute in Baghdad (q.v.). He joined the Ba'th Party (q.v.) in 1959 and was a leading opponent of the communists; he headed a ruthless drive against them during the Ba'th coup in 1963. Following the 1968 revolution (q.v.), he was appointed chief of security. He opposed the government's concessions to the Kurds (q.v.) and its rapprochement with the communists. Kazzar favored the use of force to settle the Kurdish question in 1971, and in 1972, he sponsored two attempts on the life of Mulla Mustafa al-Barzani (q.v.).

In June 1973, he attempted to overthrow the regime. While Ahmad Hasan al-Bakr (q.v.) was out of the country, Kazzar kidnapped defense minister Hammad Shihab (q.v.) and interior minister Sa'dun Ghaydan (q.v.). He planned to kill al-Bakr and Husayn when they arrived at the Baghdad airport. Kazzar panicked when the flight was delayed and fled with his hostages toward Iran. He offered to meet al-Bakr at the house of 'Abd al-Khaliq al-Samarra'i (q.v.), a major rival of Husayn's, thus implicating al-Samarra'i in the conspiracy. Kazzar was captured before he could reach Iran, and his men killed Shihab and wounded Ghaydan. He was executed 7 July 1973.

KHABUR, AL-. The name of two rivers in 'Iraq. The Lesser Khabur is a fork of the Tigris River (q.v.), and the Big Khabur is the largest fork of the Euphrates River (q.v.) that extends about 320 kilometers.

KHADDURI, MAJID. (1908–). A prominent 'Iraqi–American educator and writer and a leading authority on Islamic law and jurisprudence, modern Islam, modern 'Iraqi history, and Arab politics and personalities. Khadduri taught at the Law and Higher Teachers Colleges in Baghdad (q.v.) between 1939 and 1947. He was a member of the 'Iraqi delegation to the founding of the United Nations. In 1947, he returned to the United States, where he began a teaching career at a number of American universities, including the University of Chicago, Columbia, Harvard, the University of Virginia, and Georgetown.

Khadduri established and directed the first graduate center for Middle East Studies in the United States at the Johns Hopkins University School of Advanced International Studies (SAIS). He is the author of over 35 scholarly books and hundreds of articles on Islamic law and on the history and politics of the modern Middle East. He is president emeritus of the Shaybani Society of International Law, former president of the International Association of

Middle East Studies, and a corresponding member of the Academy of Arabic Language in Egypt and of the Iraqi Academy.

KHAMSA. An important social unit among the Arab nomads and, to a much lesser extent, among those nomads who settled. *Khamsa* means "group of five"; it usually refers to the people who are within five degrees of patrilineal relations and usually includes relatives as distant as the grandfather of the brother's grandson. It is the traditional group that functions in case of a conflict in blood feuds. Tribesman who have had relatives murdered within the khamsa would be bound to avenge the death, and the members of the murderer's khamsa are also considered to share responsibility.

KHAN MIRJAN. Building still standing in Baghdad (q.v.), dating from c. 1359. It was built by Amin Mirjan, the governor of Baghdad, as a trading center and lodging place for merchants. The revenue from the building was given as an endowment to the nearby Mirjan school. One of Baghdad's most architecturally unique buildings, it is covered by a roof supported by 14-meter-high vaults. It has been remodeled as one of Baghdad's best restaurants.

KHARIJITES. An Islamic splinter group that emerged in 658 during the conflict between 'Ali and Mu'awiya. The Kharijites opposed 'Ali's acceptance of arbitration during the Battle of Siffin (q.v.). They believed that 'Ali was the legitimate caliph (q.v.) and his opponents unjust; the Koran (q.v.) says that rebels must be fought until they are obedient. Moreover, the Kharijites insisted that the right of judging belonged only to God. They believed that by submitting to human arbitration, 'Ali had renounced his rights to the caliphate and therefore continued support of 'Ali was contrary to the spirit of Islam. The Kharijites promoted choosing the best-qualified Muslim as caliph, regardless of his race or ethnic origin, and not simply a member of the Quraysh tribe. They nominated 'Abd Adullah bin Wahab al-Rasidi as caliph in 658, the first non-Qurayshi nominated to head an Islamic group. 'Ali attempted to regain their support, but the Kharijites demanded that he resign. 'Ali sent his troops to Nahrawan, where the besieged Kharijite forces were crushed in 659. A Kharijite assassin ultimately killed 'Ali in 661.

After the Battle of Nahrawan, remnants of the Kharijites escaped to Persia, where they fought against Mu'awiya and the Umayyads. The Kharijites regrouped under the leadership of Dhahak, capturing Kufa in 745 and subjugating the rest of 'Iraq. The Umayyad caliph Marwan led his armies against Dhahak, defeating the Kharijite forces near Masibin in 746. Dhahak was killed during the battle and his supporters dispersed. The Kharijites also rebelled against the Abbasids. The Kharijites divided into a number of sects, generally over the question of the degree of moderation to be shown toward their enemies. These sects include the Azraquites, followers of Nafi' bin al-Azraq, which broke away in 685; and the Ibadhis, followers of 'Abd Allah bin Ibadh, which broke away in 705. Remnants of these groups remain today in Oman and in small parts of North Africa.

The Kharijites believed in the sanctity of the office of the Imam or Caliph, considering him to be God's representative on Earth. They accepted the caliphates of al-Bakr and 'Umar but recognized only the early periods of 'Uthman and 'Ali's caliphates. All other caliphs were considered illegitimate because they were not installed in accordance with Islamic principles. The Kharijites insisted that the caliph be the best-qualified Muslim and that he be elected by the entire Muslim community. Once elected, the caliph could neither abdicate nor withdraw from his office. Should an elected caliph commit an impious act though, he was to be impeached and dismissed. Murder was permissible if the caliph resisted. The Kharijites called for constant revolution and opposition to any illegitimate or unjust caliph or government. They also believed that mere faith in God and the Prophet was insufficient for a believer to be worthy of Paradise. Only when a believer had achieved a certain level of piety could he claim to be worthy of eternal life. The Kharijites believed that if a Muslim committed certain impious acts, he was not to be considered a Muslim but as worse than an infidel. While extremely pious and modest in their behavior, the Kharijites were tough warriors. This stemmed from their belief that they were God's own standard-bearers and defenders of the faith. Therefore, they had a duty to execute God's judgment on those who they believed had deviated from the right path. Their fanatical acts were often accompanied by daring and self-sacrifice, as they opposed the accumulation of personal riches.

KHATIB, MUHYI AL-. Senior advisor to the Foreign Ministry and a prominent former 'Iraqi diplomat who was dismissed by the regime because his brother, a prominent Ba'thist figure, was suspected of anti-Saddam activities.

KHAWRIZM SHAHS. A Persian dynasty that exercised authority over the Abbasid caliphs from 1118 to 1215. At the instigation of the Abbasid caliph (q.v.) al-Nasir (r. 1180–1225), the Khawrizm Shahs moved against the Seljuks (q.v.). They killed the Seljuk sultan, ending Seljuk rule in Persia. When their relations with al-Nasir deteriorated, they appointed a rival 'Ali caliph in Khorasan. Gengis Khan, leader of the Mongol Empire in central Asia, captured Khawrizm and much of Transcaucasia, bringing an end to the Khawrzim Shahs.

KHAYRALLA, 'ADNAN (1940–1987). Defense minister during the Iran–'Iraq war (q.v.) and cousin of Saddam Husayn (q.v.). He was born in Tikrit and attended the Baghdad Military College and the Staff College. He also received a degree from the School of Law and Politics at Baghdad University in 1975. He joined the Ba'th Party (q.v.) in 1956 and was arrested in 1959 after the Ba'th unsuccessfully attempted to assassinate 'Abd al-Karim

Qasim (q.v.). Khayralla played a role in both the 1963 and 1968 Ba'thist seizures of power. In 1977, he was appointed minister of defense and minister of state, and he held membership in the Regional Command (q.v.) and Revolutionary Command Council (q.v.). He became deputy prime minister in 1979. In 1987, he was appointed deputy supreme commander of the armed forces and played a crucial role in rebuilding and modernizing the 'Iraqi military. Khayralla had close personal ties with Ahmad Hasan al-Bakr (q.v.) and Saddam Husayn. Khayralla's father and Saddam's mother were siblings, and the Khayralla family raised Saddam. Saddam married one of Khayralla's sisters, Sajida, and Khayralla married al-Bakr's daughter. Saddam and Khayralla reportedly had a falling out over a family matter. Khayralla died in a helicopter accident, an incident that opposition forces claim was very suspicious. A huge monument has been erected in Baghdad (q.v.) to Khayralla's memory. *See also* TALFAH, KHAYRALLA.

KHAZA'I, RAJA HABIB AL-. A gynecologist from a prominent family in the Diwaniyya region in southern 'Iraq. Al-Khaza'i was the head of a maternity hospital in southern 'Iraq. She studied and lived in Britain in the 1960s and 1970s before retuning to 'Iraq in 1977.

KHOSHNOW, MUSTAFA (?–1949). Kurdish politician and military officer from Bitwata. He was an officer in the 'Iraqi army and a leading member of the Hewa Party (q.v.). He participated in the 1943–1945 uprising in 'Iraq led by Mulla Mustafa al-Barzani (q.v.) and fled with the Barzanis to Iran when the revolt collapsed in 1945. Khoshnow helped form the Mahabad Republic's army and led it in an important battle against the Iranian army. He was one of the founders of the Kurdistan Democratic Party (q.v.) in 1946. He returned to 'Iraq and was executed in Baghdad (q.v.) in 1949.

KHOSHOI, ASS'AAD (?–1977). Kurdish nationalist and military leader. He came from a family that had close ties to the Barzani clan (q.v.), and he was very active in the Kurdish movement in the 1930s. A close associate of Mulla Mustafa al-Barzani (q.v.), he joined in most of al-Barzani's military activities and followed him to Iran and then the Soviet Union. Khoshoi learned to speak Russian while in exile in the Soviet Union. Widely respected and a popular leader, he was an efficient administrator as well as a highly effective military leader.

KHUDHAYR, AHMAD HUSAYN. A Ba'thist official and cabinet minister. From Samarra, he became director-general of the Revolutionary Command Council (q.v.) in 1968. He served as minister of foreign affairs from September 1991 through July 1992, when he was appointed minister of finance. Khudhayr became prime minister in September 1993; he also served as acting minister of finance. He was removed from his post as prime minister in May 1994 and replaced by Saddam Husayn (q.v.).

KHUI, AYAT-ALLAH AL- (1899–1992). Considered the leading Shi'i (q.v.) religious authority, a grand ayatollah, and one of the greatest scholars of Shi'i Islam at the time of his death. He became, after the death of Sayid Mushin al-Hakim, the first marja' (q.v.) not only in 'Iraq but in the Shi'i world. Al-Khui was born in Khoi in Iranian Azerbaijan and later studied under Ayatollah Naini, Shaykh al-Isfahani, and al-'Iraqi. He taught literature (q.v.), philosophy, and jurisprudence and authored several books on jurisprudence. He established several charitable organizations, including the Khui Center in New York and cultural centers in Pakistan. He was considered more popular than Ayatollah Khumaini, and after the Islamic revolution in Iran, many of Khumaini's political followers looked to al-Khui for scholarly interpretations and religious perceptions. Al-Khui represented a current among Shi'i clergymen who disliked political involvement by the clergy and thus were naturally opposed to Khumaini and Muhammad Bakr al-Sadr (q.v.). His neutrality during the Iran–'Iraq war (q.v.), which he denounced as a war between brothers, greatly influenced loyal 'Iraqi Shi'is.

He shied away from siding with any 'Iraqi regime and did not allow himself to be photographed with government officials who visited the shrines in Najaf (q.v.). However, after the Shi'i uprising in March 1991 in the aftermath of Desert Storm (q.v.), al-Khui became a center of controversy. Shi'i opponents of the regime claimed that he had issued a *fatwa* calling on 'Iraqis to struggle against the regime, refuse the authority of the government and ordering the formation of a committee of religious scholars to run the affairs of the cities. The 'Iraqi government reportedly placed him under house arrest. On 20 May 1991, he appeared on 'Iraqi television with Saddam Husayn (q.v.), the first time a prominent marja' had appeared publicly with an 'Iraqi leader since 1964, and al-Khui denied issuing the fatwa. Al-Khui decried the disruptions of the sanctuaries that occurred in Najaf (q.v.) during the uprising, saying that such acts were prohibited by Islam. He called on all Muslims not to incite revolt and told Saddam that he was grateful to God that the troubles had come to an end. The program greatly angered Shi'i clergymen in Lebanon and Iran. Some believe that al-Khui's life was in danger and that he was forced to appear on television with Saddam. Others claim that 14 close collaborators of al-Khui's were arrested shortly before 20 May and that he appeared on the television program to spare them. He was returned to Najaf following his appearance, and he died there in 1992.

KHUI, FOUNDATION AL-. A religious party established by the late Ayatollah al-Khui (q.v.) and run as a charitable organization by his son, Abd al-

Majid, who was killed following his return to Najaf on 10 April 2003. The foundation cooperates with the 'Iraqi opposition.

KINDI, ABU YUSUF YA'QUB ISHAQ AL- (801–865). Famous philosopher, scientist, and musician. He was a member of the prominent Kinda tribe that established a powerful kingdom in the pre-Islamic Arabian peninsula. He was raised and educated in Baghdad (q.v.) and came under the patronage of caliph al-Mamun (r. 813–833) (q.v.). He was persecuted by caliph al-Mutawakkil (r. 847–861) (q.v.) because of his Mu'tazilite (q.v.) religious views. It is believed that al-Kindi wrote nearly 265 books, including an astronomical study proving that the Earth was round, a book on how to measure the distance between the moon and Earth, and a study of the human brain. He was a serious student and champion of Greek learning and the first great Islamic scholar to wrestle with the issue of harmony between the dogma of faith and philosophy. Al-Kindi sought to give philosophical support to fundamental Islamic religious concepts. He also prepared a compilation of music and a thesis on arranging Arabic melodies. He was familiar with Greek, Syriac, and Persian works and encouraged their translation. He was known for his tolerance of other views and ideas regardless of the source.

KIRKUK. The fourth-largest city in 'Iraq, the capital of the province of the same name, and the center of the northern oil (q.v.) fields. Serious disputes have risen about its demographic composition following the end of the 2003 war. The city is mainly inhabited by Kurds and Turkuman, with a susbstantial Arab community and a small Assyrian-Chaldean one, although the countryside around Kirkuk is populated by Kurds (q.v.) and some Arabs. Kirkuk witnessed bloody communal fighting in 1959 between the Turkuman and the Kurds. At one time, it had a number of Jews (q.v.). It is built on the ancient village of Arrafa and Corcura, which dates from Parthian times (first century B.C.). Later it became an important center of the Eastern Christian Church during the Abbasid and Sassafid time. The town is the seat of the Chaldean (q.v.) archbishop and a number of other Christians (q.v.), Armenians, Assyrians (q.v.), and Jacobites (q.v.) live there. The development of the oil fields by the 'Iraqi Petroleum Company (q.v.) in the early 20th century brought new attention to Kirkuk and greatly increased its importance. Control of the city and its oil reserves has been a source of continuing friction between Baghdad (q.v.) and the Kurds. It is also the center of an agricultural area that grows fruit, vegetables, wheat, and barley (*see* AGRICULTURE). The conflicting Kurdish and Turkuman claims have soured Turkey's ties with the Kurds of 'Iraq. Turkey supports the Turkumans while the Kurds aspire to have Kirkuk in the Kurdish region.

KITTANI, 'ISMAT (1929–2001). A politician, diplomat, and international civil servant. He was born in al-'Imadiyya to a Kurdish family. He attended Knox College in the United States and then returned to 'Iraq. After teaching high school for a short time, he joined the foreign service. Kittani served at the permanent 'Iraqi mission to the United Nations from 1957 to 1960 and became the permanent representative from 'Iraq to Geneva. He eventually became secretary of the Economic and Social Council of the UN and director of the office of the secretary general from 1968 to 1969. He was then recalled to the Foreign Ministry, where he held several high positions. In 1981, Kittani was appointed 'Iraq's ambassador to the UN and was elected president of the General Assembly. He later served as deputy foreign minister but retired for health reasons. In 1992, he was appointed the UN secretary-general's special representative to Somalia.

KOMALA. A secretive Kurdish political party founded on 10 June 1970 by a group of Marxist and communist youth. Komala formed in opposition to the Kurdistan Democratic Party (KDP) (q.v.) and outside the Kurdish section of the 'Iraqi Communist Party (q.v.). It operated in secrecy because of its fear of reprisals by the KDP, which controlled most of Kurdistan at that time. When the KDP and the Ba'th Party (q.v.) regime began full-scale fighting again in 1974, Komala fought with the KDP. After the collapse of the KDP's forces in 1975, Komala continued its resistance, fighting to prevent the deportation of Kurdish villagers by the Ba'th regime. It formed small groups in the villages that disseminated information and propaganda. In 1975, the group joined with Jalal Talabani's (q.v.) group and the Socialist Movement of Kurdistan (q.v.) to establish the Patriotic Union of Kurdistan (q.v.).

KORAN (QURAN). The Holy Book of the Muslims. Muslims believe it is the literal word of God as revealed to Muhammad by the angel Gabriel. As the Word of God, the Koran is considered to have achieved the unattainable ideal of perfection of the Arab language and style. It preaches the oneness of God, the giver of life and creator of the world and condemns polytheism and idolatry. It provides religious and legal precepts defining the Muslim way of life as well as rules and rituals for conducting worship. The Koran contains 114 *suras* (chapters) of varying length, with the longer ones at the beginning and the shorter ones at the end. It is divided according to time and place of origin. During Muhammad's life, the text of the Koran was preserved mainly by memory. The first transcriptions were made by Muhammad's Companions after his death in 632. In 650, caliph 'Uthman established a special board to compile a text of the Koran based on the material written down by the Companions, other transcriptions, and the testimony of persons who knew the sermons by heart. The board prepared an official text that continues to be recognized by the overwhelming majority of Muslims as the true text.

KUBBA, LAYTH. Democracy and human rights activist, he is currently the senior program officer for the Middle East and North Africa at the National Endowment for Democracy. Dr. Kubba previously served on the 'Iraqi Joint Action Committee, the first broad alliance of the 'Iraqi opposition, and coordinated the 'Iraqi National Congress (q.v.) meeting in Vienna while acting as its spokesperson and serving on its first executive committee. From 1993 until 1998, he was the director of international relations at the Al Khui Foundation in London. He has also served on the boards of regional institutions including the 'Iraq Foundation and the Arab Organization for Human Rights. He holds a B.A. from the University of Baghdad and a Ph.D. from the University of Wales.

KUBBA, MUHAMMAD MAHDI AL- (1900–). Cabinet minister during the monarchy. He was a strong activist against British policy in 'Iraq and played a leading role in the revolt of 1920 (q.v.). He was one of the leaders of the nationalist Nadi al-Muthanna club (q.v.) as well as of the Independence Party (q.v.). He served as minister of supply in 1948. Al-Kubba was elected to Parliament in 1937 but eventually resigned in opposition to the manner in which the elections had been held and to the oil (q.v.) agreement of 1950. He was reelected to Parliament in 1954 and 1955. After the 1958 revolution (q.v.), he was one of two members of the Presidency Council. *See also* ANGLO–'IRAQI TREATY OF 1922.

KURDAN, TREATY OF. The treaty of Kurdan reaffirmed the boundary arrangement set up in the 1639 Treaty of Zuhab (q.v.) between the Ottoman and Persian Empires. Concluded on 4 September 1746, it ended over a decade of renewed fighting between the two empires for control of parts of 'Iraq. *See also* ERZURUM, FIRST TREATY OF.

KURDISH CONSERVATIVE PARTY. A small Kurdish grouping, composed of the younger members of some Kurdish tribes. It has sought in the past to establish an independent Kurdish state in Mawsil (q.v.).

KURDISH HIZBULLAH. Kurdish Islamic group led by Shaykh Muhammad Khalid al-Barzani, the eldest son of Shaykh Ahmad al-Barzani (q.v.) and a spiritual leader of the Barzani clan (q.v.). Al-Barzani's influence among the Barzanis has declined, and his party has tense relations with the Kurdistan Democratic Party (q.v.). During 1982–1983, Iran began to support and encourage this party, and the two continue to have close ties.

KURDISH TRIBAL ASSOCIATION. A Kurdish tribal leadership group, established by younger followers of traditional tribal leaders in the summer of 1991. It involves members of 20 powerful tribes under the leadership of Shaykh Husayn. Many of its members supported the 'Iraqi government in the

1970s and 1980s against the Kurdistan Democratic Party (q.v.) and the Patriotic Union of Kurdistan (q.v.) and fought with the regime against both the Iranians and the Kurds (q.v.) during the Iran–'Iraq war (q.v.). In the aftermath of Operation Desert Storm (q.v.), the group broke ranks with the government, and its leaders moved to the Kurdish zone and took positions against the regime.

KURDISTAN DEMOCRATIC PARTY (KDP). Kurdish party founded in 1946 that is generally considered the strongest of the Kurdish groups. The KDP was founded by Mulla Mustafa al-Barzani (q.v.) in the Kurdish Republic of Mahabad in Iran. Mulla Mustafa assumed the presidency, and the party developed in accordance with his preferences. After the fall of Mahabad, Barzani took refuge in the Soviet Union and did not play a direct role in the activities of the party until his return in 1958. The party was led by Ibrahim Ahmad, a leftist lawyer and intellectual, during this period. The KDP worked with other groups, including the 'Iraqi Communist Party (ICP) (q.v.), and followed a leftist line. In 1956, it was reorganized as the Patriotic Democratic United Party of Kurdistan and published a journal, *Khebat* (Struggle). After the 1958 revolution (q.v.), Barzani returned to 'Iraq, and the KDP was allowed to operate legally. However, the honeymoon with 'Abd al-Karim Qasim (q.v.) was short-lived, and relations quickly deteriorated. A split began to emerge in the KDP between the more traditional Barzani clan and the leftists, led by Ahmad and his future son-in-law Jalal Talabani (q.v.). This rivalry would plague the Kurdish movement for many years to come. In 1964, Barzani succeeded in expelling Ahmad and his followers from the KDP; Ahmad went into exile in Iran.

The KDP negotiated the 1970 March Manifesto (q.v.) with the Ba'th Party (q.v.) regime, which granted autonomy to the Kurdish region. Although some of the agreement's provisions were implemented, relations between the KDP and the Ba'th steadily deteriorated. Fighting broke out again in 1974, and the rebellion collapsed in 1975. In the aftermath of the revolt, Ahmad and Talabani formed the Patriotic Union of Kurdistan (PUK) (q.v.). The KDP and the PUK began fighting, culminating in bloody confrontations in 1978 that left hundreds dead but that clearly established the supremacy of the KDP. Mulla Mustafa died in the United States in 1979, and control of the KDP passed to his son, Idris. The KDP reopened its military struggle against the Ba'th regime in 1983, during the Iran–'Iraq war (q.v.). The Ba'th waged a brutal campaign of repression against the Kurds (q.v.) once the war with Iran was over, including the use of chemical weapons. The KDP participated in the 1991 uprisings against the regime, which eventually led to the creation of a Western-sponsored "safe haven" in northern 'Iraq. (*See* KUWAIT, INVASION OF.)

The KDP, led by Idris's brother Mas'ud (q.v.) since 1987, is one of the largest and most powerful Kurdish organizations. In the May 1992 elections, the KDP gained slightly over 50 percent of the vote; Barzani and Talabani, whose party had garnered nearly as many votes as the KDP, agreed to cooperate in running the autonomous zone. In 1993, the KDP merged with the Unity Party of Kurdistan (q.v.), which is composed of three small parties: the Kurdistan Popular Democratic Party (q.v.), the Socialist Party of Kurdistan (q.v.), and the Popular Alliance of Socialist Kurdistan (q.v.). The KDP joined the 'Iraqi National Congress (INC) (q.v.) in 1992, and Barzani is a member of the INC's three-member executive council. The party is committed to an autonomous Kurdistan within a federated, democratic 'Iraq. It continues to be based on tribal support and is especially strong in the northern areas of Kurdistan. It commands roughly 15,000 *pesh mergas* (q.v.) and has its own radio station, *Voice of 'Iraqi Kurdistan*, as well as its own television station.

KURDISTAN POPULAR DEMOCRATIC PARTY. Established in July 1981, it held its first congress in Vienna and elected as its general secretary Sami 'Abd al-Rahman, a former member of the Kurdistan Democratic Party's (KDP) (q.v.) Politburo and close aide to Mulla Mustafa al-Barzani (q.v.) during the 1975 Kurdish revolt. In May 1992, it established the Unity Party of Kurdistan (q.v.) with the Socialist Party of Kurdistan (q.v.) and the Popular Alliance of Socialist Kurdistan (q.v.), which in turn joined the KDP in August 1993. In 1994, the party joined the Kurdish National Front. It received 1 percent of the vote in the 1992 elections.

KURDS. The Kurds are an ancient people who are mentioned by a variety of old sources. They inhabit the northeastern part of 'Iraq, in the provinces of Dohuk, Arbil (q.v.), and Sulaymaniyya. Small numbers of Kurds also live in other parts of 'Iraq. Many Kurds also live in Iran, Turkey, and several parts of the former Soviet Union. The majority of the Kurds are Sunnis (q.v.), but there are large percentages of Shi'is (q.v.) as well as Ghulat and other esoteric sects.

Many theories explain the origins of the Kurds. The most widely accepted theories claim that the Kurds are of Indo-European origins, primarily of Mede and Iranian stock who moved from the area near Lake Urmeia and Bhutan around the seventh century A.D. It is believed that they then mixed with the Keyrti and Marid tribes. Another theory says that the Kurds are not an Iranian people but rather mountain dwellers of the Caucasus and related to the Armenians, Georgians, and Chaldeans (q.v.). The Kurds' original language resembled that of the Georgians, but it changed under the influence of neighboring Iranians and Armenians. This view is strengthened by an old Kurdish tradition that claims that they left their old language and embraced a new one. A third theory traces the Kurds to the Guti tribes located in northwestern Iran around the third millennia B.C. Still others believe that they originated from the ancient Assyrians and Babylonians and mixed with the other peoples inhabiting the area at that time. Modern Kurdish writers claim that they are of Mede origins and not related to the Iranians.

The Kurds, like most peoples in the area, are in fact of mixed origins, owing to the migrations, invasions, and dominations by various groups who ruled the area at different times. The region has come under the control of the Assyrians, Akkadians, Casites, Hitites, Persians, Greeks, Armenians, various Iranian groups, Turkuman (q.v.), Mongols, and Turks. Ancient records paint a picture of a tough and proud people, unresponsive to foreign authority. The Kurds have remained a distinct and separate people from their neighbors. This may be attributed to their mountainous territory that forms a geographic barrier between them and their neighbors and to their ferocity in defending their territory as well as to their self-sufficient economy, which reduces the need for contact with outsiders. The Kurds, however, have never possessed an independent political entity, and they have been ruled and oppressed by outsiders.

The factors that have helped to preserve the Kurds' identity have also helped divide them. Isolationism has led to the growth of strong tribal and feudal systems. The tribal system, the Kurds' geographic isolation, and the difficulties in communication resulting from the remoteness and inaccessibility of their territory have contributed to the rise of intra-Kurdish rivalries and suspicions. The variety of spoken dialects has also at times impeded communication. In 'Iraq, the Kurds speak several different dialects depending on the region. There are three basic dialects: Kurmanji, Surani, and Zaza. Another dialect is known as Guarani. Kurmanji is used in the northern part of 'Iraq, while the Surani dialect is spoken by the Kurds in the southern area of 'Iraqi Kurdistan. The Kurdish language does not have its own letters. In 'Iraq and Iran, writing is in Arabic or Farsi; in the former Soviet Union, Cyrillic letters are used; and in Turkey, Latin letters are used when the Kurdish language is allowed to be used.

Socially the Kurds can be divided into urban dwellers, rural villagers and peasants, and seminomadic and nomadic tribesmen. The numbers of nomads and seminomads have been on the decline since the beginning of the 20th century. The vast majority of Kurds have lived in small villages until recent decades, retaining their tribal social structure. However the tribal, feudal society of the Kurds is breaking down as a result of contact with the outside world. Moreover, the mass deportations that took place in the wake of the 1975 Kurdish rebellion, where hundreds of thousands of Kurds were moved from the border areas to other parts of 'Iraq, have weakened the traditional ties between the Kurds and their tribal and feudal leaders, although it did not eliminate them.

Kurdish nationalism began to develop in the latter part of the 19th century and early 20th century. Kurdish nationalists living in Istanbul and Cairo emulated the example of Arab and Turkish nationalists. They began to organize small political groups and to publish Kurdish journals. The nationalists represented only a tiny minority and did not penetrate deeply into Kurdish society. The second stage of Kurdish nationalism began in the aftermath of World War I, when Kurdish committees were formed in Cairo and Istanbul. The Kurds joined hands with the Armenians at the Paris Peace Conference in order to avoid further conflict with the Armenians, and they reached an agreement that was presented to the conference as a joint memorandum outlining their borders. Articles 62, 63, and 64 of the 1920 Treaty of Sevres (q.v.) recognized the rights of the Kurds, Armenians, and other subject peoples, including the Assyrians (q.v.), to run their own affairs. The Allies were determined to break up the Ottoman Empire and create smaller entities that they would be able to control. The Treaty of Sevres, though, was never ratified, largely due to the military successes of Mustafa Kemal (Ataturk) of Turkey and his ability to preserve the unity of the Turkish Republic. The Kurds led a number of uprisings against Ataturk's government at this time.

Kurdish aspirations have been expressed in a variety of forms. The Kurds have made attempts at dialogue with the national governments of the countries that they inhabit, with international bodies, and within the Kurdish community itself. They have also traveled the road of violent struggle. The Kurds though have not been a unified community with an organized program for action, but instead one torn apart by feudal, tribal, religious, and political differences. *See also* BARZANI CLAN; KURDISH DEMOCRATIC PARTY; KUWAIT, INVASION OF; PATRIOTIC UNION OF KURDISTAN; TALABANI, JALAL.

KUWAIT, INVASION OF. On 2 August 1990, 'Iraqi forces struck across the border into Kuwait, conquering the emirate in a matter of hours. 'Iraq's decision to invade Kuwait has roots both in a long-standing territorial dispute and in 'Iraq's deteriorating financial and political situation in the spring of 1990. Baghdad (q.v.) maintains that Kuwait was and always has been part of 'Iraq, basing its claim on Kuwait's status as part of the Basra (q.v.) wilayet during the last years of the Ottoman Empire. Since the Basra wilayet was incorporated into 'Iraq, Kuwait is rightfully part of 'Iraq. This claim was advanced in the 1930s by King Faysal I (q.v.) and revived by 'Abd al-Karim Qasim (q.v.) in 1961. Second, Baghdad maintains that it has never agreed to any borders with Kuwait. While there is some justice to the first strand of 'Iraq's argument, the second point is untenable. In 1963, the short-lived Ba'th (q.v.) government signed an agreement with Kuwait in which it recognized the "independence and complete sovereignty of the state of Kuwait with its boundaries as specified in the 1932 exchange of letters." The real issue centers around 'Iraq's desire to gain a secure outlet to the Persian Gulf. The Kuwaiti islands of Warba and Bubiyan guard the entrance to the Khor Abdullah channel, which leads to the ports at Umm Qasr and Khor al-Zubair. 'Iraq has for years attempted to lease the islands from Kuwait, and its demands increased in urgency when the Shatt al-Arab (q.v.), 'Iraq's only other outlet to the Gulf, was closed in 1980 as a result of the Iran–'Iraq war (q.v.). (*See* 'IRAQI–KUWAITI SPECIAL AGREEMENT OF 1963.)

'Iraq emerged from its war with Iran believing that it was on the verge of establishing itself as the leader of the Arab world. However, its position steadily eroded in the year before its invasion of Kuwait. Weak oil (q.v.) prices kept 'Iraqi revenue low even as the regime struggled to meet the demands of 'Iraqi consumers and pursue Saddam Husayn's (q.v.) industrial and development schemes. Furthermore, 'Iraq's debt had grown to an estimated $80 to $100 billion. Complicating 'Iraq's financial difficulties was the sharp erosion in its international standing created by a series of controversies in the spring of 1990. In February, the U.S. State Department released a report lambasting 'Iraq's human rights record; on 15 March, 'Iraq executed British journalist Farzad Barzoft on charges of spying for Israel; on 28 March, several people were arrested in Britain for attempting to smuggle high-speed capacitors, or "nuclear switches," to 'Iraq; on 1 April, Saddam delivered a speech in which he pledged to use binary chemical weapons against Israel should Israel attack 'Iraq; and on 11 April, the first in a series of shipments bound for 'Iraq was seized by British officials, who claimed the shipments were components of a "supergun" the 'Iraqis were developing.

The Arab world rallied to 'Iraq's side, convening an extraordinary summit in Baghdad on 28–30 May at which it expressed solidarity with the beleaguered 'Iraqi regime. Saddam gave a secret speech at the summit, warning the delegates that an economic war was being waged against 'Iraq and that 'Iraq could no longer stand the pressure. This is a clear reference to the overproduction by Kuwait and the United Arab Emirates that had driven oil prices down 30 percent over the course of the spring. Throughout July, 'Iraq detailed its charges against Kuwait, finally moving troops to the border on 20 July. With 100,000 'Iraqi troops massed on its border, Kuwait agreed to abide by its quota with the Organization of Petroleum Exporting Countries (OPEC) on 25 July, but at talks scheduled on 30 July to discuss the border issue, Kuwait refused to compromise.

'Iraq's invasion was greeted with demands for an immediate withdrawal by the United Nations, and on 6 August, the United States announced Operation Desert Shield, designed to protect Saudi Arabia from a possible 'Iraqi assault. 'Iraq annexed Kuwait on 8 August. In response, the administration of George H. Bush defined U.S. objectives as achieving the immediate, unconditional, and complete withdrawal of all 'Iraqi forces from Kuwait and the restoration of Kuwait's legitimate government. As the months passed, 'Iraq and the international coalition organized by the United States drew closer to war. On 29 November, the UN passed Resolution 678, which authorized the use of all necessary means to eject 'Iraq from Kuwait and set a deadline for 'Iraqi withdrawal of 15 January 1991. The air campaign against

'Iraq commenced on 16 January and struck targets in both 'Iraq and Kuwait. After weeks of bombing, the coalition forces initiated ground hostilities on 24 February. The fighting was over within 100 hours; Kuwait was declared liberated on 27 February 1991.

'Iraq's terrible defeat at the hands of the allied coalition precipitated uprisings in 'Iraq; the rebellion started in the Shi'i (q.v.) south on 28 February and spread to the Kurdish north on 5 March. Despite early successes, the fighting turned against the rebels, and by 3 April, forces loyal to Saddam had crushed the uprisings. Fear of Saddam's reprisals caused a massive exodus of refugees from 'Iraq; within a week, there were over a million Kurdish refugees in Turkey and Iran and tens of thousands of Shi'is in Iran and Saudi Arabia. With hundreds of refugees dying every day, the Bush administration was finally pressured into launching a major humanitarian effort. Under the authority of UN Resolution 688, the United States created "safe havens" in northern 'Iraq to be policed by allied troops. Eventually the safe havens would become an autonomous Kurdish region, beyond the control of Baghdad; a Kurdish government was elected in May 1992. (*See* KURDISTAN DEMOCRATIC PARTY; PATRIOTIC UNION OF KURDISTAN.)

The allied bombing campaigns in 'Iraq created terrible devastation. A UN report stated that 'Iraq had been bombed back to "the preindustrial age" yet suffered all the vulnerabilities of an industrial society. For example, nearly all of 'Iraq's electrical power grid was damaged or destroyed by the bombing. As a result of the scarcity of food and the physical damage to its infrastructure, 'Iraq's infant mortality rate soared. 'Iraq's difficulties were compounded by the economic sanctions (q.v.) that were imposed by the United Nations in August 1990 and maintained until 2003. Despite calls by some to lift the sanctions on humanitarian grounds, the United States and its coalition allies insisted that 'Iraq must satisfactorily fulfill the terms of the cease-fire accord before the sanctions could be lifted.

– L –

LATIF, 'ABD AL-SATTAR 'ABD AL- (1926–). Military officer and politician. He was born in al-Adhamiyya and attended the Baghdad Military College and the Staff College. A member of both the Ba'th Party (q.v.) and the Free Officers (q.v.), he helped plan the overthrow of 'Abd al-Karim Qasim (q.v.). Al-Latif was a member of the National Command of the Revolutionary Council and was appointed minister of communications following the Ba'thist takeover in 1963. He broke with the Ba'th in late 1963 and affiliated himself with the Nasirites. He briefly held the post of minister of interior in 1967.

LATIF, WAIL ABD AL- (1950–). A Shi'a, Latif has served as judge since the early 1980s and is currently deputy head of the Basrah court. He was imprisoned for one year under the regime.

LAUSANNE, TREATY OF. Signed on 24 July 1923 between Turkey and the Entente Powers, the Treaty of Lausanne replaced the unratified Treaty of Sevres (q.v.). Article III, section 2, provided that Britain and Turkey would agree to the frontier between 'Iraq and Turkey within nine months; if they could not reach an agreement, the dispute would go to the League of Nations for a final decision. The clause was necessitated by Turkey's insistence on keeping the Mawsil (q.v.) province, which it had lost under the Treaty of Sevres. The dispute eventually went to the League on 6 August 1924; Britain and its 'Iraqi mandate were awarded Mawsil. Lausanne is also notable for the conspicuous absence of a clause governing Kurdish independence, which had been present in the Treaty of Sevres. *See* ANGLO–'IRAQI TREATY OF 1926; ANKARA, TREATY OF.

LAW 80 OF 1961. Law 80, announced by 'Abd al-Karim Qasim (q.v.) in December 1961, expropriated 99.5 percent of the 'Iraqi Petroleum Company's (IPC) (q.v.) original concession area without compensation. The expropriated areas, which included the Rumaila field, were not in production. The 'Iraqi government wanted the IPC to expand production in 'Iraq; negotiations opened in the spring of 1959. Although the initial discussions largely concerned technical issues, Qasim eventually made more fundamental demands. The 'Iraqi government wanted a 20 percent ownership in the IPC, a higher percentage of the company's profits, and the return of the unexplored portions of the concession. Qasim proclaimed Law 80 following the breakdown of negotiations in October 1961. While Law 80 was undeniably popular, it took years for 'Iraq to experience any substantive gains. Output from 'Iraqi fields remained lower than that of other Arab oil (q.v.) producers, as did the price per barrel revenues accruing to the 'Iraqi government. 'Iraq was unable to develop a national oil industry and exploit the expropriated fields until 1969. Meanwhile, 'Iraq and the IPC remained in conflict over Law 80 until 'Iraq finally nationalized the oil industry in 1972. *See also* ECONOMY IN THE INTRODUCTION; LAW 69 OF 1972.

LAW 11 OF 1964. Law 11, announced in February 1964, established the 'Iraq National Oil Company (INOC). The INOC was charged with the development of the 'Iraqi national oil (q.v.) industry. The INOC, however, lacked both the technical and financial means to fulfill its mission without substantial outside assistance, resources, and expertise. In 1967, the Soviet Union signed an agreement with 'Iraq in which it pledged to assist the INOC in developing an 'Iraqi national oil industry. Beginning in June 1969, the Soviet Union extended loans and training to the INOC. The cooperation culminated in 1972 with the opening of the Rumaila field and the nationalization of the 'Iraqi Petroleum Company (q.v.). *See also* ECONOMY IN THE INTRO-DUCTION; LAW 97 OF 1967.

LAW 97 OF 1967. Law 97, announced in August 1967, granted the 'Iraq National Oil Company the exclusive rights to develop the areas expropriated under Law 80 of 1961 (q.v.), specifically prohibiting the return of the rich Rumaila field to the 'Iraqi Petroleum Company (q.v.). *See also* ECONOMY IN THE INTRODUCTION.

LAW 69 OF 1972. Law 69, announced in June 1972, nationalized the 'Iraqi Petroleum Company (IPC) (q.v.) and established the 'Iraqi Company for Oil Operations to take over the nationalized assets. The immediate cause of the dispute between the government and the IPC was a cutback in production from the northern fields, but the issue of compensation for the concession area expropriated under Law 80 of 1961 (q.v.) was also a point of contention. *See also* ECONOMY IN THE INTRODUCTION; 'IRAQI–SOVIET TREATY OF FRIENDSHIP AND COOPERATION.

LIBERAL PARTY (HIZB AL-AHRAR). A conservative political grouping formed in 1946. Its founders included 'Ali Mumtaz and 'Abd al-Wahhab Mahmud. The party advocated moderate social reform. Although headed by Tawfiq al-Suwaydi (q.v.), real power lay with Sa'id Salih. After the death of Sa'id Salih in 1948, it was led by 'Abd al-Wahhab Mahmud. It published a newspaper, *Sawat al-Ahrar*.

LITERATURE. In the 20th century, the first influences of modern, Western thought and culture began to be seen in 'Iraq. Two world wars and the British occupation of 'Iraq imported Western influences but simultaneously fueled the nationalist feelings among 'Iraqis that eventually drove the British out and gained independence for 'Iraq in 1932. The social and political upheavals in the early 20th century profoundly affected the beginnings of the 'Iraqi short story. Although influenced by the British, 'Iraq also felt the impact of Egypt, Syria, and Lebanon, which at the time were more advanced than 'Iraq. Missionaries and foreign visitors also brought Western ways to' Iraqi society. Western visitors and their ideas generated a huge response, especially in the younger 'Iraqi generations, who sought to emulate these new social behaviors and different ways of eating and dressing in a westernization craze. This imitation of the West troubled many in 'Iraq, and these concerns contributed to the growing calls for independence. During the 1920s, many people in 'Iraq began to read books and novels, and more printing houses, bookstores, and newspapers were produced, further increasing the number of readers. Many bookstores carried foreign literary works, most of which had been translated into Arabic. These works frequently came from Egypt, and stress was placed in entertaining the reader. In fact, much of the early 'Iraqi literature was based on Egyptian influences. Unfortunately, the British occupation of 'Iraq stressed primary education more than higher echelons of learning, and as a result this weakened the chances that the cultural changes produced by increasing consumption of reading material would be great or lasting. Although a few individuals wrote and spoke about the social and philosophical issues of the day, many 'Iraqis at the time simply did not have the level of education required to understand deep philosophical and intellectual issues. Most of the novels written in 'Iraq in the 1920s were based on the models found in Egyptian literature. These types of novels stressed two main themes: love and adventure. Some Western works were translated, often from the Romanticism period (late 18th and early 19th centuries), including the German writer Johan Wolfgang von Goethe's work, *The Sufferings of Young Werther*, as well as other tragic love stories such as *Camille* by Alexander Dumas.

Mahmoud Ahmed al-Sayyid is considered to be the first 'Iraqi writer to produce a work of fiction, *For the Sake of Marriage* in 1921. Al-Sayyid wrote a love story about two ideal lovers who face difficulties as well as danger and adventure. In *For the Sake of Marriage*, many quotations are made from other books, and, typical of the Arabic writing style, al-Sayyid juxtaposes verses of poetry between sections of writing. Al-Sayyid's novel has a tone of desperation and depression, reflecting the reactions of many 'Iraqis to the influence of Western ways on the younger generation. The characters are portrayed as outsiders in society, who criticize the ways of society and the unfair rules it imposes. This early prototype of 'Iraqi fiction is representative of the Iraqi desire for independence, and although the writing may not have been as directly politically motivated as much of the poetry (q.v.) was, it still indicates the level of unrest and dissatisfaction in the country during the British mandate, as well as the desire for change.

In its early stages, 'Iraqi fiction faced many obstacles, which reflected the nature of society at the time. Many writers were unable to produce mature literary works. Second, a similar deficiency could be seen in newspaper editors, who mainly published stories that were common instead of those that might have brought a new light to the literary scene. In any case, newspapers were very politicized, and much space was allocated to political issues. Finally, much early 'Iraqi fiction was influenced by Egyptian writers and rarely showed any artistic value as it was pitched to the tastes of the masses. In short, the 'Iraqi novel in the 1920s received little attention in comparison to political events, few 'Iraqis were producing novels, and it was not until the end of the decade that the novel would begin to gain more popularity in 'Iraq.

Beginning in the 1930s, events such as World War II and the Palestinian problem caused many 'Iraqis, as well as many other concerned Arabs, Muslims, and Jews (q.v.) from that region, to take a more political stand in their writing. Many modernist writers in 'Iraq believed that the only way literature could change was when the writer became truly outraged at the status quo, and, not surprisingly, many intellectuals moved into opposition to the government. The efforts of writers to resist traditions included more emphasis on the everyday, real concerns of the 'Iraqi people and on the individual. Many 'Iraqi writers took great interest in Western literature, particularly the works of Flaubert, Tolstoy, Steinbeck, and Sartre, to name only a few. The influence of realism and existentialism from these Western writers showed up in the writings of 'Iraqis. 'Iraqi writers were also interested in Tolstoy's and Dostoevsky's criticisms of society. Predominant themes included a focus on the urban lifestyle. This emphasis on city life discusses the issues of crime, thievery, as well as prostitution. These stories of loneliness, desperation, and failures resonated with the experiences of ordinary 'Iraqis.

After the 1968 revolution (q.v.), literary changes paralleled the new ideology brought by the Ba'th Party (q.v.). Literature retained its political tone, but the short story focused more on new social models promoted by the Ba'th. Over the next decade the 'Iraqi short story went through several changes, much in line with the social changes evident in 'Iraq. One of the most important changes in the short story concerned the decision by writers to abandon colloquialism and instead adopt standard Arabic. Like the revival of folklore, it was hoped the use of standard Arabic in the short story would encourage a common culture and language that would strengthen 'Iraqi identity. The serious themes, often political, that characterized much of 'Iraqi writing were joined by the introduction of children's stories in the 1960s.

– M –

MAHDI, AL-. Abbasid caliph (q.v.), r. 775–785. Al-Mahdi's assumption to the caliphate could not be achieved without the abdication of a cousin whom Abu al-Abbas al-Saffah had named as his second heir after al-Mansur (q.v.). Khalid Ibn Barmak, the caliph's Persian treasurer, convinced the cousin to withdraw his claim by offering him a fabulous sum of money. This act endeared Khalid to the new caliph (q.v.), who appointed Khalid and two of his sons to high positions in the empire. Al-Mahdi released many Umayyads and 'Alids from prison and returned their wealth and property. He fortified a number of cities, constructed rest stations with water supplies along the route from Baghdad (q.v.) to Makka, and greatly improved the mail service. He divided the caliphate into three *diwans* or departments—Finance, Justice, and Defense—and appointed a chief to head each one. This relieved him of some of the heavy responsibilities of managing the vast affairs of the empire. Most of these departmental chiefs were non Arabs. The Abbasid caliphs felt a strong inhibition against placing Arabs in high positions because they had fought with the Umayyads and 'Alids against the Abbasids. Al-Mahdi fought a number of battles against the Byzantines. His army reached the outskirts of Constantinople itself in 782, forcing the Empress Irene to pay 70,000 gold dinars in annual tribute. He waged a tough campaign against the Manichaeans, a sect that followed the teaching of Mani (216–277) and combined elements of Zoroastrianism, Christianity, and paganism, but Manichaeism survived despite efforts to uproot it. Al-Mahdi died after his horse reportedly ran into a building.

MAHDI, 'ABD AL- (1889–?). Cabinet minister during the monarchy. He was born in Shatra to a Shi'i (q.v.) family that belonged to the Muntafiq Bedouin tribe. He received a traditional education and acquainted himself with Arab history and literature (q.v.). An ardent nationalist, he was very active during the 1920 revolt (q.v.) against Britain and opposed the Anglo–'Iraqi treaties of 1922 and 1930 (qq.v.). He was a member of the Constituent Assembly that wrote the 'Iraqi constitution. In 1924 al-Mahdi was elected deputy to the first Parliament and was reelected several times; he served in both the House and Senate. He held several cabinet portfolios: minister of education (1926–1928, 1932–1933), minister of works (1937, 1938, 1941–1943), and minister of the economy (1941, 1941–1942). Early in his career, al-Mahdi cooperated closely with nationalists Rashid 'Ali al-Kaylani and Yasin al-Hashimi (qq.v.), but he broke away from them during the mid-1930s over the harsh suppression of tribal uprisings in the mid-Euphrates (q.v.) region by al-Hashimi's government. As the tribal chief of the mid-Euphrates' districts, he was greatly angered by al-Hashimi's policy. Al-Mahdi drifted to Nuri al-Sa'id's (q.v.) faction and adopted pro-British sympathies. He favored an affirmative action-type policy for getting Shi'is into government colleges and universities.

MAHMUD, MUHAMMAD (?–1949). An officer in the 'Iraqi army. He belonged to a number of Kurdish parties and was very active in the Hewa Party (q.v.). A political writer and an excellent speaker, he wrote most of the editorials for the underground *Hewa* magazine. He joined Mulla Mustafa al-Barzani's (q.v.) 1943–1945 uprising and helped found the Kurdistan Democratic Party (q.v.) in 1946. When the Barzanis withdrew to Iran in 1945, he was the Mulla Mustafa's official spokesman. Mahmud was one of the organizers of the Mahabad Republic's army. He returned with Shaykh Ahmad (q.v.) to 'Iraq in 1947 and was executed in 1949 at Baghdad's (q.v.) central prison. On the day of his execution, he wrote a political testament to the Kurdish people calling on them to continue their fight to liberate Kurdistan and not to be led astray by ignorant leaders.

MAHMUD, NUR AL-DIN (1899–1981). Prime minister and military officer during the monarchy. He was born in Mawsil (q.v.) to one of the city's leading families. He graduated from the Military College in Istanbul in 1917 and joined the 'Iraqi army in 1921. He taught at the cavalry school and the Staff College. Mahmud was promoted to the rank of colonel in 1939, when he was the commander of the Staff College. He was appointed commander of the Second Division in 1941 and assistant chief of staff in 1943. He was promoted to general in 1944 and major general in 1948. Mahmud headed the 'Iraqi forces and later the Arab forces in the 1948–1949 Palestine war. He was appointed chief of staff in 1951. He served briefly as prime minister (November 1952–January 1953); he also held the portfolios of defense and interior in that cabinet. In January 1953, Mahmud was appointed to the Senate, where he remained until the 1958 revolution (q.v.). He was considered a professional soldier and an honorable, courageous man.

MAHMUD, SAMIR SHAKIR. A Sunni Muslim who belongs to the al-Sumaidy clan, which believes its origins can be traced back to the Prophet Muhammad. He is described as both a writer and an entrepreneur. He is from the western city of Haditha.

MAJID, 'ALI HASAN AL- (1941–). Ba'thist security and defense official, and cousin of Saddam Husayn (q.v.) and Husayn Kamil (q.v.). Born in Tikrit, he graduated from the National Defense Academy in 1978. He joined the Ba'th Party (q.v.) in 1958 and was arrested several times following the November 1963 countercoup for party activities. Al-Majid served in a number of Ba'th Party posts after 1968; he became the director general of the Regional Secretariat Office in 1976 and a member of the Military Bureau in 1978. He was elected to the Regional Command (q.v.) in 1982 and to the Revolutionary Command Council (q.v.) in October 1991. From 1984 to 1987, he was director-general of general security. Al-Majid served as minister of local administration (1989–1991), minister of interior (1991–1993), and minister of defense in the early 1990s. He is known for his ruthless crackdowns on opponents of the regime. As the security situation deteriorated in Kurdistan in 1987, Saddam named al-Majid as governor of the Kurdish region. Al-Majid was responsible for the use of chemical weapons at Halabja (q.v.), earning him the nickname "Chemical 'Ali," and he oversaw the Anfal (q.v.) campaign against Kurdish opponents, which involved mass killings, the use of chemical weapons, population transfers, and the destruction of numerous Kurdish villages and hamlets. Al-Majid was in charge of Kuwait during the occupation (1990–1991) and played a major role in crushing the Kurdish and Shi'i (q.v.) uprisings that followed Operation Desert Storm in March 1991. During the 2002–2003 crisis, Saddam divided 'Iraq into four zones, and the southern zone was placed under al-Majid's control. He was arrested by U.S. forces in August 2003 (*see* KUWAIT, INVASION OF.)

MAJID, RAJAB 'ABD AL- (1921–). A leading figure in the Free Officer (q.v.) movement. He was born in Ana and attended the School of Engineering (1936–1939) and Loughborough College in Britain (1947–1951). He also attended the Baghdad Military College. Al-Majid founded the Free Officers with Rif'at al-Hajj Sirri (q.v.) in 1952 and became the secretary of the Supreme Committee of the Free Officers in 1956. He was the primary link between the Free Officers and the civilians opposed to the monarchy. He held the posts of deputy prime minister and minister of interior from August 1966 until May 1967.

MALAIKA, NAZIK AL- (1923–). Poet, literary critic, and a leader of the free verse movement in 'Iraq. She was born to a wealthy family in Baghdad (q.v.) noted for its literary members. Her mother was Salma al-Kadhimiyya, a poet and vanguard of the early nationalist movement. Al-Malaika graduated from Baghdad's Higher Teachers College in 1943 with a degree in Arabic language and literature (q.v.). She also studied English literature at Princeton University. She taught at many 'Iraqi and Arab universities. Al-Malaika is one of the leading figures in the free verse movement. Her poetry is characterized by thematic variations and the use of imagery; in the 1970s, her verse took on strong Islamic overtones. Her collections include *Lover of the Night*, *Sparks and Ashes*, and *Bottom of the Waves*. She also wrote *The Case of Contemporary Poets*, considered a major contribution to Arab literary criticism.

MALKI, SHABIB AL-. Ba'thist administrator and cabinet minister. He was born in Baghdad (q.v.) and received a B.S. in law from the University of Baghdad. He held the positions of governor of Karbala (q.v.) and Nineveh provinces and was a consultant to the Revolutionary Command Council (q.v.). He held the post of minister of justice from March 1991 to 2001.

MAMAND, 'ABBAS AGHA. Leader of the Ako tribe that lives in the Rania area. Under the leadership of Mamand, the Ako tribe cooperated with Shaykh Mahmud's movement. They took part in fighting against the British forces, and its leaders sympathized with the Kurdish revolts. 'Abbas Agha was fair in his dealings with members of his tribe and received a great deal of respect from his acquaintances and relatives. He maintained good ties with the leaders of the Kurdish parties in 'Iraq and the 'Iraqi Communist Party (ICP) (q.v.) under the monarchy. He had a good relationship with Mulla Mustafa al-Barzani (q.v.); Barzani depended on Abbas Agha, and he is the one who encouraged him to create an armed group in Rania in 1961. He actively participated in starting the Kurdish uprising, took part in its battles, and worked diligently for its success. Abbas Agha participated in the Qoisanjaq meeting that chose the Kurdish team that would negotiate with the Ba'th (q.v.) government in 1963. He worked very hard to solve the differences between Barzani and the Ibrahim Ahmad faction and to avoid internal conflict. He became a member of the Revolutionary Council formed by Barzani in 1964. He encouraged the leaders of the Ahmad faction who had been placed under house arrest to escape. *See also* KURDS.

MAMAND, RASUL. Kurdish political leader. He was one of the founders of the Socialist Movement of Kurdistan (q.v.), which later merged with two other parties to form the Patriotic Union of Kurdistan (PUK) (q.v.). In 1979, he broke with the PUK in the wake of its costly clashes with the Kurdistan Democratic Party (q.v.) and formed the United Socialist Party of Kurdistan (USPK) (q.v.) with Mahmud 'Uthman (q.v.). In 1981, Mamand split with 'Uthman, taking with him the majority of the USPK fighters and formed the Socialist Party of Kurdistan (q.v.). Mamand served as the party's general secretary until August 1992, when the party merged with two others to form the Unity Party of Kurdistan (q.v.). *See also* KURDS.

MAMUN, AL-. Abbasid caliph (q.v.), r. 813–833. Al-Mamun rose to the caliphate by defeating the armies of his brother al-Amin (q.v.) in 813. The son of a Persian mother, he adopted the city of Marw in Persia as his capital. Some of the people of 'Iraq were angry at al-Mamun's abandonment of his Arab ancestry for his Persian maternal relatives. A revolt broke out, forcing the governor al-Hasan bin Sahl to escape to Wasit. Similar uprisings took place in Kufa, Basra (q.v.), Makka, Medina, and Yemen by the Shi'i (q.v.) and other opponents of the Abbasids. Al-Mamun invited the Shi'i Imam 'Ali al-Ridha to Marw for negotiations in an effort to reconcile the 'Alids to his rule. Al-Mamun was so impressed by al-Ridha that he designated him successor in 817, thereby approving the transfer of the caliphate from the house of Abbas to that of 'Ali. The Shi'is hailed al-Mamun's decision as the most gratifying news in all of their history. (*See also* BATTLE OF THE CAMEL.)

This news rocked Baghdad (q.v.); the residents of the city named a rival caliph (q.v.), Ibrahim, the brother of al-Rashid (q.v.), and practically severed all ties with al-Mamun's government. A similar rebellion took place in northern 'Iraq. Faced with open revolt in 'Iraq, al-Mamun decided in 818 to return to Baghdad. But during the trip from Marw to Baghdad, al-Ridha died under mysterious circumstances. By the time al-Mamun reached Baghdad in 819, Ibrahim had fled. (He was pardoned in 825.) Al-Mamun declared a general amnesty for all political prisoners. His return restored peace and prosperity to Baghdad, which had suffered from neglect since al-Amin's rule.

In 826, al-Mamun married the daughter of al-Hasan bin Sahl, his loyal commander and vassal, in what was one of the most extravagant weddings in history. Fabulous sums of money were spent on lavish decorations, and generous gifts were thrown to the crowd. The caliph's mother showered the bridegroom with 1,000 matched pearls, which were collected and given to the bride.

Al-Mamun became enamored with Mu'tazilism (q.v.), a doctrine that promoted the createdness of the Koran. Traditional Muslim belief held that the Koran was uncreated and eternal. Mu'tazilism also placed emphasis on the preeminence of the leader of the community. Al-Mamun declared his adherence to Mu'tazilism in 827 and ordered leading theologians and jurists to publicly declare their adherence to this doctrine. He led an inquisition against opponents of Mu'tazilism; Ibn Hanbal, the great jurist, was flogged and thrown in prison for his refusal to subscribe to the doctrine.

Al-Mamun is considered among the strongest and wisest of the Abbasid caliphs. Well known for his intellectual interests, he allowed scholars of various schools to debate their positions before him. He established al-Bayt al-Hikma (House of Wisdom) (q.v.) in Baghdad in 830 where translations into Arabic of Greek, Persian, Sanskrit, and Syriac works were undertaken. He died in 833 while on a military campaign against the Byzantines in Taurus.

MANSUR, ABU JA'FAR AL-. Abbasid caliph (q.v.), r. 754–775, and the founder of the Abbasid dynasty; all succeeding Abbasid caliphs were his descendants. Al-Mansur, meaning "the Victorious," successfully crushed all challenges to Abbasid rule, establishing a secure and prosperous empire. In 754, his uncle 'Abd Allah, a military commander who had ambitions to become caliph, rebelled against him. With the support of Abu Muslim, al-Mansur defeated his uncle, and 'Abd Allah fled into hiding. Al-Mansur offered him a house where he could live safely, but the house was constructed of blocks of salt. When the rainy season came, the whole house collapsed, killing 'Abd Allah and his entire household. Al-Mansur later turned on Abu Muslim, whom he saw as a potential rival, and had him killed. He also faced a rebellion by the 'Alids, the descendants of 'Ali, in 762. The revolt was led by Muhammad, known as the Pure Soul, a great-grandson of Hasan, the son of 'Ali. Muhammad was killed during fighting in Medina, but his brother Ibrahim continued the revolt in Basra (q.v.). Ibrahim was killed in 763, and the Abbasids regained control of the region.

One of al-Mansur's lasting achievements was the construction of Baghdad (q.v.). Al-Mansur decided to build a new capital whose location would be acceptable to him as well as to his commanders. He chose a site near the old capital of Madain on the western bank of the Tigris River (q.v.) where the small village of Baghdad existed. Al-Mansur himself laid the foundation stone with great ceremony in 762, calling the new city *Madinat al-Salam* (the City of Peace). The ancient name of Baghdad continued to prevail, though.

The city was circular in shape and about 2.4 kilometers in diameter with double-thick walls surrounding it. Its circumference had four equidistant gates named Kufa, Syria, Khorasan, and Basra. In the center stood the caliph's palace and the city's main mosque.

Al-Mansur's long rule was primarily a peaceful one devoted to internal reform. He encouraged agriculture (q.v.) and patronized artists and poets. He died on a pilgrimage to Makka in 775 and was succeeded by his son al-Mahdi (q.v.).

MAQAMAT (ASSEMBLIES). These were models of high Arabic prose in which the author was more concerned with demonstrating his mastery of the language and his verbal virtuosity than with content. The most famous maqamat authors are Badi al-Ziman, al-Hamathani (d. 1008), and al-Hariri of Basra (q.v.) (d. 1122), who invented his own narrator-hero, a rogue whom the reader meets in various contrived circumstances and disguises. Al-Hariri's maqamat were illustrated by Yahya al-Wasiti. The style became too formalistic, which ultimately contributed to its decline.

MARCH MANIFESTO. A far-reaching autonomy proposal offered by the Ba'thist government at the instigation of Saddam Husayn to the Kurds (qq.v.) in 1970. The Ba'th Party (q.v.) saw a settlement with the Kurds as a prerequisite for stability, development, and regime survival, and the Kurds saw the agreement as a sweeping recognition of their rights. Moreover, younger, more progressive elements within the Kurdish leadership were willing to cooperate with the Ba'th, and both sides were weary of the fighting. The proposals contained in the March Manifesto, and codified in the Autonomy Law of 11 March 1974, acknowledged a number of important points, including the recognition of the Kurdish people as a distinct national group within 'Iraq that possessed its own language and culture. Other provisions of the agreement included the formation of a Kurdish self-governing area; the recognition of the Kurdish language as official in those areas where Kurds constituted a majority; the teaching of Kurdish and Arabic in all schools; the participation of Kurds in government, including their appointment to important state posts; the appointment of a Kurdish vice president; the furtherance of Kurdish education and culture; the appointment of Kurdish-speaking officials in Kurdish areas; the right to establish Kurdish organizations (student, youth, women, teachers, etc.); economic development and agrarian reform in Kurdish areas; a constitutional amendment recognizing that 'Iraq includes the Arab and Kurdish nationalities; the return to the government of clandestine radios and heavy weapons held by the Kurds; and an amendment of provincial laws in accordance with this declaration. A list of the steps taken by the 'Iraqi regime between 1968 and 1970 to guarantee Kurdish rights was also included: the recognition of the Kurdish language, the establishment of

Sulaymaniyya University, the teaching of Kurdish in all schools, the recognition of Nawruz (the traditional New Year celebration of the Kurds) as a national holiday, and the promulgation of decentralization laws.

Despite difficulties, the two sides remained committed to the March Manifesto during 1971 and 1972. However, mutual suspicions and violations of the agreement by both sides eventually led to the outbreak of hostilities again in 1974. External machinations and promises of support to Kurdish leaders by Iran, Israel, and the United States, coupled with Mulla Mustafa al-Barzani's (q.v.) desire for an independent or confederal Kurdish state, led him to escalate his demands. He insisted that the Kurdish area should include Kirkuk (q.v.) and all its resources and that the Kurdish area have its own army and conduct its own foreign relations. The government rejected these proposals and unilaterally enacted the Manifesto on 11 March 1974. The subsequent fighting pitted 60,000 government troops against about 12,000 *pesh mergas* (q.v.), backed by Iranian troops.

On 6 March 1975, the shah of Iran and 'Iraq's Saddam Husayn signed the Algiers Agreement (q.v.), in which 'Iraq agreed to the *thalweg* (midpoint) as the boundary of the Shatt al-Arab (q.v.), and Iran promised to cut off aid to the Kurdish rebels. 'Iraq offered the Kurds a cease-fire from 13 March until 1 April, to allow Kurdish forces either to go to Iran or to surrender. Barzani gave orders to stop the fighting and withdrew with his family, close associates, and several thousand pesh mergas and their families to Iran. This marked the collapse of the Kurdish movement in the 1970s.

MARSH ARABS (AL-MA'DAN). The population of Arabs, known as *al-Ma'-dan*, who live in and around the marsh areas and are believed to be a mixture of many races. Six tribes have lived in the marsh areas for centuries. They have little contact with the outside world and have been considered untrustworthy by their neighbors and by the foreign powers that have ruled the area. Ironically, the marsh Arabs are also known for their generosity and hospitality. Some specialists believe the population migrated to the area after the sea that covered the region receded to the Gulf, which indicates that they have lived in the region for close to 6,000 years. However, there is no written record of them until about the ninth century. The records of the Abbasid caliphs (q.v.) refer to them as bands of robbers, gypsies, and other fugitives from justice, including rebels against the caliph. Many of the slaves who took part in the Zanj revolt of 889 also fled to the marshes after the collapse of the revolt. Opponents of many governments including army deserters and outlaws have sought refuge in the area. More recently, opponents of the Ba'th (q.v.) government and deserters from the Iran–'Iraq war (q.v.) have taken refuge there. Saddam Husayn's (q.v.) government undertook a project to drain the marshes in the 1990s; Baghdad (q.v.) claimed it was reclaiming the land, but many critics believe the government was trying to eliminate a center of opposition to its rule.

MA'RUF, TAHA MUHYI AL-DIN (1924–). A Kurdish government official under the Ba'thist regime. He was born in Sulaymaniyya province to a middle-class Kurdish family. He attended Baghdad University, receiving a law degree in 1947. A Kurdish nationalist, he was one of the founders of the Kurdistan Democratic Party (q.v.) in 1946. Ma'ruf later became close to the Kurdish faction led by Jalal Talabani (q.v.) and Ibrahim Ahmad. He joined the Foreign Ministry and served as director of public affairs. He was appointed minister of housing (1968–1969) and minister of state (1968–1970) and later served as charge 'd'affaires in London. He held ambassadorial posts to Italy (1970), Albania (1971), and Malta (1972). Ma'ruf was appointed vice president of the Republic in fulfillment of one of the provisions of the 1970 March Manifesto (q.v.), although he allied himself with the Ba'th Party (q.v.) during the 1974–1975 Kurdish war. In 1982, he became a member of the Revolutionary Command Council (RCC) (q.v.); he may be the only non-Ba'thist to have served on the RCC. Ma'ruf was still serving as vice president and RCC member when he was captured by U.S. forces in May 2003.

MASHAT, MUHAMMAD AL- (1930–). Diplomat and academician. He graduated from the University of Baghdad and received an M.A. from the University of California–Berkeley and a Ph.D. in sociology from the University of Maryland. He taught at both the University of Baghdad and Muhammad IV University in Morocco. Al-Mashat worked at the Ministry of Education, rising to become an undersecretary and then minister of higher education and scientific research (1977–1979). He served as ambassador to the United Nations and as ambassador to the United States, a post he held during 'Iraq's invasion of Kuwait (q.v.) and its aftermath. Al-Mashat was recalled to Baghdad (q.v.) in 1991 but sought asylum in Canada, where he now lives.

MASQUF. A famous 'Iraqi dish consisting of freshly caught river fish roasted over an open fire of tamarisk branches. An ancient dish (there are references in Syriac to the dish over 1,000 years ago), it is considered a gourmet meal in 'Iraq. It is available only in the summer. In Arabic, the name means "roofed over," although the Syriac term means "crucified," which is what literally happens to the fish.

MATHHAB. A school of Islamic jurisprudence. *Mathhab* means "path, form of action or sect." There are four schools of Sunni (q.v.) jurisprudence that emerged in the eighth and ninth centuries: the Hanafi, the Maliki, the Shafi'i, and the Hanbali. Established by Abu Hanifa (c. 700–767), the Hanafi school uses personal opinion in the application of liberal methods in the use of analogy. The Hanafis are more tolerant of the possibility of utilizing individual components of the common law and recognize the administrative regulations of the state authorities.

Established by Malik ibn Anas (c. 715–795), the Malikis place more em phasis than the other schools on the *hadith*, or Traditions (the acts and sayings of the Prophet). The Malikis view any analogy as valid as long as it is based on a valid *hadith*. This school is slightly more rigorous than the Hanafi school in its choice of the Traditions on which it bases its decisions.

The Shafi'is represent a compromise between the Hanafis and the Malikis. Established by Muhammad ibn Idris ibn al-Shafi (767–820), this school emphasizes the rational use of analogy in jurisprudence. The Shafi'i school believes that the outstretched parallelisms employed by the Hanafis and the Malikis were erroneous and therefore unfit for precedents in Islamic jurisprudence. Al-Shafi'i composed a manual for Islamic law in which he set forth rigorous principles by which analogy could be used.

The Hanbali school is the most conservative of the four Sunni schools of jurisprudence, stressing maximum strictness in all forms of the Sharia (q.v.). Established by Ahmad ibn Hanbal (780–855), it uses extreme conservatism in making legal judgments. The Hanbali school proscribes the use of personal opinion based on analogy, unlike the other three schools of jurisprudence, and permits only the use of the Koran (q.v.) and the Traditions when reaching a legal judgment. Ibn Hanbal himself collected some 80,000 hadiths that he considered valuable for Islamic jurisprudence.

MAWARDI, ABU AL-HASAN AL- (972–1058). A famous Sunni (q.v.) jurist and theorist on public administration from Basra (q.v.). He taught in Basra and served as a judge in Nishapur. He later went to Baghdad (q.v.) and became a judicial advisor to the caliph (q.v.) and his court. Al-Mawardi wrote *The Principles of Government*, in which he presented his own theory of government as well as a detailed account of the rules and relations between the ruler and his subjects. Some scholars believe that he advocated the need for a position similar to that of the modern-day ombudsman to mediate between the people and government officials.

MAWSIL (MOSUL). Mawsil is 'Iraq's third-largest city and the capital of Ninawa (Nineveh) province in north 'Iraq. It was a major commercial and cultural center with a large Christian (q.v.) population until recent times. Its population is estimated at 1.5 million people; it is 'Iraq's most ethnically mixed city, with Arabs, Kurds (q.v.), Assyrians (q.v.), and Turkumen (q.v.). It lies near the ancient site of the famed city of Nineveh, on the Tigris River (q.v.). It was a leading city of northern Mesopotamia by the time of the Abbasid caliphate because of its location along the Mediterranean–India caravan route. Sacked by the Mongol invader Hulagu in 1258, it later fell to the Ottoman Turks in 1508. The city thrived as an important commercial center but lost prominence during the last period of the Ottoman Empire. Its central role was regained when oil (q.v.) was commercially found in the region during the first decades of the 20th century. Oil and agriculture (q.v.) are its primary occupations. Mawsil, like many other 'Iraqi cities, has suffered greatly from neglect and from the impact of the Gulf wars and the UN sanctions (q.v.).

MEDIA. The first 'Iraqi newspaper *al-Zawra* was established in Baghdad (q.v.) on 15 June 1869 by the Ottoman governor Midhat Pasha and continued to publish in Arabic and Turkish until the end of World War I. After the war, a number of relatively free and influential newspapers appeared and flourished under the monarchy (1920–1958). The press became more restricted under the various republican regimes (1958–1968) where different revolutionary leaders wanted the media to mobilize the public. Under the Ba'th Party (1968–2003), this trend became more apparent as only Ba'thist newspapers and newspapers of allied parties were published. The only exceptions were the Kurdish media that emerged after the 1970 March Manifesto (q.v.) and some opposition leaflets and publications issued in the Kurdish area. Under the Ba'th regime, six national dailies and numerous magazines, journals, and children's magazines were published. These included *Afaq 'Arabiya*, which focused on politics, art, and literature (q.v.); *al-Turath al-Sha'bi*, a magazine that centered on folk culture and traditions; *al-Mawrid*, which focused on Muslim and Arab culture and heritage; and *Gilgamesh*, an English-language journal that covered Iraqi art, literature, and culture. Journals on contemporary literature and culture included *al-Thaqafa al-Jadida* and *al-Adab al-Mua'asir*. There were also several Kurdish journals and magazines that focused on Kurdish literature, culture, and heritage in Iraq, as well as journals and magazines published in the Aramaic (Syriac) (q.v.) and Turkic languages for the Assyrian–Chaldean and Turkuman (q.v.) communities. In addition, professional magazines and journals focusing on issues related to women, peasants, students, youth, and sports were published.

The Gulf War of 1990–1991 and the harsh UN sanctions (q.v.) on 'Iraq led to the interruption of many of these activities, and only recently has 'Iraq begun to witness a very modest revival in this area. As of 2003, there were seven newspapers in 'Iraq, including the government organ, *al-Jumhuriya*; the Ba'th Party newspaper *al-Thawra*; the Armed Forces newspaper *al-Qadissiya*; *al-Iraq*, which speaks for progovernment Kurdish parties and newspapers since the closure of the Kurdistan Democratic Party (q.v.) newspaper *al-Taakhi* in 1974; the publications run by Uday Husayn (q.v.), the newspaper *Babil* and the sports magazine *al-Ba'th al-Riyadhi*; and the English-language newspaper *Baghdad Observer*. The newspapers were forced, due to the lack of paper resulting from the sanctions, to reduce the number of pages as well their size to a quarter of their old format. In 1999, the newspapers began to publish in their normal size twice a week.

Professional organizations and unions produce a number of publications, including the weekly magazine *Alif Ba*, established in 1967 and published by the Ministry of Information and Culture; *Nabadh Al-Shabab*, published by the General Union of Youth; *Sawt al-Talaba*, published by the Youth and Student Union; *al-Ittihad*, published by the Union of Iraqi Industries (Chamber of Commerce); *al-I'lam*, published by the College of Communications of the University of Baghdad; *al-Ray*, which focuses on contemporary Islamic and Arab affairs; *al-Zawra*, published by the Union of Iraqi Journalists; *Alwan*, published by the Iraqi Theater Committee; and *al-Musawir al-'Arabi*, the organ of 'Iraqi photographers run by Uday Husayn.

The main radio stations are Baghdad Radio, Sawt Al-Jamahir Radio, and a new religious station launched in 1997, Itha'at al-Quran al-Karim. In addition to 'Iraqi Television, a station, al-Shabab, was owned and run by Uday Husayn. 'Iraq now has a satellite TV channel.

In the Kurdish region, two satellite television stations run by the KDP and by the Patriotic Union of Kurdistan (q.v.) broadcast mainly in Kurdish but have hours in Arabic, Turkic, and Assyrian. There are also a number of Kurdish-language newspapers published in the Kurdish region as well as Kurdish, Arabic, Assyrian, and Turkic magazines.

MIDFA'I, JAMIL AL- (1890–1958). Prime minister during the monarchy. He was born in Mawsil (q.v.). He studied at the Military College and the Engineering College in Istanbul and graduated as an artillery officer. His real name was Jamil bin Mohammad Abbas; al-Midfa'i, meaning "the Gunner," was the title he earned as an officer. He participated in the Balkans War and was imprisoned by the Greeks in 1912. He later taught at the military school in Baghdad (q.v.). During World War I, al-Midfa'i fought in the Caucasus and Palestine, and he was wounded and imprisoned by the British. He joined the Arab Revolt in 1916. He was the commander of the Damascus Garrison and one of Faysal I's (q.v.) military advisers during Faysal's rule in Syria. He returned to 'Iraq in 1920 where he took an active part in the revolt against the British. He led a band of officers and soldiers that crossed the Euphrates (q.v.) and captured Tal 'Afar on the road to Mawsil, but his group did not advance to Mawsil itself. Al-Midfa'i was excluded from the amnesty declared after the revolt, and he went to Jordan. While in Jordan, he served as the military governor of Karak district and the director-general of public security in al-Salt. He returned to 'Iraq in 1923 after he had been granted a pardon and served as the governor of several provinces.

Al-Midfa'i's attitude toward the British changed once he returned to 'Iraq. He was considered a pro-Hashimite (q.v.), pro-British politician, and he frequently was called in to head cabinets after periods of unrest. He was named prime minister several times (1933–1934, 1935, 1937–1938, 1941, 1953).

He also held the portfolios of interior (1930, 1934, 1948) and defense (1934–1935, 1937–1938). Al-Midfa'i and Nuri al-Sa'id (q.v.) were bitter rivals. There was suspicion that members of al-Midfa'i's cabinet had been accessories to the murder of Nuri's ally Rustum Haydar (q.v.) in 1940. In 1941, al-Midfa'i agreed to form a cabinet only if Nuri left the country. When al-Midfa'i became the president of the Senate in 1943, he turned it into a bulwark against Nuri. He was president of the Senate again from 1955 to 1958. He was killed during the 1958 revolution (q.v.).

MIKHAIL, SHAMUIL IRMYA (1941–). An intellectual and university professor of Chaldean (q.v.) origin and a member of the National Assembly (q.v.). He was born in 'Imadiyya in northern 'Iraq and attended schools there and in Baghdad (q.v.). He is a member of the Board of the Union of Writers. Mikhail has played an important role in preserving the Syriac language, in which he is fluent, and is a member of the Syriac Academy. *See also* ARAMAIC.

MILITARY AGREEMENT OF THE 1922 ANGLO–'IRAQI TREATY. Under Article VII of the 1922 Anglo–'Iraqi Treaty (q.v.), 'Iraq and Britain concluded a separate agreement governing their military relationship, signed on 25 March 1924. The agreement stipulated that 'Iraq would provide for its own internal and external defense within four years (Article I) and that it would devote at least 25 percent of its annual revenues to the defense budget (Article IV). Until 'Iraq was able to defend itself, Britain would extend support and assistance to 'Iraq in the form of the presence of British forces; training in Britain for 'Iraqi officers; provision of arms, ammunition, equipment, and airplanes to the 'Iraqi armed forces; and the provision of British officers (Article II). British officials had the right to inspect the 'Iraqi army and make recommendations; if 'Iraq failed to act on any recommendation, it would forfeit Britain's military assistance (Article VII).

MOSUL. *See* MAWSIL.

MOUSA, HAMID MAJID (1941–). A Shi'a and secretary-general of the 'Iraqi Communist Party (ICP) (q.v.) since 1993. An economist by training, he lived for several years in northern 'Iraq after the 1991 Gulf War.

MUGHIRA, AL-. A prominent Muslim general sent to 'Iraq by the caliph (q.v.) 'Umar. He served as the governor of Basra (q.v.) for a short time. His slave, Abu Lulua, assassinated 'Umar.

MUJTAHID. A religious scholar who practices *ijtihad* (q.v.), or the interpretation of religious law. The mujtahids have reached a high level of knowledge and have gained the recognition of their peers as possessing the right to interpret legal and religious questions independently. In Sunni (q.v.) Islam, they are regarded as the founders of the Mathhab (q.v.), the four schools of jurisprudence. In Shi'i (q.v.) Islam, the mujtahids represent the most influential circles of the higher clergy. As intermediaries between the community and the Hidden Imam, they have the authority to interpret the law and direct the affairs of the community.

MUHAMMADAWI, 'ABD AL-KARIM MAHOUD. *See* HATIM, ABU.

MUHARRAM. The first month of the Muslim year, when Husayn's death (d. 680) is commemorated in a ritualized funeral procession. *See also* KARBALA.

MUHSIN, 'ABD AL-JABBAR (1937–). Journalist and Ba'thist spokesman. Born to a Shi'i (q.v.) family of modest means, he graduated from the College of Literature with a degree in sociology. He joined the Ba'th Party (q.v.) in the early 1950s and served in a number of party posts after 1963. Muhsin worked as a journalist for *al-Thawra* newspaper as well as for the Ministry of Information. During the Iran–'Iraq war (q.v.), he served as the military spokesman. He later served as spokesman for Saddam Husayn (q.v.).

MUKHAYLIF, HIKMAT 'UMAR (1937–). An influential Ba'thist technocrat and financial expert. Prior to his government service, he taught at the University of Baghdad. He served as an adviser to the Presidential Office. In October 1984, he became the chair of the powerful Audit Bureau, which supervises expenditure by all state concerns. He was appointed minister of finance in September 1987; when he was removed from this post in October 1989, he was publicly and harshly criticized by Saddam Husayn (q.v.). It is believed that Saddam was angry with Mukhaylif's inability to obtain more funds for 'Iraq's nonconventional weapons programs.

MUKHLIS, HATIM (1951–). Medical doctor and opposition activist. Dr. Mukhlis received his medical degree from Baghdad Medical School in 1973. Mukhlis has been politically active since 1993, participating in opposition activities and conferences. He helped to establish the 'Iraq National Liberal Movement (INL) in 2002. His grandfather, Mawlud Mukhlis, considered by many to be the father of the town of Tikrit, was one of the officers who participated in the Arab Revolt during World War I. He later participated in the establishment of the 'Iraqi monarchy and served as speaker of the 'Iraqi Parliament. Jasim Mukhlis, his father, was an army officer, lawyer, and ambassador. He was executed by the regime, together with other members of the family, in 1993 after a failed coup against the regime.

MUKHLIS, MAWLUD (1886–1951). Military leader and political figure during the monarchy. He was born in Mawsil (q.v.), although his family is originally from Tikrit. He attended preparatory military school in Baghdad (q.v.) but was expelled and imprisoned. He escaped and went to Istanbul where he was a classmate of Nuri al-Sa'id's (q.v.) at the Istanbul War College (1903–1906). An ardent Arab nationalist, Mukhlis joined the Covenant Party (q.v.) in 1914–1915. During World War I, he commanded Ottoman cavalry units at Shu'aybah and Kut before he was arrested by the Ottomans in 1916 on charges of spying for the English. He escaped and joined Faysal's (q.v.) Arab army. He was wounded eight times. Mukhlis became Faysal's aide de campe and served as a military adviser during Faysal's rule in Syria. He actively participated in the 1920 revolt (q.v.) in 'Iraq, launching a number of campaigns against the British in 'Iraq. He served as governor of Karbala (q.v.) in 1923. In 1925, he was appointed to the Senate, where he served for many years, becoming its vice president in 1936. Mukhlis resigned from the Senate after he was elected as a deputy to Parliament from Baghdad in 1937; he was reelected in 1939 and in 1943. He headed the House of Representatives from 1937 to 1941. He was later reappointed to the Senate. As a protégé of Faysal I and an extremely well-connected individual, Mukhlis wielded a great deal of influence. It is as a result of his patronage that so many Tikritis were introduced into the officer corps of the 'Iraqi army, the beginning of a trend that allowed Tikritis to play leading political and military roles in the Ba'th (q.v.) regimes since the 1960s. He died in Lebanon.

MUKHTAR, AL- *See* PENITENTS.

MULLA. A Farsi (Persian) word that means "religious scholar or learned man." It can also be used to refer to lower-ranking members of the clergy, and Sunni Kurds (qq.v.) sometimes use the term to refer to members of the clergy or as a given name.

MUNTAFIQ CONFEDERATION. *See;* NOMADIC TRIBES; SETTLED TRIBES.

MUQAFFA', IBN AL- (?–757). One of the leading figures of the Abbasid period. Although he was born into a Persian, Zoroastrian family, he is generally considered a master of the Arabic language. A Tahlawi scholar, he translated many works from that language into Arabic. Al-Muqaffa''s most famous work is *Kalila wa Dimna*, which is still considered a classic in the Arab world and is one of the few of his works that survived in its entirety.

MUSAWI, MUHSIN AL- (1944–). Academic and editor. He studied in 'Iraq and Canada and taught at the University of Baghdad, where he also chaired the mass communications department. He was elected secretary-general of the 'Iraqi Writers Union. Al-Musawi at one time edited the *Afaq 'Arabiyya*, a prominent 'Iraqi historical, political, and literary journal. He also authored a number of books on Arabic literature (q.v.). He later left 'Iraq to live and teach abroad.

MUSTAFA, BURHAN (1942–). A Ba'thist activist and lawyer from Tikrit. He joined the Ba'th Party (q.v.) in the late 1950s and was arrested several times for his party activities by the governments of 'Abd al-Karim Qasim (q.v.) and the 'Arif brothers (q.v.). He served as head of the 'Iraq Ports Authority. Mustafa held membership in the Revolutionary Command Council (q.v.) and the Regional Command (q.v.) from 1977 to 1982.

MUSTAFA, 'IZZAT (1925–1981). A physician and Ba'thist politician. He was born in Ana and received his M.D. from Damascus University in the late 1940s. During the first Ba'th (q.v.) government in 1963, he held the post of minister of health. He reportedly was one of the main supporters of the party when it operated underground after the 1963 countercoup by 'Abd al-Salam 'Arif (q.v.). When the Ba'th regained power in 1968, he was again appointed minister of health, a post he held until 1976. From 1976 to 1977, Mustafa served as minister of labor and social affairs, and from January to March 1977, he was minister of municipalities. He held membership in the Regional Command (1966–1968, 1974–1977) (q.v.) and in the Revolutionary Command Council (1969–1977) (q.v.). He was one of Ahmad Hasan al-Bakr's (q.v.) closest associates, and al-Bakr sent him on a number of critical missions abroad. Mustafa was relieved of his positions in March 1977, apparently because of his leniency in dealing with Shi'i (q.v.) protestors. He was exiled to a village near Mawsil (q.v.), where he reportedly died in 1981.

MUSTAFA, 'UMAR (DABABA) (?–1991). Kurdish politician and activist. He graduated from the Law College in Baghdad (q.v.). He gained his nickname, Dababa, which means "tank" in Arabic, because during the 1958 revolution (q.v.) he climbed on a tank and took it over. Mustafa was a close associate of Jalal Talabani (q.v.), Ibrahim Ahmad, 'Ali 'Askari (q.v.), and Khalid Sa'id (q.v.).

MUTANABBI, ABU AL-TAYYIB AHMAD BIN AL-HUSAYN AL- (815–900). One of the greatest poets in Arab history. He was born in Kufa, the son of a water carrier, and educated in Syria. He grew up living among the Bedouins of the Syrian–'Iraqi desert and later traveled in Egypt and Iran. A proud and arrogant man, his motto was "Live honorably or die heroically." Many of his poems glorified the values of the Bedouin, such as friendship, chivalry, integrity, loyalty, bravery, and honor. On his return from Iran, al-Mutanabbi and a few retainers were attacked between Kufa and Baghdad (q.v.) by a party of Bedouins who were seeking vengeance for a verse attacking one of their leaders. Defeated in combat, al-Mutanabbi was preparing to flee when one of his attendants reminded him of a line from one of his poems: "I am known to the horse troop, the night and the desert expanse, not more to paper and pen than the sword and the lance." Al-Mutanabbi turned again to the battle and met his death like a desert warrior. He is considered one of the finest panegyric poets, and his style is a combination between the simple and the exaggerated or contrived. His exaggerated expressions of flattery and extravagant hyperbole have caused some Western writers to question his talents, but his artistic mastery is widely acknowledged in the Arab world. His poems are still taught in schools all over the Arab world.

MU'TASIM, AL-. Abbasid caliph (q.v.), r. 833–842. Al-Mu'tasim assumed the caliphate at a crucial time: increasing regionalism was opening serious divisions within the empire. The rivalry between Persians and Arabs was especially serious. Upon his appointment, al-Mu'tasim rushed to Baghdad (q.v.), where a group of army commanders had nominated his nephew al-Abbas as caliph. Al-Abbas abandoned his claim to the caliphate following negotiations, and the movement surrounding him collapsed. Al-Mu'tasim took firm control of the state, defeating a number of opponents. He imprisoned enemies of the Mu'tazilites (q.v.). He brought the war against the Khoramites to a complete success and defeated Byzantine forces. Al-Mu'tasim also faced plots instigated by his military commander al-Afshin. Al-Afshin sympathized with a Persian-oriented movement led by Mazyar that had emerged in Tabaristan. The movement reflected growing concern among some Persians about their loss of status in the empire. Al-Afshin encouraged Mazyar's movement so that an independent Persian state free from Arab domination could be established. Al-Mu'tasim immediately jailed his commander; al-Afshin reportedly died of poisoning, and his body was hung in the public square.

Following these events, al-Mu'tasim introduced a new element into the Abbasid state. He had sought to remain neutral in the struggle between Arabs and Persians, but he soon discovered that he could not trust either side. The son of a Turkish concubine, and acquainted with the warlike nature of the

Turkish tribes, al-Mu'tasim decided to establish a contingent of Turkish mercenaries whose loyalties to the caliph could be well assured. He sent orders to officials in Samarkand and other outposts in Transcaucasia to recruit Turkish bondsmen, who were sent to Baghdad and trained for military service. When conflicts erupted between his Arab subjects and his Turkish bodyguards, al-Mu'tasim built his mercenaries a new city north of Baghdad. Samarra, named as al-Mu'tasim's second capital in 836, grew rapidly. It was populated mainly by Turkish warriors who enjoyed the full confidence of the caliph. The Turkish groups ultimately gained dominant control of the Abbasid state. *See also* AL-MUTAWAKKIL.

MUTAWAKKIL, AL-. Abbasid caliph (q.v.), r. 847–861. During al-Mutawakkil's rule, the Mu'tazilite (q.v.) doctrine was renounced, and the Abbasid state again began to persecute the Shi'is (q.v.). Al-Mutawakkil also attempted to reassert Arab control of the caliphate; Turkish mercenaries imported during the rule of al-Mu'tasim (r. 833–842) (q.v.) were growing increasingly powerful. The Turkish mercenaries plotted al-Mutawakkil's assassination with his son al-Muntasir. Al-Muntasir was angered and humiliated by his father's designation of another son, al-Mu'tazz, as his successor. In 861, al-Muntasir and two Turks brutally murdered the caliph. This event ushered in the period of Turkish control of the caliphate.

MU'TAZILITES. A group of thinkers who tried to submit religious doctrine and faith to rational examination. The Mu'tazilites gained preeminence during the rule of Caliph al-Mamun (r. 813–833) (q.v.). They believed that the Koran (q.v.) was created, whereas orthodox Muslim beliefs held that the Koran was uncreated and eternal. The Mu'tazilite doctrine implied that the Koran could not be associated with the essence of God, whereas traditional Muslim theologians believed that the Koran belonged to God's essence. The Mu'tazilites also believed that Muslims who committed grave sins were believers who had transgressed; traditional views held that such people were still believers, while the Kharijites (q.v.) maintained such people were infidels. The Mu'tazilites argued that there was an intermediate state in which a believer was a transgressor but not an infidel. They also began to give a new interpretation to the Koran; when faced with a clear text that would contradict their beliefs, they would explain it away as the outward meaning of the Koran, the *dhahir*, which required an inner meaning, the *batin*. Such interpretations gave way to innovations that were viewed as heretical by Sunni (q.v.) Muslims. Caliph al-Mutawakkil (q.v.) renounced the Mu'tazilite doctrine during his rule (r. 847–861).

MUTHANNA, AL-. *See* AL-QADISSIYA.

– N –

NADI AL-MUTHANNA. A pan-Arab society established in Baghdad (q.v.) in 1935. It took its name from al-Muthanna ibn Haritha, the brilliant general whose Muslim Arab forces in 'Iraq fought and defeated the Persians at al-Qadissiya (q.v.) in 637. Nadi al-Muthanna and other secret societies disseminated and promoted Arab nationalist views in an attempt to mobilize public opinion in support of their ideas. The club gained a great deal of influence as its ideas began to spread in government schools. Led by Saib Shawkat and Muhammad Mahdi al-Kubba (q.v.), it came to be dominated by ultranationalists. The emergence of the club reflected the rise of Arab nationalist activities in the wake of the 1936 Bakr Sidqi (q.v.) coup. Many Arab nationalists and reformers who had supported the coup became disenchanted with Bakr Sidqi's authoritarian and arbitrary policies. The club's members joined followers of Rashid 'Ali al-Kaylani (q.v.) following World War II and formed the Independence Party (q.v.).

NAJAF. Shi'i (q.v.) holy city and famous center of religious and language studies. It is also the capital of the al-Najaf province, created in 1976, a flat region that extends from the Euphrates River (q.v.) to the Saudi border. The city itself lies on a ridge west of the Euphrates River. It is said to have been founded by caliph Harun al-Rashid (q.v.) in 791, although the city did not begin to grow rapidly until the 10th century. In the city's center is a mosque containing the tomb of Imam 'Ali, one of Shi'i Islam's (qq.v.) holiest shrines. The city has been the major spiritual and educational capital of Shi'i Islam, and it is famous for its religious and linguistic schools. Najaf has been a temptation for Iranian rulers over the recent centuries. It has suffered from Bedouin raids, particularly a Wahhabi raid in 1810. It has also historically been the center of Shi'i resistance to 'Iraq's Sunni (q.v.) rulers and of anti-British resistance during colonial rule. There are deep cellars underground the city, which traditionally have provided sanctuary to political dissidents. In February 1977, antiregime demonstrations in Najaf and Karbala (q.v.), another Shi'i holy city, led to the dispatch of 'Iraqi troops and the closing of the region to outsiders. Najaf was also a center of the Shi'i uprising in March 1991 following 'Iraq's defeat in Operation Desert Storm (q.v.).

NAMIQ, JAWHAR. A Kurdish activist. He graduated from the School of Economics at Baghdad University. He was a member of the Provisional Command of the Kurdistan Democratic Party (KDP) (q.v.) from 1975 to 1979, and he actively helped rebuild and reorganize the party after the collapse of the 1975 Kurdish revolt. One of the younger and more progressive elements in the KDP, he left 'Iraq in 1989 and moved to Sweden.

NAQIB, HASAN AL-. Former 'Iraqi military officer and member of the Executive Council of the opposition 'Iraqi National Congress (INC) (q.v.). A pan-Arabist officer, al-Naqib commanded 'Iraqi forces in Jordan during the 1967 Arab–Israeli war and called for support for the Palestinians during the September 1970 Palestine Liberation Organization (PLO)–Jordan conflict. He also served as military attaché to the United States. He was dismissed from his post as deputy chief of staff of the 'Iraqi army in 1970. Al-Naqib later served as ambassador to Spain and Sweden. He defected from the Ba'th (q.v.) regime in 1978 and became a military adviser to the PLO. Since 1990 he has led the opposition group, the 'Iraqi Independent Alliance (q.v.). He is based in Damascus and considered a moderate nationalist. A Sunni (q.v.), he is one of three members of the INC's executive council.

NAQIB, T'ALIB AL- (1862–1929). Cabinet minister and nationalist leader during the monarchy. He was born in Basra (q.v.) to a wealthy and religious family. He became a member of the Ottoman Parliament in 1909. In 1913, he was accused of plotting the assassination of a Turkish military commander in Basra. During World War I, al-Naqib opposed the British and was exiled to India following the British occupation of 'Iraq. He moved to Baghdad (q.v.) at the end of the occupation. He became the minister of interior (1920–1921) in the first cabinet established by the provisional government of 'Iraq and was a major competitor of Faysal's (q.v.) for the throne of 'Iraq. He established ties with St. John Philby, a strong opponent of the Hashimites (q.v.) who encouraged al-Naqib in his aspirations to become king of 'Iraq. Disappointed when the British chose Faysal, al-Naqib openly aired his belief that the British had made an unwise choice. He organized some tribal leaders and condemned Britain's policies, warning against the consequences if Britain's plans were implemented. His opposition led to his arrest and exile to Sri Lanka. He was allowed to return to 'Iraq after three years. He died in Munich, where he had gone to seek medical treatment.

NATION PARTY (HIZB AL-UMMA). A liberal 'Iraqi nationalist party established in 1924 by Naji al-Suwaydi and Muhammad al-Shabibi (q.v.). Its goals were to complete the 'Iraqi constitution as soon as possible and to strengthen the role of Parliament. It did not have much of an impact on 'Iraqi politics.

NATIONAL ASSEMBLY. The legislative branch of the government, established in 1980. It has 250 members, each of whom represents 50,000 citizens. The term of office is four years. The Assembly meets for two sessions every year and can be called into extraordinary session. It has the power to consider draft laws presented by the Revolutionary Command Council (RCC), the president (qq.v.), or its own members. Draft laws must be endorsed by one-quarter of Assembly members and may not deal with military or public security issues. If the Assembly approves a draft law, it is submitted to the RCC to be considered within 15 days; if approved, the law is sent to the president to be ratified. If the draft law is rejected or amended by the RCC or the president, it is returned to the Assembly. If the Assembly and the RCC cannot reach agreement, a joint session of both is usually convened wherein a final decision is reached through a two-thirds majority vote. The Assembly's other duties include the discussion of 'Iraq's general domestic and foreign policies, the enactment of international treaties and agreements, and the supervision and investigation of government bureaus. In 1988, the RCC expanded the powers of the National Assembly. It was given the power to inspect government and public sector offices, to summon the prime minister and cabinet ministers to question them about any matter, and to recommend whatever measures it thinks necessary against any persons it finds responsible for a particular problem.

NATIONAL BROTHERHOOD PARTY (HIZB AL-IKHA AL-WATANI). An opposition party formed by Yasin al-Hashimi (q.v.) and Naji al-Suwaydi in 1930. It favored national industrialization and cooperated with Ja'far abu al-Timman's (q.v.) National Party to oppose Nuri al-Sa'id (q.v.). This cooperation lasted until 1933 when Rashid 'Ali al-Kaylani (q.v.) formed his first cabinet and issued his own newspaper, *al-Ikha al-Watani* (The National Brotherhood). It was dissolved along with other political parties when al-Hashimi reached power in 1935.

NATIONAL COMMAND. It is the highest leadership entity, in the absence of the National Congress, of the Ba'th Party (q.v.) and includes Ba'th leaders from different Arab countries. It has the authority to supervise all the party's activities. The party's various entities and organizations must obey its directives in organizational, political, cultural, and representative matters. The National Conference elects from among its members a political bureau that has the authority to make decisions between the two yearly meetings of the conference. Terms in the National Command run for two years and are renewable. Due to the split in the Ba'th Party in 1966, there are rival National Commands in 'Iraq and Syria. Saddam Husayn (q.v.) was the secretary general of the National Command and the Regional Command ('Iraq). However, the Revolutionary Command Council (RCC) and the Regional Command (qq.v.) held the real levers of power, although members of the RCC was usually on the National Command.

NATIONAL DEMOCRATIC FRONT (AL-JABHA AL-WATANIYYA AL-DIMQRATIYYA). An opposition front formed in 1982. It is composed of the 'Iraqi Communist Party (q.v.), the Kurdistan Democratic Party (q.v.), and the Socialist Party of Kurdistan (q.v.). It was supported by Libya.

NATIONAL DEMOCRATIC AND PATRIOTIC FRONT (AL-JABHA AL-QAWAMIYYA WA AL-WATANIYYA WA AL-DIMQRATIYYA). An opposition front established on 17 November 1980 with the support of the Syrian government. It entailed a number of small 'Iraqi opposition groups, including the 'Iraqi Communist Party (q.v.), led by 'Aziz Muhammad; the Patriotic Union of Kurdistan (q.v.), led by Jalal Talabani (q.v.); the Arab Socialist Movement, led by Jawad Dush; the pro-Syrian branch of the 'Iraqi Ba'th Party (q.v.), led by Jabar al-Kubaisi; the Socialist Party, led by Rashid Muhsin; the Popular Liberation Army, led by Hani Hasan al-Nahr; the Independent Democrats; and the Socialist Party of Kurdistan (q.v.), led by Mahmud 'Uthman (q.v.).

NATIONAL DEMOCRATIC PARTY (NDP) (AL-HIZB AL-WATANI AL-DIMQRATIYYA). A moderate, socialist party led by Nasir Kamil al-Chadirchi (q.v.), which began its legal operations in 1946. It functioned mainly as an extension of the 1930s al-Ahali group (q.v.). Its members included Muhammad Hadid (q.v.), 'Abd al-Karim al-Uzari, Husayn Jamil (q.v.), Yusuf al-Hajj Ilyas, and Sadiq Kammunah. The NDP did not have a clear philosophy; the principles of its leaders, rather than a specific set of ideological beliefs, guided the party. Its main emphasis was the achievement of major reforms in the political, economic, social, and cultural life of 'Iraq in accordance with scientific principles and the transformation of 'Iraq from an underdeveloped, backward society to a modern, democratic one. Through its newspaper *Sawt al-Ahali* (Voice of the People), it promoted the ideas of democracy and reform. It opposed cooperation with the military as well as clandestine political activities, preferring to suspend its activities whenever parties were dissolved. It played a minor role in the preparation of the 1958 revolution (q.v.).

NATIONAL INDEPENDENCE PARTY (HIZB AL-ISTIQLAL AL-WATANI). A nationalist movement formed in 1924 by 'Abd Allah al-'Umari in Mawsil (q.v.). It primarily focused on supporting 'Iraq's position in the struggle for Mawsil province between 'Iraq and Turkey by asserting Mawsil's Arab character. It also established a National Defense Society to achieve the same objectives. It issued a newspaper *al-Ahd* (The Covenant). *See also* ANKARA, TREATY OF.

NATIONAL UNION FRONT (JABHAT AL-ITTIHAD AL-WATANI). A nationalist front established in 1956 by the Ba'th Party (q.v.), the 'Iraqi Communist Party (q.v.), the Independence Party (q.v.), and the National Democratic Party (q.v.) to oppose the policies of the government. These parties had increasingly recognized that they could not challenge the regime individually and thus needed to communicate and coordinate among themselves. Following the 1956 Tripartite attack against Egypt, representatives from the four parties and several independent politicians met and decided that unified actions had to be taken. A Higher Committee was established in February 1957.

The National Front's first program called for the dismissal of Nuri al-Sa'id's (q.v.) cabinet and the dissolution of Parliament; withdrawal from the Baghdad Pact (q.v.), which it viewed as damaging to 'Iraqi sovereignty and independence; unifying the policies of the liberated Arab countries; opposition to colonial interference in all its forms; the adoption of an independent Arab policy based on nonalignment; the adoption of full democratic and constitutional freedoms; the abolition of martial law; and the freeing of political prisoners. Overall, the National Front aligned itself with the policies of Egypt and Syria, displaying great sympathy for Arab nationalist regimes and for national liberation movements within the Arab world, especially in Algeria. The emergence of the National Front paved the way for the 1958 revolution (q.v.). The Kurdistan Democratic Party (q.v.) joined the Front after the revolution but splits within the government between 'Abd al-Karim Qasim (q.v.) and 'Abd al-Salam 'Arif (q.v.), Qasim and the nationalists, and the Arab nationalists and the communists led to the National Front's dissolution.

NATIONAL UNION PARTY (HIZB AL-ITTIHAD AL-WATANI). A left-of-center political grouping established in 1946 under 'Abd al-Fattah Ibrahim, a former founding member of al-Ahali (q.v.). The National Union Party professed socialist ideas and placed even more emphasis on democracy than the National Democratic Party (q.v.). Its objectives were to strengthen the national links between 'Iraq and other Arab countries; to expand the political solidarity and cultural and economic cooperation among Arab countries; to support Arab countries in their struggle for independence and sovereignty; to oppose the Zionist movement, which it considered a threat to the Arab countries; and to achieve a solution to the Palestine problem by achieving Palestinian independence. Its members included Nasir al-Kilani, Edwar Qulayan, and Muhammad Mahdi al-Jawahiri (q.v.). It published a newspaper, the *Politics*. It was dissolved by the government in 1947.

NATIONAL UNITED PATRIOTIC FRONT (AL-JABHA AL-WATANIYYA AL-MUTTAHIDA). The National United Patriotic Front was formed in May 1954 to test the degree to which the government planned to allow free elections following the dissolution of Parliament. It included the Independence Party (q.v.), the National Democratic Party (q.v.), members of the 'Iraqi Communist Party (q.v.), and independent politicians. It issued a charter calling for full democratic freedoms, the right to organize politically, the right to organize workers, the abolition of the 1930 Anglo–'Iraqi Treaty (q.v.) and all military alliances, and a rejection of American military aid, which the Front viewed as an attempt to limit 'Iraq's sovereignty. Of the 37 candidates fielded by the National United Patriotic Front, only 11 succeeded in being elected to Parliament. Despite this small number, the National Patriotic Front reflected the significant growth of the opposition in Parliament. Two months after these elections, Parliament was dissolved. With the exception of the Independence Party, which won two seats, opposition parties boycotted the new elections. The government then issued legislation banning political parties, forcing many to pursue their activities clandestinely.

NATIONAL UNITY PARTY (HIZB AL-WIDHA AL-WATANIYYA). A political grouping established by 'Ali Jawdat al-Ayubi (q.v.) after he became prime minister in August 1934. Having dissolved Parliament, forcing new elections, Jawdat hoped to use the party to promote the establishment of new political parties more sympathetic to his positions. The National Unity Party called for understanding and cooperation among the different political parties, with the best elements of the old parties forming new parties. It did not gain much support and disappeared after Jawdat's cabinet resigned in February 1935.

NAWAB, MUZAFFAR, AL- (1934–). One of the leading revolutionary poets in 'Iraq and the Arab world. He was born in Baghdad (q.v.) to an aristocratic Shi'a family of Indian origin that appreciated art and literature (q.v.) as well as music. He showed talent in poetry (q.v.) at an early age. His family suffered through difficult financial times as he was going to college, and during this period, he joined the 'Iraqi Communist Party (ICP) (q.v.). After graduation from the College of Literature, al-Nawab became a teacher. However, he was expelled for political reasons in 1955. He remained unemployed until the 1958 revolution (q.v.), when he was appointed as an inspector at the Ministry of Education. He fled 'Iraq in 1963 as a result of the fighting between the communists and the pan-Arabists. Al-Nawab went to Iran through Basra (q.v.) and has written about the experience in a number of his poems. He was arrested and tortured by SAVAK, the Iranian secret police, before being surrendered to the 'Iraqi government. His death sentence, handed down for one of his poems, was changed to life imprisonment. He escaped from prison by digging a tunnel under the prison and fled to Ahwar, where he joined a communist faction that sought to overthrow the government. Al-Nawab was arrested again and later released. He traveled to many countries, including Syria, Egypt, Lebanon, and Eritrea, where he stayed with the Eritrean rebels, before returning to 'Iraq secretly. He left the ICP in the mid-1970s and followed a more independent line. He completed his graduate work in Paris; traveled to Iran in 1982; went on to Algeria and Libya, where he settled for a while; visited a number of Latin American countries; and finally went back to Syria.

Al-Nawab was deeply involved in the political life of 'Iraq and the Arab world, and he was persecuted, imprisoned, and exiled by various 'Iraqi, Iranian, and Arab governments. His poetry is full of Arab, Islamic, and international leftist and revolutionary symbols, and he tried to incite public emotions against political corruption, decadence, and injustice, in harsh and sometimes profane words. In his early work, he used the dialect of southern 'Iraq because he believed this area was pregnant with revolution. However, because of the limited nature of his audience, he switched to classical language.

NAWSHIRWAN, MUSTAFA (1944–). Kurdish nationalist leader and intellectual from Sulaymaniyya. He joined the Kurdistan Democratic Party (KDP) (q.v.) in 1960, becoming very active in the Kurdish student movement. He allied himself early on with Mulla Mustafa al-Barzani's (q.v.) opponents in the KDP Politburo. After the split in the party, he moved to Baghdad (q.v.) and attended Baghdad University. Nawshirwan published *Razgari* magazine in 1968, which reflected the views of leftist Kurds (q.v.) like Jalal Talabani (q.v.). After the 1970 March Manifesto (q.v.), he helped establish the Toilers of Kurdistan Organization. This would become one of the main forces within Talabani's Patriotic Union of Kurdistan (PUK) (q.v.), established in 1976. Under Talabani's leadership, Nawshirwan became assistant secretary-general of the PUK. After the collapse of the Kurdish revolt in 1975, he helped launch new antigovernment military activity in Kurdistan. Nawshirwan was one of the main organizers of the March 1991 uprisings in Kurdistan. He is the author of a number of books on Kurdish history and the international relations of the Kurdish movement.

NAWWAS, ABU AL- (793–821). One of the best-known Arab poets in history. The Abbasid caliph (q.v.) al-Mu'tazz mentions Abu Nawwas in his anthology of the poets of his time as surpassing all others in metaphors and innovations. His original name was al-Hassan ibn Hani. He attained his peak during the reign of caliph Harun al-Rashid (q.v.). Abu Nawwas was known for his erotic poetry (q.v.) and his poems praising wine, women, and love. He is reported to have been a humorous and witty entertainer.

NAYIF, 'ABD AL-RAZZAQ AL- (1933–1978). A leading military officer and politician from al-Ramadi. He headed military intelligence at the time of the 1968 revolution (q.v.). He reported to President 'Abd al-Rahman 'Arif (q.v.) on all military activities (plots, etc.) and had a great deal of influence with 'Arif due to his direct access. Al-Nayif was one of two military officers who cooperated with the Ba'th Party (q.v.) to overthrow the 'Arif regime. Following the successful takeover on 17 July 1968, he became prime minister and a member of the Revolutionary Command Council (RCC) (q.v.). Disagreements quickly surfaced, however. Al-Nayif was considered pro-Western, and his opposition to socialism branded him a reactionary. On 30 July 1968, he was arrested by a group led by Saddam Husayn (q.v.), dropped from the RCC, and sent to Madrid. He was appointed ambassador in residence abroad and eventually retired in 1970. In 1971, an 'Iraqi court sentenced him to death in absentia. Al-Nayif survived one assassination attempt in 1972 but was shot to death in London in July 1978.

NEW VISION. An avant-garde group of young 'Iraqi painters and artists established in 1969 by Dhia al-'Azzawi, Rafi' al-Nasiri, Salih al-Jumay'i, Hashim al-Samarchi, Isma'il Fattah, and Muhammad Mahr al-Din. They signed a manifesto declaring the need for new and daring ideas based on modern artistic and cultural values.

NOMADIC TRIBES (BEDOUINS). Arab nomads who lived in the desert in the west and southwest regions of 'Iraq. Since prerecorded history, 'Iraq has attracted tribal migrations from the Arabian peninsula and desert as well as from the northern Syrian–'Iraqi desert. All of the major nomadic tribes that existed in 'Iraq at the beginning of the century—the Aniza, Dhafir, and Shammar tribes—were part of the last wave of migration in the 19th century. Most of these tribes are originally believed to have come from the Nejd area in central Arabia. In 1867, nomadic tribes accounted for about 35 percent of 'Iraq's population, but by 1905, the nomadic population had declined to 17 percent. By the late 1940s, it had fallen to less than 5 percent, and has since declined to less than 1 percent of the population.

The drastic decline in the number of nomadic tribesmen can be traced to Ottoman policies in the 19th century. The Ottoman authorities attempted to introduce direct rule of the region beginning in 1831 in an effort to collect taxes. This brought on a policy of subjugation of the tribes, which frequently resisted Ottoman tax collection. Turkish authorities offered financial subsidies and grants as incentives to the Bedouin leaders, in return for pledges to cease raids on other Bedouin camps or Turkish property and to protect the lines of communication across the desert. The most successful method the Turks used was to grant land to tribal chiefs, thus inducing them to settle. Another effective tactic was the favoring of one tribe over another, which subsequently led to fighting among the tribes. This fighting weakened the unity of the tribes as they split into warring factions. When a tribal leader refused to pay taxes or caused trouble locally, the Turks would try to destroy the power of that leader by moving in a tribal leader who was willing to cooperate. The introduction of the Ottoman land code in 1885 also undermined tribal institutions by installing a system of land titles. These land titles changed the lifestyle of the tribes, making them settled cultivators with legal ownership to the land. The land code also established the state as the land granting authority, thus bypassing tribal leaders and undermining their authority.

Each tribe was generally ruled by a shaykh, who was usually succeeded by a member of his family. The shaykh exercised traditional authority in conjunction with a tribal council consisting of his relatives and tribal elders. The council meets in the guest tent of the shaykh when the tribe is encamped. Sometimes there is also a judicial council composed of tribesman with special knowledge of tribal customs and rules. Tribe members gave their full allegiance to their shaykh, even after the nomadic tribes had been settled. Usually the tribe is related by blood or a common ancestor, but some tribes are confederated under one leader. The head of such a confederation is referred to as the *shaykh al-mashayikh* (shaykh of the shaykhs). Although the authority of the shaykhs has declined greatly, they continue to hold some moral influence. Despite the erosion of the historic functions of tribal organization, the absence of alternative social links has helped preserve the tribal character of individual and group relations, and in many cases supremacy is still given to tribal values. Tribal values and influence had declined in recent decades, but Saddam cultivated the tribes for security reasons following his confrontations with Iran and the U.S.-led coalition. The United States sought to improve ties with the tribes before and after the 2003 war. *See also* KHAMSA; SETTLED TRIBES.

– O –

OIL. Oil was discovered in 'Iraq on 15 October 1927 when the 'Iraqi Petroleum Company's (IPC) (q.v.) first major well came in at Baba Gurgur, located in the Kirkuk (q.v.) field; this was the first major field discovered in the Middle East. 'Iraqi oil is high quality and inexpensive to produce, offering a wide profit margin. 'Iraq's proven oil reserves are estimated at 112 billion barrels, second only to those of Saudi Arabia. Due to a combination of factors, much of 'Iraq has yet to undergo exploratory drilling, so its actual reserves may be nearly double the current figure. Its main producing fields are Kirkuk (q.v.), Jambur, and Bai Hussan in the northern part of the country, and Rumaila and Zubair in the south. Only 20 percent of 'Iraq's 70 fields have been developed, adding to the enormous potential for substantially greater exploitation of its oil. However, the oil industry has suffered from the combined effects of several wars and UN sanctions (q.v.). Production fell from a high of 3.5 million barrels per day (mbd) in 1991 to the current capacity of 2.5 mbd. Its facilities, from pipelines to refineries, have significantly deteriorated due to lack of spare parts and poor maintenance. Beginning in December 2000, 'Iraq was able to use revenues from the oil-for-food program (OFP) to purchase necessary parts and equipment. Oil infrastructure repair will cost an estimated $5 billion, and production increases are likely to be small even then.

'Iraq granted an oil concession to the 'Iraqi Petroleum Company, a consortium of American, British, French, and private interests, in 1925. Prolonged negotiations over new concession terms led the Qasim (q.v.) government to pass Public Law 80 in 1961 (q.v.), which expropriated 99.5 percent of the concession area, essentially leaving the IPC with only the areas it had under production. Significantly, this placed the rich and as of yet-undeveloped field at Rumaila under 'Iraqi control. The Iraqi National Oil Company, which had been created in 1964, was given exclusive rights to develop Rumaila under the provisions of Public Law 97 of 1967 (q.v.). In 1972, again during a dispute with the IPC, 'Iraq nationalized most of its oil industry, a process it completed in December 1975.

'Iraqi production reached its peak in 1979, when it produced roughly 3.5 mbd. Following its invasion of Iran in 1980 and the subsequent loss of its offshore oil terminals in the Persian Gulf, 'Iraq's production slumped to 900,000 barrels/day (b/d) in 1981, and it dropped even further with Syria's closure of the Banias pipeline in April 1982. A combination of upgrading existing pipelines, building new lines, and trucking oil through Jordan and Turkey allowed 'Iraq to regain much of its production capacity by the end of the Iran–'Iraq war (q.v.) in August 1988. During the first six months of 1990, 'Iraq was producing slightly over 3 mb/d, and its production capacity had reached 4.5 mb/d. The UN sanctions effectively halted the export of 'Iraqi oil between August 1990 and December 1996, although some sales were made to Jordan, Iran, and Turkey. Beginning in December 1996, 'Iraq exported 3.4 billion barrels of oil through the OFP, and a lucrative black market thrived, although the revenue from the northern trade with Turkey went to the Kurds (q.v.) and not to Baghdad.

'Iraq's first major pipeline was completed by the 'Iraqi Petroleum Company in 1934; the 12-inch parallel lines run from Kirkuk to Haditha and then to Tripoli, Lebanon (distance = 530 miles), and Haifa, Israel (620 miles). After World War II, parallel 16-inch lines were built; because of the 1948 Arab–Israeli War, the 16-inch line to Haifa was never completed, and use of the 12-inch line was discontinued. In April 1952, a 30-inch line was completed from Kirkuk to Banias, Syria (555 miles), with a 900,000 b/d capacity. The Tripoli spur was closed from 1975 until 1981 due to the Lebanese civil war, and the Banias line has been subject to several closures as well, usually during disputes over transit fees. Syria's support for Iran in the Iran–'Iraq war led it to close the Banias line in April 1982, and the line remained in disuse until November 2000, when 'Iraq began exporting oil to Syria. In October 1976, 'Iraq completed work on the so-called strategic pipeline, which links Kirkuk and Basra (545 kilometers) (q.v.), giving it the option of exporting Kirkuk crude from the Persian Gulf as well as from the Mediterranean. The strategic line can handle 900,000 b/d. 'Iraq officially opened another Mediterranean line in January 1977; the 40-inch line runs from Kirkuk to Ceyhan in Turkey (981 kilometers). The pipeline's initial capacity of 800,000 to 900,000 b/d has since been expanded to 1.6 mbd. With the closure of the Banias line, Iraq for several years was forced to rely almost exclusively on the Ceyhan line to export its oil. Turkey closed the pipeline in August 1990 in response to Iraq's invasion of Kuwait (q.v.), although it subsequently reopened to handle exports under the OFP.

The outbreak of the Iran–'Iraq war and 'Iraq's subsequent loss of much of its export capacity led it to put in motion several new pipeline projects to the Red Sea. IPSA 1, completed in 1985 with a capacity of 500,000 b/d, is a spur line from Basra to the Saudi Petroline, which runs from eastern Saudi Arabia to the Red Sea port of Yanbu. IPSA 2 officially opened on 19 September 1989 (960 kilometers) and replaces IPSA 1; the 56-inch pipeline runs parallel to Petroline and ends at an 'Iraqi complex south of Yanbu that includes an offshore loading terminal. At the time of its closure by Saudi Arabia in August 1990, IPSA 2 had a capacity of 1.6 mbd. The pipelines remain closed.

Prior to 1990, 'Iraq had three principal refineries and six other small plants, giving it a total refining capacity of 650,000 b/d. Its largest refinery, Salaheddin, was located at the Baiji complex; completed in 1983, it had a 290,000 b/d capacity. The Basra refinery, completed in 1974, had a capacity of 142,000 b/d; and the Doura refinery, completed in 1955, could handle 92,000 b/d. The Basra refinery suffered immense damage during the Iran–'Iraq war, and it did not reopen until January 1989. All three of the major refineries were bombed during the Desert Storm (q.v.) campaign; allied commanders reported that over three-quarters of 'Iraq's refining capability had been destroyed. However, on 15 April 1991, 'Iraqi officials announced that the refineries at Baiji and Doura were back in operation. Doura was operating at full capacity by mid-May, and Baiji reached capacity in June 1991.

'Iraq's two offshore oil terminals, Mina al-Bakr and Khor al-Amaya, are located in the Persian Gulf. Both are deep-water terminals located roughly 25 miles offshore, connected to Fao by 48-inch underwater pipelines. Mina al-Bakr had a capacity of 2.7 mb/d at the start of the Iran–'Iraq war, and Khor al-Amaya could handle 1.8 mb/d. The terminals were put out of action in the early days of fighting, forcing 'Iraq to rely solely on its pipeline network to export its oil. When the war ended, 'Iraq moved quickly to repair these facilities. Work on Mina al-Bakr commenced in March 1989, and exports resumed in June 1989, with the facility operating at 50 percent of its prewar capacity; by August 1990, the repairs had nearly been completed. Mina al-Bakr was bombed during Desert Storm and once again heavily damaged.

'Iraq has three major ports, Basra, Khor al-Zubair, and Umm Qasr, all with access to the Persian Gulf. At the time of the Iran–'Iraq war, the biggest port was Basra, which accesses the Persian Gulf through the Shatt al-Arab (q.v.) waterway. Basra had 15 berths with four more under construction, but it has been inoperative since September 1980. Some 75 ships were trapped in the Shatt al-Arab, along with unexploded ordinance and other debris. The issue of who has sovereignty over the Shatt al-Arab helped deadlock the negotiations between Iraq and Iran from August 1988 until August 1990 and prevented dregging operations, which will take one year to complete, from commencing. Despite 'Iraq and Iran coming to terms, the Shatt al-Arab is still unusable.

The controversy over the Shatt al-Arab led 'Iraq to concentrate its developmental efforts on its two other ports, Khor al-Zubair and Umm Qasr, after the Iran–'Iraq war. Access to both ports is through the Khor Abdullah channel, which was built in the late 1970s; the Kuwaiti islands of Warba and Bubiyan dominate the mouth of the channel, a situation that has caused considerable tension between 'Iraq and Kuwait and contributed to 'Iraq's decision to invade Kuwait in 1990. In the months before the cease-fire was reached in the Iran–'Iraq war, 'Iraq had begun a secret clearance program of the Khor Abdullah channel. Thus, within hours of the cease-fire announcement, 'Iraq sent vessels to both ports, a signal of its commitment to regaining an export capacity through the Persian Gulf. It also undertook an ambitious $900 million developmental program, including deepening the Khor Abdullah channel and constructing a new dockyard at Khor al-Zubair and 13 new berths at Umm Qasr, which had previously been a naval facility. However, after Operation Desert Storm, the United Nations redrew the boundary between 'Iraq and Kuwait, moving the border several miles to the north. This resulted in the loss of part of Umm Qasr for 'Iraq, and the demarcation remains controversial. Oil production declined following the 1990–1991 war and the sanctions regime. After the 2003 war, 'Iraqi production declined further as a result of the looting of oil facilities and sabotage. The Coalition Provisional Authority (CPA) (q.v.) is seeking to upgrade and privatize the oil industry. *See also* ECONOMY.

OIL-FOR-FOOD PROGRAM. *See* SANCTIONS.

ORGANIZATION OF ISLAMIC AMAL. Islamic opposition movement led by Muhammad Taqi Mudarrisi, Ayatollah Muhammad Shirazi, and Shaykh Muhsin al-Hussayni. It has a large membership within the Supreme Assembly for the Islamic Revolution in 'Iraq (SAIRI) (q.v.), but it believes that SAIRI has too much authority.

– P –

PACHACHI, 'ADNAN (1923–). Member of the 'Iraqi Governing Council (IGC) (q.v.) and a former 'Iraqi foreign minister from 1965–1967 under the Arif government, he served as 'Iraq's ambassador to the United Nations in the 1960s. Pachachi belongs to a prominent Sunni family whose members play major roles in the politics of modern 'Iraq. He has worked in the Persian Gulf as an advisor to the government of the United Arab Emirates and is also a leader of the Independent 'Iraqi Democrats Group. An elder statesman, he is backed, respected, and supported by some of the Arab Gulf states. Pachachi formed the Independent Democratic Movement with hopes of creating a nonreligious, democratic government. He was in exile for 32 years.

PACHACHI, HAMDI AL- (1886–1948). Prime minister during the monarchy. He was born to a well-to-do family in Baghdad (q.v.). He studied law at the Royal School in Istanbul, graduating in 1909. He taught at the Baghdad Law College from 1913 to 1916. During his stay in Istanbul, he joined Jam'yat al-Ahd, the Covenant Society (q.v.) and became active in the Arab nationalist movement. Upon his return to Baghdad, he cooperated with the nationalists, who were demanding the decentralization of the Ottoman Empire. As a result of his activities during the 1920 Revolt (q.v.) against the British, al-Pachachi was arrested and exiled to Hanja, an island in the Persian Gulf. After his release, he continued to take part in anti-British activities. In 1925, he dropped his opposition to the British and began cooperating with 'Abd al-Muhsin al-Sa'dun (q.v.). Al-Pachachi served as minister of *waqf* (q.v.) in one of al-Sa'dun's cabinets (1925–1926). He then retired from politics for many years. A large landowner, he concentrated on business matters and agriculture. In 1935, al-Pachachi was elected deputy to Parliament, but he did not play a major role. He held the portfolio of Social Welfare in 1941 and was elected president of the Chamber of Commerce in 1943. Al-Pachachi served as prime minister twice (1944–1946) and later was appointed minister of foreign affairs (1948). He died during his tenure as foreign minister in March 1948.

PACHACHI, MUZAHIM AL- (1890–1982). Prime minister and diplomat during the monarchy. He graduated from the Baghdad School of Law. He organized the Arab nationalist Cultural Club in Baghdad (q.v.) in 1912; its members included T'alib al-Naqib (q.v.), Hamdi al-Pachachi (q.v.), and Muhammad Ridha (q.v.). He worked for the British occupation forces after they entered Baghdad in 1917, first as a translator and then as a lawyer. In 1924, al-Pachachi was elected as a member of the Constituent Assembly, which had the responsibility of drafting the 'Iraqi constitution. He held a number of cabinet and diplomatic positions. He served as minister of works (1924–1925) before becoming a member of Parliament (1925–1927). He was appointed ambassador to Britain (1927–1928) and briefly held the post of minister of interior (1930). Al-Pachachi opposed the 1930 Anglo–'Iraqi Treaty (q.v.) because it failed to meet nationalist demands. He held a succession of ambassadorial posts: ambassador to the League of Nations (1933–1935), ambassador to Italy (1935–1939), and ambassador to France (1939–1942). During the occupation of France in World War II, al-Pachachi stayed in Switzerland. He became active in the 1930s and 1940s in pro-Palestinian activities and opposed the 1948 United Nations' truce in Palestine. In June 1948, he became prime minister, but his cabinet fell in January 1949. He was later appointed deputy prime minister (1949–1950) and minister of foreign affairs (1949–1950). Al-Pachachi opposed the 1951 law that allowed 'Iraqi Jews (q.v.) to leave the country, although he himself left 'Iraq in 1951, returning after the 1958 revolution (q.v.). His son, 'Adnan, later served as a diplomat and cabinet minister.

PACHACHI, NADIM AL- (1914–1976). Cabinet minister and technocrat during the monarchy. He was born to an old, wealthy, property-owning Baghdad (q.v.) family. He received a doctorate in petroleum engineering and worked in the Romanian oil (q.v.) fields as a young man. He became the director-general of petroleum affairs. Al-Pachachi was named secretary-general of the Organization of Petroleum Producing Countries and was later appointed minister of state (1953). He served as minister of the economy (1952–1957), minister of finance (1954–1957), and acting minister of construction (1957). He was arrested following the 1958 revolution (q.v.) and left 'Iraq for Libya and then Abu Dhabi, where he became an adviser to these governments. From January 1971 to December 1972, he served as OPEC's secretary-general. Al-Pachachi was considered one of the most brilliant figures in prerevolutionary politics and an accomplished technocrat.

PARTY OF PROGRESS (AL-TAQADDUM). A conservative political group organized in 1925 by 'Abd al-Muhsin al-Sa'dun (q.v.), it was one of the first 'Iraqi parties to display pro-British sympathies. Al-Sa'dun formed the party to strengthen his position as prime minister following the defeat of his candidate, Hikmat Sulayman (q.v.), for president of Parliament by Rashid 'Ali al-Kaylani (q.v.). The party lent support to the cabinets of al-Sa'dun (1925–1926, 1928–1929) and Ja'far al-'Askari (1926–1928) (q.v.).

PATRIOTIC UNION OF KURDISTAN (PUK). Kurdish political party founded in July 1975. The PUK was established after the collapse of the Kurdish rebellion led by Mulla Mustafa Barzani (q.v.), by Kurds (q.v.) who had broken with al-Barzani. Three groups comprised the PUK. The first group represented Barzani's traditional Kurdish opponents who had established the PUK Preparatory Committee in June 1975 under the leadership of Jalal Talabani (q.v.). This group included old members of the Kurdistan Democratic Party (KDP) (q.v.) who had broken with Barzani in the early 1960s, led by Talabani and Ibrahim Ahmad. The other two components were 'Iraqi Komala and the Socialist Movement of Kurdistan (qq.v.). These groups tried to reorganize and to reestablish antigovernment Kurdish nationalist activities. Initially the PUK was more of a front or coalition group, although Talabani enjoyed widespread support and greatly influenced the movement.

The PUK is generally considered to be pragmatic, and in the past it demonstrated a strong leftist, anti-Western, anti-imperialist, anti-Zionist and antitribal line. The party entered into a bloody confrontation with the KDP in the late 1970s. One clash in 1978 resulted in the death or arrest of hundreds of PUK leaders and supporters. This established the clear supremacy of the KDP. In 1983, while the KDP was fighting the regime, the PUK entered into negotiations with Baghdad (q.v.) and reached a cease-fire agreement. When the regime failed to implement an agreement it had signed with the PUK in 1985, the party began military operations against the government. By the end of the Iran–'Iraq war (q.v.), the PUK had almost as many *pesh mergas* (q.v.) as the KDP. In June 1988, the PUK joined with the other main Kurdish opposition groups to form the 'Iraqi Kurdistan Front, an effort to unite the Kurdish movement in pursuit of autonomy for Kurdistan. Talabani traveled widely on behalf of the Front. In the May 1992 elections, the PUK finished a close second to the KDP (with over 49 percent of the vote), and Talabani shares a leading role with the KDP's Mas'ud Barzani (q.v.). The PUK draws much of its backing from the Sulaymaniyya area and from young, urban, and intellectual elements. The PUK and KDP were involved in serious clashes in the spring and summer of 1994, which left hundreds dead. The PUK also engaged in clashes with the Turkish Kurdish Workers Party (PKK) and with the Kurdistan Islamic Movement (q.v.). *See also* KUWAIT, INVASION OF; MARCH MANIFESTO.

PENITENTS. A group of Shi'is (q.v.) in 'Iraq who led a revolt against the Umayyads in 685. The Penitents wanted to atone for their failure to protect Husayn at Karbala (q.v.) by avenging his death. Several thousand warriors attacked Ubayd Allah ibn Ziyad, the commander who had ordered the murder of Husayn, at 'Ayn al-Warda near the Syrian–'Iraqi border in 685. The Umayyads overwhelmed the Penitents in a fierce battle. Some Penitents who fled during the fighting returned and requested martyrdom so that they could enter Paradise; they were obliged by the Umayyads. The remnants of the group retreated to Kufa. After their defeat in 685, a popular movement began to crystallize among the supporters of the House of 'Ali in 'Iraq with the sole purpose of avenging the blood of Husayn. Led by al-Mukhtar, the survivors of 'Ayn al-Warda overthrew the Umayyad governor of Kufa and took control of the city. In 686, Caliph 'Abd al-Malik sent an army under the command of Ubayd Allah to suppress al-Mukhtar's rebellion. Al-Mukhtar's forces, led by Ashtar, took Ubayd Allah's army by surprise, and 300 Shi'i fighters succeeded in crossing the Umayyad lines. They fought their way to Ubayd Allah's headquarters and killed him. Al-Muhktar received his severed head in Kufa where a few years before 'Ubayd Allah had received the severed head of Husayn. Having revenged Husayn, the Shi'i forces occupied all of northern 'Iraq. However, they did not show much support or sympathy for al-Mukhtar's desire to become caliph (q.v.), perhaps due to the fact that he was not a descendant of 'Ali. Al-Mukhtar was defeated by another contender to the caliphate, 'Abd Allah bin al-Zubayr, in 687. *See also* HAJJAJ BIN YUSUF, AL-.

PEOPLE'S GROUP. *See* AHALI, JAM'AT AL-.

PEOPLE'S PARTY (HIZB AL-SHA'B). A leftist political party led by 'Aziz Sharif that began as a clandestine organization in 1942 and obtained a license in 1946. Following its suppression by the Arshad al-'Umari (q.v.) government later that same year, it continued its activities clandestinely. The party proved to be one of the most outspoken political organizations against British policy and 'Iraq's relations with Britain. It coupled hostility against British imperialism with sympathy toward the Soviet Union. 'Aziz Sharif lost his citizenship because of his opposition to the regime's policies and he was heavily criticized for acting in the interests of a foreign country. The party attracted support in the cities, appealing to those who found the monarchy oppressive and subservient to Western interests. It issued an official daily paper, *al-Watan* (The Homeland). In 1948, it participated in al-Wathba (The Uprising) (q.v.), joining the Committee for National Cooperation (q.v.). Its members included Tawfiq Munir, 'Amir 'Abdullah, Jirjis Fathallah, and Salim 'Issa. Many of its members later joined the 'Iraqi Communist Party (q.v.).

PESH MERGAS. Kurdish warriors. The term means "self-sacrificers" or "those who face death." It is popularly used to denote the Kurdish nationalist forces that have fought against numerous Iraqi governments, particularly since the 1961 revolt.

PISHDARI, BABAKR AL- (1937–). A Kurdish nationalist activist. He broke with Mulla Mustafa al-Barzani (q.v.) in 1973 over al-Barzani's opposition to the government's autonomy plans for Kurdistan. A lawyer by profession, he served in a number of administrative and governmental positions: district governor of Qala Diza, governor of Sulaymaniyya (1974–1975), and minister of labor and social affairs (1977–1979). Al-Pishdari served as a member of the Higher Popular and Nationalist Committee, edited the magazine *Labor and Social Development*, and was president of the Arab Labor Organization. He has represented 'Iraq at various international organizations.

POETRY. The beginnings of early 'Iraqi poetry are found in the Bedouin culture, which existed before the advent of Islam (q.v.). Idealistic themes such as simplicity, courage, and independence were common to the Bedouin lifestyle, but with the introduction of Islam and the advent of the Abbasid caliphate in 740, culture became more centered in the towns. Poetry reflected the wishes of the Abbasids to build and strengthen the Islamic community around a strong urban center. Abbasid contributions to poetry included the romantic epic and a style that allowed the full elaboration of mystical themes, most of which were based on verses in the Koran (q.v.). Koranic verses also began to be found in architecture, and it was common to see the exterior and interior walls of buildings adorned with calligraphy. The art of calligraphy is important in itself, but it also served to make poetry not only a spoken treasure but also a visual form of art. The use of calligraphy and poetry together was established by Ibn Muqla, and in the 10th century A.D. this method of verse and art reached its height. Text and image became inseparable. Islamic mysticism, or Sufism (q.v.), also influenced the early developments of 'Iraqi poetry by introducing a poetic method whose repeated verses and sounds would enable the listener or reader to go beyond the immediate surroundings and reach a higher level of being. Sufism stresses the inner relationship between man and God, although this relationship does not ignore the outer or exoteric reflections of God. The recitation of poetry in such a repetitive way enabled the reader to reach a desired state of ecstasy. In modern 'Iraq, however, Sufi poets are not widely known and their style is not as much in use. After the Mongol invasion of 'Iraq in 1258 A.D. poetry returned to earlier bedouin themes.

The traditional poetic form typical not only in 'Iraq but in the Islamic world as well is the *diwan*. The diwan is a collection of poems, dealing with various moral and ethical lessons, philosophy, politics and metaphysics, and Koranic commentary. It could also include commemorative poems for wedding ceremonies and reverences of the prophet Muhammad or various governors and leaders of the time. Famous 19th-century poets writing in this traditional style include 'Abd al-Baqi, 'Abd al-Ghaffar al-Akhras, Haydar al-Hilli, and Muhammad Sa'id al-Habburi (q.v.).

Modern poetry in 'Iraq draws on its traditional foundation but also strongly follows critical social and political issues of the day. Unlike the traditional form, modern poetry cannot be confined to a certain framework or style; many different styles of poetry developed in 'Iraqi in the 19th century. In the early 20th century, poetic form remained traditional. However 'Iraqi society witnessed tremendous changes: the collapse of the Ottoman Empire and the imposition of the British mandate. After World War I, 'Iraqi nationalism became more anti-European, and in the spirit of Arab emancipation several revolts were led against the British occupation. Eventually 'Iraq achieved its independence in 1932. Earlier poetry employed bedouin themes and was concerned with form and style, but the purpose of poetry during this period of great social and political change was to inform people of the ongoing and dynamic situation in 'Iraq. This movement is in large part attributed to two of 'Iraq's most famous poets, Ma'ruf al-Rasafi (1875–1945) and Jamil Sidiq al-Zahawi (1863–1936).

During and after World War II, the poetic landscape changed once again, although the traditional form still maintained some small appeal with the younger generations. The content and style of Western literature proved a major influence during this period. The tumultuous events of revolution and war have remained important poetic themes from the 1950s to the present day, including predominant ideas such as 'Iraqi national identity, pan-Arabism, and socialism. 'Iraq has produced in recent years a number of well-known poets and pioneers in free verse poetry. The Iran–'Iraq war (q.v.) in the 1980s stressed themes of death, destruction, sorrow, and loss, as many of these poets themselves had taken part in the war.

POPULAR ALLIANCE OF SOCIALIST KURDISTAN (PASOK). Kurdish party established in the 1960s that has tended to be more nationalist than socialist. More or less a continuation of the Kajik Organization to Free Kurdistan, it was led by Shwan Karkuki. The party was reorganized in 1975 and placed under the leadership of Azad Mustafa, who died in 1982. It joined the Kurdish National Front in 1985. In the May 1992 elections it received less than 1 percent of the votes. In August 1992, it merged with the Socialist Party of Kurdistan and the Kurdistan Popular Democratic Party to form the Unity Party of Kurdistan (qq.v.).

POPULAR REFORM GROUP (JAM'IAT AL-ISLAH AL-SHA'BI). A nationalist, progressive party established in 1936. Most of its members emerged from the al-Ahali (q.v.) group. Its objectives were to achieve political, economic, and social reform, including agricultural reform and industrialization, which would end exploitation and modernize 'Iraqi society; to achieve democratic freedoms; to establish stronger ties with other political parties; and to strengthen inter-Arab relations, particularly among Arab popular groups.

POPULAR RESISTANCE FORCES. In an effort to achieve popular support for the regime, the Ba'th Party (q.v.) organized units of young men inspired by Ba'thist principles and trained them in military techniques to maintain public order and other tasks for the sake of the security of the regime. The Popular Resistance Forces was one such unit organized in 1963.

PORTSMOUTH TREATY. Signed on 15 January 1948 following eight months of negotiations, the Portsmouth Treaty was meant to revise the unpopular 1930 Anglo–'Iraqi Treaty (q.v.). The new agreement eliminated the provision calling for close consultation with Britain in foreign policy; it called for the evacuation of British troops from 'Iraqi soil, although 'Iraq pledged to continue consulting British military advisers; it established a Joint Defense Board to discuss the common defense interests of the two countries; and Britain's use of the Habbaniya and Shuaybi air bases became dependent on an invitation from 'Iraq. These changes addressed most of the issues criticized by the nationalists. However, when the treaty was made public in Baghdad (q.v.) in January 1948, it caused an uprising known as *al-Wathba* (q.v.). The uprising led to the repudiation of the treaty and the resignation of Salih Jabr's (q.v.) government. *See also* COMMITTEE FOR NATIONAL COOPERATION.

PRESIDENT. Head of the 'Iraqi state and commander in chief of the armed forces. The president is the chief executive authority. He exercises this authority either directly or through the cabinet. He is responsible for maintaining 'Iraq's independence, territorial integrity, security, and preserving the people's rights and freedoms. He is entrusted with implementing the constitution and the laws. The president has the authority to appoint and dismiss his vice presidents and ministers and to supervise and coordinate the ministries and other public institutions. Saddam Husayn (q.v.) was president from 1979–2003. *See also* NATIONAL ASSEMBLY; REVOLUTIONARY COMMAND COUNCIL.

PROCES VERBAUX. The *proces verbaux*, or the proceedings of the Delimitation Commission established by the 1913 Constantinople Protocol (q.v.), affirmed the 1913 agreement. It entails numerous subsidiary protocols and maps recording the boundary line between the Ottoman Empire and Persia. It was never ratified. *See also* FRONTIER TREATY OF 1937.

PROTOCOL TO THE 1922 ANGLO–'IRAQI TREATY. Even before the 1922 Anglo–'Iraqi Treaty (q.v.) came into force, its provisions were altered.

On 30 April 1923, 'Iraq and Britain signed a protocol: the 1922 treaty would terminate upon 'Iraq becoming a member of the League of Nations and, in any case, not later than four years from the ratification of peace with Turkey. The reduction in the treaty's operative period from 20 to 4 years reflected both 'Iraq's intense dislike of the mandatory relationship and Britain's desire to cut its financial and manpower commitment. *See also* ANGLO–'IRAQ TREATY OF 1926.

– Q –

QADDURI, FAKHRI (1932–). Economist and educator. He became active in the Ba'th Party (q.v.) in the early 1950s when he attended the College of Commerce and Economics. He became the secretary-general of the Ba'th in 1953. He served as minister of the economy from 1968 to 1972.

QADHI. Term meaning "a judge." It was initially used to refer to individuals who dispensed justice in accordance with Islamic law (*shari'a*). In recent times, the term has come to mean a judge who dispenses the civil law of the state.

QADISSIYA, AL-. An 'Iraqi governorate and the site of battle in 637 between an Arab Muslim army and the army of the Persian Sassanid dynasty. Although not the final battle between the two, it marked the beginning of the decline of the Persian Empire and its inclusion in the Islamic–Arab caliphate. Saddam Husayn (q.v.) frequently referred to the Iran–'Iraq war (q.v.) as his Qadissiya, an attempt to play up the Arab–Persian nature of the conflict. The Sassanids had established a client state in 'Iraq, and a number of minor battles occurred between the Arabs and the Persians for control of the area. Caliph Abu Bakr (r. 632–634) sent an Arab army to 'Iraq under the leadership of al-Muthanna that imposed Arab control over the tribes of the southern Euphrates (q.v.) and over the regions of al-Hira and al-Anbar. But the Arab army was pushed back to the edge of the desert when the new Sassanid ruler Yazdagird sent an army of 100,000 men into the area. When internal rivalries within Persia began to weaken the Sassanid dynasty, al-Muthanna told caliph 'Umar (r. 634–644) that the time was opportune to launch another war. 'Umar sent new forces to the region under the command of Sa'd bin Abi Waqqas. He led the Arab forces after the death of al-Muthanna to al-Qadissiya, known as the gate to 'Iraq. There they met the Persian forces under the leadership of Rustum, who had an army of 30,000, while the Muslims had 8,000. Rustum offered aid to the Arab army if it went back, but it refused and called on him to submit to the new religion or fight. The battle lasted for three days, and Rustum himself was killed, demoralizing his supporters. The Arabs continued their attacks, and by 643, they were able to occupy Persia.

Al-Qadissiya governorate is one of the most important centers for industry and agriculture (qq.v.). Many agricultural and irrigation projects are undertaken in the province, which is also known for the production of dairy products, rubber, and cotton textiles.

QADRI, TAHSIN (1894–199?). Politician and diplomat during the monarchy. He was born in Ba'albeck, Lebanon, and graduated from the Military College in Istanbul as a second lieutenant in 1914. He served in the Ottoman army but deserted during World War I to join the Arab Revolt. Qadri rose to become Faysal's (q.v.) aide de camp. He followed Faysal to 'Iraq and played an important role in the conduct of 'Iraqi domestic politics until Faysal's death in 1933. He was appointed master of ceremonies at the Royal Palace in 1931. In 1936, he transferred to the ministry of foreign affairs and represented 'Iraq in a number of countries.

QASIM, 'ABD AL-KARIM (1914–1963). Military officer and ruler of 'Iraq from 1958 to 1963. He was born to an Arab family in Baghdad (q.v.). He completed one year of secondary education before entering the military, although he later completed his secondary school work. He worked as a teacher in 1931 and became an officer in the military school in 1932. He joined the Staff Officers in 1933. Qasim was cited for courage during the fight against the 1943–1945 Kurdish uprisings. He served as the deputy to the commander of the 'Iraqi forces in Jordan during the 1948 Arab–Israeli war and commanded a battalion himself. In 1950, he was sent to Britain for further training. A member of the Free Officers (q.v.), Qasim was one of the leaders of the 1958 revolution (q.v.). He took power after the overthrow of the monarchy, serving as prime minister, commander in chief, and acting minister of defense.

His humble background and life in the countryside led Qasim to be concerned about exploitation by both foreign powers and the wealthy. He believed that reform was necessary to alleviate the suffering of the poor and that the only way this could be done was to rid the country of British imperialism and the dependent, backward monarchy. Qasim was also influenced by the ideas of Bakr Sidqi (q.v.), who emphasized unity and cooperation, and the Turkish leader Mustafa Kemal (Ataturk). A charismatic ruler, he was able to win the confidence of many people because of his numerous achievements and because of his independence and honesty. He was able to maintain himself in power by removing rivals from positions of power and by manipulating the media. Qasim ruled supreme in Baghdad from 1958 to 1963; he was known in the media as "The Sole Leader."

During his rule, Qasim introduced important agricultural reforms, including the Agrarian Reform Law of 1958, which instituted a land reform program. He also took steps toward the eventual nationalization of 'Iraqi oil (q.v.). His regime and the 'Iraqi Petroleum Company (IPC) (q.v.) negotiated from August 1960 until October 1961 over terms for a new relationship that would have given 'Iraq a greater share of control over the oil industry. Following the breakdown of the talks, Baghdad declared Law 80 (q.v.), which expropriated 99.5 percent of the IPC's concession. Qasim withdrew 'Iraq from the Baghdad Pact (q.v.) and diligently tried to keep 'Iraq outside Gamal 'Abd al-Nasir's influence. Consequently, he allied himself with opponents of union with the United Arab Republic. To combat the influence of the Arab nationalists, Qasim leaned heavily on the communists for support, especially during the rebellion led by 'Abd al-Wahhab al-Shawwaf (q.v.) in March 1959. Hundreds of people were killed by the communists in the aftermath of this revolt in Mawsil (q.v.). Qasim confronted the Kurdish rebellion in 1961, and fighting continued in Kurdistan until his overthrow in 1963. Following Kuwait's independence in 1961, Qasim claimed Kuwait belonged to 'Iraq. This claim met with widespread opposition, including from the Arab League, and Britain landed troops in Kuwait to deal with the threat. Qasim's refusal to recognize Kuwait's independence led to Baghdad's isolation in the diplomatic community. (*See also* 'IRAQI–KUWAITI AGREEMENT OF 1963.)

Qasim was overthrown by a group including Ba'thists, Arab nationalists, and conservative noncommunist officers on 8 February 1963. He was arrested on the following day, court-martialed, and executed by firing squad. His regime collapsed because Qasim had become more and more dictatorial and isolated. He was an ardent 'Iraqi nationalist and had a genuine commitment to the poor. He in general displayed a tolerant attitude toward 'Iraq's various ethnic and religious groups. A private and cautious individual, Qasim used close relatives and friends as advisers, including his infamous cousin Mahdawi. *See also* 'ABD AL-SALAM 'ARIF.

QAYSI, RIYADH AL- (1939–). Diplomat, lawyer, and academic from Baghdad (q.v.). He studied at al-Mustansiriya University and the College of Law and Politics at the University of Baghdad, where he received his L.L.M. degree. In 1966, he received a Ph.D. in international law from the University of London. Al-Qaysi taught law at both the University of Baghdad and al-Mustansiriya University before joining the Ministry of Foreign Affairs. He later headed the ministry's legal department and was involved in the 1975–1976 boundary negotiations with Iran. In 1982, he became 'Iraq's ambassador to the United Nations. In 1985, al-Qaysi returned to Baghdad to become the director of international conferences and organizations at the Ministry of Foreign Affairs.

QAZZAZ, SA'ID AL- (?–1959). Cabinet official under the monarchy. He was governor of Mawsil (q.v.) during the late 1940s and early 1950s. Considered an able and straightforward administrator, he served as minister of social affairs from December 1952 to January 1953, before becoming minister of interior in March 1954, a position he held until July 1958 with only a brief hiatus in 1957–1958. After the 1958 revolution (q.v.), al-Qazzaz was arrested and gave a defiant speech in the Mahdawi Court even though he was surrounded by a mob of opponents waving ropes and threatening to drag him into the streets. He was hanged in 1959 to please the communists.

QUSARY, KHALID AL-. (?–707). A governor of 'Iraq under the Umayyads. He was famed for the elegance and correctness of his oratory and for his generosity. His father was an associate of the prophet Muhammad, and his mother was a Christian (q.v.). Doubts were raised about his religious beliefs because he built a church for his mother to pray in. He was deposed and tortured to death by his successor, Abu Yusuf al-Thaqafy.

– R –

RADHI, HUSAYN AL- (SALAM 'ADIL) (?–1963). Prominent leader of the 'Iraqi Communist Party (q.v.) in 1956. He was killed in the 1963 coup that ended 'Abd al-Karim Qasim's (q.v.) regime.

RAHHAL, KHALID AL-. A well-known painter. He came from a poor family, and his works reflect this background, emphasizing elements of ordinary life. He spent considerable time in the streets of Baghdad (q.v.) to become acquainted with the culture and life of average people. He studied sculpture in Rome and has completed works in stone, plastic, and metal. One of his stone sculptures of a woman and child was erected in Baghdad National Park.

RAMADHAN. A month of fasting for devout Muslims, where eating, drinking, or smoking are forbidden from dawn until dusk.

RAMADHAN, TAHA YASIN (1936–). Ba'thist politician and close associate of Saddam Husayn (q.v.). He was born and educated in Mawsil (q.v.). He graduated from the Military College and was commissioned as a second lieutenant just before the 1958 revolution (q.v.). During this period, he joined the Ba'th Party (q.v.) and became active in party affairs. In 1959, Ramadhan was arrested and dismissed from the military for his Ba'thist leanings. He returned to the military after the 1963 coup brought the Ba'th back into power, but following 'Abd al-Salam 'Arif's (q.v.) countercoup in November 1963, he was again dismissed and placed under house arrest for two years. In 1966, he was elected to the Regional Command (q.v.) and became a close associate of Saddam. Working in the party's military section, Ramadhan was one of the leading figures during the 1968 revolution (q.v.). With the Ba'th in power again in 1968, he returned to the army as a special aide to the chief of staff of the party's military committee, where he played an important role in ensuring army loyalty to the regime. He became a member of the Revolutionary Command Council (RCC) (q.v.) in 1969. Ramadhan chaired the RCC's Arab Affairs Bureau and the Ba'th's Military Affairs Bureau, which sought to ensure the party's control over the military. In 1973, he headed the special court set up to try the leaders of the failed coup attempt by Nazim Kazzar (q.v.); 37 accused plotters were executed and 15 imprisoned. From 1976 to 1979, Ramadhan served as minister of housing and construction. In 1976, he also became head of the Popular Army, the auxiliary military force of the Ba'th entrusted with ensuring the survival of the regime.

After Saddam came to power in 1979, Ramadhan was named first deputy prime minister. He has undertaken many visits abroad seeking to improve 'Iraq's foreign relations; during the events surrounding Operation Desert Storm (q.v.), he traveled widely to get support for 'Iraq. A major figure in the economic planning of 'Iraq, Ramadhan reportedly lost some of his influence due to the liberalization and privatization of the economy since the late 1980s. He was seen as a loyal ally and supporter of Saddam and a tough defender of the regime and the party. Remadan was captured by Kurdish pesh mergas in August 2003 and was handed over to U.S. authorities in 'Iraq.

RASAFI, MA'RUF AL- (1875–1945). Poet. He was born to a mixed Kurdish–Arab family in Baghdad (q.v.). He learned the Koran (q.v.) at school and became a Sufi (q.v.), and he decided to devote himself to literature (q.v.) as a young man. He taught Arabic in Baghdad secondary schools and composed poetry (q.v.) that was published in Lebanon, Syria, and Egypt. After the 1908 revolt in Istanbul, al-Rasafi was invited to Istanbul and he later edited an Arabic-language daily *Sabil al-Rashad*. He represented an 'Iraqi district in the Ottoman Chamber of Deputies. From 1924 until 1929, al-Rasafi served in government posts and became active in politics as a nationalist. Like other poets of his generation, he was deeply involved in the political life of 'Iraq and the Arab world. His poetry expressed the aspirations felt by many Arabs and displayed a concern with social issues, particularly the need to improve the living conditions of the workers and the poor and the extension of greater rights and educational opportunities to women. Al-Rasafi's best poems are characterized by a purity of style, a passionate appeal, and a rhetorical grandeur well suited to his role as a populist poet. His poetry has been collected into one large volume entitled *Diwan al-Rasafi*.

RASHID 'ALI. *See* KAYLANI, RASHID 'ALI AL-.

RASHID, HARUN AL-. Abbasid caliph (q.v.), r. 786–809. Al-Rashid pursued policies similar to those of his father al-Mahdi (q.v.). He released many of the Umayyads and 'Alids his brother al-Hadi (q.v.) had imprisoned and declared amnesty for all political groups of the Quraysh. Al-Rashid also released from prison his teacher and counselor Yahya, the son of Kh'alid Barmak. He appointed Yahya *wazir* (q.v.) and gave Yahya's sons Ja'far and al-Fadhl high positions in the administration of the state. This ushered in the era of Barmakid supremacy as Yahya and his sons governed the empire for 17 years. But al-Rashid eventually turned on the Barmakids. Ja'far's marriage to al-Rashid's sister was seen as an attempt to disgrace the caliph. In 803, al-Rashid ordered Ja'far, his close adviser and friend, to be put to death, and he threw Yahya, al-Fadhl, and two other Barmakids into jail and confiscated their fortune.

Large-scale hostilities broke out with Byzantium during al-Rashid's rule. Byzantine emperor Nicephorus refused to pay the tribute to the Umayyads established by Empress Irene in 782. In 804, al-Rashid organized a force said to have totaled 135,000 troops and pushed all the way to the Black Sea. Nicephorus sued for peace and agreed to pay the tribute to al-Rashid. When Nicephous reneged once more on the tribute, al-Rashid's army ravaged large parts of Asia Minor. The peace treaty signed in 806 was much more punitive than the previous tribute, and thousands of Christians (q.v.) were taken as slaves. Al-Rashid extended friendship to Charlemagne, sending him exotic gifts. The two leaders exchanged diplomatic representatives, united by a common dislike for the Umayyad dynasty in Spain.

During al-Rashid's rule, the Abbasid Empire reached its peak. It is his court that is immortalized in *The Arabian Nights* (q.v.). Prosperity returned to many cities, including Baghdad (q.v.), as a result of al-Rashid's emphasis on security and trade. The first free public hospital in the Islamic world was founded in Baghdad in 809. Al-Rashid initiated a number of agricultural and trade reforms and encouraged literary and learned guilds. Al-Rashid appointed the noted jurist Abu Yusuf, a student of the great Abu Hanifa, to be the supreme judge of the empire. He allowed poets, jurists, and theologians to debate their theories with one another without fear of reprisal. Al-Rashid died on an expedition to put down a revolt in Khorastan in 809.

RAUF, YUNIS (DALDAR) (1918–1948). Kurdish poet and writer. He was born in Qoisanjaq and graduated from the Baghdad Law College. He wrote the Kurdish national anthem. He and a group of his friends played a major role in the establishment of the Hewa Party (q.v.).

RAZZAQ, 'ARIF 'ABD AL- (1924–). Military figure and opposition politician. Well-known for his Nasirist, Arab nationalist views, he opposed the regime of 'Abd al-Karim Qasim (q.v.) after the 1958 revolution (q.v.). He also opposed the Ba'th Party (q.v.) when it took power in 1963. He closely collaborated with 'Abd al-Salam 'Arif, serving as commander of the air force (1963) and minister of agriculture (1964). Al-Razzaq became prime minister in 1965 but was removed after two weeks and exiled to Egypt in 1966. He returned to 'Iraq that same year, attempted a coup, and was arrested. He was released in 1967 and attempted another coup in 1968. He was arrested again, and after his release, he distanced himself from politics for many years. Al-Razzaq emerged as one of the leading opposition figures against Saddam Husayn (q.v.). He is one of three members on the executive council of the 'Iraqi National Congress (q.v.).

RAZZAQ, MUHAMMAD ZIMAN 'ABD AL- (1942–). Ba'thist activist and official from Dhi Qar. He received a law degree from Baghdad University and a graduate degree from al-Bakr University for Higher Military Studies. He joined the Ba'th Party (q.v.) in 1956. Al-Razzaq headed the party organization in a number of governorates, including Baghdad (q.v.), Sulaymaniyya, and al-Najaf (q.v.). He commanded the Popular Army and served as governor of Salah al-Din in 1983. At the time of the U.S. occupation in April 2003, al-Razzaq was Ba'th Party chairman and commander of its militia in the Ta'min and Nineveh governorates. He remained at large as of September 2003.

REGIONAL COMMAND (RC). Theoretically, the Ba'th Party's (q.v.) highest executive authority is the National Command (q.v.), which includes representatives of the Ba'th Party from other Arab countries and is responsible for directing the Regional Commands in those Arab countries in which it has branches. In practice, however, the Regional Command in 'Iraq has the real authority. It appoints or dismisses its members and monitors the affairs of government departments in 'Iraq. It has major responsibilities in running party affairs, but it usually operates in the shadow of the Revolutionary Command Council (RCC) (q.v.). Usually, members of the Ba'th Party's National Command are members of the Regional Command and of the RCC.

REVOLT OF 1920. *See* AL-THAWRA.

REVOLUTION, 1958. On 14 July 1958, military forces led by 'Abd al-Karim Qasim (q.v.) overthrew the 'Iraqi monarchy. Jordan had requested 'Iraqi military units to help it keep control in the face of civil war in Lebanon. Instead of going to Jordan, the troops entered Baghdad (q.v.). King Faysal II (q.v.) and his family, including the regent 'Abd al-Ilah (q.v.), were killed at the palace, bringing an end to Hashimite (q.v.) rule in 'Iraq. Many other leading members of the former regime were also killed during the fighting or hung after public trials held by the Mahdawi Court. The 1958 revolution ended 'Iraq's close relationship with the West and ushered in the first in a series of Arab nationalist regimes.

REVOLUTION, 1968. On 17 July 1968, the Ba'th Party (q.v.) cooperated with military leaders to overthrow the regime of 'Abd al-Rahman 'Arif (q.v.). Colonel Ibrahim 'Abd al-Rahman al-Dawud (q.v.), the head of the Republican Guard, and Colonel 'Abd al-Razzaq al-Nayif (q.v.), the head of military intelligence, agreed to cooperate with the Ba'th in overthrowing 'Arif. The two men saw themselves as the logical successors to 'Arif and wanted Ba'th support because they believed it would provide legitimacy for their rule. The Ba'th agreed to cooperate with them, but party leaders planned to get rid of the powerful men once they had overthrown 'Arif. On the eve of the revolution, al-Dawud and al-Nayif sent word to the Ba'th that they did not deem a military uprising possible. They had either changed their minds or had thought of a way to successfully carry out their mutiny single-handedly. Ba'th leader Ahmad Hasan al-Bakr (q.v.) decided to go ahead with the planned uprising but changed the date from 14 July to the 17th. On 16 July, al-Dawud sent word to al-Bakr that he and al-Nayif were prepared to go ahead if al-Nayif was assured the premiership of the new regime. Al-Bakr and the leaders of the Ba'th agreed without consulting the rest of the party. Their acceptance was prompted by fears that al-Nayif, as the head of military intelligence, would reveal their plot. But the Ba'thists remained determined to get rid of al-Nayif and al-Dawud at the first possible opportunity.

After the successful coup on 17 July, the Ba'th formed a coalition with the Nayif-Dawud group consisting of al-Nayif, al-Dawud, Colonel Hammad Shihab (q.v.), and Colonel Sa'dun Ghaydan (q.v.), and al-Nayif became president. There was a great deal of tension between the Ba'thists and their erstwhile allies. Al-Nayif made several antisocialist statements to the press. His group was pro-Western, did not believe in Arab unity, and favored the policies of Kurdish leader Mulla Mustafa al-Barzani (q.v.). The Ba'th refused to offer the Kurds (q.v.) any concessions that would affect national unity. Since the portfolios of defense, finance, and foreign affairs were controlled by his group, al-Nayif felt that he was safe from the Ba'th.

The Ba'th designed an elaborate plan to get rid of al-Nayif's group. Al-Dawud was called to Jordan for a visit on 29 July. While he was out of the country, Hardan al-Tikriti (q.v.) took control of the army, depriving the Nayif-Dawud group of their control over the armed forces. On 30 July, al-Nayif was called to the palace for a meeting and arrested there by a group led by Saddam Husayn (q.v.). Al-Dawud and Al-Nayif were first appointed as ambassadors in residence abroad and then retired in 1970. The 1968 revolution, a bloodless one, is at times referred to as the White Revolution.

REVOLUTIONARY COMMAND COUNCIL (RCC). The supreme government body in 'Iraq under the Ba'th Party (q.v.) regimes; it was both the highest executive and legislative body in the country. The chairman of the RCC is elected from among its members, and he has authority over all governmental decisions and activities. Saddam Husayn (q.v.) has held this position since 1979. Established following the Ba'th Party's (q.v.) seizure of power in 1968, all of its members have been Ba'thists, with the possible exception of Taha Muhyi al-Din Ma'ruf (q.v.). The number of members in the RCC has fluctuated from as many as 17 in 1977 to a low of 5 in 1991.

RIDHA, KARIM HASSAN (1944–). He was born in Khulays and educated at Baghdad Law College. He joined the Ba'th Party (q.v.) in 1966. He served as governor of Maysan (1983–1987) and Nineveh (1987). Following the merger of the agriculture (q.v.) and irrigation ministries in September 1987, he was appointed as the minister of agriculture and irrigation (1987–1989).

RIKABI, FUAD AL- (1931–1971). The founder of the 'Iraqi branch of the Ba'th Party (q.v.). He was born in Nasiriyya to a Shi'i (q.v.) family and attended the engineering school in Baghdad (q.v.). He founded the 'Iraqi branch of the Ba'th in 1952. From 1952 until 1959, al-Rikabi was the secretary of the Regional Command ('Iraq) (q.v.) and a member of the National Command (q.v.) from 1954 to 1960. He briefly held the position of minister of development during 'Abd al-Karim Qasim's (q.v.) regime; he resigned in February 1959. Al-Rikabi broke with Qasim, and, following the Ba'th's unsuccessful attempt to assassinate Qasim in 1959, he was forced to flee to Syria. In June 1961, al-Rikabi broke with the Ba'th and supported the Nasirites. He briefly held the position of minister of rural affairs under 'Abd al-Salam 'Arif (q.v.); he resigned in July 1965. He was arrested in 1971 and died in prison.

ROYALIST CONSTITUTIONAL MOVEMENT. A group that supports the Hashimite (q.v.) family and Sharif 'Ali ibn al-Husayn, the cousin of King Faysal II (q.v.), who was killed in the Revolution, 1958 (q.v.). Sharif 'Ali ibn al-Husayn is a descendant of Sharif 'Ali, the last Hashimite king of the Hijaz. He lives in London, and while he has a measure of support from the opposition, he does not have wide backing within 'Iraq.

RUBAY'I, MUHAMMAD NAJIB AL- (1904–). Military officer. He was born in Baghdad (q.v.) and attended military school in 'Iraq and Britain. He was respected as a career officer for his discipline, bravery, and honesty. He was promoted to general in 1957 and became a member of the Free Officers (q.v.). After the 1958 revolution (q.v.), he was appointed head of the Presidency Council.

RUBAY'I, MUWAFAQ AL-. British-educated doctor who lived for many years in London. A Shi'a, he is the author of a book on 'Iraqi Shi'a and a human rights activist.

– S –

SAB'AWI, YUNIS AL- (1909–1942). Political figure and radical nationalist from Mawsil (q.v.). He graduated from the War College in Baghdad (q.v.). An active nationalist, he was a close friend of the Golden Square (q.v.) colonels and Yasin al-Hashimi (q.v.). He became involved in the Nadi al-Muthanna (q.v.) club and was a member of the Palestine Defense Committee. Al-Sab'awi ardently opposed British policy both in 'Iraq and Palestine, favoring total independence for 'Iraq and Arab unity. He cooperated with Rashid 'Ali al-Kaylani (q.v.) in 1941, serving as minister of justice for five days in January and as minister of the economy from 12 April until the collapse of Rashid 'Ali's movement on 29 May. Al-Sab'awi fled to Persia, but he was extradited to 'Iraq, tried, and executed in 1942.

SABBAGH, SALAH AL-DIN AL- (1889–1945). Military figure and Arab nationalist. He was born in Mawsil (q.v.) and studied in Beirut, Mawsil, and Istanbul. He graduated as an officer from the Turkish military college in 1917. He was taken prisoner during World War I but was released to join Faysal's (q.v.) army. After the collapse of Faysal's government in Syria in 1920, al-Sabbagh was arrested by the French. He joined the military in 'Iraq and taught at the Baghdad Military Academy and later at the Staff College. He became director of operations at the Ministry of Defense in 1937 and assistant chief of staff and chief of operations in 1940. He was closely connected with the Golden Square colonels (q.v.) and played a major role in the struggle between the nationalist and pro-British officers. Al-Sabbagh figured prominently in all the military coups staged between 1937 and 1945. During the conflict between Britain and the Rashid 'Ali al-Kaylani (q.v.) government in 1941, he formed the Council for Defense to run 'Iraq. When the Rashid 'Ali movement collapsed in May 1941, he fled to Persia. He was arrested in Turkey, extradited to 'Iraq, and executed in 1945.

SABEANS MANDEANS. An ancient but small sect that has survived in southern 'Iraq, Baghdad, and Iran. The sect is generally secretive, and its numbers have greatly declined over the centuries. Questions about their origins remain unanswered, although they are generally recognized as being Semites. One theory about their origin traces them to the Kingdom of Saba (Sheba) in Yemen. Assyrian (q.v.) writers referred to them as Chaldeans (q.v.), and other names have been given to the group, such as Subba or Mandeans. Sabeans have been recognized by Islam (q.v.) as a protected group. Mandea, which has been said to refer to them, comes from the Aramaic (q.v.) word for knowledge. The Sabeans have been historically known for their learning and produced great scholars and scientists under the Abbasids. The term *Sabi'a* or *Subb* also comes from the Aramaic for "immersion in water." One of the basic religious tenets of the group has been baptism in water and the veneration of St. John the Baptist, which has led some Western scholars to describe them as the Baptists of St. John. Historically, there have been two distinct groups of Sabeans: the Mandeans, who appear to have been greatly influenced by the Manichaeans' Jewish and Christian beliefs in addition to ancient beliefs; and the Sabi'a of Harran in the northern part of 'Iraq, who were believed to have been more influenced by ancient Babylonian and Manichaean belief. This famed northern community was tolerated by the caliphs (q.v.) because of their great learning and scholarship. Under the Abbasids, the Sabeans were widely recognized as translators, mathematicians, and ministers.

One of the best-known Sabean heurists was Thabit ibn Qurra, the mathematician, astrologer, translator, and philosopher who moved from Harran to Baghdad (q.v.). He was excommunicated at Harran and established a Sabean sect in Joyeda. His son, Sinan, was also a famous physician and astrologer, as was his son Thabit, who was pressured to convert to Islam by the caliph al-Qahir.

Sabean had generally been tolerated under Islam, but under al-Qahir they became more and more victims of intolerance. All traces of Harran's Sabeans community seems to have disappeared around the middle of the 11th century, although small communities also live in Iran and the United States. The southern Mandean community has survived in tiny numbers to the present. A number of them joined the 'Iraqi Communist Party (q.v.), and a handful joined the Ba'th Party (q.v.).

The Sabean faith embraces elements of ancient Babylonian and other Mesopotamian religions as well as Judaism, Christianity, and Islam. It also borrows from ancient Chaldean customs of star worship and astrology. The Sabeans have the reputation for telling fortunes; they are master craftsmen and silversmiths. They accept 12 saviors and wear white clothes as a reflection of their emphasis on spiritual and physical purity. They traditionally lived near sources of running water to ensure that they could baptize their children and perform their ritual ablutions. They generally refrain from eating the flesh of pigs, dogs, pigeons, and birds of prey. Sabeans do not circumcise their children or marry more than one wife. Divorce is forbidden except when special permission is granted by their judges. The Sabeans are believed to have influenced Yazidi (q.v.) beliefs. Aramaic was the language of the Sabeans' religious texts.

SABRI, NAJI. 'Iraqi foreign minister from 2001 to 2003. Sabri is known as a pragmatic and sophisticated diplomat who raised his country's profile in the international community, especially in the Arab and Islamic worlds. He was appointed foreign minister in April 2001 to improve 'Iraq's ties with Arab countries and the outside world. With a doctorate in linguistics and translation, he used his English-language skills to make friends for 'Iraq and as a powerful tool in the battle of words between Baghdad (q.v.) and Washington.

In 1980, his diplomatic career almost came to a halt when his once-powerful family lost its influence. He was recalled from his post at the 'Iraqi embassy in London after two of his brothers were jailed on charges of conspiring against the regime. One of his brothers, the director-general of the foreign ministry, died in prison. The other survived and was freed after six years. Sabri taught English at Baghdad University after his recall. He later edited the *Baghdad Observer*, 'Iraq's English-language daily newspaper, and an arts journal in Baghdad. He translated three books from English into Arabic, including Michael Holroyd's biography of George Bernard Shaw.

By 1990, he had regained the trust of the regime and was appointed deputy minister at the Information Ministry. He became an adviser to Saddam Husayn (q.v.) in 1995, before he was appointed ambassador to Austria in 1998. He reportedly had close ties with Saddam's influential younger son, Qusay (q.v.). However, his relations with Saddam's elder son, Uday (q.v.), became strained after the newspaper owned by Uday, *Babil*, criticized his handling of relations with Russia and Syria as foreign minister. He is believed to have left 'Iraq at the end of the 2003 war.

S'ADABAD PACT. A forerunner to the Baghdad Pact (q.v.), the S'adabad Pact established a nonaggression arrangement among Afghanistan, Iran, 'Iraq, and Turkey. A draft treaty had been initialed by Iran and Turkey on 2 October 1935, but the 'Iraqi–Iranian dispute over the Shatt al-Arab (q.v.) prevented the pact from being signed until 8 July 1937. The pact provided for nonaggression among its signatories, the inviolability of the signatories' common frontiers, noninterference in domestic affairs, and joint consultations on disputes. The outbreak of World War II, however, rendered it a dead letter. *See also* FRONTIER TREATY OF 1937.

SA'DI, 'ALI SALIH AL- (1928–1980). A politician and a leading figure in the 1963 Ba'th coup. He was born in Baghdad (q.v.) to an Arabized Kurdish family. While at the College of Commerce in the early 1950s, he joined the Ba'th Party (q.v.). His popularity among the students allowed him to advance within the party. He became one of the leading figures in the Ba'th after the 1958 revolution (q.v.). At a time when a number of party officials were forced to leave 'Iraq, al-Sa'di remained and led party activities against the

'Iraqi Communist Party (ICP) (q.v.) and 'Abd al-Karim Qasim's (q.v.) regime. He aligned himself with the Michel Aflaq (q.v.)-Salah al-Din Bitar faction of the party and was secretary-general of the Regional Command (q.v.) between 1960 and 1963. One of the architects of the successful 1963 Ba'th coup, he was arrested several months before the implementation of the plan.

Al-Sa'di was minister of interior and deputy prime minister in the 1963 Ba'th government and took a tough position against the communists. However, he became embroiled in the internal divisions that shook the party and ultimately contributed to its loss of power in November 1963. As the rightist elements of the party appeared to be gaining the upper hand, he aligned himself with some of the leftist elements. He attempted to block the holding of the Seventh National Congress in 1964 in Damascus, an action that furthered the divisions within the 'Iraqi branch of the Ba'th. Al-Sa'di was expelled from the party and attempted to create his own separate branch. He did not play a major role after the 1968 revolution (q.v.).

SADI, 'AMIR AL- (1941–). An eloquent and prominent British-educated 'Iraqi chemist who served as a scientific adviser to Saddam Husayn (q.v.). He emerged in 2002 as 'Iraq's top armament official and its point man during the confrontation with the United States and Britain about 'Iraq's arms programs. When the Ba'th Party (q.v.) came to power in 1968, Sa'di was dismissed from the army because of his marriage to a German woman and because he was not a party member. His professionalism and his scientific and organizational skills led to his rehabilitation with the regime. Al-Sa'di was on the U.S. wanted list and surrendered to the occupation authorities on 12 April 2003. He denied Western claims of 'Iraq's posession of weapons of mass destruction and of programs to acquire them.

SADR, MUMAMMAD AL- (1883–1956). Shi'i (q.v.) religious and political figure during the monarchy. He was born in Kadhimiya, the Shi'i center of northwest Baghdad (q.v.), and studied in the religious schools in Najaf and Karbala (qq.v.). He later returned to Baghdad, where he continued his studies under the supervision of his father, the prominent religious authority, Husayn al-Sadr (1856–1935). Al-Sadr became a religious scholar and returned to Kadhimiya in 1906. Regarded as one of the most ardent nationalists among the Shi'is, he began his political career by playing a major role in mobilizing the Shi'i community in the Central Euphrates (q.v.) area against the British mandate during the revolt of 1920 (q.v.). Following the suppression of the revolt, he fled to Syria and then to Cairo and Jedda, returning to 'Iraq after King Faysal I (q.v.) announced a general amnesty in 1921.

Upon his return, al-Sadr cooperated with a number of other nationalists— including Yusuf al-Suwaydi, Hamdi al-Pachachi (q.v.), and Shaykh Mahdi al-Basir—in calling for an end to the mandate. He issued a manifesto opposing the mandate and British policies and calling for 'Iraq's full independence. A meeting of the opposition in 1922 led by al-Sadr issued an address to King Faysal and Britain demanding an end to the mandate and the establishment of a new cabinet. Following demonstrations against British high commissioner Sir Percy Cox, Britain demanded that the organizers be punished, and many of the opposition leaders were exiled to an island in the Persian Gulf. Somewhat protected by his status as a religious scholar, al-Sadr was not exiled but was asked to leave the country. He went to Persia in 1923 and did not return until 1924, after the ratification of the 1922 Anglo–'Iraqi Treaty (q.v.).

After his return to 'Iraq, al-Sadr did not take a strong stand against the British. He was appointed a senator in the first 'Iraqi Parliament in 1925, and in 1929, he was elected president of the Senate. With the exception of 1937, he was elected president of the Senate until 1944, and he remained a member of the Senate until his death. In 1948, following the uprisings that took place in opposition to the Portsmouth Treaty (q.v.) and the resignation of the Salih Jabr (q.v.) government, he was asked to form a government to calm the situation. Al-Sadr's cabinet lasted until 21 June 1948; after its collapse, he became president of the Senate once again. He was seen as someone who was both traditional and modern in his ideas, and he had a smooth, charming, and dignified manner. He died in 1956.

SADR, MUHAMMAD BAQIR AL- (1931–1980). One of the most influential of the contemporary Shi'i (q.v.) scholars and political leaders in 'Iraq, and the author of *Our Philosophy*, *Our Economics*, *Logical Basis of Induction*, and *The Usurious Bank and Islam*. He was born in Najaf (q.v.) to a prominent religious Shi'i family. He studied logic and Islamic law (*Sharia*) (q.v.) and later taught in Islamic schools. His views are in part the product of traditional Muslim propositions and a reaction to socialism and Marxism.

Al-Sadr adhered to the traditional view that God is the source of all power, the sole legislator, and the sole owner of the Earth's resources. The principle of God's sole ownership of wealth involves, in al-Sadr's view, the prohibition of property and every form of exploitation by man. He further argues that there is a need for a social revolution against injustice and exploitation. This revolution must be a universal one that allows the virtuous rich and the virtuous poor to stand together. His books on Islamic economics, such as *Our Economics*, tried to demonstrate that Islam (q.v.) does have the answers to the problems of the modern world and that Islam offers a third choice between capitalism and Marxism. These books were published in the late 1950s when the 'Iraqi Communist Party (q.v.) was making strong gains among the Shi'i.

Al-Sadr advocated an organized Islamic movement, a centralized party that could work with the varying units in the Islamic world to bring about the desired social change. He believed that the objective of the Islamic revolution was the realization of the Islamic polity, which would in turn derive its force from the application of Islamic principles and values to all spheres of life. He called on Muslims to recognize the rich legacy of Islam and to avoid coming under foreign influences, especially capitalism and Marxism. He also warned Muslims to be wary of imperialist states that were attempting to undermine Islam by spreading their ideologies among Muslims. He declared that Muslims must stand together and oppose any interference in their political, economic, and cultural affairs, and he favored the establishment of an Islamic Republic.

There were reports that al-Sadr called for the revival of the Society of Scholars (q.v.) as a means to oust the Ba'th Party (q.v.) regime. As of 1972, al-Sadr had become the leader of the militant religious leaders and was arrested for the first time. During this period, he wrote two books in which he called on the religious leadership to guide the destiny of the nation. He tried to transcend differences between the Sunnis (q.v.) and the Shi'i by quoting and using sources from both sects to offer a distinct Islamic view. After 1979, al-Sadr became more radical than other elements of the Shi'i leadership. His works emphasized the need for Islamic independence and condemned the Ba'th regime for its human rights violations and for being opposed to Islam. He reportedly sent many of his students throughout 'Iraq and Iran to broaden his base of support and to strengthen ties with the Islamic revolution in Iran.

In 1979, al-Sadr was arrested and taken from Najaf, accused of organizing riots and demonstrations in Najaf and Karbala (q.v.) to congratulate the Ayatollah Khumaini on his coming to power in Iran, despite a government ban on such processions. It is generally believed that he knew he was going to be arrested and that he planned to leave 'Iraq; there were reports that Khumaini himself urged al-Sadr to flee. His arrest triggered demonstrations in Najaf in his support. His sister Bint al-Huda, also an Islamic scholar, organized a protest against his arrest, and many other protests were organized outside 'Iraq. These protests may have contributed to his early release from prison, but al-Sadr remained under house arrest for several months.

In April 1979, al-Sadr issued a *fatwa* stating that it was prohibited for a Muslim to join the Ba'th Party because it was un-Islamic. Iranian radio, calling al-Sadr the "Khumaini of 'Iraq," reported that Khomeini had appointed al-Sadr as the head of the Islamic revolution in 'Iraq. On 5 April 1980, al-Sadr and his sister Bint al-Huda were arrested and taken to Baghdad after Tariq 'Aziz (q.v.) was nearly assassinated. Saddam Husayn (q.v.), promising to punish those responsible for the demonstrations in Najaf and the assassination attempt, ordered the execution of al-Sadr and Bint al-Huda three days later. After al-Sadr's death, the Shi'i movement in 'Iraq deteriorated due to the leadership vacuum. Shi'i activists sought to establish a plan of action which would fit both al-Sadr's ideas and those of the Iranian revolution; this effort led in part to the formation of the Supreme Assembly for the Islamic Revolution in 'Iraq (q.v.).

SADR, MUQTADA AL- (1973 or 1978–). Leader of the Sadr faction in Najaf and son of Ayatollah Muhammad Sadiq al-Sadr (q.v.), he has emerged as a charismatic leader with a significant Shi'a faction opposed to the policies of the quietist traditional Shi'a religious leaders. He appears to have a strong following in al-Sadr, a city named after his father and his uncle, and appears to have support among such influential clergymen as Muhammad al-Fartusi. He has adopted a policy of political activism since the end of the war. His supporters say he represents the activist Hawza (q.v.), unlike Sistani's (q.v.) quietist Hawza. He has criticized the 'Iraqi Governing Council (IGC) (q.v) as not being a truly representative body for 'Iraqis and declared his intention to form a more representative body. He has also formed his own army of al-Mahdi (q.v). His group has occupied hospitals in Baghdad, filled them with armed guards (ostensibly to protect the buildings from lawlessness), and has entered into confrontation with opponents inside 'Iraq. He has opposed U.S. presence but has refrained from calls on his followers to violently resist U.S. forces. Muqtada al-Sadr has recognized the conservative Ayatollah Kazim al-Hairi (q.v) who remains in Iran as his marja', or source of emulation, but not the foru marja's in 'Iraq.

SA'DUN, 'ABD AL-MUHSIN AL- (1879–1929). Prime minister during the monarchy. He was born in Nasiriyya to a prominent Arab family descended from the Ashraf family, which had come to Basra (q.v.) from the Hijaz in the 16th century. His family had ruled an emirate for 300 years until it was brought down in 1869. It also provided the paramount chiefs of the Muntafiq Tribal Confederation (q.v.). Al-Sa'dun attended Tribal College and the Military Academy in Istanbul. He was appointed as aide de camp to Sultan 'Abd al-Hamid. After the rise of the Committee for Union and Progress, of which he was a member, he was demoted, and he resigned from the military. He served as a member of the Ottoman parliament from 1908–1918. He returned to 'Iraq in 1920 and was able to win the confidence of the British during their occupation of 'Iraq.

Al-Sa'dun held numerous important cabinet portfolios. He served as prime minister four times (1922–1923, 1925–1926, 1928–1929, 1929). He held the portfolios of defense (1922), interior (1922, 1922–1923, 1924–1925), justice (1922–1923), foreign affairs (1925–1926, 1928–1929) and finance

(1925–1926). During his tenure in office, he reached a border agreement with the Nejd in 1922 and dealt firmly with the 1926 tribal uprisings. As the chair of the Constituent Assembly, he presided over the ratification of the 1922 Anglo–'Iraqi Treaty (q.v.), and he reached a protocol with the British modifying the terms of the treaty in 1923. Al-Sa'dun mobilized opinion around the issue of 'Iraq's claim to Mawsil (q.v.) and gained Britain's support in defending this claim. He was elected as head of Parliament in 1927, but he insisted that the assembly be dissolved before he would form a cabinet in 1928. During this period, al-Sa'dun came to believe with King Faysal I (q.v.) in the need to decrease British influence by modifying the Anglo–'Iraqi treaties. He favored conscription, but British opposition to the policy led to his resignation as prime minister in 1929. Backed by the king and national public opinion, he insisted that he would not return to the prime ministership.

Britain attempted to alleviate the situation by appointing a new high commissioner, Gilbert Clayton, to replace Henry Dobbs, but al-Sa'dun continued to insist that he would not change his position. He nominated Tawfiq al-Suwaydi (q.v.) to form the new government, although he continued to direct the policy of the government. When al-Suwaydi's cabinet fell in August 1929, Faysal asked al-Sa'dun to form a government. Despite his poor health and fears about British opposition to his policies, al-Sa'dun formed his fourth and last cabinet in September 1929. Family and personal problems compounded his political problems, and he committed suicide in November 1929. He wrote in Turkish that he was fed up with his life, saying that "the nation was waiting for service. . . . [T]he British do not agree and I have no support." He was seen as one of the most competent and sincere leaders to emerge in 'Iraq during this period.

SA'DUN, ZIMAM AL- (1942–). Ba'thist activist. He was born in the Thiqar governorate and attended secondary schools and the military academy. He joined the Ba'th Party (q.v.) in 1956 and was expelled after the party was ousted from power in 1963. He graduated from al-Bakr University with degrees in law and politics and higher military studies. Al-Sa'dun was active in the Peasant's Bureau and the head of the party in Najaf (q.v.) province. He also commanded the Popular Army in Najaf province. He was elected to the Regional Command (q.v.) in 1991.

SAFWAT, NAJDAT (1923–). Writer and diplomat. He attended universities in Baghdad (q.v.) and London before joining the Foreign Ministry. He served in many Arab countries and eventually became an assistant undersecretary in the Ministry of Foreign Affairs. He now lives in London, where he writes for Arab publications. He has authored works on Western literature, the Arab-American literary movement, and 'Iraqi diplomats.

SAHAF, MUHAMMAD SA'ID, AL- (1963–). 'Iraq's last information minister under Saddam Husayn (q.v.). During the 2003 war, he became the regime's spokesman. He gained notoriety for his early accurate reporting and his tart language and unusual rhetoric. However, the statements during the last week of the war showed that his daily televised briefings incited admiration and interest in the Arab world and, later on, confusion and condemnation because of his handling of the briefings.

Sahaf is a Shi'a from Hilla who had joined the Ba'th Party in 1963 after studying journalism and English. After heading 'Iraqi broadcasting, he was sent as ambassador to Burma, Sweden, and the United Nations. Sahaf was appointed foreign minister in 1992, a position which he held until 2001. Sahaf was criticized for his performance, especially by Uday Husayn. He, however, maintained close ties to Saddam, who appointed him to the Ministry of Information. After the war, Sahaf appeared as a guest on a number of Arabic satellite television channels such as al-Arabiya and Abu-Dhabi but refused to be drawn into discussion about the final days before the collapse of the regime. Sahaf surrendered to U.S. forces and was reportedly released.

SA'ID, FAHMI (1898–1942). 'Iraqi nationalist officer. He was born in Sulaymaniyya to a Kurdish family and served as an officer in the Ottoman and Syrian armies. He joined the 'Iraqi army and became the commanding officer of a mechanized force in 1940. During the 1941 Anglo–'Iraqi crisis, Sa'id commanded the Third Division. He was known as an opponent of Bakr Sidqi (q.v.) and the British. A supporter of Rashid 'Ali al-Kaylani's (q.v.) coup in 1941, he fled to Persia when the movement collapsed. He was extradited to 'Iraq and executed in 1942.

SA'ID, KHALID (1932–1978). Kurdish military leader from Koisanjaq. He joined the Kurdish Democratic Party (q.v.) at a very young age. He ascended the military ranks, eventually commanding a *pesh merga* (q.v.) group. He played a major role in founding the Patriotic Union of Kurdistan (q.v.) and commanded the pesh merga in the province of Arbil (q.v.). Sa'id was killed in PUK-KDP fighting in 1978, along with 'Ali al-'Askari and Husayn Babal (qq.v.).

SA'ID, NURI AL- (1888–1958). One of the founders of the modern 'Iraqi state and a dominant political figure, especially during the two decades preceding the 1958 revolution (q.v.). He created many of the institutions that survived the revolution, including the military and the bureaucracy. However, his failure to meet rising popular demands for social reform in the 1950s and his conservative pro-Western policies contributed to the monarchy's downfall. Nuri, whose family is of mixed Arab, Kurdish, and Turkuman (q.v.) origins, was born in Baghdad (q.v.) to a civil servant in the Ottoman government. He spoke Arabic, Turkish, Persian, and English. He graduated from a military college in Istanbul in 1906; attended the staff college there in 1911; and fought in the 1912–1913 Balkan war in Thrace.

During his years in Istanbul, he became devoted to the ideals of Arab independence. Nuri was one of the founding members of al-'Ahd (q.v.), a secret society whose aim was to free the Arab world from Ottoman domination. As Ottoman pressures mounted against Arab nationalists, he fled to Egypt and then to Basra (q.v.) to establish branches of the society with the help of T'alib al-Naqib (q.v.). He was taken prisoner by the British during their occupation of Basra and sent to India. After the 1916 Arab Revolt, Nuri joined the Arab army in the Hijaz, where he became chief of staff. He was later transferred to the Arab forces in northern Syria. After the armistice, he joined Faysal I's (q.v.) forces and accompanied him to the Paris Peace Conference and London in 1919 and 1920.

Nuri went back to 'Iraq, where he became the first chief of staff of the army after Faysal's collapse in Syria. He played an active role in the campaign that brought Faysal to power as king of 'Iraq. Sa'id became minister of defense in 1922 and served until 1930. During this time, he established an army based on the loyalty of Sharifian officers (q.v.)—former Ottoman soldiers—who formed the backbone of the regime. Although he believed in Arab ideals, including independence, he was also a pragmatist who felt that the Arabs needed the support of a superpower because of their weakness and lack of unity. Nuri saw Britain as the perfect candidate since its interests were compatible with 'Iraqi interests, unlike those of other great powers. In addition, Nuri, who saw the Western mode of thought as superior to Eastern ways, admired and respected the British.

In 1930, he was promoted to major general and became prime minister. He resigned in 1932, the year 'Iraq gained independence. As soon as the terms of the 1930 Anglo–'Iraqi Treaty (q.v.) were revealed, a public outrage ensued, which put partial blame on Nuri, leading to his resignation. He was later appointed to several cabinet posts and acted as 'Iraq's representative to the League of Nations in Geneva. He fled to Egypt and then London after the 1936 coup by Bakr Sidqi (q.v.). Nuri returned to 'Iraq upon Sidqi's assassination in December 1937 and spent most of the following year abroad as he focused on finding a solution to the Palestine problem.

Nuri returned to 'Iraq in 1938, the year the Golden Square (q.v.) officers launched a coup against Jamil al-Midfa'i (q.v.). Following King Ghazi's (q.v.) death in 1939, he was appointed prime minister, a post that he alternated with that of foreign minister with Rashid 'Ali al-Kaylani and 'Ali Jawdat (qq.v.). During World War II, Nuri favored entering the war on the British side but was strongly opposed by the Golden Square officers who had helped bring him back to power. As a result, he softened his position but did succeed in severing relations with Germany. When it became evident that Rashid 'Ali was trying to reestablish relations with the Germans, Nuri resigned from his post as foreign minister and left for Egypt, then Palestine.

After the Rashid 'Ali movement was crushed and Midfa'i resigned, Nuri was called back and became prime minister several times, during which cooperation with the British was reinforced. As a result, he became increasingly unpopular among the younger political generation. The Golden Square officers demanded some concessions from the British in return for 'Iraq's severance of relations with the Axis powers; Nuri saw this as unrealistic. His activities on behalf of the British discredited him and the Hashimites (q.v.) in the eyes of the populace, especially among the middle class, the left, and the nationalists. As the government asserted 'Iraq's pro-Western policy and took action against the communist and leftist opposition, a number of uprisings and demonstrations took place.

Nuri encouraged both Shi'is and Kurds (qq.v.) to participate more actively in public and social life. As a result, they gained greater access to official positions in the government, although they were still underrepresented. In addition, their position within the social hierarchy and their standard of living increased because of several development programs. Following the oil (q.v.) agreements of 1951, Nuri sponsored the development of several major projects, including the establishment of a Development Board composed of 'Iraqi and foreign experts who worked jointly on devising five-year plans. During this period, revenues from the 'Iraqi Petroleum Company (q.v.) doubled, and a number of irrigation, industrialization, and infrastructure projects were undertaken by the government. However, Nuri paid little attention to short-term programs, such as land and housing reforms, which increased complaints from the workers and the peasants

Nuri was representative of the landed class that benefited greatly under the monarchy. In fact, in 1958, less than 2 percent of landowners owned 63 percent of the agricultural land. Nuri's policies, which preserved the interests of the tribal shaykhs, would provide fertile ground for the rise of radicals and communist supporters. Although he favored a local policy focusing on 'Iraq's resources and development, Nuri did advocate a plan of Arab unity starting in 1942. He proposed to unite the Fertile Crescent into one Arab state, in which the Jews of Palestine and the Maronites of Lebanon would be granted autonomous status. He also called for the formation of an Arab league with a permanent council for defense and foreign affairs. When the Israeli state was established, he became more of a regionalist, emphasizing the emergence of a strong independent Arab state that would cooperate with the West.

Nuri led 'Iraq into the 1955 Baghdad Pact (q.v.) with Turkey, Pakistan, and Britain. This move, which led to widespread opposition, has come to be considered a fatal mistake. As a result of domestic protests to the pact, Nuri dismissed a relatively freely elected Parliament to establish one of his own and initiated a harsh crackdown on his opponents, many of whom had infiltrated the military. The Baghdad Pact, which led to the severance of relations with the Soviet Union, isolated 'Iraq from much of the Arab world at a time when Egypt's Jamal 'Abd al-Nasir promoted Arab nationalism. This widespread opposition reached new heights after the nationalization of the Suez Canal, which led Nuri to declare martial law. On the other hand, he was angered by the formation of the United Arab Republic because he saw unity between 'Iraq and Syria as natural because of historical and geographic commonalities. In response, he turned to Jordan and formed the Arab Union (q.v.), of which he became prime minister. He had hoped to convince Kuwait to join the federation, but the British opposed it.

Nuri's attempts to preserve the loyalty of the military through generous benefits failed. As the civil war in Lebanon in 1958 intensified, Jordan requested the help of 'Iraqi troops. The troops feigned to be en route to Jordan; instead they moved on Baghdad and launched a coup on 14 July 1958, during which the king was killed. Nuri fled and took refuge in a friend's house. The next day, he was either killed in the street, after he was discovered wearing women's clothes and men's shoes, or he committed suicide upon realizing he could not escape. His dead body was shot and dragged through the streets.

SALIH, BARHAM (1960–). Prime minister of the Kurdish Regional Government (KRG) in Sulaymaniyya led by Jalal Talabani's (q.v.) Patriotic Union of Kurdistan (PUK) (q.v.). He joined the PUK in 1976 when it was still an underground movement. He was arrested twice by the 'Iraqi security forces before leaving 'Iraq in 1979. He received a B.S. in civil and structural engineering from the University of Cardiff and a Ph.D. in statistics and computer modeling from the University of Liverpool. Salih served as the PUK's spokesman in London from 1985 to 1991. He became a member of the PUK's Political Bureau. He served for 10 years as the representative of the PUK and then of the KRG in Washington, D.C. On 21 January 2001, he was appointed by Talabani as the prime minister of the KRG in Sulaymaniya. He has used his command of English and his knowledge of the West to further the cause of the PUK and of Kurds (q.v.) living in North America.

SALIH, MUHAMMAD MAHDI (1947–). A leading economist, educator, and technocrat from Takrit. He attended and taught at Baghdad University until 1973. He holds a doctorate in regional planning from the University of Manchester. Salih joined the Ba'th Party (q.v.) in 1966. He was appointed as a presidential advisor and member of the Regional Command (q.v.) in 1982.

The following year, he became the head of the Economic Office of the Revolutionary Command Council (q.v.). He was appointed acting minister of finance from 1989 to 1991 and served as minister of trade from August 1987 until April 2003. He was captured by U.S. forces in April 2003.

SALIHI, NAJIB AL-. A Sunni military figure and an activist in the opposition to the Husayn regime. He is former divisional commander of the Republican Guard forces who defected in 1995. He headed the 'Iraqi Free Officers' Movement (IFOM), which included a number of officers who defected and/or opposed the regime.

SALIM, 'IZZ AL-DIN. A leader of the Da'wa Shi'ite Islamic Party. Salim is also a historian and a political activist from Basrah.

SALIM, JAWAD (1919–1961). Sculptor and painter who is generally considered the greatest 'Iraqi artist of the 20th century. He was born in 1919 to a family of well-known painters. He studied in Rome, Paris, and Istanbul. His work at the Baghdad Archeological Museum gave him a thorough knowledge of ancient Mesopotamian art and sculpture, and he was able to make modern 'Iraqis aware of the style and traditions of ancient 'Iraq. Salim also drew on local customs and symbols of folklore for his work. He contributed a number of drawings, paintings, book cover designs, and jewelry designs to local artisans. He created the Monument of Liberty, the largest work by an 'Iraqi artist in 2,500 years, in Florence before his sudden death in 1961. The Monument of Liberty, now standing near the south gate of Baghdad (q.v.), is a 30.47-meter work consisting of 14 groups of low-relief bronzes that stand 7.3 meters high.

SALMAN, MAHMUD (1889–1942). A nationalist officer from Baghdad (q.v.). He served as an officer in the Ottoman and later the Sharifian army (q.v.). He joined the 'Iraqi army in 1925 and became an aide de camp to both King Faysal I (q.v.) and King Faysal II (q.v.). He commanded a cavalry regiment and the Royal Air Force in 1940. Salman was a close friend and follower of Salah al-Din al-Sabbagh (q.v.). An ardent nationalist, he supported Rashid 'Ali al-Kaylani's (q.v.) coup in 1941. After its collapse he fled to Persia, but he was extradited to 'Iraq and executed in 1942.

SAMAD, MUSA 'ABD AL- (1919–). An educator and politician of Kurdish origin. He graduated from the Higher Teacher's College in Baghdad (q.v.) and taught in various cities, especially in the Kurdish areas of 'Iraq. He was active in the teacher's union movement and the campaign to wipe out illiteracy in 'Iraq. Samand was elected to the Kurdish section of the 'Iraqi Academy and as a board member of Sulaymaniyya University. He served as secretary-general of education in the government-created Kurdish autonomous region. *See also* KURDS.

SAMARRA. An ancient city located on the east bank of the Tigris River (q.v.) dating back to 5000 B.C. The present town, which was established in the third century A.D., reached its peak when Caliph al Mu'tasim (q.v.) abandoned Baghdad (q.v.) as the capital of the Abbasid Empire in 836 A.D. in its favor. Its landmarks include its famous malwiya (the spiral minaret) and the ruins of Great Friday Mosque—both built around 852. It also holds the tombs of two Shi'i, the 10th Al-Hadi and the 11th Hadi Al-'Askari.

SAMARRAI, 'ABD AL-KHALIQ AL- (1935–1979). A Ba'thist intellectual and political activist. He was born in Samarra (q.v.) and only received a secondary school education. He joined the Ba'th Party (q.v.) in 1952. He became a member of the Regional Command (q.v.) in 1964, the National Command (q.v.) in 1968, and the Revolutionary Command Council (RCC) (q.v.) in 1969. Al-Samarrai also headed the Cultural Bureau of the RCC in 1972. In the wake of party rivalries and splits, he supported Michel Aflaq (q.v.), and he always favored dialogue and reconciliation with the Kurds (q.v.) and other ethnic groups. He was considered the only credible rival to Saddam Husayn (q.v.) for control of the civilian wing of the party because of his reputation for integrity, intellectualism, and a simple way of life.

Nazim Kazzar (q.v.) implicated al-Samarra'i in his 1973 coup attempt. Al-Samarra'i was arrested, found guilty of treason, and condemned to death. Many doubt he was involved in the coup attempt. He was placed under house arrest instead because President Ahmad Hasan al-Bakr (q.v.) did not ratify the sentence and because of intercession on his behalf by prominent non-'Iraqis, including Ba'th leader Michel Aflaq and Lebanese Druze leader Kamal Junblatt. However, al-Samarra'i was executed in August 1979, during a purge carried out ostensibly because Saddam had discovered a plot to overthrow him.

SAMARRA'I, 'ABDULLAH SALLUM AL- (1932–). An educator, Ba'thist, and government figure. He was born in Samarra (q.v.) in 1932 to a lower-middle-class family. He received a B.A. and an M.A. in Islamic history from Baghdad University. He was a member of the Independence Party (q.v.) and joined the Ba'th Party (q.v.) in 1956. Al-Samarra'i held a series of cabinet and diplomatic posts: director-general, Ministry of Work and Social Affairs (1963); minister of culture and information (1968–1969); minister of state (1969–1970, 1970–1972); and ambassador to India. He held membership in the Regional Command (1964–1970) and in the Revolutionary Command

Council (1969–1970) (qq.v.). He is believed to have been an opponent of Saddam Husayn (q.v.), but he has not been active in politics since the mid-1970s.

SAMARRA'I, FAIQ AL-. A prominent Arab nationalist, conservative politician, lawyer, and Sunni (q.v.) intellectual. He is widely admired by nationalists and was one of the leaders of the Independence Party (q.v.), for which he served as deputy leader from 1946 to 1959. He was deputy chair of Nadi al-Muthanna (q.v.) in the late 1940s. Al-Samarra'i supported Rashid 'Ali al-Kaylani (q.v.) in 1941 and closely cooperated with him during the 1930s. He sided with the Ba'th Party (q.v.) in pressing for an immediate merger with the United Arab Republic in the late 1950s. He served as ambassador to Cairo and later remained in residence in Egypt.

SANCTIONS. Following 'Iraq's 1990 invasion of Kuwait (q.v.), the United Nations slapped 'Iraq with comprehensive economic sanctions, which, with some modifications, continued into 2003. The UN Security Council imposed sanctions on 'Iraq under Resolution 661 (6 August 1990) in an effort to force 'Iraq to withdraw from Kuwait. After 'Iraq's defeat, the sanctions were maintained under UNR 687 (3 April 1991) until 'Iraq complied with the resolution's other paragraphs dealing with disclosure and destruction of its weapons of mass destruction programs, demarcation of the border with Kuwait, release of Kuwaiti prisoners, and the establishment of a Compensation Commission for reparations claims.

UNR 986 (15 April 1995) established the oil-for-food program (OFP), envisioned as a short-term program and not as a solution to 'Iraq's dire humanitarian situation. 'Iraq was permitted to sell $1 billion worth of oil (q.v.) every six months. Disputes between the UN and 'Iraq delayed the start of OFP until December 1996. Proceeds went into a UN-controlled escrow account, and 'Iraqi requests were vetted to ensure that forbidden goods and equipment were not imported. Only 53 percent of revenues were available to purchase food, medicine, and other supplies for the part of the country under Baghdad's control; the other 47 percent went to the UN Compensation Fund (30 percent), the Kurdish Autonomous Zone (13 percent), the operations of UN programs including the administration of OFP and weapons inspections, and transit fees to Turkey for use of the oil pipeline.

In response to the continuing criticism of the harmful effect of sanctions on 'Iraqi civilians, the Security Council lifted the cap on oil sales in UNR 1284 (17 December 1999). But OFP was plagued by delivery delays, blocks and holds on contracts (often imposed by the United States), and 'Iraqi obstructionism. The ban on imports of equipment for the oil sector, by now badly deteriorated, was lifted in 2000. Support for the sanctions began waning given their devastating impact on the Iraqi people, and as of 2000 more and more countries were flouting the sanctions. Upon taking office in 2001, the Bush administration pushed for so-called smart sanctions, meant to expedite the delivery of food and humanitarian supplies while tightening the focus on items with a possible military use. UNR 1409 (14 May 2002) established a Goods Review List, but as the list of suspected items runs to over 300 pages, delays continued to be a problem.

Under OFP, 'Iraq earned $64 billion from oil exports. By early 2003, the UN had authorized $36 billion in expenditures, yet only $23.5 billion in food and supplies had been delivered. Although food generally received quick approval, equipment and supplies for the water, sanitation, electrical, communications, agricultural, and oil sectors frequently encountered holds or blocks. With war looming, the UN suspended OFP on 17 March 2003, and UNR 1472 transferred the authority to facilitate delivery of items already in the pipeline to the UN secretary-general for 45 days. Sixteen million 'Iraqis were entirely reliant on government food rations in 2003.

Sanctions took a terrible toll on 'Iraqi civilians. Reputable studies by American and international relief and human rights organizations, including specialized UN bodies, consistently documented the desperate conditions created by war and sanctions. The United Nations Children's Fund (UNICEF) reported that child mortality rates in 2000 were 160 percent higher than in 1990, and 70 percent of child deaths attributed to diarrheal diseases and chronic respiratory infections. Some 4,500 children under the age of five died each month from malnutrition and preventable diseases. An estimated 800,000 children were chronically malnourished. The World Health Organization reported that "half of the population has been on a semi starvation diet." Monthly food rations only supplied about 50 percent of necessary calories and were deficient in protein and many vitamins (rations included wheat flour, sugar, vegetable oil, tea, pulses, and dried milk). CARE stated that "children, mothers, the sick and the aged which were well cared for before 1990 are now dying while the outside world mistakenly believes that the deal [OFP] has solved 'Iraq's problems." The terrible humanitarian situation led to the resignation of several UN officials involved with OFP, including the two senior-most officials implementing the program.

The sanctions prohibited the import of chlorine to purify polluted water, leaving 60 percent of 'Iraqis without access to clean water in 2003. Bans on agricultural pesticides for crops and vaccines for livestock greatly harmed the agricultural sector. The criteria for banning some items was difficult to discern; forbidden items included lead pencils and pencil sharpeners, sewing machines, children's clothes, and a whole range of medical materials. Although food and most medicines were not banned, 'Iraq was unable to export products other than oil, and 'Iraqi assets were frozen overseas. Consequently, a country that before the war had a thriving middle class and one of the most advanced medical and educational systems in the Middle East was close to a state of collapse. The struggle for survival became the sole driving force in society. Crime skyrocketed, and the whole fabric of civil society disintegrated. Sanctions were lifted when the United States overthrew Saddam Husayn's (q.v.) regime, but humanitarian conditions remain grim. *See also* AGRICULTURE; ECONOMY.

SAN REMO, TREATY OF. Signed on 25 April 1920, the Treaty of San Remo appointed trustees for the former Ottoman territories, now classified as mandates in keeping with the provisions of Article 22 of the League of Nations Covenant. Britain received the mandate for 'Iraq; despite contrary provisions in the Sykes–Picot agreement (q.v.), the Mawsil (q.v.) province was included within 'Iraqi territory. 'Iraqis greeted the announcement of the mandate on 3 May 1920 with a full-fledged rebellion against British control. It would take until early 1921 before Britain regained full administrative control over 'Iraq, and the revolt of 1920 (q.v.) led the British to couch the mandate relationship with 'Iraq in the form of a treaty of alliance. *See also* ANGLO–'IRAQI TREATY OF 1922.

SARLIYAS. A small group, which with the Kakais and Bajilans and Shabak (q.v.), are often said to be extreme Shi'i (q.v.) (Ghulat) sects or Qizilbash. The Sarliyas traditionally lived in villages north of the Zab River, while the Kakais lived in villages mainly to the south of the Zab River and west of Tawq near Kirkuk (q.v.), east of Halabja (q.v.), and near the borders with Iran in the Khanaqin area. The Sarliyas, Kakais, and Bajilans speak the Gorani Kurdish dialect. Their religious beliefs are said to be influenced by Yarsanism and are akin to the 'Ali-Ilahis. Every adept has a *pir* or religious guide who usually belongs to one of the 10 families of *sayyids* (descendants of 'Ali). Five of the families claim descent from the Sultan Ishaq (or Zonak) (the fourth manifestation of the divinity) and five from the families who guard their tombs. The Bajilans traditionally lived in the Khanaqin area.

SAWERS, JOHN. British diplomat and deputy to the U.S. civilian administrator in 'Iraq, Paul Bremer (q.v.). He is the top British civilian in Baghdad, a former ambassador to Egypt, and a Downing Street advisor. The appointment of such a senior diplomat (he is set to become political director at the U.K. foreign office on his return) was a mark of the importance the British government attaches to the task of setting in place an interim administration in 'Iraq. Sawers is regarded as well placed to work with the United States, having served in Washington, D.C. He was foreign policy advisor to Tony Blair during the Kosovo conflict.

SAYIGH, YUSUF AL- (1934–). A prominent poet, novelist, and painter from Mawsil (q.v.). He attended Baghdad University and received an M.A. in Arabic literature (q.v.). Since the mid-1950s, he has published a number of poetic works and anthologies. In 1956, along with two other poets, he published *Poems Not Fit for Publication*, and he has since published several other collections, including *Lady of the Four Apples* and *Confessions of Malik ibn al-Rib*. Al-Sayigh also published two novels, *The Game* and *The Distance*. He is a well-known book illustrator and has had several painting exhibitions.

SAYYAB, BADR SHAKIR AL- (1926–1964). One of the best-known Arab poets of this century and a pioneer in the free verse movement. He was born in a small village in southern 'Iraq. He joined the 'Iraqi Communist Party (ICP) (q.v.) in 1944, and his political activism led to his suspension from school. He was active in the student demonstrations demanding a British withdrawal from 'Iraq and in anti-Zionist demonstrations demanding a favorable solution to the Palestinian problem.

Al-Sayyab began writing free verse in 1946 in a revolt against traditional forms and content and in an attempt to instill new values that echoed the requirements of modern life. He began teaching English in 1948 but was arrested during the crackdown on the ICP in 1948–1949. Barred from teaching after his release from prison, al-Sayyab took a position with the Directory of Imports and Exports. He continued to write poetry (q.v.), much of which had an anti-imperialist flavor. In 1952, he participated in the demonstrations against the government demanding political, social, and economic reforms. He fled to Iran and then Kuwait in the wake of the government's crackdown against the protestors.

Upon his return to 'Iraq in 1954, al-Sayyab formally broke with the ICP because of what he considered the party's rigid tactics and ideology, and he moved toward Arab nationalism. He worked for a newspaper before returning to his old job at the Directory of Imports and Exports in 1957. He supported the overthrow of the monarchy in 1958, but once 'Abd al-Karim Qasim (q.v.) became closely allied with the communists, al-Sayyab wrote a number of poems critical of the new regime. In 1961, he moved to Basra (q.v.), where his health began to fail. He sought treatment in both 'Iraq and Britain over the next several years, but he died in 1964 of a degenerative nerve disorder.

Al-Sayyab revolutionized numerous elements of the poem; the publication of his third volume of poetry, *Song of Rain*, was instrumental in drawing attention to the use of myth in poetry. Al-Sayyab's poems draw heavily on the symbols and myths of ancient Mesopotamian civilization. His work also draws on the Christian (q.v.) themes of sacrifice and crucifixion. His most famous works include *The Blind Prostitute*, *The Song of Rain*, *The Gravedigger*, *Myths*, *Weapons and Children*, and *Stranger in the Gulf*.

SELJUKS. A Turkish tribe that gained influence over the Abbasid caliphs (q.v.) following their occupation of Baghdad (q.v.) in 1055. This tribe, the Ghuzz, came from the eastern mountains of Khorasan and was led by the Seljuk family. The Seljuk regime reached the height of its power and influence under Tughril Beg's nephew Alp Arslan. Its authority expanded to include much of Syria after taking Damascus. The Seljuks were known as sultans and called their chief ministers *atabegs*. The Abbasids granted the Seljuks the title of "kings of the East and West." Seljuk authority and prestige actually increased to such an extent that it overshadowed that of the caliphs themselves, although certain caliphs did try to regain their independence. Al-Mustarshid (r. 1118–1135) sought to divide the Seljuk sultans in a bid to regain his authority. His son al-Rashid (r. 1135–1136) attempted to follow in his footsteps. In response, the Seljuks besieged Baghdad, forcing the city to surrender and the caliph to abdicate. *See also* ZANKID STATE.

SETTLED TRIBES. The seminomadic and settled tribes usually lived in central and southern 'Iraq along the river banks, where they relied mostly on cultivation and the breeding of cattle. The al-Muntafiq confederation (q.v.), one of the largest tribal groupings in the south, lived along the Euphrates River (q.v.) from the Qurna to Samawa and along the Gharaf River. Their prominent units included the al-Ajwad, al-BuSalih, al-Hamid, Bani Malik, Bani Sa'id, Bani Hisham Khaffaja, Hajiam, and Bani Asad. The leaders of this confederation did not come from these tribes but from a family of Nejdi origin, the Sa'dun. In the middle Euphrates, there was another series of tribal confederations.

The Zubayd confederation settled between the Tigris (q.v.) and Euphrates Rivers; the Bani Hisham lived between Karbala (q.v.) and Kufa; al-Fatla, which lived along the Mushkhab and Shamiya Rivers; the Khazail confederation, which lived between Diwaniya and Kifl; and the Aqra and Afij who lived on the Shatt al-Arab (q.v.), as did the al-Busultan and the al-Jubur. The Zubayd and Bani Tamim lived along the Euphrates River from Musayib to Ramadi. From Qorna to Baghdad (q.v.) along the Tigris River lived the Bani Kaab, who usually owed allegiance to the shaykh of Muhammara. In the Diyala area resided the al-Bu Muhammad, al-Uzayrij Bani Lam, Rabia, Shammar al-Tuqa, part of the Zubayd tribe, Bani Tamim, al-Ubayd, and al-Izza tribes. The Ubayd and Shammar al-Jarba tribes lived around the towns of Samarra (q.v.) and Tikrit, as did other tribes, such as Juwari, al-Bu Badri, and the Daraj. Other northern tribes include al-Uqardat, al-Jubur, Tay, al-Dulaym, Zawba, Unayza, and Bayat.

The Kurdish tribes are also divided into northern tribes and southern tribes. The northern tribes traditionally lived in the areas around Aqra, Dahuk, and Imadiyya and included the Doski, Sindi, Gali, Barzan Mizuri,

Suruhi, Zibar, Birwari Bala, and the Birwaris. The southern tribes traditionally inhabited the areas near Sulaymaniyya, Kirkuk (q.v.), and Arbil (q.v.) and included the Pishdar, Baradost, Bajillan, Dizai, Kakai, Hamawand, Jaf, Talabani, Hirki, and Khoshnao tribes. *See also* KURDS; NOMADIC TRIBES.

SEVRES, TREATY OF. Signed on 10 August 1920, the Treaty of Sevres ended the state of hostilities between Turkey and the Entente powers in World War I. Articles 62, 63, and 64 recognized the rights of the Kurds (q.v.) and the Armenians to form independent states. Moreover, it would have permitted the voluntary union between an independent Kurdish state and that part of the Mawsil (q.v.) province where Kurds formed a majority. The rise of Mustafa Kemal in Turkey nullified Sevres, and a new treaty was signed—the Treaty of Lausanne (q.v.)—that made no mention of a Kurdish state.

SHABAK. A tiny and unique religious community of people who number about 50,000 to 70,000 and live between the Mawsil (q.v.) plain and Ba'shiqa. Some of the Shabak speak Gorani, a dialect of Kurdish close to the Persian language, while others speak a Turkic dialect. There have been different theories about their origins and their religious beliefs. They have been described as *Ahl al-Haqq* (q.v.). The members of this sect venerate 'Ali as the second manifestation of the Universal Spirit, or divinity. Others say that 'Ali is only venerated and is not as important as Sultan Ishaq (or Zohak), the Kurds' (q.v.) ancient mythical nemesis who brought in the fourth divine epoch. Others believe they are extreme Shi'is (Ghulat) (q.v.) affected with the teachings of Bektashi Sufi (q.v.) orders or are Qizilbash (Red-Head) Shi'is. Still others believe they are followers of Yarsanism. They are said to share with Yarsanism the belief in seven good and seven evil spirits who run the world. They are also said to believe in a universal spirit or God or al-Haqq (truth) and practice some Christian (q.v.) rites.

The Shabaks' ethnic origins are also somewhat obscure. They are said to be of a Turkic, Persian, or Kurdish origin and supposedly they are remnants of the Mongol invasion. Many of the Turkuman (q.v.) villagers near Kirkuk are Qizilbash. The Qizilbash are said to be descendants of Shi'is of Turkish origin who were resettled from Iran during the reigns of Salim I and Sulayman I and of the original native inhabitants who had embraced Islam (q.v.) during the Seljuks (q.v.) period, after having been believers in the great goddess Ma and who converted to Christianity and were influenced later by Manichaeanism. All of these creeds have left an impact on their religious beliefs and practices. In recent decades, many Shabak have become culturally and linguistically Arabized.

SHABIB, KAMIL (1895–1942). A nationalist officer from Baghdad (q.v.) and a member of the Golden Square (q.v.). He served in both the Ottoman and Sharifian armies (q.v.). He joined the 'Iraqi army when 'Iraq was established, graduated as an officer from the 'Iraqi Staff College, and rose to command the 'Iraqi First Division. An active Arab nationalist, Shabib opposed the policies of Britain and the regent, 'Abd al-Ilah (q.v.). He was one of the primary figures who staged the 1941 coup that brought Rashid 'Ali al-Kaylani (q.v.) to power. When Rashid 'Ali's regime collapsed, Shabib fled to Persia. He was extradited, tried, and executed for his role in 1942.

SHABIBI, MUHAMMAD RIDHA AL- (1889–1975). Statesman, educator, poet, and nationalist figure. A member of the prominent Shabibi family of Najaf (q.v.), he studied religion and literature (q.v.) in Najaf. As a young man he published poetry (q.v.) in Syrian, Lebanese, and Egyptian publications. He played a major role in the efforts of 'Iraq to achieve independence after World War I; he carried petitions and messages from 'Iraqi political and religious figures to Sharif Husayn to explain the desire of 'Iraqis to achieve freedom and independence in 1919. Al-Shabibi served in Parliament from the 1920s through the 1940s and as minister of education in several cabinets (1924–1925, 1935, 1937–1938, 1941, 1948). He was elected president of the 'Iraqi Academy in 1928–1929 and became a member of the Arab Language Academy in Cairo. He authored a number of books on 'Iraqi history, the 'Iraqi dialect, and education.

SHAHIR, NURI FAYSAL (1939–). A Ba'th Party (q.v.) and government official from Haditha. He was educated at the Military Academy and joined the Ba'th Party in 1955. He held a variety of party posts from 1969–1979. He served as minister of waqfs (1979–1982), governor of Babil (1982–1983), and minister of youth (1982–1986). He became a member of the Regional Command (q.v.) in 1991.

SHAIKHALY, 'ABD AL-KARIM AL- (1937–1980). A Ba'thist activist and politician. He was born in Baghdad (q.v.) to a Kurdish family. He attended medical school for two years at Damascus University. He joined the Ba'th Party (q.v.) in 1956. The Mahdawi Court sentenced him to death in 1960 although he was in Cairo. Al-Shaikhaly held a diplomatic post in Lebanon in 1963 but was arrested by the 'Abd al-Salam 'Arif (q.v.) regime in 1965. He escaped from prison the following year. He became a member of the Regional Command (q.v.) in 1966 and of the Revolutionary Command Council (RCC) (q.v.) in 1969. After the Ba'th's successful seizure of power in 1968, al-Shaikhaly was appointed minister of foreign affairs. He was relieved of his cabinet post and his membership in the RCC in 1971. He then became the chief delegate to the

United Nations from 'Iraq, a post he held until 1978. An advocate of rapprochement with the Syrian Ba'th regime, he was arrested in 1979 when Saddam Husayn (q.v.) took power. He was murdered in Baghdad in 1980.

SHAIKHALY, SALAH AL-. Economist, diplomat, and journalist, he was born in Baghdad and completed his primary and secondary education in Baghdad and later in Kirkuk. He later completed his B.Sc., M.Sc., and Ph.D. at Manchester University. He taught at Baghdad and Mustansirya Universities in 'Iraq, as well as at the London School of Economics, Oxford University, and Leeds University in the United Kingdom, where he was a visiting professor in the management studies department. In 'Iraq he held the positions of head of the central statistical organization, acting governor of the Central Bank of 'Iraq, and president of the 'Iraqi Fund for External Development. For six years he served as assistant secretary general at the United Nations in New York and regional director for the Bureau of Arab States, UNDP. He also served as consultant to UNICEF, UNESCO, FAO, OPEC Fund, UNDRO, and AGFUND. He served as a leading member of the Political Bureau of the 'Iraqi National Accord (INA) in charge of media and external affairs. He was also the editor-in-chief of the INA's official newspaper, *Baghdad*.

SHAKIR, SA'DUN (1939–). A Ba'thist politician and security official. He graduated from the College of Law and Political Science at al-Mustansiriya University in 1975. He joined the Ba'th Party (q.v.) in the early 1950s and was arrested several times for party activities. Prior to the 1968 revolution (q.v.), he was responsible for Ba'th Party security. After the coup, he headed the special agency entrusted with protecting the party and the regime. Shakir served as director-general of intelligence (1972), minister of state (1977), and minister of interior (1979–1987). He also held membership on the Regional Command (q.v.) and the Revolutionary Command Council (q.v.) from 1977 to 1991. He was removed as minister of interior in 1987 because of increasing problems in the Kurdish areas. He is a close friend of Saddam Husayn (q.v.).

SHANSHAL, 'ABD AL-JABBAR (1920–). A prominent career military officer from Mawsil (q.v.). He was appointed chief of staff in 1970 when Hardan al-Tikriti (q.v.) and Salih Mahdi Ammash (q.v.) were appointed vice presidents. He served as minister of defense (1989–1990) and has held the post of minister of state for military affairs since 1984. He is generally viewed as a professional officer who does not favor military interference in politics.

SHANSHAL, SIDDIQ (1919–). Cabinet minister. He was born to a Mawsil (q.v.) commercial family and studied law in Damascus and Paris. He was the brother-in-law of Yunis al-Sab'awi (q.v.) and a close friend of Faiq al-Samarra'i (q.v.). He served as the director of information during the Rashid 'Ali al-Kaylani (q.v.) coup in 1941 and was a member and secretary of Nadi al-Muthanna (q.v.). In 1957, Shanshal acted as a liaison between the National Union Front (q.v.) and the Free Officers (q.v.). He briefly served as minister of guidance (1958–1959).

SHARIA. Islamic law that formed from the seventh to the 10th centuries. *Sharia* literally means "the correct path of action." It is the compilation of the religious, legal, and ethical precepts of Islam based on the Koran (q.v.), the habits of the prophet Muhammad, and *fiqh* (jurisprudence) (q.v.). It includes the norms of criminal, civil, and procedural law. From 1869 to 1877, the Ottoman authorities issued a civil code known as *al-Majalah*, which was based on a modification of the sharia with special attention paid to social relations. It was adhered to in 'Iraq until 1951, when a combination of Islamic and secular principles were introduced into the new constitution. In recent times, there have been calls by the Islamic parties and groups to establish an Islamic government based on the sharia.

SHARIF, 'ABD AL-SATTAR TAHIR (1933–). Kurdish leader. He joined the Kurdistan Democratic Party (q.v.) in 1958 and became a reserve member of its central command. He was arrested for his nationalist activities. He helped found the Kurdistan Revolutionary Party in 1972, one of the groups that opposed Mulla Mustafa al-Barzani's (q.v.) leadership, and became its secretary general. Resentful of al-Barzani's traditional methods, Sharif cooperated with the Ba'th Party (q.v.) in an attempt to play a role in developing the Kurdish provinces along socialist lines. The Ba'th invited Sharif to represent his party in the Progressive National Front. He held the posts of minister of municipalities (1974–1976) and minister of transport (1976–1977). He served as the vice president of the Kurdish Cultural Society and authored a number of books on Kurdish national movements and Kurdish culture. *See also* KURDS.

SHARIFIAN ARMY. A group of Arab officers serving in the Ottoman military who were the main supporters of the Arab Revolt and who played a major role in 'Iraqi politics until the 1958 revolution (q.v.). Many of these officers belonged to the Covenant Society (q.v.), a secret military society influenced by the Young Turks, secular nationalism, and Western modernization. They were seeking Arab independence and social change, which they believed had to be directed from above. Most of these officers were Sunni (q.v.) Arabs from middle-class and lower-middle-class families. A small number of officers came from wealthy families.

Many Sharifian officers fought in the Arab Revolt and later joined Faysal (q.v.) in Syria and in 'Iraq. A number of them became prominent officers or ministers in 'Iraq, including Nuri al-Sa'id, Ja'far al-'Askari, Jamil al-Midfa'i, 'Ali Jawdat al-Ayubi, and Jamal Baban (qq.v.). They played a major role in demanding that Faysal become king of 'Iraq, and they formed his main base of support. They supported Faysal's demand that the British mandate be replaced by a treaty of friendship and alliance, a stand that allied them with nationalist and religious opponents of the British. They received the support of the Shi'i (q.v.) community in this as well as in their effort to establish a strong 'Iraqi military.

When Nuri al-Sa'id formed his first cabinet in 1930, five of the six posts were given to Sharifian officers. The influence of these officers increased as the palace's role in political affairs declined in the wake of Faysal's death in 1933. The Sharifian officers began to interfere in a more direct manner in politics, which ultimately negatively affected their unity and cooperation. Bakr Sidqi (q.v.) and 'Abd al-Latif Nuri, two of the officers who led the first coup in the Arab world in 1936, and the four officers who led the 1941 Rashid 'Ali al-Kaylani (q.v.) movement were Sharifian officers. In the wake of the British defeat of the Rashid 'Ali regime, many of the officers became closely tied to the British. Many of them also gained the support of the large landowners as well as the foreign companies operating in the country, allowing them to become the dominant ruling elite until the monarchy's overthrow in 1958. *See also* HASHIMITES.

SHATT AL-ARAB. 'Iraq's main outlet to the sea, formed by the confluence of the Euphrates and Tigris Rivers (qq.v.), which continues for about 110 kilometers and is joined by the Karun River before emptying into the Persian Gulf near the city of al-Fao. The Shatt provides access to Basra (q.v.) as well as the Iranian refinery at Abadan, the port of Khoramshahr (Muhammara), and the industrial area of Ahwaz. The Shatt al-Arab is the most contentious part of the 'Iraq–Iran border and has been the subject of boundary disputes since the Treaty of Zuhab (q.v.) in 1639. However, with the exception of a few kilometers around Abadan, the Shatt was wholly under Ottoman and later 'Iraqi sovereignty until the 1975 Algiers Agreement (q.v.). Beginning in the 1930s, the Iranians insisted that the border should follow the *thalweg* (midpoint) of the channel, and tensions were high throughout the 1960s.

In 1969, the shah of Iran abrogated the Frontier Treaty of 1937 (q.v.), unilaterally declaring the thalweg as the border. The Ba'th regime, beset by internal problems, could not challenge the Iranian action. Iran ratcheted up the pressure by supporting the Kurdish revolt in 1974–1975. In 1975, Saddam Husayn (q.v.) and the shah of Iran signed the Algiers Agreement (q.v.), in which 'Iraq conceded the thalweg as the boundary in return for a cessation of Iranian support to the Kurds (q.v.). Saddam declared the Algiers Agreement "null and void" a few days before 'Iraq invaded Iran in September 1980, and a favorable resolution of the boundary issue became a major point for both sides. The Shatt was rendered useless within a few days of the outbreak of fighting, and it remains clogged with about 75 sunken ships, debris, unexploded ordinance, and years of silting. 'Iraq conceded the thalweg as the border in August 1990, as part of the treaty that formally ended the Iran–'Iraq war (q.v.). *See also* KURDAN, TREATY OF.

SHAWKAT, MUDHAR (1950–). Chief coordinator and operating officer of the 'Iraqi National Movement (INM). He received his diploma from Baghdad College in 1968, his B.Sc. from the University of Mosul in 1973, and his Ph.D. from the University of Newcastle Upon Tyne (U.K.) in 1979. From a politically influential family, Dr. Shawkat has been a political opponent of the 'Iraqi regime since 1968. He escaped 'Iraq in 1986 when he became an active opponent of the Saddam Husayn (q.v.) regime.

SHAWKAT, NAJI (1891–1980). Prime minister during the monarchy. He was born in Baghdad (q.v.) to a prominent family of mamluk descent. His father was Shawkat Pasha, a deputy in the Ottoman Parliament from Baghdad. He studied in Turkey and graduated from the Law College in Istanbul. In 1940, Shawkat was appointed a public prosecutor in the civil courts in Hilla.

During World War I, he served in the Ottoman army but was taken prisoner and sent to India. He later joined the Arab army in Hijaz and served with Lawrence of Arabia in 'Aqaba. After his return to Baghdad in 1919, he became the assistant to the governors of Baghdad, Kut, Mawsil (q.v.), and Hilla. Shawkat served as minister of the interior (1928, 1931) and as minister of justice (1929). After the admission of 'Iraq into the League of Nations in 1932, Shawkat served as prime minister for four months. He also held the post of minister of interior (1933–1934) and head of 'Iraq's mission to Turkey (1934–1938). He briefly served as minister of interior again in 1938–1939.

During World War II, Shawkat established a very good relationship with the German ambassador Fritz Grobba and displayed sympathy for Germany in the hopes of undermining British influence in 'Iraq. He was appointed minister of justice (1940–1941) in Rashid 'Ali al-Kaylani's (q.v.) first cabinet and served as minister of defense during Rashid 'Ali's 1941 coup. There are reports that he attempted to reach a compromise with Britain using Turkey as the mediator, but these efforts failed. After the collapse of the Rashid 'Ali regime, Shawkat went to Berlin, Italy, and then South Africa, where he was arrested and handed over to 'Iraq in 1945. Although tried and sentenced to 15 years of hard labor for his role in the 1941 events, he was placed under house arrest in 1947 and amnestied in 1948. He continued to submit memos to the king protesting the 'Iraqi government's pro-British policies until the 1958 revolution (q.v.). He was the brother of Sami Shawkat (q.v.).

SHAWKAT, SAMI. Cabinet minister during the monarchy. He was a descendant of the Kolamand, the mamluks of Georgian origin who dominated 'Iraq under the Ottomans. He was quite influential in the later part of the 1930s as a strong pan-Arab nationalist. He established al-Futuwa, an ultranationalist youth group. He served as minister of social affairs (1939–1940) and minister of education (1940). He was the brother of Naji Shawkat (q.v.).

SHAWWAF, 'ABD AL-WAHHAB AL- (1916–1959). Arab nationalist and opponent of 'Abd al-Karim Qasim's (q.v.) regime. He was born in Baghdad (q.v.) to a religious and landowning family. He attended the Baghdad Military College, the Staff College, and the Senior Officer's School in Britain. A member of the Free Officers (q.v.), he was one of the seven officers who decided to overthrow the monarchy. Following the 1958 revolution (q.v.), al-Shawwaf was appointed commander of the Mawsil (q.v.) garrison. He felt slighted by the post and became further frustrated when he was passed over for the post of minister of interior in September 1958. A junior officer who was not a Free Officer, Ahmad Muhammad Yahya, was given the post instead. Qasim's reliance on the communists also alienated al-Shawwaf.

In March 1959, he joined the conspiracy against Qasim led by Rif'at al-Hajj Sirri (q.v.). On his own initiative, al-Shawwaf announced a revolt in Mawsil on 8 March following a huge communist rally there. His coconspirators did not rally to his call. Some were caught off guard by his surprise announcement; others were being watched by the government, including Sirri. Al-Shawwaf was seriously wounded during the subsequent fighting and was reportedly killed by a communist at the local hospital, where he went seeking treatment for his wounds. The revolt was defeated by Qasim's forces.

SHAYBANI, MUHAMMAD IBN AL-HASSAN AL- (750–804). The father of Islamic international law. He was born at Wasit, although he spent most of his later life as a teacher and jurist in Kufa. In his major work, *Siyar al-Shaybani*, he presented in a full and systematic way the Muslim theory of international law and relations. This included matters such as the conduct of war, the conduct of the army in enemy territory, the intercourse between the territory of Islam (q.v.) and the territory of war, peace treaties, safe conduct, apostasy, and dissension.

SHIHAB, HAMMAD (1922–1973). A Ba'thist officer and politician. He was born in Tikrit and attended the Baghdad Military College. He was the head of the Baghdad (q.v.) garrison at the time of the 1968 revolution (q.v.), which helped ensure its success. Following the Ba'th's (q.v.) seizure of power, he was appointed chief of staff and became a member of the Revolutionary Command Council (q.v.). He was appointed minister of defense in April 1970. Shihab was taken hostage during Nazim Kazzar's (q.v.) coup attempt. He was shot to death on 30 June 1973 by Kazzar's followers after Kazzar was apprehended by the 'Iraqi regime.

SHI'I. Shi'i Muslims form a majority of the population in 'Iraq, ranging between 55 and 58 percent. There are several Shi'i sects. The Zaydis follow 5 of the Imams, while the Isma'ilis (Seveners) follow 7 Imams; the Twelvers, who form the majority of Shi'is in 'Iraq, Iran, and the rest of the world, recognize 12 Imams. They believe that the 12th Imam disappeared (went to occultation) and will return one day as the *al-Mahdi*, or "the rightly guided one," to bring justice to the world. The original differences between Shi'is and Sunnis (q.v.) were primarily political rather than doctrinal or ethnic.

The term *Shi'i* refers to Shi'i 'Ali or the Partisans of 'Ali, the fourth Muslim caliph (q.v.), the cousin of the prophet Muhammad, and the husband of his daughter Fatimah. Shi'i believed that 'Ali was the rightful successor to the Prophet. After the death of the Prophet, Abubaker was selected as his temporal successor; some Muslims, however, believe that 'Ali was the rightful successor. His supporters later advocated that his descendants are the legitimate Imams, the spiritual and the temporal leaders of the Muslim community. After the assassination of the caliph 'Uthman, conflicts erupted between Mu'awiya (q.v.), the Umayyad governor of Damascus, and 'Ali. When 'Ali was assassinated in 661 A.D., Mu'awiya established a hereditary caliphate in Damascus.

'Ali's second son Husayn was called on by the people of Kufa to assume the mantle of his father. He was later killed along with a small number of relatives and companions on the plain of Karbala (q.v.) in 'Iraq during a confrontation with forces loyal to the Umayyads. This event became a major religious, historical, and emotional event for the Shi'i. The Shi'i went into opposition, a position they have maintained for centuries of rule by Sunni governments. Husayn and his brother al-Abbas were buried in Karbala. His father was buried in Najaf (q.v.), making these two cities holy sites for the Shi'i. Other Shi'i holy cities include Kazimain, which holds the Shrine of the 7th and the 9th Imams, and Samarra (q.v.), which holds the shrine of the 10th and 11th Imams.

'Iraqi Shi'i are the largest Arab Shi'i community, and 'Iraq has been closely tied to Shi'i history since the early days of Islam. 'Ali himself moved his capital from Hijaz to Kofa in 'Iraq. After the dawn of the 16th century, the new Safavid dynasty in Iran made Shi'ism the religion of the state. The Safavid looked to the Shi'i religious centers at Najaf and Karbala for religious guidance and sought to bring 'Iraq under their control. The Sunni Ottoman dynasty opposed Safavid ambitions, and 'Iraq became an arena for battles between the two empires. 'Iraq mostly remained under Ottoman control; during centuries of Ottoman rule, the Shi'is were excluded from service in the government and the military. The Ottoman period contributed to tension between the Sunni and Shi'i communities because political power largely rested in Sunni hands.

After the creation of the modern 'Iraqi state, King Faysal I (q.v.) was generally accepted by the Sunnis because of his faith and by the Shi'i because of his lineage as a descendant of the Prophet. Faysal, who understood the complexity and diversity of 'Iraqi society, sought to forge a new 'Iraqi identity among 'Iraq's different ethnic and religious groups. His efforts met with limited success. The Shi'i remained relatively isolated, owing partly to the reluctance of many to embrace a secular outlook, but mainly because the Sunnis had longer experience in political and military service and dominated the state's administrative system.

During the revolt of 1920 (q.v.), Sunni and Shi'i together opposed British control and demanded independence. The Shi'i *mujtahid* (q.v.) played an instrumental part in the revolt. The British and some secular Sunni leaders were opposed to a strong role for the religious establishment, and the 'Iraqi government expelled a number of Shi'i ulama to Iran. However, beginning in 1922, Faysal tried to integrate Shi'i into the government. During the 1940s and 1950s, the status of the Shi'is showed some improvements, and an increasing number participated in the political system. Four Shi'i headed five of the cabinets during the last decade of the monarchy. From the eve of the 1958 revolution (q.v.) through the early 1960s, many Shi'is were opposed to a possible union with Egypt and Syria, because they were afraid of becoming a minority in a larger Sunni-dominated state.

Shi'i consciousness and activism began to rise in this period in response to the success of 'Iraqi communists in recruiting Shi'is, including members of prominent clerical families, and because rural-urban migration improved Shi'is' lives. Nonetheless they continued to suffer economic deprivation in the urban slums. Economic and social conditions led many Shi'i to join the 'Iraqi Communist Party (ICP) (q.v.). The Ba'th Party (q.v.) also made inroads among the Shi'i. One of the first party cells was established in Karbala, and many party leaders were Shi'i. During the short-lived 1963 Ba'th government, 53. 8 percent of the civilian leaders were Shi'i, and only 38.5 percent were Sunni. However, by the 1970s, only 5.7 percent of party leaders were Shi'is, making the Ba'th more homogeneous but less representative.

The successes of the ICP led some Shi'i clergy to launch religious political parties such as the al-Dawa Party, which was popular among those with the strongest religious loyalties. Under the Qasim (q.v.) government, Ayatullah Muhsen al-Hakim issued a *fatwa* against joining the ICP. Two young clerics, Mahdi al-Hakim and Muhammad Baqr al-Sadr (q.v.), became active in the new Dawa Party. Hakim traveled widely, established contacts, and organized activities. The Dawa was involved in an attempted coup in 1970, and Hakim fled the country to avoid arrest. He was assassinated in Sudan in 1999 allegedly by government agents.

The deteriorating relations between 'Iraq and Iran after the 1979 Iranian revolution prompted Iran to use the Shi'i card to pressure the 'Iraqi government and encouraged greater Shi'i activism in 'Iraq. The Dawa, the Islamic Action Organization (q.v.), and the mujahidin as well as a number of small groups launched well-organized antiregime campaigns in response to the rising repression between 1974 and 1977. This led to a harsh response by the Ba'th regime, particularly toward those Shi'i of Iranian origins. 'Iraq expelled over 250,000 'Iraqi Shi'i of Iranian origins during the 1970s and 1980s. Al-Sadr, who was described on Iranian radio as the "Ayatullah Khumaini of 'Iraq," issued a fatwa against joining the Ba'th Party.

The repression worsened after Saddam Husayn (q.v.) assumed power. All Shi'i endowments were placed under government control, and al-Sadr was arrested and later executed with his sister in 1980. Repression, however, was not the only response to Shi'i activities. The Ba'th continued to recruit Shi'is, some of whom reached high positions in the party and in the government. Shi'i peasants and workers benefited from the regime's social and economic welfare programs. Large sums of money were spent repairing Shi'i shrines during the Iran–'Iraq war (q.v.). Saddam's carrot-and-stick policy succeeded in maintaining the loyalty of most Shi'is during the war.

In spite of the effort to subordinate religious national symbols, the traditional tensions between Sunnis and Shi'is were too deep to be superseded in a relatively short time. The regime's repression also contributed to the alienation of many devote Shi'is. Thus it came as no surprise that as soon as the Ba'th regime appeared on the verge of collapse during the 1991 Gulf War, the Shi'is spearheaded an uprising to bring down the regime. The Supreme Assembly for the Islamic Revolution in 'Iraq (SAIRI) (q.v.), which was based in Iran and headed by Ayatullah Baqr al-Hakim (q.v.), joined the uprising. The brutal and rapid respond of the regime crushed the uprising.

Saddam's regime strengthened its grip on power after the uprisings. Although it rebuilt the damaged holy Shi'i shrines, it worked to reduce the influence of Najaf and Karbala as religious centers. Nevertheless, the religious leaders at Najaf continued to draw the support of Shi'i within 'Iraq and the Arab and Islamic worlds despite the growing influence of Qum and Mashad in Iran. Important 'Iraqi marjas include Ayatullah al-Khui (q.v.) and his successor Ali al-Sistani (q.v.), both of whom were of Iranian origin; Seyyed Muhammad Sa'id al-Hakim; and Seyyed Muqtada al-Sadr, the son of Ayatullah Muhammad Sadiq al-Sadr, who was assassinated in 1999. Ayatullah Muhammad Baqir al-Hakim (q.v.) emerged as a major figure with wide backing. He was later assassinated in Najaf in a car bomb attack. His brother, 'Abd al-'Aziz has emerged as the leader of SAIRI (q.v.). SAIRI has 12 to 15 thousand armed men, some of whom were moved into 'Iraq during the 2003 war. The majority of Shi'i appeared to oppose a U.S. presence in 'Iraq and to favor political methods to oppose them. Following the end of hostilities in April 2003, Shi'i activism again was on the rise, and the American forces reported being surprised by the strength and organization of the Shi'i religious leaders.

SIDQI, BAKR (1885–1937). The leader of the first military coup d'état in the Arab world in 1936. Bakr Sidqi was born to a Kurdish family in 'Askar. He studied at the Military College in Istanbul and graduated as a second lieutenant. He fought in the Balkans war and joined the Staff College in Istanbul, graduating in 1915. He joined Faysal's (q.v.) army in Syria and served in Aleppo with a number of other Sharifian officers (q.v.). After the collapse of Faysal's kingdom in Syria, Sidqi joined the 'Iraqi army in 1921. He attended the British Staff College and was considered one of 'Iraq's most competent officers. He lectured in the military school and achieved the rank of colonel in 1928 and brigadier general in 1933. Sidqi brutally repressed the Assyrian (q.v.) uprising in 1933 by ordering a massacre in which civilians, including women and children, were killed in the village of Smayl. In 1935, he cracked down on the tribal rebellions at al-Rumaitha and al-Diwaniya with unprecedented harshness.

In October 1936, Sidqi launched a coup against the government of Yasin al-Hashimi (q.v.). 'Iraqi planes distributed leaflets that called for the overthrow of the cabinet and the appointment of Hikmat Sulayman (q.v.) as prime minister. The leaflets warned that the military under the leadership of Sidqi would march on Baghdad (q.v.) if these steps were not implemented. Ja'far al-'Askari (q.v.), the minister of defense, attempted to dissuade Sidqi from his activities, but Sidqi arranged for al-'Askari's murder. Al-Hashimi subsequently resigned and left the country.

Hikmat Sulayman formed a new cabinet and Bakr Sidqi became the commander of the armed forces. However, the murder of al-'Askari created strong feelings against the new government, and Sulayman's cabinet did not survive for long. Bakr Sidqi was assassinated in Mawsil (q.v.) in 1937 on his way to Turkey by a dissident group of army officers. Recognized as one of the most brilliant officers in the 'Iraqi army, he was known for his intelligence, ambition, and self-confidence. He also believed in the need to use the army to bring about reform and achieve order. In this respect, he was influenced by Mustafa Kemal in Turkey and Reza Pahlavi in Iran.

SINJARI, 'ALI AL- (1932–). Founder of the Kurdistan Democratic Union. He was born in the Sinjar area of northern 'Iraq. After completing secondary school, he became active in the Kurdistan Democratic Party (KDP) (q.v.). He became a member of the KDP Central Committee in 1963. In 1964, al-Sinjari became a member of the KDP Political Bureau, a post he held until the collapse of the Kurdish movement in 1975. In 1977, he established the Kurdish Democratic Union and became its secretary-general. During the Iran–'Iraq war (q.v.), the KDU strongly opposed fighting the 'Iraqi army.

SIRRI, RIF'AT AL-HAJJ (1917–1959). A major figure in the 1958 revolution (q.v.). He was born in Baghdad (q.v.) to a military family and educated at the Baghdad Military College (1937–1939). He founded the Free Officers (q.v.), organizing the first cell in 1952. Although he was a member of the Supreme Committee of the Free Officers, he could never participate in their meetings because the government had him under surveillance. When his activities were discovered in 1956, Sirri was transferred to Kut province. He was appointed director of military intelligence after the successful overthrow of the monarchy in 1958. Sirri plotted against 'Abd al-Karim Qasim (q.v.) and planned a revolt in Mawsil (q.v.) in March 1959. Sirri was unable to participate in the failed rebellion, however, because Qasim had him under surveillance. Sirri was executed for his role in the revolt in September 1959. *See also* 'ABD AL-WAHHAB AL-SHAWWAF.

SISTANI, AYAT-ALLAH 'ALI AL- (1930–). The leading Shi'i (q.v.) *maya*, or the most senior religious scholar, for 'Iraqi and many other Shi'a. As the only grand ayatollah in the country, Sistani was under close watch at his home in the holy city of Najaf (q.v.) by Saddam Husayn's (q.v.) secret police for almost a decade. Sayyid 'Ali Husayni al-Sistani was born in the holy Shi'i city of Mashhad, Iran, to a well-known religious family of *'ulama* and religious leaders. After completing his primary and secondary studies, Sistani studied Islamic law, jurisprudence, and theology. He later moved to Najaf, where he attended Ayatullah Khui's (q.v.) lectures on the fundamentals of jurisprudence as well as lectures by prominent marjas Muhsin al-Hakim and Husayn al-Hilli. Ayatullah Sistani began to teach jurisprudence and *hadith* as well as other related subjects. He also wrote many books on jurisprudence and the judiciary. He was a close follower of al-Khui and was opposed to the politicization of religion and to the concept of the Government of the Jurisprudent adopted by Ayatullah Khumaini in Iran. Prior to the war on 'Iraq in March 2003, he issued *fatwas* urging opposition and noncooperation by the faithful to any American invasion. He was reportedly fired on when his guards fled as U.S. forces advanced on Najaf in early April. There were reports that his house had been surrounded by followers of a religious rival and that he and other non-Arab marjas were asked to leave 'Iraq, a charge that was later denied. Tribesmen and other followers rallied to Sistani's side.

SOCIALIST MOVEMENT OF KURDISTAN. Kurdish political party founded by 'Ali al-'Askari and Rasul Mamand (qq.v.) in 1976. The party established contacts with Jalal Talabani (q.v.), who was in Damascus at that time, and began to launch activities against the 'Iraqi regime. It was one of the founding components of the Patriotic Union of Kurdistan (PUK) (q.v.). Following the disastrous confrontation between the PUK and the Kurdistan Democratic Party (q.v.) in 1978, which resulted in the death or arrest of hundreds of PUK members, Mamand split from the PUK in 1979 and formed the United Socialist Party of Kurdistan (q.v.) with Mahmud 'Uthman (q.v.).

SOCIALIST PARTY OF KURDISTAN (SPK). Party formed in 1981 when Rasul Mamand (q.v.) split from the United Socialist Party of Kurdistan (q.v.), taking most of its fighters with him. It has allied itself with the Kurdistan Democratic Party (q.v.) and engaged in military clashes with the Patriotic Union of Kurdistan (q.v.), notably in 1983 when the party suffered heavy losses. It received 2.6 percent of the vote in the May 1992 elections. In August 1992, it merged with the Kurdistan Popular Democratic Party (q.v.) and the Popular Alliance of Socialist Kurdistan (q.v.) to form the Unity Party of Kurdistan (q.v.). *See also* SOCIALIST MOVEMENT OF KURDISTAN.

SOCIALIST UNION PARTY (HIZB AL-UMMA AL-ISHTIRAKI). A conservative political party established in 1951 that included a number of feudal landowners and political leaders who had broken away from Nuri al-Sa'id's (q.v.) Constitutional Union Party (q.v.). Led by Salih Jabr (q.v.) and supported by the regent 'Abd al-Ilah (q.v.), the Socialist Union Party (SUP) did not differ greatly from the Constitutional Union Party. Both agreed on foreign policy and drew support from large landowners and tribal leaders, particularly in southern 'Iraq. While the SUP opposed some of the policies of Nuri's government, the differences were based more on personality and personal ambition than on ideology. The SUP supported the establishment of democracy, direct elections, and the accountability of the cabinet before Parliament in accordance with the constitution. It also called for the coordination of relations between 'Iraq and other Arab states on the basis of a political union that potentially could include all of these parties; the Arab League was the vehicle by which this goal would be achieved. Despite its name, the SUP was not socialist. It was dissolved in 1952.

SOCIETY FOR ISLAMIC RESISTANCE (JAM'IYAT AL-NADHA AL-ISLAMIYYA). Established in 1917 by prominent tribal and religious leaders in southern 'Iraq, it was in many ways the forerunner of modern Islamic groups. It called for the establishment of an Arab-Islamic movement to oppose the British occupation and to establish Islamic unity. It also called for the establishment of a government totally independent from foreign influence and for modernization without westernization. It was unique for setting up a separate military wing.

SOCIETY OF SCHOLARS (JAM'IYAT AL-'ULAMA). The Society of Scholars emerged in 1959 to combat the rising influence of the communists under 'Abd al-Karim Qasim (q.v.), and it actively participated in the opposition to Qasim until his overthrow in 1963. It initially welcomed the Ba'th (q.v.) government but quickly moved into opposition against this regime as well. A number of clergymen who were members of the movement, including Shaykh 'Abd al-'Aziz al-Badri and Mahdi al-Hakim, were executed by the Ba'th in 1969, accused of spying or collaborating with Iran. A number of others were expelled to Iran. After these events, the Society of Scholars ceased to be a viable organization. *See also* SUPREME ASSEMBLY FOR THE ISLAMIC REVOLUTION IN 'IRAQ (SAIRI).

SOLDIERS OF THE IMAM (JUND AL-IMAM). A small Shi'i (q.v.) opposition party led by Dr. Sami al-Badri. Other leaders include al-Sayyid Abu Zaynab al-Shahbandar, Shaykh al-Khafaji, and Shaykh Abu 'Abd al-Rahman. The party split from al-Dawa (q.v.) in the 1970s over the need for the activity of an Islamic military and political party. It is a political movement that has not participated in any major way in armed action. The group believes in the need for a *faqih* (jurisprudent) at the head of every form of Islamic action, be it social or political. Its maximum goal is a program of action that indicates that its members want to be soldiers for the Imam. It does not see itself as an interim or temporary organization preparing the believers until the return of the Mahdi. It is politically close to the views of the Society of Scholars (*Jam'yat al-Ulama*) (q.v.) and is willing to cooperate with any Islamic group that sees itself moving along the path of historic Shi'i movements beginning with the era of prophecy and ending with the establishment of the state by the Mahdi. The goal of this group is to unify the 'Iraqi Islamic opposition movement within the framework of one group that would include all Muslim sects and ethnic groups in 'Iraq seeking the ouster of Saddam Husayn (q.v.). The group claims to seek a democratic 'Iraq that would be ruled in accordance with the rules of the *sharia* (q.v.). However, one of its leaders has stated that the group is willing to accept any democratically elected leader. The party is part of a Tehran-based umbrella organization called the Supreme Assembly for the Islamic Revolution in 'Iraq (SAIRI) (q.v.).

SUFIS. The mystics of Islam (q.v.). The name comes from *suf*, which means "wool" in Arabic, because many Sufis wore coarse wool garments to symbolize their rejection of worldly pleasures. The movement arose in the eighth century in 'Iraq and Syria and quickly spread to other parts of the Islamic world. Some scholars have explained the rise of mysticism as being influenced by Christianity; others have traced Zoroastrian and Buddhist influences as well. Sufism may also be seen as a natural development within Islam itself, part of an attempt to seek a closer understanding and relationship with God.

Sufis strive to achieve *fana* (oneness with God). They believe that *ibat* (the duties of worship) are ways to bring man closer to his Creator; these include penitence, love of God, meditation, and self-denial. There are different *tariqa* (mystical paths) (q.v.) by which an individual can achieve his own nothingness so that he can gain illumination, ecstasy, and union with God. Orthodox Muslims regarded Sufism with disapproval and suspicion, often finding the ecstatic sayings of Sufis to be blasphemous. Al-Hallaj (q.v.), one of the most famous Sufis, was found guilty of blasphemy in 922 and put to death by the caliph (q.v.) al-Muqtadir. Sufism lost some of its heretical traits following its reformation by the Persian jurist Abu Hamid al-Ghazali (1058–1111) (q.v.), ending the persecution of Sufis by orthodox Muslim clergy. 'Iraq is an important center for a number of Sufi orders. The Naqshabandiyya follow the path of Muhammad ibn Muhammad Baha al-Din, the Qadiriya follow al-Gaylani (d. 1166), and the Rifayia follow Ahmad al-Rifai (d. 1182). The Naqshabandiyya and the Qadiriya have a wide following among the Kurds.

SULAYMAN, 'ALI HAYDAR (1905–). Diplomat and cabinet minister during the monarchy. He was born in Rawanduz to a Kurdish family and educated at the American University of Beirut. He served as an official at various ministries, including education, foreign affairs, and interior, from 1930 to 1941. He worked in private business until 1947, when he was elected as a deputy to Parliament. Sulayman held a number of cabinet and diplomatic positions. He served as minister of the economy (1948–1949, 1954), minister of works (1949–1950, 1951–1952), and minister of construction (1953–1954). He held ambassadorial posts in West Germany (1956–1959), the United States (1959–1964), and Switzerland (1964–1966). Sulayman was undersecretary of state for foreign affairs for brief periods in 1959 and 1964. He also served numerous times as the 'Iraqi delegate to the United Nations.

SULAYMAN, AMIN ZAKI (1887–199?). Army officer. He was born in Baghdad (q.v.) to a Kurdish family. He studied in Istanbul and was appointed second lieutenant in the Ottoman army in 1905. He joined the 'Iraqi army in 1921. Sulayman was promoted to major in 1926 and colonel in 1930. He served as the commander of the Fourth 'Iraqi Infantry Battalion. He was appointed acting chief of staff in 1940. Sulayman played a significant role in the 1941 Rashid 'Ali al-Kaylani (q.v.) coup and fled with Rashid 'Ali and the Golden Square colonels (q.v.) to Persia following the movement's collapse.

SULAYMAN, HIKMAT (1889–1964). Prime minister and cabinet official during the monarchy. His father was governor of Basra (q.v.) and the author of a number of historical works in Turkish. Sulayman is believed to be of Christian (q.v.) origin, although his grandfather was kidnapped from the Caucasus and raised as a Muslim. He studied law at Istanbul College and graduated from the infantry school as a reserve officer in 1911. He served as an assistant to the governor of Istanbul in 1912. In 1914, he was appointed director of the School of Law and became head of the Department of Education in Baghdad (q.v.) the following year.

Sulayman served in the Ottoman army during World War I. After the war, he held a number of positions in 'Iraq: director of posts and telegraphs (1922–1925), speaker of Parliament (1925), minister of interior (1926), and minister of justice (1928–1929). As minister of interior in 1933, Sulayman supported Bakr Sidqi's (q.v.) repression of the Assyrian (q.v.) rebellion. He joined Sidqi in the overthrow of Yasin al-Hashimi's (q.v.) government in 1936, becoming prime minister after al-Hashimi's resignation. However, Sidqi's interference made it difficult for Sulayman's regime to achieve many of its objectives, and the cabinet resigned in 1937 following Sidqi's murder. Sulayman was then arrested and imprisoned in a comfortable home in Sulaymaniyya. He was released in 1940 by Rashid 'Ali al-Kaylani's (q.v.) government and he left for Iran the same year. He returned to Baghdad in 1942 and became involved in private affairs, including supervising the translation and publication of some of his father's works.

SUNNIS. The principal sect in Islam (q.v.). Sunnis comprise roughly 40 percent of the population of 'Iraq and have dominated the political and economic life of the county since 1920. There are no substantial theological differences among Sunnis, although divisions over understanding and applying the *sharia* (q.v.) have produced four schools of *mathhab* (jurisprudence) (q.v.). Most Sunni doctrines have emerged in response to attacks by other sects, particularly the Mu'tazilites (q.v.). Sunnis believe in the miraculous revelation and the eternal nature and message of the Koran (q.v.). They view its miraculous revelation to Muhammad as evidence of his prophetic call. They also believe that Muslims are candidates for Paradise as long as they maintain their faith; only apostasy excludes a Muslim from Paradise.

Sunnis rely on *ijma* (consensus) to select the head of the community and therefore recognize the Orthodox as well as the Umayyad and Abbasid caliphs (q.v.). The Shi'is (q.v.) split with the Sunnis over the question of the assumption of the caliphate. Shi'is recognize 'Ali and his descendants as the rightful caliphs and do not accept the assumption of the caliphate by the Umayyads. Makka and Medina are the holiest sites in Sunni Islam. Since the fall of the Saddam Husayn regime, a growing resistance movement emerged among the Sunnis in what is described as the "Sunni triangle" to the north and west of Baghdad. Many Sunnis (secular, nationalist, Ba'thist, and Islamist) came to believe they were the losers in the Gulf War, were being targeted by the Coalition, and began to fight back against U.S. and Coalition forces. *See also* BATTLE OF SIFFIN.

SUPREME ASSEMBLY OF THE ISLAMIC REVOLUTION IN 'IRAQ (SAIRI) (AL-MAJLIS AL-'ALA LI AL-THAWRA AL-ISLAMIYYA FI AL-'IRAQ). SAIRI is an umbrella group or a parliament representing different Islamic movements. The group's headquarters is located in Tehran, with additional offices in Damascus and London. SAIRI issues a publication known as *Martyrdom*. Other publications, such as *al-Jihad* and *al-Amal al- Islami*, are issued by individual member groups. It serves as a parliament for Islamic groups and attempts to coordinate their activities so that they have a united political and strategic position. It has its own military units known as the *Ninth of Badr*. This corps formed the brigade known as *al-Sadiq brigade*, which later became the nucleus of the Liwa Badr. The number of these units is around 10,000 to 15,000 soldiers. Most of the soldiers are 'Iraqis who participated in the Iran–'Iraq war (q.v.) on the Iranian side, and some are recruited from among 'Iraqi prisoners of war. This corps was also active in the uprisings following Operation Desert Storm (q.v.) in 1992. SAIRI maintains very close relations with Iran.

SAIRI involves 15 personalities representing different Islamic movements, including 'Abd al-'Aziz al- Hakim, the youngest brother of Muhammad Baqir al-Hakim (q.v.) and the leader of the 'Iraqi mujahhidin; Husayn al-Sadr; Kazim al-Hilli; Shaykh Muhammad Mahdi al-Asifi, the spokeman for al-Da'wa (q.v.); Muhammad Taqi al- Mudarrisi, the spiritual leader of the Islamic Action Organization; Sami al-Badri, the head of the Soldiers of the Imam (q.v.); Shaykh Muhammad Taqi, who is responsible for the military units of the council; Shaykh Jawad al- Khalisi; Dr. Ja'fari, a member of al-Dawa party; Sadr al-Din al-Qabanji; Sayid Muhammad al-Haydari; Abu Bilal al-Adib, a member of al-Da'wa; Shakyh Muhsin al-Husayni, the spokesman of the Islamic Action Organization (q.v.); 'Abd al-Zahra, a former member of al-Dawa who has broken with the party; Dr. Hamam Baqir; and Shaykh Jalal al-Din al-Saghir.

SAIRI is headed by Muhammad Baqir al-Hakim, son of the late marja', Grand Ayatullah al-Sayyid Muhsin al-Hakim. The idea for the organization grew out of the leadership vacuum in the 'Iraqi Shi'i (q.v.) community, which resulted from the execution of Muhammad Baqir al-Sadr (q.v.) by the

'Iraqi government in 1980. Shi'i leaders sought to establish a plan of action that would fit within the framework of Sadr's ideas as well as those of the Islamic revolution in Iran. The divisions that emerged within the various Islamic organizations in 'Iraq also contributed to the pressure to deal decisively with the question of who was going to lead the Islamic opposition in 'Iraq. There was a report that before his death al-Sadr had called for the revival of the Society of Scholars (*Jam'yat al-Ulama*) (q.v.), as the means to oust the Ba'th regime. Other reports claimed al-Sadr had established a five-member group to lead the opposition, and others said that he had appointed al-Hakim to lead the struggle.

With the establishment of SAIRI, the Islamic movements in Iran and 'Iraq became increasingly polarized as various factions tried to seize control of the group. The movement of this and other Islamic groups was greatly influenced by the tug and pull of the 'Iran–Iraq war and the need to increase coordination and cooperation became essential for the Islamic movement. With the arrival of Baqir al-Hakim in Damascus in 1980 after he was expelled from 'Iraq, the Society of Scholars was officially established in 1980. The failure of this group to become effective, however, led to an evolution of its activities with the establishment of the Bureau of the Islamic Revolution in 1982, which in turn established Liwa al-Sadiq, the al-Sadiq brigade.

The time coincided with the huge Iranian preparations for the liberation of Khoramshahr when Iranian president 'Ali Khameini and Ayatullah Muntazari, at the direction of Ayatullah Khomeini, supported the establishment of a unified Islamic group to lead the fight inside 'Iraq as Iran was leading it from the outside to oust the Ba'th regime. The bureau, however, was unable to resolve the internal conflicts among its members until 1983, when SAIRI was established. The organization was declared the sole legitimate representative of the 'Iraqi Islamic movement.

SAIRI does not count any secular or nationalist figures among its members, despite its call on nationalist parties to join. Al-Hakim was the spokesman of the council when it was first established under the leadership of Mahmud al-Hashimi, born in al-Nayaf in 1945. However, governmental institutions in Iran were directed to deal with al-Hakim when it came to 'Iraqi matters. Al-Hakim benefited from 'Ali Khameini's personal friendship, the support of Syrian president Hafiz al-Asad, and the desire of Ayatullah Khomeini that the son of Ayatullah Muhsin al-Hakim become the leader of the group.

SUSA, AHMAD (1902–1980s). Engineer and author. He was born in al-Hilla to a leading Jewish family, but he eventually converted to Islam (q.v.). He attended the American University of Beirut and completed his graduate work at George Washington University and Johns Hopkins University. He received a prize from George Washington University in 1929 for writing the best article on how to strengthen peace among the countries of the world. Susa returned to 'Iraq and worked as an irrigation specialist until 1957. He represented 'Iraq at international conferences dealing with irrigation and engineering. He was elected to the 'Iraqi Academy. He wrote more than 20 books in Arabic and English on irrigation, the Euphrates River (q.v.) valley, and on the history of Arabs and Jews (q.v.).

SUWAYDI, TAWFIQ AL- (1891–1968). Politician and diplomat during the monarchy. He was born in Baghdad (q.v.), the son of a former president of the 'Iraqi Senate. He studied law at the University of Istanbul and at the Sorbonne. He represented 'Iraq at the Arab conference organized in Paris in June 1913 where he called for the revival of the Arab nation and for reform. Al-Suwaydi was appointed dean of the Baghdad Law College in 1923, served with the British delegation at the Lausanne Conference, and served as legal adviser to the 'Iraqi government from 1921 to 1929. He was appointed director-general of the Ministry of Justice in 1925 and minister of education in 1928. He became prime minister in 1929, during which he also held the foreign affairs portfolio, but resigned after four months and was elected president of the chamber. Al-Suwaydi held a succession of government and diplomatic posts: 'Iraq's representative to the League of Nations (1934); comptroller and auditor-general of Accounts (1935); minister of foreign affairs (1934, 1937–1938, 1941); and deputy prime minister (1943–1944). He became prime minister in 1946 and again in 1950, both times also holding the foreign affairs portfolio. He served as minister of foreign affairs in 1953. In 1958, he was appointed deputy prime minister before becoming the foreign minister in the Joint Arab Cabinet of the Hashimite (q.v.) Union. Following the 1958 revolution (q.v.), he was sentenced to hard labor for life but was amnestied in 1961. Al-Suwaydi was known for his liberalism, tolerance, and intelligence. A brilliant jurist, his lectures at the Law College were combined and published as a book. A strong anticommunist, he called for close cooperation with the West. He died in Beirut.

SYKES–PICOT AGREEMENT. Britain and France entered into a secret arrangement on 16 May 1916, effectively dividing the Middle East into spheres of influence. According to the agreement, 'Iraq was divided into three zones: France took Mawsil (q.v.), Britain took southern 'Iraq and Baghdad (q.v.), and the area between Baghdad and Mawsil was to be shared jointly. The presence of oil (q.v.) in Mawsil made its eventual disposition an extremely contentious issue in the post–World War I period, with Britain, France, Turkey, the United States, and 'Iraq all making claims and counterclaims to the administration of the territory. *See also* ANKARA, TREATY OF.

SYRIAC CHURCH. *See* JACOBITES.

– T –

TAAMIM, AL-. The name of the former governorate of Kirkuk (q.v.); the name was changed in 1972 after the nationalization of foreign oil (q.v.) companies. The capital city of Kirkuk is one of 'Iraq's oldest cities and contains numerous oil wells. The city is inhabited by Arabs, Kurds (q.v.), and Turkumans (q.v.) and is at the center of a dispute over whether it belongs in the autonomous Kurdish region. The regime wishes to exclude it, while the Kurds insist it be included. *See also* MARCH MANIFESTO.

TALABANI, JALAL (1933–). One of the key leaders of the Kurdish nationalist movement since the early 1960s, and the secretary-general of the Patriotic Union of Kurdistan (PUK) (q.v.). He was born in the village of Kelkan in Arbil (q.v.) province. His father was a religious shaykh who headed the Talabani *taqiyya* (religious center). He attended secondary schools in Arbil and Kirkuk (q.v.) and the Law College in Baghdad (q.v.) from 1952 to 1955. Talabani was forced to leave school and go into hiding because of his political activities. After the 1958 revolution (q.v.), he reenrolled and graduated in 1959. He later served in the 'Iraqi army and became the commander of a tank unit. He joined the Kurdistan Democratic Party (KDP) (q.v.) of Mulla Mustafa al-Barzani (q.v.) while in college and organized the Kurdish Student Union.

In 1953 Talabani became a member of the KDP's Central Committee, and in 1959, he became a member of the Politburo. He worked as a journalist for Kurdish publications from 1958 to 1961 and was elected to the administration committee of the 'Iraqi Journalist Union. In 1961, he joined al-Barzani's forces in the uprising against the government and took charge of the fighting in the Kirkuk and Sulaymaniyya areas. Talabani led the Kurdish delegation in 1963 in negotiations with the Ba'thist regime. During this time, he met with Egyptian president Gamal 'Abd al-Nasir.

In 1964, Talabani and his future father-in-law Ibrahim Ahmad led a leftist KDP faction that split with the main KDP group led by al-Barzani. In the ensuing fighting, the Talabani-Ahmad group was defeated. Talabani and al-Barzani would have a stormy relationship for decades, leading to armed confrontations between their followers. He cooperated with the Ba'th Party (q.v.) from 1968 to 1970 but returned to an opposition stance when these contacts failed to produce results. After the collapse of the Kurdish revolt in 1975, Talabani formed the PUK. He rejected the regime's autonomy law and launched armed resistance against the regime. He attempted negotiations with Baghdad again in 1983–1984, although he returned to armed resistance when the contacts failed. Talabani has been a charismatic and articulate defender of the Kurdish cause, and he favors a democratic socialist system for 'Iraq.

A skillful and pragmatic leader, he has successfully established ties with Western leaders and media as well as with the late Turgut Ozal of Turkey and the late Hafiz al-Assad of Syria. After 1988, Talabani had better relations with KDP leader Mas'ud al-Barzani, and the PUK and KDP coordinated their actions during the 1991 uprisings. In May 1992, elections in the Kurdish area gave a slight edge to the KDP. Talabani and Barzani agreed to share power, but the two parties continued to disagree over turf and leadership leading to serious confrontations. In recent years, the two sides have worked to coordinate their efforts to oppose the Husayn regime and to adopt some common stands. He was named to the 25-person 'Iraqi Governing Council (IGC) (q.v.) in July 2003. *See also* MARCH MANIFESTO.

TALABANI, MUKARRAM AL- (1925–). Kurdish communist politician. Al-Talabani broke with Mulla Mustafa al-Barzani (q.v.) in 1963, after al-Barzani made peace with the government before he had been given assurances that his demand for Kurdish autonomy had been accepted. He later joined the 'Iraqi Communist Party (ICP) (q.v.). He served in several Ba'thist cabinets, holding the posts of minister of irrigation (1972–1977) and minister of transport (1977–1978). Al-Talabani was dismissed from his post in 1978 when the ICP fell out of favor with the regime, and he went into exile in Eastern Europe. He later served as a mediator between the government and Kurdish opposition leaders, including the period after the 1991 Kurdish uprisings.

TALFAH, KHAYRALLA (1910–). Government official and military figure from Tikrit. He is the maternal uncle of Saddam Husayn (q.v.) and his father-in-law. His nationalist views and activities influenced the young Saddam, who lived in Talfah's home from the time he was 10. He served as governor of Baghdad (1958) (q.v.), as a member of the Higher Education and Scientific Research Council (1972), and as head of the Civil Service Board (1973–1982). His son, 'Adnan Khayralla (q.v.), served as minister of defense under Saddam.

TAL HARMAL. Site of an early agricultural town, which lies today in Baghdad (q.v.). The earliest settlement can be traced back to the Akkadians and the third Ur dynasty, although the area is believed to have reached its peak around 1850 B.C. when it became the administrative center of the kingdom of Eshnuma. Tal Harmal had an advanced city planning system, detailed in the clay tablets found on the site whose inscriptions contained various administrative documents, commercial letters, contracts, and literary texts. An important legal text known as the Eshnuma Code of Laws was also found at the site. These laws predate Hammurabi's (q.v.) Code of Laws by about two centuries.

Some archeologists believe that the world's oldest college was founded in Tal Harmal and that it was concerned with the study of mathematics. A number of math texts have been found in this area, including one near Tal al-Dhiba', where a tablet was found solving a geometric problem through the use of triangles, which predated Euclides by about 1,700 years.

TALIB, NAJI (1917–). A member of the Free Officers movement (q.v.). He was born in Nasiriyya to a landed Shi'i (q.v.) family. His father was the mayor of Nasiriyya and a member of Parliament. He was educated at the Baghdad Military College (1936–1938), the British Military Academy (1938–1939), and the British Staff College (1950–1951). Talib attended the Baghdad Law College but did not finish his degree. He joined the Free Officers and in 1956 became a member and second deputy chair of the Supreme Committee of the Free Officers. He was one of seven officers involved in the decision to overthrow the monarchy in 1958.

Talib was appointed minister of social affairs during 'Abd al-Karim Qasim's (q.v.) regime, a post he resigned from in February 1959. During the 1963 Ba'th (q.v.) government, he held the post of minister of industry. He became prime minister under 'Abd al- Rahman 'Arif (q.v.) following the resignation of 'Abd al-Rahman al-Bazzaz (q.v.). He held the posts of prime minister and minister of oil from August 1966 until May 1967.

TAQA, SHATHIL (1929–1974). Diplomat, poet, and journalist. He was born in Mawsil (q.v.) and graduated from the Higher Teacher's College with a degree in Arabic literature (q.v.). He taught in Mawsil before moving to Baghdad (q.v.), where he worked at the Ministry of Information. In the 1950s, Taqa joined the Ba'th Party (q.v.) and was arrested in 1959 for his Ba'thist activities. He became head of the 'Iraqi News Agency after the 1963 Ba'thist coup and began to write for the *Baghdad Observor*, an English-language daily. When the Ba'th returned to power in 1968, he became the undersecretary to the minister of information. Taqa was appointed ambassador to the Soviet Union. He was undersecretary to the minister of foreign affairs, a post he held in 1974. He died of a heart attack during the Arab Foreign Ministers Conference in Rabat.

TARIQA. The system of rituals and practices developed by the Sufis (q.v.), who sought to attain knowledge of or unity with God through meditation, asceticism, or communal worship practices. More recently, the term has referred to Sufi orders that developed their own initiation rituals, communal worship, rites, and hierarchy. Some orders historically played not only a religious role but a social one in providing social welfare services. 'Iraq is an important center of Sufi orders, particularly the Naqshabandi and Qadiriyya orders that flourish among the Kurds (q.v.).

TAWFIQ, DARA. Prominent Kurdish nationalist and close aide to Mulla Mustafa al-Barzani (q.v.). He studied in 'Iraq and Britain and was the director of the Marine Transport Company in 'Iraq. An engineer by training, he spent most of his time in political activity. Tawfiq was initially a communist and served as a conduit between the Kurdistan Democratic Party (KDP) (q.v.) and the Soviet Union in the 1970s. Popular within the Kurdish movement, he wrote extensively in support of liberation movements and peace and served as editor of the KDP's newspaper. He headed the information effort after the resumption of fighting in 1974–1975 between the KDP and the Ba'th (q.v.) regime. After the collapse of the rebellion, Tawfiq returned to Baghdad (q.v.). He disappeared after the outbreak of the Iran–'Iraq war (q.v.), which he opposed.

TEHRAN PROTOCOL. Concluded on 21 December 1911, the Tehran Protocol established a joint Turko–Persian Delimitation Commission to delimit the border based on the 1847 Second Treaty of Erzurum (q.v.), although Persia refused to accept the validity of the Explanatory Note. In the event of disagreements, the dispute would be submitted to the Hague Court of Arbitration. *See also* CONSTANTINOPLE PROTOCOL.

THABEEHI, 'ABD AL-RAHMAN. Kurdish politician from Mahabad. He was a founding member of the Komala (q.v.) Party and became its secretary. He was also a leader in the Iranian Kurdish Democratic Party (KDP), which founded the 1946 Mahabad Republic. After its fall, he returned to 'Iraq where he worked with the 'Iraqi Kurdish Democratic Party (q.v.). He was subjected to harassment under the monarchy and fled to Syria. Thabeehi returned to 'Iraq following the 1958 revolution (q.v.), when he became a member of the central committee of the KDP and settled in Baghdad (q.v.). In 1970, he retired from politics and concentrated all his efforts on writing a Kurdish dictionary, of which only 2 of 26 volumes were published. Thabeehi returned to politics after the fall of the shah of Iran in 1979 by working with Shaykh 'Iz al-Din Husayni, a Kurdish leader. He suddenly disappeared in 1979. It is rumored that he was assassinated by the 'Iraqi secret service.

THAWRAT, AL-'ISHRIN (1920 REVOLT). A major revolt that broke out in 1920 against the British occupation of 'Iraq that forced the British government to reassess its mandatory policies. The direct causes of the revolt stem from a combination of regional and domestic factors. Despite the British promise in the Husayn–McMahon correspondence (q.v.) to create an Arab state after the defeat of the Ottoman Empire, the Arab territories were divided into mandates and assigned to Britain and France at the San Remo Conference (q.v.). Nationalist sentiments—fueled by the Arab Revolt, broken British promises, American President Woodrow Wilson's declaration on self-determination, and the actions of inexperienced British agents in 'Iraq—were inflamed by the announcement of 'Iraq's status as a British mandate on 3 March 1920. 'Iraqis who had expected to gain independence or to become part of a larger independent Arab state reacted with mass protests. Led by nationalist and religious leaders in cooperation with the tribes of the Middle Euphrates (q.v.) region, the protests erupted into a full-scale revolt in June 1920. British forces occupied most of 'Iraq in order to quell the uprising and moved to occupy Mawsil (q.v.) province, which was still in Turkish hands. The 'Iraqis suffered 8,000 casualties, and the British lost about 2,000 men and £40 million. In the aftermath of the revolt, Britain appointed a new high commissioner in 'Iraq, Sir Percy Cox, who arrived in October 1920. Cox announced Britain's intention to form an independent Arab government in 'Iraq under British trusteeship. A referendum was scheduled to determine whether 'Iraqis would support the ascension of Faysal (q.v.) to the 'Iraqi throne; Faysal received overwhelming support. *See also* ANGLO–'IRAQI TREATY OF 1922; GUARDIANS OF INDEPENDENCE.

THAWRAT AL-ZANJ (THE NEGRO REVOLT) (870–883). A major rebellion flared among the black slaves in southern 'Iraq during the rule of caliph al-Mu'tamid (r. 870–892). The movement was led by 'Ali bin Muhammad, who called on the slaves brought from East Africa to declare their freedom and start a revolt. Several thousand slaves rallied to his call in 870. They seized Basra (q.v.) in 871, took Wasit in 878, and threatened Baghdad (q.v.). Al-Mu'tamid charged his brother with suppressing the revolt. Short of money and equipment, the Abbasids were forced to request financial assistance from Ahmad ibn Tulun, the semiautonomous governor of Egypt. Even with this aid, the war dragged on for several years. In 883, 'Ali bin Muhammad was captured and executed. The slaves surrendered and asked for al-Mu'tamid's pardon. Many of them were returned to the homes of their masters.

TIGRIS RIVER. One of two major rivers in 'Iraq, the other being the Euphrates (q.v.). The river is roughly 1,840 kilometers long. It arises in the mountains of northeastern Anatolia before flowing through Turkey, Syria, and on to southern 'Iraq, where it joins the Euphrates northwest of Basra (q.v.) to form the Shatt al-Arab (q.v.). It is fed by four major tributaries, the Greater Zab, the Lesser Zab, the Adhaim, and the Diyala Rivers. It is heavily dammed for hydroelectric, irrigation, and flood control purposes. The Tigris has been used for irrigation since ancient times; the earliest farmlands were along its banks. By the time it reaches the Shatt al-Arab, 70 to 80 percent of its flow has been diverted by irrigation. The river is infamous for its flooding, and the 'Iraq government uses both dams and a diversion channel to the Euphrates to control this problem.

TIKRITI, 'ABD AL-GHAFFAR HARDAN AL- (1925–1971). Military and political figure from Tikrit. He was educated at the Flight and Staff Academies in Baghdad (q.v.). He joined the Ba'th Party (q.v.) in 1961 and was a principal figure in planning both the 1963 and the 1968 revolutions (q.v.). During the 1963 Ba'thist government, al-Tikriti was appointed commander of the air force and was a member of the ruling National Council of the Revolutionary Command. However, he supported 'Abd al-Salam 'Arif (q.v.) in his November 1963 move against the Ba'th. He became defense minister in the new regime, a position he held from November 1963 until March 1964. During the 1968 revolution, al-Tikriti went to the Presidential Palace, informed President 'Abd al-Rahman 'Arif (q.v.) that a coup was under way, and escorted 'Arif to the airport, where the deposed leader was flown out of the country.

In the new Ba'th regime, al-Tikriti held the positions of minister of defense, deputy prime minister, chief of staff, and deputy commander in chief. He also belonged to the ruling Revolutionary Command Council (RCC) (q.v.). His rivalry with interior minister Salih Mahdi 'Ammash (q.v.) for leadership of the military resulted in both men being relieved of their cabinet positions and appointed as vice presidents on 3 April 1970. Following the failure of 'Iraqi troops to support the Palestinian commandos in Jordan during Black September in 1970, al-Tikriti was relieved of his post as vice president and dropped from the RCC on 9 October. He went to Algeria and then moved to Kuwait in February 1971. He was gunned down by unknown assassins in Kuwait City in March 1971. It was widely speculated the assassins were 'Iraqi government agents.

TIMMAN, JA'FAR ABU AL- (1881–1945). A prominent politician and businessmen of Shi'i (q.v.) origin. An ardent nationalist, he played an important role in mobilizing public support during the 1920 revolt (q.v.) opposing British control. He served as treasurer of the committee responsible for collecting public contributions to support the nationalist movement and led the revolt in the Central Euphrates (q.v.). After the collapse of the revolt, he fled to Iran, returning when Faysal I (q.v.) took the throne.

Throughout his career, abu al-Timman strove to bring Sunnis (q.v.) and Shi'is together and fought British control, carrying the banner of full independence and democratic institutions and freedoms. As a result of his stubborn opposition to the British, he was exiled in 1922. He headed the National Party and served as President of the Baghdad Chamber of Commerce from 1935 to 1945. In 1935, he became a leader of al-Ahali (q.v.), the main opposition group to the government besides the military. Abu al-Timman cooperated with the military during the Bakr Sidqi (q.v.) coup because he believed that the military would stay out of politics once a new government was formed. He served as minister of finance in the new cabinet (1936–1937) but became increasingly upset with the interference of Sidqi and other officers. This tension reached a boiling point over the handling of the Diwaniya uprising. In June 1937, abu al-Timman resigned in protest along with three other cabinet members, thus virtually paralyzing the cabinet.

TURKUMAN (TURKUMEN). An ancient Turkic community whose presence in Iraq dates to the Abbasid and particularly the Seljuk (q.v.) periods. Today they number close to half a million people. Traditionally, they have lived in Kirkuk, Arbil (qq.v.), and Diyala provinces and Baghdad (q.v.). A small community lives in Mandali. These include Qaratapi, Tuz Khurmatu, Tawq, Altun Kupri, and Tal 'Afar. Some of the Turkuman have become Arabized, while others cling to their traditions. Many have held high government posts and prospered as businessmen and professionals. Tensions have surfaced in the past between the Turkuman and the Kurds (q.v.) because of economic reasons, as was the case in 1959 and because both groups lay claim to the city of Kirkuk. The Turkuman speak a dialect of Turkish that is closer to Azeri than it is to the standard Turkish of Turkey. They include Sunnis (q.v.) and some Shi'is (q.v.), particularly Qizilbash, among their members.

– U –

'ULUM, MUIIAMMAD BAHR AL- (1923–). A member of the Executive Council of the 'Iraqi National Congress (q.v.). Although a Shi'i (q.v.) cleric, he has not been known as an advocate of the establishment of an 'Iraqi Islamic Republic. He is a member of a prominent Shi'a clerical family from Najaf and is generally seen as a liberal cleric. He fled 'Iraq in 1991 after several members of his family were killed by Saddam's regime. He enjoys some support among secular and moderate Shi'is, but he is not well known and does not have much support inside 'Iraq. Al-'Ulum served as an aide to the late Shi'i *marja'* Muhsin al-Hakim, the father of Muhammad Baqir al-Hakim (q.v.), who is the head of the Supreme Assembly of the Islamic Revolution in 'Iraq (q.v.). He is based in London where he led the Ahl-al-Bayt charitable organization. He was named to the 25-person 'Iraqi Governing Council (IGC) (q.v.) in July 2003.

'UMAR, CHANKUL HABIB (1968–). The lone Turkuman member of the 'Iraqi Governing Council (IGC) (q.v.). She is a trained engineer, artist, and teacher. She is married to a lawyer and lives in Kirkuk (q.v.) where she has been active in women's affairs and in Turkuman politics as a member of the 'Iraqi Turkuman Front.

'UMARI, ARSHAD AL- (1888–?). Prime minister and cabinet official during the monarchy. He was born in Mawsil (q.v.) to the prominent 'Umari family. He graduated as a civil engineer from the Royal Engineering School in Istanbul. He was a member of the Senate in 1936 and was elected mayor of Baghdad (q.v.) in the early 1940s. Al-'Umari held numerous cabinet posts and twice served as prime minister (1946, 1954). He held the portfolios of defense (1944–1946, 1948), foreign affairs (1944–1946), supply (1944), interior (1946), and construction (1954). As the minister of foreign affairs, al-'Umari served as 'Iraq's delegate to the San Francisco Conference in 1945. He was removed as minister when he refused to sign the United Nations' charter because of his personal disagreements with some of the phraseology.

'UMARI, MUSTAFA AL- (1895–1960). Prime minister and cabinet official during the monarchy. He was born in Mawsil (q.v.) and studied at the Baghdad Law College. After graduation, he served in the Ottoman administration of 'Iraq. He joined the Ottoman army during World War I. He was taken prisoner by the British and sent to India in 1917. Al-'Umari returned to 'Iraq in 1919.

He served in a number of administrative and cabinet positions over the next several decades. He held positions in both the Interior and Finance Ministries, including assistant secretary to the minister of interior (1921), director-general of interior (1933), inspector-general of finance (1935), and accountant-general of finance (1936). He was prime minister for several months in 1952. Al-'Umari also held the portfolios of justice (1937–1938), interior (1937–1938, 1941, 1944–1946, 1948, 1952), and the economy (1948). Al-'Umari was often accused of working to dissolve cabinets so that he could be prime minister. Although he was an excellent administrator, many believed he was corrupt and abused his offices. Following the 1958 revolution (q.v.), the 'Abd al-Karim Qasim (q.v.) government confiscated his land, froze his assets, and placed him under house arrest. He later left 'Iraq for London.

UNITED 'IRAQI DEMOCRATIC UNION. An opposition group composed of the Islamic League (al-Rabitah al-Islamiya), the Islamic Union, and Communist Youth. This group held discussions with 'Iraqi government officials in December 1997.

UNITED NATIONS MONITORING, VERIFICATION, AND INSPECTION COMMISSION (UNMOVIC). Successor commission to the United Nations Special Commission on 'Iraq (q.v.). UNMOVIC was established in 1999 under UN Security Council Resolution 1284 and headed by Swedish diplomat Hans Blix. It was to set up and reinforce a system of inspections and ongoing monitoring of 'Iraq's weapons of mass destruction and missile programs, verify 'Iraq's compliance with the relevant UN resolutions, and address unresolved issues related to these tasks. Like UNSCOM, UN-MOVIC cooperated with the International Atomic Energy Agency (IAEA), headed by Muhammad al-Barade'i. UNMOVIC began renewed inspections in November 2002 after a four-year hiatus, but its efforts to complete its task were aborted by the United States' and Britain's decision to launch war against Iraq in March 2003.

UNITED NATIONS SPECIAL COMMISSION ON 'IRAQ (UNSCOM). Commission created by the UN secretary general to undertake inspections in 'Iraq for chemical, biological, and missile facilities and to work with the International Atomic Energy Agency (IAEA) on inspecting 'Iraq's nuclear programs and capabilities. UNSCOM was established in accordance with UN Security Council Resolution 687 adopted in 1991. It set up a monitoring system to verify 'Iraq's nuclear capabilities and its commitments under UNR 687 and UNR 715. UNSCOM was originally headed by the Swedish diplomat Rolf Ekeus and then by Australian Richard Butler. There were accusations that UNSCOM or some of its members were spying on 'Iraq and advancing specious or extraneous examples of 'Iraqi noncompliance to further the agenda of the United States. On the eve of the Desert Fox attack in 1998, Butler withdrew UNSCOM from 'Iraq. Following the attack, 'Iraq refused to allow the inspectors back in to the country, leading to a long confrontation with the UN and the absence of inspectors for four years. See also UNITED NATIONS MONITORING, VERIFICATION, AND INSPECTON COMMISSION (UNMOVIC).

UNITED SOCIALIST PARTY OF KURDISTAN. Established in the winter of 1979 by Rasul Mamand (q.v.), who broke from the Patriotic Union of Kurdistan (q.v.), and Dr. Mahmud 'Uthman (q.v.), formerly a close aide to Mulla Mustafa al-Barzani (q.v.). 'Uthman became the general secretary of the party at its first congress. In November 1980, it joined the Kurdish National Front with the Kurdistan Democratic Party (q.v.) and the 'Iraqi Communist Party (q.v.). Mamand and 'Uthman split however in 1981, with the bulk of the fighters following Mamand, who established the Socialist Party of Kurdistan (q.v.).

UNITY PARTY OF KURDISTAN. Party formed in August 1992 by the Kurdistan Popular Democratic Party (q.v.), the Popular Alliance of Socialist Kurdistan (q.v.), and the Socialist Party of Kurdistan (q.v.). Led by Sami 'Abd al-Rahman, it merged with the Kurdistan Democratic Party (q.v.) in August 1993.

'UQAYLI, 'ABD AL-'AZIZ AL-. Military officer. He served as minister of defense in 1965–1966. After the 1967 Six-Day War, he joined a group demanding free elections, the relaxation of restrictive collectivist measures, and policies independent of those of the United Arab Republic. He was imprisoned in

January 1969 as a result of one of the spy network trials. A former member of Parliament testified that al-'Uqayli, 'Abd al-Rahman al-Bazzaz, and Khalil Kanna (qq.v.) had formed a group to overthrow the Ba'th Party (q.v.) regime. Despite his alleged connections to a spy network, al-'Uqayli was not executed.

'URAYBI, QASIM AHMAD TAQI AL- (1936–). An engineer and technocrat from Mawsil (q.v.). He received an engineering degree from Baghdad University. He held the post of minister of oil from 1982 until March 1987, when he was appointed minister of heavy industry. He also served as acting minister of light industry (1986–1987).

'UTHMAN, MAHMUD (1943–). A Sunni Kurdish member of the 'Iraqi Governing Council (IGC) (q.v.), nationalist and physician from Sulaymaniyya. He played a major role in the Kurdistan Democratic Party (KDP) (q.v.) in the 1960s and 1970s. He was one of the primary negotiators for Mulla Mustafa al-Barzani (q.v.) in the Kurdish-Ba'th talks that produced the 1970 March Manifesto (q.v.). Although one of al-Barzani's closest aides in the early 1970s, 'Uthman came to feel he was being overshadowed by other supporters.

After the 1975 collapse of the Kurdish rebellion, he called for a comprehensive reassessment of the Kurdish situation and established the Kurdistan Democratic Party—Provisional Committee. 'Uthman cooperated with Rasul Mamand (q.v.) in the establishment of the United Socialist Party of Kurdistan (q.v.); control remained largely in Mamand's hands, though, because he commanded the party's *pesh mergas* (q.v.). He broke with Mamand in 1981 and established his own group. His group formed a coalition with the KDP after the May 1992 Kurdish elections, and merged with the KDP in the summer of 1993. 'Uthman has lived in Damascus, Tehran, and London.

– W –

WAHBI, TAWFIQ (1892–1984). Kurdish politician from Sulaymaniyya. He attended schools in his hometown, in Baghdad (q.v.), and later at the Military College in Istanbul. He became a captain in the Ottoman army. After World War I, he served as an aide to Shaykh Mahmud al-Hafid. After the defeat of the shaykh's first uprising, he joined the 'Iraqi army, in which he was promoted to the rank of colonel. Wahbi also taught at the Military College and became its director in 1923. In 1930, he was appointed governor of Sulaymaniyya but was sent to Lebanon shortly thereafter. He was transferred in 1935 to the civil service, probably as a result of his Kurdish nationalist activities. In 1936, he was appointed governor of Sulaymaniyya under the Bakr Sidqi (q.v.) government.

Wahbi held several government posts, including director-general of irrigation and director of land survey (1942). He was appointed minister of the economy in 1944 because of his pro-British leanings and his prestige among educated Kurds (q.v.). He later became a member of the 'Iraqi Senate. He was out of the country when the 1958 revolution (q.v.) occurred, and he remained in London until his death. Wahbi was a moderate Kurdish nationalist with strong pro-British positions, known for his liberal, prodemocratic views. He was also an intellectual who promoted Kurdish language and culture. He laid down a Kurdish grammar and coauthored a Kurdish –English dictionary with C. J. Edmonds. He was a member of the Baghdad PEN Club.

WAHHAB, SAMIR MUHAMMAD 'ABD AL- (1945–). A Ba'thist activist and security official. He joined the Ba'th Party (q.v.) in 1959 and was imprisoned under both the 'Abd al-Karim Qasim and 'Abd al-Salam 'Arif (qq.v.) regimes. In 1963, he participated in the Ba'thist coup. His home was the hiding place from which the Ba'thists moved against the presidential palace in 1968. In the 1970s, most of his party activities were with the Baghdad (q.v.) branch. Al-Wahhab served as mayor of Baghdad in 1979 and was a member of the senior command of the Baghdad party militia. He became a member of the Regional Command (q.v.) in 1982 and was appointed a presidential adviser with ministerial rank. He held the post of minister of higher education from 1985–1987, when he was appointed minister of interior (1987–1991).

A party activist and Saddam Husayn (q.v.) loyalist, al-Wahhab has frequently been assigned special missions for the regime. In 1987, he was appointed head of police and charged with restoring public order and dealing with deserters. He served as head of the first investigative body in the directorate of intelligence. During the Iran–'Iraq war (q.v.), al-Wahhab was a member of a special committee headed by Saddam and entrusted with launching a guerrilla war in the event Iranian forces penetrated Baghdad. He was not reelected to the Regional Command in 1991.

WAHID, 'ABD AL-RAZZAQ 'ABD AL- (1932–). Poet and playwright from Baghdad (q.v.). He studied Arabic literature (q.v.) at the University of Baghdad where he worked as a teacher before taking a position as assistant to the dean of the Arts Academy. In 1970, he transferred to the Ministry of Information and Culture, holding several positions before becoming director of the National Library in Baghdad. Al-Wahid's first collection of poetry (q.v.) appeared in 1956, and he has published several more collections, including *Leaves on the Sidewalk of Memory* (1969), *A Tent at the Threshold of Forty* (1970), and *Where Is Your Calmness Now?* (1983). He has also written several verse plays.

WAQF. Religious endowments or charitable trusts. The income of these endowments or trusts may be applied to some charitable purpose or to the use of specified individuals and/or their families and descendants. The declaration of property as waqf must be done in perpetuity and not for a specified time period.

WARDI, 'ALI AL- (?–1995). A prominent sociologist and intellectual. He was a liberal reformer who advocated the liberation of the common people from religious practices and legends that had been intended to represent ethical values but that had lost their original meaning. He stressed the ethical and cultural values of Islam (q.v.), which he believed were the most important elements affecting life and society. He asserted that the 'Iraqi personality consisted of a "dual character" and that urban 'Iraqis hold tribal bedouin values at heart. Al-Wardi authored *The Sultan's Preacher*, *The Comedy of Man's Mind*, and a study of 'Iraqi society that is considered one of the most important works in Arabic on the history and culture of 'Iraq.

WATHBA, AL-. An uprising in 1948 sparked by the signing of the Portsmouth Treaty (q.v.) on 15 January by 'Iraqi prime minister Salih Jabr (q.v.) and representatives of Britain. The text of the treaty was released in Baghdad (q.v.) on 16 January, setting off three days of student demonstrations and strikes. 'Iraqi opposition parties joined in the Committee for National Cooperation (q.v.) and agitated against the treaty. A mass demonstration by the students and wide segments of the 'Iraqi public on 20 January resulted in several casualties when police and the demonstrators fired at each other. On 21 January, the regent 'Abd al-Ilah (q.v.) issued a proclamation repudiating the treaty, putting a temporary end to the disturbances. Jabr returned to Baghdad from London on 26 January. He refused to heed calls for his resignation and announced that no final decision had been taken on the status of the treaty. Violent clashes between the police and demonstrators demanding Jabr's resignation on 27 January resulted in scores of deaths and hundreds wounded, according to official sources. Jabr resigned later the same day.

Al-Wathba was the culmination of 'Iraqi anger over several issues, not merely a reaction to a revised treaty of alliance with Britain. The new agreement was being negotiated as events in Palestine neared their conclusion, with Britain receiving the majority of the blame; economic conditions were worsening; and Jabr was an unpopular leader who had antagonized the nationalists and clamped down on political parties. With many sectors of the public already alienated, the Portsmouth Treaty tipped the balance against the government and led to its downfall.

WAZIR. A title given to the administrative assistant of the caliph (q.v.) during the rule of the Abbasids from 750 to 1258. The word has come to mean "minister" or "member of the cabinet." Wazirs had great authority under the caliphs; they were in charge of the budget, maintaining the army, and employing or dismissing officials. They also supervised the functions of the special departments that handled various services.

WILSON, SIR ARNOLD (1884–1940). British civil servant who was acting commissioner for 'Iraq in 1918–1920. During Wilson's tenure, Britain faced the most serious threat to its rule in 'Iraq and in the region during the revolt of 1920 (q.v.). Upon learning that 'Iraq had been assigned to Britain as a mandate, 'Iraqis erupted into rebellion against the League of Nations mandate system and British control of their affairs. In the aftermath of the revolt, Wilson was replaced by Sir Percy Cox. Wilson suggested that Faysal (q.v.) should head an 'Iraqi administration. He wrote one of the first books on the history of the Persian Gulf.

– Y –

YAHYA, TAHIR (1913–1986). Prime minister and military officer from Tikrit. He was educated at the Baghdad Military College and the Staff College. A member of the Free Officers (q.v.), Yahya was one of the seven people involved in the decision to launch the 1958 revolution (q.v.). He joined the Ba'th Party (q.v.) in 1963. He was appointed chief of the general staff during the 1963 Ba'th government and was also a member of the ruling National Council for the Revolutionary Command. He favored cooperation with other nationalist groups and postponing the introduction of socialism.

Yahya supported 'Abd al-Salam 'Arif's (q.v.) countercoup against the Ba'th in November 1963. He became prime minister in 'Arif's government, a post he held from November 1963 until September 1965. He also held the defense portfolio following the removal of Hardan al-Tikriti (q.v.) in March 1964. During his tenure, a satisfactory agreement was worked out with the oil (q.v.) companies. He also opened negotiations with the Kurds (q.v.). Yahya resigned as prime minister on 3 September 1965; his cabinet had suffered a rash of resignations by its Nasirite elements, and the military had swung its support behind 'Arif 'Abd al-Razzaq (q.v.). Yahya was appointed deputy prime minister in May 1967, and he became prime minister and minister of interior in July 1967, a position he held until the Ba'thist takeover in July 1968.

YAMALKY, MUSTAFA (1856–1936). Kurdish leader from Sulaymaniyya. He was educated in Sulaymaniyya, Baghdad (q.v.), and Istanbul, where he became an officer in the Ottoman army in 1877. He held several high military positions but was forced to resign when the Kemalists came to power in

Turkey. Active in the Kurdish nationalist movements, he returned to Sulay-maniyya after the failure of Shaykh Mahmud's (q.v.) first uprising in 1919. Yamalky published a weekly newspaper, *Bomki Kurdistan*, in Kurdish, Turk-ish, and Persian. He helped pave the way for the return of Shaykh Mahmud from exile. He became minister of information during Shaykh Mahmud's second term in office, but they disagreed on issues concerning the British and the Kamaleen. Yamalky went back to Baghdad and continued publishing his newspaper. He never held any government positions in Baghdad.

YASIN, 'ABD AL-FATTAH AL- (1932–). An economist and politician. He completed secondary schooling in Tikrit and graduated from the College of Commerce and Economy in Baghdad (q.v.) in 1955. He joined the Ba'th Party (q.v.) in the 1960s and was arrested for his activities and exiled to Sulay-maniyya. In 1963, al-Yasin served in a number of administrative and eco-nomic positions but was arrested again after the fall of the Ba'th government in November 1963. When the Ba'th returned to power in 1968, he was ap-pointed ambassador to Lebanon. He held a variety of posts, including under secretary of the Ministry of the Economy and member of a presidential com-mittee. In 1973, he became a member of the National Union Front (q.v.) and in 1974 chaired the Northern Affairs Bureau, where he dealt with the Kurdish situation. Al-Yasin was elected to the Regional Command (q.v.) in 1974, be-came a member of the Higher Agricultural Committee in 1976, and became a member of the Revolutionary Command Council (RCC) (q.v.) in 1977. After Saddam Husayn's (q.v.) assumption of power in 1979, he served as minister of local government (1979–1982). Al-Yasin was an adviser in the office of the Popular Organizations in 1982 and minister of youth (1986–1988). He lost his membership in both the Regional Command and the RCC in 1982.

YAWAR, GHAZI MASH'AL AJIL AL-. A member of the Shaykhli family in northern 'Iraq. He is a civil engineer who spent 15 years based in Saudi Ara-bia. A Sunni Muslim, he is a close relative of Sheikh Muhsin 'Adil al-Yawar, head of the powerful Shammar tribe, which includes both Sunnis and Shi'is.

YAZDI, MUHAMMAD KAZIM (1831–1919). Leading Shi'i *marja'* in Najaf (qq.v.) until his death. He was born near Yezd and later studied in Isfahan and Najaf. He began to teach at Najaf, where he became the main marja' in 1911. As a religious authority, he was a traditionalist and eschewed the mixing of religion and politics. Unlike most *'ulama* (religious scholars), he was op-posed to the constitutional movement in Iran. When the leaders of Najaf met with British high commissioner Sir Arnold Wilson (q.v.) to discuss their views on the future of 'Iraq, specifically whether to establish a constitutional Arab government or to continue British control, the majority of the clergymen favored the establishment of an Arab government. Yazdi, though, said that although the question was an important matter that had to be discussed by all, he did not understand politics, and his information was limited to matters of right and wrong. He was accused of cooperation with the British authorities and criticized by some of his opponents for looking the other way when the British suppressed the 1918 uprising in Najaf.

YAZIDI, SHAYKH TAHSIN AL-. One of the most influential and widely respected figures in the Yazidi (q.v.) sect. Accused of participating in a 1969 coup attempt, he joined Mulla Mustafa al-Barzani's (q.v.) forces in Kurdistan. He was eventually pardoned by Saddam Husyan (q.v.) and continues to live in 'Iraq.

YAZIDIS. A religious sect practicing angel worship, found mainly in northern 'Iraq. Smaller groups live in Turkey, Syria, Armenia, and Azerbaijan. Scholars estimate the number of Yazidis at 100,000. Most Yazidis speak a Kurdish dialect, although some of their sacred books are in Arabic. Because of their language, some scholars believe that the Yazidis have Kurdish origins. Others contend that the sect's roots go back to southern 'Iraq and the lower Euphrates (q.v.) region. The origin of the religion is also relatively obscure. Some scholars believe the sect is an Islamic one descended from supporters of the Umayyad caliph (q.v.) Yazid in 686 A.D. Others trace the name to the Adestan god Yazdan, or Ized, the angel deity. The Yazidis have absorbed elements from many religions: the prohibition of certain foods from Judaism; baptism, the drinking of wine, and eucharistic rites from Zoroastrianism and Christianity; fasting, sacrifice, and pilgrimage from Islam (q.v.); Sufi (q.v.) and Ismaili beliefs such as ecstasy, the synthetic doctrine, and reverence for a large number of initiate shaykhs; and Sabean (q.v.) and Babylonian mystic features. There are also elements of nature worship and worship of the sun.

Yazidis have often been inaccurately portrayed by their enemies as devil worshippers; in fact, they practice angel worship. They believe that the Supreme Being, the Spirit of Good, delegated power over the world for 10,000 years to Shaytan (the devil), after his fall from heaven. They do not worship but rather placate one who is regarded as a lord of power, not as the author of evil, an ancient Mesopotamian and Semitic idea. Yazidis do not utter the name *Shaytan*, nor do they utter words beginning with the letter *sheen*. A special place in their pantheon is given to Malak Tawus (the Peacock angel), who is sometimes mistakenly identified as Shaytan. They consider Jesus to be an angel and Muhammad a prophet. Their patron saint, Shaykh Adi bin Musafir, died about 1162. His tomb at Bathra is a shrine of pilgrimage. Others see a link to Mar Adi who helped bring Christianity to Mesopotamia. The Yazidis hold a festival in the spring and an assembly at the shrine of Shaykh

Adi in October. During the assembly, a bull is sacrificed and neighborhoods are illuminated with oil lanterns. The Yazidis do not seek converts.

The Yazidis traditionally set themselves apart from the mainstream of the societies in which they live. Nevertheless, the sect has suffered severe persecution for its religious beliefs. Massacres at the hands of the Ottoman Turks and Kurdish princes almost wiped out the Yazidis during the 19th century. Many of those who survived went to Syria or to what is now Armenia and Azerbaijan. Yazidi society is strongly communal. It is divided into laity and clergy. The religious hierarchy is strictly guarded, with a priestly caste and a single shaykh recognized as the religious authority. Most Yazidis are farmers and herdsmen, although some seminomadic tribes continue to exist.

YUSUF, SA'DI (1943–). A well-known contemporary poet and a communist intellectual from Basra (q.v.). He graduated from the Higher Teachers College in Baghdad (q.v.) and held various positions in cultural institutions in 'Iraq. He also taught in Algeria and worked as a journalist in several Arab countries. His greatest attribute as a poet has been his capacity to speak in direct and simple, yet highly poetic terms about life's daily experiences and routines and to portray them with intimacy and familiarity. In this respect, his poetry (q.v.) is remarkably different from that of many of his contemporaries. Yusuf has published several volumes, including *Collected Works*, which contains all his former *diwans*; *The Pirate*; *51 Poems*; *Visible Poems*; *Far from First Heaven*; *Al-Akhdhar bin Yusuf*; and *His Worries*. He has been living outside 'Iraq in recent years.

YUSUFI, SALIH AL- (1915–1982). A judge, writer, journalist, and Kurdish activist from the Dohuk area. He participated in negotiations with the 'Iraqi government in the 1960s and 1970s and favored cooperation and agreement with the central government. A popular and well-respected individual, al-Yusufi was a member of the International Peace Council. He returned to 'Iraq after the collapse of the 1975 Kurdish revolt and was welcomed by the 'Iraqi government although he did not receive an official political or military position.

– Z –

ZAHAWI, JAMIL SIDQI AL- (1863–1936). A liberal thinker, poet, and Ottoman official. He was born in Baghdad (q.v.) to parents of Kurdish origin. He studied the Koran (q.v.), grammar, and logic under his father and studied modern literature (q.v.) translated into Arabic on his own. He mastered Arabic, Kurdish, Persian, and Turkish, among other languages. He served in the Ottoman administration in Baghdad, Istanbul, and Yemen and taught philosophy in Istanbul. In 1886, al-Zahawi was appointed a teacher at Sulaymaniyya and later became a member of the Baghdad *wilayet* (province) Majlis. In 1888, he became the director of the press for the Baghdad wilayet and editor of the Arabic section of the official newspaper, *al-Zawra*.

Al-Zahawi was later arrested and his travels limited to Baghdad. He supported the Ottoman constitution of 1908. He went to Egypt in 1924 and returned after four months. A liberal thinker and agnostic, al-Zahawi advocated the adoption of Western science and technology and was one of the strongest advocates of the emancipation of women. His work stood for modernism and progress, for personal and national freedom, and for scientific experiment. His most impressive work is *Revolt in Hell*, which shows the influence of Dante. Al-Zahawi portrays hell as primarily inhabited by scientists, philosophers, and poets. Al-Zahawi portrays damned intellectuals revolting, suppressing the fires, and arresting the Guardians of Hell.

ZAINY, MUHAMMAD ALI (1939–). Senior advisor to the Ministry of Oil. He trained at Colorado School of Mines and was an engineer and mid-ranking official of 'Iraq's Ministry of Oil until he left 'Iraq in 1982. Two of his nephews were executed in 1980 for joining an Islamist group. He has worked with OPEC (as a representative of the 'Iraqi government) as an oil company executive and energy consultant in Colorado and with the Center for Global Energy Studies in London as an analyst. He is an American citizen.

ZAKI, MUHAMMAD (1894–1937). Cabinet official during the monarchy. He was born in a small village in the Basra (q.v.) province to a family of modest background. His father died while he was young; his uncle married his mother and took care of him. He was educated in Basra and began studying at the Baghdad Law College before his studies were interrupted by World War I. Zaki served as a reserve officer in the Ottoman army and was wounded at Salman Pak. After the war, he finished his law degree and began practicing in 'Iraq. He was the youngest deputy elected to Parliament in 1924. Zaki was reelected a number of times as a deputy from Basra and was elected head of Parliament in 1935.

With Rashid 'Ali al-Kaylani and Yasin al-Hashimi (qq.v.), he founded the National Brotherhood Party (q.v.) in 1930. He served as minister of justice in three cabinets (1933, 1935–1936). Zaki was well known for his extensive legal knowledge and his support of the parliamentary system in 'Iraq. He authored a number of articles on both subjects. He strongly believed that the parliamentary system was the best system of government that mankind had achieved in recent history because it allowed the citizenry to pay close attention to the political decision-making process.

ZAKI, MUHAMMAD AMIN (1880–1948). Kurdish nationalist and cabinet official. He was born in Sulaymaniyya to a prominent Kurdish family. He was educated at the Military and Staff Colleges in Istanbul and graduated with the rank of captain in 1902. He served in the Ottoman government as an engineer and fought on the Ottoman side in both the Balkan Wars and World War I. In 1924, Zaki returned to 'Iraq, where he was appointed as an instructor at the Military College, where he eventually became commandant. He was elected deputy to Parliament from Sulaymaniyya in 1925. He served in numerous cabinets, indicating the need of successive governments regardless of their political views to have a Kurdish member. Zaki held the portfolios of works (1926–1928, 1929–1930, 1930–1932, 1935–1936, 1941–1942), education (1926–1928), defense (1928–1929), and the economy (1940–1941). A Kurdish nationalist, he wanted to revive the Kurdish nation through the spread of Kurdish culture.

ZAKI, SHUKRI SALIH (1920–). Lawyer, politician, and more recently an opposition figure. He was born in Baghdad (q.v.) and became active in politics in the 1940s, when he began contributing articles to newspapers. Zaki held a number of positions during the rule of 'Abd al-Salam 'Arif (q.v.): minister of commerce (1963), ambassador to Cairo (1964), minister of the economy (1965), minister of finance (1965–1966), and minister of oil (1965–1966). He practiced as a lawyer for a while before moving to Abu Dhabi in 1969, where he still resides. He was active in establishing secondary and evening schools from which a number of prominent politicians, including Ahmad Hasan al-Bakr (q.v.), have graduated. These schools were nationalized in 1973.

ZANKID STATE. A state established by the Atabegs of Mawsil (q.v.), the chief ministers of the Seljuk (q.v.) sultan, which lasted from 1127 to 1250. The Atabegs gained influence as the Seljuk sultans declined. In response to attacks by the Crusaders, the Seljuk sultan appointed 'Imad al-din Zanki as the ruler of the district of Mawsil in 1127. Zanki participated in the wars against the Crusaders and was hailed as a hero by the Muslims of Syria and 'Iraq.

Zanki became virtually independent in Mawsil when the Seljuks were defeated. He united Damascus and Mawsil, moving his capital first to Damascus and then to Aleppo to lead the campaign against the Crusaders. Zanki was killed by one of his own people in 1146. His son Nur al-Din took over the Zanki state. Nur al-Din was recognized as a tough and brave leader. He gained control of the al-Raha from the Crusaders. He sent an army under Shirkuh that brought the Potomites in Egypt under Nur al-Din's control. Ruling Egypt as Nur al-Din's viceroy, Shirkuh defeated the Crusaders near Alexandria. Shirkuh was succeeded by his nephew Salah al-Din (q.v.), who founded the Ayyubid (q.v.) state.

ZAYD BIN 'ALI (698–740). Jurisprudent, religious scholar and orator, and the grandson of Imam al-Husayn bin 'Ali. He was raised in Medina but lived most of his life in Kufa. He led the revolutionary faction among the household of the prophet Muhammad. His faction rejected the idea of simply having the Imamate as a religious post and sought to make it politically active in the struggle against the Umayyads. Caliph Hisham (r. 724–743) had him arrested and imprisoned for several months. People began to follow him secretly and he announced a revolt in Kufa in 740. The revolt was put down easily by the authorities, who had known in advance about the uprising, and Zayd bin 'Ali was killed. His son carried the banner of revolt after his death, but he also was killed by the authorities. Zayd bin 'Ali is considered the head of the Zaydi Shi'i (q.v.) sect; many of its followers today live in Yemen.

ZAYD BIN AL-HUSAYN (1889–1970). The youngest son of Sharif Husayn, the leader of the Hijaz and the Arab Revolt. He assumed a military role during the Arab Revolt and represented Faysal (q.v.) abroad when he was king of Syria and then 'Iraq. For personal and political reasons, he was not named as regent for Faysal II (q.v.) following the death of King Ghazi (q.v.) in 1939; the post went instead to 'Abd al-Ilah (q.v.). Zayd bin al-Husayn died in Istanbul in 1970. *See also* HASHIMITES.

ZIYAD BIN ABIH (622–673). A political and military leader during the orthodox Umayyad state. His mother was from a leading Arab tribe, but the identity of his father was unknown, hence his name, which means "the son of his father." He was sent to Basra (q.v.) after its establishment by caliph 'Umar (r. 634–644) to divide the spoils among the soldiers because of his knowledge of reading and writing. Caliph 'Ali (r. 656–661) appointed him governor of Basra. In 661, Ziyad bin Abih refused to give allegiance to Mu'awiya (r. 661–680), the founder of the Umayyad state. Mu'awiya sent him a special messenger recognizing him as his half-brother in 662. Mu'awiya appointed him governor of Basra in 665 and of Kufa in 670. Eventually, Ziyad bin Abih came to rule the eastern half of the empire, including Bahrain, India, Oman, and Kuhfa. (*See also* BATTLE OF SIFFIN.)

Ziyad was widely recognized as a skilled orator and mediator. He consulted military and tribal leaders in most of his decisions, which helped him maintain his control over governmental affairs. He also launched an important attempt to strengthen loyalty to the state as opposed to the tribe by putting fighters from various tribes together in different military units.

ZUBAYDI, MUHAMMAD HAMZA AL- (1938–). A Ba'th Party (q.v.) activist and government official from Babil governorate. A Shi'i (q.v.), he joined the Ba'th Party in 1954 and was arrested, deported, and put under house arrest at various times for party activities. He held his first party branch command position in 1962 and came to hold leading party positions in all parts of the country. Al-Zubaydi was appointed adviser to the Revolutionary Command Council (RCC) (q.v.) following the 1968 revolution (q.v.) and became the director-general of the Ba'th Secretariat and head of the RCC's Arab Affairs Bureau until 1977. In 1977, he served as governor of Tamim province and was also elected as a candidate member of the Regional Command (q.v.). He became a full member of the Regional Command and a presidential adviser with the rank of minister in 1982. Al-Zubaydi served as minister of transport and communications (1987–1991). In March 1991, he was appointed deputy prime minister and became prime minister in September 1991—a position he held until September 1993. In 1994, he once again became deputy prime minister; he was removed from his ministerial and Regional Command posts in 2001. He played a major role in suppressing the uprisings in the south in the wake of Operation Desert Storm (q.v.). He was captured by U.S. forces in April 2003.

ZUHAB, TREATY OF. The Treaty of Zuhab was concluded on 17 May 1639 between the Ottoman sultan Murad IV and Shah Safi of the Persian Safavid dynasty, ending the two empires' battle for control of Baghdad (q.v.) and Mesopotamia. The treaty, referred to as a *sulh* (truce) and not as a *silm* (peace), defined the boundary between Ottoman and Persian territory in accordance with the loyalties of the tribes inhabiting the 161-kilometer wide frontier zone. This left the Ottoman Empire in control of the whole of Mesopotamia, including the Shatt al-Arab (q.v.) waterway. *See also* TREATY OF KURDAN.

UN Security Council Resolutions

UNSCR 660 (2 AUGUST 1990)

The Security Council, Alarmed by the invasion of Kuwait on 2 August 1990 by the military forces of Iraq, Determining that there exists a breach of international peace and security as regards the Iraqi invasion of Kuwait, Acting under Articles 39 and 40 of the Charter of the United Nations,

1. Condemns the Iraqi invasion of Kuwait;
2. Demands that Iraq withdraw immediately and unconditionally all its forces to the positions in which they were located on 1 August 1990;
3. Calls upon Iraq and Kuwait to begin immediately intensive negotiations for the resolution of their differences and supports all efforts in this regard, and especially those of the League of Arab States;
4. Decides to meet again as necessary to consider further steps to ensure compliance with the present resolution. Adopted by 14 votes to none, with one abstention (Yemen)*

UNSCR 661 (6 AUGUST 1990)

The Security Council, Reaffirming its resolution 660 (1990) of 2 August 1990, Deeply concerned that the resolution has not been implemented and that the invasion by Iraq of Kuwait continues with further loss of human life and material destruction, Determined to bring the invasion and occupation of Kuwait by Iraq to an end and to restore the sovereignty, independence and territorial integrity of Kuwait, Noting that the legitimate Government of Kuwait has expressed its readiness to comply with resolution 660 (1990), Mindful of its responsibilities under the Charter of the United Nations for "the maintenance of international peace and security," Affirming the inherent right of individual or collective self-defence, in response to the armed attack by Iraq against Kuwait, in accordance with Article 51 of the Charter, Acting under Chapter VII of the Charter of the United Nations,

1. Determines that Iraq so far has failed to comply with paragraph 2 of Resolution 660 (1990) and has usurped the authority of the legitimate Government of Kuwait;

2. Decides, as a consequence, to take the following measures to secure compliance of Iraq with paragraph 2 of Resolution 660 (1990) and to restore the authority of the legitimate Government of Kuwait;

3. Decides that all States shall prevent: (a) The import into their territories of all commodities and products originating in Iraq or Kuwait exported therefrom after the date of the present resolution; (b) Any activities by their nationals or in their territories which would promote or are calculated to promote the export or transshipment of any commodities or products from Iraq or Kuwait; and any dealings by their nationals or their flag vessels or in their territories in any commodities or products originating in Iraq or Kuwait and exported therefrom after the date of the present resolution, including in particular any transfer of funds to Iraq or Kuwait for the purposes of such activities or dealings; (c) The sale or supply by their nationals or from their territories or using their flag vessels of any commodities or products, including weapons or any other military equipment, whether or not originating in their territories but not including supplies intended strictly for medical purposes, and, in humanitarian circumstances, foodstuffs, to any person or body in Iraq or Kuwait or to any person or body for the purposes of any business carried on in or operated from Iraq or Kuwait, and any activities by their nationals or in their territories which promote or are calculated to promote such sale or supply of such commodities or products;

4. Decides that all States shall not make available to the Government of Iraq or to any commercial, industrial or public utility undertaking in Iraq or Kuwait, any funds or any other financial or economic resources and shall prevent their nationals and any persons within their territories from removing from their territories or otherwise making available to that Government or to any such undertaking any such funds or resources and from remitting any other funds to persons or bodies within Iraq or Kuwait, except payments exclusively for strictly medical or humanitarian purposes and, in humanitarian circumstances, foodstuffs;

5. Calls upon all States, including States non-members of the United Nations, to act strictly in accordance with the provisions of the present resolution notwithstanding any contract entered into or license granted before the date of the present resolution;

6. Decides to establish, in accordance with rule 28 of the provisional rules of procedure of the Security Council, a Committee of the Security Council consisting of all the members of the Council, to undertake the fol-

lowing tasks and to report on its work to the Council with its observations and recommendations:

(a) To examine the reports on the progress of the implementation of the present resolution which will be submitted to the Secretary-General; (b) To seek from all States further information regarding the action taken by them concerning the effective implementation of the provisions laid down in the present resolution;

7. Calls upon all States to co-operate fully with the Committee in the fulfillment of its task, including supplying such information as may be sought by the Committee in pursuance of the present resolution;

8. Requests the Secretary-General to provide all necessary assistance to the Committee and to make the necessary arrangements in the Secretariat for the purpose;

9. Decides that, notwithstanding paragraphs 4 through 8 above, nothing in the present resolution shall prohibit assistance to the legitimate Government of Kuwait, and calls upon all States: (a) To take appropriate measures to protect assets of the legitimate Government of Kuwait and its agencies; (b) Not to recognize any regime set up by the occupying Power;

10. Requests the Secretary-General to report to the Council on the progress of the implementation of the present resolution, the first report to be submitted within thirty days;

11. Decides to keep this item on its agenda and to continue its efforts to put an early end to the invasion by Iraq. Adopted by 13 votes to none, with two abstentions (Cuba and Yemen)

UNSCR 662 (9 AUGUST 1990)

The Security Council, Recalling its resolutions 660 (1990) and 661 (1990), Gravely alarmed by the declaration by Iraq of a "comprehensive and eternal merger" with Kuwait, Demanding once again that Iraq withdraw immediately and unconditionally all its forces to positions in which they were located on 1 August 1990, Determined to bring the occupation of Kuwait by Iraq to an end and to restore the sovereignty, independence and territorial integrity of Kuwait, Determined also to restore the authority of the legitimate Government of Kuwait,

1. Decides that annexation of Kuwait by Iraq under any form and whatever pretext has no legal validity, and is considered null and void;

2. Calls upon all States, international organizations and specialized agencies not to recognize that annexation, and to refrain from any action or dealing that might be interpreted as an indirect recognition of the annexation;

3. Further demands that Iraq rescind its actions purporting to annex Kuwait;
4. Decides to keep this item on its agenda and to continue its efforts to put an early end to the occupation. Adopted by unanimous vote

UNSCR 664 (18 AUGUST 1990)

The Security Council, Recalling the Iraqi invasion and purported annexation of Kuwait and resolutions 660, 661 and 662, Deeply concerned for the safety and well being of third state nationals in Iraq and Kuwait, Recalling the obligations of Iraq in this regard under international law, Welcoming the efforts of the Secretary-General to pursue urgent consultations with the Government of Iraq following the concern and anxiety expressed by the members of the Council on 17 August 1990, Acting under Chapter VII of the United Nations Charter,

1. Demands that Iraq permit and facilitate the immediate departure from Kuwait and Iraq of the nationals of third countries and grant immediate and continuing access of consular officials to such nationals;
2. Further demands that Iraq take no action to jeopardize the safety, security or health of such nationals;
3. Reaffirms its decision in resolution 662 (1990) that annexation of Kuwait by Iraq is null and void, and therefore demands that the Government of Iraq rescind its orders for the closure of diplomatic and consular missions in Kuwait and the withdrawal of the immunity of their personnel, and refrain from any such actions in the future;
4. Requests the Secretary-General to report to the Council on compliance with this resolution at the earliest possible time. Adopted by unanimous vote

UNSCR 665 (25 AUGUST 1990)

The Security Council, Recalling its resolutions 660 (1990), 661 (1990), 662 (1990) and 664 (1990) and demanding their full and immediate implementation, Having decided in resolution 661 (1990) to impose economic sanctions under Chapter VII of the Charter of the United Nations, Determined to bring an end to the occupation of Kuwait by Iraq which imperils the existence of a Member State and to restore the legitimate authority, and the sovereignty, independence and territorial integrity of Kuwait which requires the speedy implementation of the above resolutions, Deploring the loss of innocent life stemming from the Iraqi invasion of Kuwait and determined to prevent further such losses, Gravely alarmed that Iraq continues to refuse to comply with resolutions 660 (1990), 661 (1990), 662 (1990) and 664 (1990) and in particular at the conduct of the Government of Iraq in using Iraqi flag vessels to export oil,

1. Calls upon those Member States co-operating with the Government of Kuwait which are deploying maritime forces to the area to use such measures commensurate to the specific circumstances as may be necessary under the authority of the Security Council to halt all inward and outward maritime shipping in order to inspect and verify their cargoes and destinations and to ensure strict implementation of the provisions related to such shipping laid down in resolution 661 (1990);

2. Invites Member States accordingly to co-operate as may be necessary to ensure compliance with the provisions of resolution 661 (1990) with maximum use of political and diplomatic measures, in accordance with paragraph 1 above;

3. Requests all States to provide in accordance with the Charter such assistance as may be required by the States referred to in paragraph 1 of this resolution;

4. Further requests the States concerned to co-ordinate their actions in pursuit of the above paragraphs of this resolution using as appropriate mechanisms of the Military Staff Committee and after consultation with the Secretary-General to submit reports to the Security Council and its Committee established under resolution 661 (1990) to facilitate the monitoring of the implementation of this resolution; S. Decides to remain actively seized of the matter. Adopted by 13 votes to none, with two abstentions (Cuba and Yemen)

UNSCR 666 (13 SEPTEMBER 1990)

The Security Council, Recalling its resolution 661 (1990), paragraphs 3 (c) and 4 of which apply, except in humanitarian circumstances, to foodstuffs, Recognizing that circumstances may arise in which it will be necessary for foodstuffs to be supplied to the civilian population of Iraq or Kuwait in order to relieve human suffering, Noting that in this respect the Committee established under paragraph 6 of that resolution has received communications from several Member States, Emphasizing that it is for the Security Council, alone or acting through the Committee, to determine whether humanitarian circumstances have arisen, Deeply concerned that Iraq has failed to comply with its obligations under Security Council resolution 664 (1990) in respect of the safety and well-being of third State nationals, and reaffirming that Iraq retains full responsibility in this regard under international humanitarian law including where applicable, the Fourth Geneva Convention, Acting under Chapter VII of the Charter of the United Nations,

1. Decides that in order to make the necessary determination whether or not for the purposes of paragraph 3 (c) and paragraph 4 of resolution 661 (1990)

humanitarian circumstances have arisen, the Committee shall keep the sit
uation regarding foodstuffs in Iraq and Kuwait under constant review;

2. Expects Iraq to comply with its obligations under Security Council resolution 664 (1990) in respect of third State nationals and reaffirms that Iraq
   remains fully responsible for their safety and well-being in accordance
   with international humanitarian law including, where applicable, the
   Fourth Geneva Convention;

3. Requests, for the purposes of paragraphs 1 and 2 of this resolution, that
   the Secretary-General seek urgently, and on a continuing basis, information from relevant United Nations and other appropriate humanitarian
   agencies and all other sources on the availability of food in Iraq and
   Kuwait, such information to be communicated by the Secretary-General
   to the Committee regularly;

4. Requests further that in seeking and supplying such information particular attention will be paid to such categories of persons who might suffer
   specially, such as children under 15 years of age, expectant mothers, maternity cases, the sick and the elderly;

5. Decides that if the Committee, after receiving the reports from the Secretary-General, determines that circumstances have arisen in which there is
   an urgent humanitarian need to supply foodstuffs to Iraq or Kuwait in order to relieve human suffering, it will report promptly to the Council its
   decision as to how such needs should be met;

6. Directs the Committee that in formulating its decisions it, should bear in
   mind that foodstuffs should be provided through the United Nations in cooperation with the International Committee of the Red Cross or other appropriate humanitarian agencies and distributed by them or under their
   supervision in order to ensure that they reach the intended beneficiaries;

7. Requests the Secretary-General to use his good offices to facilitate the delivery and distribution of foodstuffs to Kuwait and Iraq in accordance
   with the provisions of this and other relevant resolutions;

8. Recalls that resolution 661 (1990) does not apply to supplies intended
   strictly for medical purposes, but in this connection recommends that
   medical supplies should be exported under the strict supervision of the
   government of the exporting State or by appropriate humanitarian agencies. Adopted by 13 votes to two (Cuba and Yemen)

UNSCR 667 (16 SEPTEMBER 1990)

The Security Council, Reaffirming its resolutions 660 (1990), 661 (1990), 662
(1990), 664 (1990), 665 (1990) and 666 (1990), Recalling the Vienna Conventions of 18 April 1961 on diplomatic relations and of 24 April 1963 on consular

relations, to both of which Iraq is party, Considering that the decision of Iraq to order the closure of diplomatic and consular missions in Kuwait and to withdraw the immunity and privileges of these missions and their personnel is contrary to the decisions of the Security Council, the international Conventions mentioned above and international law, Deeply concerned that Iraq, notwithstanding the decisions of the Security Council and the provisions of the Conventions mentioned above, has committed acts of violence against diplomatic missions and their personnel in Kuwait,

Outraged at recent violations by Iraq of diplomatic premises in Kuwait and at the abduction of personnel enjoying diplomatic immunity and foreign nationals who were present in these premises, Considering that the above actions by Iraq constitute aggressive acts and a flagrant violation of its international obligations which strike at the root of the conduct of international relations in accordance with the Charter of the United Nations, Recalling that Iraq is fully responsible for any use of violence against foreign nationals or against any diplomatic or consular mission in Kuwait or its personnel, Determined to ensure respect for its decisions and for Article 25 of the Charter of the United Nations, Further considering that the grave nature of Iraq's actions, which constitute a new escalation of its violations of international law, obliges the Council not only to express its intermediate reaction but also to consult urgently to take further concrete measures to ensure Iraq's compliance with the Council's resolutions, Acting under Chapter VII of the Charter of the United Nations,

1. Strongly condemns aggressive acts perpetrated by Iraq against diplomatic premises and personnel in Kuwait, including the abduction of foreign nationals who were present in those premises;
2. Demands the immediate release of those foreign nationals as well as all nationals mentioned in resolution 664 (1990);
3. Further demands that Iraq immediately and fully comply with its international obligations under resolutions 660 (1990), 662 (1990) and 664 (1990) of the Security Council, the Vienna Conventions on diplomatic and consular relations and international law;
4. Further demands that Iraq immediately protect the safety and well-being of diplomatic and consular personnel and premises in Kuwait and in Iraq and take no action to hinder the diplomatic and consular missions in the performance of their functions, including access to their nationals and the protection of their person and interests;
5. Reminds all states that they are obliged to observe strictly resolutions 661 (1990), 662 (1990), 664 (1990), 665 (1990) and 666 (1990);
6. Decides to consult urgently to take further concrete measures as soon as possible, under Chapter VII of the Charter, in response to Iraq's continued

violation of the Charter, of resolutions of the Council and of international law. Adopted by unanimous vote

UNSCR 669 (24 SEPTEMBER 1990)

The Security Council, Recalling its resolution 661 (1990) of 6 August 1990, Recalling also Article 50 of the Charter of the United Nations, Conscious of the fact that an increasing number of requests for assistance have been received under the provisions of Article 50 of the United Nations, Entrusts the Committee established under resolution 661 (1990) concerning the situation between Iraq and Kuwait with the task of examining requests for assistance under the provisions of Article 50 of the Charter of the United Nations and making recommendations to the President of the Security Council for appropriate action. Adopted by unanimous vote

UNSCR 670 (25 SEPTEMBER 1990)

The Security Council, Reaffirming its resolutions 660 (1990), 661 (1990), 662 (1990), 664 (1990), 665 (1990), 666 (1990) and 667 (1990), Condemning Iraq's continued occupation of Kuwait, its failure to rescind its actions and end its purported annexation and its holding of third State nationals against their will, in flagrant violation of resolutions 660 (1990), 662 (1990), 664 (1990) and 667 (1990) and of international humanitarian law, Condemning further the treatment by Iraqi forces of Kuwaiti nationals, including measures to force them to leave their own country and mistreatment of persons and property in Kuwait in violation of international law, Noting with grave concern the persistent attempts to evade the measures laid down in resolution 661 (1990), Further noting that a number of States have limited the number of Iraqi diplomatic and consular officials in their countries and that others are planning to do so, Determined to ensure by all necessary means the strict and complete application of the measures laid down in resolution 661 (1990), Determined to ensure respect for its decisions and the provisions of Articles 25 and 48 of the Charter of the United Nations, Affirming that any acts of the Government of Iraq which are contrary to the above-mentioned resolutions or to Articles 25 or 48 of the Charter of the United Nations, such as Decree No. 377 of the Revolution Command Council of Iraq of 16 September 1990, are null and void, Reaffirming its determination to ensure compliance with Security Council resolutions by maximum use of political and diplomatic means, Welcoming the Secretary-General's use of his good offices to advance a peaceful solution based on the relevant Security Council resolutions and noting with appreciation his continuing efforts to this end, Underlining to the Government of Iraq that its continued failure to comply with the terms of resolutions 660 (1990), 661 (1990), 662 (1990), 664 (1990), 666 (1990) and 667 (1990) could lead to further serious action by the Council under the Charter of the United Nations, including under Chapter VII, Recalling the provisions of Article 103 of the Charter of the United Nations, Acting under Chapter VII of the Charter of the United Nations,

1. Calls upon all States to carry out their obligations to ensure strict and complete compliance with resolution 661 (1990) and in particular paragraphs 3, 4 and 5 thereof;
2. Confirms that resolution 661 (1990) applies to all means of transport, including aircraft;
3. Decides that all States, notwithstanding the existence of any rights or obligations conferred or imposed by any international agreement or any contract entered into or any license or permit granted before the date of the present resolution, shall deny permission to any aircraft to take off from their territory if the aircraft would carry any cargo to or from Iraq or Kuwait other than food in humanitarian circumstances, subject to the authorization by the Council or the Committee established by resolution 661 (1990) and in accordance with resolution 666 (1990), or supplies intended strictly for medical purposes or solely for UNIIMOG [United Nations Iran-Iraq Military Observer Group];
4. Decides further that all States shall deny permission to any aircraft destined to land in Iraq or Kuwait, whatever its State of registration, to overfly its territory unless: (a) The aircraft lands at an airfield designated by that State outside Iraq or Kuwait in order to permit its inspection to ensure that there is no cargo on board in violation of resolution 661 (1990) or the present resolution, and for this purpose the aircraft may be detained for as long as necessary; or (b) The particular flight has been approved by the Committee established by resolution 661 (1990); or (c) The flight is certified by the United Nations as solely for the purposes of UNUMOG;
5. Decides that each State shall take all necessary measures to ensure that any aircraft registered in its territory or operated by an operator who has his principal place of business or permanent residence in Iraqi territory complies with the provisions of resolution 661 (1990) and the present resolution;
6. Decides further that all States shall notify in a timely fashion the Committee established by resolution 661 (1990) of any flight between its territory and Iraq or Kuwait to which the requirement to land in paragraph 4 above does not apply, and the purpose for such a flight;
7. Calls on all States to co-operate in taking such measures as may be necessary, consistent with international law, including the Chicago Convention,

to ensure the effective implementation of the provisions of resolution 661 (1990) or the present resolution;

8. Calls upon all States to detain any ships of Iraqi registry which enter their ports and which are being or have been used in violation of resolution 661 (1990), or to deny such ships entrance to their ports except in circumstances recognized under international law as necessary to safeguard human life;

9. Reminds all States of their obligations under resolution 661 (1990) with regard to the freezing of Iraqi assets, and the protection of the assets of the legitimate Government of Kuwait and its agencies, located within their territory and to report to the Committee established under resolution 661 (1990) regarding those assets;

10. Calls upon States to provide to the Committee established by resolution 661 (1990) information regarding the action taken by them to implement the provisions laid down in the present resolution;

Affirming the inherent right of individual or collective self-defence, in response to the armed attack by Iraq against Kuwait, in accordance with Article 51 of the Charter, Acting under Chapter VII of the Charter of the United Nations,

1. Determines that Iraq so far has failed to comply with paragraph 2 of resolution 660 (1990) and has usurped the authority of the legitimate Government of Kuwait;

2. Decides, as a consequence, to take the following measures to secure compliance of Iraq with paragraph 2 of resolution 660 (1990) and to restore the authority of the legitimate Government of Kuwait;

3. Decides that all States shall prevent: (a) The import into their territories of all commodities and products originating in Iraq or Kuwait exported therefrom after the date of the present resolution; (b) Any activities by their nationals or in their territories which would promote or are calculated to promote the export or transshipment of any commodities or products from Iraq or Kuwait; and any dealings by their nationals or their flag vessels or in their territories in any commodities or products originating in Iraq or Kuwait and exported therefrom after the date of the present resolution, including in particular any transfer of funds to Iraq or Kuwait for the purposes of such activities or dealings; (c) The sale or supply by their nationals or from their territories or using their flag vessels of any commodities or products, including weapons or any other military equipment, whether or not originating in their territories but not including supplies intended strictly for medical purposes, and, in humanitarian circumstances, foodstuffs, to any person or body in Iraq or Kuwait or to any person or body for the purposes of any business carried on in or operated from Iraq

or Kuwait, and any activities by their nationals or in their territories which promote or are calculated to promote such or supply of such commodities or products;

4. Decides that all States shall not make available to the Government of Iraq or to any commercial, industrial or public utility undertaking in Iraq or Kuwait, any funds or any other financial or economic resources and shall prevent their nationals and any persons within their territories from removing from their territories or otherwise making available to that Government or to any such under any such funds or resources and from remitting any other funds to persons or bodies within Iraq or Kuwait, except payments exclusively for strictly medical or humanitarian purposes and, in humanitarian circumstances, foodstuffs;

5. Calls upon all States, including States non-members of the United Nations, to act strictly in accordance with the provisions of the present resolution notwithstanding any contract entered into or license granted before the date of the present resolution;

6. Decides to establish, in accordance with rule 28 of the provisional rules of procedure of the Security Council, a Committee of the Security Council consisting of all the members of the Council, to undertake the following tasks and to report on its work to the Council with its observations and recommendations:

   1. Affirms that the United Nations Organization, the specialized agencies and other international organizations in the United Nations system are required to take such measures as may be necessary to give effect to the terms of resolution 661 (1990) and this resolution;

   2. Decides to consider, in the event of evasion of the provisions of resolution 661 (1990) or of the present resolution by a State or its nationals or through its territory, measures directed at the State in question to prevent such evasion;

   3. Reaffirms that the Fourth Geneva Convention applies to Kuwait and that as a High Contracting Party to the Convention Iraq is bound to comply fully with all its terms and in particular is liable under the Convention in respect of the grave breaches committed by it, as are individuals who commit or order the commission of grave breaches.
   Adopted by 14 votes to one (Cuba)

UNSCR 674 (29 OCTOBER 1990)

The Security Council, Recalling its resolutions 660 (1990), 661 (1990), 662 (1990), 664 (1990), 665 (1990), 666 (1990), 667 (1990) and 670 (1990), Stressing the urgent need for the immediate and unconditional withdrawal of all Iraqi forces from Kuwait, for the restoration of Kuwait's sovereignty, independence and territorial integrity and of the authority of its legitimate government, Condemning the actions by the Iraqi authorities and occupying forces to take third-State nationals hostage and to mistreat and oppress Kuwaiti and third-State nationals, and the other actions reported to the Security Council, such as the destruction of Kuwaiti demographic records, the forced departure of Kuwaitis, the relocation of population in Kuwait and the unlawful destruction and seizure of public and private property in Kuwait, including hospital supplies and equipment, in violation of the decisions of the Council, the Charter of the United Nations, the Fourth Geneva Convention, the Vienna Conventions on Diplomatic and Consular Relations and international law, Expressing grave alarm over the situation of nationals of third States in Kuwait and Iraq, including the personnel of the diplomatic and consular missions of such States, Reaffirming that the Fourth Geneva Convention applies to Kuwait and that as a High Contracting Party to the Convention Iraq is bound to comply fully with all its terms and in particular is liable under the Convention in respect of the grave breaches committed by it, as are individuals who commit or order the commission of grave breaches, Recalling the efforts of the Secretary-General concerning the safety and well-being of third-State nationals in Iraq and Kuwait, Deeply concerned at the economic cost and at the loss and suffering caused to individuals in Kuwait and Iraq as a result of the invasion and occupation of Kuwait by Iraq, Acting under Chapter VII of the Charter of the United Nations, Reaffirming the goal of the international community of maintaining and security by seeking to resolve international disputes international peace and conflicts through peaceful means, and its Secretary, Recalling the important role that the United Nations General have played in the peaceful solution of disputes and conflicts in conformity with the provisions of the Charter, Alarmed by the dangers of the present crisis caused by the Iraqi invasion and occupation of Kuwait, which directly threaten international peace and security, and seeking to avoid any further worsening of the situation, the relevant resolutions of the Security Council Calling upon Iraq to comply with Council, in particular resolutions 660 (1990), 662 (1990) and 664 (1990), Reaffirming its determination to ensure compliance by Iraq with Security Council resolutions by maximum use of political and diplomatic means,

1. Demands that the Iraqi authorities and occupying forces immediately cease and desist from taking third-State nationals hostage, mistreating and oppressing Kuwaiti and third-State nationals and any other actions, such as those reported to the Security Council and described above, that violate the decisions of the Council, the Charter of the United Nations, the Fourth Geneva Convention, the Vienna Conventions on Diplomatic and Consular Relations and international law;

2. Invites States to collate substantiated information in their possession or submitted to them on the grave breaches by Iraq as per paragraph 1 above and to make this information available to the Security Council;

3. Reaffirming its demand that Iraq immediately fulfil its obligations to third-State nationals in Kuwait and Iraq, including the personnel of diplomatic and consular missions, under the Charter, the Fourth Geneva Convention, the Vienna Conventions on Diplomatic and Consular Relations, general principles of international law and the relevant resolutions of the Council;

4. Also reaffirms its demand that Iraq permit and facilitate the immediate departure from Kuwait and Iraq of those third-State nationals, including diplomatic and consular personnel, who wish to leave; Demands that Iraq ensure the immediate access to food, water and basic services necessary to the protection and well-being of Kuwaiti nationals and of nationals of third States in Kuwait and Iraq, including the personnel of diplomatic and consular missions in Kuwait;

5. Reaffirms its demand that Iraq immediately protect the safety and well-being of diplomatic and consular personnel and premises in Kuwait and in Iraq, take no action to hinder these diplomatic and consular missions in the performance of their functions, including access to their nationals and the protection of their position and interests and rescind its orders for the closure of diplomatic and consular missions in Kuwait and the withdrawal of the immunity of their personnel;

6. Requests the Secretary-General, in the context of the continued exercise of his good offices concerning the safety and well-being of third-State nationals in Iraq and Kuwait, to seek to achieve the objective of paragraphs 4, 5 and 6 above and in particular the provision of food, water and basic services to Kuwaiti nationals and to the diplomatic and consular missions in Kuwait and the evacuation of third-State nationals;

7. Reminds Iraq that under international law it is liable for any loss, damage or injury arising in regard to Kuwait and third States, and their nationals and corporations, as a result of the invasion and illegal occupation of Kuwait by Iraq;

8. Invites States to collect relevant information regarding their claims, and those of their nationals and corporations, for restitution or financial compensation by Iraq with a view to such arrangements as may be established in accordance with international law;

9. Requires that Iraq comply with the provisions of the present resolution and its previous resolutions, failing which the Security Council will need to take further measures under the Charter;

1. Decides to remain actively and permanently seized of the matter until Kuwait has regained its independence and peace has been restored in conformity with the relevant resolutions of the Security Council;

2. Reposes its trust in the Secretary-General to make available his good offices and, as he considers appropriate, to pursue them and to undertake diplomatic efforts in order to reach a peaceful solution to the crisis caused by the Iraqi invasion and occupation of Kuwait on the basis of Security Council resolutions 660 (1990), 662 (1990) and 664 (1990), and calls upon all States, both those in the region and others, to pursue on this basis their efforts to this end, in conformity with the Charter, in order to improve the situation and restore peace, security and stability;

3. Requests the Secretary-General to report to the Security Council on the results of his good offices and diplomatic efforts. Adopted by 13 votes to none, with two abstentions (Cuba and Yemen)

UNSCR 677 (28 NOVEMBER 1990)

The Security Council, Recalling its resolutions 660 (1990) of 2 August 1990, 662 (1990) of 9 August 1990 and 674 (1990) of 29 October 1990, Reiterating its concern for the suffering caused to individuals in Kuwait as a result of the invasion and occupation of Kuwait by Iraq, Gravely concerned at the ongoing attempt by Iraq to alter the demographic composition of the population of Kuwait and to destroy the civil records maintained by the legitimate Government of Kuwait, Acting under Chapter VII of the Charter of the United Nations,

1. Condemns the attempts by Iraq to alter the demographic composition of the population of Kuwait and to destroy the civil records maintained by the legitimate Government of Kuwait;

2. Mandates the Secretary-General to take custody of a copy of the population register of Kuwait, the authenticity of which has been certified by the legitimate Government of Kuwait and which covers the registration of the population up to 1 August 1990;

3. Requests the Secretary-General to establish, in co-operation with the legitimate Government of Kuwait, an Order of Rules and Regulations governing access to and use of the said copy of the population register. Adopted by unanimous vote

UNCSR 678 (29 NOVEMBER 1990)

The Security Council, Recalling and reaffirming its resolutions 660 (1990) of 2 August 1990, 661 (1990) of 6 August 1990, 662 (1990) of 9 August 1990, 664 (1990) of 18 August 1990, 665 (1990) of 25 August 1990, 666 (1990) of 13

September 1990, 667 (1990) of 16 September 1990, 669 (1990) of 24 September 1990, 670 (1990) of 25 September 1990, 674 (1990) of 29 October 1990 and 677 (1990) of 28 November 1990, Noting that, despite all efforts by the United Nations, Iraq refuses to comply with its obligation to implement resolution 660 (1990) and the above-mentioned subsequent resolutions, in flagrant contempt of the Security Council, Mindful of its duties and responsibilities under the Charter of the United Nations for the maintenance and preservation of international peace and security, Determined to secure full compliance with its decisions, Acting under Chapter VII of the Charter,

1. Demands that Iraq comply fully with resolution 660 (1990) and all subsequent relevant resolutions, and decides, while maintaining all its decisions, to allow Iraq one final opportunity, as a pause of goodwill, to do so;
2. Authorizes Member States co-operating with the Government of Kuwait, unless Iraq on or before 15 January 1991 fully implements, as set forth in paragraph 1 above, the foregoing resolutions, to use all necessary means to uphold and implement resolution 660 (1990) and all subsequent relevant resolutions and to restore international peace and security in the area;
3. Requests all States to provide appropriate support for the actions undertaken in pursuance of paragraph 2 of the present resolution;
4. Requests the States concerned to keep the Security Council regularly informed on the progress of actions undertaken pursuant to paragraphs 2 and 3 of the present resolution;
5. Decides to remain seized of the matter. Adopted by 12 votes to two (Cuba and Yemen), with one abstention (China)

UNSCR 686 (2 MARCH 1991)

The Security Council, Recalling and reaffirming its resolutions 660 (1990), 661 (1990), 662 (1990), 664 (1990), 665 (1990), 666 (1990), 667 (1990), 669 (1990), 670 (1990), 674 (1990), 677 (1990) and 678 (1990), Recalling the obligations of Member States under Article 25 of the Charter, Recalling paragraph 9 of resolution 661 (1990) regarding assistance to the Government of Kuwait and paragraph 3 (c) of that resolution regarding supplies strictly for medical purposes and, in humanitarian circumstances, foodstuffs, Taking note of the letters of the Foreign Minister of Iraq confirming Iraq's agreement to comply fully with all of the resolutions noted above (S/22275), and stating its intention to release prisoners of war immediately (S/22273), Taking note of the suspension of offensive combat operations by the forces of Kuwait and the Member States co-operating with Kuwait pursuant to resolution 678 (1990), Bearing in mind the need to be assured of Iraq's peaceful intentions, and the objective in resolution

678 (1990) of restoring international peace and security in the region, Underlining the importance of Iraq taking the necessary measures which would permit a definitive end to the hostilities, Affirming the commitment of all Member States to the independence, sovereignty and territorial integrity of Iraq and Kuwait, and noting the intention expressed by the Member States co-operating under paragraph 2 of Security Council resolution 678 (1990) to bring their military presence in Iraq to an end as soon as possible consistent with achieving the objectives of the resolution, Acting under Chapter VII of the Charter,

1. Affirms that all twelve resolutions noted above continue to have full force and effect;
2. Demands that Iraq implement its acceptance of all twelve resolutions noted above and in particular that Iraq: (a) Rescind immediately its actions purporting to annex Kuwait; (b) Accept in principle its liability under international law for loss, damage, or injury arising in regard to Kuwait and third States, and their nationals and corporations, as a result of the invasion and illegal occupation of Kuwait by Iraq; (c) Immediately release under the auspices of the International Committee of the Red Cross, Red Cross Societies, or Red Crescent Societies, all Kuwaiti and third country nationals detained by Iraq and return the remains of any deceased Kuwaiti and third country nationals so detained; and (d) immediately begin to return all Kuwaiti property seized by Iraq, to be completed in the shortest possible period;
3. Further demands that Iraq: (a) Cease hostile or provocative actions by its forces against all Member States, including missile attacks and flights of combat aircraft; (b) Designate military commanders to meet with counterparts from the forces of Kuwait and the Member States co-operating with Kuwait pursuant to resolution 678 (1990) to arrange for the military aspects of a cessation of hostilities at the earliest possible time; (c) Arrange for immediate access to and release of all prisoners of war under the auspices of the International Committee of the Red Cross and return the remains of any deceased personnel of the forces of Kuwait and the Member States co-operating with Kuwait pursuant to resolution 678 (1990); and (d) Provide all information and assistance in identifying Iraqi mines, booby traps and other explosives as well as any chemical and biological weapons and material in Kuwait, in areas of Iraq where forces of Member States co-operating with Kuwait pursuant to resolution 678 (1990) are present temporarily, and in the adjacent waters;
4. Recognizes that during the period required for Iraq to comply with paragraphs 2 and 3 above, the provisions of paragraph 2 of resolution 678 (1990) remain valid;

5. Welcomes the decision of Kuwait and the Member States co-operating with Kuwait pursuant to resolution 678 (1990) to provide access and to commence immediately the release of Iraqi prisoners of war as required by the terms of the Third Geneva Convention of 1949, under the auspices of the International Committee of the Red Cross;

6. Requests all Member States, as well as the United Nations, the specialized agencies and other international organizations in the United Nations system, to take all appropriate action with the Government and people of Kuwait in the reconstruction of their country;

7. Decides that Iraq shall notify the Secretary-General and the Security Council when it has taken the actions set out above;

8. Decides that in order to secure the rapid establishment of a definitive end to the hostilities, the Security Council remains actively seized of the matter. Adopted by 11 votes to one (Cuba), with three abstentions (China, India and Yemen)

UNSCR 687 (3 APRIL 1991)

The Security Council, Recalling its resolutions 660 (1990), 661 (1990), 662 11990), 664 (1990), 665 (19901, 666 (1990), 667 (1990), 669 (1990), 670 (1990), 674 (1990), 677 (1990), 678 (1990) and 686 (1990), Welcoming the restoration to Kuwait of its sovereignty, independence and territorial integrity and the return of its legitimate government, Affirming the commitment of all Member States to the sovereignty, territorial integrity and political independence of Kuwait and Iraq, and noting the intention expressed by the Member States co-operating with Kuwait under paragraph 2 of resolution 678 (1990) to bring their military presence in Iraq to an end as soon as possible consistent with paragraph 8 of resolution 686 (1991), Reaffirming the need to be assured of Iraq's peaceful intentions in light of its unlawful invasion and occupation of Kuwait,

Taking note of the letter sent by the Foreign Minister of Iraq on 27 February 1991 (S/22275) and those sent pursuant to resolution 686 (1990) (S/22273, S/22276, S/22320, S/22321, and S/22330), Noting that Iraq and Kuwait, as independent sovereign States, signed at Baghdad on 4 October 1963 "Agreed Minutes Regarding the Restoration of Friendly Relations, Recognition and Related Matters", thereby recognizing formally the boundary between Iraq and Kuwait and the allocation of islands, which were registered with the United Nations in accordance with Article 102 of the Charter and in which Iraq recognized the independence and complete sovereignty of the State of Kuwait within its borders as specified and accepted in the letter of the Prime Minister of Iraq dated 21 july 1932, and as accepted by the Ruler of Kuwait in his letter dated 10 August 1932, Conscious of the need for demarcation of the said boundary,

Conscious also of the statements by Iraq threatening to use weapons in violation of its obligations under the Geneva Protocol for the prohibition of the Use
in War of Asphyxiating, Poisonous or Other Gases, and of Bacteriological
Methods of Warfare, signed at Geneva on 17 june 1925, and of its prior use of
chemical weapons and affirming that grave consequences would follow any
further use by Iraq of such weapons, Recalling that Iraq has subscribed to the
Declaration adopted by all States participating in the Conference of States Parties to the 1925 Geneva Protocol and Other Interested States, held at Paris from
7 to 11 January 1989, establishing the objective of universal elimination of
chemical and biological weapons, Recalling further that Iraq has signed the
Convention on the Prohibition of the Development, Production and Stockpiling
of Bacteriological (Biological) and Toxin Weapons and on Their Destruction,
of 10 April 1972, Noting the importance of Iraq ratifying this Convention, Noting moreover the importance of all States adhering to this Convention and encouraging its forthcoming Review Conference to reinforce the authority, efficiency and universal scope of the convention, Stressing the importance of an
early conclusion by the Conference on Disarmament of its work on a Convention on the Universal Prohibition of Chemical Weapons and of universal adherence thereto, Aware of the use by Iraq of ballistic missiles in unprovoked attacks and therefore of the need to take specific measures in regard to such
missiles located in Iraq, Concerned by the reports in the hands of Member
States that Iraq has attempted to acquire materials for a nuclear-weapons program contrary to its obligations under the treaty on the Non-Proliferation of
Nuclear Weapons of 1 July 1968, Recalling the objective of the establishment
of a nuclear-weapons-free zone in the region of the Middle East,

Conscious of the threat which all weapons of mass destruction pose to peace,
and security in the area and of the need to work towards the establishment in
the Middle East of a zone free of such weapons, Conscious also of the objective of achieving balanced and comprehensive control of armaments in the region, Conscious further of the importance of achieving the objectives noted
above using all available means, including a dialogue among the states of the
region, Noting that resolution 686 (1991) marked the lifting of the measures
imposed by resolution 661 (1990) in so far as they applied to Kuwait, Noting
that despite the progress being made in fulfilling the obligations of resolution
686 (1991), many Kuwaiti and third country nationals are still not accounted
for and property remains unreturned, Recalling the International Convention
against the taking of hostages, opened for signature at New York on 18 December 1979, which categorizes all acts of taking hostages as manifestations of
international terrorism, Deploring threats made by Iraq during the recent conflict to make use of terrorism against targets outside Iraq and the taking of
hostages by Iraq, Taking note with grave concern of the reports of the Secretary-General of 20 March 1991 (S/22366) and 28 March 1991 (S/22409), and

conscious of the necessity to meet urgently the humanitarian needs in Kuwait and Iraq, Bearing in mind its objective of restoring international peace and security in the area as set out in recent Council resolutions, Conscious of the need to take the following measures acting under Chapter VII of the Charter,

1. Affirms all thirteen resolutions noted above, except as expressly changed below to achieve the goals of this resolution, including a formal cease-fire;

2. Demands that Iraq and Kuwait respect the inviolability of the international boundary and the allocation of islands set out in the "Agreed Minutes Between the State of Kuwait and the Republic of Iraq Regarding the Restoration of Friendly Relations, Recognition and Related Matters", signed by them in the exercise of their sovereignty at Baghdad on 4 October 1963 and registered with the United Nations and published by the United Nations in document 7063, United Nations Treaty Series, 1964;

3. Calls on the Secretary-General to lend his assistance to make arrangements with Iraq and Kuwait to demarcate the boundary between Iraq and Kuwait, drawing on appropriate material including the map transmitted by Security Council document S/22412 and to report back to the Security Council within one month;

4. Decides to guarantee the inviolability of the above-mentioned international boundary and to take as appropriate all necessary measures to that end in accordance with the Charter;

5. Requests the Secretary-General, after consulting with Iraq and Kuwait, to submit within three days to the Security Council for its approval a plan for the immediate deployment of a United Nations observer unit to monitor the Khor Abdullah and a demilitarized zone, 10 kilometres into Iraq and 5 kilometres into Kuwait from the boundary referred to in the "Agreed Minutes Between the State of Kuwait and the Republic of Iraq Regarding the Restoration of Friendly Relations, Recognition and Related Matters" of 4 October 1963; to deter violations of the boundary through its presence in and surveillance of the demilitarized zone; to observe any hostile or potentially hostile action mounted from the territory of one State to the other; and for the Secretary-General to report regularly to the Council on the operations of the unit, and immediately if there are any serious violations of the zone or potential threats to peace;

6. Notes that as soon as the Secretary-General notifies the Council of the completion of the deployment of the United Nations observer units conditions will be established for the Member States co-operating with Kuwait in accordance with resolution 678 (1990) to bring their military presence in Iraq to an end consistent with resolution 686 (1991);

7. Invites Iraq to reaffirm unconditionally its obligations under the Geneva Protocol for the Prohibition of the Use in War of Asphyxiatin & Poisonous or Other Gases, and of Bacteriological Methods of Warfare, signed at Geneva on 17 June 1925, and to ratify the Convention on the Prohibition of the Development, Production, and Stockpiling of Bacteriological (Biological) and Toxin Weapons and on Their Destruction, of 10 April 1972;

8. Decides that Iraq shall unconditionally accept the destruction, removal, or rendering harmless, under international supervision, of: (a) all chemical and biological weapons and all stocks of agents and all related subsystems and components and all research, development, support and manufacturing facilities; (b) all ballistic missiles with a range greater than 150 kilometres and related major parts, and repair and production facilities;

9. Decides for the implementation of paragraph 8 above, the following: (a) Iraq shall submit to the Secretary-General, within fifteen days of the adoption of this resolution, a declaration of the locations, amounts and types of all items specified in paragraph 8 and agree to urgent, on-site inspection as specified below; (b) the Secretary-General, in consultation with the appropriate Governments and, where appropriate, with the Director-General of the World Health Organization (WHO), within 45 days of the passage of this resolution, shall develop, and submit to the Council for approval, a plan calling for the completion of the following acts within 45 days of such approval: (i) the forming of a Special Commission, which shall carry out immediate on-site inspection of Iraq's biological, chemical and missile capabilities, based on Iraq's declarations and the designation of any additional locations by the Special Commission itself; (ii) the yielding by Iraq of possession to the Special Commission for destruction, removal or rendering harmless, taking into account the requirements of public safety, of all items specified under paragraph 8 (a) above including items at the additional locations designated by the Special Commission under paragraph 9 (b) (i) above and the destruction by Iraq, under supervision of the Special Commission of all its missile capabilities including launchers as specified under paragraph 8 (b) above; (iii) the provision by the Special Commission of the assistance and co-operation to the Director-General of the International Atomic Energy Agency (IAEA) required in paragraphs 12 and 13 below;

10. Decides further that Iraq shall unconditionally undertake not to use, develop, construct or acquire any of the items specified in paragraphs 8 and 9 above and requests the Secretary-General, in consultation with the Special Commission, to develop a plan for the future ongoing monitoring and verification of Iraq's compliance with this paragraph, to be sub-

mitted to the Council for approval within 120 days of the passage of this resolution;

11. Invites Iraq to reaffirm unconditionally its obligations under the treaty on the Non-Proliferation of Nuclear Weapons, of 1 July 1968;

12. Decides that Iraq shall unconditionally agree not to acquire or develop nuclear weapons or nuclear-weapons-usable material or any subsystems or components or any research, development, support or manufacturing facilities related to the above; to submit to the Secretary-General and the Director General of the International Atomic Energy Agency (IAEA) within 15 days of the adoption of this resolution a declaration of the locations, amounts and types of all items specified above; to place all of its nuclear-weapons-usable material under the exclusive control, for custody and removal, of the IAEA, with the assistance and cooperation of the Special Commission as provided for in the plan of the Secretary-General discussed in paragraph 9 (b) above; to accept in accordance with the arrangements provided for in paragraph 13 below, urgent on-site inspection and the destruction, removal and rendering harmless as appropriate of all items specified above; and to accept the plan as discussed in paragraph 13 below for the future ongoing monitoring and verification of its compliance with these undertakings;

13. Requests the Director General of the International Atomic Energy Agency (IAEA) through the Secretary-General, with the assistance and co-operation of the Special Commission as provided for in the plan of the Secretary-General in paragraph 9 (b) above, to carry out immediate on-site inspection of Iraq's nuclear capabilities based on Iraq's declarations and the designation of any additional locations by the Special Commission; to develop a plan for submission to the Security Council within 45 days calling for the destruction, removal, or rendering harmless as appropriate of all items listed in paragraph 12 above; to carry out the plan within 45 days following approval by the Security Council; and to develop a plan, taking into account the rights and obligations of Iraq under the Treaty on the Non-Proliferation of Nuclear Weapons, of 1 July 1968, for the future ongoing monitoring and verification of Iraq's compliance with paragraph 12 above, including an inventory of all nuclear material in Iraq subject to the Agency's verification and inspections to confirm that IAEA safeguards cover all relevant nuclear activities in Iraq, to be submitted to the Council for approval within 120 days of the passage of this resolution;

14. Takes note that the actions to be taken by Iraq in paragraphs 8 to 13 represent steps towards the goal of establishing in the Middle East a zone free from weapons of mass destruction and all missiles for their delivery and the objective of a global ban on chemical weapons;

15. Requests the Secretary-General to report to the Security Council on the steps taken to facilitate the return of all Kuwaiti property seized by Iraq, including a list of any property which Kuwait claims has not been returned or which has not been returned intact;

16. Reaffirms that Iraq, without prejudice to the debts and obligation of Iraq arising prior to 2 August 1990, which will be addressed through the normal mechanisms, is liable under international law for any direct loss, damage, including environmental damage and the depletion of natural resources, or in to foreign Governments, nationals and corporations, as a result of Iraq's unlawful invasion and occupation of Kuwait;

17. Decides that all Iraqi statements made since 2 August 1990, repudiating its foreign debt are null and void, and demands that Iraq scrupulously adhere to all of its obligations concerning servicing and repayment of its foreign debt;

18. Decides to create a Fund to pay compensation for claims that fall within paragraph 16 above and to establish a Commission that will administer the Fund;

19. Directs the Secretary-General to develop and present to the Council for decision, no later than 30 days following the adoption of this resolution, recommendations for the Fund to meet the requirement for the payment of claims established in accordance with paragraph 18 above and for a program to implement the decisions in paragraphs 16, 17, and 18 above, including: administration of the Fund; mechanisms for determining the appropriate level for Iraq's contribution to the Fund based on a percentage of the value of the exports of petroleum and petroleum products from Iraq not to exceed a figure to be suggested to the Council by the Secretary-General, taking into account the requirement of the people of Iraq, Iraq's payment capacity as assessed in conjunction with the international financial institutions taking into consideration external debt service, and the needs of the Iraqi economy; arrangements for ensuring that payments are made to the Fund; the process by which funds will be allocated and claims paid; appropriate procedures for evaluating losses, listing claims and verifying their validity and resolving disputed claims in respect of Iraq's liability as specified in paragraph 16 above; and the composition of the Commission designated above;

20. Decides, effective immediately, that the prohibitions against the sale or supply to Iraq of commodities or products, other than medicine and health supplies, and prohibitions against financial transactions related thereto, contained in resolution 661 (1990) shall not apply to foodstuffs notified to the Security Council Committee established by resolution 661 (1990) concerning the situation between Iraq and Kuwait or, with

the approval of that Committee, under the simplified and accelerated "no-objection" procedure, to materials and supplies for essential civilian needs as identified in the report of the Secretary-General dated 20 March 1991 (S/22366), and in any further findings of humanitarian need by the Committee;

21. Decides that the Council shall review the provisions of paragraph 20 above every sixty days in light of the policies and practices of the Government of Iraq, including the implementation of all relevant resolutions of the Security Council, for the purposes of determining whether to reduce or lift the prohibitions referred to therein;

22. Decides that upon the approval by the Council of the program called for in paragraph 19 above and upon Council agreement that Iraq has completed all actions contemplated in paragraphs 8, 9, 10, 11, 12, and 13 above, the prohibitions against the import of commodities and products originating in Iraq and the prohibitions against financial transactions related thereto contained in resolution 661 (1990) shall have no further force or effect;

23. Decides that, pending action by the Council under paragraph 22 above, the Committee established by resolution 661 (1990) shall be empowered to approve, when required to assure adequate financial resources on the part of Iraq to carry out the activities under paragraph 20 above, exceptions to the prohibition against the import of commodities and products originating in Iraq;

24. Decides that, in accordance with resolution 661 (1990) and subsequent related resolutions and until a further decision is taken by the Council, all States shall continue to prevent the sale or supply, or promotion or facilitation of such sale or supply, to Iraq by their nationals, or from their territories or using their flag vessels or aircraft, of: (a) arms and related material of all types, specifically including conventional military equipment, including for paramilitary forces, and spare parts and components and their means of production, for such equipment; (b) items specified and defined in paragraph 8 and paragraph 12 above not otherwise covered above; (c) technology under licensing or other transfer arrangements used in production, utilization or stockpiling of items specified in subparagraphs (a) and (b) above; (d) personnel or materials for training or technical support services relating to the design, development, manufacture, use, maintenance or support of items specified in subparagraphs (a) and (b) above;

25. Calls upon all States and international organizations to act strictly in accordance with paragraph 24 above, notwithstanding the existence of any contracts, agreements, licenses, or any other arrangements;

26. Requests the Secretary-General, in consultation with appropriate Governments, to develop within sixty days, for approval of the Council, guidelines to facilitate full international implementation of paragraphs 24 and 25 above and paragraph 27 below, and to make them available to all States and to establish a procedure for updating these guidelines periodically;

27. Calls upon all States to maintain such national controls and procedures and to take such other actions consistent with the guidelines to be established by the Security Council under paragraph 26 above as may be necessary to ensure compliance with the terms of paragraph 24 above, and calls upon international organizations to take all appropriate steps to assist in ensuring such full compliance;

28. Agrees to review its decisions in paragraphs 22, 23, 24, and 25 above, except for the items specified and defined in paragraphs 8 and 12 above, on a regular basis and in any case 120 days following passage of this resolution, taking into account Iraq's compliance with this resolution and general progress towards the control of armaments in the region;

29. Decides that all States, including Iraq, shall take the necessary measures to ensure that no claim shall lie at the instance of the Government of Iraq, or of any person or body in Iraq, or of any person claiming through or for the benefit of any such person or body, in connection with any contract or other transaction where its performance was affected by reason of the measures taken by the Security Council in resolution 661 (1990) and related resolutions;

30. Decides that, in furtherance of its commitment to facilitate the repatriation of all Kuwaiti and third-State nationals, Iraq shall extend all necessary cooperation to the International Committee of the Red Cross by providing lists of such persons, facilitating the access of the International Committee to all such persons wherever located or detained and facilitating the search by the International Committee for those Kuwaiti and third country nationals still unaccounted for;

31. Invites the International Committee of the Red Cross to keep the Secretary-General appraised as appropriate of all activities undertaken in connection with facilitating the repatriation or return of all Kuwaiti and third country nationals or their remains present in Iraq on or after 2 August 1990;

32. Requires Iraq to inform the Council that it will not commit or support any act of international terrorism or allow any organization directed towards commission of such acts to operate within its territory and to condemn unequivocally and renounce all acts, methods, and practices of terrorism;

33. Declares that, upon official notification by Iraq to the Secretary-General and to the Security Council of its acceptance of the provisions above, a formal cease-fire is effective between Iraq and Kuwait and the Member States co-operating with Kuwait in accordance with resolution 678 (1990);

34. Decides to remain seized of the matter and to take such further steps as may be required for the implementation of this resolution and to secure peace and security in the area. Adopted by 12 votes to one (Cuba), with two abstentions (Ecuador and Yemen)

UNSCR 688 (5 APRIL 1991)

The Security Council, Mindful of its duties and responsibilities under the Charter of the United Nations for the maintenance of international peace and security, Recalling Article 2, paragraph 7, of the Charter of the United Nations, Gravely concerned by the repression of the Iraqi civilian population in many parts of Iraq, including most recently in Kurdish populated areas which led to a massive flow of refugees towards and across international frontiers and to cross border incursions, which threaten international peace and security in the region, Deeply disturbed by the magnitude of the human suffering involved,

Taking note of the letters sent by the representatives of Turkey and France to the United Nations dated 2 April 1991 and 4 April 1991, respectively (S/22435 and S/22442), Taking note also of the letters sent by the Permanent Representative of the Islamic Republic of Iran to the United Nations dated 3 and 4 April 1991, respectively (S/22436 and S/22447), Reaffirming the commitment of all Member States to the sovereignty, territorial integrity and political independence of Iraq and of all States in the area, Bearing in mind the Secretary-General's report of 20 March 1991 (S/22366),

1. Condemns the repression of the Iraqi civilian population in many parts of Iraq, including most recently in Kurdish populated areas, the consequences of which threaten international peace and security in the region;

2. Demands that Iraq, as a contribution to removing the threat to international peace and security in the region, immediately end this repression and expresses the hope in the same context that an open dialogue will take place to ensure that the human and political rights of all Iraqi citizens are respected;

3. Insists that Iraq allow immediate access by international humanitarian organizations to all those in need of assistance in all parts of Iraq and to make available all necessary facilities for their operations;

4. Requests the Secretary-General to pursue his humanitarian efforts in Iraq and to report forthwith, if appropriate on the basis of a further mission to the region, on the plight of the Iraqi civilian population, and in particular the Kurdish population, suffering from the repression in all its forms inflicted by the Iraqi authorities;

5. Requests further the Secretary-General to use all the resources at his disposal, including those of the relevant United Nations agencies, to address urgently the critical needs of the refugees and displaced Iraqi population;

6. Appeals to all Member States and to all humanitarian organizations to contribute to these humanitarian relief efforts;

7. Demands that Iraq co-operate with the Secretary-General to these ends;

8. Decides to remain seized of the matter. Adopted by 10 votes to three (Cuba, Yemen and Zimbabwe), with two abstentions (China and India)

UNSCR 689 (9 APRIL 1991)

The Security Council, Recalling its resolution 687 (1991), Acting under Chapter VII of the Charter of the United Nations,

1. Approves the report of the Secretary-General on the implementation of paragraph 5 of Security Council resolution 687 (1991) contained in document S/22454 and Add. 1-3 of 5 and 9 April 1991, respectively;

2. Notes that the decision to set up the observer unit was taken in paragraph 5 of resolution 687 (1991) and can only be terminated by a decision of the Council; the Council shall therefore review the question of termination or continuation every six months;

3. Decides that the modalities for the initial six-month period of the United Nations Iraq-Kuwait Observation Mission shall be in accordance with the above-mentioned report and shall also be reviewed every six months. Adopted by unanimous vote

UNSCR 692 (20 MAY 1991)

The Security Council, Recalling its resolutions 674 (1990), 686 (1990) and 687 (1991), concerning the liability of Iraq, without prejudice to its debts and obligations arising prior to 2 August 1990, for any direct loss, damage, including environmental damage and the depletion of natural resources, or injury to foreign Governments, nationals and corporations, as a result of Iraq's unlawful invasion and occupation of Kuwait,

Noting the Secretary-General's report of 2 May 1991 (S/22559), submitted in accordance with paragraph 19 of resolution 687 (1991), Acting under Chapter VII of the Charter,

1. Expresses its appreciation to the Secretary-General for his report of 2 May 1991 (S/22559);
2. Welcomes the fact that the Secretary-General will now undertake the appropriate consultations requested by paragraph 19 of 687 so that he will be in a position to recommend to the Security Council for decision as soon as possible the figure which the level of Iraq's contribution to the Fund will not exceed;
3. Decides to establish the Fund and Commission referred to in paragraph 18 of resolution 687 (1991) in accordance with Part I of the Secretary-General's report and that the Governing Council shall be located at the Offices of the United Nations in Geneva and that the Governing Council may decide whether some of the activities of the Commission shall be carried out elsewhere;
4. Requests the Secretary-General to take the action necessary to implement paragraphs 2 and 3 above in consultation with the members of the Governing Council;
5. Directs the Governing Council to proceed in an expeditious manner to implement the provisions of Section E of resolution 687 (1991), taking into account the recommendations in Part II of the Secretary-General's report;
6. Decides that the requirement for Iraqi contributions shall apply in the manner to be prescribed by the Governing Council with respect to all Iraqi petroleum and petroleum products exported from Iraq after 3 April 1991 as well as petroleum and petroleum products exported earlier but not delivered or not paid as a specific result of the prohibitions contained in resolution 661 (1990);
7. Requests the Governing Council to report as soon as possible on the actions it has taken with regard to the mechanisms for determining the appropriate level of Iraq's contribution to the Fund and the arrangements for ensuring that payments are made to the Fund, so that the Security Council can give its approval in accordance with paragraph 22 of resolution 687 (1991);
8. Requests that all States and international organizations co-operate with the decisions of the Governing Council taken pursuant to paragraph 5 of this resolution and further requests that the Governing Council keep the Security Council informed on this matter;
9. Decides that if the Governing Council notifies the Security Council that Iraq has failed to carry out decisions of the Governing Council taken pursuant to paragraph 5 of this resolution, the Security Council intends

to retain or to take action to reimpose the prohibition against the import of petroleum and petroleum products originating in Iraq and financial transactions related thereto;

10. Decides to remain seized of this matter and that the Governing Council will submit periodic reports to the Secretary-General and the Security Council. Adopted by 14 votes to none, with one abstention (Cuba)

UNSCR 699 (17 JUNE 1991)

The Security Council, Recalling its resolution 687 (1991), Taking note of the report of the Secretary-General of 17 May 1991 (S/22614), submitted to it in pursuance of paragraph 9 (b) of resolution 687 (1991), Also taking note of the Secretary-General's note of 17 May 1991 (S/22615), transmitting to the Council the letter to him under paragraph 13 of the resolution by the Director-General of the International Atomic Energy Agency (IAEA), Acting under Chapter VII of the Charter,

1. Approves the plan contained in the report of the Secretary-General;
2. Confirms that the Special Commission and the IAEA have the authority to conduct activities under section C of resolution 687 (1991), for the purpose of the destruction, removal or rendering harmless of the items specified in paragraphs 8 and 12 of that resolution, after the 45-day period following the approval of this plan until such activities have been completed;
3. Requests the Secretary-General to submit to the Security Council progress reports on the implementation of the plan referred to in paragraph 1 every six months after the adoption of this resolution;
4. Decides to encourage the maximum assistance, in cash and in kind, from all Member States to ensure that activities under section C of resolution 687 (1991) are undertaken effectively and expeditiously; further decides, however, that the Government of Iraq shall be liable for the full costs of carrying out the tasks authorized by section C; and requests the Secretary-General to submit to the Council within 30 days for approval recommendations as to the most effective means by which Iraq's obligations in this respect may be fulfilled. Adopted by unanimous vote

UNSCR 700 (17 JUNE 1991)

The Security Council, Recalling its resolutions 661 (1990) of 6 August 1990, 665 (1990) of 25 August 1990, 670 (1990) of 25 September 1990 and 687 (1991) of 3 April 1991, Taking note of the Secretary-General's report of 2 June

1991 (S/22660) submitted pursuant to paragraph 26 of resolution 687 (1991), Acting under Chapter VII of the Charter of the United Nations,

1. Expresses its appreciation to the Secretary-General for his report of 2 June 1991 (S/22660);
2. Approves the Guidelines to Facilitate Full International Implementation of paragraphs 24, 25 and 27 of Security Council resolution 687 (1991), annexed to the report of the Secretary-General (S/22660);
3. Reiterates its call upon all States and international organizations to act in a manner consistent with the Guidelines;
4. Requests all States, in accordance with paragraph 8 of the Guidelines, to report to the Secretary-General within 45 days on the measures they have instituted for meeting the obligations set out in paragraph 24 of resolution 687 (1991); Entrusts the Committee established under resolution 661 (1990) concerning the situation between Iraq and Kuwait with the responsibility, under the Guidelines, for monitoring the prohibitions against the sale or supply of arms to Iraq and related sanctions established in paragraph 24 of resolution 687 (1991);
6. Decides to remain seized of the matter and to review the Guidelines at the same time as it reviews paragraphs 22, 23, 24 and 25 of resolution 687 (1991) as set out in paragraph 28 thereof. Adopted by unanimous vote

UNSCR 949 (15 OCTOBER 1994)

The Security Council, Recalling all its previous relevant resolutions, and reaffirming resolutions 678 (1990) of 29 November 1990, 686 (1991) of 2 March 1991, 687 (1991) of 3 April 1991, 689 (1991) of 9 April 1991 and 833 (1993) of 27 May 1993, and in particular paragraph 2 of resolution 678 (1990), Recalling that Iraq's acceptance of resolution 687 (1991) adopted pursuant to Chapter VII of the Charter of the United Nations forms the basis of the ceasefire, Noting past Iraqi threats and instances of actual use of force against its neighbours, Recognizing that any hostile or provocative action directed against its neighbours by the Government of Iraq constitutes a threat to peace and security in the region, Welcoming all diplomatic and other efforts to resolve the crisis, Determined to prevent Iraq from resorting to threats and intimidation of its neighbours and the United Nations, Underlining that it will consider Iraq fully responsible for the serious consequences of any failure to fulfil the demands in the present resolution, Noting that Iraq has affirmed its readiness to resolve in a positive manner the issue of recognizing Kuwait's sovereignty and its borders as endorsed by resolution 833 (1993), but underlining that Iraq must unequivocally commit itself by full and formal constitutional procedures to respect Kuwait's sovereignty, territorial integrity and borders, as required by resolutions 687 (1991) and 833 (1993), Reaffirming the commitment of all Member States to the sovereignty, territorial integrity and political independence of Kuwait and Iraq, Reaffirming its statement of 8 October 1994 (S/1994/PRST/58), Taking note of the letter from the Permanent Representative of Kuwait of 6 October 1994 (S/1994/1137), regarding the statement by the Revolution Command Council of Iraq of 6 October 1994, Taking note also of the letter from the Permanent Representative of Iraq of 10 October 1994 (S/1994/1149), announcing that the Government of Iraq had decided to withdraw the troops recently deployed in the direction of the border with Kuwait, Acting under Chapter VII of the Charter of the United Nations,

1. Condemns recent military deployments by Iraq in the direction of the border with Kuwait;
2. Demands that Iraq immediately complete the withdrawal of all military units recently deployed to southern Iraq to their original positions;
3. Demands that Iraq not again utilize its military or any other forces in a hostile or provocative manner to threaten either its neighbours or United Nations operations in Iraq;
4. Demands therefore that Iraq not redeploy to the south the units referred to in paragraph 2 above or take any other action to enhance its military capacity in southern Iraq;
5. Demands that Iraq cooperate fully with the United Nations Special Commission;
6. Decides to remain actively seized of the matter.

UNSCR 986 (14 APRIL 1995)

The Security Council, Recalling its previous relevant resolutions, Concerned by the serious nutritional and health situation of the Iraqi population, and by the risk of a further deterioration in this situation, Convinced of the need as a temporary measure to provide for the humanitarian needs of the Iraqi people until the fulfilment by Iraq of the relevant Security Council resolutions, including notably resolution 687 (1991) of 3 April 1991, allows the Council to take further action with regard to the prohibitions referred to in resolution 661 (1990) of 6 August 1990, in accordance with the provisions of those resolutions, Convinced also of the need for equitable distribution of humanitarian relief to all segments of the Iraqi population throughout the country, Reaffirming the commitment of all Member States to the sovereignty and territorial integrity of Iraq, Acting under Chapter VII of the Charter of the United Nations,

1. Authorizes States, notwithstanding the provisions of paragraphs 3 (a), 3 (b) and 4 of resolution 661 (1990) and subsequent relevant resolutions, to permit the import of petroleum and petroleum products originating in Iraq, including financial and other essential transactions directly relating thereto, sufficient to produce a sum not exceeding a total of one billion United States dollars every 90 days for the purposes set out in this resolution and subject to the following conditions:

   (a) Approval by the Committee established by resolution 661 (1990), in order to ensure the transparency of each transaction and its conformity with the other provisions of this resolution, after submission of an application by the State concerned, endorsed by the Government of Iraq, for each proposed purchase of Iraqi petroleum and petroleum products, including details of the purchase price at fair market value, the export route, the opening of a letter of credit payable to the escrow account to be established by the Secretary-General for the purposes of this resolution, and of any other directly related financial or other essential transaction;

   (b) Payment of the full amount of each purchase of Iraqi petroleum and petroleum products directly by the purchaser in the State concerned into the escrow account to be established by the Secretary-General for the purposes of this resolution;

2. Authorizes Turkey, notwithstanding the provisions of paragraphs 3 (a), 3 (b) and 4 of resolution 661 (1990) and the provisions of paragraph 1 above, to permit the import of petroleum and petroleum products originating in Iraq sufficient, after the deduction of the percentage referred to in paragraph 8 (c) below for the Compensation Fund, to meet the pipeline tariff charges, verified as reasonable by the independent inspection agents referred to in paragraph 6 below, for the transport of Iraqi petroleum and petroleum products through the Kirkuk-Yumurtalik pipeline in Turkey authorized by paragraph 1 above;

3. Decides that paragraphs 1 and 2 of this resolution shall come into force at 00.01 Eastern Standard Time on the day after the President of the Council has informed the members of the Council that he has received the report from the Secretary-General requested in paragraph 13 below, and shall remain in force for an initial period of 180 days unless the Council takes other relevant action with regard to the provisions of resolution 661 (1990);

4. Further decides to conduct a thorough review of all aspects of the implementation of this resolution 90 days after the entry into force of paragraph 1 above and again prior to the end of the initial 180 day period, on receipt of the reports referred to in paragraphs 11 and 12 below, and expresses its intention, prior to the end of the 180 day period, to consider favourably

renewal of the provisions of this resolution, provided that the reports referred to in paragraphs 11 and 12 below indicate that those provisions are being satisfactorily implemented;

5. Further decides that the remaining paragraphs of this resolution shall come into force forthwith;

6. Directs the Committee established by resolution 661 (1990) to monitor the sale of petroleum and petroleum products to be exported by Iraq via the Kirkuk-Yumurtalik pipeline from Iraq to Turkey and from the Mina al-Bakr oil terminal, with the assistance of independent inspection agents appointed by the Secretary-General, who will keep the Committee informed of the amount of petroleum and petroleum products exported from Iraq after the date of entry into force of paragraph 1 of this resolution, and will verify that the purchase price of the petroleum and petroleum products is reasonable in the light of prevailing market conditions, and that, for the purposes of the arrangements set out in this resolution, the larger share of the petroleum and petroleum products is shipped via the Kirkuk-Yumurtalik pipeline and the remainder is exported from the Mina al-Bakr oil terminal;

7. Requests the Secretary-General to establish an escrow account for the purposes of this resolution, to appoint independent and certified public accountants to audit it, and to keep the Government of Iraq fully informed;

8. Decides that the funds in the escrow account shall be used to meet the humanitarian needs of the Iraqi population and for the following other purposes, and requests the Secretary-General to use the funds deposited in the escrow account:

    (a) To finance the export to Iraq, in accordance with the procedures of the Committee established by resolution 661 (1990), of medicine, health supplies, foodstuffs, and materials and supplies for essential civilian needs, as referred to in paragraph 20 of resolution 687 (1991) provided that:

        (i) Each export of goods is at the request of the Government of Iraq;

        (ii) Iraq effectively guarantees their equitable distribution, on the basis of a plan submitted to and approved by the Secretary-General, including a description of the goods to be purchased;

        (iii) The Secretary-General receives authenticated confirmation that the exported goods concerned have arrived in Iraq;

    (b) To complement, in view of the exceptional circumstances prevailing in the three Governorates mentioned below, the distribution by the Government of Iraq of goods imported under this resolution, in order to ensure an equitable distribution of humanitarian relief to all seg-

ments of the Iraqi population throughout the country, by providing
between 130 million and 150 million United States dollars every 90
days to the United Nations Inter-Agency Humanitarian Programme
operating within the sovereign territory of Iraq in the three northern
Governorates of Dihouk, Arbil and Suleimaniyeh, except that if less
than one billion United States dollars worth of petroleum or petroleum products is sold during any 90 day period, the Secretary-General may provide a proportionately smaller amount for this purpose;

(c) To transfer to the Compensation Fund the same percentage of the
funds deposited in the escrow account as that decided by the Council
in paragraph 2 of resolution 705 (1991) of 15 August 1991;

(d) To meet the costs to the United Nations of the independent inspection agents and the certified public accountants and the activities associated with implementation of this resolution;

(e) To meet the current operating costs of the Special Commission, pending subsequent payment in full of the costs of carrying out the tasks
authorized by section C of resolution 687 (1991);

(f) To meet any reasonable expenses, other than expenses payable in
Iraq, which are determined by the Committee established by resolution 661 (1990) to be directly related to the export by Iraq of petroleum and petroleum products permitted under paragraph 1 above or
to the export to Iraq, and activities directly necessary therefor, of the
parts and equipment permitted under paragraph 9 below;

(g) To make available up to 10 million United States dollars every 90
days from the funds deposited in the escrow account for the payments envisaged under paragraph 6 of resolution 778 (1992) of 2 October 1992;

9. Authorizes States to permit, notwithstanding the provisions of paragraph
3 (c) of resolution 661 (1990):

(a) The export to Iraq of the parts and equipment which are essential for
the safe operation of the Kirkuk-Yumurtalik pipeline system in Iraq,
subject to the prior approval by the Committee established by resolution 661 (1990) of each export contract;

(b) Activities directly necessary for the exports authorized under sub-
paragraph (a) above, including financial transactions related
thereto;

10. Decides that, since the costs of the exports and activities authorized under
paragraph 9 above are precluded by paragraph 4 of resolution 661 (1990)
and by paragraph 11 of resolution 778 (1991) from being met from funds
frozen in accordance with those provisions, the cost of such exports and activities may, until funds begin to be paid into the escrow account established
for the purposes of this resolution, and following approval in each case by

the Committee established by resolution 661 (1990), exceptionally be financed by letters of credit, drawn against future oil sales the proceeds of which are to be deposited in the escrow account;

11. Requests the Secretary-General to report to the Council 90 days after the date of entry into force of paragraph 1 above, and again prior to the end of the initial 180 day period, on the basis of observation by United Nations personnel in Iraq, and on the basis of consultations with the Government of Iraq, on whether Iraq has ensured the equitable distribution of medicine, health supplies, foodstuffs, and materials and supplies for essential civilian needs, financed in accordance with paragraph 8 (a) above, including in his reports any observations he may have on the adequacy of the revenues to meet Iraq's humanitarian needs, and on Iraq's capacity to export sufficient quantities of petroleum and petroleum products to produce the sum referred to in paragraph 1 above;

12. Requests the Committee established by resolution 661 (1990), in close coordination with the Secretary-General, to develop expedited procedures as necessary to implement the arrangements in paragraphs 1, 2, 6, 8, 9 and 10 of this resolution and to report to the Council 90 days after the date of entry into force of paragraph 1 above and again prior to the end of the initial 180 day period on the implementation of those arrangements;

13. Requests the Secretary-General to take the actions necessary to ensure the effective implementation of this resolution, authorizes him to enter into any necessary arrangements or agreements, and requests him to report to the Council when he has done so;

14. Decides that petroleum and petroleum products subject to this resolution shall while under Iraqi title be immune from legal proceedings and not be subject to any form of attachment, garnishment or execution, and that all States shall take any steps that may be necessary under their respective domestic legal systems to assure this protection, and to ensure that the proceeds of the sale are not diverted from the purposes laid down in this resolution;

15. Affirms that the escrow account established for the purposes of this resolution enjoys the privileges and immunities of the United Nations;

16. Affirms that all persons appointed by the Secretary-General for the purpose of implementing this resolution enjoy privileges and immunities as experts on mission for the United Nations in accordance with the Convention on the Privileges and Immunities of the United Nations, and requires the Government of Iraq to allow them full freedom of movement and all necessary facilities for the discharge of their duties in the implementation of this resolution;

17. Affirms that nothing in this resolution affects Iraq's duty scrupulously to

adhere to all of its obligations concerning servicing and repayment of its foreign debt, in accordance with the appropriate international mechanisms;

18. Also affirms that nothing in this resolution should be construed as infringing the sovereignty or territorial integrity of Iraq;

19. Decides to remain seized of the matter.

UNSCR 1051 (27 MARCH 1996)

The Security Council, Reaffirming its resolution 687 (1991) of 8 April 1991, and in particular section C thereof, its resolution 707 (1991) of 15 August 1991 and its resolution 715 (1991) of 11 October 1991 and the plans for ongoing monitoring and verification approved thereunder, Recalling the request in paragraph 7 of its resolution 715 (1991) to the Committee established under resolution 661 (1990), the Special Commission and the Director General of the International Atomic Energy Agency (IAEA) to develop in cooperation a mechanism for monitoring any future sales or supplies by other countries to Iraq of items relevant to the implementation of section C of resolution 687 (1991) and other relevant resolutions, including resolution 715 (1991) and the plans approved thereunder, Having considered the letter of 7 December 1995 (S/1995/1017) to the President of the Council from the Chairman of the Committee established under resolution 661 (1990), annex I of which contains the provisions for the mechanism for export/import monitoring called for in paragraph 7 of resolution 715 (1991), Recognizing that the export/import monitoring mechanism is an integral part of ongoing monitoring and verification by the Special Commission and the IAEA, Recognizing that the export/import mechanism is not a regime for international licensing, but rather for the timely provision of information by States in which companies are located which are contemplating sales or supplies to Iraq of items covered by the plans for ongoing monitoring and verification and will not impede Iraq's legitimate right to import or export for non-proscribed purposes, items and technology necessary for the promotion of its economic and social development, Acting under Chapter VII of the Charter of the United Nations,

1. Approves, pursuant to the relevant provisions of its resolutions 687 (1991) and 715 (1991), the provisions for the monitoring mechanism contained in annex I of the aforementioned letter of 7 December 1995 (S/1995/1017), subject to the terms of this resolution;

2. Approves also the general principles to be followed in implementing the monitoring mechanism contained in the letter of 17 July 1995 from the Chairman of the Special Commission to the Chairman of the Committee established under resolution 661 (1990) which is contained in annex II

of the aforementioned letter of 7 December 1995 (S/1995/1017);

3. Affirms that the mechanism approved by this resolution is without prejudice to and shall not impair the operation of existing or future non-proliferation agreements or regimes on the international or regional level including arrangements referred to in resolution 687 (1991), nor shall such agreements or regimes impair the operation of the mechanism;

4. Confirms, until the Council decides otherwise under its relevant resolutions, that requests by other States for sales to Iraq or requests by Iraq for import of any item or technology to which the mechanism applies shall continue to be addressed to the Committee established under resolution 661 (1990) for decision by that Committee in accordance with paragraph 4 of the mechanism;

5. Decides, subject to paragraphs 4 and 7 of this resolution, that all States shall:

   (a) Transmit to the joint unit constituted by the Special Commission and the Director General of the IAEA under paragraph 16 of the mechanism the notifications, with the data from potential exporters, and all other relevant information when available to the States, as requested in the mechanism on the intended sale or supply from their territories of any items or technologies which are subject to such notification in accordance with paragraphs 9, 11, 13, 24, 25, 27 and 28 of the mechanism;

   (b) Report to the joint unit, in accordance with paragraphs 13, 24, 25, 27 and 28 of the mechanism, any information they may have at their disposal or may receive from suppliers in their territories of attempts to circumvent the mechanism or to supply Iraq with items prohibited to Iraq under the plans for ongoing monitoring and verification approved by resolution 715 (1991), or where the procedures for special exceptions laid down in paragraphs 24 and 25 of the mechanism have not been followed by Iraq;

6. Decides that the notifications required under paragraph 5 above shall be provided to the joint unit by Iraq, in respect of all items and technologies referred to in paragraph 12 of the mechanism, as from the date agreed upon between the Special Commission and the Director General of the IAEA and Iraq, and in any event not later than sixty days after the adoption of this resolution;

7. Decides that the notifications required under paragraph 5 above shall be provided to the joint unit by all other States as from the date the Secretary-General and the Director General of the IAEA, after their consultations with the members of the Council and other interested States, report to the Council indicating that they are satisfied with the preparedness of States for the effective implementation of the mechanism;

8. Decides that the information provided through the mechanism shall be

treated as confidential and restricted to the Special Commission and the IAEA, to the extent that this is consistent with their respective responsibilities under resolution 715 (1991), other relevant resolutions and the plans for ongoing monitoring and verification approved under resolution 715 (1991);

9. Affirms, if experience over time demonstrates the need or new technologies so require, that the Council would be prepared to review the mechanism in order to determine whether any changes are required and that the annexes to the plans for ongoing monitoring and verification approved under resolution 715 (1991), which identify the items and technologies to be notified under the mechanism, may be amended in accordance with the plans, after appropriate consultations with interested States and, as laid down in the plans, after notification to the Council;

10. Decides also that the Committee established under resolution 661 (1990) and the Special Commission shall carry out the functions assigned to them under the mechanism, until the Council decides otherwise;

11. Requests the Director General of the IAEA to carry out, with the assistance and cooperation of the Special Commission, the functions assigned to him under the mechanism;

12. Calls upon all States and international organizations to cooperate fully with the Committee established under resolution 661 (1990), the Special Commission and the Director General of the IAEA in the fulfilment of their tasks in connection with the mechanism, including supplying such information as may be sought by them in implementation of the mechanism;

13. Calls upon all States to adopt as soon as possible such measures as may be necessary under their national procedures to implement the mechanism;

14. Decides that all States shall, not later than 45 days after the adoption of this resolution, be provided by the Special Commission and the Director General of the IAEA with information necessary to make preparatory arrangements at the national level prior to the implementation of the provisions of the mechanism;

15. Demands that Iraq meet unconditionally all its obligations under the mechanism approved by this resolution and cooperate fully with the Special Commission and the Director General of the IAEA in the carrying out of their tasks under this resolution and the mechanism by such means as they may determine in accordance with their mandates from the Council;

16. Decides to consolidate the periodic requirements for progress reports under its resolutions 699 (1991), 715 (1991) and this resolution and to request the Secretary-General and the Director General of the IAEA to submit such consolidated progress reports every six months to the Council, commencing on 11 April 1996;

17. Decides to remain seized of the matter.

UNSCR 1060 (12 JUNE 1996)

The Security Council, Recalling all its previous relevant resolutions, and in particular its resolutions 687 (1991) of 3 April 1991, 707 (1991) of 15 August 1991 and 715 (1991) of 11 October 1991, Recalling also the letter from the Executive Chairman of the United Nations Special Commission to the President of the Security Council of 9 March 1996 (S/1996/182), the letter from the President of the Security Council to the Executive Chairman of the Special Commission of 12 March 1996 (S/1996/183), the statement made at its 3642nd meeting on 19 March 1996 by the President of the Security Council (S/PRST/1996/11), and the report of the Chairman of the Special Commission of 11 April 1996 (S/1996/258), Reiterating the commitment of all Member States to the sovereignty, territorial integrity and political independence of Kuwait and Iraq, Recalling in this context the notes from the Secretary-General of 21 July 1993 (S/26127) and 1 December 1993 (S/26825), Noting the progress made in the work of the Special Commission towards the elimination of Iraq's programmes of weapons of mass destruction, and outstanding problems, reported by the Chairman of the Special Commission, Noting with concern the incidents on 11 and 12 June 1996, reported to members of the Council by the Executive Chairman of the Special Commission, when access by a Special Commission inspection team to sites in Iraq designated for inspection by the Commission was excluded by the Iraqi authorities, Emphasizing the importance the Council attaches to full compliance by Iraq with its obligations under resolutions 687 (1991), 707 (1991) and 715 (1991) to permit immediate, unconditional and unrestricted access to the Special Commission to any site which the Commission wishes to inspect, Emphasizing the unacceptability of any attempts by Iraq to deny access to any such site, Acting under Chapter VII of the Charter of the United Nations,

1. Deplores the refusal of the Iraqi authorities to allow access to sites designated by the Special Commission, which constitutes a clear violation of the provisions of Security Council resolutions 687 (1991), 707 (1991) and 715 (1991);
2. Demands that Iraq cooperate fully with the Special Commission in accordance with the relevant resolutions; and that the Government of Iraq allow the Special Commission inspection teams immediate, unconditional and unrestricted access to any and all areas, facilities, equipment, records and means of transportation which they wish to inspect;
3. Expresses its full support to the Special Commission in its efforts to ensure implementation of its mandate under the relevant resolutions of the Council;
4. Decides to remain seized of the matter.

UNSCR 1111 (4 JUNE 1997)

The Security Council, Recalling its previous resolutions and in particular its resolution 986 (1995) of 14 April 1995, Convinced of the need as a temporary measure to continue to provide for the humanitarian needs of the Iraqi people until the fulfilment by Iraq of the relevant Security Council resolutions, including notably resolution 687 (1991) of 3 April 1991, allows the Council to take further action with regard to the prohibitions referred to in resolution 661 (1990) of 6 August 1990, in accordance with the provisions of those resolutions, Determined to avoid any further deterioration of the current humanitarian situation, Convinced also of the need for equitable distribution of humanitarian relief to all segments of the Iraqi population throughout the country, Welcoming the report submitted by the Secretary-General in accordance with paragraph 11 of resolution 986 (1995) (S/1997/419), as well as the report submitted in accordance with paragraph 12 of resolution 986 (1995) (S/1997/417) by the Committee established by resolution 661 (1990) of 6 August 1990, Reaffirming the commitment of all Member States to the sovereignty and territorial integrity of Iraq, Acting under Chapter VII of the Charter of the United Nations,

1. Decides that the provisions of resolution 986 (1995), except those contained in paragraphs 4, 11 and 12, shall remain in force for another period of 180 days beginning at 00.01 hours, Eastern Daylight Time, on 8 June 1997;

2. Further decides to conduct a thorough review of all aspects of the implementation of this resolution 90 days after the entry into force of paragraph 1 above and again prior to the end of the 180 day period, on receipt of the reports referred to in paragraphs 3 and 4 below, and expresses its intention, prior to the end of the 180 day period, to consider favourably renewal of the provisions of this resolution, provided that the reports referred to in paragraphs 3 and 4 below indicate that those provisions are being satisfactorily implemented;

3. Requests the Secretary-General to report to the Council 90 days after the date of entry into force of paragraph 1 above, and again prior to the end of the 180 day period, on the basis of observation by United Nations personnel in Iraq, and on the basis of consultations with the Government of Iraq, on whether Iraq has ensured the equitable distribution of medicine, health supplies, foodstuffs, and materials and supplies for essential civilian needs, financed in accordance with paragraph 8 (a) of resolution 986 (1995), including in his reports any observations he may have on the adequacy of the revenues to meet Iraq's humanitarian needs, and on Iraq's capacity to export sufficient quantities of petroleum and petroleum products to produce the sum referred to in paragraph 1 of resolution 986 (1995);

4. Requests the Committee established by resolution 661 (1990), in close coordination with the Secretary-General, to report to the Council 90 days after the date of entry into force of paragraph 1 above and again prior to the end of the 180 day period on the implementation of the arrangements in paragraphs 1, 2, 6, 8, 9 and 10 of resolution 986 (1995);

5. Directs the Committee established by resolution 661 (1990) of 6 August 1990 to process expeditiously contract applications submitted under the present resolution as soon as the Secretary-General has approved the new Plan submitted by the Government of Iraq, guaranteeing equitable distribution and including a description of the goods to be purchased with the revenues of the sale of petroleum and petroleum products authorized by the present resolution;

6. Decides to remain seized of the matter.

UNSCR 1115 (21 JUNE 1997)

The Security Council, Recalling all its previous relevant resolutions, and in particular its resolutions 687 (1991) of 3 April 1991, 707 (1991) of 15 August 1991, 715 (1991) of 11 October 1991 and 1060 (1996) of 12 June 1996, Recalling also the letter from the Executive Chairman of the Special Commission to the President of the Security Council of 12 June 1997 (S/1997/474), which reported to the Council the incidents on 10 and 12 June 1997 when access by a Special Commission inspection team to sites in Iraq designated for inspection by the Commission was excluded by the Iraqi authorities, Determined to ensure full compliance by Iraq with its obligations under all previous resolutions, in particular resolutions 687 (1991), 707 (1991), 715 (1991) and 1060 (1996) to permit immediate, unconditional and unrestricted access to the Special Commission to any site which the Commission wishes to inspect, Stressing the unacceptability of any attempts by Iraq to deny access to any such site, Reiterating the commitment of all Member States to the sovereignty, territorial integrity and political independence of Kuwait and Iraq, Acting under Chapter VII of the Charter of the United Nations,

1. Condemns the repeated refusal of the Iraqi authorities to allow access to sites designated by the Special Commission, which constitutes a clear and flagrant violation of the provisions of Security Council resolutions 687 (1991), 707 (1991), 715 (1991)and 1060 (1996);

2. Demands that Iraq cooperate fully with the Special Commission in accordance with the relevant resolutions; and that the Government of Iraq allow the Special Commission inspection teams immediate, unconditional and unrestricted access to any and all areas, facilities, equipment,

records and means of transportation which they wish to inspect in accordance with the mandate of the Special Commission;

3. Demands further that the Government of Iraq give immediate, unconditional and unrestricted access to officials and other persons under the authority of the Iraqi Government whom the Special Commission wishes to interview, so that the Special Commission may fully discharge its mandate;

4. Requests the Chairman of the Special Commission to include in his consolidated progress reports under resolution 1051 (1996) an annex evaluating Iraq's compliance with paragraphs 2 and 3 of this resolution;

5. Decides not to conduct the reviews provided for in paragraphs 21 and 28 of resolution 687 (1991) until after the next consolidated progress report of the Special Commission, due on 11 October 1997, after which time those reviews will resume in accordance with resolution 687 (1991);

6. Expresses the firm intention, unless the Special Commission advises the Council in the report referred to in paragraphs 4 and 5 that Iraq is in substantial compliance with paragraphs 2 and 3 of this resolution, to impose additional measures on those categories of Iraqi officials responsible for the non-compliance;

7. Reaffirms its full support to the Special Commission in its efforts to ensure the implementation of its mandate under the relevant resolutions of the Council;

8. Decides to remain seized of the matter.

UNSCR 1129 (12 SEPTEMBER 1997)

The Security Council, Recalling its previous resolutions and, in particular, its resolutions 986 (1995) of 14 April 1995 and 1111 (1997) of 4 June 1997, Reaffirming that the implementation period of resolution 1111 (1997) began at 00.01, Eastern Daylight Time, on 8 June 1997, and that the export of petroleum and petroleum products by Iraq pursuant to resolution 1111 (1997) did not require the approval by the Secretary-General of the distribution plan mentioned in paragraph 8 (a) (ii) of resolution 986 (1995), Taking note of the decision by the Government of Iraq not to export petroleum and petroleum products permitted pursuant to resolution 1111 (1997) during the period 8 June to 13 August 1997, Deeply concerned about the resulting humanitarian consequences for the Iraqi people, since the shortfall in the revenue from the sale of petroleum and petroleum products will delay the provision of humanitarian relief and create hardship for the Iraqi people, Noting that, as set out in the report of the Committee established by resolution 661 (1990) (S/1997/692), Iraq will not be able to export petroleum and petroleum products worth two billion United States dollars by the end of the period set by resolution 1111 (1997) while complying with the requirement not to produce a sum exceeding one billion United States dollars every 90 days set out in paragraph 1 of resolution 986 (1995) and renewed in resolution 1111 (1997), Acknowledging the situation with regard to the delivery of humanitarian goods to Iraq as described in the report of the Secretary-General (S/1997/685) and encouraging the continuing efforts to improve this situation, Stressing the importance of an equitable distribution of humanitarian goods as called for by paragraph 8 (a) (ii) of resolution 986 (1995), Determined to avoid any further deterioration of the current humanitarian situation, Reaffirming the commitment of all Member States to the sovereignty and territorial integrity of Iraq, Acting under Chapter VII of the Charter of the United Nations,

1. Decides that the provisions of resolution 1111 (1997) shall remain in force, except that States are authorized to permit the import of petroleum and petroleum products originating in Iraq, including financial and other essential transactions directly relating thereto, sufficient to produce a sum not exceeding a total of one billion United States dollars within a period of 120 days from 00.01, Eastern Daylight Time, on 8 June 1997 and, thereafter, a sum not exceeding a total of one billion United States dollars within a period of 60 days from 00.01, Eastern Daylight Time, on 4 October 1997;

2. Decides further that the provisions of paragraph 1 above shall apply only to the period of implementation of resolution 1111 (1997), and expresses its firm intention that under any future resolutions authorizing States to permit the import of petroleum and petroleum products originating in Iraq, the time limits within which imports may be permitted established in such resolutions shall be strictly enforced;

3. Expresses its full support for the intention of the Secretary-General, stated in his report to the Security Council (S/1997/685), to follow up his observations concerning the needs of vulnerable groups in Iraq by monitoring the actions of the Government of Iraq in respect of these groups;

4. Stresses that contracts for the purchase of humanitarian supplies submitted in accordance with resolution 1111 (1997) must be limited to items which appear on the list of supplies annexed to the second distribution plan prepared by the Government of Iraq and approved by the Secretary-General pursuant to paragraph 8 (a) (ii) of resolution 986 (1995), or appropriate amendments to the plan must be requested prior to purchasing items not on the annexed list;

5. Decides to remain seized of the matter.

UNSCR 1134 (23 OCTOBER 1997)

The Security Council, Recalling all its previous relevant resolutions, and in particular its resolutions 687 (1991) of 3 April 1991, 707 (1991) of 15 August 1991, 715 (1991) of 11 October 1991, 1060 (1996) of 12 June 1996, and 1115 (1997) of 21 June 1997, Having considered the report of the Executive Chairman of the Special Commission dated 6 October 1997 (S/1997/774), Expressing grave concern at the report of additional incidents since the adoption of resolution 1115 (1997) in which access by the Special Commission inspection teams to sites in Iraq designated for inspection by the Commission was again denied by the Iraqi authorities, Stressing the unacceptability of any attempts by Iraq to deny access to such sites, Taking note of the progress nevertheless achieved by the Special Commission, as set out in the report of the Executive Chairman, towards the elimination of Iraq's programme of weapons of mass destruction, Reaffirming its determination to ensure full compliance by Iraq with all its obligations under all previous relevant resolutions and reiterating its demand that Iraq allow immediate, unconditional and unrestricted access to the Special Commission to any site which the Commission wishes to inspect, and in particular allow the Special Commission and its inspection teams to conduct both fixed wing and helicopter flights throughout Iraq for all relevant purposes including inspection, surveillance, aerial surveys, transportation and logistics without interferences of any kind and upon such terms and conditions as may be determined by the Special Commission, and to make use of their own aircraft and such airfields in Iraq as they may determine are most appropriate for the work of the Commission, Recalling that resolution 1115 (1997) expresses the Council's firm intention, unless the Special Commission has advised the Council that Iraq is in substantial compliance with paragraphs 2 and 3 of that resolution, to impose additional measures on those categories of Iraqi officials responsible for the non-compliance, Reiterating the commitment of all Member States to the sovereignty, territorial integrity and political independence of Kuwait and Iraq, Acting under Chapter VII of the Charter of the United Nations,

1. Condemns the repeated refusal of the Iraqi authorities, as detailed in the report of the Executive Chairman of the Special Commission, to allow access to sites designated by the Special Commission, and especially Iraqi actions endangering the safety of Special Commission personnel, the removal and destruction of documents of interest to the Special Commission and interference with the freedom of movement of Special Commission personnel;

2. Decides that such refusals to cooperate constitute a flagrant violation of Security Council resolutions 687 (1991), 707 (1991), 715 (1991) and

1060 (1996), and notes that the Special Commission in the report of the Executive Chairman was unable to advise that Iraq was in substantial compliance with paragraphs 2 and 3 of resolution 1115 (1997);

3. Demands that Iraq cooperate fully with the Special Commission in accordance with the relevant resolutions, which constitute the governing standard of Iraqi compliance;

4. Demands in particular that Iraq without delay allow the Special Commission inspection teams immediate, unconditional and unrestricted access to any and all areas, facilities, equipment, records and means of transportation which they wish to inspect in accordance with the mandate of the Special Commission, as well as to officials and other persons under the authority of the Iraqi Government whom the Special Commission wishes to interview so that the Special Commission may fully discharge its mandate;

5. Requests the Chairman of the Special Commission to include in all future consolidated progress reports prepared under resolution 1051 (1996) an annex evaluating Iraq's compliance with paragraphs 2 and 3 of resolution 1115 (1997);

6. Expresses the firm intention—if the Special Commission reports that Iraq is not in compliance with paragraphs 2 and 3 of resolution 1115 (1997) or if the Special Commission does not advise the Council in the report of the Executive Chairman due on 11 April 1998 that Iraq is in compliance with paragraphs 2 and 3 of resolution 1115 (1997)—to adopt measures which would oblige all States to prevent without delay the entry into or transit through their territories of all Iraqi officials and members of the Iraqi armed forces who are responsible for or participate in instances of non-compliance with paragraphs 2 and 3 of resolution 1115 (1997), provided that the entry of a person into a particular State on a specified date may be authorized by the Committee established by resolution 661 (1990), and provided that nothing in this paragraph shall oblige a State to refuse entry into its own territory to its own nationals or persons carrying out bona fide diplomatic assignments or missions;

7. Decides further, on the basis of all incidents related to the implementation of paragraphs 2 and 3 of resolution 1115 (1997), to begin to designate, in consultation with the Special Commission, individuals whose entry or transit would be prevented upon implementation of the measures set out in paragraph 6 above;

8. Decides not to conduct the reviews provided for in paragraphs 21 and 28 of resolution 687 (1991) until after the next consolidated progress report of the Special Commission, due on 11 April 1998, after which those reviews will resume in accordance with resolution 687 (1991), beginning on 26 April 1998;

9. Reaffirms its full support for the authority of the Special Commission under its Executive Chairman to ensure the implementation of its mandate under the relevant resolutions of the Council;

10. Decides to remain seized of the matter.

UNSCR 1137 (12 NOVEMBER 1997)

The Security Council, Recalling all its previous relevant resolutions, and in particular its resolutions 687 (1991) of 3 April 1991, 707 (1991) of 15 August 1991, 715 (1991) of 11 October 1991, 1060 (1996) of 12 June 1996, 1115 (1997) of 21 June 1997, and 1134 (1997) of 23 October 1997, Taking note with grave concern of the letter of 29 October 1997 from the Deputy Prime Minister of Iraq to the President of the Security Council (S/1997/829) conveying the unacceptable decision of the Government of Iraq to seek to impose conditions on its cooperation with the Special Commission, of the letter of 2 November 1997 from the Permanent Representative of Iraq to the United Nations to the Executive Chairman of the Special Commission (S/1997/837, annex) which reiterated the unacceptable demand that the reconnaissance aircraft operating on behalf of the Special Commission be withdrawn from use and which implicitly threatened the safety of such aircraft, and of the letter of 6 November 1997 from the Minister of Foreign Affairs of Iraq to the President of the Security Council (S/1997/855) admitting that Iraq has moved dual-capable equipment which is subject to monitoring by the Special Commission, Also taking note with grave concern of the letters of 30 October 1997 (S/1997/830) and 2 November 1997 (S/1997/836) from the Executive Chairman of the Special Commission to the President of the Security Council advising that the Government of Iraq had denied entry to Iraq to two Special Commission officials on 30 October 1997 and 2 November 1997 on the grounds of their nationality, and of the letters of 3 November 1997 (S/1997/837), 4 November 1997 (S/1997/843), 5 November 1997 (S/1997/851) and 7 November 1997 (S/1997/864) from the Executive Chairman of the Special Commission to the President of the Security Council advising that the Government of Iraq had denied entry to sites designated for inspection by the Special Commission on 3, 4, 5, 6 and 7 November 1997 to Special Commission inspectors on the grounds of their nationality, and of the additional information in the Executive Chairman's letter of 5 November 1997 to the President of the Security Council (S/1997/851) that the Government of Iraq has moved significant pieces of dual-capable equipment subject to monitoring by the Special Commission, and that monitoring cameras appear to have been tampered with or covered, Welcoming the diplomatic initiatives, including that of the high-level mission of the Secretary-General, which have taken place in an effort to ensure that Iraq complies unconditionally with its obligations under the relevant resolutions, Deeply concerned at the report of the high-level mission of the Secretary-General on the results of its meetings with the highest levels of the Government of Iraq, Recalling that its resolution 1115 (1997) expressed its firm intention, unless the Special Commission advised the Council that Iraq is in substantial compliance with paragraphs 2 and 3 of that resolution, to impose additional measures on those categories of Iraqi officials responsible for the non-compliance, Recalling also that its resolution 1134 (1997) reaffirmed its firm intention, if inter alia the Special Commission reports that Iraq is not in compliance with paragraphs 2 and 3 of resolution 1115 (1997), to adopt measures which would oblige States to refuse the entry into or transit through their territories of all Iraqi officials and members of the Iraqi armed forces who are responsible for or participate in instances of non-compliance with paragraphs 2 and 3 of resolution 1115 (1997), Recalling further the Statement of its President of 29 October 1997 (S/PRST/1997/49) in which the Council condemned the decision of the Government of Iraq to try to dictate the terms of its compliance with its obligation to cooperate with the Special Commission, and warned of the serious consequences of Iraq's failure to comply immediately and fully and without conditions or restrictions with its obligations under the relevant resolutions, Reiterating the commitment of all Member States to the sovereignty, territorial integrity and political independence of Kuwait and Iraq, Determined to ensure immediate and full compliance without conditions or restrictions by Iraq with its obligations under the relevant resolutions, Determining that this situation continues to constitute a threat to international peace and security, Acting under Chapter VII of the Charter,

1. Condemns the continued violations by Iraq of its obligations under the relevant resolutions to cooperate fully and unconditionally with the Special Commission in the fulfilment of its mandate, including its unacceptable decision of 29 October 1997 to seek to impose conditions on cooperation with the Special Commission, its refusal on 30 October 1997 and 2 November 1997 to allow entry to Iraq to two Special Commission officials on the grounds of their nationality, its denial of entry on 3, 4, 5, 6 and 7 November 1997 to sites designated by the Special Commission for inspection to Special Commission inspectors on the grounds of their nationality, its implicit threat to the safety of the reconnaissance aircraft operating on behalf of the Special Commission, its removal of significant pieces of dual-use equipment from their previous sites, and its tampering with monitoring cameras of the Special Commission;

2. Demands that the Government of Iraq rescind immediately its decision of 29 October 1997;

3. Demands also that Iraq cooperate fully and immediately and without conditions or restrictions with the Special Commission in accordance

with the relevant resolutions, which constitute the governing standard of Iraqi compliance;

4. Decides, in accordance with paragraph 6 of resolution 1134 (1997), that States shall without delay prevent the entry into or transit through their territories of all Iraqi officials and members of the Iraqi armed forces who were responsible for or participated in the instances of non-compliance detailed in paragraph 1 above, provided that the entry of a person into a particular State on a specified date may be authorized by the Committee established by resolution 661 (1990) of 6 August 1990, and provided that nothing in this paragraph shall oblige a State to refuse entry into its own territory to its own nationals, or to persons carrying out bona fide diplomatic assignments, or missions approved by the Committee established by resolution 661 (1990);

5. Decides also, in accordance with paragraph 7 of resolution 1134 (1997), to designate in consultation with the Special Commission a list of individuals whose entry or transit will be prevented under the provisions of paragraph 4 above, and requests the Committee established by resolution 661 (1990) to develop guidelines and procedures as appropriate for the implementation of the measures set out in paragraph 4 above, and to transmit copies of these guidelines and procedures, as well as a list of the individuals designated, to all Member States;

6. Decides that the provisions of paragraphs 4 and 5 above shall terminate one day after the Executive Chairman of the Special Commission reports to the Council that Iraq is allowing the Special Commission inspection teams immediate, unconditional and unrestricted access to any and all areas, facilities, equipment, records and means of transportation which they wish to inspect in accordance with the mandate of the Special Commission, as well as to officials and other persons under the authority of the Iraqi Government whom the Special Commission wishes to interview so that the Special Commission may fully discharge its mandate;

7. Decides that the reviews provided for in paragraphs 21 and 28 of resolution 687 (1991) shall resume in April 1998 in accordance with paragraph 8 of resolution 1134 (1997), provided that the Government of Iraq shall have complied with paragraph 2 above;

8. Expresses the firm intention to take further measures as may be required for the implementation of this resolution;

9. Reaffirms the responsibility of the Government of Iraq under the relevant resolutions to ensure the safety and security of the personnel and equipment of the Special Commission and its inspection teams;

10. Reaffirms also its full support for the authority of the Special Commission under its Executive Chairman to ensure the implementation of its mandate under the relevant resolutions of the Council;

11. Decides to remain seized of the matter.

UNSCR 1143 (4 DECEMBER 1997)

The Security Council, Recalling its previous resolutions and in particular its resolutions 986 (1995) of 14 April 1995, 1111 (1997) of 4 June 1997 and 1129 (1997) of 12 September 1997, Convinced of the need as a temporary measure to continue to provide for the humanitarian needs of the Iraqi people until the fulfilment by Iraq of the relevant resolutions, including notably resolution 687 (1991) of 3 April 1991, allows the Council to take further action with regard to the prohibitions referred to in resolution 661 (1990) of 6 August 1990, in accordance with the provisions of those resolutions, Convinced also of the need for equitable distribution of humanitarian relief to all segments of the Iraqi population throughout the country, Welcoming the report submitted by the Secretary-General in accordance with paragraph 3 of resolution 1111 (1997) (S/1997/935) and his intention to submit a supplementary report, as well as the report submitted in accordance with paragraph 4 of resolution 1111 (1997) by the Committee established by resolution 661 (1990) of 6 August 1990 (S/1997/942), Noting with concern that, despite the ongoing implementation of resolutions 986 (1995) and 1111 (1997), the population of Iraq continues to face a serious nutritional and health situation, Determined to avoid any further deterioration of the current humanitarian situation, Noting with appreciation the recommendation of the Secretary-General that the Council re-examine the adequacy of the revenues provided by resolution 986 (1995) and consider how best to meet the priority humanitarian requirements of the Iraqi people, including the possibility of increasing those revenues, Noting also with appreciation the Secretary-General's intention to include in his supplementary report recommendations on ways to improve the processing and supply of humanitarian goods under resolution 986 (1995), Welcoming the efforts made by the Committee established by resolution 661 (1990) to refine and clarify its working procedures and encouraging the Committee to go further in that direction in order to expedite the approval process, Reaffirming the commitment of all Member States to the sovereignty and territorial integrity of Iraq, Acting under Chapter VII of the Charter of the United Nations,

1. Decides that the provisions of resolution 986 (1995), except those contained in paragraphs 4, 11 and 12, shall remain in force for another period of 180 days beginning at 00.01 hours, Eastern Standard Time, on 5 December 1997;

2. Further decides that the provisions of the distribution plan in respect of goods purchased in accordance with resolution 1111 (1997) shall continue to apply to foodstuffs, medicine and health supplies purchased in accordance with this resolution pending the Secretary-General's approval of a new distribution plan, to be submitted by the Government of Iraq before 5 January 1998;

3. Further decides to conduct a thorough review of all aspects of the implementation of this resolution 90 days after the entry into force of paragraph 1 above and again prior to the end of the 180-day period, on receipt of the reports referred to in paragraphs 4 and 5 below, and expresses its intention, prior to the end of the 180-day period, to consider favourably renewal of the provisions of this resolution, provided that the reports referred to in paragraphs 4 and 5 below indicate that those provisions are being satisfactorily implemented;

4. Requests the Secretary-General to report to the Council 90 days after the date of entry into force of paragraph 1 above, and again prior to the end of the 180-day period, on the basis of observation by United Nations personnel in Iraq, and on the basis of consultations with the Government of Iraq, on whether Iraq has ensured the equitable distribution of medicine, health supplies, foodstuffs, and materials and supplies for essential civilian needs, financed in accordance with paragraph 8 (a) of resolution 986 (1995), including in his reports any observations he may have on the adequacy of the revenues to meet Iraq's humanitarian needs, and on Iraq's capacity to export sufficient quantities of petroleum and petroleum products to produce the sum referred to in paragraph 1 of resolution 986 (1995);

5. Requests the Committee established by resolution 661 (1990), in close coordination with the Secretary-General, to report to the Council 90 days after the date of entry into force of paragraph 1 above and again prior to the end of the 180-day period on the implementation of the arrangements in paragraphs 1, 2, 6, 8, 9 and 10 of resolution 986 (1995);

6. Welcomes the intention of the Secretary-General to submit a supplementary report, and expresses its willingness, in the light of his recommendations, to find ways of improving the implementation of the humanitarian programme and to take such action over additional resources as needed to meet priority humanitarian requirements of the Iraqi people, as well as to consider an extension of the time-frame for the implementation of this resolution;

7. Requests the Secretary-General to submit his supplementary report to the Council no later than 30 January 1998;

8. Stresses the need to ensure respect for the security and safety of all persons appointed by the Secretary-General for the implementation of this resolution in Iraq;

9. Requests the Committee established by resolution 661 (1990) to continue, in close coordination with the Secretary-General, to refine and clarify working procedures in order to expedite the approval process and to report to the Council no later than 30 January 1998;

10. Decides to remain seized of the matter.

UNSCR 1153 (20 FEBRUARY 1998)

The Security Council, Recalling its previous relevant resolutions and in particular its resolutions 986 (1995) of 14 April 1995, 1111 (1997) of 4 June 1997, 1129 (1997) of 12 September 1997 and 1143 (1997) of 4 December 1997, Convinced of the need as a temporary measure to continue to provide for the humanitarian needs of the Iraqi people until the fulfilment by Iraq of the relevant resolutions, including notably resolution 687 (1991) of 3 April 1991, allows the Council to take further action with regard to the prohibitions referred to in resolution 661 (1990) of 6 August 1990, in accordance with the provisions of those resolutions, and emphasizing the temporary nature of the distribution plan envisaged by this resolution, Convinced also of the need for equitable distribution of humanitarian supplies to all segments of the Iraqi population throughout the country, Welcoming the report submitted on 1 February 1998 by the Secretary-General in accordance with paragraph 7 of resolution 1143 (1997) (S/1998/90) and his recommendations, as well as the report submitted on 30 January 1998 in accordance with paragraph 9 of resolution 1143 (1997) by the Committee established by resolution 661 (1990) of 6 August 1990 (S/1998/92), Noting that the Government of Iraq did not cooperate fully in the preparation of the report of the Secretary-General, Noting with concern that, despite the ongoing implementation of resolutions 986 (1995), 1111 (1997) and 1143 (1997), the population of Iraq continues to face a very serious nutritional and health situation, Determined to avoid any further deterioration of the current humanitarian situation, Reaffirming the commitment of all Member States to the sovereignty and territorial integrity of Iraq, Acting under Chapter VII of the Charter of the United Nations,

1. Decides that the provisions of resolution 986 (1995), except those contained in paragraphs 4, 11 and 12, shall remain in force for a new period of 180 days beginning at 00.01 hours, Eastern Standard Time, on the day after the President of the Council has informed the members of the Council that he has received the report of the Secretary-General requested in paragraph 5 below, on which date the provisions of resolution 1143 (1997), if still in force, shall terminate, except as regards sums already produced pursuant to that resolution prior to that date;
2. Decides further that the authorization given to States by paragraph 1 of resolution 986 (1995) shall permit the import of petroleum and petroleum products originating in Iraq, including financial and other essential transactions directly relating thereto, sufficient to produce a sum, in the 180-day period referred to in paragraph 1 above, not exceeding a total of 5.256 billion United States dollars, of which the amounts recommended by the Secretary-General for the food/nutrition and health sectors should

be allocated on a priority basis, and of which between 682 million United States dollars and 788 million United States dollars shall be used for the purpose referred to in paragraph 8 (b) of resolution 986 (1995), except that if less than 5.256 billion United States dollars worth of petroleum or petroleum products is sold during the 180-day period, particular attention will be paid to meeting the urgent humanitarian needs in the food/nutrition and health sectors and the Secretary-General may provide a proportionately smaller amount for the purpose referred to in paragraph 8 (b) of resolution 986 (1995);

3. Directs the Committee established by resolution 661 (1990) to authorize, on the basis of specific requests, reasonable expenses related to the Hajj pilgrimage, to be met by funds in the escrow account;

4. Requests the Secretary-General to take the actions necessary to ensure the effective and efficient implementation of this resolution, and in particular to enhance the United Nations observation process in Iraq in such a way as to provide the required assurance to the Council of the equitable distribution of the goods produced in accordance with this resolution and that all supplies authorized for procurement, including dual-usage items and spare parts, are utilized for the purpose for which they have been authorized;

5. Requests the Secretary-General to report to the Council when he has entered into any necessary arrangements or agreements, and approved a distribution plan, submitted by the Government of Iraq, which includes a description of the goods to be purchased and effectively guarantees their equitable distribution, in accordance with his recommendations that the plan should be ongoing and should reflect the relative priorities of humanitarian supplies as well as their interrelationships within the context of projects or activities, required delivery dates, preferred points of entry, and targeted objectives to be achieved;

6. Urges all States, and in particular the Government of Iraq, to provide their full cooperation in the effective implementation of this resolution;

7. Appeals to all States to cooperate in the timely submission of applications and the expeditious issue of export licences, facilitating the transit of humanitarian supplies authorized by the Committee established by resolution 661 (1990), and taking all other appropriate measures within their competence in order to ensure that urgently required humanitarian supplies reach the Iraqi people as rapidly as possible;

8. Stresses the need to ensure respect for the security and safety of all persons directly involved in the implementation of this resolution in Iraq;

9. Decides to conduct an interim review of the implementation of this resolution 90 days after the entry into force of paragraph 1 above and a thorough review of all aspects of its implementation prior to the end of

the 180-day period, on receipt of the reports referred to in paragraphs 10 and 14 below, and expresses its intention, prior to the end of the 180-day period, to consider favourably the renewal of the provisions of this resolution as appropriate, provided that the reports referred to in paragraphs 10 and 14 below indicate that those provisions are being satisfactorily implemented;

10. Requests the Secretary-General to make an interim report to the Council 90 days after the entry into force of paragraph 1 above, and to make a full report prior to the end of the 180-day period, on the basis of observation by United Nations personnel in Iraq, and on the basis of consultations with the Government of Iraq, on whether Iraq has ensured the equitable distribution of medicine, health supplies, foodstuffs and materials and supplies for essential civilian needs, financed in accordance with paragraph 8 (a) of resolution 986 (1995), including in his reports any observations he may have on the adequacy of the revenues to meet Iraq's humanitarian needs, and on Iraq's capacity to export sufficient quantities of petroleum and petroleum products to produce the sum referred to in paragraph 2 above;

11. Takes note of the Secretary-General's observation that the situation in the electricity sector is extremely grave, and of his intention to return to the Council with proposals for appropriate funding, requests him to submit urgently a report for this purpose prepared in consultation with the Government of Iraq to the Council, and further requests him to submit to the Council other studies, drawing upon United Nations agencies as appropriate and in consultation with the Government of Iraq, on essential humanitarian needs in Iraq including necessary improvements to infrastructure;

12. Requests the Secretary-General to establish a group of experts to determine in consultation with the Government of Iraq whether Iraq is able to export petroleum or petroleum products sufficient to produce the total sum referred to in paragraph 2 above and to prepare an independent report on Iraqi production and transportation capacity and necessary monitoring, also requests him in the light of that report to make early and appropriate recommendations and expresses its readiness to take a decision, on the basis of these recommendations and the humanitarian objectives of this resolution, notwithstanding paragraph 3 of resolution 661 (1990), regarding authorization of the export of the necessary equipment to enable Iraq to increase the export of petroleum or petroleum products and to give the appropriate directions to the Committee established by resolution 661 (1990);

13. Requests the Secretary-General to report to the Council, if Iraq is unable to export petroleum or petroleum products sufficient to produce the total sum referred to in paragraph 2 above, and following consultations with

relevant United Nations agencies and the Iraqi authorities, making recommendations for the expenditure of the sum expected to be available,
consistent with the distribution plan referred to in paragraph 5 above;

14. Requests the Committee established by resolution 661 (1990), in coordination with the Secretary-General, to report to the Council 90 days after the entry into force of paragraph 1 above and again prior to the end
of the 180-day period on the implementation of the arrangements in
paragraphs 1, 2, 6, 8, 9 and 10 of resolution 986 (1995);

15. Requests further the Committee established by resolution 661 (1990) to
implement the measures and take action on the steps referred to in its report of 30 January 1998, with regard to the refining and clarifying of its
working procedures, to consider the relevant observations and recommendations referred to in the report of the Secretary-General of 1 February 1998 in particular with a view to reducing to the extent possible
the delay between the export of petroleum and petroleum products from
Iraq and the supply of goods to Iraq in accordance with this resolution,
to report to the Council by 31 March 1998 and thereafter to continue to
review its procedures whenever necessary;

16. Decides to remain seized of the matter.

UNSCR 1175 (19 JUNE 1998)

The Security Council, Recalling its previous relevant resolutions and in particu
lar its resolutions 986 (1995) of 14 April 1995, 1111 (1997) of 4 June 1997, 1129
(1997) of 12 September 1997, 1143 (1997) of 4 December 1997, 1153 (1998) of
20 February 1998 and 1158 (1998) of 25 March 1998, Welcoming the letter of
the Secretary-General of 15 April 1998 (S/1998/330) annexing the summary of
the report of the group of experts established pursuant to paragraph 12 of resolution 1153 (1998) and noting the assessment that under existing circumstances
Iraq is unable to export petroleum or petroleum products sufficient to produce
the total sum of 5.256 billion United States dollars referred to in resolution 1153
(1998), Welcoming the letter of the Secretary-General of 29 May 1998
(S/1998/446) expressing his approval of the distribution plan submitted by the
Government of Iraq, Convinced of the need to continue the programme authorized by resolution 1153 (1998) as a temporary measure to provide for the humanitarian needs of the Iraqi people until fulfilment by the Government of Iraq
of the relevant resolutions, including notably resolution 687 (1991) of 3 April
1991, allows the Council to take further action with regard to the prohibitions
referred to in resolution 661 (1990) of 6 August 1990 in accordance with the provisions of those resolutions, Reaffirming its endorsement, in paragraph 5 of resolution 1153 (1998), of the recommendations of the Secretary-General in his

report of 1 February 1998 (S/1998/90) concerning an improved, ongoing and project-based distribution plan, Reaffirming also the commitment of all Member States to the sovereignty and territorial integrity of Iraq, Acting under Chapter VII of the Charter of the United Nations,

1. Authorizes States, subject to the provisions of paragraph 2 below, to permit, notwithstanding the provisions of paragraph 3 (c) of resolution 661 (1990), the export to Iraq of the necessary parts and equipment to enable Iraq to increase the export of petroleum and petroleum products, in quantities sufficient to produce the sum established in paragraph 2 of resolution 1153 (1998);

2. Requests the Committee established by resolution 661 (1990), or a panel of experts appointed by that Committee for this purpose, to approve contracts for the parts and equipment referred to in paragraph 1 above according to lists of parts and equipment approved by that Committee for each individual project;

3. Decides that the funds in the escrow account produced pursuant to resolution 1153 (1998) up to a total of 300 million United States dollars may be used to meet any reasonable expenses, other than expenses payable in Iraq, which follow directly from contracts approved in accordance with paragraph 2 above;

4. Decides also that the expenses directly related to such exports may, until the necessary funds are paid into the escrow account, and following approval of each contract, be financed by letters of credit drawn against future oil sales, the proceeds of which are to be deposited in the escrow account;

5. Notes that the distribution plan approved by the Secretary-General on 29 May 1998, or any new distribution plan agreed by the Government of Iraq and the Secretary-General, will remain in effect, as required, for each subsequent periodic renewal of the temporary humanitarian arrangements for Iraq and that, for this purpose, the plan will be kept under constant review and amended as necessary through the agreement of the Secretary-General and the Government of Iraq and in a manner consistent with resolution 1153 (1998);

6. Expresses its gratitude to the Secretary-General for making available to the Committee established by resolution 661 (1990) a comprehensive review, with comments by the group of experts established pursuant to paragraph 12 of resolution 1153 (1998), of the list of parts and equipment presented by the Government of Iraq, and requests the Secretary-General, in accordance with the intention expressed in his letter of 15 April 1998, to provide for the monitoring of the parts and equipment inside Iraq;

7. Decides to remain seized of the matter.

UNSCR 1154 (2 MARCH 1998)

The Security Council, Recalling all its previous relevant resolutions, which constitute the governing standard of Iraqi compliance, Determined to ensure immediate and full compliance by Iraq without conditions or restrictions with its obligations under resolution 687 (1991) and the other relevant resolutions, Reaffirming the commitment of all Member States to the sovereignty, territorial integrity and political independence of Iraq, Kuwait and the neighbouring States, Acting under Chapter VII of the Charter of the United Nations,

1. Commends the initiative by the Secretary-General to secure commitments from the Government of Iraq on compliance with its obligations under the relevant resolutions, and in this regard endorses the memorandum of understanding signed by the Deputy Prime Minister of Iraq and the Secretary-General on 23 February 1998 (S/1998/166) and looks forward to its early and full implementation;
2. Requests the Secretary-General to report to the Council as soon as possible with regard to the finalization of procedures for Presidential sites in consultation with the Executive Chairman of the United Nations Special Commission and the Director-General of the International Atomic Energy Agency (IAEA);
3. Stresses that compliance by the Government of Iraq with its obligations, repeated again in the memorandum of understanding, to accord immediate, unconditional and unrestricted access to the Special Commission and the IAEA in conformity with the relevant resolutions is necessary for the implementation of resolution 687 (1991), but that any violation would have severest consequences for Iraq;
4. Reaffirms its intention to act in accordance with the relevant provisions of resolution 687 (1991) on the duration of the prohibitions referred to in that resolution and notes that by its failure so far to comply with its relevant obligations Iraq has delayed the moment when the Council can do so;
5. Decides, in accordance with its responsibility under the Charter, to remain actively seized of the matter, in order to ensure implementation of this resolution, and to secure peace and security in the area.

UNSCR 1194 (9 SEPTEMBER 1998)

The Security Council, Recalling all its previous relevant resolutions, and in particular its resolutions 687 (1991) of 3 April 1991, 707 (1991) of 15 August 1991, 715 (1991) of 11 October 1991, 1060 (1996) of 12 June 1996, 1115

(1997) of 21 June 1997 and 1154 (1998) of 2 March 1998, Noting the announcement by Iraq on 5 August 1998 that it had decided to suspend cooperation with the United Nations Special Commission and the International Atomic Energy Agency (IAEA) on all disarmament activities and restrict ongoing monitoring and verification activities at declared sites, and/or actions implementing the above decision, Stressing that the necessary conditions do not exist for the modification of the measures referred to in section F of resolution 687 (1991), Recalling the letter from the Executive Chairman of the Special Commission to the President of the Security Council of 12 August 1998 (S/1998/767), which reported to the Council that Iraq had halted all disarmament activities of the Special Commission and placed limitations on the rights of the Commission to conduct its monitoring operations, Recalling also the letter from the Director General of the IAEA to the President of the Security Council of 11 August 1998 (S/1998/766) which reported the refusal by Iraq to cooperate in any activity involving investigation of its clandestine nuclear programme and other restrictions of access placed by Iraq on the ongoing monitoring and verification programme of the IAEA, Noting the letters of 18 August 1998 from the President of the Security Council to the Executive Chairman of the Special Commission and the Director General of the IAEA (S/1998/769, S/1998/768), which expressed the full support of the Security Council for those organizations in the implementation of the full range of their mandated activities, including inspections, Recalling the Memorandum of Understanding signed by the Deputy Prime Minister of Iraq and the Secretary-General on 23 February 1998 (S/1998/166), in which Iraq reiterated its undertaking to cooperate fully with the Special Commission and the IAEA, Noting that the announcement by Iraq of 5 August 1998 followed a period of increased cooperation and some tangible progress achieved since the signing of the Memorandum of Understanding, Reiterating its intention to respond favourably to future progress made in the disarmament process and reaffirming its commitment to comprehensive implementation of its resolutions, in particular resolution 687 (1991), Determined to ensure full compliance by Iraq with its obligations under all previous resolutions, in particular resolutions 687 (1991), 707 (1991), 715 (1991), 1060 (1996), 1115 (1997) and 1154 (1998), to permit immediate, unconditional and unrestricted access to the Special Commission and the IAEA to all sites which they wish to inspect, and to provide the Special Commission and the IAEA with all the cooperation necessary for them to fulfil their mandates under those resolutions, Stressing the unacceptability of any attempts by Iraq to deny access to any sites or to refuse to provide the necessary cooperation, Expressing its readiness to consider, in a comprehensive review, Iraq's compliance with its obligations under all relevant resolutions once Iraq has rescinded its above-mentioned decision and demonstrated that it is prepared to fulfil all its obligations, including, in particular on disarmament issues, by resuming full cooperation with the Special Commission and the IAEA consistent with the Memorandum of Understanding, as endorsed by the Council in resolution 1154 (1998), and to that end welcoming the proposal of the Secretary-General for such a comprehensive review and inviting the Secretary-General to provide his views in that regard, Reiterating the commitment of all Member States to the sovereignty, territorial integrity and political independence of Kuwait and Iraq, Acting under Chapter VII of the Charter of the United Nations,

1. Condemns the decision by Iraq of 5 August 1998 to suspend cooperation with the Special Commission and the IAEA, which constitutes a totally unacceptable contravention of its obligations under resolutions 687 (1991), 707 (1991), 715 (1991), 1060 (1996), 1115 (1997) and 1154 (1998), and the Memorandum of Understanding signed by the Deputy Prime Minister of Iraq and the Secretary-General on 23 February 1998;
2. Demands that Iraq rescind its above-mentioned decision and cooperate fully with the Special Commission and the IAEA in accordance with its obligations under the relevant resolutions and the Memorandum of Understanding as well as resume dialogue with the Special Commission and the IAEA immediately;
3. Decides not to conduct the review scheduled for October 1998 provided for in paragraphs 21 and 28 of resolution 687 (1991), and not to conduct any further such reviews until Iraq rescinds its above-mentioned decision of 5 August 1998 and the Special Commission and the IAEA report to the Council that they are satisfied that they have been able to exercise the full range of activities provided for in their mandates, including inspections;
4. Reaffirms its full support for the Special Commission and the IAEA in their efforts to ensure the implementation of their mandates under the relevant resolutions of the Council;
5. Reaffirms its full support for the Secretary-General in his efforts to urge Iraq to rescind its above-mentioned decision;
6. Reaffirms its intention to act in accordance with the relevant provisions of resolution 687 (1991) on the duration of the prohibitions referred to in that resolution and notes that by its failure so far to comply with its relevant obligations Iraq has delayed the moment when the Council can do so;
7. Decides to remain seized of the matter.

UNSCR 1205 (5 NOVEMBER 1998)

The Security Council, Recalling all its previous relevant resolutions on the situation in Iraq, in particular its resolution 1154 (1998) of 2 March 1998 and

1194 (1998) of 9 September 1998, Noting with alarm the decision of Iraq on 31 October 1998 to cease cooperation with the United Nations Special Commission, and its continued restrictions on the work of the International Atomic Energy Agency (IAEA), Noting the letters from the Deputy Executive Chairman of the Special Commission of 31 October 1998 (S/1998/1023) and from the Executive Chairman of the Special Commission of 2 November 1998 (S/1998/1032) to the President of the Security Council, which reported to the Council the decision by Iraq and described the implications of that decision for the work of the Special Commission, and noting also the letter from the Director General of the IAEA of 3 November 1998 (S/1998/1033, annex) which described the implications of the decision for the work of the IAEA, Determined to ensure immediate and full compliance by Iraq without conditions or restrictions with its obligations under resolution 687 (1991) of 3 April 1991 and the other relevant resolutions, Recalling that the effective operation of the Special Commission and the IAEA is essential for the implementation of resolution 687 (1991), Reaffirming its readiness to consider, in a comprehensive review, Iraq's compliance with its obligations under all relevant resolutions once Iraq has rescinded its above-mentioned decision and its decision of 5 August 1998 and demonstrated that it is prepared to fulfil all its obligations, including in particular on disarmament issues, by resuming full cooperation with the Special Commission and the IAEA consistent with the Memorandum of Understanding signed by the Deputy Prime Minister of Iraq and the Secretary-General on 23 February 1998 (S/1998/166), endorsed by the Council in resolution 1154 (1998), Reiterating the commitment of all Member States to the sovereignty, territorial integrity and political independence of Kuwait and Iraq, Acting under Chapter VII of the Charter of the United Nations,

1. Condemns the decision by Iraq of 31 October 1998 to cease cooperation with the Special Commission as a flagrant violation of resolution 687 (1991) and other relevant resolutions;
2. Demands that Iraq rescind immediately and unconditionally the decision of 31 October 1998, as well as the decision of 5 August 1998, to suspend cooperation with the Special Commission and to maintain restrictions on the work of the IAEA, and that Iraq provide immediate, complete and unconditional cooperation with the Special Commission and the IAEA;
3. Reaffirms its full support for the Special Commission and the IAEA in their efforts to ensure the implementation of their mandates under the relevant resolutions of the Council;
4. Expresses its full support for the Secretary-General in his efforts to seek full implementation of the Memorandum of Understanding of 23 February 1998;
5. Reaffirms its intention to act in accordance with the relevant provisions of resolution 687 (1991) on the duration of the prohibitions referred to in that

resolution, and notes that by its failure so far to comply with its relevant obligations Iraq has delayed the moment when the Council can do so;

6. Decides, in accordance with its primary responsibility under the Charter for the maintenance of international peace and security, to remain actively seized of the matter.

UNSCR 1210 (24 NOVEMBER 1998)

The Security Council, Recalling its previous relevant resolutions and in particular its resolutions 986 (1995) of 14 April 1995, 1111 (1997) of 4 June 1997, 1129 (1997) of 12 September 1997, 1143 (1997) of 4 December 1997, 1153 (1998) of 20 February 1998 and 1175 (1998) of 19 June 1998, Convinced of the need as a temporary measure to continue to provide for the humanitarian needs of the Iraqi people until the fulfilment by the Government of Iraq of the relevant resolutions, including notably resolution 687 (1991) of 3 April 1991, allows the Council to take further action with regard to the prohibitions referred to in resolution 661 (1990) of 6 August 1990, in accordance with the provisions of those resolutions, Convinced also of the need for equitable distribution of humanitarian supplies to all segments of the Iraqi population throughout the country, Welcoming the positive impact of the relevant resolutions on the humanitarian situation in Iraq as described in the report of the Secretary-General dated 19 November 1998 (S/1998/1100), Determined to improve the humanitarian situation in Iraq, Reaffirming the commitment of all Member States to the sovereignty and territorial integrity of Iraq, Acting under Chapter VII of the Charter of the United Nations,

1. Decides that the provisions of resolution 986 (1995), except those contained in paragraphs 4, 11 and 12, shall remain in force for a new period of 180 days beginning at 00.01 hours, Eastern Standard Time, on 26 November 1998;

2. Further decides that paragraph 2 of resolution 1153 (1998) shall remain in force and shall apply to the 180-day period referred to in paragraph 1 above;

3. Directs the Committee established by resolution 661 (1990) to authorize, on the basis of specific requests, reasonable expenses related to the Hajj pilgrimage, to be met by funds in the escrow account;

4. Requests the Secretary-General to continue to take the actions necessary to ensure the effective and efficient implementation of this resolution, and to review, by 31 December 1998, the various options to resolve the difficulties encountered in the financial process, referred to in the Secretary-General's report of 19 November 1998 (S/1998/1100), and to

continue to enhance as necessary the United Nations observation process in Iraq in such a way as to provide the required assurance to the Council that the goods produced in accordance with this resolution are distributed equitably and that all supplies authorized for procurement, including dual usage items and spare parts, are utilized for the purpose for which they have been authorized;

5. Further decides to conduct a thorough review of all aspects of the implementation of this resolution 90 days after the entry into force of paragraph 1 above and again prior to the end of the 180-day period, on receipt of the reports referred to in paragraphs 6 and 10 below, and expresses its intention, prior to the end of the 180-day period, to consider favourably renewal of the provisions of this resolution as appropriate, provided that the said reports indicate that those provisions are being satisfactorily implemented;

6. Requests the Secretary-General to report to the Council 90 days after the date of entry into force of paragraph 1 above, and again prior to the end of the 180-day period, on the basis of observations of United Nations personnel in Iraq, and of consultations with the Government of Iraq, on whether Iraq has ensured the equitable distribution of medicine, health supplies, foodstuffs, and materials and supplies for essential civilian needs, financed in accordance with paragraph 8 (a) of resolution 986 (1995), including in his reports any observations which he may have on the adequacy of the revenues to meet Iraq's humanitarian needs, and on Iraq's capacity to export sufficient quantities of petroleum and petroleum products to produce the sum referred to in paragraph 2 of resolution 1153 (1998);

7. Requests the Secretary-General to report to the Council if Iraq is unable to export petroleum and petroleum products sufficient to produce the total sum provided for in paragraph 2 above and, following consultations with relevant United Nations agencies and the Iraqi authorities, make recommendations for the expenditure of the sum expected to be available, consistent with the priorities established in paragraph 2 of resolution 1153 (1998) and with the distribution plan referred to in paragraph 5 of resolution 1175 (1998);

8. Decides that paragraphs 1, 2, 3 and 4 of resolution 1175 (1998) shall remain in force and shall apply to the new 180-day period referred to in paragraph 1 above;

9. Requests the Secretary-General, in consultation with the Government of Iraq, to submit to the Council, by 31 December 1998, a detailed list of parts and equipment necessary for the purpose described in paragraph 1 of resolution 1175 (1998);

10. Requests the Committee established by resolution 661 (1990), in close coordination with the Secretary-General, to report to the Council 90

days after the entry into force of paragraph 1 above and again prior to the end of the 180-day period on the implementation of the arrangements in paragraphs 1, 2, 6, 8, 9 and 10 of resolution 986 (1995);

11. Urges all States, and in particular the Government of Iraq, to provide their full cooperation in the effective implementation of this resolution;

12. Appeals to all States to continue to cooperate in the timely submission of applications and the expeditious issue of export licences, facilitating the transit of humanitarian supplies authorized by the Committee established by resolution 661 (1990), and to take all other appropriate measures within their competence in order to ensure that urgently required humanitarian supplies reach the Iraqi people as rapidly as possible;

13. Stresses the need to continue to ensure respect for the security and safety of all persons directly involved in the implementation of this resolution in Iraq;

14. Decides to remain seized of the matter.

UNSCR 1242 (21 MAY 1999)

The Security Council, Recalling its previous relevant resolutions and in particular its resolutions 986 (1995) of 14 April 1995, 1111 (1997) of 4 June 1997, 1129 (1997) of 12 September 1997, 1143 (1997) of 4 December 1997, 1153 (1998) of 20 February 1998, 1175 (1998) of 19 June 1998 and 1210 (1998) of 24 November 1998, Convinced of the need as a temporary measure to continue to provide for the humanitarian needs of the Iraqi people until the fulfilment by the Government of Iraq of the relevant resolutions, including notably resolution 687 (1991) of 3 April 1991, allows the Council to take further action with regard to the prohibitions referred to in resolution 661 (1990) of 6 August 1990, in accordance with the provisions of those resolutions, Convinced also of the need for equitable distribution of humanitarian supplies to all segments of the Iraqi population throughout the country, Determined to improve the humanitarian situation in Iraq, Reaffirming the commitment of all Member States to the sovereignty and territorial integrity of Iraq, Acting under Chapter VII of the Charter of the United Nations,

1. Decides that the provisions of resolution 986 (1995), except those contained in paragraphs 4, 11 and 12, shall remain in force for a new period of 180 days beginning at 00.01 hours, Eastern Standard Time, on 25 May 1999;

2. Further decides that paragraph 2 of resolution 1153 (1998) shall remain in force and shall apply to the 180-day period referred to in paragraph 1 above;

3. Requests the Secretary-General to continue to take the actions necessary to ensure the effective and efficient implementation of this resolution, and to continue to enhance as necessary the United Nations observation process in Iraq in such a way as to provide the required assurance to the Council that the goods produced in accordance with this resolution are distributed equitably and that all supplies authorized for procurement, including dual usage items and spare parts, are utilized for the purpose for which they have been authorized;

4. Takes note that the Committee established by resolution 661 (1990) is reviewing various options, in particular the proposal made by the Secretary-General, as requested by paragraph 4 of resolution 1210 (1998), to resolve the difficulties encountered in the financial process referred to in the Secretary-General's report of 19 November 1998 (S/1998/1100);

5. Further decides to conduct a thorough review of all aspects of the implementation of this resolution 90 days after the entry into force of paragraph 1 above and again prior to the end of the 180-day period, on receipt of the reports referred to in paragraphs 6 and 10 below, and expresses its intention, prior to the end of the 180-day period, to consider favourably renewal of the provisions of this resolution as appropriate, provided that the said reports indicate that those provisions are being satisfactorily implemented;

6. Requests the Secretary-General to report to the Council 90 days after the date of entry into force of paragraph 1 above and again prior to the end of the 180-day period, on the basis of observations of United Nations personnel in Iraq, and of consultations with the Government of Iraq, on whether Iraq has ensured the equitable distribution of medicine, health supplies, foodstuffs, and materials and supplies for essential civilian needs, financed in accordance with paragraph 8 (a) of resolution 986 (1995), including in his reports any observations which he may have on the adequacy of the revenues to meet Iraq's humanitarian needs, and on Iraq's capacity to export sufficient quantities of petroleum and petroleum products to produce the sum referred to in paragraph 2 of resolution 1153 (1998);

7. Requests the Secretary-General to report to the Council if Iraq is unable to export petroleum and petroleum products sufficient to produce the total sum provided for in paragraph 2 above and, following consultations with relevant United Nations agencies and the Iraqi authorities, make recommendations for the expenditure of the sum expected to be available, consistent with the priorities established in paragraph 2 of resolution 1153 (1998) and with the distribution plan referred to in paragraph 5 of resolution 1175 (1998);

8. Decides that paragraphs 1, 2, 3 and 4 of resolution 1175 (1998) shall remain in force and shall apply to the new 180-day period referred to in paragraph 1 above;

9. Requests the Secretary-General, in consultation with the Government of Iraq, to submit to the Council, by 30 June 1999, a detailed list of parts and equipment necessary for the purpose described in paragraph 1 of resolution 1175 (1998);

10. Requests the Committee established by resolution 661 (1990), in close coordination with the Secretary-General, to report to the Council 90 days after the entry into force of paragraph 1 above and again prior to the end of the 180-day period on the implementation of the arrangements in paragraphs 1, 2, 6, 8, 9 and 10 of resolution 986 (1995);

11. Urges all States, and in particular the Government of Iraq, to provide their full cooperation in the effective implementation of this resolution;

12. Appeals to all States to continue to cooperate in the timely submission of applications and the expeditious issue of export licences, facilitating the transit of humanitarian supplies authorized by the Committee established by resolution 661 (1990), and to take all other appropriate measures within their competence in order to ensure that urgently required humanitarian supplies reach the Iraqi people as rapidly as possible;

13. Stresses the need to continue to ensure respect for the security and safety of all persons directly involved in the implementation of this resolution in Iraq;

14. Decides to keep these arrangements under review, including in particular those in paragraph 2 above, to ensure the uninterrupted flow of humanitarian supplies into Iraq, and expresses its willingness to review the relevant recommendations of the report of the panel established to review humanitarian issues (S/1999/356, annex II) as appropriate with regard to the 180-day period referred to in paragraph 1 above;

15. Decides to remain seized of the matter.

UNSCR 1266 (4 OCTOBER 1999)

The Security Council, Recalling its previous relevant resolutions and in particular its resolutions 986 (1995) of 14 April 1995, 1111 (1997) of 4 June 1997, 1129 (1997) of 12 September 1997, 1143 (1997) of 4 December 1997, 1153 (1998) of 20 February 1998, 1175 (1998) of 19 June 1998, 1210 (1998) of 24 November 1998 and 1242 (1999) of 21 May 1999, Recalling also the report of the Secretary-General of 19 August 1999 (S/1999/896), in particular, paragraphs 4 and 94, Determined to improve the humanitarian situation in Iraq,

Reaffirming the commitment of all Member States to the sovereignty and territorial integrity of Iraq, Acting under Chapter VII of the Charter of the United Nations,

1. Decides that paragraph 2 of resolution 1153 (1998), as extended by resolution 1242 (1999), shall be modified to the extent necessary to authorize States to permit the import of petroleum and petroleum products originating in Iraq, including financial and other essential transactions directly related thereto, sufficient to produce an additional sum, beyond that provided for by resolution 1242 (1999), equivalent to the total shortfall of revenues authorized but not generated under resolutions 1210 (1998) and 1153 (1998), 3.04 billion United States dollars, within the period of 180 days from 0001 hours, eastern standard time, on 25 May 1999;

2. Decides to remain seized of the matter.

UNSCR 1281 (10 DECEMBER 1999)

The Security Council, Recalling its previous relevant resolutions and in particular its resolutions 986 (1995) of 14 April 1995, 1111 (1997) of 4 June 1997, 1129 (1997) of 12 September 1997, 1143 (1997) of 4 December 1997, 1153 (1998) of 20 February 1998, 1175 (1998) of 19 June 1998, 1210 (1998) of 24 November 1998, 1242 (1999) of 21 May 1999, 1266 (1999) of 4 October 1999 and 1275 (1999) of 19 November 1999, and 1280 (1999) of 3 December 1999, Convinced of the need as a temporary measure to continue to provide for the humanitarian needs of the Iraqi people until the fulfilment by the Government of Iraq of the relevant resolutions, including notably resolution 687 (1991) of 3 April 1991, allows the Council to take further action with regard to the prohibitions referred to in resolution 661 (1990) of 6 August 1990, in accordance with the provisions of those resolutions, Convinced also of the need for equitable distribution of humanitarian supplies to all segments of the Iraqi population throughout the country, Determined to improve the humanitarian situation in Iraq, Reaffirming the commitment of all Member States to the sovereignty and territorial integrity of Iraq, Acting under Chapter VII of the Charter of the United Nations,

1. Decides that the provisions of resolution 986 (1995), except those contained in paragraphs 4, 11 and 12, shall remain in force for a new period of 180 days beginning at 00.01 hours, Eastern Standard Time, on 12 December 1999;

2. Further decides that paragraph 2 of resolution 1153 (1998) shall remain in force and shall apply to the 180-day period referred to in paragraph 1 above;

3. Requests the Secretary-General to continue to take the actions necessary to ensure the effective and efficient implementation of this resolution, and to continue to enhance as necessary the United Nations observation process in Iraq in such a way as to provide the required assurance to the Council that the goods produced in accordance with this resolution are distributed equitably and that all supplies authorized for procurement, including dual usage items and spare parts, are utilized for the purpose for which they have been authorized;

4. Further decides to conduct a thorough review of all aspects of the implementation of this resolution 90 days after the entry into force of paragraph 1 above and again prior to the end of the 180-day period, on receipt of the reports referred to in paragraphs 5 and 10 below, and expresses its intention, prior to the end of the 180-day period, to consider favourably renewal of the provisions of this resolution as appropriate, provided that the said reports indicate that those provisions are being satisfactorily implemented;

5. Requests the Secretary-General to report to the Council 90 days after the date of entry into force of paragraph 1 above and again prior to the end of the 180-day period, on the basis of observations of United Nations personnel in Iraq, and o f consultations with the Government of Iraq, on whether Iraq has ensured the equitable distribution of medicine, health supplies, foodstuffs, and materials and supplies for essential civilian needs, financed in accordance with paragraph 8 (a) of resolution 986 (1995), including in his reports any observations which he may have on the adequacy of the revenues to meet Iraq's humanitarian needs, and on Iraq's capacity to export sufficient quantities of petroleum and petroleum products to produce the sum referred to in paragraph 2 of resolution 1153 (1998);

6. Requests the Secretary-General to report to the Council if Iraq is unable to export petroleum and petroleum products sufficient to produce the total sum provided for in paragraph 2 above and, following consultations with the relevant United Nations agencies and the Iraqi authorities, make recommendations for the expenditure of sums expected to be available, consistent with the priorities established in paragraph 2 of resolution 1153 (1998) and with the distribution plan referred to in paragraph 5 of resolution 1175 (1998);

7. Decides that paragraph 3 of resolution 1210 (1998) shall apply to the new 180-day period referred to in paragraph 1 above;

8. Decides that paragraphs 1, 2, 3 and 4 of resolution 1175 (1998) shall remain in force and shall apply to the new 180-day period referred to in paragraph 1 above;

9. Requests the Secretary-General, in consultation with the Government of Iraq, to submit to the Council no later than 15 January 2000 a detailed

list of parts and equipment necessary for the purpose described in paragraph 1 of resolution 1175 (1998);

10. Requests the Committee established by resolution 661 (1990), in close
coordination with the Secretary-General, to report to the Council 90
days after the entry into force of paragraph 1 above and again prior to
the end of the 180-day period on the implementation of the arrangements
in paragraphs 1, 2, 6, 8, 9 and 10 of resolution 986 (1995);

11. Urges all States, and in particular the Government of Iraq, to provide
their full cooperation in the effective implementation of this resolution;

12. Appeals to all States to continue to cooperate in the timely submission
of applications and the expeditious issue of export licences, facilitating the transit of humanitarian supplies authorized by the Committee
established by resolution 661 (1990), and to take all other appropriate
measures within their competence in order to ensure that urgently
needed humanitarian supplies reach the Iraqi people as rapidly as
possible;

13. Stresses the need to continue to ensure respect for the security and safety
of all persons directly involved in the implementation of this resolution
in Iraq;

14. Decides to keep these arrangements under review including in particular
those in paragraph 2 above, to ensure the uninterrupted flow of humanitarian supplies into Iraq, and expresses its determination to act without
delay to address the recommendations of the report of the panel established to review humanitarian and other issues in Iraq (S/1999/356) in a
further, comprehensive resolution;

15. Decides to remain seized of the matter.

UNSCR 1284 (17 DECEMBER 1999)

The Security Council, Recalling its previous relevant resolutions, including its
resolutions 661 (1990) of 6 August 1990, 687 (1991) of 3 April 1991, 699
(1991) of 17 June 1991, 707 (1991) of 15 August 1991, 715 (1991) of 11 October 1991, 986 (1995) of 14 April 1995, 1051 (1996) of 27 March 1996, 1153
(1998) of 20 February 1998, 1175 (1998) of 19 June 1998, 1242 (1999) of 21
May 1999 and 1266 (1999) of 4 October 1999, Recalling the approval by the
Council in its resolution 715 (1991) of the plans for future ongoing monitoring
and verification submitted by the Secretary-General and the Director General
of the International Atomic Energy Agency (IAEA) in pursuance of paragraphs
10 and 13 of resolution 687 (1991), Welcoming the reports of the three panels
on Iraq (S/1999/356), and having held a comprehensive consideration of them
and the recommendations contained in them, Stressing the importance of a

comprehensive approach to the full implementation of all relevant Security Council resolutions regarding Iraq and the need for Iraqi compliance with these resolutions, Recalling the goal of establishing in the Middle East a zone free from weapons of mass destruction and all missiles for their delivery and the objective of a global ban on chemical weapons as referred to in paragraph 14 of resolution 687 (1991), Concerned at the humanitarian situation in Iraq, and determined to improve that situation, Recalling with concern that the repatriation and return of all Kuwaiti and third country nationals or their remains, present in Iraq on or after 2 August 1990, pursuant to paragraph 2 (c) of resolution 686 (1991) of 2 March 1991 and paragraph 30 of resolution 687 (1991), have not yet been fully carried out by Iraq, Recalling that in its resolutions 686 (1991) and 687 (1991) the Council demanded that Iraq return in the shortest possible time all Kuwaiti property it had seized, and noting with regret that Iraq has still not complied fully with this demand, Acknowledging the progress made by Iraq towards compliance with the provisions of resolution 687 (1991), but noting that, as a result of its failure to implement the relevant Council resolutions fully, the conditions do not exist which would enable the Council to take a decision pursuant to resolution 687 (1991) to lift the prohibitions referred to in that resolution, Reiterating the commitment of all Member States to the sovereignty, territorial integrity and political independence of Kuwait, Iraq and the neighbouring States, Acting under Chapter VII of the Charter of the United Nations, and taking into account that operative provisions of this resolution relate to previous resolutions adopted under Chapter VII of the Charter,

1. Decides to establish, as a subsidiary body of the Council, the United Nations Monitoring, Verification and Inspection Commission (UNMOVIC) which replaces the Special Commission established pursuant to paragraph 9 (b) of resolution 687 (1991);
2. Decides also that UNMOVIC will undertake the responsibilities mandated to the Special Commission by the Council with regard to the verification of compliance by Iraq with its obligations under paragraphs 8, 9 and 10 of resolution 687 (1991) and other related resolutions, that UNMOVIC will establish and operate, as was recommended by the panel on disarmament and current and future ongoing monitoring and verification issues, a reinforced system of ongoing monitoring and verification, which will implement the plan approved by the Council in resolution 715 (1991) and address unresolved disarmament issues, and that UNMOVIC will identify, as necessary in accordance with its mandate, additional sites in Iraq to be covered by the reinforced system of ongoing monitoring and verification;
3. Reaffirms the provisions of the relevant resolutions with regard to the role of the IAEA in addressing compliance by Iraq with paragraphs 12

and 13 of resolution 687 (1991) and other related resolutions, and requests the Director General of the IAEA to maintain this role with the assistance and cooperation of UNMOVIC;

4. Reaffirms its resolutions 687 (1991), 699 (1991), 707 (1991), 715 (1991), 1051 (1996), 1154 (1998) and all other relevant resolutions and statements of its President, which establish the criteria for Iraqi compliance, affirms that the obligations of Iraq referred to in those resolutions and statements with regard to cooperation with the Special Commission, unrestricted access and provision of information will apply in respect of UNMOVIC, and decides in particular that Iraq shall allow UNMOVIC teams immediate, unconditional and unrestricted access to any and all areas, facilities, equipment, records and means of transport which they wish to inspect in accordance with the mandate of UNMOVIC, as well as to all officials and other persons under the authority of the Iraqi Government whom UNMOVIC wishes to interview so that UNMOVIC may fully discharge its mandate;

5. Requests the Secretary-General, within 30 days of the adoption of this resolution, to appoint, after consultation with and subject to the approval of the Council, an Executive Chairman of UNMOVIC who will take up his mandated tasks as soon as possible, and, in consultation with the Executive Chairman and the Council members, to appoint suitably qualified experts as a College of Commissioners for UNMOVIC which will meet regularly to review the implementation of this and other relevant resolutions and provide professional advice and guidance to the Executive Chairman, including on significant policy decisions and on written reports to be submitted to the Council through the Secretary-General;

6. Requests the Executive Chairman of UNMOVIC, within 45 days of his appointment, to submit to the Council, in consultation with and through the Secretary-General, for its approval an organizational plan for UNMOVIC, including its structure, staffing requirements, management guidelines, recruitment and training procedures, incorporating as appropriate the recommendations of the panel on disarmament and current and future ongoing monitoring and verification issues, and recognizing in particular the need for an effective, cooperative management structure for the new organization, for staffing with suitably qualified and experienced personnel, who would be regarded as international civil servants subject to Article 100 of the Charter of the United Nations, drawn from the broadest possible geographical base, including as he deems necessary from international arms control organizations, and for the provision of high quality technical and cultural training;

7. Decides that UNMOVIC and the IAEA, not later than 60 days after they have both started work in Iraq, will each draw up, for approval by the

Council, a work programme for the discharge of their mandates, which will include both the implementation of the reinforced system of ongoing monitoring and verification, and the key remaining disarmament tasks to be completed by Iraq pursuant to its obligations to comply with the disarmament requirements of resolution 687 (1991) and other related resolutions, which constitute the governing standard of Iraqi compliance, and further decides that what is required of Iraq for the implementation of each task shall be clearly defined and precise;

8. Requests the Executive Chairman of UNMOVIC and the Director General of the IAEA, drawing on the expertise of other international organizations as appropriate, to establish a unit which will have the responsibilities of the joint unit constituted by the Special Commission and the Director General of the IAEA under paragraph 16 of the export/import mechanism approved by resolution 1051 (1996), and also requests the Executive Chairman of UNMOVIC, in consultation with the Director General of the IAEA, to resume the revision and updating of the lists of items and technology to which the mechanism applies;

9. Decides that the Government of Iraq shall be liable for the full costs of UNMOVIC and the IAEA in relation to their work under this and other related resolutions on Iraq;

10. Requests Member States to give full cooperation to UNMOVIC and the IAEA in the discharge of their mandates;

11. Decides that UNMOVIC shall take over all assets, liabilities and archives of the Special Commission, and that it shall assume the Special Commission's part in agreements existing between the Special Commission and Iraq and between the United Nations and Iraq, and affirms that the Executive Chairman, the Commissioners and the personnel serving with UNMOVIC shall have the rights, privileges, facilities and immunities of the Special Commission;

12. Requests the Executive Chairman of UNMOVIC to report, through the Secretary-General, to the Council, following consultation with the Commissioners, every three months on the work of UNMOVIC, pending submission of the first reports referred to in paragraph 33 below, and to report immediately when the reinforced system of ongoing monitoring and verification is fully operational in Iraq;

13. Reiterates the obligation of Iraq, in furtherance of its commitment to facilitate the repatriation of all Kuwaiti and third country nationals referred to in paragraph 30 of resolution 687 (1991), to extend all necessary cooperation to the International Committee of the Red Cross, and calls upon the Government of Iraq to resume cooperation with the Tripartite Commission and Technical Subcommittee established to facilitate work on this issue;

14. Requests the Secretary-General to report to the Council every four months on compliance by Iraq with its obligations regarding the repatriation or return of all Kuwaiti and third country nationals or their remains, to report every six months on the return of all Kuwaiti property, including archives, seized by Iraq, and to appoint a high-level coordinator for these issues;

15. Authorizes States, notwithstanding the provisions of paragraphs 3 (a), 3 (b) and 4 of resolution 661 (1990) and subsequent relevant resolutions, to permit the import of any volume of petroleum and petroleum products originating in Iraq, including financial and other essential transactions directly relating thereto, as required for the purposes and on the conditions set out in paragraph 1 (a) and (b) and subsequent provisions of resolution 986 (1995) and related resolutions;

16. Underlines, in this context, its intention to take further action, including permitting the use of additional export routes for petroleum and petroleum products, under appropriate conditions otherwise consistent with the purpose and provisions of resolution 986 (1995) and related resolutions;

17. Directs the Committee established by resolution 661 (1990) to approve, on the basis of proposals from the Secretary-General, lists of humanitarian items, including foodstuffs, pharmaceutical and medical supplies, as well as basic or standard medical and agricultural equipment and basic or standard educational items, decides, notwithstanding paragraph 3 of resolution 661 (1990) and paragraph 20 of resolution 687 (1991), that supplies of these items will not be submitted for approval of that Committee, except for items subject to the provisions of resolution 1051 (1996), and will be notified to the Secretary-General and financed in accordance with the provisions of paragraph 8 (a) and 8 (b) of resolution 986 (1995), and requests the Secretary-General to inform the Committee in a timely manner of all such notifications received and actions taken;

18. Requests the Committee established by resolution 661 (1990) to appoint, in accordance with resolutions 1175 (1998) and 1210 (1998), a group of experts, including independent inspection agents appointed by the Secretary-General in accordance with paragraph 6 of resolution 986 (1995), decides that this group will be mandated to approve speedily contracts for the parts and the equipments necessary to enable Iraq to increase its exports of petroleum and petroleum products, according to lists of parts and equipments approved by that Committee for each individual project, and requests the Secretary-General to continue to provide for the monitoring of these parts and equipments inside Iraq;

19. Encourages Member States and international organizations to provide supplementary humanitarian assistance to Iraq and published material of an educational character to Iraq;

20. Decides to suspend, for an initial period of six months from the date of the adoption of this resolution and subject to review, the implementation of paragraph 8 (g) of resolution 986 (1995);

21. Requests the Secretary-General to take steps to maximize, drawing as necessary on the advice of specialists, including representatives of international humanitarian organizations, the effectiveness of the arrangements set out in resolution 986 (1995) and related resolutions including the humanitarian benefit to the Iraqi population in all areas of the country, and further requests the Secretary-General to continue to enhance as necessary the United Nations observation process in Iraq, ensuring that all supplies under the humanitarian programme are utilized as authorized, to bring to the attention of the Council any circumstances preventing or impeding effective and equitable distribution and to keep the Council informed of the steps taken towards the implementation of this paragraph;

22. Requests also the Secretary-General to minimize the cost of the United Nations activities associated with the implementation of resolution 986 (1995) as well as the cost of the independent inspection agents and the certified public accountants appointed by him, in accordance with paragraphs 6 and 7 of resolution 986 (1995);

23. Requests further the Secretary-General to provide Iraq and the Committee established by resolution 661 (1990) with a daily statement of the status of the escrow account established by paragraph 7 of resolution 986 (1995);

24. Requests the Secretary-General to make the necessary arrangements, subject to Security Council approval, to allow funds deposited in the escrow account established by resolution 986 (1995) to be used for the purchase of locally produced goods and to meet the local cost for essential civilian needs which have been funded in accordance with the provisions of resolution 986 (1995) and related resolutions, including, where appropriate, the cost of installation and training services;

25. Directs the Committee established by resolution 661 (1990) to take a decision on all applications in respect of humanitarian and essential civilian needs within a target of two working days of receipt of these applications from the Secretary-General, and to ensure that all approval and notification letters issued by the Committee stipulate delivery within a specified time, according to the nature of the items to be supplied, and requests the Secretary-General to notify the Committee of all applications for humanitarian items which are included in the list to which the export/import mechanism approved by resolution 1051 (1996) applies;

26. Decides that Hajj pilgrimage flights which do not transport cargo into or out of Iraq are exempt from the provisions of paragraph 3 of resolution 661 (1990) and resolution 670 (1990), provided timely notification of

each flight is made to the Committee established by resolution 661 (1990), and requests the Secretary-General to make the necessary arrangements, for approval by the Security Council, to provide for reasonable expenses related to the Hajj pilgrimage to be met by funds in the escrow account established by resolution 986 (1995);

27. Calls upon the Government of Iraq:
    (i) to take all steps to ensure the timely and equitable distribution of all humanitarian goods, in particular medical supplies, and to remove and avoid delays at its warehouses;
    (ii) to address effectively the needs of vulnerable groups, including children, pregnant women, the disabled, the elderly and the mentally ill among others, and to allow freer access, without any discrimination, including on the basis of religion or nationality, by United Nations agencies and humanitarian organizations to all areas and sections of the population for evaluation of their nutritional and humanitarian condition;
    (iii) to prioritize applications for humanitarian goods under the arrangements set out in resolution 986 (1995) and related resolutions;
    (iv) to ensure that those involuntarily displaced receive humanitarian assistance without the need to demonstrate that they have resided for six months in their places of temporary residence;
    (v) to extend full cooperation to the United Nations Office for Project Services mine-clearance programme in the three northern Governorates of Iraq and to consider the initiation of the demining efforts in other Governorates;

28. Requests the Secretary-General to report on the progress made in meeting the humanitarian needs of the Iraqi people and on the revenues necessary to meet those needs, including recommendations on necessary additions to the current allocation for oil spare parts and equipment, on the basis of a comprehensive survey of the condition of the Iraqi oil production sector, not later than 60 days from the date of the adoption of this resolution and updated thereafter as necessary;

29. Expresses its readiness to authorize additions to the current allocation for oil spare parts and equipment, on the basis of the report and recommendations requested in paragraph 28 above, in order to meet the humanitarian purposes set out in resolution 986 (1995) and related resolutions;

30. Requests the Secretary-General to establish a group of experts, including oil industry experts, to report within 100 days of the date of adoption of this resolution on Iraq's existing petroleum production and export capacity and to make recommendations, to be updated as necessary, on alternatives for increasing Iraq's petroleum production and export capac-

ity in a manner consistent with the purposes of relevant resolutions, and on the options for involving foreign oil companies in Iraq's oil sector, including investments, subject to appropriate monitoring and controls;

31. Notes that in the event of the Council acting as provided for in paragraph 33 of this resolution to suspend the prohibitions referred to in that paragraph, appropriate arrangements and procedures will need, subject to paragraph 35 below, to be agreed by the Council in good time beforehand, including suspension of provisions of resolution 986 (1995) and related resolutions;

32. Requests the Secretary-General to report to the Council on the implementation of paragraphs 15 to 30 of this resolution within 30 days of the adoption of this resolution;

33. Expresses its intention, upon receipt of reports from the Executive Chairman of UNMOVIC and from the Director General of the IAEA that Iraq has cooperated in all respects with UNMOVIC and the IAEA in particular in fulfilling the work programmes in all the aspects referred to in paragraph 7 above, for a period of 120 days after the date on which the Council is in receipt of reports from both UNMOVIC and the IAEA that the reinforced system of ongoing monitoring and verification is fully operational, to suspend with the fundamental objective of improving the humanitarian situation in Iraq and securing the implementation of the Council's resolutions, for a period of 120 days renewable by the Council, and subject to the elaboration of effective financial and other operational measures to ensure that Iraq does not acquire prohibited items, prohibitions against the import of commodities and products originating in Iraq, and prohibitions against the sale, supply and delivery to Iraq of civilian commodities and products other than those referred to in paragraph 24 of resolution 687 (1991) or those to which the mechanism established by resolution 1051 (1996) applies;

34. Decides that in reporting to the Council for the purposes of paragraph 33 above, the Executive Chairman of UNMOVIC will include as a basis for his assessment the progress made in completing the tasks referred to in paragraph 7 above;

35. Decides that if at any time the Executive Chairman of UNMOVIC or the Director General of the IAEA reports that Iraq is not cooperating in all respects with UNMOVIC or the IAEA or if Iraq is in the process of acquiring any prohibited items, the suspension of the prohibitions referred to in paragraph 33 above shall terminate on the fifth working day following the report, unless the Council decides to the contrary;

36. Expresses its intention to approve arrangements for effective financial and other operational measures, including on the delivery of and payment

for authorized civilian commodities and products to be sold or supplied to Iraq, in order to ensure that Iraq does not acquire prohibited items in the event of suspension of the prohibitions referred to in paragraph 33 above, to begin the elaboration of such measures not later than the date of the receipt of the initial reports referred to in paragraph 33 above, and to approve such arrangements before the Council decision in accordance with that paragraph;

37. Further expresses its intention to take steps, based on the report and recommendations requested in paragraph 30 above, and consistent with the purpose of resolution 986 (1995) and related resolutions, to enable Iraq to increase its petroleum production and export capacity, upon receipt of the reports relating to the cooperation in all respects with UNMOVIC and the IAEA referred to in paragraph 33 above;

38. Reaffirms its intention to act in accordance with the relevant provisions of resolution 687 (1991) on the termination of prohibitions referred to in that resolution;

39. Decides to remain actively seized of the matter and expresses its intention to consider action in accordance with paragraph 33 above no later than 12 months from the date of the adoption of this resolution provided the conditions set out in paragraph 33 above have been satisfied by Iraq.

UNSCR 1441 (8 NOVEMBER 2002)

The Security Council, Recalling all its previous relevant resolutions, in particular its resolutions 661 (1990) of 6 August 1990, 678 (1990) of 29 November 1990, 686 (1991) of 2 March 1991, 687 (1991) of 3 April 1991, 688 (1991) of 5 April 1991, 707 (1991) of 15 August 1991, 715 (1991) of 11 October 1991, 986 (1995) of 14 April 1995, and 1284 (1999) of 17 December 1999, and all the relevant statements of its President,

Recalling also its resolution 1382 (2001) of 29 November 2001 and its intention to implement it fully,

Recognizing the threat Iraq's noncompliance with Council resolutions and proliferation of weapons of mass destruction and long-range missiles poses to international peace and security,

Recalling that its resolution 678 (1990) authorized Member States to use all necessary means to uphold and implement its resolution 660 (1990) of 2 August 1990 and all relevant resolutions subsequent to Resolution 660 (1990) and to restore international peace and security in the area,

Further recalling that its resolution 687 (1991) imposed obligations on Iraq as a necessary step for achievement of its stated objective of restoring international peace and security in the area,

Deploring the fact that Iraq has not provided an accurate, full, final, and complete disclosure, as required by resolution 687 (1991), of all aspects of its programmes to develop weapons of mass destruction and ballistic missiles with a range greater than one hundred and fifty kilometres, and of all holdings of such weapons, their components and production facilities and locations, as well as all other nuclear programmes, including any which it claims are for purposes not related to nuclear-weapons-usable material,

Deploring further that Iraq repeatedly obstructed immediate, unconditional, and unrestricted access to sites designated by the United Nations Special Commission (UNSCOM) and the International Atomic Energy Agency (IAEA), failed to cooperate fully and unconditionally with UNSCOM and IAEA weapons inspectors, as required by resolution 687 (1991), and ultimately ceased all cooperation with UNSCOM and the IAEA in 1998,

Deploring the absence, since December 1998, in Iraq of international monitoring, inspection, and verification, as required by relevant resolutions, of weapons of mass destruction and ballistic missiles, in spite of the Council's repeated demands that Iraq provide immediate, unconditional, and unrestricted access to the United Nations Monitoring, Verification and Inspection Commission (UNMOVIC), established in resolution 1284 (1999) as the successor organization to UNSCOM, and the IAEA, and regretting the consequent prolonging of the crisis in the region and the suffering of the Iraqi people,

Deploring also that the Government of Iraq has failed to comply with its commitments pursuant to resolution 687 (1991) with regard to terrorism, pursuant to resolution 688 (1991) to end repression of its civilian population and to provide access by international humanitarian organizations to all those in need of assistance in Iraq, and pursuant to resolutions 686 (1991), 687 (1991), and 1284 (1999) to return or cooperate in accounting for Kuwaiti and third country nationals wrongfully detained by Iraq, or to return Kuwaiti property wrongfully seized by Iraq,

Recalling that in its resolution 687 (1991) the Council declared that a ceasefire would be based on acceptance by Iraq of the provisions of that resolution, including the obligations on Iraq contained therein,

Determined to ensure full and immediate compliance by Iraq without conditions or restrictions with its obligations under resolution 687 (1991) and other relevant resolutions and recalling that the resolutions of the Council constitute the governing standard of Iraqi compliance,

Recalling that the effective operation of UNMOVIC, as the successor organization to the Special Commission, and the IAEA is essential for the implementation of resolution 687 (1991) and other relevant resolutions,

Noting the letter dated 16 September 2002 from the Minister for Foreign Affairs of Iraq addressed to the Secretary General is a necessary first step toward rectifying Iraq's continued failure to comply with relevant Council resolutions,

Noting further the letter dated 8 October 2002 from the Executive Chairman of UNMOVIC and the Director General of the IAEA to General Al-Saadi of the Government of Iraq laying out the practical arrangements, as a follow-up to their meeting in Vienna, that are prerequisites for the resumption of inspections in Iraq by UNMOVIC and the IAEA, and expressing the gravest concern at the continued failure by the Government of Iraq to provide confirmation of the arrangements as laid out in that letter,

Reaffirming the commitment of all Member States to the sovereignty and territorial integrity of Iraq, Kuwait, and the neighbouring States,

Commending the Secretary General and members of the League of Arab States and its Secretary General for their efforts in this regard,

Determined to secure full compliance with its decisions,

Acting under Chapter VII of the Charter of the United Nations,

1. Decides that Iraq has been and remains in material breach of its obligations under relevant resolutions, including resolution 687 (1991), in particular through Iraq's failure to cooperate with United Nations inspectors and the IAEA, and to complete the actions required under paragraphs 8 to 13 of resolution 687 (1991);

2. Decides, while acknowledging paragraph 1 above, to afford Iraq, by this resolution, a final opportunity to comply with its disarmament obligations under relevant resolutions of the Council; and accordingly decides to set up an enhanced inspection regime with the aim of bringing to full and verified completion the disarmament process established by resolution 687 (1991) and subsequent resolutions of the Council;

3. Decides that, in order to begin to comply with its disarmament obligations, in addition to submitting the required biannual declarations, the Government of Iraq shall provide to UNMOVIC, the IAEA, and the Council, not later than 30 days from the date of this resolution, a currently accurate, full, and complete declaration of all aspects of its programmes to develop chemical, biological, and nuclear weapons, ballistic missiles, and other delivery systems such as unmanned aerial vehicles and dispersal systems designed for use on aircraft, including any holdings and precise locations of such weapons, components, subcomponents, stocks of agents, and related material and equipment, the locations and work of its research, development and production facilities, as well as all other chemical, biological, and nuclear programmes, including any which it claims are for purposes not related to weapon production or material;

4. Decides that false statements or omissions in the declarations submitted by Iraq pursuant to this resolution and failure by Iraq at any time to comply with, and cooperate fully in the implementation of, this resolution

shall constitute a further material breach of Iraq's obligations and will be reported to the Council for assessment in accordance with paragraphs 11 and or 12 below;

5. Decides that Iraq shall provide UNMOVIC and the IAEA immediate, unimpeded, unconditional, and unrestricted access to any and all, including underground, areas, facilities, buildings, equipment, records, and means of transport which they wish to inspect, as well as immediate, unimpeded, unrestricted, and private access to all officials and other persons whom UNMOVIC or the IAEA wish to interview in the mode or location of UNMOVIC's or the IAEA's choice pursuant to any aspect of their mandates; further decides that UNMOVIC and the IAEA may at their discretion conduct interviews inside or outside of Iraq, may facilitate the travel of those interviewed and family members outside of Iraq, and that, at the sole discretion of UNMOVIC and the IAEA, such interviews may occur without the presence of observers from the Iraqi government; and instructs UNMOVIC and requests the IAEA to resume inspections no later than 45 days following adoption of this resolution and to update the Council 60 days thereafter;

6. Endorses the 8 October 2002 letter from the Executive Chairman of UNMOVIC and the Director General of the IAEA to General Al-Saadi of the Government of Iraq, which is annexed hereto, and decides that the contents of the letter shall be binding upon Iraq;

7. Decides further that, in view of the prolonged interruption by Iraq of the presence of UNMOVIC and the IAEA and in order for them to accomplish the tasks set forth in this resolution and all previous relevant resolutions and notwithstanding prior understandings, the Council hereby establishes the following revised or additional authorities, which shall be binding upon Iraq , to facilitate their work in Iraq:

- UNMOVIC and the IAEA shall determine the composition of their inspection teams and ensure that these teams are composed of the most qualified and experienced experts available;

- All UNMOVIC and IAEA personnel shall enjoy the privileges and immunities, corresponding to those of experts on mission, provided in the Convention on Privileges and Immunities of the United Nations and the Agreement on the Privileges and Immunities of the IAEA ;

- UNMOVIC and the IAEA shall have unrestricted rights of entry into and out of Iraq, the right to free, unrestricted, and immediate movement to and from inspection sites, and the right to inspect any sites and buildings, including immediate, unimpeded, unconditional, and unrestricted access to Presidential Sites equal to that at other sites, notwithstanding the provisions of resolution 1154 (1998);

- UNMOVIC and the IAEA shall have the right to be provided by Iraq the names of all personnel currently and formerly associated with Iraq's chemical, biological, nuclear, and ballistic missile programmes and the associated research, development, and production facilities;
- Security of UNMOVIC and IAEA facilities shall be ensured by sufficient UN security guards;
- UNMOVIC and the IAEA shall have the right to declare, for the purposes of freezing a site to be inspected, exclusion zones, including surrounding areas and transit corridors, in which Iraq will suspend ground and aerial movement so that nothing is changed in or taken out of a site being inspected;
- UNMOVIC and the IAEA shall have the free and unrestricted use and landing of fixed- and rotary-winged aircraft, including manned and unmanned reconnaissance vehicles;
- UNMOVIC and the IAEA shall have the right at their sole discretion verifiably to remove, destroy, or render harmless all prohibited weapons, subsystems, components, records, materials, and other related items, and the right to impound or close any facilities or equipment for the production thereof; and
- UNMOVIC and the IAEA shall have the right to free import and use of equipment or materials for inspections and to seize and export any equipment, materials, or documents taken during inspections, without search of UNMOVIC or IAEA personnel or official or personal baggage;

8. Decides further that Iraq shall not take or threaten hostile acts directed against any representative or personnel of the United Nations or the IAEA or of any Member State taking action to uphold any Council resolution;

9. Requests the Secretary General immediately to notify Iraq of this resolution, which is binding on Iraq; demands that Iraq confirm within seven days of that notification its intention to comply fully with this resolution; and demands further that Iraq cooperate immediately, unconditionally, and actively with UNMOVIC and the IAEA;

10. Requests all Member States to give full support to UNMOVIC and the IAEA in the discharge of their mandates, including by providing any information related to prohibited programmes or other aspects of their mandates, including on Iraqi attempts since 1998 to acquire prohibited items, and by recommending sites to be inspected, persons to be interviewed, conditions of such interviews, and data to be collected, the results of which shall be reported to the Council by UNMOVIC and the IAEA;

11. Directs the Executive Chairman of UNMOVIC and the Director General of the IAEA to report immediately to the Council any interference by Iraq with inspection activities, as well as any failure by Iraq to comply with its disarmament obligations, including its obligations regarding inspections under this resolution;

12. Decides to convene immediately upon receipt of a report in accordance with paragraphs 4 or 11 above, in order to consider the situation and the need for full compliance with all of the relevant Council resolutions in order to secure international peace and security;

13. Recalls, in that context, that the Council has repeatedly warned Iraq that it will face serious consequences as a result of its continued violations of its obligations;

14. Decides to remain seized of the matter.

UNSCR 1500 (14 AUGUST 2003)

The Security Council, Recalling all its previous relevant resolutions, in particular resolution 1483 (2003) of 22 May 2003,

Reaffirming the sovereignty and territorial integrity of Iraq,

Reaffirming also the vital role for the United Nations in Iraq which was set out in relevant paragraphs of resolution 1483 (2003),

Having considered the report of the Secretary-General of 15 July 2003 (S/2003/715),

1. Welcomes the establishment of the broadly representative Governing Council of Iraq on 13 July 2003, as an important step towards the formation by the people of Iraq of an internationally recognized, representative government that will exercise the sovereignty of Iraq;

2. Decides to establish the United Nations Assistance Mission for Iraq to support the Secretary-General in the fulfilment of his mandate under resolution 1483 in accordance with the structure and responsibilities set out in his report of 15 July 2003, for an initial period of twelve months;

3. Decides to remain seized of this matter.

UNSCR 1511 (16 OCTOBER 2003)

The Security Council, Reaffirming its previous resolutions on Iraq, including resolution 1483 (2003) of 22 May 2003 and 1500 (2003) of 14 August 2003, and on threats to peace and security caused by terrorist acts, including resolution 1373 (2001) of 28 September 2001, and other relevant resolutions,

Underscoring that the sovereignty of Iraq resides in the State of Iraq, reaffirming the right of the Iraqi people freely to determine their own political future the day when Iraqis govern themselves must come quickly, and recognizing the importance of international support, particularly that of countries in the region, Iraq's neighbours, and regional organizations, in taking forward this process expeditiously,

Recognizing that international support for restoration of conditions of stability and security is essential to the well-being of the people of Iraq as well as to the ability of all concerned to carry out their work on behalf of the people of Iraq, and welcoming Member State contributions in this regard under resolution 1483 (2003),

Welcoming the decision of the Governing Council of Iraq to form a preparatory constitutional committee to prepare for a constitutional conference that will draft a constitution to embody the aspirations of the Iraqi people, and urging it to complete this process quickly,

Affirming that the terrorist bombings of the Embassy of Jordan on 7 August 2003, of the United Nations headquarters in Baghdad on 19 August 2003, of the Imam Ali Mosque in Najaf on 29 August 2003, and of the Embassy of Turkey on 14October 2003, and the murder of a Spanish diplomat on 9 October 2003 are attacks on the people of Iraq, the United Nations, and the international community, and deploring the assassination of Dr. Akila al-Hashimi, who died on 25 September2003, as an attack directed against the future of Iraq,

In that context, recalling and reaffirming the statement of its President of 20August 2003 (S/PRST/2003/13) and resolution 1502 (2003) of 26 August 2003,

Determining that the situation in Iraq, although improved, continues to constitute a threat to international peace and security,

Acting under Chapter VII of the Charter of the United Nations,

1. Reaffirms the sovereignty and territorial integrity of Iraq, and underscores, in that context, the temporary nature of the exercise by the Coalition Provisional Authority (Authority) of the specific responsibilities, authorities, and obligations under applicable international law recognized and set forth in resolution 1483 (2003), which will cease when an internationally recognized, representative government established by the people of Iraq is sworn in and assumes the responsibilities of the Authority, inter alia through steps envisaged in paragraphs 4 through 7 and 10 below;

2. Welcomes the positive response of the international community, in fora such as the Arab League, the Organization of the Islamic Conference,

the United Nations General Assembly, and the United Nations Educational, Scientific and Cultural Organization, to the establishment of the broadly representative Governing Council as an important step towards an internationally recognized, representative government;

3. Supports the Governing Council's efforts to mobilize the people of Iraq, including by the appointment of a cabinet of ministers and a preparatory constitutional committee to lead a process in which the Iraqi people will progressively take control of their own affairs;

4. Determines that the Governing Council and its ministers are the principal bodies of the Iraqi interim administration, which, without prejudice to its further evolution, embodies the sovereignty of the State of Iraq during the transitional period until an internationally recognized, representative government is established and assumes the responsibilities of the Authority;

5. Affirms that the administration of Iraq will be progressively undertaken by the evolving structures of the Iraqi interim administration;

6. Calls upon the Authority, in this context, to return governing responsibilities and authorities to the people of Iraq as soon as practicable and requests the Authority, in cooperation as appropriate with the Governing Council and the Secretary-General, to report to the Council on the progress being made;

7. Invites the Governing Council to provide to the Security Council, for its review, no later than 15 December 2003, in cooperation with the Authority and, as circumstances permit, the Special Representative of the Secretary-General, a timetable and a programme for the drafting of a new constitution for Iraq and for the holding of democratic elections under that constitution;

8. Resolves that the United Nations, acting through the Secretary-General, his Special Representative, and the United Nations Assistance Mission in Iraq, should strengthen its vital role in Iraq, including by providing humanitarian relief, promoting the economic reconstruction of and conditions for sustainable development in Iraq, and advancing efforts to restore and establish national and local institutions for representative government;

9. Requests that, as circumstances permit, the Secretary-General pursue the course of action outlined in paragraphs 98 and 99 of the report of the Secretary-General of 17 July 2003 (S/2003/715);

10. Takes note of the intention of the Governing Council to hold a constitutional conference and, recognizing that the convening of the conference will be a milestone in the movement to the full exercise of sovereignty, calls for its preparation through national dialogue and consensus-building as soon as practicable and requests the Special Representative of the

Secretary-General, at the time of the convening of the conference or, as circumstances permit, to lend the unique expertise of the United Nations to the Iraqi people in this process of political transition, including the establishment of electoral processes;

11. Requests the Secretary-General to ensure that the resources of the United Nations and associated organizations are available, if requested by the Iraqi Governing Council and, as circumstances permit, to assist in furtherance of the programme provided by the Governing Council in paragraph 7 above, and encourages other organizations with expertise in this area to support the Iraqi Governing Council, if requested;

12. Requests the Secretary-General to report to the Security Council on his responsibilities under this resolution and the development and implementation of a timetable and programme under paragraph 7 above;

13. Determines that the provision of security and stability is essential to the successful completion of the political process as outlined in paragraph 7 above and to the ability of the United Nations to contribute effectively to that process and the implementation of resolution 1483 (2003), and authorizes a multinational force under unified command to take all necessary measures to contribute to the maintenance of security and stability in Iraq, including for the purpose of ensuring necessary conditions for the implementation of the timetable and programme as well as to contribute to the security of the United Nations Assistance Mission for Iraq, the Governing Council of Iraq and other institutions of the Iraqi interim administration, and key humanitarian and economic infrastructure;

14. Urges Member States to contribute assistance under this United Nations mandate, including military forces, to the multinational force referred to in paragraph 13 above;

15. Decides that the Council shall review the requirements and mission of the multinational force referred to in paragraph 13 above not later than one year from the date of this resolution, and that in any case the mandate of the force shall expire upon the completion of the political process as described in paragraphs 4 through 7 and 10 above, and expresses readiness to consider on that occasion any future need for the continuation of the multinational force, taking into account the views of an internationally recognized, representative government of Iraq;

16. Emphasizes the importance of establishing effective Iraqi police and security forces in maintaining law, order, and security and combating terrorism consistent with paragraph 4 of resolution 1483 (2003), and calls upon Member States and international and regional organizations to contribute to the training and equipping of Iraqi police and security forces;

17. Expresses deep sympathy and condolences for the personal losses suffered by the Iraqi people and by the United Nations and the families of

those United Nations personnel and other innocent victims who were killed or injured in these tragic attacks;

18. Unequivocally condemns the terrorist bombings of the Embassy of Jordan on 7 August 2003, of the United Nations headquarters in Baghdad on 19 August 2003, and of the Imam Ali Mosque in Najaf on 29 August 2003, and of the Embassy of Turkey on 14 October 2003, the murder of a Spanish diplomat on 9 October 2003, and the assassination of Dr. Akila al-Hashimi, who died on 25 September 2003, and emphasizes that those responsible must be brought to justice;

19. Calls upon Member States to prevent the transit of terrorists to Iraq, arms for terrorists, and financing that would support terrorists, and emphasizes the importance of strengthening the cooperation of the countries of the region, particularly neighbours of Iraq, in this regard;

20. Appeals to Member States and the international financial institutions to strengthen their efforts to assist the people of Iraq in the reconstruction and development of their economy, and urges those institutions to take immediate steps to provide their full range of loans and other financial assistance to Iraq, working with the Governing Council and appropriate Iraqi ministries;

21. Urges Member States and international and regional organizations to support the Iraq reconstruction effort initiated at the 24 June 2003 United Nations Technical Consultations, including through substantial pledges at the 23–24 October 2003 International Donors Conference in Madrid;

22. Calls upon Member States and concerned organizations to help meet the needs of the Iraqi people by providing resources necessary for the rehabilitation and reconstruction of Iraq's economic infrastructure;

23. Emphasizes that the International Advisory and Monitoring Board (IAMB) referred to in paragraph 12 of resolution 1483 (2003) should be established as a priority, and reiterates that the Development Fund for Iraq shall be used in a transparent manner as set out in paragraph 14 of resolution 1483 (2003);

24. Reminds all Member States of their obligations under paragraphs 19 and 23 of resolution 1483 (2003) in particular the obligation to immediately cause the transfer of funds, other financial assets and economic resources to the Development Fund for Iraq for the benefit of the Iraqi people;

25. Requests that the United States, on behalf of the multinational force as outlined in paragraph 13 above, report to the Security Council on the efforts and progress of this force as appropriate and not less than every six months;

26. Decides to remain seized of the matter.

Appendix A
'Iraqi Cabinets, 1920–2003

PROVISIONAL GOVERNMENT

'Abd al-Rahman al-Naqib (23 October 1920–23 August 1921)

Commerce	'Abd al-Latif al-Mandil
Defense	Ja'far al-'Askari
Education	Muhammad Mahdi Tabtabai
Finance	Sasun Hisqayl
Health	Muhammad Mahdi Tabtabai
Interior	Talib al-Naqib
Justice	Mustafa al-Alusi
Waqf	Muhammad Ali Fadhil
Without Portfolio	'Abd al-Rahman al-Haydari
	'Abd al-Jabbar al-Khayyat
	Fahkri al-Jamil
	Hajj 'Abd al-Ghani Kubba
	Daud al-Yusifani
	Shaykh Ajil al-Samarmad
	Ahmad al-Sani
	'Abd al-Majid al-Shawi
	Shaykh Muhammad al-Sayhud
	Shaykh Salim al-Khayyun
	Hajj Najm al-Badrawi
	Shaykh Dhari al-Sa'dun
Works	Izzat Karkukli

'Abd al-Rahman al-Naqib (10 September 1921–14 August 1922)

Commerce	'Abd al-Latif al-Mandil (resigned 22 March 1922)
Defense	Ja'far al-'Askari
Education	Muhammad Ali al-Shahristani
Finance	Sasun Hisqayl

Health	Hanna Khayyat
Interior	Hajj Ramzi
Justice	Naji al-Suwaydi (resigned 22 March 1922)
	'Abd al-Muhsin al-Sa'dun
Waqf	Muhammad Ali Fadhil
Works	Izzat Karkukli (resigned 22 March 1922)
Replacements	Tawfiq al-Khalidi
	Sabih Nasrat
	Ja'far Abu al-Timman

'Abd al-Rahman al-Kaylani (30 August 1922–16 November 1922)

Defense	Ja'far al-'Askari
Education	Muhsin al-Shallash
Finance	Sasun Hisqayl
Interior	'Abd al-Muhsin al-Sa'dun
Justice	Tawfiq al-Khalidi
Waqf	Ali Fadhil
Works	Sabih Nasrat

'Abd al-Muhsin al-Sa'dun (20 November 1922–16 November 1923)

Defense	Nuri al-Sa'id
Education	'Abd al-Husayn al-Chalabi
Finance	Sasun Hisqayl
Interior	Naji al-Suwaydi
	'Abd al-Muhsin al-Sa'dun
Justice	'Abd al-Muhsin al-Sa'dun
	Naji al-Suwaydi
Waqf	'Abd al-Latif al-Mandil
Works	Yasin al-Hashimi

Ja'far al-'Askari (22 November 1923–2 August 1924)

Defense	Nuri al-Sa'id
Education	Ja'far al-'Askari
Finance	Muhsin al-Shallash
Interior	Ali Jawdat al-Ayubi
Other Officials	Shaykh Salih al-Bashayan
	Ahmad al-Fakhri
	Sabih Nasrat

Yasin al-Hashimi (2 August 1924–2 June 1925)

Communications/Works	Muzahim al-Pachachi
Defense	Yasin al-Hashimi
Education	Muhammad Ridha al-Shabibi
Finance	Sasun Hisqayl
Foreign Affairs (created in 1925)	Yasin al-Hashimi
Interior	'Abd al-Muhsin al-Sa'dun
Justice	Rashid 'Ali al-Kaylani (resigned 1928
Waqf	Ibrahim Effendi al-Hayda

'Abd al-Muhsin al-Sadun (26 June 1925–1 November 1926)

Defense	Nuri al-Sa'id
Finance	'Abd al-Muhsin al-Sa'dun
Foreign Affairs	'Abd al-Muhsin al-Sa'dun
Interior	Rashid 'Ali al-Kaylani
	Hikmat Sulayman
	'Abd al-'Aziz al-Qassab
Waqf	Hamdi al-Pachachi
Other Officials	Rauf al-Chadirchi
	'Abd al-Husayn al-Chalabi
	Sabih Nasrat
	Naji al-Suwaydi
	Substitution Muhammad Amin Zaki

Ja'far al-'Askari (21 November 1926–8 January 1928)

Communications/Works	Muhammad Amin Zaki
	Alwan al-Yasin
Defense	Nuri al-Sa'id
Education	'Abd al-Mahdi
	Muhammad Amin Zaki
Finance	Yasin al-Hashimi (resigned) (d.1937)
Foreign Affairs	Ja'far al-'Askari
Interior	Rashid 'Ali al-Kaylani (resigned January 1928)
Irrigation/Agriculture (created in August 1927)	'Abd al-Husayn al-Chalabi
Justice	Rauf al-Chadirchi
Waqf	Amin al-Bashayah

'Abd al-Muhsin al-Sadun (14 January 1928–20 January 1929)

Defense	
Education	Tawfiq al-Suwaydi
Finance	Yusif Ghanima
Foreign Affairs	'Abd al-Muhsin al-Sadun
Interior	'Abd al-Aziz al-Qassab
Irrigation	Salman Barrak
Justice	Hikmat Sulayman
Waqf	Shaykh Ahmad al-Daud
Works	Muhsin al-Shallash

Tawfiq al-Suwaydi (28 April 1929–25 August 1929)

Defense	Muhammad Amin Zaki
Education	Khalid Sulayman
Finance	Yusif Ghanima
Foreign Affairs	Tawfiq al-Suwaydi
Interior	'Abd al-Aziz al-Qassab
Justice	Daud al-Haydari
Works	Muhsin al-Shallash
Waqf	ceased to exist

'Abd al-Muhsin al-Sadun (19 September 1929–died 13 November 1929)

Defense	Nuri al-Sa'id
Education	'Abd al-Husayn al-Chalabi
Finance	Yasin al-Hashimi
Foreign Affairs	'Abd al-Muhsin al-Sadun
Interior	Naji al-Suwaydi
Justice	Naji Shawkat
Works	Muhammad Amin Zaki

Naji al-Suwaydi (18 November 1929–19 March 1930)

Defense	Nuri al-Sa'id
Education	'Abd al-Husayn al-Chalabi
Finance	Yasin al-Hashimi
Foreign Affairs	Naji al-Suwaydi
Interior	Naji al-Suwaydi
Justice	Naji Shawkat

Works   Muhammad Amin Zaki
Other Official   Khalid Sulayman

Nuri al-Sa'id (23 March 1930–19 October 1930)

Defense   Ja'far al-'Askari
Education   'Abd al-Husayn al-Chalabi
Finance   'Ali Jawdat al-Ayubi (resigned 30 September 1930)
                 Rustum Haydar
Foreign Affairs Nuri al-Sa'id (until June 1930)
                 'Abdullah Damluji
Interior   Jamil al-Midfa'i*
Justice   Jamal Baban
Works   Jamil al-Rawi

Nuri al-Sa'id (19 October 30–27 October 1932)

Defense   Ja'far al-'Askari
Education   'Abd al-Husayn al-Chalabi
Finance   Rustum Haydar
Foreign Affairs Ja'far al-'Askari
Interior   Naji Shawkat
Justice   Jamal Baban
Works   Muhammad Amin Zaki

Naji Shawkat (3 November 1932–18 March 1933)

Defense   Rashid al-Khawja
Education   'Abd al-Mahdi
Finance   Nasrat al-Farsi
Foreign Affairs 'Abd al-Qadir Rashid
Interior   Naji Shawkat
Justice   Jamal al-Wadi
Works   Jalal Baban

Rashid 'Ali al-Kaylani (20 March 1933–9 September 1933)

Defense   Jalal Baban
Education   'Abd al-Mahdi

*Left for Chamber of Deputies.

Finance	Yasin al-Hashimi
Foreign Affairs	Nuri al-Sa'id
Interior	Hikmat Sulayman
Justice	Muhammad Zaki al-Basri
Works	Rustum Haydar

Rashid 'Ali al-Kaylani (9 September 1933–28 October 1933)

Defense	Jalal Baban
Education	'Abd al-Mahdi
Finance	Yasin al-Hashimi
Foreign Affairs	Nuri al-Sa'id
Interior	Hikmat Sulayman
Justice	Muhammad Zaki al-Basri
Works	Rustum Haydar

Jamil al-Midfai (9 November 1933–10 February 1934)

Defense	Nuri al-Sa'id
Education	Salih Jabr
Finance	Nasrat al-Farisi
Foreign Affairs	Nuri al-Sa'id
Interior	Naji Shawkat
Justice	Jamal Baban
Works	Rustum Haydar (resigned 21 February 1934)

Jamil al-Midfai (21 February 1934–25 August 1934)

Defense	Rashid al-Khawja
Education	Jalal Baban
Finance	Naji al-Suwaydi
Foreign Affairs	'Abdullah Damluji
	Tawfiq Suwaydi
Interior	Jamil al-Midfai
Justice	Jamil Baban
Other Official	'Abd al-Mahdi

Ali Jawdat al-Ayubi (27 August 1934–23 February 1935)

Defense	Jamil al-Midfai

Finance	Yusif Ghanima
Foreign Affairs	Nuri al-Sa'id
Interior	Ali Jawdat al-Ayubi
Justice	Jamil Baban
Other Official	'Abd al-Husayn al-Chalabi

Jamil al-Midfai (4 March 1935–16 March 1935)

Defense	Rashid al-Khawja
Foreign Affairs	Nuri al-Sa'id
Interior	'Abd al-Aziz al-Qassab
Justice	Mumammad al-Bashri
Other Officials	Yusif Ghanima
	Tawfiq al-Suwaydi
	Muhammad Amin Zaki

Yasin al-Hashimi (17 March 1935–29 October 1936)

Defense	Ja'far al-'Askari
Education	Muhammad Ridha al-Shabibi
	(resigned 15 September 1935)
	Sadiq al-Bassam
Finance	Rauf Bahrani
Foreign Affairs	Nuri al-Sa'id
Interior	Rashid 'Ali al-Kaylani
Justice	Muhammad Zaki
Works	Muhammad Amin Zaki

Hikmat Sulayman (29 October 1936–16 August 1937)

Defense	'Abd al-Latif Nuri
Education	Yusif Izz al-Din (resigned June 1937)
	Ja'far Hamandi
Finance	Ja'far Abu al-Timman (resigned June 1937)
	Muhammad Ali Mahmud
Foreign Affairs	Naji al-Asil
Interior	Hikmat Sulayman
Justice	Salih Jabr (resigned June 1937)
	Ali Mahmud
Works	Kamil al-Chadirchi (resigned June 1937)
	'Abd al-Mahdi

Jamil al-Midfai (17 August 1937–25 December 1938)

Defense	Jamil al-Midfai
	Subih Najib*
Education	Muhammad Ridha al-Shabibi
Finance	Ibrahim Kamal
Foreign Affairs	Tawfiq al-Suwaydi
Interior	Mustafa al-Umari
	Jamil al-Midfai*
Justice	'Abd al-Mahdi
	Mustafa al-Umari*
Works	Jalal Baban
	'Abd al-Mahdi*

Nuri al-Sa'id (25 December 1938–4 April 1939)

Defense	Taha al-Hashimi
Education	Salih Jabr
Finance	Rustum Haydar
Foreign Affairs	Nuri al-Sa'id
Interior	Naji Shawkat
Justice	Mahmud Subhi al-Daftari
Works	Umar Nazmi

Nuri al-Sa'id (6 April 1939–21 February 1940)

Defense	Taha al-Hashimi
Economics	Sadiq al-Bassam (appointed October 1939)
Education	Salih Jabr
Finance	Rustum Haydar (died 18 January 1940)
Foreign Affairs	Nuri al-Sa'id
	Ali Jawdat al-Ayubi
Interior	Naji Shawkat (resigned 29 April 1939)
	Nuri al-Sa'id
	Umar Nazmi (appointed October 1939)
Justice	Mahmud Subhi al-Daftari
Social Affairs	Sami Shawkat (appointed October 1939)
Works	Umar Nazmi
	Jalal Baban (appointed October 1939)
Economics and Social Affairs	created in December 1939

*Named in October reconstruction.

Nuri al-Sa'id (22 February 1940–31 March 1940)

Defense	Taha al-Hashimi
Economics	Sadiq al-Bassam
Education	Sami Shawkat
Finance	Rauf Bahrani
Foreign Affairs	Ali Jawdat al-Ayubi
Interior	Umar Nazmi
Justice	Mahmud Subhi al-Daftari
Social Affairs	Salih Jabr
Works	Jalal Baban

Rashid 'Ali al-Kaylani (31 March 1940–30 January 1941)

Defense	Taha al-Hashimi
Economics	Muhammad Amin Zaki
Education	Sadiq al-Bassam
Finance	Naji al-Suwaydi
Foreign Affairs	Nuri al-Sa'id (resigned 25 January 1941)
	Ali Mahmud al-Shaykh
Interior	Rashid 'Ali al-Kaylani
Justice	Naji Shawkat (resigned 25 January 1941)
	Yunis al-Sab'Awi
Social Affairs	Rauf al-Bahrani
Without Portfolio	Muhammad Ali Mahmud
	(appointed 28 January 1941)
	Musa al-Shahbandar (appointed 28 January 1941)
Works/Transport	Umar Nazmi

Taha al-Hashimi (1 Febraury 1941–1 April 1941)

Defense	Taha al-Hashimi
Economics	'Abd al-Mahdi
Education	Sadiq al-Bassam
Finance	Ali Mumtaz
Foreign Affairs	Tawfiq al-Suwaydi
Interior	Umar Nazmi
Justice	Umar Nazmi
Social Affairs	Hamdi al-Pachachi
Works/Transport	Ali Mumtaz

Rashid 'Ali al-Kaylani (12 April 1941–29 May 1941)

Defense	Naji Shawkat
Economics	Yunis al-Sab'Awi
Education	Muhammad Hasah al-Salman
Finance	Naji al-Suwaydi
Foreign Affairs	Musa al-Shahbandar
Interior	Rashid 'Ali al-Kaylani
Justice	Ali Mahmud
Social Affairs	Rauf al-Bahrani
Works/Transport	Muhammad Ali Mahmud

Jamil al-Midfai (2 June 1941–7 October 1941)

Defense	Nazif al-Shawi
Economics	Nasrat al-Farisi
Education	Muhammad Ridhai al-Shabibi
Finance	Ibrahim Kamal
Foreign Affairs	Ali Jawdat al-Ayubi
Interior	Mustafa al-Umari
Justice	Ibrahim Kamal
Social Affairs	Ja'far Hamandi
Works/Transport	Jalal Baban

Nuri al-Sa'id (9 October 1941–8 October 1942)

Defense	Nuri al-Sa'id
Economics	'Abd al-Mahdi
Education	Tahsin Ali
Finance	Ali Mumtaz
Foreign Affairs	Salih Jabr
	Abdullah Damluji (appointed February 1942)
Interior	Salih Jabr
Justice	Sadiq al-Bassam
	Daud al-Haydari (appointed April 1942)
Social Affairs	Jamal Baban
Works/Transport	Muhammad Amin Zaki
	'Abd al-Mahdi

Nuri al-Sa'id (8 October 1942–25 December 1943)

Defense	
Economics	Muhsin al-Shallash (retired)
	Salman Barrak

Education	Tahsin 'Ali
	'Abd al-Ilah Hafiz (appointed June 1943)
Finance	Salih Jabr
	Jalal Baban (appointed June 1943;
	resigned October 1943)
	'Abd al-Ilah Hafiz
Foreign Affairs	'Abd al-Ilah Hafiz
	Nasrat al-Farisi (appointed June 1943;
	resigned October 1943)
	Tahsin al-'Askari
Interior	Tahsin al-'Askari
	Salih Jabr (appointed June 1943;
	resigned October 1943)
	'Abdullah al-Qassab
Justice	Daud al-Haydari
	Ahmad Muhktar Baban (appointed June 1943)
Social Affairs	Ahmad Muhktar Baban
	'Abd al-Razzaq al-Uzri (appointed June 1943)
Works/Transport	'Abd al-Mahdi
	Tahsin al-'Askari (appointed June 1943)

Nuri al-Sa'id (25 December 1943–3 June 1944

Defense	
Deputy P.M.	Tawfiq al-Suwaydi (resigned March 1944)
Economics	Salman Barrak
Education	'Abd al-Ilah Hafiz
Finance	Ali Mumtaz
Foreign Affairs	Mahmud Subih al-Daftari
Interior	Umar Nazmi
Justice	Ahmad Muhktar Baban
Social Affairs	Muhammad Hasan Kubba
Supply	(No one would accept the post.)
Without Portfolio	Majid Mustafa
Works/Transport	Sadiq Bassam

Hamdi al-Pachachi (4 June 1944–29 August 1944)

Defense	Tahsin 'Ali
	Arshad al-'Umari
Economics	Tawfiq Wahbi

Education	Ibrahim 'Akif al-Alusi
Finance	Salih Jabr
Foreign Affairs	Arshad al-'Umari
Interior	Mustafa al-'Umari
Justice	Ahmad Muhktar Baban
Social Affairs	Muhammad Hasan Kubba
Supply	Arshad al-'Umari
Works/Transport	'Abd al-Amir al-Uzri
	Tahsin 'Ali

Hamdi al-Pachachi (29 August 1944–January 1946)

Defense	Tahsin 'Ali (resigned September 1944)
	Arshad al-'Umari
	Isma'il Namiq (appointed December 1944)
Economics	Tawfiq Wahbi
Education	Ibrahim 'Akif al-Alusi
Finance	Salih Jabr
Foreign Affairs	Arshad al-'Umari
Interior	Mustafa al-'Umari
Justice	Ahmad Muhktar Baban
Social Affairs	Muhammad Hasan Kubba
	'Abd al-Majid al-'Alawi
Supply	Salih Jabr
	Yusif Ghanima
Works/Transport	'Abd al-Amir al-Uzri
	Tahsin 'Ali

Tawfiq al-Suwaydi (23 February 1946–3 May 1946)

Defense	Ismael Namiq
Economics	'Abd al-Hadi al-Dharir
Education	Najib al-Rawi
Finance	'Abd al-Wahhab Mahmud
Foreign Affairs	Tawfiq al-Suwaydi
	Ali Mumtaz (appointed April 1946)
Interior	Sad Salih
Justice	Umar Nazmi
Social Affairs	Ahmad Muhktar Baban
	Shawkat al-Zahawi (appointed April 1946)
Supply	'Abd al-Jabbar al-Chalabi

Works/Transport	Ali Mumtaz
	'Abd al-Jabbar al-Chalabi (appointed April 1946)

Arshad al-'Umari (1 June 1946–14 November 1946)

Defense	Sa'id Haqqi
Economics	Baba Ali
Education	Nuri al-Qadhi
Finance	Yusif Ghanima
Foreign Affairs	Fadhil Jamali
Interior	'Abdullah al-Qassab (resigned August 1946)
	Arshad al-Umari
Justice	Muhammad Hasan Kubba
Social Affairs	'Abd al-Hadi al-Pachachi
Supply	Yusif Ghanima
	'Abd al-Ilah Hafiz (appointed 26 August 1946)
Works/Transport	'Abd al-Hadi Chalabi

Nuri al-Sa'id (21 November 1946–11 March 1947)

Defense	Shakir al-Wadi
Economics	Baba Ali
Education	Sadiq Bassam
	Jamil 'Abd al-Wahhab
Finance	Salih Jabr (removed 12-46)
	'Abd al-Ilah Hafiz
Foreign Affairs	Fadhil Jamali
Interior	Mustafa al-'Umari
Justice	'Umar Nazmi
Social Affairs	Jamil 'Abd al-Wahhab
Supply	Muhammad Hadid (removed December 1946)
	'Abd al-Ilah Hafiz
Works/Transport	Ali Mumtaz
	'Abd al-Hadi Chalabi

Salih Jabr (29 March 1947–27 January 1948)

Defense	Shakir al-Wadi
Economics	Jamal Baban

Education	Tawfiq Wahbi
Finance	Yusif Ghanima
Foreign Affairs	Fadhil Jamali
Interior	Salih Jabr
Justice	Jamal Baban
Social Affairs	Jamil 'Abd al-Wahhab
Supply	'Abd al-Ilah Hafiz
Works/Transport	Dhiya Ja'far

Muhammad al-Sadr (29 January 1948–21 June 1948)

Defense	Arshad al-Umari
Economics	Mustafa al-Umari
Education	Muhammad Ridha al-Shabibi
Finance	Sadiq Bassam
Foreign Affairs	Hamdi al-Pachachi (died 17 March 1948)
	Nasrat al-Farsi
Interior	Jamil al-Midfai (removed 4 March 1948)
	Nasrat al-Farsi
	Mustafa al-Umari
Justice	Umar Nazmi (removed 4 March 1948)
	Najib al-Rawi
Social Affairs	Najib al-Rawi
	Daud al-Haydari
Supply	Muhammad Mahdi al-Kubba (removed 7 June 1948)
Without Portfolio	Nasrat al-Farsi
	Daud al-Haydari
	Muhammad al-Sayhud (removed April 1948)
Works/Transport	Jalal Baban

Muzahim al-Pachachi (26 June 1948–6 January 1949)

Defense	Sadiq Bassam (removed 27 September 1948)
	Shakir al-Wadi (appointed 20 October 1948)
Economics	'Abd al-Wahhab Mirjan (removed November 1948)
	Ali Haydar Sulayman
Education	Najib al-Rawi
Finance	Ali Mumtaz (removed 27 September 1948)
	Khalil Ismael
Foreign Affairs	Ali Jawdat al-Ayubi (appointed 20 October 1948)
Interior	Mustafa al-Umari (removed October 1948)
	Umar Nazmi

Justice	Muhammad Hasan al-Kubba
Social Affairs	Jalal Baban
Supply	Ali Mumtaz (removed 27 October 1948)
Without Portfolio	Muhammad al-Sayhud (appointed October 1948)

Nuri al-Sa'id (6 January 1949–10 December 1949)

Defense	Shakir al-Wadi
Deputy P.M.	Umar Nazmi (appointed March 1949)
Economics	Dhiya Ja'far
Education	Najib al-Rawi
Finance	Jalal Baban
	Khalil Ismael
Foreign Affairs	'Abd al-Ilah Hafiz
	Fadhil Jamali (appointed March 1949; removed September 1949)
	Shakir al-Wadi
Interior	Nuri al-Sa'id
	Tawfiq al-Naib (appointed March 1949)
	Umar Nazmi
Justice	Muhammad Hasan al-Kubba
Social Affairs	Baha al-Din Nuri
Works	Jalal Baban

Ali Jawdat (10 December 1949–1 February 1950)

Defense	Umar Nazmi
Deputy P.M.	Muzahim al-Pachachi
Economics	'Abd al-Razzaq al-Dharir
Education	Najib al-Rawi
Finance	Ali Mumtaz
Foreign Affairs	Muzahim al-Pachachi
Interior	Umar Nazmi
Justice	Sa'd Umar
Social Affairs	Husayn Jamil
Without Portfolio	Ali al-Sharqi
Works	Ali Haydar Sulayman

Tawfiq al-Suwaydi (5 February 1950–15 September 1950)

Defense	Shakir al-Wadi
Economics	Dhiya Ja'far

Education	Sad Umar
Finance	'Abd al-Karim al-Uzri
Foreign Affairs	Tawfiq al-Suwaydi
Interior	Salih Jabr
Justice	Hasan Sami Tatar (retired August 1950)
	Jamil al-Urfali
Social Affairs	Tawfiq Wahbi
Without Portfolio	Hazim Shamdin Agha
	Khalil Kunna
	Jamil al-Urfali

Nuri al-Sa'id (15 September 1950–10 July 1952)

Defense	Shakir al-Wadi
Economics	Dhiya Ja'far
	'Abd al-Majid Mahmud (appointed December 1950)
Education	Khalil Kunna
Finance	'Abd al-Wahhab Mirjan
Foreign Affairs	Shakir al-Wadi
Interior	Nuri al-Sa'id
Justice	Hasan Sami Tatar
Social Affairs	Majid Mustafa
Without Portfolio	Sadiq Bassam (appointed December 1950)
	Muhammad Hasan al-Kubba (appointed December 1950)
	Umar Nazmi (appointed December 1950)
Works	'Abd al-Wahhab Mirjan
	Dhiya Ja'far (appointed December 1950)
	Ali Haydar Sulayman

Mustafa al-Umari (12 July 1952–21 November 1952)

Agriculture	'Abd al-Jabbar al-Chalabi
Defense	Husam al-Din Jum'A
Economy	Nadim al-Pachachi
Finance	Ibrahim al-Shahbandar (removed 15 November 1952)
	Ali Mahmud
Foreign Affairs	Fadhil al-Jamali
Health	'Abd al-Rahman Jawdat

Interior   Mustafa al-Umari (acting)

Interior	Mustafa al-Umari (acting)
	Muhammad Hassan Juma'A (acting)
Justice	Jamal Baban
Social Affairs	Majid Mustafa
Transportation	'Abd al-Majid Allawi

Nur al-Din Mahmud (23 November 1952–22 January 1953)

Agriculture	Rayeh al-Attiyah
Defense	Nur al-Din Mahmud
Economy	Majid Mustafa (acting)
	Nadim al-Pachachi
	(appointed 21 December 1952)
Education	Qasim Khali
Finance	Ali Mahmud al-Shaikh
Foreign Affairs	Fadhil al-Jawali
Health	'Abd al-Majid al-Qassab
Interior	Nur al-Din Mahmud (acting)
Justice	'Abd al-Rasul al-Khalisi
Social Affairs	Majid Mustafa
	Sa'id Qazzaz(appointed 21 December 1952)
Transport/ Public Works	'Abd al-Rasul al-Khalisi (acting)
	Abd al-Rahman Jawdat (appointed 21 December 1952)

Jamil al-Midfai (29 January 1953–5 May 1953)

Agriculture	'Abd al-Rahman Jawdat
Defense	Nuri al-Sa'id
Deputy P.M.	Ali Jawdat al-Ayubi
Economy	Dhia Ja'far
Education	Khalil Kanna
Finance	Ali Mumtaz al-Daftari
Foreign Affairs	Tawfiq al-Suwaydi
Health	Muhammad Hasan Salman
Interior	Husam al-Din Jum'A
Justice	Ahmad Muhktar Baban
Social Affairs	Majid Mustafa
Transport/Public Works	'Abd al-Wahhab Murjan

Jamil al-Midfai (7 May 1953–15 September 1953)

Agriculture	'Abd al-Rahman Jawdat
Defense	Nuri al-Sa'id
Deputy P.M.	Ali Jawdat
Economy	Dhia Ja'far
Education	Khalil Kanna
Finance	Ali Mumtaz
Foreign Affairs	Tawfiq al-Suwaydi
Health	Muhammad Hasan Salman
Interior	Husam al-Din Jum'A
Justice	Muhammad Ali Mahmud
Social Affairs	Majid Mustafa
State	Ali al-Sharqi
State	Nadim al-Pachachi
Transport/Public Works	'Abd al-Wahhab Murjan

Muhammad Fadhil al-Jamali (17 September 1953–27 February 1954)

Agriculture	'Abd al-Ghani al-Dalli
Construction	Ali Haydar Sulayman
Defense	Husayn Makki Khammas
Deputy P.M.	Muhammad Ali Mahmud
Economy	'Abd al-Rahman al-Jalili
Education	'Abd al-Majid al-Qassab
Finance	'Abd al-Karim al-Uzari
Foreign Affairs	'Abdullah Bakr
Health	'Abd al-Amir 'Allawi
Interior	Muhammad Fadhil al-Jamali (acting)
Justice	Jamil al-Urfali
Social Affairs	Hasan 'Abd al-Rahman
Transport	'Abd al-Majid Abbas
Without Portfolio	Arkan 'Abbadi
Without Portfolio	Muhammad Shafiq al-'Ani
Without Portfolio	Rufayil Butti
Without Portfolio	Sadiq Kammuna

Muhammad Fadhil al-Jamali (8 March 1954–19 April 1954)

Agriculture	'Abd al-Ghani al-Dalli
Construction	'Abd al-Karim al-Uzari (removed 6 April 1954)
	Ali Haydar Sulayman
Defense	Husayn Makki Khammas

Deputy P.M.	Ahmad Muhktar Baban
Economy	Ali Haydar Sulayman
Education	Jamil al-Urfali
Finance	Ali Mumtaz
Foreign Affair	Musa al-Shahbandar
Health	'Abd al-Majid al-Qassab
Interior	Sa'id Qazzaz
Justice	Muhammad Ali Mahmud
Social Affairs	Arkan Abbadi
State	Rafayl Batti
Transport	'Abd al-Ghani al-Dalli

Arshad al-Umari (29 April 1954–17 June 1954)

Agriculture	Abd al-Ghani al-Dalli
Construction	Arshad al-Umari
Defense	Husayn Makki Khammas
Economy	Ali al-Safi
Education	Fadhil al-Jamali
Foreign Affairs	Fadhil al-Jamali
Health	Abd al-Hadi al-Pachachi
Interior	Sa'id al-Qazzaz
Justice	Fakhri al-Tabaqjali
Social Affairs	Sami Fattah
Transport/Public Works	Fakhri al-Fakhri

Nuri al-Sa'id (3 September 1954–17 December 1955)

Agriculture	'Abd al-Wahhab Murjan
Construction	'Abd al-Majid Mahmud
Defense	Nuri al-Sa'id
Economy	Nadim al-Pachachi
Education	Khalil Kanna
Finance	Dia Ja'far
Foreign Affairs	Musa al-Shabandar
Health	Muhammad Hasan Salman
Interior	Sa'id al-Qazzaz
Justice	Muhammad Ali Mahmud
Transport/Public Works	Salih Saib
Without Portfolio	Burhan Bash A'yan
Without Portfolio	Ahmad Mukhtar Baban
Without Portfolio	Rushdi al-Chalabi
Without Portfolio	Ali al-Sharqi

Nuri al-Sa'id (17 December 1955–7 June 1957)

Agriculture	Rushdi al-Chalabi
Construction	Dia Ja'far
Defense	Nuri al-Sa'id
Deputy P.M.	Ahmad Mukhtar Baban
Economy	Nadim al-Pachachi
Education	Munir al-Qadhi
Finance	Khalil Kanna
Foreign Affairs	Burhan Bash A'yan
Health	'Abd al-Amir 'Allawi
Interior	Sa'id al-Qazzaz
Justice	'Abd al-Jabbar al-Takarli
Social Affairs	'Abd al-Rasul al-Khalisi
Transport	Saib Salih al-Juliuri
Without Portfolio	Ali al-Sharqi

Ali Jawdat al-Ayubi (20 June 1957–16 December 1957)

Agriculture	Jamal Umar Nazmi
Construction	Nadim al-Pachachi (acting)
Defense	Ahmad Muhktar Baban
Economy	Nadim al-Pachachi
Education	Ahmad Muhktar Baban (acting)
Finance	Ali Mumtaz
Foreign Affairs	Ali Mumtaz (acting)
Health	'Abd al-Amir Allawi
Interior	Sami Fattah
Justice	'Abd al-Rasul al-Khalisi
Social Affairs	Arkan Abbadi
Transport/Public Works	'Abd al-Wahhab Murjan
Without Portfolio	Ali al-Sharqi

'Abd al-Wahhab Murjan (15 December 1957)

Agriculture	Jamil al-Urfali
Construction	Salih Saib
Defense	'Abd al-Wahhab Murjan
Economy	Muhammad al-Hardan
Education	'Abd al-Hamid Kazim
Finance	Nadim al-Pachachi
Foreign Affairs	Burhan Bash A'yan
Health	Mahmud Baban

Interior	Sami Fattah
Justice	'Abd al-Rasul al-Khalisi
Social Affairs	Arkan Abbadi
Transport	'Abd al-Amir Allawi
Without Portfolio	Izz al-Din al-Mulla
	Jawad al-Khatib
	Ali al-Sharqi

Nuri al-Sa'id (3 March 1958–14 July 1958)

Agriculture	Muhammad al-Hardan
Construction	Saib Salih
Defense	Nuri al-Sa'id
Deputy P.M.	Tawfiq al-Suwaydi
Economy	Dia Ja'far
Education	'Abd al-Hamid Kazim
Finance	'Abd al-Karim al-Uzari
Foreign Affairs	Muhammad Fadhil al-Janqali
Health	'Abd al-Amir Allawi
Interior	Sa'id al-Qazzaz
Justice	Jamil 'Abd al-Wahhab
Social Affairs	Sami Fattah
Transport	Rushdi al-Chalabi
Without Portfolio	Rayeh al-Attiya
Without Portfolio	Burhan Bash A'yan
Without Portfolio	Mahmud Baban

Ahmad Mukhtar Baban (19 May 1958–14 July 1958)

Agriculture	Jamil al-Urfali
Construction	Dia Ja'far
Economy	Rushdi al-Chalibi
Education	'Abd al-Hamid Kazim
Finance	Nadim al-Pachachi
Health	'Abd al-Amir Allawi
Information/Guidance	Burhan Bash A'yan
Interior	Sa'id al-Qazzaz
Justice	Jamil 'Abd al-Wahhab
Social Affairs	Sadiq Kammuna
Transport/Public Works	Salih Saib
Without Portfolio	Mahmud Baban
	Ali al-Sharqi
	'Abd al-Jabbar al-Takarli

Nuri al-Sa'id: The Arab Union Government (19 May 1958–14 July 1958)

Defense*	Sulayman Tuqan
Deputy P.M.	Ibrahim Hashim
Finance	'Abd al-Karim al-Uzari
Foreign Affairs*	Tawfiq al-Suwaydi
State/Defense	Sami Fattah
State/Foreign Affairs	Khulusi al-Khayri

'Abd al-Karim Qasim (14 July 1958–7 February 1959)

Agriculture	Hudayb al-Hajj Hammad
Defense	'Abd al-Karim Qasim
Development	Fuad al-Rikabi (removed 7 February 1959)
Economics	Ibrahim Kubba
Education	Jabir Umar (removed 7 February 1959)
Finance	Muhammad Hadid
Foreign Affairs	'Abd al-Jabbar Jumard (removed February 1959)
Guidance	Siddiq Shanshal (removed 7 February 1959)
Health	Muhammad Salih Mahmud (removed 7 February 1959)
Interior	'Abd al-Salam Arif (removed 30 September 1958)
	Ahmad Muhammad Yahya
Justice	Mustafa Ali
Social Affairs	Naji Talib (removed 7 February 1959)
Works	Baba Ali (removed 7 Febraury 1959)

'Abd al-Karim Qasim (10 February 1959–8 February 1963)

Agrarian Reform	Ibrahim Kubba (removed 16 February 1960)
Agriculture	Hudayb al-Hajj Hammad
Communications	Hasan al-Talibani
Defense	'Abd al-Karim Qasim
Development	Talat al-Shaybani
Economics	Ibrahim Kubba (removed 16 February 1960)
Education	Muhyi Din 'Abd al-Hamid
Finance	Muhammad Hadid
Foreign Affairs	Hasim Jawad

*The Ministries of Defense and Foreign Affairs were taken from the Iraqi cabinet and attached to the Union government.

Guidance	Husayn Jamil (removed 10 February 1959)
	Fuad 'Arif (acting)
	Faisal al-Samir (appointed July 1959; removed 14 May 1961)
Health	Muhammad al-Shawwaf
Industry	Muhyi al-Din Hamid
Interior	Ahmad Muhammad Yahya
Justice	Mustafa Ali (removed 5 April 1961)
Municipalities	Naziha al-Dulaymi (appointed July 1959; dropped to state on 5 March 1969)
Oil	Muhammad Salman
Planning	Talat al-Shaybani
Social Affairs	'Abd al-Wahhab Amin
State	Fuad 'Arif
	Naziha al-Dulaymi (appointed 3 May 1960; removed 15 November 1960)
Works	Baba Ali (removed 2 July 1959)
Works/Housing	Awni Yusuf (appointed July 1959; removed 15 November 1960)

President: 'Abd al-Salam 'Arif; Prime Minister: Ahmad Hasan al-Bakr (8 February 1963– 18 November 1963)

Agrarian Reform	Sadun Hammadi
Agriculture	Baba Ali
Commerce	Shukri Salih Zaki
Communications'	Abd al-Sattar 'Abd al-Latif
Defense	Salih Mahdi Ammash
Deputy P.M.	Ali Salih al-Sa'di
Education	Ahmad 'Abd al-Sattar al-Juwari
Finance	Salih Kubba
	Muhammad Jawad al-Ubasi (appointed 13 May 1963)
Foreign Affairs	Talib Husayn Shabib
Guidance	Musari al-Rawi
	Ali Salih al-Sa'di (appointed 13 May 1963)
Health	Izzat Mustafa
Industry	Naji Talib
Interior	Ali Salih al-Sa'di

	Hazim Jawad (appointed 13 May 1963)
Justice	Mahdi al-Dawlai
Municipalities	Mahmud Sheeth Khattab
Oil	'Abd al-Aziz al-Wattari
Planning	'Abd al-Karim al-Ali
Settlement	'Abd al-Sattar Ali al-Husayn
Social Affairs	Hamid al-Khalkhal (removed November 1963)
	Hamdi 'Abd al-Majid
State	Fuad Arif
State/Presidential Affairs	Hazim Jawad
State/Union Affairs	Musari al-Rawi (named 13 May 1963)

President: 'Abd al-Salam 'Arif; Prime Minister: Tahir Yahya (18 November 1963–3 September 1965)

Communications	'Abd al-Sattar 'Abd al-Latif (removed 14 December 1963)
Defense	Hardan al-Takriti (removed 2 March 1964)
	Tahir Yahya
Economics	Aziz Hafiz (removed 10 July 1965)
	Qasim 'Abd al-Hamid
Education	Khadir 'Abd al-Ghafir (appointed July 1965)
Foreign Affairs	Subih 'Abd al-Hamid
Guidance	'Abd al-Karim Farhan
	'Abd al-Rahman Khalid al-Qaysi (appointed July 1965)
Industry	Adib al-Jadir (removed 10 July 1965)
	Jamil al-Malaika
Interior	Rashid Musleh
	Subih 'Abd al-Hamid (appointed November 1964; removed 10 July 1965)
	'Abd al-Latif al-Darraji
Justice	'Abd al-Sattar Ali al-Husayn (removed 10 July 65)
Oil	'Abd al-'Aziz al-Wattari
Rural Affairs	Fuad al-Rikabi (appointed November 1964; removed 10 July 1965)
	Ahmad 'Abd al-Hadi al-Habboubi
Unity	'Abd al-Razzaq Muhyi al-Din (removed 10 July 1965)
Vice President	Ahmad Hasan al-Bakr (position abolished 4 January 1964)

President: 'Abd al-Salam 'Arif; Prime Minister: 'Arif 'Abd al-Razzaq (6 September 1965–16 September 1965)

Agrarian Reform	'Abd al-Rahman Khalid al-Qaysi
Agriculture	Akram al-Jaf
Communications	Ismael Mustafa
Culture/Guidance	Muhammad Nasir
Defense	'Arif 'Abd al-Razzaq (acting)
Deputy P.M.	'Abd al-Rahman al-Bazzaz
Economics	Shukri Salih Zaki
Education	Khidr 'Abd al-Ghafur
Finance	Salman 'Abd al-Razzaq al-Aswad
Foreign Affairs	'Abd al-Rahman al-Bazzaz
Health	'Abd al-Latif al-Badri
Industry	Mustafa 'Abdullah
Interior	'Abd al-Latif al-Darraji
Justice	Husayn Muhammad al-Sa'id
Labor/Social Affairs	Jamal Umar Nazmi
Municipal/Rural Affairs	Ismael Mustafa (acting)
Oil	'Abd al-Rahman al-Bazzaz
Planning	Mustafa 'Abdullah (acting)
State	Salman al-Safwani
Union Affairs	'Abd al-Razzaq Muhyi al-Din
Waqf	'Abd al-Rahman Khalid al Qays
Works/Housing	Ja'far Alawi

President: 'Abd al-Salam 'Arif (died 3 April 1966); Prime Minister: 'Abd al-Rahman al-Bazzaz (21 September 1965–18 April 1966)

Agrarian Reform	Faris Nasir al-Hasan (acting)
Agriculture	Akram al-Jaf
Culture/Guidance	Muhammad Nasir
Defense	'Abd al-Aziz al-Uqayli
Economics	'Abd al-Hamid al-Hilali
Education	Khidr 'Abd al-Ghafur
Finance	Shukri Salih Zaki
Foreign Affairs	'Abd al-Rahman al-Bazzaz
Health	'Abd al-Latif al-Badri
Industry	Mustafa 'Abdullah (died 3 April 1966)
Interior	'Abd al-Latif al-Darraji (died 3 April 1966)
Justice	Qasim al-Rawwaf
Labor/Social Affairs	Faris Nasir al-Hasan
Municipal/Village	Ismael Mustafa

Oil	Shukri Salih Zaki (acting)
Planning	Salman 'Abd al-Razzaq al-Aswad
State	Salman al-Safwani
Union Affairs	'Abd al-Razzaq Muhyi al-Din
Waqf	Khidr 'Abd al-Ghafur (acting)
Works/Housing	Ismael Mustafa (acting)

President: 'Abd al-Rahman 'Arif; Prime Minister: 'Abd al-Rahman al-Bazzaz (18 April 1966–6 August 1966)

Agrarian Reform	Faris Nasir al-Hasan
Agriculture	Akram al-Jaf
Culture/Guidance	Muhammad Nasir
Defense	Shakir Mahmud Shukri
Economics	'Abd al-Hamid al-Hilali
Education	Khidr 'Abd al-Ghafur
Finance	Shukri Salih Zaki
Foreign Affairs	Adnan al-Pachachi
Health	'Abd al-Latif al-Badri
Industry	Sadiq Jalal
Interior	'Abd al-Rahman al-Bazzaz
Justice	Qasim al-Rawwaf
Labor/Social Affairs	Muhammad al-Abta
Municipal/Village	Ismael Mustafa
Oil	Shukri Salih Zaki
Planning	Salman 'Abd al-Razzaq al-Aswad
State	Salman al-Safwani
Union Affairs	'Abd al-Razzaq Muhyi al-Din
Waqf	Khidr 'Abd al-Ghafur
Works/Housing	Ismael Mustafa

President: 'Abd al-Rahman 'Arif; Prime Minister: Naji Talib (6 August 1966–10 May 1967)

Agrarian Reform/ Agriculture	Ahmad Mahdi al-Dujayli
Arab Unity Affairs	Gharbi al-Hajj Ahmad
Communications	Ismael Mustafa
Culture/Guidance	Durayd al-Damluji
Defense	Shakir Mahmud Shukri
Deputy P.M.	Rajab 'Abd al-Majid
Economics	Qasim 'Abd al-Hamid
Education	'Abd al-Rahman al-Qaysi

Finance	'Abdullah al-Naqshabandi
Foreign Affairs	Adnan al-Pachachi
Health	Fuad Hasan Ghali
Industry	Khalid al-Shawi
Interior	Rajab 'Abd al-Majid
Justice	Muslih al-Naqshbandi
Labor/Social Affairs	Farid Fityan
Municipalities/Works	Dawud Sarsam
Oil	Naji Talib
Planning	Muhammad Yaqub al-Sa'idi
State/	
North Reconstruction	Ahmad Kamil Qadir
Transportation	Ismael Mustafa

President: 'Abd al-Rahman 'Arif; Prime Minister: 'Abd al-Rahman 'Arif (10 May 1967–19 July 1967)

Agrarian Reform	'Abd al-Karim Farhan
Agriculture	'Abd al-Majid al-Jumayyid
Communications	Fadhil Muhsin al-Hakim
Culture/Guidance	Ahmad Mutlab
Defense	Shakir Mahmud Shukri
Economics	Qasim 'Abd al-Hamid
Education	'Abd al-Rahman al-Qaysi
Finance	'Abd al-Rahman al-Habib
Foreign Affairs	Adnan al-Pachachi
Health	'Abd al-Karim Hani (acting)
Industry	Khalid al-Shawi
Interior	'Abd al-Sattar 'Abd al-Latif
Justice	Muslih al-Naqshbandi
Labor/Social Affairs	'Abd al-Karim Hani
Municipalities/Works	Ihsan Shirzad
Oil	'Abd al-Sattar al-Husayn
Planning	Muhammad Yaqub al-Sa'idi
Reconstruction of North	Fuad 'Arif
State	Gharbi al-Hajj Ahmad
State	Ismael Khayrallah
State/Youth/Labor	Qasim Khalil
Union	'Abd al-Razzaq Muhyi al-Din
Vice Premier	Fuad 'Arif
	Ismael Mustafa
	'Abd al-Ghani al-Rawi
	Tahir Yahya

Tahir Yahya (April 1968)

Agrarian Reform/ Agriculture	'Abd al-Karim Farhan
Arab Unity	Shamal al-Samarai
Culture/Guidance	Malik Douhane al-Hassan
Defense	Shakir Mahmud Shukri
Economics	'Abd al-Karim Kannuna
Education	Taha al-Hajj Elias
Finance	'Abd al-Rahman al-Habib
Foreign Affairs	Ismael Khayrallah
Health	Jamal Ahmad Hamdi
Industry	Adib al-Jadir
Interior	Tahir Yahya
Justice	Muslih al-Naqshbandi
Labor/Social Affairs	'Abd al-Karim Hani
Northern Affairs	'Abd al-Fattah al-Shami
Oil	'Abd al-Satter Ali al-Husayn
Planning	Muhammad Ya'qub al-Sa'idi
Public Works	Ihsan Shirzad
State	Faysal Sharhan al-Irs
State/Industry	Khalil Ibrahim
State/Presidency	Ismail Khayrallah
Youth	Yasin Khalil

'Abd al-Razzaq al-Nayif (17 July 1968–30 July 1968; removed 29 July 1968)

Agrarian Reform	'Abd al-Majid al-Jumayli
Agriculture	Muhsin al-Qazwini
Arab Unity Affairs	Jasim Kazim al-Azzawi
Communications	Mahmud Shith Khattab
Culture/Guidance	Taha al-Hajj Ilyas
Defense	Ibrahim 'Abd al-Rahman al-Dawud (removed 30 July 1968)
Economics	'Abdullah al-Naqshabandi
Education	Ahmad 'Abd al-Sattar al-Jawari
Finance	Salih Kubba
Foreign Affairs	Nasir al-Hani
Health	Izzat Mustafa
Industry	Khalid Makki al-Hashimi
Interior	Salih Mahdi 'Ammash

Justice	Muslih al-Naqshabandi
Labor/Social Affairs	Anwar 'Abd al-Qadir al-Hadithi
Municipalities/	
Rural Affairs	Ghaib Mawlud Mukhlis
Oil/Mineral Resources	Mahdi Hantush
Planning	Muhammad Yaqub al-Sa'idi
Public Works/Housing	Ihsan Shirzad
Reconstruction of North	Muhsin Dizai
State/Liason with RCC	Kazim Mu'Alla
State/Presidential Affairs	Rashid al-Rifa'i
State/Waqf	'Abd al-Karim Zaydan
Without Portfolio	Naji al-Khalaf
	Kahdim al-Mu'Alla
Youth Affairs	Dhiyab al-Alkawi

Ahmad Hasan al-Bakr (30 July 1968–31 December 1969)

Agrarian Reform	Jasim Kazim al-Azzawi
Agriculture	'Abd al-Husayn al-Attiya
Arab Unity	'Abdullah Sulayman al-Khubayr Fadhil
Culture/Information	'Abdullah Sallum al-Samarra'i
Defense	Hardan al-Takriti
Economy	Fakhri Qadduri
Education	Ahmad 'Abd al-Sattar al-Jawari
Finance	Amin 'Abd al-Karim
Foreign Affairs	'Abd al-Karim al-Shaykhli
Health	Izzat Mustafa
Housing	Taha Muhyi al-Din Ma'ruf
Industry	Khalid Makki al-Hashimi
Interior	Salih Mahdi 'Ammash
Justice	Mahdi al-Dawlai
Labor/Social Affairs	Anwar 'Abd al-Qadir al-Hadithi
Municipalities	Ghalib Mawlud Mukhlis
Oil/Mineral Resources	Rashid al-Rifa'i
Planning	Hashim Jawwad
State	Taha Muhyi al-Din Ma'ruf
State	Adnan Ayyub Sabri
State/Presidency	Hamid al-Juburi
State/Waqf	Muhammad al-Karbuli
Transport	Mahmud Shitt Khattab
Youth	Shafiq al-Kamali

Ahmad Hasan al-Bakr (31 December 1969–29 March 1970)

Agrarian Reform	Izzat Ibrahim
Agriculture	Mawlud Kamil al-'Abd
	Salah Umar Ali (appointed 7 March 1970)
Arab Unity/	
Northern Affairs	'Abdullah Sulayman Fadhil al-Khudayri
Communications	Adnan Ayyub Sabri
Culture/Information	Hamid Alwan al-Juburi
Defense	Hardan al-Takriti
Economy	Fakhri Qadduri
Education	Sad 'Abd al-Baqi
Finance	Amin 'Abd al-Karim
Foreign Affairs	'Abd al-Karim al-Shaykhli
Health	Izzat Mustafa
Higher Education/	
Research	Suad Khalil Isma'il
Industry	Khalid Makki al-Hashimi
Interior	Salih Mahdi 'Ammash
Irrigation	Taha Ibrahim 'Abdullah
Justice	Aziz Sharif
Labor/Social Affairs	Anwar 'Abd al-Qadir al-Hadithi
Municipalities	Ghalib Mawlud Mukhlis
Oil/Mineral Resources	Sadun Hammadi
Planning	Jawad Hashim
State	Taha Muhyi al-Din Ma'ruf
	Rashid al-Rifa'i
	'Abdullah Sallum al-Samarra'i
State/Presidency	Ahmad 'Abd al-Sattar Jawari
State/Waqf	Hamad Dalli al-Karbuli
Transport	Adnan Ayyub Sabri
Works/Housing	Taha Muhyi al-Din Ma'ruf
Youth	Shafiq al-Kamali

Ahmad Hasan al-Bakr (29 March 1970–3 April 1970)

Agrarian Reform	Izzat Ibrahim
Agriculture	Nafidh Jalal
Communication	Adnan Ayyub Sabri
Construction of North	Muhammad Mahmud
Culture/Information	Salah Umar Ali
Defense	Hardan al-Tikriti

Economy	Fakhri Qadduri
Education	Sa'd 'Abd al-Baqi
Finance	Amin 'Abd al-Karim
Foreign Affairs	'Abd al-Karim al-Shaykhli
Health	Izzat Mustafa
Higher Education/ Research	Suad Khalil Isma'il
Industry	Taha Yasin Ramadan
Interior	Salih Mahdi 'Ammash
Irrigation	Taha Ibrahim 'Abdullah
Justice	Aziz Sharif
Labor/Social Affairs	Murtada Sa'id al-Hadithi
Municipalities	Ihsan Shirzad
Oil/Mineral Resources	Sa'dun Hammadi
Planning	Jawad Hashim
Public Works/Housing	Nuri Shawish
State	Rashid al-Rifa'i
	Salih Yusifi
State/Military Affairs	Khalid Makki al-Hashimi
State/Presidency	Ahmad 'Abd al-Sattar al-Jawari
Transport	Anwar 'Abd al-Qadir al-Hadithi
Unity	'Abdullah Khudayri
Works/Housing	Nuri Shawish
Youth	Hamid al-Juburi

Ahmad Hasan al-Bakr (3 April 1970–15 May 1972)

Agrarian Reform	Izzat Ibrahim
Agriculture	Nafidh Jalal
Communication	Adnan Ayyub Sabri
Construction of North	Muhammad Mahmud
Culture/Information	Salah Umar Ali
Defense	Hamad Shihab
Economy	Fakhri Qadduri
Education	Sa'd 'Abd al-Baqi
Finance	Amin 'Abd al-Karim
Foreign Affairs	'Abd al-Karim al-Shaykhli
	Murtada al-Hadithi (appointed October 1971)
Health	Izzat Mustafa
Higher Education/Research	Suad Khalil Ismail

Industry	Taha Yasin Ramadan
Interior	Sa'dun Ghaydan
Irrigation	Taha Ibrahim 'Abdullah
Justice	Aziz Sharif
Labor/Social Affairs	Murtada al-Hadithi
Municipalities	Ihsan Shirzad
Oil/Mineral Resources	Sa'dun Hammadi
Planning	Jawad Hashim
	Rashid al-Rifa'I
	(appointed January 1971)
Public Works/Housing	Nuri Shawish
State	Rashid al-Rifa'i
	Salih Yusifi
	'Abdullah Sallum al-Samarra'i
State/Military Affairs	Khalid Makki al-Hashimi
State/Presidency	Ahmad 'Abd al-Sattar Jawari
Transport	Anwar 'Abd al-Qadir al-Hadithi
Unity	'Abdullah Khudayri
Works/Housing	Nuri Shawish
Youth	Hamid al-Juburi

Ahmad Hasan al-Bakr (15 May 1972–11 November 1974)

Agrarian Reform	Izzat Ibrahim*
Agriculture	Nafidh Jalal (died 10 July 1972)
	Izzat Ibrahim
Communication	Rashid al-Rifa'i
Construction of North	Muhammad Mahmud
Defense	Hammad Shihab (killed 30 June 1973)
	Rashid al-Rifa'i (acting; appointed July 1973)
Economy	Hikmat Ibrahim al-Azzawi
Education	Ahmad 'Abd al-Sattar Jawari
Finance	Amin 'Abd al-Karim
Foreign Affairs	Murtada al-Hadithi
	Shathil Taqa (appointed June 1974;
	died 20 October 1974)
Health	Izzat Mustafa
Higher Education/	
Research	Hisham al-Shawi

*The Ministries of Agrarian Reform and Agriculture merged in November 1972; Izzat Ibrahim retains the portfolio.

Industry	Taha Yasin Ramadan
Information	Hamid Alwan al-Juburi
Interior	Sa'dun Ghaydan
Irrigation	Mukarram al-Talabani
Justice	Muhammad Rida al-Safi
	'Abdullah al-Khadduri
	(appointed 24 December 1973)
Municipalities	Ihsan Shirzad
Oil/Mineral Resources	Sa'dun Hammadi
Planning	Jawad Hashim
Public Works/Housing	Nuri Shawish
	Muhsin Desayee (appointed August 1973)
State	Nazar al-Tabaqchali
	Amir 'Abdullah
	Salih Yusifi
	Nuri Shawish (appointed August 1973)
	Aziz Sharif
Transport	Khalid Makki al-Hashimi
	Nizar al-Tabaqjali (acting;
	appointed 1 July 1972)
	Nihad Kakhri al-Khaffaf
	(appointed April 1973)
Unity	'Abdullah Sulayman Fadil al-Khudayri
Work/Social Affairs	Anwar 'Abd al-Qadir al-Hadithi
Youth	Adnan Ayyub Sabri al-'Izzi

Ahmad Hasan al-Bakr (11 November 1974–10 May 1976)

Agrarian Reform/ Agriculture	Hasan Fahmi Jumaa
Communications	Sa'dun Ghaydan
Defense	Ahmad Hasan al-Bakr
Economy	Hikmat al-Azzawi*
Education	Muhammad Mahjub
Finance	Saadi Ibrahim (died 8 October 1975)
Foreign Affairs	Sa'dun Hammadi
Foreign Trade	Hikmat al-Azzawi*
Health	Izzat Mustafa

*The Ministry of Economy was abolished in January 1976, and the Ministries of Foreign Trade and Internal Trade were created in its place.

Higher Education/	
Scientific Research	Ghanim 'Abd al-Jalil
Industry	Taha Yasin Ramadan
Information	Tariq Aziz
Interior	Izzat Ibrahim
Internal Trade	Hasan Ali*
Irrigation	Mukarram al-Talbani
Justice	Munzir al-Shawi
Labor/Social Affairs	Anwar 'Abd al-Kadir al-Hadithi
Municipalities	'Abd al-Sattar Tahir Sharif
Oil	Tayih 'Abd al-Karim
Planning	Taha Yasin Ramadan (acting)
Public Works	Rashid al-Rifa'i
State	Ahmad 'Abd al-Sattar al-Jawari
	Hamed al-Jebouri
	Aziz 'Aqrawi
	Hishan al-Shawi
	'Abdullah al-Khodeir
	'Amir 'Abdullah
	Aziz Sherif
	'Abdullah Ismael Ahmad
	'Ubayd-Allah al-Barzani
State/Foreign Affairs	Hisham al-Shawi (appointed June 1975)
Transport	Adnan Ayub Subri
Unity Affairs	'Abdullah al-Khudhayri
Youth	Na'im Haddad

Ahmad Hasan al-Bakr (10 May 1976–23 January 1977)

Agrarian Reform/	
Agriculture	Hasan Fahmi Juma'a
Communications	Sa'dun Ghaydan
Defense	Ahmad Hasan al-Bakr
Education	Muhammad Mahjub
Finance	Fawzi al-Qaisi
Foreign Affairs	Sa'dun Hammadi
Foreign Trade	Hikmat al-Azzawi
Health	Riyadh Ibrahim Husayn
Higher Education/	
Scientific Research	Ghanim 'Abd al-Jalil
Industry	Fulayih Hasan Jasim
Information	Tariq Aziz

Interior	Izzat Ibrahim
Internal Trade	Hasan al-Amri
Irrigation	Mukarram al-Talabani
Justice	Munthir al-Shawi
Labor/Social Affairs	Izzat Mustafa
Municipalities	Amir 'Abd al-Qadir
Oil	Tayih 'Abd al-Karim
Planning	Adnan al-Hamdani
Public Works	Taha Yasin Ramadan
State	Aziz Aqrawi
	'Amir 'Abdullah
	'Abdullah Isma'il Ahmad
	Ubayd Allah al-Barzani
Transport	'Abd al-Sattar Tahir Sharif
Waqfs	Ahmad 'Abd al-Sattar al-Jawari
Youth	Na'im Haddad

Ahmad Hasan al-Bakr (23 January 1977–15 October 1977)

Agrarian Reform/	
Agriculture	Hasan Fahmi Juma'a
	Latif Nusayyif Jasim
	(appointed 5 April 1977)
Communications	Sa'dun Ghaydan
Defense	Ahmad Hasan al-Bakr
Education	Muhammad Mahjub
Finance	Fawzi al-Qaisi
Foreign Affairs	Sa'dun Hammadi
Foreign Trade	Hasan Ali (acting)*
Health	Riyadh Ibrahim Husayn
Higher Education/	
Scientific Research	Muhammad al-Mashat
Industry	Najib Muhammed Khalil
Information	Tariq Aziz
Interior	Izzat Ibrahim
Internal Trade	Hasan Ali*
Irrigation	Mukarram al-Talabani
Justice	Munthir al-Shawi
Labor/Social Affairs	Babakr al-Pishadari

*Ministries for Foreign Trade and Internal Trade merged into the Ministry of trade in early 1977.

Municipalities	Izzat Mustafa (dismissed March 1977) †
Oil	Tayih 'Abd al-Karim
Planning	Adnan Husayn al-Hamdani
Public Works	Taha Yasin Ramadan
State	'Ubayd Allah al-Barzani
	'Aziz 'Aqrawi
	'Abdullah Ismael Ahmad
	'Amir 'Abdullah
	Na'im Haddad ‡
	Ghanim 'Abd al-Jalil‡
	Tahir al-'Ani‡
	'Abd al-Fattah Muhammad Amin‡
	Sa'dun Shakir‡
	Ja'far Qasim Hammudi‡
	'Abdullah Fadhl‡
	Fulayih Hasan Jasim
	(dismissed March 1977)
	Hikmat Ibrahim al-'Azzawi‡
	Muhammad 'Ayish‡
State/Kurdistan	Burhanndin 'Abd al-Rahman
	(appointed 5 April 1977)
State/Foreign Affairs	Hamid Alwan al-Jebouri
Transport/	
Communications	'Abd al-Sattar Tahir Sharif
	Aziz Aqrawi (appointed 22 June 1977)
Waqfs	Ahmad 'Abd al-Sattar al-Jawari
Youth	Burhan al-Din 'Abd al-Rahman
	Karim Mahmud (appointed 5 April 1977)

Ahmad Hasan al-Bakr (15 October 1977–16 July 1979)

Agrarian Reform/	
Agriculture	Latif Nusayyif Jasim
Communications	Sa'dun Ghaydan
Culture/Arts	Sa'd Qasim Hammudi (acting)
	Karim Mahmud Shintaf
	(appointed 12 Novemebr 1977)
Defense	Adnan Khayrallah
Education	Muhammad Mahjub
Finance	Fawzi al-Qaisi

†Ministry of Municipalities abolished on 11 May 1977.
‡On 4 September 1977, these ministers were relieved of their duties by virtue of their election to the Revolutionary Command Council.

Foreign Affairs	Sa'dun Hammadi
Health	Riyadh Ibrahim Husayn
Higher Education/	
Scientific Research	Muhammad al-Mashat
	Adnan Husayn al-Hamdani
	(appointed 13 February 1978)
	Issam 'Abd Ali (appointed April 1978)
Industry	Najib Muhammad Khalil
	Muhammad Ayesh
	(appointed 13 February 1978)
Information	Sa'd Qasim Hammoudi
Interior	Izzat Ibrahim
Irrigation	Mukarram al-Talabani
	'Abd al-Wahhab Mahmud 'Abdullah
	(appointed 12 November 1977)
Justice	Munthir al-Shawi
Labor/Social Affairs	Babakr al-Pishadari
Oil	Tayih 'Abd al-Karim
Planning	Adnan Husayn al-Hamdani
Public Works	Taha Yasin Ramadan
State	Ubayd Allah al-Barzani
	Aziz Aqraq
	'Abdullah Ismael Ahmad
	Amir 'Abdullah (dismissed 25 April 1978)
	'Aziz 'Aqrawi (appointed
	12 Novemebr 1977)
	Hashim Hasan (appointed
	12 November 1977)
State/Kurdistan	Burhan al-Din 'Abd al-Rahman
	Khalid 'Abd Othman
	(appointed 13 February 1978)
State/Foreign Affairs	Hamid Alwan al-Jebouri
Transport/	
Communications	Aziz Aqzawi
	Mukarram al-Talabani
	(12 November 1977–May 1978)
Waqfs	Ahmad 'Abd al-Sattar al-Jawari
Youth	Karim Mahmud

Saddam Husayn (16 July 1979–27 June 1982)

Agrarian Reform/Agriculture	Amir Mahdi Salih
Culture/Information	Latif Nusayyif Jasim

Defense	Adnan Khayrallah
Deputy P.M./First	Taha Yasin Ramadan
Deputy P.M.	Tariq Aziz
	Sa'dun Ghaydan
	Na'im Haddad
	(removed 30 June 1980)
	Adnan Khayrallah
	Adnan Husayn al-Hamdani
Education	Muhammad Mahjub
	'Abd al-Jabbar 'Abd al-Majid
	(appointed 12 August 1979)
	'Abd al-Kadir Izzadin
	(appointed 26 July 1981)
Finance	Thamir Razzuqi
Foreign Affairs	Sa'dun Hammadi
Health	Riyadh Ibrahim Husayn
Higher Education/	
Scientific Research	Issam Abed Ali
	Jasim Muhammad Khalaf
	(appointed 12 August 1979)
	'Abd al-Razzaq Qasim al-Hashimi
	(appointed 26 July 1981)
Housing/Construction	Muhammad Fadhil Husayn
Industry	Tahir al-Ani
Interior	Sa'dun Shakir
Irrigation	'Abd al-Wahhab Mahmud 'Abdullah
Justice	Munthir Ibrahim
Labor/Social Affairs	Bakr Mahmud Rasoul
Local Government	'Abd al-Fattah al-Yasin
Oil	Tayih 'Abd al-Karim
Planning	Taha Ibrahim al-'Abdullah
	Thamir Razzuqi
	(acting; appointed 28 December 1981)
State	Hasem Hasan
	'Abdullah Ismael
	Aziz Rashid
	Arshad Ahmad al-Zibari
	(appointed 29 October 1980)
	Ubayd Allah al-Barzani
State/Foreign Affairs	Hamed Alwan al-Jiburi
State/Kurdish Affairs	Khaled 'Abd Othman
Trade	Hasan Ali

Transport/Communications	Sa'dun Ghaydan
Waqfs	Ahmad 'Abd al-Sattar
	Nuri Faysal Shahir
	(appointed 13 November 1979)
	'Abd al-Ghani 'Abd al-Ghafour
	(appointed January 1982)
Youth	'Abd al-Karim Mahmud Husayn

Saddam Husayn (27 June 1982–23 March 1991)

Agrarian Reform/	
Agriculture	Sadiq 'Abd al-Latif Yunis
	Aziz Salih Hasan al-Nu'man (appointed 10 August 1986)
Agriculture/Irrigation	Karim Hasan Ridha
	'Abdullah Badr Danoun (acting; appointed 8 March 1989; dismissed 3 October 1989)
	'Abd al-Wahhab Mahmud al-Sabbagh (appointed 3 March 1990)
Culture/Information	Latif Nusayyif Jasim
Defense	Adnan Khayrallah (5 May 1989)
	'Abd al-Jabbar Shanshal (appointed 5 May 1989)
	Saadi Tu'ma 'Abbas (appointed 12 December 1990)
Deputy P.M./First	Taha Yasin Ramadan
Deputy P.M.	Tariq Aziz
	Na'im Haddad
	Adnan Khayrallah (died 5 May 1989)
	Sa'dun Hammadi
	(appointed 5 June 1989)
Education	'Abd al-Kadir Izzadin
Finance	Thamir Razzuqi
	Hisham Hassan Tawfiq
	(appointed 14 August 1983)
	Hikmat Omar Mukhaylif
	(appointed September 1987)
	Muhammad Mehdi Salih
	(appointed 7 October 1989)
Foreign Affairs	Sa'dun Hammadi
	Tariq Aziz
	(appointed 24 January 1983)

Health   Sadiq Hamid Allush
                                   (dismissed 11 May 1988)
                               'Abd al-Salem Muhammad Saeed
                                   (appointed 1 August 1988)
Heavy Industry   Qasim Ahmad Taqi al-Uraibi
                                   (appointed March 1987)
                               'Abd al-Tawab 'Abdullah Mulla Hawaish
                                   (appointed 22 September 1987)
Higher Education/
   Scientific Research   'Abd al-Razzaq Qasim al-Hashimi
                               'Abd al-Qadir Izzadin
                                   (appointed December 1983)
                               Samir Muhammad 'Abd al-Wahhab
                                   (appointed 25 July 1985) (left 4
                                   August 1987)
                               Munthir Ibrahim (appointed
                                   16 January1988)
Housing   Muhammad Fadhil Husayn
                               Tahir Muhammad Hassun al-Marzuq
                                   (appointed 31 March 1988)
Industry   Subhi Yasin Khudhayr
Industry/Minerals   Husayn Kemil
Industry/
   Military Industry   Husayn Kemil
Interior   Sa'dun Shakir
                               Samir Muhammad 'Abd al-Wahhab
                                   (appointed 4 August 1987)
                               Ali Hasan al-Majid (appointed
                                   6 March 1991)
Irrigation   'Abd al-Wahhab Mahmud 'Abdullah
Justice   Munthir Ibrahim
                               Akram 'Abd al-Qadir Ali
                                   (appointed 16 January 1988)
Labor/Social Affairs   Bakr Mahmud Rasoul
                               Umeed Madhat Mubarak
                                   (appointed 3 January 1989)
Light Industry   Tariq al-'Abdullah
                                   (died 17 December 1986)
                               Qasim Ahmad Taqi al-Uraibi
                                   (appointed 17 December 1986)
                               Hatem 'Abd al-Rashid
                                   (appointed 1 February 1987)

Local Government	Sadi 'Ayyash 'Araym
	Kamil Yasin Rashid
	Adnan Dawud Salman
	(appointed December 1983)
	Ali Hasan al-Majid
	(appointed 2 June 1989)
Oil	Qasim Ahmad Taqi al-'Uraibi
	'Abd al-Rahman al-Chalabi
	(appointed March 1987)
	Husayn Kamil (acting; appointed
	28 October 1990)
Planning	Amal Najid Faraj
State	Hashim Hasan
	Ubayd Allah al-Barzani
	'Abdullah Ahmad
	(dismissed 11 February 1989)
	Arshad Ahmad al-Zibari
	Sa'dun Hammadi (appointed 24 January 1983;
	dismissed November 1984)
State/Foreign Affairs	Hamid Alwan (dismissed 1 October 1984)
	Sa'dun Hammadi (appointed
	25 July 1988; left 5 June 1989)
	Muhammad Sa'id al-Sahhaf
	(appointed October 1990)
State/	
Military Affairs	'Abd al-Jabbar Shanshal
	(appointed January 1984)
Trade	Hasan Ali
	Muhammad Mehdi Salih
	(appointed 4 August 1987)
Transport/	
Communications	'Abd al-Jabbar 'Abd al-Rahim al-Asadi
	Muhammad Hamza al-Zubaydi
	(appointed March 1987)
Waqfs	'Abdullah Fadhil Abbas
Without Portfolio	Muhammad Hamza al-Zubaydi
	'Abd al-Ghani 'Abd al-Ghafur
	Samir Muhammad 'Abd al-Wahhab
	'Abd al-Hasan Rahi Far 'Awn
	Sadi Mahdi Salih
	Mizban Khidr Hadi
	Khaled 'Abd al-Moneim

Youth   Ahmad Husayn al-Samarra'i
                               Nuri Faysal Shahir (died 17 June 1986)
                               'Abd al-Fattah al-Yasin
                                  (appointed 10 August 1986)*
                                  (dismissed 11 May 1988)

Agrarian Reform/
  Agriculture and
  Irrigation   Merge in September 1987
Heavy Industry
  and Industry   Merge into Industry/Minerals on
                                  26 March 1988
Industry/Military
  Industrialization   Created 13 July 1988
Youth   Dissolved on 28 September 1987
Local Government   Abolished on 6 March 1991

Sa'dun Hammadi (23 March 1991–13 September 1991)

Agriculture/Irrigation   'Abd al-Wahhab al-Sabbagh
Culture/Information   Hamad Yusuf Hammadi
Defense   Sa'di Tu'ma 'Abbas
                              Husayn Kemil (appointed 6 April 1991)
Deputy P.M.   Tariq Aziz
                              Muhammad Hamza al-Zubaydi
Education   Hikmat 'Abdullah al-Bazzaz
Finance   Majid 'Abd Ja'far
Foreign Affairs   Ahmad Husayn Khudhayr
Health   'Abd al-Salam Muhammad Sa'id
Higher Education   'Abd al-Razzaq Qasim al-Hashimi
Housing   Mahmud Dhujab al-Ahmad
Industry/Military
  Industrial   Husayn Kemil
                              Amir Hammudi al-Sadi
                                 (appointed 6 April 1991)
Interior   Ali Hasan al-Majid
Justice   Shabib al-Malki
Labor/Social Affairs   Umid Midhat Mubarak
Oil   Husayn Kemil (acting)
                              Usamah 'Abd al-Razzaq Hammadi
                                 al-Hithi (appointed 27 May 1991)
Planning   Samal Majid Faraj
State   Arshad Ahmad Uhammad al-Zibari
State/Foreign Affairs   Muhammad Sa'id Kazim al-Sahhaf

State/Military Affairs   'Abd al-Jabbar Shanshal
State/Oil Affairs   Usamah 'Abd al-Razzaq Hammadi al-Hithi
Trade   Muhammad Mahdi Salih
Transport/
  Communications   'Abd al-Sattar Ahmad al-Maini
Waqf   'Abdullah Fadhil Abbas

Muhammad Hamza al-Zubaydi
(13 September 1991–5 September 1993)

Agriculture/Irrigation   'Abd al-Wahhab al-Sabbagh
Culture/Information   Hamad Yusuf Hammadi
Defense   Husayn Kemil
                                 Ali Hasan al-Majid
                                     (appointed 13 November 1991)
Deputy P.M.   Tariq Aziz
Education   Hikmat 'Abdullah al-Bazzaz
Finance   Majid 'Abd Ja'far
                                 Ahmad Husayn Khudhayr
                                     (appointed 30 July 1992)
Foreign Affairs   Ahmad Husayn Khudhayr
                                 Muhammad Sa'id al-Sahhaf
                                     (appointed 30 July 1992)
Health   'Abd al-Salam Muhammad Sa'id
Higher Education   'Abd al-Razzaq Qasim al-Hashimi
                                 Humam 'Abd al-Khaliq 'Abd al-Ghafur
                                     (appointed 30 July 1992)
Housing   Mahmud Dhujab al-Ahmad
Industry/Minerals   Amir Hammudi al-Sa'di
Interior   Ali Hasan al-Majid
                                 Watban Ibrahim al-Hasan
                                     (appointed 13 November 1991)
Justice   Shabib al-Maliki
Labor/Social Affairs   Umid Midhat Mubarak
Oil   Usamah 'Abd al-Razzaq Hammadi al-Hiti
Planning   Samal Majid Faraj
State/Foreign Affairs   Muhammad Sa'id Kazim al-Sahhaf
State/Military Affairs   'Abd al-Jabbar Shanshal
Trade   Muhammad Mahdi Salih
Transport/
  Communications   'Abd al-Sattar Ahmad al-Maini
Waqf   'Abdullah Fadhil Abbas

Ahmad Husayn Khudhayr (5 September 1993–29 May 1994)

Agriculture	Bashir Alwan Hammadi
	Nizar Jumah Ali al-Qasir
	(appointed 25 May 1994)
Culture/Information	Hamad Yusuf Hammadi
Defense	Ali Hasan al-Majid
Deputy P.M.	Tariq Aziz
Education	Hikmat 'Abdullah al-Bazzaz
Finance	Ahmad Husayn Khudhayr (acting)
Foreign Affairs	Muhammad Sa'id al-Sahhaf
Health	Umid Midhat Mubarak
Higher Education	Human 'Abd al-Khaliq 'Abd al-Ghafur
Housing	Mahmud Dhujab al-Ahmad
Industry/Minerals	Husayn Kamil
Interior	Watban Ibrahim al-Hasan
Irrigation	Nizar Jumah Ali al-Qasir
Justice	Shabib al-Maliki
Labor/Social Affairs	Latif Nusayyif Jasim
Oil	Safa Hadi Jawad
Planning	Samal Majid Faraj
State	'Abd al-Wahhab Umar Mirza al-Atrushi
	Arshad Muhammad Ahmad Muhammad
	al-Zibari
State/Military Affairs	'Abd al-Jabbar Shanshal
Trade	Muhammad Mahdi Salih
Transport/	
Communications	Ahmad Murtadha Ahmad Khalil
Waqf	'Abd al-Mun'im Ahmad Salih

Saddam Husayn (29 May 1994–17 April 2001)

Agriculture	Nizar Jum'A Ali al-Qasir (acting)
	'Adbullah Hamid Mahmud al-Salih
Culture/Information*	Hamad Yusuf Hammadi
	Human 'Abd al-Khaliq 'Abd al-Ghafur
Culture	Hamad Yusuf Hammadi
Defense	Ali Hasan al-Majid
	Sultan Hashim Ahmad al-Jaburi Tai

*Culture and Information split into two ministries in February 2001.
†Planning Vacant in 2001.

Deputy P.M.	Tariq Aziz
	Taha Yasin Ramadan
	Muhammad Hamza al-Zubaydi
	Hikmat Mizban Ibrahim al-'Azzawi
	(appointed 30 July 1999)
Education	Hikmat 'Abdullah al-Bazzaz
	Fahd Salim Shaqrah
Finance	Ahmad Husayn Khudhayr (acting)
	Hikmat Mizban Ibrahim al-'Azzawi
Foreign Affairs	Muhammad Sa'id al-Sahhaf
Health	Umid Midhat Mubarak
Higher Education	Human 'Abd al-Khaliq 'Abd al-Ghafur
	'Abd al-Jabbar Tawfiq
	Human 'Abd al-Khaliq 'Abd al-Ghafur
Housing/	
Reconstruction	Mahmud Dhujab al-Ahmad
	Maan 'Abdullah al-Sarsam
Industry/Minerals	Husayn Kamil (defected August 1995)
	Adnan 'Abd al-Majid Jasim al-'Ani
Information	Muhammad Sa'id al-Sahhaf
	Human 'Abd al-Khaliq 'Abd al-Ghafur
Interior	Watban Ibrahim al-Hasan
	Muhammad Ziman 'Abd al-Razzaq
Irrigation	Nizar Jumah Ali al-Qasir
	(defected April 1996)
	Mahmud Dhuyab al-Ahmad
Justice	Shabib al-Maliki
	Mundhir Ibrahim al-Shawi
Labor/Social Affairs	Latif Nusayyif Jasim
	Sadi Tumah Abbas Jabburi
Oil	Safa Hadi Jawad
	'Amir Rashid Muhammad al-'Ubaydi
Planning†	Samal Majid Faraj (removed August 1994)
State	'Abd al-Wahhab Umar Mirza al-Atrushi
	Arshad Muhammad Ahmad Muhammad
	al-Zibari
State/Military Affairs	'Abd al-Jabbar Shanshal
Trade	Muhammad Mahdi Salih
Transport/	
Communications	Ahmad Murtada Ahmad Khalil
Waqf	'Abd al-Munim Ahmad Salih

Saddam Husayn (18 April 2001–9 April 2003)

Agriculture	'Adbullah Hamid Mahmud al-Salih
Culture	Hamad Yusuf Hammadi
Defense	Sultan Hashim Ahmad al-Jaburi Tai
Deputy P.M.	Tariq Aziz
	Muhammad Hamza al-Zubaydi
	(removed 23 June 2001)
	Hikmat Mizban Ibrahim al-'Azzawi
	Ahmad Hasan Khudayr
	(appointed July 2001)
	Abd al-Tawab Mullah al-Huwaysh
	(8 July 2001)
Education	Fahd Salim Shaqrah
Finance	Hikmat Mizban Ibrahim al-Azzawi
Foreign Affairs	Tariq Aziz (acting as of 18 April 2001)
	Mahmud Dhiyab al-Ahmad
	(appointed 23 June 2001)
	Naji Sabri (appointed 11 August 2001)
Health	Umid Midhat Mubarak
Higher Education	Human 'Abd al-Khaliq 'Abd al-Ghafur
Housing/	
Reconstruction	Maan 'Abdullah al-Sarsam
Industry/Minerals	Adnan 'Abd al-Majid Jasim al-'Ani
	Muyassar Raja Shalah
	(appointed August 2001)
Information	Muhammad Sa'id al-Sahhaf
Interior	Muhammad Ziman 'Abd al-Razzaq
	(removed June 2001)
	Mahmud Thiyab al-Ahmad
	(appointed 23 June 2001)
Irrigation	Nizar Jum'ah Ali al-Qasir
	(defected April 1996)
	Mahmud Dhuyab al-Ahmad
	(removed 23 June 2001)
	Rasul 'Abd al-Husayn al-Swadi
	(appointed 23 June 2001)
Justice	Mundhir Ibrahim al-Shawi
Labor/Social Affairs	Sadi Tu'ma 'Abbas al-Jaburi
	Mundhir Mudhaffar
	Muhammad Asad al-Naqshabandi
	(appointed August 2002)

Military
Industrialization   Abd al-Tawab Mullah al-Huwaysh
Oil   Amir Rashid Muhammad al-Ubaydi
                               Samir Abd al-'Aziz al-Najm
                                 (appointed 7 January 2003)
Planning   Vacant in 2001, 2002
                               Hasan Abd al-Mu'in al-Khattab
                                 (appointed August 2002)
State   'Abd al-Wahhab Umar Mirza al-Atrushi
                               Arshad Muhammad Ahmad Muhammad
                                 al-Zibari
State/Military Affairs   'Abd al-Jabbar Shanshal
Trade   Muhammad Mahdi Salih
Transport/
Communications   Ahmad Murtada Ahmad Khalil
Waqf   'Abd al-Munim Ahmad Salih

Appendix B
Revolutionary Command Councils, 1968–2003

July 1968–November 1969

Ahmad Hasan al-Bakr
Salih Mahdi 'Ammash
Hardan al-Tikriti
Sa'dun Ghaydan
Hammad Shihab

November 1969–March 1977

Ahmad Hasan al-Bakr (chairman)
Saddam Husayn (deputy chairman)
Salih Mahdi 'Ammash (dismissed 1971)
Hardan al-Tikriti (dismissed 1970)
Sa'dun Ghaydan
Hammad Shihab (murdered 1973)
'Abd al-Karim 'Abd al-Sattar al-Shaykhli (dismissed 1971)
'Abdullah Sallum al-Samarra'i (dismissed 1970)
Murtadha al-Hadithi (dismissed June 1974)
'Abd al-Khaliq al-Samarra'i (imprisoned 1973; executed 1979)
Izzat Ibrahim
Salah 'Umar al-'Ali (dismissed 1970)
Taha Yasin Ramadhan
Shafiq 'Abd al-Jabbar al-Kamali (dismissed 1970)
Izzat Mustafa (dismissed March 1977)

March 1977–September 1977

Ahmad Hasan al-Bakr (chairman)
Saddam Husayn (deputy chairman)
Sa'dun Ghaydan
Izzat Ibrahim
Taha Yasin Ramadhan

September 1977–July 1979

Ahmad Hasan al-Bakr (chairman)
Saddam Husayn (deputy chairman)
Sa'dun Ghaydan
Izzat Ibrahim
Taha Yasin Ramadhan
Na'im Haddad
Tayih 'Abd al-Karim
Muhammad Mahjub (dismissed and executed 1979)
Muhammad Ayish (executed 1979)
Adnan Husayn Abbas al-Hamdani (executed 1979)
Ghanim 'Abd al-Jalil (executed 1979)
Muhyi 'Abd al-Husayn al-Mashhadi (executed 1979)
Tahir al-'Ani
'Abd al-Fattah al-Yasin
Hasan 'Ali
Sa'dun Shakir
Ja'far Qasim Hammudi
'Abdullah Fadhil Abbas
Tariq 'Aziz
Adnan Khayralla
Hikmat Ibrahim al-'Azzawi
Burhan Mustafa

16 July 1979–29 June 1982

Saddam Husayn (chairman)
Sa'dun Ghaydan (deputy chairman)
Izzat Ibrahim
Taha Yasin Ramadhan
Na'im Haddad
Tahir al-'Ani
'Abd al-Fattah al-Yasin
Hasan 'Ali
Sa'dun Shakir
Ja'far Qasim Hammudi
'Abdullah Fadil Abbas
Tariq 'Aziz
Adnan Khayralla
Hikmat Ibrahim al-'Azzawi
Burhan Mustafa
Tayih 'Abd al-Karim

29 June 1982

Saddam Husayn (chairman)
Izzat Ibrahim
Taha Yasin Ramadhan
Na'im Haddad
Hasan 'Ali
Sa'dun Shakir
Tariq 'Aziz
Adnan Khayrallah
Taha Muhyi al-Din Ma'ruf

August 1986

Saddam Husayn (chairman)
Izzat Ibrahim
Taha Yasin Ramadhan
Sa'dun Hammadi
Hasan 'Ali
Sa'dun Shakir (retired 18 September 1990)
Tariq 'Aziz
Adnan Khayralla (died 5 May 1989)
Taha Muhyi al-Din Ma'ruf

September 1991

Saddam Husayn (chairman)
Izzat Ibrahim
Taha Yasin Ramadhan
Tariq 'Aziz
Taha Muhyi al-Din Ma'ruf
'Ali Hasan al-Majid
Muhammad Hamza al-Zubaydi
Mizban Khidr Hadi

February 1994

Saddam Husayn (chairman)
Izzat Ibrahim
Taha Yasin Ramadhan
Tariq 'Aziz
Ali Hasan al-Majid

Muhammad Hamza al-Zubaydi (removed in 2001)
Mizban Khidr Hadi
Latif Nusayyif Jasim
Muhammad Ziman Abd al-Razzaq
'Abd al-Baqi 'Abd al-Karim al-Sa'dun
Samir 'Abd al-'Aziz al-Najm
Adil 'Abdullah
Aziz Salih al-Numan

May 2001

Saddam Husayn (chairman)
Izzat Ibrahim
Taha Yasin Ramadhan
Tariq Aziz
Ali Hasan al-Majid
Mizban Khidr Hadi
Latif Nusayyif Jasim
Muhammad Ziman Abd al-Razzaq
'Abd al- Baqi 'Abd al-Karim al-Sa'dun
Samir 'Abd al-Aziz al-Najm
Adil 'Abdullah
Aziz Salih al-Numan
Qusay Husayn
Yahya 'Abdullah al-Abbudi
Uklah 'Abd Sakr
Rashid Ta'an Kazim
Fadil Mahmud Gharib
Muhsin Khadr al-Khafaji
Huda Salih Mahdi 'Ammash

Appendix C
Regional Commands, 1966–2003

October 1966–November 1968

Ahmad Hasan al-Bakr
Saddam Husayn
Salih Mahdi 'Ammash
'Abd al-Karim 'Abd al-Satar al-Shaykhli
'Abdullah Sallum al-Samarra'i
'Abd al-Khaliq al-Samarra'i
Murtada al-Hadithi
Taha Yasin Ramadhan
Salah 'Umar al-'Ali
Izzat Mustafa

November 1968–January 1974

Ahmad Hasan al-Bakr
Saddam Husayn
Salih Mahdi 'Ammash (dismissed 1971)
'Abd al-Karim 'Abd al-Satar al-Shaykhli (dismissed 1971)
'Abdullah Sallum al-Samarra'i (dismissed 1970)
'Abd al-Khaliq al-Samarra'i (imprisoned 1973)
Murtada al-Hadithi (dismissed 1974)
Taha Yasin Ramadhan
Salah 'Umar al-'Ali (dismissed 1970)
Izzat Ibrahim
Samir 'Abd al-Aziz Najam (dismissed 1971)
'Abd al-Wahhab Karim [S] (dismissed within a few months)

January 1974–December 1976

Ahmad Hasan al-Bakr
Saddam Husayn

Taha Yasin Ramadhan
Izzat Ibrahim
Na'im Haddad
Tayih 'Abd al-Karim
Muhammad Muhjub
Adnan Hasan Abbas al-Hamdani
Ghanim 'Abd al-Jalil
Tahir al-'Ani
'Abd al-Fattah al-Yasin
Hasan 'Ali
Izzat Mustafa (dismissed 1977;
    added January–March 1977)
Sa'dun Shakir
Ja'far Qasim Hammudi
'Abdullah Fadhil Samarra'i
Fulayyih Hasan Jasim (dismissed March 1977)
Tariq 'Aziz
Adnan Khayralla
Hikmat Ibrahim al-'Azzawi
Muhammad Ayish Hamad
Muhyi 'Abd al-Husayn Mashhadi
Burhan Mustafa

July 1979–June 1982

Saddam Husayn
Taha Yasin Ramadhan
Izzat Ibrahim
Na'im Haddad
Tayih 'Abd al-Karim
Tahir al-'Ani
'Abd al-Fattah al-Yasin
Hasan 'Ali
Sa'dun Shakir
Ja'far Qasim Hammudi
'Abdullah Fadhil
Tariq 'Aziz
Adnan Khayralla
Hikmat Ibrahim al-'Azzawi
Burhan Mustafa

June 1982–September 1991

Saddam Husayn
Taha Yasin Ramadhan
Izzat Ibrahim
Na'im Haddad
Hasan 'Ali
Sa'dun Shakir
Tariq 'Aziz
Adnan Khayralla
Sa'dun Hammadi
Mizban Khidr Hadi
Sa'di Mahdi Salih
'Abd al-Ghani 'Abd al-Ghafur
Muhammad Hamza al-Zubaydi
Samir Muhammad 'Abd al-Wahhab
'Abd al-Hasan Rahi Majhul al-Firawn
Kamil Yasin Rashid
'Ali Hasan al-Majid
Latif Nusayyif Jasim

September 1991–1994

Saddam Husayn
Izzat Ibrahim
'Ali Hasan al-Majid
Kamil Yasin Rashid
Sadi Mahdi Salih
Tariq 'Aziz
Muhammad Hamza al-Zubaydi
Mizban Khidr Hadi
Muhammad Zimam 'Abd al-Razzaq
Taha Yasin Ramadhan
Muhammad al-Ahmad
Khadar 'Abd al-Aziz Husayn
'Abd al-Rahman Ahmad 'Abd al-Rahman
Nuri Faysal Shahir
'Abd al-Ghani 'Abd al-Ghafur
Mizhir Matni al Awwad
Fawzi Khalaf
Reserves: 'Abd al-Rahman Hamid; Khalil Ibrahim; Anwar Mawlud Dhiban

1994–May 2001

Saddam Husayn
Izzat Ibrahim
'Ali Hasan al-Majid
Tariq 'Aziz
Mizban Khidr Hadi
Muhammad Zimam 'Abd al-Razzaq
Taha Yasin Ramadhan
Latif Nusayyif Jasim
'Abd al-Baqi 'Abd al-Karim al-Sadun
Samir 'Abd al-'Aziz al-Najm
'Aziz Abdullah
'Aziz Salih al-Numan
Muhammad Hamza al-Zubaydi
Kamil Yasin Rashid
Muhammad al-Ahmad
Fadil Ibrahim al-Mashadani
Sa'dun Hammadi
'Abd al-Ghani 'Abd al-Ghafur

May 2001–April 2003

Saddam Husayn
Izzat Ibrahim
'Ali Hasan al-Majid
Tariq 'Aziz
Mizban Khidr Hadi
Muhammad Zimam 'Abd al-Razzaq
Taha Yasin Ramadhan
Latif Nusayyif Jasim
'Abd al-Baqi 'Abd al-Karim al-Sadun
Samir Abd al-'Aziz al-Najm
'Aziz Abdullah
'Aziz Salih Numan
Qusay Husayn
Yahya 'Abdullah al-Abudi
Uqlah 'Abd Saqar
Rashid Ta'an Kazim
Fadhil Mahmud Gharib
Muhsin Khudayr al-Khafaji
Huda Salih Mahdi 'Ammash

Appendix D
Media in Post-War 'Iraq

After the fall of the regime, 'Iraq witnessed the emergence of numerous newspapers and magazines reflecting diverse points of view, ranging from the extreme left to the extreme right, encompassing both secular and religious philosophies. The papers began to face restrictions from Coalition officials, however, after some began publish sensationalist stories and stories considered by the U.S. administration authorities to be inciting violence and ethnic or religious hatred, destabilizing, and spreading rumors and inaccurate stories. A press code of conduct was introduced by U.S. authorities and regulations were introduced. The U.S. authorities and the 'Iraqi Governing Council (IGC) (q.v.) sharply criticized Arab satellite channels, such as al-Jazeera and al-Arabiyya, for incitement and spreading inaccurate information after they broadcasted interviews with masked 'Iraqis claiming to represent the anti-American 'Iraqi resistance calling on 'Iraqis to rise and attack occupation troops in 'Iraq as well as airing audio tapes from Saddam Husayn and for interviews with masked anti-CPA and anti-IGC gunmen

PRINT MEDIA

The following newspapers are being published in 'Iraq:

- *Al-Ahrar* **(The Liberals)** considers itself "the newspaper of all Arabs" and an "independent political daily". For now it is issued only on Sundays.
- *Al-Ayyam* **(The Times)** is an independent newspaper that hopes "to become a daily newspaper and a forum for writers and national educated journalists" and that does not "represent any viewpoint of any party, movement, or direction."

393

- **Baghdad** is an Arabic-language weekly connected with the 'Iraqi National Accord Movement, whose leader is Iyad 'Allawi (q.v). The newspaper moved its headquarters from London to Baghdad.
- **Brayati** is the daily Kurdish-language newspaper issued by the 'Iraqi Kurdistan Democratic Party (KDP).
- **Al Da'wah** is a Shi'a Arabic Language newspaper issued by the Islamic Da'wah (q.v) Party. The editor-in-chief is Hasan Sa'id
- **Al-Dimuqrati (The Democrat)** is a weekly newspaper published by the 'Iraqi Grouping for Democracy, and is sold in Baghdad.
- **Fajr Baghdad (Baghdad Dawn)** confirms that it is the first democratic independent newspaper in 'Iraq. Its editor-in-chief is 'Ali Al-Nashmi, a professor at the University of Baghdad.
- **Govari Gulan** is a monthly KDP (q.v) magazine issued in Kurdish Language.
- **Habazbouz** is an 'Iraqi satirical weekly edited by Jasim Ali al-Yasiri.
- **Hawlati** is an independent Kurdish-language weekly newspaper.
- **Al-Hurriya (Freedom)** is issued by the Arab National Democrats Movement. The editor-in-chief is Husam Al-Saffar.
- **Al-'Iraq Al-Jadid (New 'Iraq)** is an Arabic-language independent daily that stresses its independence from capitalism and special-interest financing.
- **Al-Ittihad (The Union),** the Arabic-language newspaper of the Patriotic Union of Kurdistan (PUK) (q.v.), which is reported to be printing 30,000 copies daily in Baghdad.
- **Jamawar** is an independent Kurdish-language weekly newspaper.
- **Kaldo-Ashur** is the Arabic language supplement of Regay Kurdistan and focuses on the Assyrian and Chaldean communities
- **Khabat** is a Kurdish-language weekly newspaper. It is sold presently in Baghdad.
- **Komala** is a Kurdish-language bimonthly newspaper of the Islamic Group of 'Iraqi Kurdistan.
- **Kurdistani Nuwe** is the Kurdish-language Daily newspaper issued by the 'Iraqi Patriotic Union of Kurdistan (PUK).
- **Al-Majd (The Glory)** is a secular weekly paper. It deplored the lack of administration and security in Baghdad.
- **Al-Naba (The News)** is a self-declared independent national paper aiming to report "without ambiguity or bias." An editorial dated 15 May called on coalition forces to leave 'Iraq.

- *Nida Al-Mustaqbal* **(Call of the Future)** is an Arabic-language daily newspaper issued by the 'Iraqi National Accord Movement. Muhammad Khurshid, its publisher, is a member in the 'Iraqi National Accord Movement Central Council.
- *Al-Nur* **(The Light)** is a Shi'a Arabic-language weekly newspaper issued by the Islamic Cultural Center in Baghdad.
- *Regay Kurdistan* is a Kurdish-language weekly newspaper of the Communist Party of 'Iraqi Kurdistan.
- *Al-Sa'ah* **(The Hour)** is biweekly newspaper issued by the United 'Iraqi National Movement. The paper is backed by Ahmed Al-Kubaysi, a Dubai-based Sunni Muslim cleric and a sharp critic of U.S. occupation, who has called for Sunni-Shi'i cooperation against U.S. and British presence in 'Iraq. The editor-in-chief is Adib Sha'ban, a former employee of Uday Husayn (q.v.).
- *Al-Sabah* **(The Dawn)** is an eight-page, twice-weekly broadsheet issued by the reconstruction office, with an initial run of 50,000 copies. It does not have opinion pieces, and does not reflect politicians' viewpoints. It is edited by Isma'il Zayer, who has pledged to adhere to international codes of journalism.
- *Al-Taakhi* **(The Brotherhood)** publishes around 20,000 copies daily in Baghdad, using a printing press recovered from the former 'Iraqi government paper *Al-'Iraq*. The paper was published previously in Baghdad between 1967 and 1974, when it was banned. It is run by the Kurdistan Democratic Party (KDP) (q.v.).
- *Tariq Al-Sha'b* is the monthly Arabic newspaper issued by the 'Iraqi Communist Party (ICP) (q.v.), currently sold in Baghdad.
- *Al-Zaman* **(Time)** is an independent Arabic-language daily printed in Baghdad as well as being printed in Basrah, in addition to the UK and Bahrain. Its owner and editor-in-chief is Sa'd al-Bazzaz, who fled 'Iraq 11 years ago, a former editor-in-chief of the now-defunct 'Iraqi government daily *Al-Jumhuriya*. Local stories are now being edited in Baghdad, the rest are produced in London.

'Iraq's emerging media scene enjoys freedoms unheard of during Saddam Husayn's (q.v.) tenure. Few foreign newspapers had been allowed in the country and satellite dishes were banned. Since the former leader was overthrown, a host of newspapers and a number of early radio and television stations have sprung up. For the residents of 'Iraq, choosing what to read, watch, or listen to is no longer a simple affair. There is apparently no shortage of paper, supplies have been located and can easily be procured from Turkey and Syria, according to an AFP report.

At least 170 newspapers have appeared in Baghdad and other major 'Iraqi cities and towns. In particular, they are giving voice to political, religious, and ethnic groupings seeking a role in shaping 'Iraq's political future. Complaints abound about general lawlessness and poor recovery of public services are directed at the U.S.-led forces. Many of the new media publish stories on Saddam's regime (accusing it of corruption, brutality, and crimes) and focus on the factors behind Saddam's rise and his ability to stay in power for 35 years. Some of the former regime's defenders and advocates among journalists have turned to critics, Shi'a media openly call for an Islamic state, while secular media say they are representing the disparate political and ethnic groups. The religious media reflect majority Shi'a opinion and are concerned at the influence of Western and secular media. The secular media has been promoting the idea of a pluralistic, democratic government and a free press as a solution to the nation's ills. At a price of 3 to 4 dinars each however, the price of a newspaper is prohibitive to many in a shattered economy. Prominent 'Iraqi journalists have returned from abroad and have started to publish or are preparing to begin publishing quality newspapers. They promise independent and democratic media. Many are small daily or weekly publications that often do not exceed eight pages. Most of the papers lack qualified staff, modern equipment, and the resources needed to produce high-quality newspapers. They suffer from poor editing and from the absence of the tools and equipment necessary to gather and produce information. Many of the former regime's papers and printing presses were damaged, destroyed, or seized by some of the former opposition parties or groups. Some of the papers represent the views of their political sponsors or are organs of political parties.

The Kurdish-language weekly *Khabat* (Struggle), published in Arbil, is the organ of the Kurdistan Democratic Party (KDP) (q.v.) and has now also made its way onto Baghdad's news stands. Other papers include *Al-Dimuqrati* (The Democrat), published by the 'Iraqi Grouping for Democracy and sold in Baghdad. Or there is *Al-Ahrar*, describing itself as an independent newspaper for "all Arabs." One recent edition of this paper carried a front-page headline reading "'Iraq is our most precious possession."

BROADCAST MEDIA

The broadcast media is also expanding, but at a slower rate than the print media. The U.S. plans to create a nationwide TV network, an AM radio channel, and an independent newspaper for 'Iraq. All will be run by previously exiled 'Iraqis, along with journalists recruited from within the country. The U.S. broadcast operations will be funded by American taxpayers and run the 'Iraqi Media Project, an offshoot of the Pentagon's Office of Reconstruction and Humanitarian Assistance (ORHA) (q.v.).

Most people still depend on the radio for news and information and former 'Iraqi opposition groups have recently set up a number of news stations. One common complaint, however, is the lack of resources, with stations obliged to operate under the most basic conditions, often without a constant electricity supply or access to the telephone network.

Politics are still determining the type of information available. News outlets are often linked to certain political, ethnic, or religious groups jostling for a say in 'Iraq's future. Kurdish leaders, for example, have capitalized on the media free-for-all by launching new radio and television stations in Baghdad. Without 'Iraq's domestic services on the air, the world's national and international broadcasters are targeting the region.

Among 'Iraq's rich, satellite television has become the new fad. Sales of satellite dishes and receiving equipment have increased as 'Iraqis seek to have an open window to the outside world. However, for the time being, only the well-off can afford satellite television.

Meanwhile, the U.S. wound down its psychological operations in the form of radio and television transmissions from *Commando Solo,* the aircraft over flying 'Iraq. Plans are afoot for a new terrestrial television service that is to broadcast first in the Baghdad area and later outside the capital. The choice of foreign news will not be limited to U.S.-backed broadcasters. The Iran-based television station Al-'Aalam (The World), broadcasts into Baghdad from across the border via terrestrial as well as satellite links. The station, which carries programs in both Arabic and English, is the only foreign channel that can be received without the need for expensive satellite equipment.

Any national 'Iraqi television station will probably have to wait for a new government to be formed in order to coordinate the installation of the technical infrastructure and to define the station's aims and objectives. A Swedish 'Iraqi, Ahmed al-Rikabi, has been appointed by the U.S. Defense Department as 'Iraqi TV's new chief.

Radio

- **Radio 'Iraq** is the voice of new 'Iraq. It was set up by Robert Reilly, formerly director of Voice of America. It is financed by the Pentagon. The director of news is Ahmad Al-Rikaby. His former job was London bureau chief at Radio Free 'Iraq, which was funded by the U.S.
- 'Iraqi Media Network, **Voice of New 'Iraq**, was operated by the U.S. Office of Reconstruction and Humanitarian Assistance. It is heard on medium wave 756 kHz and also on 909 kHz.
- Also a radio station by the name of **The Republic of 'Iraq Radio from Baghdad** started on 12 May. It issued statements by the Office of Reconstruction and Humanitarian Assistance.
- **Radio Freedom from Baghdad** broadcast in Arabic on FM 96.5 MHz.
- **Voice of Freedom, Voice of the Patriotic Union of Kurdistan,** affiliated with the PUK is radio transmitting daily in both Arabic and Kurdish languages. It broadcast on FM 95 MHz. Its programs include news bulletins, political analyses, interviews, music, and variety shows.
- **Turkumanli Radio** was launched in Kirkuk in April 2003. They present broadcasts on behalf of 'Iraqi Turkoman Front. They opened radio stations in Tall 'Afar and Mosul on 6 and 8 May.
- **Dangi Komal-Kurkuk Radio** broadcasts in Arabic and Turkic in Kurdish, Arabic, and Turkish to Kirkuk on behalf of the Kurdistan Islamic Group.
- **Radio Bopeshawa,** from the Worker's Communist Party of 'Iraq, is to broadcast for one hour daily starting half an hour in Arabic and half an hour in Kurdish to the areas of Arbil, Kirkuk, and Mosul.
- **Voice of the People of Kurdistan** is operated by the PUK. It was operating before April 2003 and continues operating.
- **Voice of 'Iraqi Kurdistan** is operated by the Kurdistan Democratic Party, KDP.
- **Ashur Radio** started operating in April 2000. It is operated by the Assyrian Democratic Movement. It broadcasts in Assyrian and Arabic on shortwave,

- **Voice of the 'Iraqi Republic from Baghdad, Voice of the 'Iraqi People** is an opposition station that has been operating since 1991. It is thought to transmit from Saudi Arabia.
- **Voice of the 'Iraqi People, Voice of the 'Iraqi Communist Party** broadcasts from northern 'Iraq.
- **Voice of the Mujahid** was the radio of the Mojahidin-e-Khalq Organization opposed to the Islamic regime in Iran. They previously broadcast by shortwave, satellite, and by uploading archive audio files to the Internet.

Television

- **KurdSat** is the television station of the PUK. It has expanded its broadcasts to Kirkuk and Khanaqin.
- **Kurdistan TV** is a KDP television station that sends its programs now to Kirkuk and Mosul.
- **Karbala** is a local TV channel that was launched on April 16, 2003.
- **'Iraqi TV Network** is a station that the U.S. plans to succeed the airborne Towards Freedom TV. There will initially be only two hours of programming, but will eventually move to full 24-hour service. It should include 30 minutes of news every night, with some local news segments. The station will be broadcast from a tower in Baghdad, then from Arbil in the north and Umm Qasr in the south, as well as via satellite. It started broadcasts on May 13, but there were ongoing conflicts between U.S. advisers, Canadian advisers, and 'Iraqi journalists, because of censorship. Ahmad Al-Rikabi, a Swedish 'Iraqi from Swedish TV and Radio, was appointed by the U.S. Defense Department as the TV's new chief, but had conflicts with U.S. censorship issues.
- **Al-Hurriya (Freedom) TV** is a television station sponsored by PUK. It began trials for transmission from Baghdad on April 30.
- **Mosul TV** was the first station to resume transmission after Saddam Husayn's fall.
- **Kirkuk TV Channel** started to broadcast on April 23, under supervision of coalition forces.
- **Turkomanli TV** started in Kirkuk in April 2003, broadcasts on behalf of 'Iraqi Turkuman Front.

- **Vision of Resistance TV (Sima-ye Moqavemat) is the TV of Mojahedin-e-Khalq Organization**, used to have their studios in Ashraf, North of Baghdad. At present, they are sent via satellite, but are not located in 'Iraq.

IRANIAN BROADCAST MEDIA ACCESSIBLE IN 'IRAQ

Radio

- **Voice of the Mujahidin** is possibly supported by the Supreme Assembly for Islamic Revolution In 'Iraq (SASIRI). The station was transmitting on some frequencies used by Islamic Republic of Iran Broadcast (Al-Alam).
- **Voice of the Islamic Republic of Iran (VIRI)** an Arabic service broadcast on mediumwave and shortwave inside 'Iraq.
- **Voice of Rebellious 'Iraq** supports the Supreme Council of the Islamic Revolution in 'Iraq (SCIRI), the Shia group sponsored by Iran. It is assumed to transmit from Iran.

Television

- **Al-'Alam (The World)** is a satellite TV channel in Arabic and English, based in Iran. It is a 24-hours news channel transmitted over four satellites: Arabsat, Asiasat, Telstar, and Hot Bird. It can also be viewed by 'Iraqis without a satellite dish. It is widely viewed because average 'Iraqis cannot afford a satellite dish and receiver. It can be received in Europe, the Middle East, Asia, and America.
- **The Arabic Channel** began broadcasting in February 2003. The English segment is limited to horizontal news subtitles or news tickers.
- **Sahar Universal Network 1 and 2 television** is Iran's external satellite TV service on the Hot Bird 1–6 satellites. It is widely viewed in 'Iraq. It includes Arabic programming.
- **Resistance Channel (Al-Istiqama TV)** was believed to be using Iran TV facilities, including Iran's Education Channel to broadcast to 'Iraq. It was opened in April 2003 by Ayat Allah Hakim, the head of the Supreme Assembly for Islamic Revolution (SAIRI) in 'Iraq. It was also available via satellite in the Middle East via Iran's digital multiplex.

Appendix E
Important 'Iraqis in Post-War 'Iraq

'IRAQI GOVERNING COUNCIL MEMBERS

The U.S.-appointed 'Iraqi Governing Council (IGC) is made up of 25 individuals representing 'Iraq's different ethnic and religious groups. The governing council has only three female members.

Shi'is

Ahmad Chalabi
Abu Hatim ('Abd al-Karim Mahoud Muhammadawi) Muwafaq al-
   Rubay'i Muhammad Bahr al-'Ulum
Iyad 'Allawi
Wail 'Abd al-Latif
'Abd al-'Aziz al-Hakim
Ahmad al-Barrak
Ibrahim al-Ja'fari
Raja Habib al-Khaza'i
'Aquila al-Hashimi
'Izz al-Din Salim
Ghazi Mash'al Ajil al-Yawar Hamid Majid Mousa

Kurds

Mas'ud al-Barzani
Jalal Talabani
Baha al-Din
'Uthman, Mahmud

Sunnis

Muhsin 'Abd al-Hamid 'Adnan Pachachi
Nasir Kamil al-Chadirchi
Dara Nur-al-Din Samir Shakir Mahmud

Assyrian Christian

Younadim Yusuf Kannu

Turkuman

Chankul Habib 'Umar

'IRAQI CABINET MEMBERS

Ministry	Minister	Ethnic Group
Communication	Hayder al-Ibadi	Shi'ite
Public Works	Nisrin Mustafa Siddiq Barwari	Kurd
Housing and Reconstruction	Bayan Baqir Solagh	Shi'ite
Environment	Abd al-Rahman Siddiq Karim	Kurd
Trade	'Ali 'Alawi	Shi'ite
Planning	Mahdi al-Hafiz	Shi'ite
Education	'Alaa al-Alwan	Shi'ite
Higher Education	Ziad Abd al-Razzaq Muhammad Aswad	Sunni
Culture	Mufid Muhammad Jawad al-Jazairy	Shi'ite
Human Rights	Abd al-Basit Turki	Sunni
Foreign Affairs	Hushiar Mahmoud Mahmmed al-Zibari	Kurd
Interior Affairs	Nuri al-Badran	Shi'ite
Agriculture	Abd al-Amr Abood Rhayma	Shi'ite
Youth and Sports	Ali Fa'iq al-Ghaban	Shi'ite
Health	Khudhair Abbas	Shi'ite
Industry and Minerals	Muhammad Tawfeoq Rahim	Kurd
Justice	Hasim Abd al-Rahman al-Shibli	Sunni
Science and Technology	Rashad Mindan Omar	Turk
Labor and Social Affairs	Sami Azara al-Ma'joun	Shi'ite
Electricity	Ayham al-Samarraiy	Sunni
Finance	Kamil Mubdir al-Kaylani	Sunni
Immigration	Muhammad Jassim Khudhair	Shi'ite
Water Resources	Latif Rashid	Kurd
Oil	Ibrahim Muhammad Bahr al-'Ulum	Shi'ite
Transportation	Bahnam Zia Bulus	Assyrian Christian

'IRAQ RESISTANCE GROUPS

Following the fall of Baghdad and the establishment of the Coalition Provisional Authority (CPA), U.S. forces encountered a small number of attacks. These attacks began to escalate following the decision by Ambassador L. Paul Bremer, the head of the CPA, to disband the civil servants: the 'Iraqi military, police, and security services, the Special Republican Guards, and the Ba'th party. These actions angered regime loyalists, Ba'thists, Islamists, and 'Iraqi nationalists, many of whom left with their arms and were without income or hope for the future. They became ripe recruits for the opposition. Some of the groups are believed to be small and local and operate with the help or support of family and clan members.

There have been reports in the Arab media that Saddam Husayn, knowing he could not face the overwhelming superiority of U.S. forces in a conventional conflict, began to prepare for a protracted guerilla war against U.S. and allied forces if they invade 'Iraq. Consequently, he prepared for the confrontation by creating parallel organizations to the traditional military in 2002. Other interpretations have disagreed with this view.

Some nationalist and patriotic 'Iraqis resented the presence of U.S. forces and the harsh U.S. operational methods they saw as bringing dishonor or humiliation upon 'Iraqis. In addition, the collapse of law and order, the failure of coalition forces to restore security as well as basic services, such as water, electricity, and hospitalization, added fuel to the fire and greatly contributed to the rise of these opposition groups. Some of them seek to drive the invaders out and establish a new regime, while others want a return of the old regime. The exact identities of these groups remain unclear and little is known about their organizational structures and their numbers and affiliations.

Some of these groups are Islamic fundamentalists who have gained greater freedom since the collapse of the Ba'th regime. Many have little military experience, while others appear to have considerable experience or benefit from the experience of other Islamic groups. A small number of Islamist fighters have infiltrated 'Iraq to fight the United States. They are believed to have come from Syria, Jordan, Saudi Arabia, Egypt, Sudan, Algeria, and Yemen. While some of these fighters had little military experience, others appeared to be experienced and they fought well against U.S. forces during the war itself. Some, in order to sow confusion, are different names for the same groups.

Over 30 groups have claimed responsibility for the attacks against U.S. and allied forces, UN and international organizations, foreign missions, 'Iraqi police, and 'Iraqi Governing Council (IGC) officials. The resistance began in the Sunni areas in the central part of the country and in Baghdad. So far, there have been few incidents of attacks on U.S. or allied forces in the predominantly Shi'i southern part of 'Iraq. Supreme Assembly for the Islamic Revolution in 'Iraq (SAIRI) is represented in the government, and Muqtada al-Sadr's followers in Jaysh al-Mahdi (The Mahdi's Army) have generally refrained from attacks on Coalition forces.

U.S. authorities have generally categorized these groups as remnants of the old regime, criminals who had been released by Saddam, Arab fighters infiltrating 'Iraq, or terrorists allied to Osama bin Laden's al-Qaeda organization. The insurgents appear to include a mix of Saddam loyalists, Ba'thists, 'Iraqi nationalists, tribal elements, Islamic groups, and Arab fighters who had gone to 'Iraq to fight U.S. forces. The nationalist, Ba'thist, and Saddam loyalists are believed to include the General Command of the Armed Forces and the Popular Resistance for the Liberation of 'Iraq. These groups are most likely composed of former 'Iraqi military personnel, particularly from the Special Republican Guards, security and intelligence, Ba'thists, and the paramilitary Fida'iyin.

Other groups believed to have similar orientations are al-'Awda (The Return) or al-Awda al-Thaniya (the Second Return), Jihaz al-I'lam al-siyasi li Hizb al-Ba'th (Political Information Organ of the Ba'th Party), and Harakat Ra's al-Af 'a (Snake's Head Movement). The first is a group that came into prominence in mid-June 2003. It is generally thought these groups are made up of former security service members and soldiers of the former 'Iraqi armed forces organized in cells spread throughout cities such as Baghdad, Mawsil, and Ramadi. There are reports that the pro-Saddam Ba'thists have actually renamed the party "al-'Awda al-Thaniya (the Second Return)." The second group has described itself as the political and media organ of the Ba'th party. The third named group is also Ba'thist and has links to Sunni Arab tribes.

Revolutionary Groups in 'Iraq

Al-Ansar (the Partisans): A highly motivated group of Ba'thists established by Saddam in 1998

Saddam's Fidayin (Saddam's Commandos): Established in 1991 and was headed by 'Uday Saddam Husayn

Nassirites: A small group of non-Ba'thist pan-Arab nationalists. Their only claim to fame apart from allegedly successful attacks on U.S. forces is their success of making enemies of almost all other 'Iraqi political groups.

Thuwar al-'Iraq—Kataib al-Anbar al-musallahah ('Iraq's Revolutionaries—al-Anbar Armed Brigades): An anti-Saddam nationalist insurgent group from al-Anbar province.

The Mujahidin (the Holy Combatants): Believed to be a group of non-Ba'thist 'Iraqi and foreign fighters with nationalist and religious backgrounds.

General Secretariat for a Democratic and Liberated 'Iraq: Thought to be a leftist nationalist group opposed to Saddam and sharply condemns the CPA for failing to provide security and basic services.

Munazamat al-'Alam al-Aswad (the Black Banner Organization): An organization that indicates that it has nationalist and religious elements. The color of the Abbasid dynasty based in Baghdad was black. It has called for sabotaging the oil industry to prevent it from falling under foreign control.

Jabhat al-Tawhid li-Tahrir al-'Iraq (the United Front for the Liberation of 'Iraq): Very little is known about this group except that it is an anti-Saddam and anti-Ba'thist organization that has called upon all 'Iraqi forces to fight the U.S. occupation.

Jabhat Tahrir al-'Iraq (the National Front for the Liberation of 'Iraq): Believed to be made up of nationalist and religious elements and has former Republican Guards in its ranks. It was also one of the first to appear during the war. It issued its first communiqués in April and actually claimed that it had tried to assassinate Ahmad Chalabi, an IGC member, but only succeeded in killing some of his supporters in an attack in al-Najaf.

Jaysh Tahrir al-'Iraq (the 'Iraq Liberation Army): A group that has issued warnings to UN officials and foreign governments against sending peacekeeping forces to 'Iraq to support the U.S. forces.

Groups with Varying Islamic Orientations

Alwiyat al-Faruq (al-Faruq Brigades): Believed to be a Sunni group with Islamic tendencies and refers to itself as the military arm of an Islamic resistance organization called the Islamic Movement in 'Iraq, or al-Haraka al-Islamiya fi al-'Iraq. The Brigades emerged in early June and might include secular Sunni Arabs and individuals from now defunct organizations of the former regime. The al-Faruq Brigades have set up small units or "squadrons," which they give Islamic names.

Mujahidi al-Taifa al-Mansura (Combatants or Mujahidin of the Victorious Sect): A group believed to be made up of 'Iraqi and non-'Iraqi Sunni Islamist elements or even Sunni Salafi revivalist elements. Its military wing is known as the "Martyr Khattab Brigade."

Munazamat Alwiyat al-Jihad (Organization of the Jihad Brigades): Believed to be a group targeting collaborators with the U.S. and allied forces. It isn't clear whether this is solely an Islamist group since some of the nationalist groups use religious symbols.

Jaysh Ansar al-Sunna (the Army of Sunna Partisans): A new islamist group claiming to operate all over 'Iraq. It adopts Islamist discourse against the "foreign infidel invaders" and emerged in October 2003

Kataib al mujahidin fi al-jama'a al-Salafiya fi al-'Iraq (Mujahidin Battalions of the Salafi Group of 'Iraq): A Sunni Islamist group that claims as its spiritual mentor the Palestinian Islamist, 'Abdallah 'Azzam, who fought with the Afghan Mujahidin and who inspired the Arabs fighting there and eventually became known as the "Afghan Arabs."

Armed Vanguards of Muhammad's Second Army: An Islamic group that has declared that its mission is to expel foreign forces from 'Iraq. It has vowed to attack foreigners as well as Arabs and Muslims who cooperate with U.S. authorities and with the IGC in 'Iraq. This group claimed responsibility for the attack on UN headquarters in Baghdad on 19 August 2003. The group was highly critical of the UN for its alleged support of the sanctions and war on 'Iraq.

Ansar al-Islam (Partisans of Islam): A Kurdish group that was based in the PUK-controlled area of northern 'Iraq near the border of Iran. Its leader, Mulla Krekar, has denied any links with the Saddam Husayn regime, and the group had entered into bloody confrontations with the Poking in 2001. Some of its members are believed to have fought in Afghanistan against the Soviets, and its leaders maintained ties to Osama bin Laden's al-Qaeda. Al-Ansar was attacked by U.S. forces during the war, and many fled to Iran. The U.S.-led CPA has said that al-Ansar had begun to move back to Baghdad and other areas in 'Iraq to attack U.S. forces and other targets.

Bibliography

A select group of Iraqi authors contributed to *Hadharat al-Iraq* (1985), 13 volumes, one of the most comprehensive works dealing with 'Iraqi geography, climate, history, culture, economy, as well as the country's physical and ethnic landscape. *Encyclopaedia Brittanica* also provides wide-ranging background information both on the ancient as well as the modern periods in Iraq's history and development. Useful works on Iraq's wildlife include Evan Guest (ed.), *Flora of Iraq,* vol. 1 (1988), and Gavin Young, *Iraq, Land of Two Rivers* (1980), which offers a guide to the people and landscape. Wilfrid Thesiger, *The Marsh Arabs* (1964), is an important work on a unique Iraqi community and their historical origins, role in 'Iraq's political and economic history, and recent position. Alvin Cottrell, *The Persian Gulf States: A General Survey* (1980), offers useful chapters on the country's physical landscape. Guy Le Strange, *The Lands of the Eastern Caliphate* (1905), is an important book relying on the writings of Arab geographers of the period. The economy, society, and foreign policy are discussed in a number of works, including Tim Niblock (ed.), *Iraq: The Contemporary State* (1982); Michael Szaz (ed.), *Domestic and Foreign Policy Issues in Iraq* (1986); and Kathleen M. Langley, *The Industrialization of Iraq* (1961), which focuses on the early development of modern industry, its impact on society, and the future potential of the 'Iraqi oil industry.

With regard to Iraq's history, Helen Chapin Metz (ed.), *Iraq: A Country Study*, fourth edition (1990), provides a useful overall survey of the country; and Christine Moss Helms, *Iraq: Eastern Flank of the Arab World* (1984), discusses 'Iraq's geopolitical significance considering its position on the fringes of the Arab world. *Hadharat al-'Iraq* offers significant scholarly work reviewing the history of 'Iraq during its early era, the Islamic period, and into the modern era. Hugh Kennedy, *The Prophet and the Age of the Caliphates* (1986), provides special emphasis on the conditions in 'Iraq from the time of the Prophet to the Caliph 'Ali and the rise of Shi'ism, while Michael G. Morony, *Iraq after the Muslim Conquest* (1984), focuses more on the post-caliphal period with special emphasis on the changes that Islam produced. Heribert Busse, *Chalif und Grosskönig: Die Buyiden im Iraq (945–1055)* (1969), concentrates on the rise of the Buyids and their struggle for power in ʿIraq. W. Barthold, *Turkestan Down to the Mongol Invasion* (1977), and ʿAbbas al-ʾAzzawi, *Tˉarˉikh al-ʿIrˉaq bayna ihtilˉalayn [taʾlˉif] ʿAbbˉas al-ʿAzzˉawˉi,* eight volumes (1935–1956), offer comprehensive works on the period between the 11th and 16th centuries. Tom Nieuwenhuis documents the end of mamluk rule and the short-lived attempts to establish local self-rule in *Politics and Society in Early Modern Iraq: Mamluk Pashas Tribal Shayks and Local Rule between 1802 and 1831* (1982). Stephen Longrigg, *Four Centuries of Modern Iraq* (1925), provides a political narrative of ʿIraqi history under the Ottomans. Longrigg follows up his work with *Iraq: 1900–1950* (1953). See also *Encyclopaedia Britannica* (1997) and the comprehensive work of ʿAlˉi Wardˉl, *Lamahˉat ijtimˉaʿˉiyah min tˉarˉikh al-ʿIrˉaq al-hadˉith* (1991).

Other works reviewing the first half of the 20th century include Philip Ireland, *Iraq: A Study in Political Development* (1937), a useful work on the period of the British Mandate. The most significant book on the country's political development since ʿIraq's emergence as an independent state is Majid Khadduri, *Independent Iraq 1932–1958: A Study in Iraqi Politics*, second edition (1960). A complement to Khadduri's work is ʿAbd al-Razzaq al-Hassani, *Tarikh al-Wazarat al-Iraqiya*, 10 volumes (1953–1961), which focuses on ʿIraq under the Hashimite monarchy, including the review of numerous documents. See also Abid al-Marayati, *A Diplomatic History of Iraq* (1961).

Several works discuss the Republican period and the subsequent establishment of Baʾthist rule, including Majid Khadduri, *Republican Iraq: A Study in Iraqi Politics since the Revolution of 1958* (1969); Majid Khadduri, *Socialist Iraq: A Study in Iraqi Politics since 1968* (1969); Eberhard Kienle, *Baʾth vs. Baʾth: The Conflict Between Syria and Iraq 1968–1989* (1990); and Hanna Batatu, *The Old Social Classes and Revolutionary Movements in Iraq: A Study of Iraq's Old Landed and Commercial Classes and Its Communists, Baʾthists and Free Officers* (1978), which offers a comprehensive study of the political and class history of modern ʿIraq and provides the most authoritative study on the history of the ʿIraqi communists. An important historical book covering ʿIraqi history and society from the Ottoman to the modern period is ʿAli al-Wardi, *Lamahat Ijtimaʾiya min Tarikh al-Iraq al-Hadith*, eight volumes (1969–1972). Other important works on modern history and politics are Christine Helms, *Iraq: The Eastern Flank of the Arab World* (1984), and Phoebe Marr, *The Modern History of Iraq* (1985).

The Iran–ʿIraq War has been well covered in Majid Khadduri, *The Gulf War: The Origins and Implications of the Iraq–Iran Conflict,* which offers a comprehensive historical, legal, and political study of this conflict. Other useful works on this conflict include Kaiyan Homi Kaikobad, *The Shatt al-Arab Boundary Question: A Legal Appraisal* (1988), and Efraim Karsh (ed.), *The Iran–Iraq War: Impact and Implications* (1989). The Kuwait crisis and the second Gulf war are covered in a number of works. Majid Khadduri and Edmund Ghareeb, *War in the Gulf: The Origins and Implications of the Iraq–Kuwait Conflict* (1997), provide an analysis of the historical, legal, and political aspects and ramifications of this conflict. Dilip Hiro, *Desert Shield to Desert Storm* (1992), also offers a balanced and comprehensive view of the war. Other useful works focusing on the military and other aspects of the conflict include James Ridgeway, *The March to War: From Day One to End and Beyond* (1991); Colin Powell, *My American Journey* (1995); Jeffery McCausland, *The Gulf Conflict: A Military Analysis* (1993); and Bob Woodward, *The Commanders* (1991).

Edmund Ghareeb, *The Kurdish Question in Iraq* (1981), traces the history of Kurdish relations with the government, with special emphasis on the period under the Ba'th. Michael Gunter, *The Kurds of Iraq* (1992), focuses on the most recent developments. The history of the Jews in Iraq is adequately discussed by Nissim Rejwan, *The Jews of Iraq: 3000 Years of History and Culture* (1985), and Abbas Shiblaq, *The Lure of Zion: The Case of Iraqi Jews* (1986). For information on the history of the Christian and other communities in Iraq, see George Perecy Badger, *The Nestorians and Their Rituals* (1851); Harry Charles Luke, *Mossul and Its Minorities* (1925); J. M. Fiey, *Assyrie Chrétienne*, two volumes (1967); and Pierre Rondot, *Les Chrétiens d'Orient* (1955). For useful studies on the Shi'is of Iraq, see Pierre-Jean Luizard, *La Formation de l'Iraq contemporain: Le rôle politique des Ulemas Chiittes à la fin de la domination Ottomane au moment de la construction de l'ètat Iraqien* (1992); Joyce Wiley, *The Islamic Movement of Iraq Shi'as* (1991); Yitzhaq Nakash, *The Shi'is of Iraq* (1994); and Chibli Mallat, *The Renewal of Islamic Law: Mohammed Baquer al-Sadr, Najaf and the Shi'i International* (1993).

A number of books and articles are useful for information on 'Iraqi culture, including May Mudhaffar, "Modern Iraqi Art and Poetry," *Gilgamesh* 2 (1986); Amatzia Baram, *Culture, History and Ideology in the Formation of Ba'thist Iraq 1968–89* (1991); Abdul Ilah Ahmed, "Fiction in Iraq between the Two World Wars," *Gilgamesh* 3 (1987); Muhsin Jassim al-Musawi, "The Modernist Trend in the Iraqi Short Story in the 1950's," *Gilgamesh* 2 (1986); Bassim A. Hamoudi, "The Iraqi Short Story: The Artistic and Social Changes," *Gilgamesh* 2 (1986); Ahmed F. Al-Mafraji, "Iraqi Theater 1921–1958," *Gilgamesh* 2 (1986); Bassim Hanna Petros, "Some Aspects of Iraqi Music," *Gilgamesh* 2 (1986); and As'ad Mohammed Ali, "Musical Composition in Iraq," *Gilgamesh* 2 (1987).

CONTENTS

Assyrians
Jews
Kurds
Shiʻis
Yazidis

GENERAL

Encyclopaedia Brittanica, 2001.
Hadharat al-Iraq, 1971.

Adams, Michael. *The Middle East: A Handbook.* London: Blond, 1971.
Ani, Khaled A. M. al-. *The Encyclopedia of Modern ʻIraq.* Baghdad: Arab Encyclopedia House, 1977.
Helms, Christine Moss. *Iraq: Eastern Flank of the Arab World.* Washington, D.C.: Brookings Institution, 1984.
Izzeddin, Nejla. *The Arab World: Past, Present, and Future.* Chicago: Regnery, 1953.
Maubec, Paul. *Irak.* Baghdad: Ministry of Information, Tourism Administration; Boulogne: Delroisse, c. 1974.
Metz, Helen Chapin, ed. *ʻIraq: A Country Study.* Washington, D.C.: Federal Research Division, 1990.
Niblock, Tim. *Iraq, the Contemporary State.* New York: St. Martin's, 1982.
Wardī, ʻAlī. *Lamahāt ijtimāʻīyah min tārīkh al-ʻIrāq al-hadīth.* Landan: Kūfān lil- Nashr, 1991.

Travel and Guide Books

Bell, Gertrude. *From Amurath to Amurath.* London: Heinemann, 1911.
Buckingham, J. S. *Travels in Mesopotamia, Including a Journey from Aleppo, across the Euphrates to Orpha.* London: Colburn, 1827; reprinted, Farnborough, England: Gregg International, 1971.
Budge, E. A. Wallis. *By Nile and Tigris: A Narrative of Journeys in Egypt and Mesopotamia on Behalf of the British Museum between the Years 1886 and 1913.* London: Murray, 1920; reprinted, New York: AMS Press, 1975.
Chesney, R.A. *The Expedition for the Survey of the River Euphrates and Tigris, Carried on by Order of the British Government, in the Years 1835, 1836, and 1837.* London: Longman, Brown, Green, & Longsmans, 1850; reprinted, New York: Greenwood, 1969.
Dickson, Mora. *Baghdad and Beyond.* London: Dobson, 1961.
Drower, E. S. Stevens, Lady. *By Tigris and Euphrates.* London: n.p., 1923.
Goold-Adams, Richard. *Middle East Journey.* London: Murray, 1947.
Heyerdahl, Thor. *The Tigris Expedition: In Search of Our Beginnings.* London: Allen & Unwin, 1980.
Jebb, Louisa. *Desert Way to Baghdad.* London: Fisher Unwin, 1909.

Lawley, Arthur. *Message from Mesopotamia*. London: Hodder & Stoughton, 1917.
Perera, Judith. "'Iraq." In *Travellers' Guide to the Middle East*, ed. Richard Synge. London: I.C. Magazine, 1980.
Raswan, Carl R. *Escape from Baghdad*. London: Hutchinson, 1978.
Stark, Freya. *East Is West*. London: Murray, 1945.
———. *Baghdad Sketches*. London: Murray, 1937.
Wellsted, J. R. "Mesopotamia and the Shores of the Mediterranean." In *Travels to the City of the Caliphs*. London: Longman, Brown, Green & Longsmans, 1850; reprinted, New York: Greenwood, 1969.
Young, Gavin. *'Iraq: Land of the Two Rivers*. London: Collins, 1980.

Bibliographies

Abdulrahman, Abdul Jabber. *'Iraq*. Oxford: Clio, 1984.
———. *A Bibliography of 'Iraq*. Basra: Center for Arab Gulf Studies, University of Basra, 1977.
Boxer, Rosemary. *A Bibliography of Material on Development of Modern 'Iraq*. Baghdad: Rabita, 1953.

Statistical Abstracts

Annual Abstract of Statistics. Baghdad: 'Iraqi Ministry of Planning, Central Statistical Organization, annual.
Annual Foreign Trade Statistics. Baghdad: 'Iraqi Ministry of Planning, Central Statistical Organization, annual.
Demographic Yearbook. New York: United Nations, Statistical Office, annual.
'Iraq in Figures. Baghdad: 'Iraqi Ministry of Planning, Central Statistical Organization, annual.

Climate and Geography

Beumont, Peter, H. Blake, and J. Malcolm Wagstaff. *The Middle East: A Geographical Study*. New York: Wiley, 1976.
Buringh, P. *Soils and Soil Condition in 'Iraq*. Baghdad: 'Iraqi Ministry of Agriculture, 1960.
Cressey, George B. "'Iraq: Twin Rivers, the People of 'Iraq, Climate and Land Use, Development Potentials." In *Asia's Lands and Peoples: A Geography of One Third of the Earth and Two Thirds of Its People*, ed. George B. Cressey. New York: McGraw-Hill, 1963.
Cottrell, Alvin. *The Persian Gulf States: A General Survey*. Baltimore, Md.: Johns Hopkins University Press, 1980.
Feel, Muhammad Rashid al-. "The Historical Geography of 'Iraq between Mongolian and Ottoman Conquest (1258–1534 A.D.)." Ph.D. diss., University of Reading, 1959.
———. *'Iraq: A Geographical Study, Social and Economic Development*. Baghdad: Ministry of Culture and Guidance, 1964.
Fisher, W. B. "'Iraq: Physical and Social Geography." In *The Middle East and North Africa, 1977–78*. London: Europa, 1977.

Le Strange, Guy. *Lands of the Eastern Caliphate: Mesopotamia, Persia, and Central Asia, from the Moslem Conquest to the Time of Timur.* Cambridge: University Press, 1905.

Lovejoy, Bajhija Fattuhi. *The Land and the People of 'Iraq.* Philadelphia: Lippincott, 1964.

Ramzl, N. *'Iraq: The Land and the People.* Baghdad: National Printing and Advertising, 1964.

Shalash, 'Ali al-. *The Climate of 'Iraq.* Amman: Cooperative Printing, 1966.

Flora and Fauna

Allouse, Bashir E. *The Avifauna of 'Iraq.* Baghdad: 'Iraqi Natural History Museum, 1953.

Chakravarty, H. L. *The Plant Wealth of 'Iraq: A Dictionary of Economic Plants.* Baghdad: 'Iraqi Ministry of Agriculture and Agrarian Reform, 1976.

Guest, Evan, ed. *Flora of 'Iraq.* Baghdad: 'Iraqi Ministry of Agriculture, 1966–1974.

Hingston, R. W. G. *Nature at the Desert's Edge; Studies and Observations in the Baghdad Oasis.* London: Witherby, 1925.

Khalaf, Kamel T. *The Marine and Fresh Water Fish of 'Iraq.* Baghdad: n.p., 1963.

——. *Reptiles of 'Iraq with Some Notes on the Amphibians.* Baghdad: n.p., 1959.

Rzoska, Julian. *Euphrates and Tigris: Mesopotamian Ecology and Destiny.* The Hague: Junk, 1980.

Young, Gavin. *Iraq, Land of Two Rivers.* London: Collins, 1980.

Biography and Memoirs

Aburish, Said. *Saddam Hussein: The Politics of Revenge.* New York: Bloomsbury, 2000.

Arif, Ismail. *'Iraq Reborn: A Firsthand Account of the July 1958 Revolution and After.* New York: Vantage, 1982.

Baram, Amatzia. "Saddam Husayn: A Political Profile." *Jerusalem Quarterly* 17 (Fall 1980): 115–4.

Bell, Florence, ed. *The Letters of Gertrude Bell.* London: Benn, 1927.

Birdwood, Lord. *Nuri al-Said, a Study in Arab Leadership.* London: 1959.

Erskine, Stuart. *King Faisal of 'Iraq: An Authorized and Authentic Study.* London: Hutchinson, 1933.

Gallman, Waldemar J. *'Iraq under General Nuri: My Recollections of Nuri al-Said, 1954–1958.* Baltimore, Md.: Johns Hopkins University Press, 1964.

Iskandar, Amir. *Saddam Husayn: Soldier, Scholar, Human Being.* Paris: Hachette Realities, 1980.

Karsh, Efraim, and Inari Rautsi. *Saddam Hussein: A Political Biography.* New York: Free Press, 1991.

Lawrence, T. E. *Seven Pillars of Wisdom.* London, 1935.

Mattar, Fuad. *Saddam Hussein: A Biography.* London: Highlight P.D.I., 1990.

——. *Saddam Hussein: The Man, the Cause and the Future.* London: Third World Press, 1981.

Maxwell, Donald. *A Dweller in Mesopotamia, Being the Adventures of an Official Artist in the Garden of Eden.* London: John Lane, 1921.

Powell, Colin L. *My American Journey.* New York: Random House, 1995.

Sinderson, Harry C. *Ten Thousand and One Nights: Memoirs of 'Iraq's Sharifian Dynasty*. London: Hodder & Stoughton, 1973.

CULTURE

General

Roaf, Michael. *Cultural Atlas of Mesopotamia and the Ancient Near East*. New York: Facts on File, 1990.

Archeology

Armstrong, James A. "West of Edin: Tell al-Deylam and the Babylonian City of Dilbat." *Biblical Archeologist* 55 (December 1992): 219–26.

Baqir, Taha. *Agar Quf*. Baghdad: Directorate General of Antiquities, 1959.

———. *Babylon and Borsippa*. Baghdad: Government Press, 1959.

———. *Baghdad*. Baghdad: Directorate General of Antiquities, 1959.

Campbell, Stuart. "The Halaf Period in 'Iraq: Old Sites and New." *Biblical Archeologist* 55 (December 1992): 182–87.

Daniel, Glyn. *The First Civilizations: The Archeology of Their Origins*. London: Thames & Hudson, 1968.

Dittman, Reinhard. "The Ubaid Period in 'Iraq: Recent Excavations in the Hamrin Region." *Bulletin of the American Schools of Oriental Research* 286 (May 1992): 91–94.

Finegan, Jack. *Archaeological History of the Ancient Middle East*. Boulder, Colo.: Westview, 1979.

George, A. R. "Babylon Revisited: Archeology and Philology in Harness." *Antiquity* 67 (December 1993): 734–46.

Hansen, Donald P. "Royal Building Activity at Sumerian Lagash in the Early Dynastic Period." *Biblical Archeologist* 55 (December 1992): 206–11.

Huot, Jean-Louis. "The First Farmers at Ouelli." *Biblical Archeologist* 55 (December 1992): 188–95.

Lloyd, Seton. *The Archaeology of Mesopotamia from the Stone Age to the Persian Conquest*. London: Thames & Hudson, 1978.

———. *Foundations in the Dust: A Story of Mesopotamian Exploration*. New York: AMS Press, 1978.

———. *Ruined Cities of 'Iraq*. London: Oxford University Press, 1947.

Matthews, Roger J. "Jemdat Nasr: The Site and the Period." *Biblical Archeologist* 55 (December 1992): 196–203.

Nashef, Khaled. "Archeology in 'Iraq." *American Journal of Archeology* 96 (April 1992): 301–23.

Stone, Elizabeth C., and Paul Zimansky. "Mashkan-shapir and the Anatomy of an Old Babylonian City." *Biblical Archeologist* 55 (December 1992): 212–18.

Stronach, David, and Stephen Lumsden. "UC-Berkeley's Excavations at Ninevah." *Biblical Archeologist* 55 (December 1992): 227–33.

Watkins, Trevor. "Pushing Back the Frontiers of Mesopotamian Prehistory." *Biblical Archeologist* 55 (December 1992): 176–81.

Architecture

Amid, Tahir al-. *The Abbasid Architecture of Samarra in the Reign of Both Al-Mutasim and Al- Mutawakkil.* Baghdad: Al-Ma'aref, 1973.
Crawford, Harriet E. W. *The Architecture of 'Iraq in the Third Millennium B.C.* Copenhagen: Akademisk Forlag, 1977.
Daniel, Glyn. *The First Civilizations: the Archaeology of Their Origins.* London: Thames & Hudson, 1968.
Janabi, Tariq Jawad al-. *Studies in Medieval 'Iraqi Architecture.* Baghdad: Ministry of Culture and Information, State Organization of Antiquities and Heritage, 1982.
Philon, Helen. "'Iraq." in *Architecture of the Islamic World: Its History and Social Meaning with a Complete Survey of the Monuments.* London: Thames & Hudson, 1978.

Arts, Literature, and Folktales

Ahmed, Abdul Ilah. "Fiction in Iraq between the Two World Wars." *Gilgamesh Baghdad* 3 (1987.)
Ali, As'ad Mohammed. "Musical Composition in Iraq." *Gilgamesh Baghdad* 2 (1986).
Barnet, R. D. *Assyrian Palace Reliefs in the British Museum.* New York: British Museum Publications, 1970.
Basmachi, Faraj. *Treasures of the 'Iraq Museum.* Baghdad: 'Iraqi Ministry of Information, Directorate General of Antiquities, 1976.
Campbell, Charles G. *Tales from the Arab Tribes.* New York: Arno, 1980.
Cassimy, 'Ali M., and W. McClung Frazier, trans. *Modern 'Iraqi Short Stories.* Baghdad: Ministry of Information, Directorate General of Culture, 1971.
Grimal, Pierre. *Stories from Babylon and Persia.* London: Burke, 1964.
Hamoudi, Bassim A. "The Iraqi Short Story: The Artistic and Social Changes." *Gilgamesh Baghdad* 2 (1986).
Hussein, Ronak, and Yasir Suleiman. "Death in the Early Poetry of Nazik al-Malaika." *British Journal of Middle Eastern Studies* 20, no. 2 (1993): 214–25.
Mafraji, Ahmed F. al-."Iraqi Theater 1921–1958." *Gilgamesh Baghdad* 2 (1986).
Mudhaffar, May. "Modern Iraqi Art and Poetry." *Gilgamesh Baghdad* 2 (1986).
Musawi, Muhsin Jassim al-. "The Modernist Trend in the Iraqi Short Story in the 1950's." *Gilgamesh Baghdad* 22 (1986.)
Stevens, E. S. *Folk-tales of 'Iraq, Set Down and Translated from the Vernacular.* London: Oxford University Press, 1931.

Language and Dictionaries

Clarity, Beverly E. A. *Dictionary of 'Iraqi-Arabic and English-Arabic.* Washington, D.C.: Georgetown University Press, 1964.
Ervin, Wallace E. *A Basic Course in 'Iraqi Arabic.* Washington, D.C.: Georgetown University Press, 1969.

MacKenzie, D. N. *Kurdish Dialect Studies I and II.* London: Oxford University Press, 1961.
McCarthy, R. J. *Spoken Arabic of Baghdad.* Beirut: Librairie Orientale, 1965.
Woodhead, D. R. *A Dictionary of 'Iraqi Arabic: Arabic-English.* Washington, D.C.: Georgetown University Press, 1967.

ECONOMY

General

Ameen, Abdul Wahab. *External Trade and Economic Growth in Developing Countries, with Special Reference to 'Iraq.* Baghdad: al-Huriyah Print House, 1975.
Brozoska, Michael. "Profiteering on the Iran–'Iraq War." *Bulletin of the Atomic Scientist* 43 (June 1987): 42–45.
Campbell, B., and D. Newcomb. *Impact of the Freeze of Kuwaiti and 'Iraqi Assets on Financial Institutions and Financial Transactions.* London: Graham & Trotman, 1990.
Ellis, Howard S. *Private Enterprise and Socialism in the Middle East.* Washington, D.C.: American Enterprise Institute, 1970.
Fenelon, K. G. *National Income In 'Iraq: Selected Studies.* Baghdad: Ministry of Planning, Central Statistical Organization, 1970.
Hall, L. J. *The Inland Water Transport in Mesopotamia.* London: Constable, 1921.
Hardan, Adai. "Sharing the Euphrates." *Research and Exploration* 9 (November 1993): 72–79.
Haseeb, K. *The National Income of 'Iraq, 1953–1961.* London: Oxford University Press, 1964.
Issawi, Charles. *The Fertile Crescent, 1800–1914: A Documentary Economic History.* New York: Oxford University Press, 1988.
Kanovsky, Eliyahu. *The Economic Consequences of the Persian Gulf War.* Washington, D.C.: Washington Institute for Near East Policy, 1992.
Kelidar, Abbas, ed. *The Integration of Modern 'Iraq.* New York: St. Martin's, 1979.
McKeirle, Joseph O. "'Iraq." In *The Arab World: a Guide to Business, Economics, and Industrial Information Sources.* Dallas, Tex.: Inter Crescent, 1980.
Mofid, Kamran. *The Economic Consequences of the Gulf War.* New York: Routledge, 1990.
Qubain, Fahim I. *The Reconstruction of 'Iraq: 1950–1957.* New York: Praeger, 1958.
Sassoon, Joseph. *Economic Policy in 'Iraq, 1932–1950.* London:Cass, 1987.
Sayigh, Yusif A. *The Economics of the Arab World: Development since 1945.* London: Croom Helm, 1978.
Simonds, S. *'Iraq: Economic and Commercial Conditions in 'Iraq.* London: Her Majesty's Stationery Office, 1953.

Agriculture and Land Reform

Adams, Robert McCormick. *Irrigation's Impact on Society.* Tucson: University of Arizona Press, 1974.

Dahiri, Abdul Wahab M. al-. *The Economics of the Agricultural Sector in 'Iraq.* Baghdad: University of Baghdad Press, 1976.

Gabbay, Rony. *Communism and Agrarian Reform in 'Iraq.* London: Croom Helm, 1978.

Hashimi, M. al-, and M. M. El-Imam. "'Iraq." In *Report on FAO/UNFPA Seminar on Agricultural Planning and Population.* Rome: Food and Agriculture Organization, 1975.

Hussain, 'Ali A. *Date Palms and Dates with Their Pests in 'Iraq.* Baghdad: University of Baghdad Press, 1974.

Kessler, J. *Drainage and Salinity Control for Land Development: A Report to the Government of 'Iraq.* Rome: Food and Agriculture Organization, 1970.

McAdams, Robert. *Land behind Baghdad: A History of Settlement on the Diyala Plains.* Chicago: University of Chicago Press, 1965.

Main, Ernest. *In and around Baghdad.* Baghdad: Times Press, 1975.

Ockerman, Herbert W., and Shimoon G. Samano. "The Agricultural Development of 'Iraq." In *Agricultural Development in the Middle East*, ed. K. S. McLachlan and Peter Beaumont. New York: Wiley, 1985, 189–207.

Springborg, Robert. "'Iraqi Intifah: Agrarian Transformation and Growth of the Private Sector." *Middle East Journal* 40, no. 1 (Winter 1986): 33–52.

———. "Ba'thism in Practice: Agriculture, Politics, and Political Culture in Syria and 'Iraq." *Middle Eastern Studies* 17, no. 2 (1981): 191–209.

Treakle, Hugh Charles. *The Agricultural Economy of 'Iraq.* Washington, D.C.: n.p., 1965.

Warriner, Doreen. *Land Reform and Development in the Middle East: A Study of Egypt, Syria and 'Iraq.* London: Oxford University Press for the Royal Institute of International Affairs, 1962.

Development and Industry

Buckley, Arthur B. *Mesopotamia as a Country for Future Development.* Cairo: Government Press, 1919.

Cooper, Charles A. *Economic Development and Growth in the Middle East.* New York: Elsevier, 1972.

Gerke, Gerwin. "The 'Iraq Development Board and British Policy, 1945–50." *Middle Eastern Studies* 27 (April 1991): 231–55.

Iverson, Carl. *A Report on the Monetary Policy of 'Iraq.* Copenhagen: Munksgaard, 1954.

Jalal, Ferhang. *The Role of Government in the Industrialization of 'Iraq, 1950–1965.* London: Cass, 1972.

Langley, Kathleen M. *The Industrialization of 'Iraq.* Cambridge, Mass.: Harvard University Press, 1967.

Looney, Robert E. "Economic Development in 'Iraq: Factors Underlying the Relative Deterioration of Human Capital Formation." *Journal of Economic Issues* 26 (June 1992): 615–22.

Perdikis, Nicholas, and Hassan Saluom. "An Analysis of the Error between Forecast and Actual Expenditure in the Budgetary System of 'Iraq." *International Journal of Middle East Studies* 19, no. 2 (May 1987): 131–54.

Salter, Lord. *The Development of 'Iraq: A Plan of Action.* Baghdad: 'Iraq Development Board, 1955.

Labor

Bade, Albert Y., and Simon G. Siksek. *Manpower and Oil in Arab Countries.* Beirut: Economic Research Institute, American University of Beirut, 1959.

Birks, J. S. "The Republic of 'Iraq." In *Arab Manpower: Crisis of Development.* London: Croom Helm, 1980.

Hameed, K. A. "Manpower and Employment Planning in 'Iraq and the Syrian Arab Republic." In *Manpower and Employment in Arab Countries: Some Critical Issues.* Geneva: International Labour Office, May 1975.

Oil

Abdul-Rasool, Faik. "Growth and Stuctural Change of Output in the Economy of 'Iraq." *OPEC Review* 6 (1982): 27–40.

Adams, Walter, James W. Brock, and John M. Blair. "Retarding the Development of 'Iraq's Oil Resources: An Episode in Oleaginous Diplomacy, 1927–1939." *Journal of Economic Issues* 27 (March 1993): 69–93.

Brown, Michael E. "The Nationalization of the 'Iraqi Petroleum Company." *International Journal of Middle East Studies* 10 (1979): 107–24.

Eyd, Kadhim A. al-. *Oil Revenues and Accelerated Growth: Absorption Capacity in 'Iraq.* New York: Praeger, 1979.

Hussein, Adel. *'Iraq: The Eternal Fire: 1972 'Iraqi Oil Nationalization in Perspective.* London: Third World Center for Research and Publishing, 1981.

Longhurst, H. *Adventure in Oil: The Story of British Petroleum.* London, 1959.

Longrigg, Stephen H. *Oil in the Middle East: Its Discovery and Development.* London: Oxford University Press, 1968.

Mejcher, Helmut. *Imperial Quest for Oil: 'Iraq 1910–1928.* London: Ithaca, 1976.

Mosawi, Muhsen al-. *'Iraq's Oil: The People's Struggle.* Baghdad: 'Iraqi Ministry of Information, 1973.

Nasrawi, Abbas al-. *Financing Economic Development in 'Iraq: The Role of Oil in a Middle Eastern Economy.* New York: Praeger, 1967.

Stivers, William. *Supremacy and Oil: 'Iraq, Turkey, and the Anglo-American World Order, 1918–1930.* Ithaca, N.Y.: Cornell University Press, 1982.

Stocking, George W. "'Iraq and the 'Iraq Petroleum Company's Concessions." In George W. Stocking, *Middle East Oil: A Study in Political and Economic Controversy.* Nashville, Tenn.: Vanderbilt University Press, 1970.

Suleyman, H. S. *The Story of Oil in 'Iraq.* London, 1958.

4. HISTORY

General

Farouk-Sluglett, Marion, and Peter Sluglett. *'Iraq since 1958: From Revolution to Dictatorship.* New York: St. Martin's, 1990.

——. "The Historiography of Modern 'Iraq." *American Historical Review* 96 (December 1991): 1408–21.

Lloyd, Seton. *'Iraq*. London: Oxford University Press, 1943.

——. *Twin Rivers: A Brief History of 'Iraq from the Earliest Times to the Present Day*. London: Oxford University Press, 1947. Longrigg, Stephen. *Four Centuries of Modern 'Iraq*. Oxford: Clarendon s, 1968.

——. *Iraq, 1900–1950: A Political, Social, and Economic History*. Oxford: Oxford University Press, 1953.

Longrigg, Stephen H., and Frank Stoakes. *'Iraq*. London: Benn, 1958.

Marayati, Abid A. al-. *A Diplomatic History of Modern 'Iraq*. New York: Speller, 1961.

Marr, Phebe. *The Modern History of 'Iraq*. Boulder, Colo.: Westview, 1985.

Penrose, Edith, and E. F. Penrose. *'Iraq: International Relations and National Development*. London: Benn, 1978.

Sacher, Howard. *The Emergence of the Middle East, 1914–19*. London: Lane, 1970.

Saleh, Zaki. *Mesopotamia 1600–1914: A Study in Britain's Foreign Affairs*. Baghdad: al-Ma'aref, 1957.

Simons, Geoff. *Iraq: From Summer to Saddam*. London: Macmillan, 1994.

Stewart, Desmond, and John Haylock. *New Babylon: A Portrait of 'Iraq*. London: Collins, 1956.

Thesiger, Wilfrid. *The Marsh Arabs*. London: Longmans, 1964.

Tripp, Charles. *A History of 'Iraq*. New York: Cambridge University Press, 2000.

Ward⁻i, 'Al⁻i. *Lamah⁻at ijtim⁻a'⁻iyah min t⁻ar⁻ikh al-'Ir⁻aq al-had⁻ith*. Baghd⁻ad: Matba'at al-Irsh⁻ad, 1969.

Ancient

Adams, Robert McCormick. *The Evolution of Urban Society: Early Mesopotamia and Pre- Hispanic Mexico*. London: Weidenfeld & Nicolson, 1966.

Ahmad, Sami Said. *Southern Mesopotamia in the Time of Ashurbanipal*. The Hague: Mouton, 1968.

Baumann, Hans. *The Land of Ur*. London: Oxford University Press, 1969.

Beek, Martin A. *Atlas of Mesopotamia*. Trans. D. R. Welsh; ed. H. H. Rowley. London: Nelson, 1962.

Braidwood, Robert, and Bruce Howe. *Prehistoric Investigations in 'Iraqi Kurdistan*. Chicago: University of Chicago Press, 1960.

Carleton, Patrick. *Buried Empires: The Earliest Civilizations of the Middle East*. London: Arnold, 1939; reprinted, London: Arnold, 1948.

Crawford, Harriet E. W. *Sumer and the Sumerians*. New York: Cambridge University Press, 1991.

Hall, H. R. "The Early History of Babylonia." In H. R. Hall, *The Ancient History of the Near East: From the Earliest Times to the Battle of Salmis*. London: Methuen, 1950.

Hyma, Albert. "The Kingdom of Ancient Mesopotamia." In *Ancient History*. New York: Barnes & Noble, 1940.

Jacobsen, Thorkild. *Toward the Image of Tammuz and Other Essays on Mesopotamian History and Culture*. Cambridge, Mass.: Harvard University Press, 1970.

King, Leonard W. *A History of Babylon from the Foundation of the Monarchy to the Persian Conquest*. London: Chatto & Windus, 1919.

———. *A History of Sumer and Akkad: An Account of the Early Races of Babylonia from Prehistoric Times to the Foundation of the Babylonian Monarchy.* London: Chatto & Windus, 1910.

Laessoe, Jorgen. *People of Ancient Assyria: Their Inscriptions and Correspondence.* Trans. from Danish by F. S. Leigh-Browne. London: Routledge & Kegan Paul, 1963.

Lansing, Elizabeth. *The Sumerians: Inventors and Builders.* London: Cassell, 1974.

Oates, David. *Studies in the Ancient History of Northern 'Iraq.* London: Oxford University Press, 1968.

Oppenheim, A. Leo. *Ancient Mesopotamia: Portrait of a Dead Civilization.* Chicago: University of Chicago Press, 1977.

Postgate, N. J. *Early Mesopotamia: Society and Economy at the Dawn of History.* New York: Routledge, 1992.

Roux, Georges. *Ancient 'Iraq.* London: Allen & Unwin, 1964.

Severy, Merle. "'Iraq: Crucible of Civilization." *National Geographic* 179 (May 1991): 102–15.

Smith, Sidney. *Early History of Assyria to 1000 B.C.* London: Chatto & Windus, 1928.

Starr, Chester G. "Civilization in Babylon." In Chester G. Starr, *Early Man, Prehistory and the Civilizations of the Ancient Near East.* London: Oxford University Press, 1973.

Thompson, R. Cambell. *Late Babylonian Letters: Transliterations and Translations of a Series of Letters Written in Babylonian Cuneiform.* New York: AMS Press, 1976.

Weiss, H., M. A. Courty, and W. Wetterstrom. "The Genesis and Collapse of Third Millennium North Mesopotamian Civilization." *Science* 261 (August 20, 1994): 995–1004.

Whitehouse, Ruth. *The First Cities.* Oxford: Phaidon, 1977.

Medieval and Ottoman Periods

Ashtor, E. "'Iraq under Mongol and Turcoman Feudal Lords." In E. Ashtor, *A Social and Economic History of the Near East in the Middle Ages.* London: Collins, 1976.

'Azzawi, 'Abbas al-. *Tᵃrīkh al-'Irᵃaq bayna ihtilᵃalayn [ta'lᵢf] 'Abbᵃas al-'Azzᵃawī.* Baghdad: Matba'at Baghdᵃad, 1353–1376/1935–1956.

Bartol'd, V. V. (Vasilii Vladimirovich). *Turkestan Down to the Mongol Invasion.* Philadelphia: distributed in the United States by Porcupine Press, 1977.

Busse, Heribert. *Chalif und Grosskönig; die Buyiden im Iraq (945–1055).* Beirut; In Kommission bei F. Steiner, Wiesbaden, 1969.

Cole Juan. "Indian Money and the Shia Shrine-cities of 'Iraq, 1786–1850." *Middle Eastern Studies* 22 (October 1986): 461–80.

Haj, Samira. "The Problems of Tribalism: The Case of Nineteenth Century 'Iraqi History." *Social History* 16 (January 1991): 45–58.

El-Hibri, Tayeb. "Harun al-Rashid and the Mecca Protocol of 802: A Plan for Division or Succession?" *International Journal of Middle Eastern Studies* 24 (August 1992): 461–80.

Kennedy, Hugh. *The Prophet and the Age of the Caliphates: The Islamic Near East from the Sixth to the Eleventh Century.* London: Longman, 1986.

Morony, Michael. *'Iraq after the Muslim Conquest.* Princeton, N.J.: Princeton University Press, 1984.

Nieuwenhuis, Tom. *Politics and Society in Early Modern Iraq: Mamluk Pashas Tribal Shayks and Local Rule between 1802 and 1831.* The Hague: Martinus Nijhoff, 1982.

Shields, Sarah D. "Sheep, Nomads and Merchants in Nineteenth Century Mosul: Creating Transformations in an Ottoman Society." *Journal of Social History* 25 (Summer 1992): 773–89.

———. "Regional Trade and Nineteenth Century Mosul: Revising the Role of Europe in the Middle East Economy." *International Journal of Middle East Studies* 23 (February 1991): 19–37.

Vaglieri, Laura Veccia. "The Patriarchal and Umayyad Caliphates." In *The Cambridge History of Islam, Vol. I,* ed. P. M. Holt, Ann K. S. Lambton, and Bernard Lewis. Cambridge: Cambridge University Press, 1970.

Monarchial (1900–1958)

Antonius, George. *The Arab Awakening: The Study of the Arab National Movement.* London: Hamilton, 1938.

Atiyyah, Ghassan R. *'Iraq, 1908–1921: A Socio-Political Study.* Beirut: Arab Institute for Research and Publishing, 1973.

Baram, Phillip J. "Policy towards the British Sphere of Influence: 'Iraq." In *The Department of State in the Middle East, 1919–1945.* Philadelphia: University of Pennsylvania Press, 1978.

Barker, A. J. *The Neglected War, Mesopotamia 1914–1918.* London, 1967.

Buchanan, George. *The Tragedy of Mesopotamia.* London: Blackwell, 1938.

Cohen, Stuart A. *British Policy in Mesopotamia, 1903–1914.* London: Ithaca, 1976.

De Gaury, Gerald. *Three Kings in Baghdad, 1921–1958.* London: Hutchinson, 1961.

Earle, Edward Mead. *Turkey, the Great Powers and the Baghdad Railway: A Study in Imperialism.* New York, Macmillan, 1923.

Eppel, Michael. "The Hikmat Sulayman-Bakr Sidqi Government in 'Iraq, 1936–37, and the Palestine Question." *Middle Eastern Studies* 24 (January 1988): 25–41.

Ewing, William. *From Gallipoli to Baghdad.* London: Hodder & Stoughton, 1919.

Foster, Henry A. *The Making of Modern 'Iraq.* Norman: University of Oklahoma Press, 1935.

Glubb, John Bagot. "'Iraq between the Wars." In *Britain and the Arabs: A Study of Fifty Years 1908–1958.* London: Hodder & Stoughton, 1959.

Haldane, Sir James L. *The Insurrection in Mesopotamia, 1920.* London: Blackwood, 1932.

Ireland, Philip. *'Iraq: A Study in Political Development.* London: Cape, 1937.

Jasse, Richard L. "The Baghdad Pact: Cold War or Colonialism?" *Middle Eastern Studies* 27 (January 1991): 140–56.

Khadduri, Majid. *Independent 'Iraq.* Oxford: Oxford University Press, 1951.

Khan, M. A. Saleem. *The Monarchic 'Iraq.* Aligarth, India: Centre of West Asian Studies, Aligarth Muslim University, 1987.

MacCallum, Elizabeth P. *'Iraq and the British Treaties.* New York: Information Service of the Foreign Policy Association, 1930.

Main, Ernest. *'Iraq from Mandate to Independence.* London: Allen & Unwin, 1935.

Masalha, N. "Faisal's Pan-Arabism." *Middle Eastern Studies* 27 (October 1991): 679–93.

Moberly, F. J. *The Campaign in Mesopotamia 1914–1918.* London: His Majesty's Stationery Office, 1923.

Porath, Yehoshua. "Nuri al-Said's Arab Unity Program." *Middle Eastern Studies* 20 (October 1984): 76–98.

Saleh, Zaki. *Origins of British Influence in Mesopotamia.* New York: Columbia University Press, 1941.

Shawdran, Benjamin. *The Power Struggle in 'Iraq.* New York: Council for Middle Eastern Affairs Press, 1960.

Shikara, Ahmed Abdul Razzaq. *'Iraqi Politics 1921–1941: The Intersection between Domestic Politics and Foreign Policy.* London: Laam, 1987.

Silverfarb, Daniel. *Britain's Informal Empire in the Middle East: A Case Study of 'Iraq, 1929–1941.* New York: Oxford University Press, 1986.

Simon, Reeva S. *'Iraq between the Two World Wars: The Creation and Implementation of a Nationalist Ideology.* New York: Columbia University Press, 1986.

Sluglett, Peter. *Britain in 'Iraq.* London: Ithaca, 1976.

Vinogradov, Amal. "The 1920 Revolt in 'Iraq Reconsidered: The Role of Tribes in National Politics." *International Journal of Middle East Studies* 3 (1972): 123–39.

Wilson, Sir Arnold. *Mesopotamia, 1917–1920: A Clash of Loyalties.* London: Oxford University Press, 1931.

——. *Loyalties: Mesopotamia, 1914–1917.* London: Oxford University Press, 1930.

Zamir, Mier. "Faisel and the Lebanese Question, 1918–20." *Middle Eastern Studies* 45 (Winter 1991): 51–70.

Republican (1958–1968)

Dann, Uriel. *'Iraq under Qassem: A Political History, 1958–1963.* New York: Praeger, 1969.

Khadduri, Majid. *Republican 'Iraq: A Study in 'Iraqi Politics since the Revolution of 1958.* New York: Oxford University, 1969.

Lenczowski, George. "'Iraq: Seven Years of Revolution." *Current History* 49 (May 1965): 281–89.

Ba'thist (1968–2003)

Baram, Amatzia. *Culture, History, and Ideology in the Formation of Ba'thist Iraq, 1968–69.* Houndmills, England: Macmillan in association with St. Antony's College, Oxford, 1991.

Farouk-Sluglett, Marion, and Sluglett, Peter. *Iraq Since 1958: From Revolution to Dictatorship.* New York: Tauris, 2001.

Khadduri, Majid. *Socialist 'Iraq: A Study in 'Iraqi Politics since 1968.* Washington, D.C: Middle East Institute, 1978.

5. POLITICS

General

'Ali, Sadeq M. *Response to Challenges: An Outline of 'Iraq's Stand towards Arab and International Issues.* Baghdad: 'Iraqi Ministry of Culture and Information, 1980.

Amnesty International. *'Iraq: Evidence of Torture.* London: Author, 1981.

Axelgard, Frederick W., ed. *'Iraq in Transition.* Boulder, Colo.: Westview, 1986.

Baram, Amatzia. "Neo-Tribalism in 'Iraq: Saddam Hussein's Tribal Policies 1991–96." *International Journal of Middle East Studies* 29 (1997): 1–31.

———. *Culture, History, and Ideology in the Formation of Ba'thist 'Iraq, 1968–1989.* New York: St. Martin's, 1991.

———. "The Future of Ba'thist 'Iraq: Power Structure, Challenges, and Prospects." In *The Politics of Change in the Middle East*, ed. Robert Satloff. Boulder, Colo.: Westview, 1993, 31–62.

———. "The Ruling Political Elite in Ba'thi 'Iraq, 1968–1986: The Changing Features of a Collective Profile." *International Journal of Middle East Studies* 21, no. 4 (November 1989): 447–93.

———. "Mesopotamian Identity in Ba'thi 'Iraq." *Middle Eastern Studies* 19, no. 4 (1983): 426–55.

Batatu, Hanna. *The Egyptian, Syrian and 'Iraqi Revolutions: Some Observations on Their Underlying Causes and Social Character.* Washington, D.C.: Georgetown University, 1984.

———. *The Old Social Classes and the Revolutionary Movement in 'Iraq: A Study of 'Iraq's Old Landed and Commercial Classes and Its Communists, Ba'thists and Free Officers.* Princeton, N.J.: Princeton University Press, 1978.

Bengio, Ofra. "Saddam Husayn's Quest for Power and Survival." *Asian and African Studies* 15 (1981): 323–41.

Central Intelligence Agency. *Directory of 'Iraqi Officials.* Washington, D.C.: CIA, Directorate of Intelligence, Document Expediting Project, Exchange and Gift Division, Library of Congress, 1986.

Committee against Repression and for Democratic Rights in 'Iraq (CARDRI). *Saddam's 'Iraq: Revolution or Reaction?* London: Zed, 1989.

Fernea, Robert A., and William Rodger Louis, eds. *The 'Iraqi Revolution of 1958: The Old Social Classes Revisited.* London: Tauris, 1991.

Ghareeb, Edmund. "'Iraq and Gulf Security." In *The Impact of the Iranian Events upon Persian Gulf and United States Security*, Michael Szaz. Washington, D.C.: American Foreign Policy Institute, 1979, 39–64.

———. "'Iraq: Emergent Gulf Power." In *The Security of the Persian Gulf*, ed. Hossein Amirsadeghi. New York: St. Martin's, 1981, 197–230.

Helms, Christine Moss. *'Iraq: Eastern Flank of the Arab World.* Washington, D.C.: Brookings Institution, 1984.

Ireland, Philip Willard. *'Iraq: A Study in Political Development.* London: Cape, 1937.

Ismael, Tareq Y. *Government and Politics of the Contemporary Middle East.* Homewood, Ill.: Dorsey, 1970.

Ismael, Tareq Y., and Jacqueline S. Ismael. "'Iraq's Interrupted Revolution." *Current History* 84, no. 488 (1985): 29+.

Kelidar, Abbas. "The Wars of Saddam Hussein." *Middle Eastern Studies* 28, no. 4 (October 1992): 778–98.

———. "'Iraq: The Search for Stability." *Conflict Studies* 59 (July 1975): 1–21.

Khadduri, Majid. *Arab Contemporaries: The Role of Personalities in Politics.* Baltimore, Md.: Johns Hopkins University Press, 1973.

Khafaji, Isam al-. "State Terror and the Degradation of Politics in 'Iraq." *Middle East Reports* 22, no. 3 (May/June 1992): 15–21.

Khalil, Samir al-. *The Monument: Art, Vulgarity and Responsibility in 'Iraq.* Berkeley: University of California Press, 1991.

———. *The Republic of Fear.* Berkeley: University of California Press, 1989.

Kimball, Lorenzo K. *The Changing Pattern of Political Power in 'Iraq, 1958 to 1971.* New York: Speller, 1972.

Korn, David A. *Human Rights in 'Iraq.* New Haven, Conn.: Yale University Press, 1990.

Luizard, Pierre-Jean. *La formation de l'Irak contemporain: Le rôle politique des ulémas chiites à la fin de la domination ottomane et au moment de la construction de l'état irakien.* Paris: Editions du Centre national de la recherche scientifique, 1991.

Makiya, Kanan. "The Anfal," *Harper's* 284 (May 1992): 53–61.

———. *Cruelty and Silence: War, Tyranny, Uprising and the Arab World.* New York: Norton, 1993.

Marayati, Abid A. al-. *The Middle East: Its Governments and Politics.* Belmont, Calif: Duxbury, 1972.

Marr, Phoebe. "'Iraq's Uncertain Future." *Current History* 90, no. 552 (January 1991): 1–4+.

———. "The Political Elite in 'Iraq." In *Political Elites in the Middle East*, ed. George Lenczowski. Washington, D.C.: American Enterprise Institute, 1975, 109-149.

———. "'Iraq's Leadership Dilemma: A Study in Leadership Trends, 1948–1968." *Middle East Journal* 24, no. 3 (Summer 1970): 283–99.Mattair, Thomas R., and Stephen Brannon. "UN Sanctions against 'Iraq," *Middle East Policy* 3, no. 1 (1994): 27–43.

McLaurin, R. D. *Foreign Policy Making in the Middle East: Domestic Influences on Policy in Egypt, 'Iraq, Israel, and Syria.* New York: Praeger, 1977.

Miller, Judith. "'Iraq Accused: A Case of Genocide." *New York Times Magazine* 3 (January 1993): 12–17.

Mostyn, Tevor. *Major Political Events in Iran, 'Iraq and the Arabian Peninsula 1945–1990.* New York: Facts on File, 1991.

Niblock, Tim, ed. *'Iraq: The Contemporary State.* New York: St. Martin's, 1982.

Pelletiere, Stephen. *Winds of Death: 'Iraq's Use of Poison Gas against Its Kurdish Population—Report of a Medical Mission to Turkish Kurdistan.* Somerville, Mass: Physicians for Human Rights, 1989.

Pelletiere, Stephen, et al. *'Iraqi Power and US Security in the Middle East.* Carlisle Barracks, Penn.: Strategic Studies Institute, U.S. Army War College, 1990.

Reid, Donald Malcolm. "The Postage Stamp: A Window on Saddam Hussein's 'Iraq." *Middle East Journal* 47, no. 1 (Winter 1993): 77–89.

Samiuddin, Abida. "The Beginning of Parliamentary Democracy in 'Iraq—A Case Study." *Middle Eastern Studies* 18 (October 1982): 445–48.

Szaz, Z. Michael, ed. *Sources of Domestic and Foreign Policy in 'Iraq.* Washington, D.C.: American Foreign Policy Institute, 1986.
Turner, Arthur Campbell. "'Iraq: Pragmatic Radicalism in the Fertile Crescent." *Current History* 81, no. 471 (1982): 14–17.
Wahib, Hani. *The Democratic Experience and the National Assembly Elections.* Baghdad: Dar al-Hurriya, 1981.
Wright, Claudia. "'Iraq: New Power in the Middle East." *Foreign Affairs* 58, no. 2 (Winter 1979–1980): 257–77.
Wright, Quincy. "The Government of 'Iraq." *American Political Science Review* 20 (November 1926).

Boundary Disputes

Biger, Gideon. "The Shatt al-Arab River Boundary: A Note." *Middle Eastern Studies* 25 (April 1989): 249–52.
Edmonds, C. J. "The 'Iraqi-Persian Frontier: 1639–1938." *Asian Affairs* 62 (June 1975): 147–54.
Finnie, David H. *Shifting Lines in the Sand: Kuwait's Elusive Frontier with 'Iraq.* Cambridge, Mass.: Harvard University Press, 1992.
Kaikobad, Kaiyan Homi. *The Shatt al-Arab Boundary Question: A Legal Reappraisal.* New York: Oxford University Press, 1988.
Izzi, Khalid al-. *The Shatt al-Arab River Dispute in Terms of Law.* Baghdad: Ministry of Information, 1972.
Tauber, Eliezer. "The Struggle for Dayr al-Zur: The Determination of Borders between Syria and 'Iraq." *International Journal of Middle East Studies* 23, no. 3 (August 1991): 361–85.

Foreign Relations

Axelgard, Frederick W. "US-'Iraqi Relations: A Status Report." *American-Arab Affairs* 13 (Summer 1985): 1–9.
Baram, Amatzia. "Israeli Deterrence, 'Iraqi Responses." *Orbis* 36 (Summer 1992): 397–409.
——. "Baathi 'Iraq and Hashemite Jordan: From Hostility to Alignment." *Middle East Journal* 45 (Winter 1991): 51–70.
Brand, Laurie. "Economics and Shifting Alliances: Jordan's Relations with Syria and 'Iraq." *International Journal of Middle Eastern Studies* 26, no. 3 (August 1994): 393–413.
Dawisha, Adeed. "'Iraq: The West's Opportunity." *Foreign Policy* 41 (Winter 1980–1081): 134–53.
Dickey, Christopher. "Assad and His Allies: Irreconcilable Differences." *Foreign Affairs* 66 (Fall 1987): 58–76.
Eberhard, Kienle. *Ba'th v. Ba'th : The Conflict Between Syria and Iraq, 1968-69.* New York: Tauris; distributed in the United States and Canada by St. Martin's Press, 1990.
Eppel, Michael. "'Iraqi Politics and Regional Policies." *Middle Eastern Studies* 28 (January 1992): 108–19.

———. *The Conflict Between the Ba'th Regimes of Syria and 'Iraq prior to Their Consolidation: From Regime Survival to Regional Domination*. Berlin: Verlag das Arabische Buch, 1986.

Kimche, Jon. "'Iraq and Transjordan." In *The Second Arab Awakening*. New York: Holt, Rinehart & Winston, 1970.

Lemarchand, Philippe, ed. *'Iraq, the Gulf, and the Arab World*. Boulder, Colo.: Westview Press, 1992.

Maddy-Weitzman, Bruce. "Jordan and 'Iraq: Efforts at Intra-Hashemite Unity." *Middle Eastern Studies* 26 (January 1990): 65–75.

Marayati, Abid A. al-. *A Diplomatic History of Modern Iraq*. New York: Speller, 1961.

Mylroie, Laurie. "After the Guns Fell Silent." *Middle East Journal* 43, no. 1 (Winter 1989): 51–67.

———. "'Iraq's Changing Role in the Persian Gulf." *Current History* 88 (February 1989): 89–92+.

Podeh, Elie. "The Struggle over Arab Hegemony after the Suez Crisis." *Middle Eastern Studies* 29 (January 1993): 91–110.

Shemesh, Haim. *Soviet-'Iraqi Relations, 1968–1988: In the Shadow of the 'Iraq–Iran Conflict*. Boulder, Colo.: Rienner, 1992.

Sirriya, Hussein. "Development of the 'Iraqi-Iranian Dispute, 1847–1975." *Journal of Contemporary History* 20 (July 1985): 483–92.

Smolansky, Oles M., with Bettie M. Smolansky. *The USSR and 'Iraq: The Soviet Quest for Influence*. Durham, N.C.: Duke University Press, 1991.

Terrill, W. Andrew. "Saddam's Closest Ally: Jordan and the Gulf War." *Journal of South Asian and Middle Eastern Studies* 9, no. 2 (Winter 1985): 43–54.

Tomasek, Robert D. "The Resolution of Major Controversies between Iran and 'Iraq." *World Affairs* 139, no. 3 (Winter 1976–77): 206–30.

Warner, Geoffrey. *'Iraq and Syria, 1941*. London: Davis-Poynter, 1974.

Legal System

Amin, Syed Hassan. *Legal System of 'Iraq*. Glasgow: Royston, 1989.

Chibli, Mallat. *The Renewal of Islamic Law: Muhammad Baqer as-Sadr, Najaf, and the Shi'i International*. New York: Cambridge University Press, 1993.

Jwaideh, Zuhair E. *Nature and Scope of Marriage and Divorce Laws in Egypt and 'Iraq*. N.p.: 1976.

Ziadeh, Farhat J. *Property Law in the Arab World: Real Rights in Egypt, 'Iraq, Jordan, Lebanon, Libya, Syria, Saudi Arabia and the Gulf States*. London: Graham & Trotman, 1979.

Military in Politics

Badeeb, Saeed M. "The Impact of Military Power in 'Iraq since the 1958 Revolution." *American-Arab Affairs* 34 (Fall 1990): 17–28.

Haddad, George M. *Revolution and Military Rule in the Middle East*. New York: Speller, Vol. I, 1965; Vol. II, 1971; Vol. III, 1973.

Heller, Mark. "Politics and the Military in 'Iraq and Jordan, 1920–1958: The British In-fluence." *Armed Forces and Society* 4, no. 1 (Fall 1977): 75–100.

Tarbush, Muhammad A. *The Role of the Military in Politics: A Case Study of 'Iraq to 1941.* London: Kegan Paul, 1982.

Political Parties

Amin, Muddaffar. "The Origin and Growth of the Ahali Party in 'Iraq 1932–1945." Ph.D. diss., Durham University.

Batatu, Hanna. *The Old Social Classes and the Revolutionary Movements of Iraq: A Study of Iraq's Old Landed and Commercial Classes and of Its Communists, Ba'thists and Free Officers.* Princeton, N.J.: Princeton University Press, 1978.

Devlin, John. *The Ba'th Party.* Stanford, Calif.: Hoover Institution Press, 1976.

———. "The Ba'th Party: Rise and Metamorphosis." *American Historical Review* 96 (December 1991): 1396–1407.

Haji, Aziz al-. *With the Years: Pages from the History of the Communist Movement in 'Iraq between 1958–1969.* Beirut: al-Mu'assanasa al-'Arabiya lil-Dirasat wa'l-Nashr, 1980.

Jabir, Kamil Abu. *Arab Ba'th Socialist Party.* Syracuse, N.Y.: Syracuse University Press, 1966.

Torrey, Gordon. "The Baath Ideology and Practice." *Middle East Journal* 23 (Autumn 1969): 445–70.

Wiley, Joyce N. *The Islamic Movement of Iraqi Shi'as.* Boulder, Colo.: Rienner, 1992.

Iran–'Iraq War

Abdulghani, Jasim M. *'Iraq and Iran: The Years of Crisis.* Baltimore, Md.: Johns Hop-kins University Press, 1984.

Axelgard, Frederick W. "'Iraq and the War with Iran." *Current History* 86, no. 523 (1987): 574+.

Aziz, Tareq. *The 'Iraq-Iran Conflict: Questions and Discussions.* London: Third World Centre for Research and Publishing, 1981.

Central Intelligence Agency. "Iraq: Chemical Agents and The Kurdish Experience." *Science and Weapons Review* (23 September 1988): 1–2 (MORI DocID: 121671).

Chubin, Shahram, and Charles Trip. *Iran and 'Iraq at War.* London: Tauris, 1988.

Cordesman, Anthony H. *The Iran-'Iraq War and Western Security, 1984–1987.* London: Jane's, 1987.

———. "Lessons of the Iran–'Iraq War: The First Round." *Armed Forces Journal* 119, no. 8 (April 1982): 32–47.

———. "Lessons of the Iran-'Iraq War: Part Two—Tactics, Technology, and Training." *Armed Forces Journal* 119, no. 10 (June 1982): 68–85.

Devlin, John. "'Iraqi Military Policy: From Assertiveness to Defence." In *Gulf Security and the Iran-'Iraq War,* ed. Thomas Naff. Washington, D.C.: National Defense University Press, 1985, 129–56.

El-Azhary, M. S. *The Iran-'Iraq War: An Historical, Economic and Political Analysis.* New York: 1984.

Ghareeb, Edmund. "The Forgotten War." *American-Arab Affairs* 5 (Summer 1983): 59–75.

Helms, Christine Moss. "The 'Iraqi Dilemma: Political Objectives versus Military Strategy." *American-Arab Affairs* 5 (Summer 1983): 76–85.

Hiro, Dilip. *The Longest War: The Iran–'Iraq Military Conflict*. London: Grafton, 1989.

Ismael, Tareq Y. *'Iraq and Iran: Roots of Conflict*. Syracuse, N.Y.: Syracuse University Press, 1982.

Jawdat, Nameer 'Ali. "Reflections on the Gulf War." *American-Arab Affairs* 5 (Summer 1983): 86–98.

Joyner, Christopher, ed. *The Persian Gulf War*. New York: Greenwood, 1990.

Karsh, Efraim. *The Iran–'Iraq War: A Military Analysis*. London: Adelphi Paper 220, Spring 1987.

Khadduri, Majid. *The Gulf War*. New York: Oxford University Press, 1988.

Moberly, John. "'Iraq in the Aftermath of the Gulf War." *Asian Affairs* 20 (October 1989): 306–14.

Mylroie, Laurie. "The Superpowers and the Iran–'Iraq War." *American-Arab Affairs* 21 (Summer 1987): 15–26.

Nonneman, Gerd. *'Iraq, the Gulf States and the War*. London: Ithaca, 1989.

O'Ballance, Edgar. *The Gulf War*. London: Brassay's Defense Publishers, 1988.

Pelletiere, Stephen, and Douglas V. Johnson II. *Lessons Learned: The Iran–'Iraq War*. Carlisle Barracks, Penn.: Strategic Studies Institute, U.S. Army War College, 1990.

Rajaee, Farhang. *The Iran–'Iraq War: The Politics of Aggression*. Gainesville: University Press of Florida, 1993.

Segal, David. "The Iran–'Iraq War: A Military Analysis." *Foreign Affairs* 66 (Summer 1988): 946–64.

Sick, Gary. "Trial by Error: Reflections on the Iran–'Iraq War." *Middle East Journal* 43, no. 2 (Spring 1989): 230–45.

Stauffer, Thomas. "Economic Warfare in the Gulf." *American-Arab Affairs* 14 (Fall 1985): 98–116.

Tahir-Kheli, Shirin, and Ayubi Shaheen, eds. *The Iran–'Iraq War: New Weapons, Old Conflicts*. New York: Praeger, 1983.

Viorst, Milton. "'Iraq at War." *Foreign Affairs* 65, no. 2 (Winter 1986–1987): 349–65.

Invasion of Kuwait/Operation Desert Storm

Axelgard, Frederick W. *A New 'Iraq? The Gulf War and Implications for US Policy*. New York: Praeger, 1988.

Baram, Amatzia, and Barry Rubin, eds. *'Iraq's Road to War*. New York: St. Martin's, 1993.

Bishku, Michael B. "'Iraq's Claim to Kuwait: A Historical Overview." *American-Arab Affairs* 37 (Summer 1991): 77–88.

Bulloch, John, and Harvey Morris. *Saddam's War: The Origins of the Kuwait Conflict and the International Response*. London: Faber & Faber, 1991.

Darwish, Adel, and Gregory Alexander. *Unholy Babylon: The Secret History of Saddam's War*. London: Gollancz, 1991.

Draper, Theodore. "The Gulf War Reconsidered." *New York Review of Books* 39 (16 January 1992): 46–53.

Ehteshami, Anoushiravant, and Gerd Nonneman with Charles Trip. *War and Peace in the Gulf*. Reading, England: Ithaca, 1991.

Finkelstein, Norman. "Israel and 'Iraq: A Double Standard." *Journal of Palestine Studies* 20, no. 2 (Winter 1991): 43–56.

Freedman, Lawrence, and Efraim Karsh. *The Gulf Conflict, 1990–1991*. Princeton, N.J.: Princeton University Press, 1993.

Ghabra, Shafeeq. "The 'Iraqi Occupation of Kuwait: An Eyewitness Account." *Journal of Palestine Studies* 20, no. 2 (Winter 1991): 112–25.

Greer, Edward. "The Hidden History of the 'Iraq War." *Monthly Review* 43 (May 1991): 1–14.

Gregg, Robert W. *About Face? The United States and the United Nations*. Boulder, Colo.: Rienner, 1993.

Hashim, Ahmed. "'Iraq, the Pariah State." *Current History* 91, no. 561 (January 1992): 11–16.

Henderson, Simon. *Instant Empire: Saddam Hussein's Ambition for 'Iraq*. San Francisco: Mercury House, 1991.

Hilsman, Roger. *George Bush vs. Saddam Hussein: Military Success! Political Failure?* Novato, Calif.: Presidio, 1992.

Hiro, Dilip. *Desert Shield to Desert Storm: The Second Gulf War*. New York: Routledge, 1992.

Jabbar, Faleh Abd al-. "Why the Uprisings Failed." *Middle East Reports* 22, no. 3 (May/June 1992): 2–14.

Joyner, Christopher C. "Sanctions, Compliance and International Law: Reflections on the United Nation's Experience Against 'Iraq." *Virginia Journal of International Law* 32 (Fall 1991): 1–46.

Khalidi, Walid. "The Gulf Crisis: Origins and Consequences." *Journal of Palestine Studies* 20, no. 2 (Winter 1991): 5–28.

Kono, Tom. "The Economics behind the Invasion," *Middle East Insight* 7, no. 4 (1990): 36–41.

———. "Road to the Invasion," *American-Arab Affairs* 34 (Fall 1990): 29–45.

Lauterpacht, Elihu, ed. *The Kuwait Crisis: Basic Documents*. Cambridge: Grotius, 1991.

McCausland, Jeffrey. *The Gulf Conflict: A Military Analysis*. N.p.: 1993.

Miller, Judith, and Laurie Mylroie. *Saddam Hussein and the Crisis in the Gulf*. New York: Times Books, 1990.

Mylroie, Laurie. "How We Helped Saddam Survive." *Commentary* 92 (July 1991): 15–18.

Neff, Donald. "The US, 'Iraq, Israel, and Iran: Backdrop to War." *Journal of Palestine Studies* 20, no. 4 (Summer 1991): 23–41.

Newell, Clayton R. *Historical Dictionary of the Persian Gulf War*. Lanhom, Md.: Scarecrow, 1998.

Ridgeway, James. *The March to War*. New York: Four Walls Eight Windows, 1991.

Salinger, Pierre, and Eric Laurent. *Secret Dossier: The Hidden Agenda Behind the Gulf War*. New York: Penguin, 1991.

Schofield, Richard. *Kuwait and 'Iraq: Historical Claims and Territorial Disputes*. London: 1991.

Sciolino, Elaine. *The Outlaw State: Saddam Hussein's Quest for Power and the Gulf Crisis*. New York: Wiley, 1991.

Simpson, John. "The Aftermath of the Gulf War." *Asian Affairs* 23 (June 1992): 161–70.

Summers, Harry G. *On Strategy II: A Critical Analysis of the Gulf War*. New York: Dell, 1992.

Tripp, Charles. "The Gulf Crisis and the Politics of 'Iraq." *Middle East Insight* 7, no. 4 (1990): 4–10.

Woodward, Bob. *The Commanders*. New York: Simon & Schuster, 1991.

'Iraq's Strategic and Nuclear Weapons' Programs

Albright, David. "Supplier-spotting." *Bulletin of the Atomic Scientist* 49 (January/February 1993): 8–9.

Albright, David, and Mark Hibbs. "'Iraq and the Bomb: Were They Even Close?" *Bulletin of the Atomic Scientist* 47 (March 1991): 16–25.

Bishara, Ghassan. "The Political Repercussions of the Israeli Raid on the 'Iraqi Nuclear Reactor." *Journal of Palestine Studies* 11, no. 3 (Spring 1992): 58–76.

Cohen, Avner, and Marvin Miller. "'Iraq and the Rules of the Nuclear Game." *Bulletin of the Atomic Scientist* 47 (July/August 1991): 10–11.

Davis, Jay C., and David A. Kay. "'Iraq's Secret Nuclear Weapons Program." *Physics Today* 45 (July 1992): 21–27.

Eisentadt, Michael. *The Sword of the Arabs': 'Iraq's Strategic Weapons*. Washington, D.C.: Washington Institute for Near East Policy, 1990.

Feldman, Shai. "The Bombing of Os'Iraq—Revisited." *International Security* 7, no. 1 (Fall 1982): 114–42.

Lowther, William. *Arms and the Man: Dr. Gerald Bull, 'Iraq, and the Supergun*. London: Macmillan, 1991.

Pilate, Joseph F. "'Iraq and the Future of Nuclear Nonproliferation: The Roles of Inspections and Treaties." *Science* 244 (6–11 March 1992): 1224–29.

Ramberg, Bennett. "Attacks on Nuclear Reactors: The Implications of Israel's Strike on Os'Iraq." *Political Science Quarterly* 97 (Winter 1982–1983): 653–69.

Ruthen, Russel. "'Iraq's Nuclear Threat: Is the US Underestimating Hussein's Nuclear Capability?" *Scientific American* 264 (February 1991): 14+.

Snyder, Jeb C. "The Road to Os'Iraq: Baghdad's Quest for the Bomb." *Middle East Journal* 37, no. 4 (Autumn 1983): 565–93.

Timmerman, Kenneth R. *The Death Lobby: How the West Armed 'Iraq*. Boston: Houghton Mifflin, 1991.

Wilson, Richard. "Nuclear Proliferation and the Case of 'Iraq." *Journal of Palestine Studies* 20, no. 3 (Spring 1991): 5–15.

6. POPULATION, RELIGION, AND SOCIETY

General

Badger, George Percy. *The Nestorians and Their Rituals: With the Narrative of a Mission to Mesopotamia and Coordistan in 1842–44, and of a Late Visit to Those Countries in 1850; also Researches the Present Condition of the Syrian Jacobites, Papal Syrians, and Chaldeans, and an Inquiry into the Religious Tenets of the Yazeedees.* London: Masters, 1852.

Edmonds, C. J. *Kurds, Turks and Arabs: Politics, Travel and Research in North-Eastern 'Iraq 1919–1925.* London: Oxford University Press, 1957.

Gotlieb, Yosef. "Sectarianism and the 'Iraqi State." In *Religion and Politics of the Middle East,* ed. Michael Curtis. Boulder, Colo.: Westview, 1981, 153–61.

Joseph, John. *The Nestorians and Their Muslim Neighbors.* Princeton, N.J.: Princeton University Press, 1961.

Hourani, Albert. *Minorities in the Arab World.* London: Oxford University Press, 1947.

Luke, Henry Charles. *Mosul and Its Minorities.* London: Hopkinson, 1925.

Mallat Chibli. *The Renewal of Islamic Law: Muhammad Baqer as-Sadr, Najaf, and the Shi'i International.* New York: Cambridge University Press, 1993.

Melkonian, Vartan. *An Historical Glimpse of the Armenians in 'Iraq, from Earliest Times to the Present Day.* Basra: Times Press, 1957.

Nakash, Yitzhaq. *The Shi'is of Iraq.* Princeton, N.J.: Princeton University Press, 1994.

Nasser, Munir H. "'Iraq: Ethnic Minorities and Their Impact on Politics." *Journal of South Asian and Middle Eastern Studies* 8, no. 3 (Spring 1985): 22–37.

Rondot, Pierre. *Les Chrétiens d'Orient.* Paris: Payronnet, 1955.

Thesiger, Wilfrid. *The Marsh Arabs.* London: Longmans, 1964.

Wardi, 'Ali, al-. *Lamahat ijtima'iyah min tarikh al-'Iraq al hadith.* Baghdad: Ma -tba'at al- Irshad, 1969.

Wiley, Joyce N. *The Islamic Movement of Iraqi Shi'as.* Boulder, Colo.: Rienner, 1992.

Assyrians

Fiey, J. M. *Assyrie chrétienne.* Beyrouth: Imprimerie Catholique, 1965.

Husry, Khaldun S. "The Assyrian Affair of 1933." *International Journal of the American Oriental Society* 75, no. 1 (January–March 1955): 1–13.

Wigram, William A. *The Assyrians and Their Neighbors.* London: Bell, 1929.

Jews

Darvish, Tikva. *The Jews in the Economy of 'Iraq.* Ramat-Gan, Israel: Bar-Ilan University Press, 1987.

Nakash, Yitzhaq. *The Shi'is of Iraq.* Princeton, N.J.: Princeton University Press, 1994.

Rejwan, Nissim. *The Jews of 'Iraq: Three Thousand Years of History and Culture.* Boulder, Colo.: Westview, 1985.

Shiblak, Abbas. *The Lure of Zion: The Case of the 'Iraqi Jews.* London: Al Saqi, 1986.
Shiloah, Amnon. *The Musical Tradition of 'Iraqi Jews.* Or Yehuda, Israel: 'Iraqi Jews' Traditional Culture Center, 1983.

Kurds

Adamson, David C. *The Kurdish War.* London: Allen & Unwin, 1964.
Arfa, Hassan. *The Kurds: An Historical and Political Study.* London: Oxford University Press, 1966.
Backer, Ralf, and Ronald Ofteringer. "Iraqi Kurdistan: A Republic of Statelessness." *Middle East Report* (March–June 1994): 40–45.
Barth, Fredrik. *Principles of Social Organization in Southern Kurdistan*: Oslo: Jorgensen, 1953.
Bois, Thomas. *The Kurds.* Trans. from the French by M. W. M. Welland. Beirut: Khayats, 1966.
Bruinessen, Martin van. *Agha, Shaikh and State: The Social and Political Structures of Kurdistan.* London: Zed, 1992.
——. 'The Kurds between Iran and 'Iraq." *Middle East Report* 16, no. 4 (July–August 1986).
Bulloch, John, and Harvey Morris. *No Friends but the Mountains: The Tragic History of the Kurds.* New York: n.p., 1992.
Central Intelligence Agency. *Iraq-Turkey-Iran: The Kurdish Insurgencies: An Intelligence Assessment.* MORI DocID: 705726. Washington, D.C.: Author, 1988.
——. *The Kurdish Minority Problem.* MORI DocID: 258376. Washington, D.C.: Author, 1948.
——. *The Kurdish Problem in Perspective: A Research Paper.* MORI DocID: 626727. Washington, D.C.: Author, 1979.
——. *The Kurdish War—Round Four.* MORI DocID: 119556. Washington, D.C.: Author, 1965.
——. "Iraq: Chemical Agents and the Kurdish Experience." *Science and Weapons Review* (23 September 1988): 1–2 (MORI DocID: 121671).
Chaliand, Gerard, ed. *People without a Country: The Kurds and Kurdistan.* London: Zed, 1980.
Dann, Uriel. "The Kurdish Nationalist Movement in 'Iraq." *Jerusalem Quarterly* 9 (Fall 1978): 131–44.
Edmonds, C. J. "Kurdish Nationalism." *Journal of Contemporary History* 6, no. 1 (1971): 87–107.
——. "The Kurds and the Revolution in 'Iraq." *Middle East Journal* 13, no. 1 (Winter 1959): 1–10.
——. "The Kurds of 'Iraq." *Middle East Journal* 11, no. 1 (Winter 1957): 52–62.
Entessar, Nadar. *Kurdish Ethnonationalism.* Boulder, Colo.: Reinner, 1992.
Ghareeb, Edmund. *The Kurdish Question in 'Iraq.* Syracuse, N.Y.: Syracuse University Press, 1981.
Ghassemlou, Abdul Rahman. *Kurdistan and the Kurds.* London: Collet's, 1965.
Gunter, Michael. *The Kurdish Predicament in 'Iraq.* New York: St. Martin's, 1999.

——. "The KDP-PUK Conflict in Northern Iraq." *Middle East Journal* 50, no. 2 (Spring 1996).

——. *The Kurds of Iraq: Tragedy and Hope.* New York: St. Martin's, 1992.

Hassanpour, Amir. "The Kurdish Experience." *Middle East Report* (July–August 1994): 3–7+.

Izady, Mehrdad R. *A Concise Handbook of the Kurds.* Washington, D.C.: Taylor & Francis, 1992.

Jawad, Saad. *'Iraq and the Kurdish Question, 1958–1970.* London: Ithaca, 1981.

Jwaideh, Wadie. "The Kurdish National Movement: Its Origins and Development." Ph.D. diss., Syracuse University, Syracuse, N.Y., 1960.

Kinnane, Derk. *The Kurds and Kurdistan.* London: Oxford University Press, 1964.

Kreyenbroek, Philip G., and Stefan Sperl, eds. *The Kurds: A Contemporary Overview.* London: Routledge, 1992.

Kutschera, Chris. *Le Mouvement National Kurde.* Paris: Flammarion, 1979.

MacDonald, Charles. "The Kurds." *Journal of Political Science* 19 (1991): 121–39.

McDowell, David. *A Modern History of the Kurds.* New York: Taurus, 1996.

——. *The Kurds: A Nation Denied.* London: Minority Rights Group, 1992.

O'Balance, Edgar. *The Kurdish Revolt 1961–1970.* London: Faber & Faber, 1973.

Pelletiere, Stephen. *The Kurds: An Unstable Element in the Gulf.* Boulder, Colo.: Westview, 1984.

Randall, Jonathan. *After Such Knowledge, What Forgiveness?* Boulder, Colo.: Westview, 1999.

Schmidt, Dana Adams. *Journey among Brave Men.* Boston: Atlantic Monthly Press, 1964.

Vanly, Ismet Cherif. *Le Kurdistan Irakien Entité Nationale.* Neuchâtel, Switzerland: La Baconnière, 1970.

Wenner, Lettie M. "Arab-Kurdish Rivalries in 'Iraq." *Middle East Journal* 17, nos. 1–2 (Winter/Spring 1963): 68–82.

Epilogue

As this epilogue was being written, news of Saddam Husayn's capture was revealed. On December 13, 2003, American forces captured Saddam during a nighttime raid on Al-Dawr, a small village roughly 15 kilometers from Tikrit. Close questioning of Saddam's former bodyguards and members of his family were said to have produced the intelligence that led to the raid. He was reported to be living in a two-room mud shack, with a small hole in the ground outside disguised with Styrofoam and dirt. When soldiers uncovered the spider hole, Saddam was reported by U.S. officials to have emerged with his hands raised, stating he was the 'Iraqi president and wanted to negotiate. He was armed with a pistol; soldiers also recovered $750,000 in one hundred dollar bills and two AK-47 rifles. To prove that Saddam was now in U.S. custody, footage of him undergoing a medical examination was released. He appeared haggard and exhausted, with a long beard and disheveled hair. The airing of the photos, as was the case with the airing on TV of photos of the bodies of his dead sons Qusay and Uday, were controversial and were criticized by some in 'Iraq, as well as the region and the world as a violation of the Geneva Convention on the treatment of prisoners of war. Many jubilant 'Iraqis, however, took to the streets to celebrate, although some simultaneously expressed a sense of humiliation at the failure of their former leader to defend himself. Saddam is being questioned by American military and intelligence personnel, a process expected to extend to at least June 2004. He has reportedly denied directing the insurgency against the American occupation, and also denied that 'Iraq had weapons of mass destruction. He will likely be tried before the newly established 'Iraq tribunal for genocide, crimes against humanity, and war crimes, or by a hybrid tribunal composed of 'Iraqis and international prosecutors and judges.

Saddam's capture ended the career of one of the most controversial leaders in 'Iraq. Saddam had wanted to modernize his country and to make it a regional leader and an international player, but his accelerated use of violence domestically and his military interventions abroad had the opposite effect. His capture is likely to help open a new page in the history of 'Iraq and the region. However, it will resolve few of the questions concerning 'Iraq's futureænamely the future of federalism, the nature of Kurdish–Arab relations, the role of the 'Iraqi Governing Council, the timetable for ending occupation, the question of direct elections, the future of the resistance to the United States in 'Iraq, and more importantly, the future of the 'Iraqi state established in 1921. Despite the capture of Saddam, the insurgency, so far, has continued to inflict almost daily casualties on American and international troops as well as on 'Iraqi police and civilians.

The arrest will not necessarily end the conflict in 'Iraq, the Middle East, or the one between radical Islamists and nationalists and the United States. It has, however, brought a psychological and political boost to the Bush administration, which was facing increasing criticism domestically and internationally about its 'Iraq policies. The small number of casualtiesæless than 500 killedæhad led to new questions in some sectors. The failure to find the weapons of mass destruction, the premature declaration of Mission Accomplished and the failure to adequately plan for the postwar period have raised questions in the minds of many. The long-term nature of this boost is likely to depend to a great extent on the unfolding events in 'Iraq and especially on the ability of the Coalition Provisional Authority (CPA) to establish a sense of normalcy and stability and hope in 'Iraq.

Since the Bush administration's assumption of power in 2000, U.S. foreign policy has undergone a dramatic transformation and the war on terrorism provided neoconservatives in the administration with a new opportunity to implement policies and doctrines, some of which they had begun to develop under the first Bush administration. These policies involved the pursuit of unilateralism and preemptive strikes if U.S. interests were to be threatened. The neoconservatives and their allies had begun to focus on 'Iraq and to call for regime change both before and immediately after the election of President Bush to office. The terrorist attacks of September 11, 2001, were a catalyst that accelerated their efforts to bring down the Saddam Husayn regime by linking 'Iraq to the war on terrorism.

Disagreements emerged between the neo-conservative hard-liners in the Department of Defense and the White House on the one hand, and the State Department and National Security Council (NSC) officials on the other, who had raised questions about some of the policies and views expressed by the neoconservatives. The State Department and certain NSC officials favored cooperation with groups and individuals they considered to be more representative than the 'Iraqi National Congress, which was supported by the neoconservatives in the Department of Defense.

There were also statements and accusations by neoconservatives implying a link between 'Iraq and the anthrax-laced letters that were distributed to a number of high-profile individuals and groups in the government and media. U.S. officials also began to focus on the dictatorial nature of the 'Iraqi regime and the danger posed by its efforts to acquire weapons of mass destruction (WMD).

In his January 28, 2002, State of the Union Address, President George Bush listed 'Iraq along with North Korea and Iran as members of the Axis of Evil countries that must be dealt with. He threatened to take unspecified actions to prevent 'Iraq from threatening U.S. national security interests. Furthermore, President Bush insisted that it was U.S. policy to bring about a change of regime in 'Iraq, and that unless the 'Iraqi regime was removed, it may provide terrorists with WMD to attack U.S. and Israeli targets. The reaction to the speech in Europe and the Middle East ranged from lukewarm to critical. Senator Tom Daschle (D-SD), who led the Democrats in the U.S. Senate, warned that this policy would anger allies and friends and furthermore isolate the United States. The U.S. public, which was becoming increasingly concerned about terrorist threats, appeared to support the administration, which had been warning against serious and imminent threats posed by the 'Iraqi regime.

Administration officials, including President Bush, Vice President Richard Cheney, Secretary of Defense Donald Rumsfeld, NSC adviser Condoleeza Rice, and Secretary of State Colin Powell continued to hammer on the theme that 'Iraq posed a threat to national security and had to be disarmed. Some neoconservative intellectuals and officials further argued that the war would be a cakewalk and that the 'Iraqi military and people would rise up and welcome U.S. forces as liberators, once they were assured that the United States was serious in its efforts to bring down the regime. In early 2002, the United States and its British allies issued dossiers to the UN and the media purporting to show that 'Iraq was beginning to resume its WMD buildup. They pointed out that 'Iraq had resorted to these weapons against Iran and its Kurdish people and that the 'Iraqi rogue regime continued to pose a serious threat to the security and well-being of its people, its neighbors, and the United States. 'Iraq was also accused of violating UN resolutions and refusing to allow the return of international inspectors.

Vice President Cheney visited the Middle East in early 2002 to build a coalition for the war on terrorism and a possible coalition for the war on 'Iraq. Most regional leaders publicly expressed their opposition to, or reservations against, any war against 'Iraq, but they expressed a willingness to cooperate on the war on terrorism. Several said that the threat to the region came from Israeli leader Ariel Sharon and his policies toward the Palestinians and warned that an invasion of 'Iraq would be seen in the region as a war against Arabs and Muslims.

The administration, however, was unrelenting in its insistence that 'Iraq posed a threat to its national security and had to be disarmed. The debate in Washington continued within the administration and the Republican Party. Former Secretaries of State James Baker and Lawrence Eagleburger, and former National Security Advisor Brent Scowcroft, favored Secretary of State Powell's view of going to the UN to seek a new resolution and held that it was necessary to build an effective coalition against 'Iraq in case war was unavoidable. Opposing views were offered by former Secretaries of State Alexander Haig, George Schultz, and Henry Kissinger, who warned against the consequences and difficulties that may emerge as a result of a war on 'Iraq. Gen. Scowcroft, however, called for some movement toward resolving the Arab–Israeli conflict before taking any action against 'Iraq. Some U.S. military officials indicated that the United States had succeeded in containing 'Iraq. General Eric Shinseki, the Army's chief of staff had warned in a congressional testimony that an attack on 'Iraq might require from 200,000 to 300,000 soldiers to do the job. Secretary Rumsfeld and his deputy Paul Wolfowitz, however, said these estimates were off the mark and they also spoke of differing scenarios being discussed by officials. Secretary Rumsfeld warned that 'Iraq was seeking to hide its chemical and biological weapons by moving them around or storing them underground.

Vice President Cheney, in a speech on August 29, 2002, claimed that Husayn's regime continued to pursue an aggressive nuclear weapons program. U.S. officials also accused Husayn of providing support for Palestinian suicide bombers by giving their families $25,000.

The administration decided to go the UN to gain support of its 'Iraq policy. On September 12, 2002, President Bush addressed the UN General Assembly and called for a new resolution to disarm 'Iraq. He said that if the UN was not prepared to assume its responsibilities, the United States was ready to do its duty alone. He repeated many of the charges against 'Iraq.

On September 16, 2002, 'Iraqi officials expressed their agreement to allow UN weapons inspectors to return to 'Iraq without any preconditions. This decision was relayed in a letter to the Secretary General of the UN. 'Iraq also called upon the UN to shoulder its responsibilities toward 'Iraq. France, Russia, and China urged 'Iraq to comply with relevant UN resolutions and to cooperate with the inspectors as a way to avoid a destructive war. The Arab League and its Secretary General also played a role in the negotiations. 'Iraq, in the meantime, had launched a diplomatic campaign to gain support for its position and to avoid a U.S.-British war on 'Iraq. The 'Iraqi decision led to negotiations between 'Iraq and the UN in Vienna, which in turn led to the signing of a Memorandum of Agreement concerning the return of inspectors. These efforts appeared to slow down the U.S. campaign.

In the meantime, the Bush administration called upon Congress to approve a resolution giving the administration the authority to launch a war against 'Iraq if it became necessary. The United States rejected the agreement signed by Chief Inspector Hans Blix in Vienna and called for a more intrusive resolution to allow for the return of the inspectors. The administration had also distributed a new dossier on 'Iraqi transgressions. The Bush administration appeared to be critical of the agreement and of the statement of the Secretary General of the UN. On September 12, 2002, before the General Assembly of the UN, the Secretary General declared that inspections were only one step toward a comprehensive solution, which included lifting the sanctions on 'Iraq, as well as 'Iraq's implementation of relevant UN resolutions including 687. The Secretary General also called for respecting 'Iraq's sovereignty, independence, and territorial integrity. In the meantime, the administration, followed by the British government, issued a new document, which emphasized 'Iraq's oppression of its population and its previous use of chemical weapons, its attempts to acquire weapons of mass destruction, and its violation of UN resolutions. However, this document was later shown to rely on a paper written in the early '90s by an 'Iraqi graduate student in the United States. 'Iraq issued a document of its own, responding to the British and U.S. accusations.

On November 11, 2002, Congress passed a resolution, by a large margin, giving the president the authority to use force against 'Iraq. This was seen as a major victory for the administration and was intended in part to strengthen its hand in negotiations at the UN. Several countries in the UN Security Council, including permanent Security Council members, opposed any unilateral use of force by the United States and required a new specific Security Council resolution authorizing such force.

Neoconservative intellectuals in the United States had argued that a war on 'Iraq was "doable." It would not only bring down a dictatorial regime but it would also transform 'Iraq into an important ally of the United States. This would lead to benefits in the form of increased access to oil, and would change the regional dynamics in the Middle East by weakening anti-American radical forces and promoting democratic and tolerant societies and institutions. A pro-American and democratic regime in Baghdad would make 'Iraq a model for the democratic transformation of the Middle East. Politically and diplomatically, a successful war would also strengthen the administration's hand in defeating radical Islamic fundamentalists and terrorists, and it would also weaken rejectionists who oppose the peace process in the Middle East and would provide a new opportunity to resolve the Israeli–Palestinian conflict in a more acceptable way. Such a transformation would make Israel more secure. It would also increase cooperation in the war against terrorism. Additionally, a new 'Iraqi regime with a free-market economy would undoubtedly be an ally of the United States, thus creating an environment that would be more receptive to American values and policies.

In terms of oil, this outcome would give the United States access to the second-largest oil reserve in the Middle East. A pro-U.S. government in Baghdad would further help the United States influence world oil prices and production. In terms of security, 'Iraq was a major regional power and its transformation into an American ally would strengthen the U.S. strategic position vis-à-vis some of 'Iraq's neighbors, particularly Iran and Syria. Furthermore, Washington needed access to new strategic military facilities in the region at a time when the United States was under pressure to close down bases in Saudi Arabia.

Opponents argued that a war could be counterproductive and would instead create additional negative anti-American reactions in the Arab and Islamic worlds and alienate the United States from its allies. They feared that a destabilized 'Iraq would inflame radicalism, thus increasing the terrorism the United States was seeking to combat. Also, some feared that increased attacks against U.S. targets and against its allies in the region could embroil the United States in an 'Iraqi quagmire. Others argued that the United States would be seen by many in the world, as well as within the United States, as waging an imperial war against a relatively defenseless third-world country that has been suffering under sanctions. Some argued that a war on 'Iraq would also be seen as a colonial war motivated by oil and strategic designs and would be inconsistent with traditional U.S. policies, values, and interests. Many feared that the opposition to the United States in 'Iraq would be more persistent and determined, even if it quickly succeeded in bringing down the Husayn regime. Some also warned against the danger of the collapse of the 'Iraqi state, which could open a regional Pandora's box with devastating consequences for 'Iraq and the entire region.

In the meantime, the 'Iraqi regime continued to seek ways to avoid a confrontation, which it knew it could not win, by providing concessions to the UN, complying with the inspections process, and seeking back channels to Washington. The *New York Times* reported a curious episode on November 6, 2003, in which 'Iraqi leaders, in an effort to prevent a war, offered the Bush administration major concessions on the eve of the start of the war. They made a last-minute overture through a Lebanese American businessman who had contacts with both the U.S. Department of Defense and with top 'Iraqi intelligence officials. The 'Iraqis offered to cooperate with the United States in fighting terrorism, to support U.S. peace plans, to promote U.S. strategic plans in the region, and to allow American soldiers and inspectors to search for weapons of mass destruction. They also offered to surrender an 'Iraqi, Ahmad Yasin, who was accused of involvement in the 1993 attack on the World Trade Center in New York. They promised to hold elections in two years. The contacts were made through the office of Under Secretary Douglas Feith at the Defense Department and through Richard Perle, a neoconservative intellectual and member of the influential Defense Policy Board at the Pentagon. Both figures were well known for their hawkish views in favor of a regime change in 'Iraq. The offers were not taken seriously and Perle later said he feared it was a trap. It is not clear how high this information reached.

In November 2002, the UN Security Council passed Resolution 1441, which was designed to force 'Iraq to give up all weapons of mass destruction. The resolution threatened serious consequences if 'Iraq was noncompliant. 'Iraq accepted the terms of the resolution and weapons inspections resumed on November 27, 2002. In response to UN demands 'Iraq, on December 7, 2002, submitted a massive 12,000-page declaration of its chemical, biological, and nuclear activities, and declared that it had no nuclear, chemical, or biological weapons or weapons programs.

In December, the United States began deploying troops to the Persian Gulf region. The international community, however, was still skeptical. On January 27, 2003, Chief UN Weapons Inspector Hans Blix stated that 'Iraq appeared not to have come to a genuine acceptance of the disarmament that was demanded of it. Nevertheless, he cited significant cooperation and called for the continuation of the inspections and for major powers to cooperate and provide intelligence information on 'Iraqi weapons. The following day, President Bush claimed that Saddam Husayn has shown utter contempt for the United Nations and the opinion of the world. On February 5, 2003, U.S. Secretary of State Colin Powell told the UN that inspections were not achieving the disarmament of 'Iraq. However, in subsequent weeks Hans Blix stated that 'Iraq had made genuine progress in terms of cooperation with UN inspectors.

On February 24, 2003, the United States, Great Britain, and Spain submitted a proposed resolution to the UN Security Council that stated, among other things, that 'Iraq had failed to take the final opportunity afforded to it in Resolution 1441. France, Russia, and Germany opposed the proposed resolution, contending that inspections in 'Iraq needed to be extended and intensified to ensure a peaceful resolution to the crisis. The three nations also believed that military action against 'Iraq should only be used as a last resort. The United States lobbied intensively in the UN but it later decided, along with its allies, not to call for a vote on the resolution.

In a live television broadcast on March 17, 2003, President Bush is-sued an ultimatum demanding that Saddam Husayn and his sons depart 'Iraq within 48 hours. This demand went unanswered by the 'Iraqis. On March 19, 2003, the United States began the war, dubbed Operation 'Iraqi Freedom, with an initial aerial attack on a target of opportunity in Baghdad where it was thought that senior members of the 'Iraqi regime—possibly Saddam Husayn and his sons, Uday and Qusay— were present. Ground forces invaded from Kuwait, with U.S. troops moving rapidly toward Baghdad while British troops moved to secure key towns in the south, most notably Basra. On March 21, 2003, Bagh-dad and other cities were hit with overwhelming aerial attacks meant to instill shock and awe. Many of these assaults destroyed or damaged 'Iraqi infrastructure, which has proven to be hard to repair following the fall the regime, and inflicted heavy casualties on 'Iraqi forces in the area. After initial fierce resistance, mainly from 'Iraqi units and Saddam Commandos in Um Qasr, Nasiriya, and other southern areas, U.S. forces reached the outskirts of Baghdad in early April and eventually took Saddam Husayn International Airport. During the war, no weapons of mass destruction were used by 'Iraqi forces and, to date, no weapons stockpiles have been found.

After a period of initial resistance, the poorly equipped and organized 'Iraqi units in and around Baghdad melted away into the general popu-lationæsome taking their own light arms with them. Confusion and poor coordination were rampant. On April 9, 2003, U.S. Marines helped a small crowd to topple a giant statue of Saddam Husayn in the heart of Baghdad. At the same time, major looting and vandalism broke out in the city. The National Archives and the 'Iraqi National Museum were also looted, sparking an international outcry over why these sites did not receive U.S. military protection. A crime wave quickly followed so that many 'Iraqis, particularly women, feared venturing outside their homes. An independent report of U.S. combat data, battlefield press re-ports, and 'Iraqi hospital surveys produced by The Project on Defense Alternatives at Commonwealth Institute in Cambridge, Massachusetts, has found that approximately 13,000 'Iraqis (plus or minus 16.5 percent or 2,150) were killed during the major combat phase of the war. The re-port covers the period from March 19 to the end of April 2004. Among the 'Iraqi dead were between 3,200 and 4,300 civilians who did not take up arms. The casualty rates among 'Iraqis continued to mount after the war, but no official count was given. U.S. casualties were around 500 dead and over 10,000 who were evacuated for medical reasons, including wounded soldiers. Other figures said that the number of 'Iraqi casualties until the late fall reached over 50,000 'Iraqis killed, including over 9,000 civilians.

On May 1, 2003, President Bush declared an end to major combat operations in 'Iraq following a dramatic tail-hook landing on an aircraft carrier off the coast of San Diego. A few weeks after this announcement, L. Paul Bremer III took over as the new administrator of the Coalition Provisional Authority (CPA) in 'Iraq, replacing the first administrator General Jay Garner.

Soon after the beginning of the war, the United States moved to help establish a new 'Iraqi government. A meeting was organized on April 26, 2003, in Nasiriya to which different 'Iraqi opposition groups were invited. The meeting was mainly attended by representatives of some tribal groups, as well as representatives of some Shi'ite opposition groups such as SAIRI. Al-Da'wa boycotted the meeting and called for an Islamic government and for the withdrawal of U.S. forces. Meanwhile, the United States had begun, prior to the launching of the war, to expand its ties beyond the INC and the other opposition groups with which it was working to include some of the Shi'i groups said to be close to Iran, along with ex-security and ex-military officials.

These groups included the 'Iraqi National Movement (founded in 2001 and led by former military officer Hasan al-Naqib and by Hatim Mukhlis), the 'Iraqi National Front (set up in 2000 by a former Shi'i General Tawfiq al-Yasiri who had actively participated in the 1991 uprising), the Free Officers and Civilians Movement (headed by former Republican Guard General Najib al-Salhi), the Higher Council for National Salvation (established in Denmark by Wafiq al-Samarrai, the former head of military intelligence and by General Nizar al-Khazraji, a former 'Iraqi chief of staff) and the Islamic Accord (based in Damascus and led by Ayat Allah Shirazi, who headed a group that had allegedly sought to bring down the Bahraini government). Contacts were also expanded to include the 'Iraqi Turkuman Front and the Assyrian Democratic Movement representing some Turkuman and Assyrian factions.

Another meeting, attended by U.S. officials, was held by the five main representatives with whom Washington was working—the KDP, PUK, SAIRI, INA, and the INC. A decision was made to expand the group to include the Islamic al-Dews Party and Nasir al-Chadirchi of the National Democratic Party of 'Iraq, who had close ties to Adnan al-Pachachi. The group reversed an earlier U.S. decision to delay the formation of a self-rule authority.

On July 13, 2003, the United States also moved to give a degree of power back to the 'Iraqi people through the establishment of the 'Iraqi Governing Council (IGC) composed of 25 'Iraqis from various religious and ethnic groups. The IGC included three women, thirteen Shi'is, five Sunnis, five Kurds, including one Christian and one Turkuman. The Council decided to have rotating membership for each month from among nine of its members. One of the IGC women members Dr. 'Aquila al-Hashimi, a Shi'ite and prominent 'Iraqi diplomat who headed the office of Tariq Aziz under the Ba'th was later assassinated. Another major assassination occurred on August 29, 2003, when a car bomb exploded outside the Imam Ali shrine at al-Najaf, which killed about a hundred people but which was aimed at Ayat Allah Muhammad Baqir al-Hakim, the head of the SAIRI and a prominent Shi'i leader.

On May 1, the Bush administration claimed an end to major combat operations but conditions in 'Iraq began to quickly deteriorate. Immediately after the end of major fighting and the fall of Baghdad, the 'Iraqi State established by Faysal I appeared to be collapsing. Most state institutions collapsed, particularly after the decision by U.S. authorities to dissolve the Ba'th Party, the armed forces, and the police. The U.S. authorities, which had proved to be well prepared for war, were generally unprepared for what came afterward. The whole social contract appeared to be falling apart. Looting, crime, and unemployment were on the rise. Basic water, electricity, banking, education, and health services were unavailable in many parts of the country. Millions of people had lost their jobs. These factors, along with the lack of understanding of 'Iraqi culture and mores, have contributed to the rapid rise of a violent resistance. Also, what was seen as heavy-handed measures employed by some Coalition forces in their efforts to restore order and to root out Saddam loyalists, nationalists, and religious opponents of U.S. occupation was an additional contributing factor to a rise in violent resistance.

This resistance to U.S.–British occupation emerged quickly, although at a low level. U.S. officials blamed the resistance on Ba'thist dead-enders and Arab volunteers with ties to Al-Qaeda, and from Ansar al-Islam, a radical Kurdish Islamist faction. By July 17, 2003, General John

Abizaid of the Central Command said the United States was facing a classic guerilla war in 'Iraq.

Beginning in June 2003, resistance groups began to issue statements declaring their intent to fight against U.S. forces with names such as: Al-'Awda (The Return), Al-Awda al-Thaniya (The Second Return, a probable reference to the return of the Ba'th or of Saddam to power), the Armed Islamic Movement of Al-Qaeda, the Army of Muhammad, The Black Banners, Jaush Ansar al-Sunnah (The Army of the Supporters of Sunnah), and the Nasirite Group. Some Shi'ite organizations, such as the Sadrist faction of Muqtada al-Sadr, also began to mobilize nonviolent opposition by organizing demonstrations in Baghdad and Basra. Al-Sadr also began to organize his Jaysh (Army) of al-Mahdi. There were also signs of limited contact and talk of cooperation between some Shi'i and Sunni religious leaders (Ahmad al-Kubaisi).

The rapid emergence of the insurgents pointed to prior planning and preparation. The resistance is widely believed to be made up of some Ba'thists, former regime loyalists, nationalists, and Islamists. The participation of some of these groups may also indicate that other groups outside the regimes' circle were preparing for resistance. Immediately after the fall of the regime, a group calling itself the 'Iraqi National Liberation Front declared that it would fight against the occupation. The front is said to have a coalition of ten small groups operating in various governorates independently of each other and of the Ba'thists. Since then, more than 35 groups have announced their presence on the ground. It is not clear, however, how many of these groups are real or are the same groups operating under multiple names.

Guerilla attacks on U.S. forces increased by mid-June and insurgent tactics began to change in July and August. Saddam Husayn also reemerged via a taped message sent to Arab satellite channels on July 4th, U.S. Independence Day, to applaud the resistance offered against infidel foreign invaders. Attacks were also launched against the oil pipelines and other infrastructures. In August 2003 the financial cost of U.S. occupation was estimated around $4 billion a month.

In July and August, a series of bombings occurred in tandem with periodic attacks on U.S. soldiers. On July 22, 2003, the killing of Saddam's sons, Uday and Qusay, in a firefight at their hideout in the northern 'Iraqi town of Mawsil did not end or reduce the resistance activities. Sabotage of 'Iraqi infrastructure continued unabated.

At the same time, prewar claims by Prime Minister Tony Blair and President Bush on 'Iraqi possession and development of weapons of mass destruction were called into question. Also questioned were many of the accusations used as justifications for the war, such as 'Iraq's alleged purchase of uranium yellowcake from Niger, the aluminum tubes that Washington claimed were to be used in 'Iraq's nuclear program, and 'Iraq's ties to Osama bin Laden's Al-Qaeda organization.

The White House eventually acknowledged that President Bush's claim that 'Iraq was actively seeking uranium in Africa, delivered during his State of the Union Address, was inaccurate.

Meanwhile, a new phase of violent escalation was initiated on August 19, 2003, when a truck bomb slammed into UN headquarters in Baghdad killing 20, including Sergio Vieira de Mello, the UN High Commissioner for Human Rights. Attacks against U.S. interests and troops continues to date and numerous NGOs, including the International Committee of the Red Cross and UN agencies, have either pulled out or scaled back their operations in Baghdad.

Additionally, the insurgents appeared to be showing more sophistication, determination, and skill. They were pursuing a strategy of undermining the tactics of CPA by turning public opinion against it, as well as creating a wedge among the nations that make up the Coalition by attacking their contingents in 'Iraq. By August 2003, guerilla attacks reached about 500 a month with over 95 percent aimed at U.S forces. The resistance was also targeting nongovernmental organizations. The Bush administration, however, argued that the attacks actually showed that progress was being made in 'Iraq and against the insurgents.

The new methods were reflected in the car-bomb attack on the Jordanian Embassy on August 7, 2003, and the more powerful attack against UN headquarters in Baghdad, as well as the attack on the Turkish Embassy following reports that Turkey might send troops to 'Iraq. Suicide bomb attacks also occurred at the Baghdad headquarters of the International Committee of the Red Cross. 'Iraqis, who had been working with the coalition, including police recruits, interpreters, and translators, as well as judges, became targets. These actions led to the withdrawal of the UN and the International Red Cross and many foreign embassy staff, except for skeleton crews. A number of countries also expressed hesitancy about sending troops to 'Iraq without UN cover, or refused to do so outright. Another development was the increasing sophistication and lethality of insurgent attacks against U.S. forces. A number of attacks occurred against CPA's headquarters in Baghdad as mortars and rockets landed within the secure green zone. There were also rocket attacks on the Al-Rashid Hotel in Baghdad, where Deputy Defense Secretary Paul Wolfowitz was staying at the time.

The strategy of the insurgents appeared to be aimed at inflicting casualties among CPA forces and their supporters, and at undermining morale and support for the Bush administration's 'Iraq policy at home and abroad. This would make it difficult for other countries to aid the U.S. effort. The resistance also may have sought to put CPA forces in situations where they would be forced to react harshly so as to inflict collateral damage, thereby alienating the 'Iraqi public. Several attacks have also been motivated by the desire to drive away international organizations, such as the UN, which was criticized for its failure to stop the war and for the decade-long sanctions, although its humanitarian efforts were deeply appreciated. A message was being sent to the UN not to cooperate with, or to help legitimize U.S. occupation. In addition, these attacks were intended to send the message that the United States was not in control.

Meanwhile, reports surfaced in the Arab press that Saddam Husayn might have been involved in some of the resistance activities, and that he had begun to lay plans for a long-term, unconventional resistance once he realized that his forces could not defeat American forces in a conventional war. Others argued that the poor planning for the postwar period by U.S. authorities had contributed to the deterioration, and to mounting 'Iraqi anger and frustration, particularly in Baghdad and in the area dubbed by U.S. officials as the Sunni Triangle.

The strength of the resistance movement, which was being increasingly described as terrorist by the IGC and some U.S. officials, has been reflected in its ability to continue daily operations since the fall of Baghdad. This strength has continued despite the arrest and/or the death of numerous members of the old 'Iraqi leadership and of suspected fighters and commanders. The early rise of resistance made it difficult for the Coalition forces to have a breathing period to benefit from the quick military victory and to better administer 'Iraq. The anti-CPA efforts, as well as attacks on 'Iraqis accused of cooperating with occupation authorities, have helped to isolate the CPA from average 'Iraqis and reduced the number of 'Iraqis willing to work with the U.S. and IGC authorities.

Nevertheless, the resistance seemed to suffer from a number of weaknesses. Although the insurgents had launched operations in most 'Iraqi governorates, they appeared to be better organized in Baghdad and the center of the country (dubbed as the Sunni Triangle). They were much less developed in the south and almost nonexistent in the Kurdish region. The concern of some Shi'ite groups about Saddam's return to power may have contributed to the reluctance among some Shi'i opponents of occupation. Some also believed that it was only a matter of time before the Shi'i majority gained its rightful political place in the country. Some of the Shi'i religious leaders had expressed opposition to the occupation but favored a nonviolent approach at this time. The Kurdish position has also been an important factor. Most Kurds, who form close to a fifth of the population, had suffered greatly under the regime and had benefited from the protection offered by the Allies after the 1990-1991 Gulf War. Tiny Kurdish Islamist groups, such as Ansar al-Islam, appeared to support the insurgency. In addition, the resistance suffers from limited funding and lacks international and regional support. Concern about possible U.S. reaction, previous differences with the former 'Iraqi regime, and a desire to benefit from the reconstruction effort in 'Iraq have been among the factors leading to the reluctance on the part of different governments to assist the insurgents.

On another front, the collapse of the regime has led to a media free-for-all in different parts of 'Iraq with numerous 'Iraqi exiles, political groups, and businessmen launching their own media outlets, leading to the launching of close to 160 newspapers. 'Iraqis who have dishes also have had access to Arab and other satellite channels, such as al-Jazeera, al-Arabiya, Abu Dhabi TV, and the Iranian-based al-Alam (which can be easily seen by 'Iraqi viewers) in addition to the BBC, MBC, and Monte Carlo radios that closely follow the 'Iraqi scene. Both al-Jazeera and al-Arabiya have been banned from covering the IGC for stories covering Saddam's and insurgent's statements calling for attacks on those cooperating with the CPA. In order to respond to what was generally viewed as critical regional satellite TV and radio coverage of 'Iraq, and as part of the U.S. public diplomacy campaign to win hearts and minds in 'Iraq and the Middle East, the U.S. Defense Department launched the Middle East Television Network, in addition to the 'Iraq Media Network. A new U.S.-funded television channel, Al-Hurra, is scheduled for launching in February 2004. Radio SAWA, a region-wide

Arabic language music and news station, was launched by the VOA and
has special programs for 'Iraq.

Various scenarios have been put forward concerning the future of
'Iraq. Some have hypothesized that the United States could pull out of
'Iraq after a brief period of institution building and the drafting of a constitution. An early U.S. pullout would most likely take place with UN
involvement. The United States could also stay to help establish a democratic regime and to maintain troops in 'Iraq indefinitely. The motives
for staying would be strategic considerations, oil, U.S. service company
interests, and the hope of turning 'Iraq into a Middle Eastern model of
democracy. The United States could leave 'Iraq, however, if high levels
of casualties are sustained, if high economic costs are experienced, or if
the United States is otherwise unable to bring stability and a level of
normalcy to 'Iraq. Currently, the U.S. strategy seems to be to turn over
responsibility for security to 'Iraqis. A key step in this effort would be
the drafting of a new 'Iraqi constitution that would be agreed upon by
the different communities and domestic factions, and which could be
backed by a national referendum.

Another U.S. objective, in addition to establishing a viable pro-
American 'Iraqi government, is the privatization of 'Iraq's economy. In
an effort to accomplish this at a faster pace, the United States is promoting debt forgiveness and international development aid for 'Iraq.
The United States might also put pressure on 'Iraq's neighbors to prevent interference in 'Iraq's internal affairs.

The CPA, in agreement with the IGC, has prepared a timetable for sur-
rendering sovereignty to the 'Iraqis. On February 28, 2004, the IGC is expected to produce a provisional constitution. One month later, U.S. military authorities and the IGC are expected to reach an agreement giving
U.S. forces long-term basing rights. On May 31, 2004, caucuses are to be
held in which prominent figures in religious, ethnic, tribal, and professional groups choose members of a transitional legislative council. The
legislative council is expected to number between 250 and 275 members.
'Iraq would appoint a three-member presidency, chosen by the council,
along with a new cabinet, which would assume power, by June 30, 2004.
The provisional constitution would serve until October 2005, when a nationwide referendum is supposed to be held on a permanent constitution.

The United States faces a Herculean task in 'Iraq. The challenges include accommodating the myriad of rival domestic interests and avoid-

ing being seen as seeking to control 'Iraq's natural resources. A major challenge will also surround the legitimacy of an unelected government appointed through caucuses resting on the foundation of U.S. military authority. The highest Shi'i Marja' in 'Iraq, Grand Ayat Allah Ali al-Sistani, has called for direct election for fear that the caucuses might dilute the Shiite numerical majority. At the same time, the failure to meet the deadline would be a setback for the CPA. Other challenges include establishing and maintaining security, suppressing, or at least containing, the resistance movement, making a deal with the Islamist forces, particularly among the Shi'is, bringing in the alienated Sunnis, satisfying Kurdish autonomist aspirations, and drafting a constitution while dealing with some members of the IGC who are maneuvering to hold on to power.

The challenges also include the creation of an environment that is likely to encourage the growth of democratic institutions in a country that has not had much recent experience with such institutions. Dealing with rising ethnic, tribal, and religious communities and groups where the emphasis on differences may become a self-fulfilling prophecy also contribute to the challenges.

Seeking to regain stability and a normal life for 'Iraqis by providing improvement in the peoples' daily lives and respecting their basic human rights and traditions may contribute toward stabilizing the country. Achieving these objectives is highly unlikely without the strengthened role for the 'Iraqi middle class, which numbers about twenty percent of the population. The middle class, which has been greatly weakened as a result of the devastating sanctions, the harsh policies of the old regime, immigration, and more recently as a result of the dissolution of state institutions and their consequences, could become the backbone of a new 'Iraq. Its members cut across religious, sectarian, tribal, and ethnic lines and have a strong sense of their 'Iraqi identity. The middle class could also help overcome the increasing emphasis on sectarian loyalty and identity which, if it continues unchecked, could open a Pandora's box for most 'Iraqis. The middle class could also play a role in overcoming the increasing ruralization and retribalization of some 'Iraqi towns and cities, and might reverse the trend toward emphasizing the primacy of ethnic and religious identities.

U.S. policy makers have been warned to avoid the mistakes made by British colonial powers. The British had helped set up some democratic institutions such as a constitutional monarchy, a parliament, separation of powers, and a relatively free press. However, their constant maneuvering to maintain a dominant role in 'Iraq in order to protect their economic, political, and strategic interests led to numerous overt and covert interventions in 'Iraqi affairs that alienated the 'Iraqis. The British also contributed to increased radicalization, which ultimately led to the bloody overthrow of the Hashimite monarchy that they had helped set up in 'Iraq.

Despite the quick defeat of 'Iraqi forces, the fall of the Ba'th regime, and the arrest of its leading members, the United States has been unable to bring the prerequisite stability necessary for establishing a new political order. An existing state was destroyed but a new one has not yet been created. Instead, the disintegration of 'Iraqi society and institutions was pervasive. The whole social contract was in a state of disarray. Many citizens lack basic services. Many civil servants and public workers have been dismissed and are unable to draw their salaries. Religious and ethnic tensions are on the rise. Women are facing serious pressures and threats, which have forced many to stay at home and undermined the progress they had achieved in the past. U.S. authorities that had proven that they were well prepared for war planning appear to have made few coherent plans for the postwar period. Such circumstances complicated the resumption of economic development and growth in the country.

The war and its aftermath have led to the rise of internal as well as external forces and to the rapid metamorphosis of these forces and interests leading to the rise of several possible trends. The possible emergence of a strong anti-U.S. coalition is one such trend. The formation of a pro-U.S. 'Iraqi government is another. Another possible trend is the possible slide toward civil war and the disintegration of the country if solutions are not found to the complex and difficult problems 'Iraq is now facing.

Some elements of the former opposition are being pushed to the forefront, although some appear to have little popular support. Such a scenario doesn't reflect the real dynamics in the country. If it is not modified, it could accelerate the rise of a new anti-occupation coalition composed of 'Iraqi nationalists as well as Shi'i, Sunni, and other elements who feel they have not been represented in the government. External intervention by neighboring states that have strong interests in the future of 'Iraq, and some of whom are allied to political forces inside 'Iraq cannot be excluded, particularly if these states believe that anarchy or civil war in 'Iraq are likely outcomes. 'Iraq's communities have strong ethnic, religious, or tribal links to the neighboring countries, which have strong interests in 'Iraq and its future. Turkey has close ties with some members of the Turkuman community and is greatly concerned about any potential impact of the 'Iraqi Kurds' success in gaining autonomy and self-expression in the new 'Iraq. They fear its impact on Turkey's large and restive Kurdish population. Iran, for its part, claims close ties and interests in the mainly Shi'i south as well as in the Kurdish region. Iran has a large Kurdish minority of its own and has expressed concern about Kurdish demands for a federal arrangement. Turkey and Iran are likely to keep wary eyes on each other's activities inside 'Iraq. Intervention by Turkey and/or Iran might also push some of the Kurdish forces to join an anti-occupation coalition if they conclude that their aspirations to self-rule are not going to be realized. Syria and Saudi Arabia also have strong interests and historic ties with 'Iraq, and numerous 'Iraqi tribes have kin across the borders of these countries. Both countries would also be concerned about the active involvement of Turkey and Iran in 'Iraqi affairs. Other countries that have strong interests in 'Iraq's future include Egypt, Israel, and Jordan, as well as France, Russia, Germany, China, and India.

One of the ideas that has been put forward to keep 'Iraq united involves the creation of a federation along ethnic and/or administrative lines. These communities would consist of five or seven or nine divisions, one or two Kurdish units in the north, one or two mainly Arab Sunni units, including Mawsil, in the north and the center, a separate unit consisting of Baghdad, and two or three predominantly Shi'i units in the south. Others see this prescription as a recipe for future conflict.

The issue of federalism is likely to be one of the most sensitive for the U.S., the new 'Iraqi leaders, and the neighboring states. The major Kurdish leaders and political parties insist on a federal arrangement allowing for Kurdish and Arab regions in 'Iraq with significant degrees of authority over political, economic, and security issues. They also insist that the new constitution guarantee linguistic and cultural autonomy for the Kurds and for the minorities inhabiting the Kurdistan region. They are also likely to call for Kurdish political participation in the executive, legislative, and judicial branches of the central government and a share in the national resources in accordance with their percentage of the population. Kurdish leaders also favor a more secular government and constitutional guarantees for the federal arrangement. The most difficult aspect in the negotiations between the Kurds and the central government may not be about the nature of self-government for any Kurdish region. The Ba'th government had offered the Kurds wide-ranging cultural and political rights as early as 1970. It is likely to be over the borders of this region. Oil-rich Kirkuk is claimed by the Kurds, but the Turkuman community, supported by Turkey, rejects this claim, thus making for an explosive situation if the issue is not dealt with through peaceful negotiations.

The invasion of 'Iraq by the United States and Britain is a watershed in 'Iraqi, Middle Eastern, and world history. It has changed the 'Iraqi political, social, and economic landscape. It may be the most important event since the collapse of the Soviet communist empire. This war and its aftermath have unleashed centrifugal forces with unknown consequences for 'Iraq, the United States, and for the Arab and Islamic worlds.

The fall of Saddam Husayn and the U.S. occupation of 'Iraq have also brought to the fore some new and old social, economic, and political forces. The fall of the regime has brought down the Ba'th Party and the ruling power structure, but new as well as old forces long suppressed by the Ba'th have resurfaced. The collapse of the state institutions, of the Ba'th Party, the loss millions of jobs as well as the policies pursued by the CPA and some 'Iraqi political forces, have accentuated a trend among many to revert to older, more primordial loyalties, based on religion, sect, tribe, family, or ethnic identity. The collapse of basic social, health, and educational services, and the absence of strong national and civic institutions have led to a loss of confidence among many citizenry and pushed many to search for belonging and security in these identities. This climate, however, makes an agreed solution within 'Iraq's complex and diverse ethnic and religious landscape hard to achieve. The new political landscape encompasses secular as well as religious Shi'i forces, Sunni religious and secular forces, monarchists, independent democrats, Kurdish nationalists, 'Iraqi nationalists, and independent 'Iraqi democrats. 'Iraq's survival and development require a minimum level of cooperation among these myriad forces to allow for the creation of civil society, rule of law, and representative government institutions, which, although representing the majority, protect the rights and interests of the minorities as well. 'Iraq may see the emergence of a new authoritarian regime, or 'Iraq may slide toward civil war and a possible breakup of the country.

About the Authors

Edmund Ghareeb is a resident scholar on Kurdish studies at American University in Washington, D.C. He is also an adjunct professor of Iraq studies at Georgetown University, and he has taught at the University of Virginia and George Washington University. Dr. Ghareeb was born and educated in Lebanon, where, as a journalist, he followed and wrote on events in the Middle East, including Iraq. He has written articles, chapters, and books dealing with the issues of Iraq. His most recent work is *Split Vision: Portrayal of Arabs in the American Media.*

Beth K. Dougherty is the Manger Professor of International Relations at Beloit College and the chair of the international relations program. She received her M.A. and Ph.D. in foreign affairs from the University of Virginia. She specializes in nationalism and ethnic conflict, as well as human rights, with a focus on Africa and the Middle East. She is the recipient of the 1999 Underkofler Excellence in Teaching Award at Beloit College and the corecipient of the 2001 Rowman and Littlefield Award for Innovative Teaching in Political Science, awarded through the National Political Science Association.